HAMPSHIRE & ISLE OF WIGHT
BIBLIOGRAPHIES

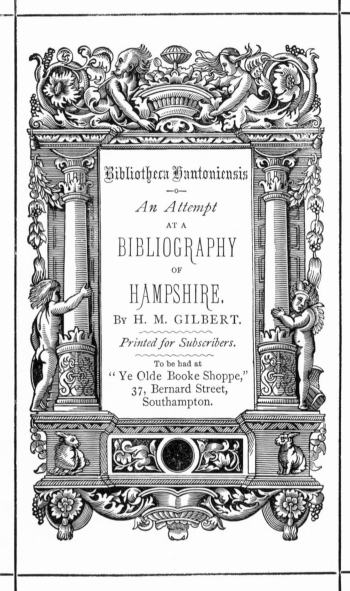

Bibliotheca Hantoniensis
—o—
An Attempt
AT A
BIBLIOGRAPHY
OF
HAMPSHIRE.
By H. M. GILBERT.

Printed for Subscribers.

To be had at
" Ye Olde Booke Shoppe,"
37, Bernard Street,
Southampton.

[Figure 1; 18.5 x 25.4 cm]

HAMPSHIRE & ISLE OF WIGHT BIBLIOGRAPHIES

Selected Nineteenth Century Sources

Edited by
Raymond V. Turley
Southampton University Library

Barry Shurlock

BARRY SHURLOCK
& Co. (Publishers) Ltd.,
174 Stockbridge Road,
WINCHESTER,
Hants, SO22 6RW

This edition is limited to 250 copies

Printed in Great Britain by
The Scolar Press Ltd ,
Ilkley, Yorkshire

To Eric F. Dadson, Esq.
formerly of Ashcliff, Bonchurch;
who,
by stimulating my appreciation of prints and
other works of art, has added a new dimension
to my enthusiasm for, and knowledge of the
Isle of Wight,
this book is gratefully dedicated.

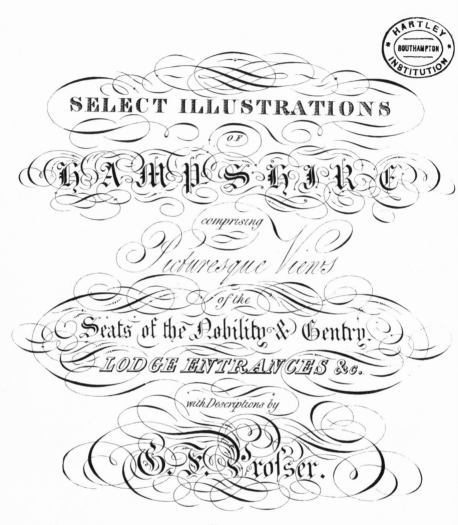

SELECT ILLUSTRATIONS

OF

HAMPSHIRE

comprising

Picturesque Views

of the

Seats of the Nobility & Gentry,

LODGE ENTRANCES &c.

with Descriptions by

G. F. Prosser.

London.

Published by J & A Arch, 61, Cornhill Carpenter & Son, Old Bond Street,
Hampshire, Jacobs & Johnson, Winchester Joyce & Co. Southampton;
1833.
And G. F. Prosser, 10, Grosvenor Terrace, St. George's, Camberwell.
Printed by C. Hullmandel.

[Figure 2; 22.7 x 29.2 cm]

CONTENTS

LIST OF ILLUSTRATIONS

The illustrations are reproduced from title-pages (unless otherwise stated) of books recorded in one or other of the bibliographies. In each case the size of the original is given in centimetres on the figure itself.

All illustrations are taken from copies of books in the Cope Collection,
Southampton University Library.

BATT upon BATT.

A
POEM

UPON

The Parts, Patience, and Pains,

OF

Barth.Kempster,

CLERK, POET, CUTLER,

OF

Holy-Rood–Parifh in *Southampton*.

By a Perfon of Quality.

To which is annexed the VISION,

Wherein is defcribed *Batt's* Perfon and Ingenuity ;

With an Account of the Antient and Prefent State and Glory of
Southampton.
By the fame AUTHOR.

Dedicated to the Gentry of *Hampfhire*, for their Diverfion :
But more efpecially to the Inhabitants of *Southampton.*

LONDON: Printed for *Samuel Crouch.* 1680.

[Figure 3; 13.6 x 18.8 cm]

INTRODUCTION

This work brings together a selection of important bibliographies covering Hampshire* and the Isle of Wight, most of which are both difficult and expensive to procure in their original states; indeed one of them, Cope (1879), has previously been published only in a private edition of 25 copies. These bibliographies have been comprehensively indexed by place, name and subject (see page 389 for further details), since this volume is intended for use as a working tool by the librarian, local historian, antiquarian bookseller, private collector, genealogist, school-teacher, etc. However, notwithstanding its obvious value as a major guide to pre-1900 literature on the county, the uncorrected reprinting of a collection of nineteenth century bibliographies may call for a measure of justification as far as the modern bibliographer is concerned.

Little defence need be advanced on purely historical grounds. In addition to their subject importance, the sources reflect some typical bibliographical forms of their period, comprising, as they do, the catalogue of a gentleman's library; a county bibliography compiled by a provincial bookseller and one of the local clergy; supplements to the latter (also assembled by priests — one Church of England, the other Roman Catholic) published in the proceedings of the county's Field Club; a section from one of the most significant English topographical bibliographies; two extracts from London booksellers' catalogues of material arranged by county; and lastly, part of another general bibliography, based this time on the holdings of a great public library (the British Museum). To compare their different approaches, methods of arrangement, amounts of detail given, and degrees of accuracy, may well prove a fascinating exercise for the student of historical bibliography.

Nevertheless it is hoped that this collection will serve a far wider purpose, in the absence of a more recent compilation. The present work is not an ideal substitute for the new Hampshire bibliography which is so badly needed. Of course it would have been better to correct all the errors in the original sources, eliminate the duplication and reduce the number of serious omissions; but the less-than-perfect arrangement of material ought then to have been improved, and why

* As defined prior to the local government reorganization of April 1974.

should the items for inclusion remain limited to those published before about 1900? In other words, there seemed no point in embarking on a minor tidying-up operation (desirable though it might at first sight appear), especially since no sensible line could be drawn between this and the full scale reconstruction and expansion really required.

As an aside, it can be argued that the task of establishing a comprehensive, up-to-date Hampshire bibliography is almost certainly beyond the capability of a single person. Enough work is involved to occupy a team of bibliographers for a number of years (particularly if the entries were to be similar in standard to those of Upcott), and the publication of the final result would scarcely be an economic proposition. The county bibliography of today must serve a wide range of users. Entries consisting merely of author, title, date of publication and few other details may be acceptable for a bibliographical check-list, but are inadequate to fulfil many needs. The field to be covered is vast. A good Hampshire bibliography would list individually *every* paper in the Field Club's *Proceedings*, not to mention articles in the county's other magazines and those of local interest in general periodicals. Some attempt was made in this direction by several of the bibliographies reprinted here; but despite their undoubted virtues, none of them is in any sense 'complete' and surprising omissions are not hard to find. For example, there is no reference (in the appropriate sources) to Lewis's invaluable *A Topographical Dictionary of England* – the first edition of which, being printed at Andover, additionally qualifies as a local imprint. Furthermore, there are the quite different problems posed by manuscripts and other archival material.

The inescapable conclusion is that there may never be an exhaustive new Hampshire bibliography (unless, perchance, the appearance of this work should prove sufficient stimulus for a latter-day Cope or Gilbert). What are the practical alternatives? Here are two.

(i)   The selective publication of library catalogues:

Several libraries in the county have substantial, well-organised local history collections. These have been professionally catalogued, usually with author and subject entries, and there is no great difficulty in reproducing standard catalogue cards on printed pages (though the end product is functional rather than elegant). This option has an extra advantage: the user knows that every item in the bibliography is held by the library in question.

(ii)   The preparation of specialised bibliographies on relatively narrow aspects of the county:

Other things being equal, the narrower the topic, the better the chance of completeness. In this area, attention may be drawn to the series of guides to historical records produced by the Hampshire Archivists' Group, as examples of one possible approach.

Whatever shortcomings the bibliographies reprinted here may possess, it cannot be denied that they form an essential corpus of source material, with much to offer the present-day user.

The Sources

Each of the sources reproduced here in facsimile (but with revised pagination) has its own peculiar strengths and weaknesses. They combine to give a fairly broad account of the available material; though again it must be emphasised that there are gaps in the coverage, just as there is a certain amount of duplication. Some background information about the bibliographies and their original compilers may not be without interest.

Cope (1879)

The Rev. Sir William Henry Cope, Bt., only son of Lieut.-Gen. Edmund Reilly Cope (1765-1835), was born in 1811. He obtained a bachelor's degree at Trinity College, Dublin in 1831, which was later incorporated at Magdalen Hall, Oxford and led to an M.A. in 1840. W. H. Cope's professional career began in the army; it was as a lieutenant in the Rifle Brigade that he purchased his discharge in 1839 to become ordained as a priest. For a short time he was curate at Easton, near Winchester, but then came the appointments of minor canon and librarian of Westminster Abbey. Cope was also chaplain of Westminster Hospital for ten years until 1851, when he succeeded to the baronetcy. A moderate literary output includes a history of Bramshill, his home, *A Glossary of Hampshire Words and Phrases* published by the English Dialect Society in 1883, and *The History of the Rifle Brigade* (1877). He died at Southsea, from the effects of a chill, in 1892.

Unfortunately it is not known when Cope began to collect Hampshire books. The catalogue reprinted here, of which 25 copies were produced in 1879, lists 717 publications (allowing for the fact that several numbers are used more than once — see page 72, for example); but the collection had certainly doubled in size before his death, as the manuscript catalogue now held by Southampton University Library shows one of the last books to be added, Gilbert & Godwin's *Bibliotheca Hantoniensis* (1891), became item number 1524 according to his revised and enlarged schedule. Due, it is said, to the influence of the then principal (T. W. Shore), Cope's Hampshire collection was bequeathed to the Hartley Institution, which evolved into the University of Southampton. There seems to have been a little difficulty at first regarding some books which could not be accounted for, and the decision to accept the collection as it stood was not finally taken until 1894. For this reason, therefore, it is impossible to trace *every* item listed in Cope (1879); however most of the baronet's books are still available for consultation in the University Library.

Cope's annotated copy of his printed catalogue has also been preserved. Interestingly enough it exhibits very few major corrections: that of greatest importance concerns item 455 (page 53), which is reattributed to Charlotte Yonge. The relationship between Cope (1879) and Gilbert & Godwin (1891) is discussed below, on pages *xv-xvii*.

Gilbert & Godwin (1891)

The firm of H. M. Gilbert, which still exists, was founded by Henry Gilbert (a printer and bookseller formerly of Halstead, Essex) in Bernard Street, Southampton during the year 1859. The business migrated to the High Street for a while around 1875, before establishing itself in Above Bar, where it remained until 1939 (then moving to its present location in Portland Street). In 1895 a Winchester branch was opened.

Henry March Gilbert, son of the founder, was born *c.* 1846. After spending some time with the London bookseller Sotheran, he returned to take over the family business in 1869, following his father's death. H. M. Gilbert lived in Southampton for the next 30 years or so, successively occupying addresses in Millbrook Road, Belmont Road, Hill Lane, and Archers Road (among others). In 1898, or thereabouts, he moved to Winchester, ultimately becoming a City Magistrate, and residing in Grafton Road until his death in 1931 at the age of 85. Apart from his involvement with *Bibliotheca Hantoniensis* he wrote little; but did compile a *Catalogue of the Library, R. Y. S. Castle, Cowes* which was published in 1893, and contributed 'A short sketch of the rise and progress of Nonconformity in Wandsworth' (1882) to a book written by the dissenting minister John Park.

The Rev. George Nelson Godwin, born in 1846, was a native of Winchester. Qualification at the London College of Divinity led to his ordination as a priest in 1870, and subsequently he too was educated at Trinity College, Dublin, obtaining a B.A. in 1884 and his B.D. three years later. In 1877, G. N. Godwin was appointed chaplain of the forces, and continued in the army until 1890 (serving part of this time at Netley Hospital), when he became vicar of East Boldre for three years, and vicar of Popham, near Micheldever for the next five. He was well known as an antiquary and local historian, being a founder member of the Hampshire Field Club, as well as editor of *Hampshire Notes and Queries* for a time. However his most important book is *The Civil War in Hampshire* (1882), of which a new and revised edition was published by H. M. Gilbert & Son in 1904. Godwin's other works include *Materials for English Church History* (1895), an account of Silchester written jointly with John Plummer (1879), and volumes on Southampton and Southsea in the Mate's Illustrated Guides series. He died at Little Walsingham, Norfolk in 1907.

In 1872, H. M. Gilbert (then a young man of about 26) brought out a volume 'printed for subscribers' entitled *Bibliotheca Hantoniensis: an attempt at a Bibliography of Hampshire*, which must be regarded as the first edition of the work later revised and greatly enlarged by Gilbert & Godwin. Although Gilbert's book is undated, it may be safely ascribed to 1872 since a review was printed in the *Southampton Times* for 2nd November of that year. The preface opens with the words

> In sending forth this little volume, the compiler would offer his sincere thanks to those gentlemen who have so kindly come forward to help, including Sir Wm. Heathcote, Bart., the Rev. E. Kell, the Rev. T. L. O. Davies, M.A., S. Shaw, Esq., and especially to Sir Wm. Cope, Bart., who, by his untiring efforts, has rendered so material an assistance in the getting up of this work.

This seems straightforward enough, but the statement concerning the part played by Cope may be responsible for the impression created in some quarters that the baronet himself was the true author. Thus the following note occurs inside a copy of the book held by the Bodleian Library, Oxford (shelf mark 258.d.93)

> A small paper copy was given by Mr. Gilbert. This large paper by Sir W. Cope, Bart. who was really the compiler of the work. H.O.C. [presumably Henry Octavius Coxe – Librarian of the Bodleian, 1860-81].

Studying the annotation in his own copy yields no indication that Cope ever claimed to be the author of this book. The question which immediately springs to mind is: how many of the items in Gilbert's (1872) bibliography are also to be found in Cope's (1879) library catalogue? A survey reveals that about 65% of Gilbert's material is present in Cope (1879), and 40% of Cope's material is also in Gilbert (1872). These figures tend to reinforce this supposition: Cope's rôle went no further than that of a major supplier of information, and certainly did not extend to being 'really the compiler'.

Equally, there is evidence to show how Gilbert drew on data which must have been supplied by Cope. Compare the explanatory notes relating to *Batt upon Batt: a Poem on the Parts, Patience, and Pains of Bartholomew Kempster, Clerk, Poet, and Cutler of Holy Rood Parish, Southampton* as they appear in Cope (1879) and Gilbert (1872):

> *Cope* (1879). The Printer's preface to the 1st Edition is signed T.A., but it is printed for Samuel Crouch. Gough (in a MS. note in the Bodleian Library) says that there was an earlier edition in folio, of 8 pp., and that the Poem has been attributed to Mr. John Rooke, of Southampton. But there seems little doubt that it is by John Speed, M.D., of Southampton, a grandson of the historian.
>
> C. Johnson in his life of Mrs. Elizabeth Mann, states that this satire was said to have broken Batt's heart, and that he printed an answer under the title of "Jack upon Jack," wherein the wit turned on playing on the Doctor's verses. Doctor Speed's enemies asserted that he bought up Batt's impression (I have never seen a copy) and purchased its author's silence with a suit of black.
>
> *Gilbert* (1872). Gough says this work has been ascribed to Mr. John Rooke, of Southampton, who was said to have broken Batt's head. Capt. Johnson, in his life of Mrs. Elizabeth Nash, says Batt printed it under the title of "Jack upon Jack."
>
> The Doctor's enemies asserted that he bought up Batt's impression, and its author's silence, with a suit of black. Batt's wit turned chiefly in playing upon the Doctor's verses. The printer's Preface to the first edition is signed T. A. Gough (in a MS. note) says there was an earlier edition in folio, of eight pages. John Speed, M.D., of Southampton, the reputed author, was grandson of the historian.

There can be little doubt that one of these is derived from the other, and Cope's is clearly the less corrupt version (even though it was published seven years afterwards). In making his note, Gilbert has introduced substantial errors:

(a)   'this satire was said to have broken Batt's *heart*' (Cope) makes more sense in the present context than 'Mr. John Rooke, of Southampton, who was said to have broken Batt's *head*' (Gilbert).

(b)   C. Johnson wrote a life of Mrs. Elizabeth *Mann*, as correctly stated by Cope, not Mrs. Elizabeth *Nash*, as recorded by Gilbert.

(c)   one can safely assume that Batt did not print 'it' (the work — i.e. *Batt upon Batt*) under the title *Jack upon Jack*, but may reasonably conjecture, with Cope, whether he produced an *answer* satirising John (= Jack) Speed with this title.

All these mistakes have been corrected by the baronet in his own copy of Gilbert (1872). As it happens, a portion of the same note in Cope's handwriting (which may date from before the publication of his printed catalogue, since he intended to add the item number of Mrs. Mann's biography but left the space blank) now forms part of his manuscript catalogue. By a stretch of the imagination, 'Batt's heart' might be misread as 'Batt's head' and 'Mrs. Elizabeth Mann' similarly misinterpreted as 'Mrs. Elizabeth Nash'. Independently of this, however, the fact remains that, taken in isolation, Gilbert's version simply does not make sense.

A further decline in accuracy may be observed between Gilbert (1872) and Gilbert & Godwin (1891) where, according to the latter (see page 149), 'the printer's preface to the first edition is signed "T. A. Gough" (in a MS. note)'; the biographer of Mrs. Nash (= Mann) is now called Johns*t*on; and John Speed has become an M.O. The perpetuation of these errors is all the more surprising when it is realised that Gilbert & Godwin made direct use of Cope (1879) in compiling their revised bibliography (indeed a pre-publication announcement of the new edition to members of the Hampshire Field Club specifically mentions Sir William's list). Proof takes the form of their occasional oversight in failing to omit the baronet's library shelf marks: see, for example, the entries for Henry Doman's *Songs of Lymington* (shelf mark Mus.D.ix.) on pages 25 and 111; or those for Humphry Ellis's *Pseudo-Christus* (shelf mark Mus.C.vii.6.) on pages 21 and 113. No shelf marks appear in Gilbert (1872). A rather more alarming result of using Cope (1879) occurs on page 131, in the shape of *Mason's Poetical Excursions in the Isle of Wight* (1777). The latter presumably comes into being through a misunderstanding of the heading for item 288 on page 35, *Mason's* having been taken (inappropriately) from no. 286; especially since Gilbert (1872) correctly enters this anonymous work as *POETICAL EXCURSIONS in the Isle of Wight*. 4to. 1777, and files it under 'P'.

Cope (1879) may not have priority over Gilbert (1872) as far as publication date is concerned, but enough has now been said to defend its position as the first source in this volume and to indicate that, in all probability, the baronet was an active bibliographer long before the bookseller. The reprinting of Gilbert & Godwin (1891) rather than Gilbert (1872) is further justified by the vastly increased content of the later edition, whose major additions include a 35-page section of *Books & Periodicals containing References to Hampshire*, a *List of Hampshire Newspapers* compiled by F. A. Edwards, and a specialised bibliography of *Works on the Natural History & Geololgy* [sic] *of Hampshire*. Its arrangement of material, which would not be adopted today, renders the work sometimes less than easy to use, though the index supplied with this volume should help overcome most difficulties.

Wilson (1896/7)

The Rev. Sumner Wilson (1831-1917) was the only son of Canon William Wilson, D.D., vicar of Holy Rood, Southampton from 1824 to 1873. Sumner Wilson attended Christ Church, Oxford where he obtained his B.A. in 1853 and an M.A. seven years later. He was ordained as a priest in 1856: after a period as curate at Nately Scures came his appointment as vicar of Preston Candover, in 1862, which he held until his death.

Like Cope, he was a collector of Hampshire books. The *Supplementary Hampshire Bibliography* which he contributed to the *Proceedings* of the Hampshire Field Club (for 1896/7) was based on material in his own library. A few of the items listed in this *Supplement*, which was intended mainly to cover pre-1891 publications, are also to be found in Gilbert & Godwin (1891). These include T. W. Shore's article on Hampshire boroughs (pages 193 and 241), Oglander's account of Charles I in the Isle of Wight (pages 170 and 243), and the paper on alien priories by Venables (pages 181 and 243). That they occur here is doubtless due to their having been 'lost' in Gilbert & Godwin's arrangement

Davis (1904-5)

The Rev. Richard George Davis, London born in 1837, was educated partly at Downside and partly in Belgium. Ordained as a Roman Catholic priest in 1862, he held appointments at Southampton, Portsmouth and Aldershot, among other places, before ill health caused his departure for Buckland (1882). In 1885 he became rector of Cowes, and remained there until his retirement in 1909. R. G. Davis was an active member of the Hampshire Field Club: he contributed a number of papers, including *A Second Supplement to Hampshire Bibliography* published in the *Proceedings* for 1904 and 1905 (years during which he was also a vice-president). It is said that, owing to his efforts, Cowes is one of the best documented parishes in the diocese. Davis died at Southampton in 1914.

This second supplement to Gilbert & Godwin (1891) is the only source reprinted here which definitely excludes the Isle of Wight; perhaps because, around 1895, Davis produced an as yet unpublished bibliography of the Island. A copy of the latter was deposited in the British Museum (now the British Library – shelf mark 2330.g.2) and its title-page reads as follows

Bibliotheca Vectensis: a preliminary Catalogue of Books relating to the Isle of Wight, compiled by the Rev. R. G. Davis, Cowes, Isle of Wight. Jas. P. Witham, Typewriter-copyist, &c., Pyle-Ho., Newport, I.W.

Bibliotheca Vectensis, the major part of which is arranged chronologically, covers material published between 1551 and 1894: it includes a significant number of items not listed by any of the sources reproduced in this volume. The general standard of entries is similar to that of Gilbert & Godwin (1891) and its supplements.

Upcott (1818)
The antiquary and collector William Upcott was born in 1779, a native of Oxfordshire. At first he intended becoming a bookseller, but in 1806 came the appointment of sub-librarian at the London Institution, a post he was to hold till his resignation in 1834. Upcott spent the rest of his life at Islington, where he died eleven years later. His house became known as 'Autograph Cottage', for he amassed a huge collection of manuscripts, books, prints, drawings etc. and, after he died, many of the 32,000 autograph letters were bought by the British Museum (Add. MS. 15841-15957).

Upcott's most important work *A Bibliographical Account of the Principal Works relating to English Topography* (3 volumes) was published in 1818. Compiled with the requirements of collectors of county history very much in mind, its value lies in the wealth of detail supplied with each entry. Full collations are given, enabling one to tell whether a particular copy of a book is complete, or lacking plates, maps, or text. The author remarks in the preface that his labours

> have required a close and specific examination of more than fifteen hundred publications of various sizes; whilst in numerous instances several copies of each have been collated and compared, in order to ensure every possible accuracy and correctness; in the course of which he [i.e. Upcott] has been obliged to investigate and examine the great *public*, and some of the most valuable *private libraries* in the kingdom.

Here was no armchair bibliographer! The original edition, limited to 250 copies (50 on large paper), was oversubscribed before publication.

Smith (1878)
John Russell Smith, the London bookseller and publisher, was born at Sevenoaks in 1810 and died at Kentish Town in 1894. Occupying premises in Old Compton Street (1834-52) and Soho Square (1852-88), he was responsible for a variety of bibliographies or catalogues on subjects as diverse as dialects, angling, America and Shakesperiana. J. R. Smith also compiled a *Bibliotheca Cantiana* (1837) and, for a time, issued the Library of Old Authors reprint series. His son, Alfred Russell Smith, worked with him in the business.

The year 1878 saw the appearance of a substantial volume, described on its title-page as

A Catalogue of Ten Thousand Tracts and Pamphlets, and Fifty Thousand Prints and Drawings, illustrating the Topography and Antiquities of England, Wales, Scotland, and Ireland. Collected during the last thirty-five years by the late William Upcott and John Russell Smith. Now offered for sale . . . by Alfred Russell Smith.

The contents of this catalogue were arranged topographically and it was decided, in addition, to issue the section for each county separately. In a brief introduction, John Russell Smith explained that the foundation of this collection was a purchase made in 1841 from William Upcott. It had been Upcott's desire to produce a more comprehensive bibliography of British topography than that published in 1818, so he had gathered material towards this end. Having acquired the collection, J. R. Smith himself added to it during the intervening years. Probably the most valuable feature of this source is the inclusion of prints: naturally the lists are incomplete, but they provide data which is not readily available elsewhere.

Hotten (1863)

Another London publisher and bookseller, John Camden Hotten (originally named John William Hotten), born at Clerkenwell in 1832, was of Cornish extraction. He entered the bookselling trade at the age of 14, but left England for America two years later and stayed there until 1856, when he returned to set up business in Piccadilly, London. Hotten's affairs flourished: in 1866 he became Swinburne's publisher, after Moxon had refused to continue handling the first series of *Poems and Ballads* because of their supposed indecency, and continued to act in this capacity till his death at Hampstead in 1873 (whereupon the poet chose to remain with his successors, Chatto & Windus). He published the first edition of W. S. Gilbert's *Bab Ballads* (1868), collaborated with Jacob Larwood (pseud.) on *The History of Signboards* (1867), and himself wrote *A Dictionary of Modern Slang, Cant and Vulgar Words* (1859 etc.), as well as biographies of Charles Dickens and Mark Twain. Hotten was also associated with literature of a less respectable kind, of which it would be inappropriate to give further details.

The catalogue partly reprinted here, *A Hand-Book to the Topography and Family History of England and Wales*, dates from 1863. According to the introduction, its preparation had taken thirteen hours daily labour for nine long months, though the compiler assures us this was a pleasant task. Perhaps the pleasure is to some extent reflected in the annotation. A few prints were included, but the work's main value lies in the rarity of certain tracts and pamphlets described therein. Item 1951 (page 371) from Hotten's list seems to be identical with no. 2198 (page 330) in Smith's catalogue: if this is indeed the case, note the price has *fallen* from 18s. 6d. in 1863 to 5s. in 1878. Whilst on the subject of prices, it is hardly necessary to state that those occurring in this volume bear no relation whatsoever to present-day market values. Nevertheless, the curious may care to observe (page 373) how Mudie's 3-volume *History of Hampshire* once sold at £2. 12s. 6d. could be bought for 19s. 6d.; or that Englefield's *Isle of Wight* published at £7. 7s. might be purchased for £1. 16s.

Anderson (1881)

John Parker Anderson was born in 1841. He spent over 41 years serving the British Museum, which he entered (aged 18) as an Attendant of the Third Class, being placed almost immediately in the Department of Printed Books. Promotions to Attendant of the Second and First Classes followed when he was 23 and 34 years old, respectively. In 1882, the Trustees recommended that a 'Clerk of the Reading Room' position should be created for him, but this was refused by the Treasury. However the succeeding year saw him appointed 'Assistant of the Second Class for special service in the Reading Room' — a new post. Anderson retired on his 60th birthday.

His published work consists mainly of bibliographies commissioned by other authors: thus he contributed to late-nineteenth century books about the Rossettis, Charles Darwin, Cardinal Manning and Arthur Young. *The Book of British Topography*, which came out in 1881, constitutes a major exception. Writing in the preface, Anderson is careful to point out that his book is in no sense an official publication, based though it is entirely upon the fine collection of topographical material preserved in the British Museum. He explains why poll books and most civil war tracts had to be omitted; also informing the reader how each item is entered using the precise heading under which it will be found when referring to the Museum's own catalogue (the letters 'P.P.', see page 377 for example, denote the 'Periodical Publications' section of the British Museum catalogue). Anderson's arrangement by place makes the bibliography easy to use from this point of view, and there is the extra advantage of knowing the books listed are all held by one (identified) library.

How to Use this Book

There are, no doubt, many ways of using this volume: it is impossible to enumerate them all. The first point to appreciate, though, is that each source may still be used in the manner intended by its original compiler(s). Thus the Gilbert & Godwin (1891) section can be exploited quite independently of the rest of this book, if the reader so chooses. However, for many purposes it will be better to begin with the index — whose arrangement is described on page 389. Do not forget there may be more than one mention of a name or topic on any page to which you are directed.

(1)   If you are looking for a book by a given **author**, or about a particular **person**, it will normally be quickest to use the index.

(2)   If you want material on a specified **subject**, there is little alternative to using the index, unless your requirement falls within the scope of the Natural History & Geology division of Gilbert & Godwin (1891).

(3)   For items concerning a particular **place**, again there is much to be said for using the index; but for a limited amount of information it may be quicker to look under the appropriate heading in Anderson (1881) or, sometimes, to try Gilbert & Godwin (1891) direct.

(4)   Should you require **illustrative material**, the index ought to be used as page numbers for prints are given in **bold type**, making them easy to pick out.

(5)   If your problem is to determine whether a given copy of a Hampshire book is complete, or has something missing, this can be solved providing the item appears in Upcott (1818) — which may be searched without using the index.

(6)   Some antiquarian booksellers have acquired the habit of quoting Anderson (1881) as a reference source in their own catalogues, generally in the form 'Very rare, not in Anderson': to evaluate such comments, it is desirable to know exactly what this bibliography does, and does not contain (e.g. poll books were specifically excluded).

(7)   It may be necessary, on occasion, for serious users to examine every page corresponding to an index entry (with the consequent frustration of encountering duplication of material between the various

sources); most readers, however, will only be looking for 'a few references' or a selection of representative items – sometimes, perhaps, just for an alternative work to one which is not locally available.

How NOT to use this book
(1)   This is a reference book (designed to be consulted, not read from cover to cover), but it is neither a county handbook, nor an encyclopedia, nor a gazeteer: do not attempt to use it as a substitute for these quite different kinds of reference work.

(2)   Do not assume merely because this volume fails to produce something on your chosen place or topic that nothing has been published; there are many *general* books on Hampshire and its regions, not to mention periodical articles, so the information you need may well be buried in one of these – consider browsing in a well-stocked local history collection, or seeking the advice of subject experts, or both.

(3)   The sources reprinted here were compiled mainly during the nineteenth century; therefore this work *cannot* lead you to the latest (or even recent) information on most subjects, neither is it 'complete' for the period which it does cover: do not forget these limitations.

How to get Further Information

People and organizations
The more complicated your information requirement, the wiser it is to seek expert advice. There are centres of local history expertise (in the widest sense) distributed throughout the county: among them are libraries, record offices and museums, which all have qualified staff whose job it is to help you, if you ask. The larger public libraries usually maintain a 'local history' collection of printed material relating to their own area; they may even be able to provide special facilities – an index of relevant articles appearing in newspapers and magazines, for example. Record offices acquire and preserve manuscript or other (unpublished) archive material; such as deeds, wills, family papers, parish and civic records, etc. It is less easy to generalise about museums, since they often concentrate on a particular field (e.g. archaeology, natural history, naval or military history); but their collections may include paintings, prints, photographs and other pictures of local interest, as well as documents (remember most have insufficient space to keep their entire stock on permanent display). Your telephone

directory will guide you to some of these organizations — it is sensible to make contact before your visit as opening hours are often restricted, and professional staff are not always available to deal with problems — alternatively you may enquire at the nearest public library or town hall. Details of several important examples are given below.

Libraries

Hampshire County Library
Headquarters
81 North Walls, Winchester
(Tel: Winchester 3301)

> The staff may be able to advise you whether copies of a specific 'Hampshire' book are held by any of the public libraries within the county.

Isle of Wight County Library
Headquarters
Parkhurst, nr. Newport (I.W.)
(Tel: Newport 2324)

> This library holds the principal 'local history' collection on the island.

Portsmouth Central Library
Guildhall Square, Portsmouth
(Tel: Portsmouth 21441)

Southampton Central Library
Civic Centre, Southampton
(Tel: Southampton 23855)

Southampton University Library
The University, Southampton
(Tel: Southampton 559122)

> The Cope Collection (covering Hampshire and the Isle of Wight) may be used by special arrangement; prior application should be made to the Librarian.

Winchester District Library
Jewry Street, Winchester
(Tel: Winchester 3909)

Record Offices

Hampshire County Record
Office
20 Southgate Street, Winchester
(Tel: Winchester 63153)

Isle of Wight County Record
Office
26 Hillside, Newport (I.W.)
(Tel: Newport 4031)

Portsmouth City Record Office
The Guildhall, Portsmouth
(Tel: Portsmouth 21771)

Southampton City Record
Office
Civic Centre, Southampton
(Tel: Southampton 23855)

Museums

Carisbrooke Castle Museum
Carisbrooke Castle, nr. Newport
(I.W.)
(Tel: Newport 3112)
> This is the island's chief museum, though there is also a geological museum at Sandown.

Portsmouth City Museum and Art Gallery
Museum Road, Portsmouth
(Tel: Portsmouth 811527)
> There are other museums in the city, including Cumberland House Museum and Aquarium (natural history), and Southsea Castle and Museum (naval and military history, archaeology).

Tudor House Museum
St. Michael's Square,
Southampton
(Tel: Southampton 24216)
> Other Southampton museums include the Bargate Guildhall Museum, the Museum of Archaeology, and the Maritime Museum.

Winchester City Museum
The Square, Winchester
(Tel: Winchester 3361)
> The other museums in this city include the Westgate Museum, the Regimental Museum of the Royal Hampshire Regiment, and the Royal Greenjackets Museum.

Finally, do not forget that there are individuals such as writers of local history articles, private collectors, and antiquarian booksellers who might be prepared to supply you with information if approached in the right way.

Guides to printed Sources

To compile a short, well-balanced list of major guides to printed sources of local history information is rather difficult. The present attempt may be justly criticised as incomplete and uneven; it merely represents a very limited, personal choice of items thought to be of potential use.

A Handbook to County Bibliography, being a Bibliography of Bibliographies relating to the Counties and Towns of Great Britain and Ireland, by Arthur L. Humphreys. London, 1917.
> A standard work which, although out of date, has not yet been superseded: it was reprinted in 1974. Entries are arranged (mainly) chronologically by county, but there is also a general section. The index lists names (of people and places) and subjects. N.B. this is a guide to *other* bibliographies, and thus covers material like that reproduced here.

A Bibliography of British Municipal History, including Gilds and Parliamentary Representation, by Charles Gross. New York, 1897. Harvard Historical Studies, 5.
> Another standard work, also out of date. A reprint, with a new introduction, was published by Leicester University Press in 1966. Some

two-thirds of the book consists of entries arranged by town; part of the remaining (general) material being listed by county. There is an index of names (people and places) and subjects.

A Bibliographical Account of the works relating to English Topography in the Library of J. T. Spalding, J.P., Nottingham. 5 vols. Exeter, 1912-13.

The entries in Spalding's catalogue (which was privately printed) are similar in kind to those of Upcott (1818), and more Hampshire items are included.

Scenery of Great Britain and Ireland in Aquatint and Lithography, 1770-1860; from the Library of J. R. Abbey: a Bibliographical Catalogue. London, 1952.

This volume and its companion, *Life in England in Aquatint and Lithography, 1770-1860* (London, 1953), can be extremely helpful when dealing with illustrated books or loose prints. Abbey's *Scenery* has entries arranged by place (the alphabetical sequence for England being a mixture of towns and counties) and they include a full list of the plates in each book. Abbey's *Life* arranges its material in broad subject groups, such as 'Drawing Books and Artists' Sketch Books' or 'Magazines' (listing all the plates ever published in Ackermann's *Repository of Arts*, for example). The following indexes are provided in each volume: artists and engravers; authors; printers, publishers and booksellers; titles. Both works were reprinted in 1972.

It is worth noting that 'local bibliography' theses are occasionally submitted by candidates for Fellowship of the Library Association (F.L.A.). In due course they may be published but, if not, arrangements can be made to consult the original documents at the Library Association, 7 Ridgmount Street, London WC1E 7AE (Tel: 01-636 7543). One example of interest here is *Isle of Wight Local History – a Guide to Sources* by A. G. Parker, which was accepted during 1972/73.

Those concerned with historical maps of the region are referred to a series of articles by E. G. Box entitled 'Hampshire in early Maps and early Road-books' published in *Papers and Proceedings of the Hampshire Field Club and Archaeological Society* (v. 12, pt. 3, pp. 221-235, 1934; v. 13, pt. 1, pp. 61-68, 1935; v. 13, pt. 2, pp. 165-169, 1936), and to a paper by R. V. Turley on 'Printed County Maps of the Isle of Wight, 1590-1870: a check-list and guide for students (and collectors)' also in the Field Club *Proceedings* (v. 31, 1974 – pagination not available at the time of going to press).

Two useful bibliographies dealing with our earlier history, both compiled by Wilfrid Bonser, are *A Romano-British Bibliography*

(55 B.C.-A.D. 449) (2 vols. Oxford, 1964) and *An Anglo-Saxon and Celtic Bibliography (450-1087)* (2 vols. Oxford, 1957): these are well indexed, name and subject approach being provided for. The *Index of Archaeological Papers, 1665-1890* edited by George Laurence Gomme (2 vols. London, 1907) is of more limited use, as it is arranged alphabetically by author and has no subject index; but details of some Hampshire Field Club papers appear in *A Guide to the Historical and Archaeological Publications of Societies in England and Wales, 1901-1933* compiled by E. L. C. Mullins (London, 1968), which has indexes covering names and subjects. Publications of local record societies are listed in *Texts and Calendars: an analytical guide to serial publications* by E. L. C. Mullins (Royal Historical Society Guides and Handbooks, no. 7: London, 1958); and a few Hampshire directories will be found via *Guide to the National and Provincial Directories of England and Wales, excluding London, published before 1856* by Jane E. Norton (Royal Historical Society Guides and Handbooks, no. 5: London, 1950).

Perhaps the most elusive category of all local literature, though, is 'topographical fiction' — elusive because it is often written by minor authors and, in the past at any rate, little effort has been made to systematically identify and preserve it. One of the comparatively few sources of information about this neglected field is the popular series of illustrated guide-books published by Ward, Lock & Co., especially during the earlier years of this century. These guides (with their distinctive red covers) usually have a literary note near the beginning, which gives details of novels whose background is set in the area concerned: the idea being, presumably, to suggest some appropriate holiday reading.

Lastly, it must be re-emphasised that only a handful of sources and guides have been mentioned here; therefore you are urged to get in touch with the staff at one of the larger libraries if you experience difficulty in obtaining the information you require.

Acknowledgements

A number of people have helped me with the preparation of this work, and I wish to extend my thanks to them all. However, I am particularly grateful to the following: The Librarians of Southampton and Leicester Universities, for kind permission to use books from their Libraries in the making of this reprint; G. Hampson, Esq., librarian responsible for the Cope Collection (Southampton University Library), for his friendly advice and encouragement at all times; Barry Shurlock, my publisher, for enthusiastically accepting the basic idea of this book and converting it into reality; B. L. Gilbert, Esq., D.F.C., J.P., of Southampton, for studying the introduction (especially that portion dealing with his family business) and according a welcome to the reappearance of his grandfather's pioneer bibliography; Robert Burrell, of Southampton Central Library, for assisting with the investigation of some Hampshire worthies; C. W. F. Skrimshire, Esq., of Southampton, for sparing time from his genealogical researches to pursue an enquiry at the Bodleian Library on my behalf; Mrs. A. Hopley of the Director's Office, The British Museum, for supplying information about the career of J. P. Anderson; and last, but definitely not least, J. Munro, Esq., of Northampton, for his helpful comments on bibliographical sources (which led, among other things, to the inclusion of the extract from Hotten's catalogue in this volume). To my wife and family I can only apologise, for depriving them of my attention for so many long hours.

R.V.T.
Southampton University Library
28th June, 1975.

A CANDID

REVIEW of FACTS,

In the LITIGATION between

PETER BARFOOT, Efq.

A N D

RICHARD BARGUS, and OTHERS,

W I T H T H E

BISHOP of WINCHESTER,

Concerning the RIGHT of

FAREHAM QUAY.

D E C I D E D

By the FINAL AWARD

O F

ROBERT POPE BLACHFORD, Efq.

Of OSBORNE, in the ISLE of WIGHT.

RARO ANTECEDENTEM SCELESTUM
DESERUIT PEDE POENA, CLAUDO.———HORACE.

L O N D O N:

PRINTED FOR GREEN AND CO. No. 176, NEAR SURRY STREET,
STRAND.
MDCCLXXXVIII.

[Figure 4; 13.6 x 22.6 cm]

THE

ISLE OF WIGHT

𝕲𝖆𝖗𝖑𝖆𝖓𝖉.

IN THREE PARTS.

PART I. *The Outlandish Lady's Love to an English Sailor.*

PART II. *The Lady's Love discovered by her Waiting-Maid to her Father.*

PART III. *The Wandering Lady's Return; or the Stony Heart Softened.*

RYDE, ISLE OF WIGHT.

1839.

[Figure 5; 10.0 x 16.1 cm]

A

LIST

OF BOOKS RELATING TO

HAMPSHIRE,

ITS

PLACES, PERSONS, AND HISTORY;

IN THE LIBRARY AT

BRAMSHILL,

COLLECTED BY

SIR WILLIAM H. COPE, Bart.

[Not Published.]

PRINTED BY W. J. GOTELEE,

WOKINGHAM.

1879.

[1]

Twenty-five copies printed.

A LIST,

&ca.

1 ACCOUNT of the character of the Right Honble.
Henry Bilson Legge [with letters and particulars
relating to the Hampshire Election, 1759].
4to., Lond., 1764.

2 ACT confirming an Agreement between the principal
Officers of the Ordnance and Thomas Missing,
Esq., for Exchange of Lands at Portsmouth.
fol., Lond., 1723.

3 ACT for repairing the Highways from Street Bridge,
Petersfield, to Portsmouth.
fol., Lond., 1726.

4 ACT for repairing the Highways from Crown Corner,
Reading, to Basingstoke.
fol., Lond., 1736.

5 ACT for inclosing the Common fields in Abbots Ann.
fol., Lond., 1774.

6 ACT for inclosing the Common fields in Kingsomborn.
fol., Lond., 1783.

7 ACT for inclosing the Common fields in Andover.
fol., Lond., 1784.

8 ACT for inclosing the Common fields in Upper
Clatford.
fol., Lond., 1785.

9 ACT for inclosing Frodington, otherwise Fradding-
ton, otherwise Fratton Common and Southsea
Common in Portsea.
fol., Lond., 1785.

10   Act for inclosing the Common fields in Broughton.
fol., Lond., 1789.

11   Act for inclosing the Common fields of Odiham, Northwarnborough, Hillside, Rye, and Stapely in Odiham.   fol., Lond., 1789.

12   Act for inclosing the Common fields in Dibden.
fol., Lond., 1790.

13   Act for inclosing the Common fields in Shipton.
fol., Lond., 1792.

14   Act for inclosing the Common fields in Monk Sherborne.   fol., Lond., 1792.

15 Act for inclosing Lands in Elvetham.
fol., Lond., 1813.

16   Act for confirming an agreement between the Warden and Scholars of Saint Mary College, Winchester, and Robert Pope Blachford, Esq., for exchange of Lands in Whippingham, Isle of Wight.   fol., Lond., n.d.

17   Act for repairing the Road from the Golden Farmer, near Bagshot, to Hertfordbridge Hill.
KK.iv. $\frac{7}{3}$ 16mo., Lond., 1757.

18   Act for repairing the Road from the Golden Farmer, near Bagshot to Hertfordbridge Hill, Basingstoke, and Odiham.
Mus. B.iv. $\frac{17}{3}$ 8vo., Lond., 1819.

19   Act for repairing and improving the Road from Stockbridge to Winchester and Southampton.
fol., Lond., 1823.

20   Act for maintaining the Road from Winchester, through Whitchurch, &ca., to Andover.
fol., Lond., 1823.

21 ACT for making a railway from London to Southampton.
    Mus. C.ii., 6.   fol., Lond., 1834.

22 ADAMS (W. H. DAVENPORT). The Garden Isle ; the History, Topography, and Antiquities of the Isle of Wight.
    Mus. C.ii. 23.   4to., Lond., 1856.

23 ———— Nelson's Handbook of the Isle of Wight.   8vo., Lond., 1866.

———— *See* Briddon.

24 ADKINS, (THOMAS). Records of the Church of Christ of the Independent denomination at Southampton, from its establishment to the present time.
    Mus. B.v. 16. 12mo., Southampton, 1836.

25 ———— Jubilee of The Rev. T. Adkins ; Proceedings of Public Meetings. Edited by John Bullar.
    Mus. B.v. 17. 12om., Southampton, [1860.]

AITKEN, (T. J.) *See* Bournemouth.

26 AKERMAN, (JOHN YONGE). Account of Excavations on the site of some ancient Potteries in the New Forest.
    Mus.   4to., Lond., 1853.

27 AKERMAN, (R.) History of Winchester College.
    Mus. C.ii. 2.   4to., Lond., 1816.

28 ALBIN, (J.) Companion to the Isle of Wight.
    Mus. D.ix. 12. 12mo., Newport., 1802.

29 ———— The same.
    Mus. B.v. 13. 12mo., Newport, 1813.

30 ———— The same.
    Mus. D.ix. 9. 12mo., Newport, 1823.

31　ALBIN, (J.)　History of the Isle of Wight.
　　　　Mus. B.iii., 13.　　8vo., Newport, 1795.

32　ALLEN, (LAKE).　History of Portsmouth, with the
　　towns of Portsea and Gosport, &ca.
　　　　Mus. B.v. 10.　　12mo., Lond., 1817.

33　ANDOVER Union.　Two letters to the Right Honble.
　　Sir George Grey, Bart., (by H. W. Parker).
　　　　Mus. D.ix. $\frac{1}{18}$　　8vo., Lond., 1847.

34　ASHBURNER, (ED.)　Sermon at the Ordination of
　　Sir Harry Trelawny, at Southampton, with Sir
　　Harry's confession of faith.
　　　　　　　　　　8vo., Southampton, 1777.

35　ASHLEY, (JOHN).　Mr. Moberly and the letter which
　　appeared at Mr. Pearce's bank, at Southampton.
　　A short answer of the matter.
　　　　Mus. D., ix. $\frac{10}{7}$　12mo., Southampton, 1857.

36　ATCHESON, (R. S.)　History of Churcher's College
　　at Petersfield, with Life of Churcher.
　　　　Mus. B.iii. 5.　　8vo., Lond., 1823.

37　————　Report of the case of the Borough of
　　Petersfield, tried by the House of Commons
　　in 1820.
　　　　Mus. B.iii., 23.　　8vo., Lond., 1831.

38　ATKINS, (HENRY).　The Isle of Wight.　A Poem.
　　　　Mus. D.ix.　8vo., Lond. [Chichester], 1832.

39　————　The Isle of Wight ; a Poem, with other
　　pieces in verse.
　　　　Mus. D.ix.　12mo. Lond. [Chichester], 1837.

40　BAIGENT, (FRANCIS JOSEPH).　The family of De
　　Lymerston, and its heiress, the foundress of the
　　Tichborne dole.
　　　　Mus. B.iii. $\frac{3}{6}$　　　8vo., n.p. or d.

41 BAIGENT, (F. J.) Locks on pews [in Elvetham Church].
>   Mus. D.ix. $\frac{2}{24}$ 8vo., Broadsheet.

42 ———— On the Martyrdom of St. Thomas of Canterbury, and other paintings, discovered at St. John's Church, Winchester.
>   Mus. B.iii. $\frac{3}{4.5.}$ 8vo., n.p. or d.

43 ———— Sheriff's Seals in Hampshire.
>   Mus. B.iii. $\frac{3}{7}$ 8vo., Lond., n.d.

44 ———— Unlearned Clerks [in Hants].
>   Mus. D.ix. $\frac{2}{23}$ 8vo., Broadsheet.

45 ———— Winchester in 1852 and 1865.
>   Mus. D.ix. $\frac{2}{21}$ 3 pp., 8vo., 1865.

46 ———— History and Antiquities of the Parish Church of Wyke, near Winchester.
>   Mus. B.iii. $\frac{3}{3}$ 8vo., Winchester. 1865.

47 ———— Another copy.
>   Mus. D.ix. $\frac{3}{7}$

48 BAILEY, (CHARLES). Transcripts from the Municipal archives of Winchester, and other documents, elucidating the government, manners, and charters of the same city.
>   Mus. D.ix. 7.   8vo., Winchester, 1856.

49 BALL, (CHARLES). Historical Account of Winchester, with descriptive walks.
>   Mus. B.iii. 1.   4to, Winchester, 1818.

50 BARBER, (T.) Picturesque Illustrations of the Isle of Wight.
>   Mus. B.iii. 4.   8vo., Lond., n.d.

51 BARING, (WILLIAM BINGHAM). Letter to the Inhabitants of Winchester, on his conduct as a Magistrate, in the arrest of Mr. and Mrs. Deacle.
>   Mus. D.ix. $\frac{1}{4}$ 8vo., Lond. [Winchester], 1831.

52 BARING, (W. B.) Answer to Mr. Bingham Baring's letter to the Inhabitants of Winchester on his conduct as a Magistrate, &ca.
Mus. D.ix. $\frac{1}{6}$ 8vo., Winchester, 1831.

53 ———— Reply to a letter of, in justification of the arrest of Mr. and Mrs. Deacle ; by the Rev. D. Williams.
Mus. D.ix. $\frac{1}{5}$ 8vo., Lond., 1832.

54 ———— Letter to the Hon. W. B. Baring, being a defence of his more active friends at the late election for Winchester, and a protest on their behalf against some of the views contained in his published, "Vindication." By a Conservative Reformer.
Mus. D.ix. $\frac{1}{7}$ 8vo., Winchester, 1835.

55 ———— Correspondence between the Hon. W. B. Baring and his election committee, upon their requisition that agreeably to the tenor of a written pledge he should resign his seat as one of the representatives of Winchester.
Mus. D.ix. $\frac{1}{3}$ 8vo., Winchester, 1837.

56 BARNES, (JOHN, of Winchester). An essay on Fate, and other Poems, by John Barnes, 14 years of age.
Mus. D.ix.   12mo., Winchester, 1807.

57 BARTLETT, (J. PEMBERTON). Ancient Potteries in the New Forest (plates).
Mus. D.ix. $\frac{3}{9}$ 6pp., 8vo.

58 BASING HOUSE : The History of ; with an account of the siege.   10th edit., 8vo., Basingstoke, 1858.
Mus. B.ix. $\frac{18}{5}$

59 BASING CHURCH *See* Wyatt.

60 BASINGSTOKE. Abstract of an Act for enlarging the Market-place in Basingstoke.

Mus. D.ix. $\frac{3}{5}$ 8vo., Basingstoke, 1829.

———————— *See* Jefferson.—Loggon.—Millard.

61 [BASKETT, (HERBERT).] The Island Minstrel, by H. FitzHerbert. 12mo., Lond. [Ryde], 1842.

The writer of this volume of poems was Herbert Baskett, a journeyman gardener, son of Thomas Baskett, for many years a resident and owner of a lodging house and garden, on the West side of George Street, Ryde.

Herbert Baskett was born in Ryde, and received his very limited education at the National Schools, in Melville Street. His natural talent for a long time was known only to his own family, to whom he was in the habit of reading the poems, which, composed while working with his spade in his father's garden, he committed to paper during the leisure of the evening. The MSS. were written in a hand, almost as illegible to himself as to others, but the fame of their contents after a time becoming known beyond the humble circle for which they were intended —publication followed. The refinement of taste and ideas, which would appear to be inseparable from poetry, had not their civilizing effect on Baskett, who died a victim to drinking.—J.H.H.

MS. note in my copy of these poems.

62 BATT UPON BATT : a Poem on the Parts, Patience, and Pains of Barth. Kempster, Clerk, Poet, Cutler, of *Holy Rood*-Parish, in *Southampton*. By a Person of quality [Dr. John Speed] to which is annexed the Vision, wherein is described *Batt's* Person and Ingenuity ; with an account of the antient and present state and glory of *Southampton*. By the same Author.

Mus. B.v. 6. 4to., Lond., 1680.

63 ———————— Another copy. Mus. C.vii. $\frac{3}{6}$

64 ———————— 5th Edition.
Mus. 8vo., Lond, 1706.

65 ———————— 5th Edition.
Mus. Reprint. 8vo., Dublin, 1709.

The Printer's preface to the 1st Edition is signed T.A., but it is printed for Samuel Crouch. Gough (in a MS. note in the Bodleian Library) says that there was an earlier edition in folio, of 8 pp., and that the Poem has been attributed to Mr. John Rooke, of Southampton. But there seems little doubt that it is by John Speed, M.D., of Southampton, a grandson of the historian.

C. Johnson in his life of Mrs. Elizabeth Mann, states that this satire was said to have broken Batt's heart, and that he printed an answer under the title of "Jack upon Jack," wherein the wit turned on playing on the Doctor's verses. Doctor Speed's enemies asserted that he bought up Batt's impression (I have never seen a copy) and purchased its author's silence with a suit of black.

66 BEAL, (SAMUEL BENONI). Church of Saint Thomas, Newport, Isle of Wight. Elizabeth Stuart, the Prisoner of Carisbrook (plates).
4to., Lond., 1856.

67 BEARDMORE, (J.) Catalogue of the Collection of Ancient Arms and Armour, at Uplands, near Fareham (plates).
Mus. A. 4.   fol., Lond., 1844.

68 BERRY, (WILLIAM). Pedigrees of the Families of the County of Hants.
Mus. C.ii. 4.   fol., Lond., 1833.

69 BERTHON, (E. L.) The Fareham Life Boat (plates).
8vo., Fareham, 1853.

70 BEVIS. History of the famous and extraordinary Sir Bevis of Southampton, carefully revised from a very ancient copy in black letter.
Mus. C.ix. 2. 8vo., Southampton, 1775.

71 ——— The Adventures of Sir Bevis of Hamptown; with an Historical Preface, by E. H. Jones.
Mus. D.ix. 12mo., Southampton, 1870.

72 BINGLEY, (WILLIAM). Topographical account of the Hundred of Bosmere, comprising the Parishes of Havant, Warblington, and Hayling (plates).
Mus. B.iii. 21. 4to., Havant Press, 1817.

A note at the end of the Introduction states that this work was compiled for the use of an intended History of Hampshire, undertaken by the Rev. William Bingley, under the patronage of the Right Hon. George Rose; but as that work was laid aside, a few copies only were printed for the author's friends.

73 BLACK'S Guide to Hampshire and the Isle of Wight.
XX.vii. 14.   8vo., Edinburgh, 1861.

74 BLAIR, (WILLIAM).   Letter to Dr. Jenner, on the
supposed failures of vaccination at Ringwood,
Hants.
Mus. C.vi. 7.   8vo., Lond., 1808.

75 BLOME, (RICHARD).   Hantshire.   (From his Brit-
tannia.)   (Map.)   fol., Lond., 1673.

76 BONCHURCH.   A Remembrance of Bonchurch, Isle
of Wight, [by Harriet Sewell].
Mus. D.ix. 8.   8vo., Lond., 1849.

77 BONNER, (G. W.)   Picturesque Views in the Isle
of Wight, Hampshire, &c.   Letterpress by C.
Mackenzie.
Mus. C.ii. 13.   Oblong 4to., Lond., n.d.

78 BOURNEMOUTH, Visitor's Guide to.   2nd Edition
with Appendix, by Thomas Johnstone Aitkin, M.D.
Mus. D.ix. $\frac{6}{4}$ 8vo., Poole, 1842.

79 BRAMSHILL.   Pictures in the Reredos of the Chapel
of Bramshill House.
Mus. D.ix. $\frac{10}{9}$ 12mo.

80 ———— Recollections of a visit to Bramshill.
Mus. B.iv. $\frac{18}{6}$ 8vo., Lond., n.d.

Reprinted, for private circulation, from Sir Bernard Burke's " Visitation
of the Seats of Noblemen and Gentlemen in Great Britain."

81 ———— Account of Bramshill House.   From
" The Antiquary."   4to., Lond., June, 1873.

82 BRANDER, (GUSTAVUS).   Fossilia Hantoniensia
(plates).
Mus. C.ii. 11.   4to., Lond., 1766.

83 BRANNON, (GEORGE). Graphic delineations of the
    most prominent objects in the Isle of Wight.
                            Oblong, Wootton, I.W., n.d.

84 —————— Picture of the Isle of Wight.
    (Map and plates.)   8vo., Wootton, 1842.
    Mus. D.ix. $\frac{4}{10}$

85 —————— Pleasure Visitors' Companion to the
    Isle of Wight.
    Mus. D.ix. 13.   8vo., Wootton, 1843.

86 —————— Sketches of the Isle of Wight, illustra-
    tive of Leigh Richmond's " Annals of the Poor."
    (plates.)
    Mus. B.iii. $\frac{4}{2}$ 8vo., Wootton, 1832.

87 —————— Vectis Scenery : Views of the Picturesque
    beauties of the Isle of Wight.
    Mus. C.ii. 26.   4to., Wootton, 1842.

88 BRANNON, (PHILIP). Stranger's Guide to Netley
    Abbey.
    Mus. C.viii. $\frac{7}{3}$ 8vo., Southampton.

89 —————— Stranger's Guide to Southampton.
    Mus. C.viii. $\frac{7}{2}$ 8vo., Southampton.

90 BRETTELL, (T.) Handbook to the Isle of Wight,
    comprising its History, Topography, &c.   3rd
    Edition.
    Mus. C.viii. $\frac{2}{2}$ 8vo., Lond., 1849.

91 BRIDDON, (J.) Handbook to the Isle of Wight.
    Mus. D.ix. $\frac{8}{3}$ 8vo., Ryde, n.d.

91* —————— An earlier Edition ; adds by W. H.
    D. Adams, Esq.

92 BRION and WILKIN. Geology, Topography, and
    Antiquities of the Isle of Wight (Geological map).
    Mus. C.ii. 16.   8vo., Newport, 1859.

93 BRISTOW, (H. W.) Geology of the Isle of Wight.
   Mus. B.iii. $\frac{19}{2}$ 8vo., Lond., 1862.

94 ———— and WHITAKER, (W.) Geology of parts
   of Berkshire and Hampshire.
   Mus. B.iii. $\frac{19}{3}$ 8vo., Lond., 1862.

95 BRITISH Topography. Views in Hampshire (plates
   only, in various states).
   Mus. C.ii. 28.   4to., Lond., 1800.

96 BRITTON and BRAYLEY. Topographical and Histori-
   cal description of Hampshire and the Isle of
   Wight. From the " Beauties of England and
   Wales."
   Mus. B.iv. 11.   8vo., Lond., 1805.

   This copy belonged to Sir Henry Ellis ; has a MS. Index and some
   notes and corrections by him ; and has some plates inserted.

97 BROMFIELD, (W. A.) List of Plants likely to be
   found growing wild in the Isle of Wight.
   Mus. B.vi. 1.   12mo., Ryde, 1840.

98 ———— Flora Vectensis : a description of the
   Flowering Plants of the Isle of Wight. Edited
   by Hooker and Bell (with Map).
   Mus. B.vi. 1.   8vo., Lond., 1856.

99 BROMLEY, (S.) Southampton and the Isle of
   Wight, a Poem, in four books.
   Mus. D.ix.   12mo., 1849.

100 BROWNE, (JOHN, [of Whitchurch].) Poetical Trans-
    lations from various authors.
    4to., Lond., 1786.

101 BROWNE, (SAMUEL, [of Tadley].) Travels of
    Seektruth.
    Mus. D.viii. 26. 12mo., Basingstoke, 1805.

102   BUCKLAND, (FRANK).   Reminiscences of Winchester College. [From " Temple Bar Magazine."]
　　　　　Mus. D.ix. $\frac{3}{17}$　10pp., 8vo., Lond., 1873.

103   BULLAR, (JOHN).   Companion in a visit to Netley-Abbey, to which is annexed Mr. Keate's Elegy. 4th Edition.　　　12mo., Southampton, 1812.

104　——— 7th Edition.
　　　　　Mus. C.viii. $\frac{5}{5}$　12mo., Southampton, 1833.

105　——— 9th Edition, enlarged.
　　　　　Mus. D.ix. $\frac{10}{3}$　12mo., Southampton, 1844.

106　——— Another copy.
　　　　　Mus. D.ix. $\frac{11}{3}$

107　——— Companion in a tour round Southampton.   2nd Edition.
　　　　　Mus. C.viii. 2.   12mo., Southampton, 1801.

108　——— 4th Edition.
　　　　　Mus. C.viii. 3.   12mo., Southampton, 1819.

109　——— Historical and Picturesque Guide to the Isle of Wight.
　　　　　Mus. C.viii. $\frac{5}{3}$　12mo., Southampton, 1806.

110　——— 9th Edition.
　　　　　Mus. D.ix. $\frac{7}{2}$　　12mo., Lond., n.d.

111　——— Historical Particulars relating to Southampton.
　　　　　Mus. B.iv. $\frac{18}{2}$　8vo., Southampton, 1820.

112　——— and DREW, (JOHN).   Hints to assist Visitors to Southampton and the Isle of Wight.
　　　　　Mus. B.iv. $\frac{17}{5}$　8vo., Southampton, 1846.

BURLEY, (Capt. JOHN).   *See* Civil War pamphlets.

113 CALVERT, (F.) The Isle of Wight ; pictorially illustrated and accompanied by Topographical, Geographical, and Historical descriptions.
Mus. C.ii. 22. 4to., Lond., 1846.

114 CAMDEN, (WILLIAM). Hampshire (from his " Britannia "). fol., Lond., 16 ...

115 ———— Hampshire and the Isle of Wight (from his " Britannia "), with additions by Richard Gough, (Map and Plate).
fol., Lond., 1806.

116 CARISBROOKE. Historical recollections of Carisbrooke Castle.
Mus. D.ix. $\frac{10}{2}$ 12mo., Lond., 1849.

117 ———— Carisbrooke Castle. From the " Sixpenny Magazine."
Mus. D.ix. $\frac{2}{14}$ 8vo., Lond., 1862.

118 ———— The case of Breeks v. Woolfrey [relating to the setting up a monument in Carisbrooke Churchyard], with the judgment of Sir Herbert Jenner thereon added in MS.
Mus. D.ix. $\frac{1}{12}$ 8vo., Lond., 1838.

119 CARNARVON, (HENRY, Earl of). Hampshire : its early and later History ; being two Lectures delivered at the Basingstoke Literary Institute.
KK. iv. $\frac{3}{6}$ 12mo, 1857.

120 CARTER, (O. B.) Ancient painted glass of Winchester Cathedral, traced from the windows (coloured plates).
Mus. C.ii. 25. 4to., Lond., 1845.

121 CASE of Appellants and Respondents before the House of Lords, between James Middleton and others and Richard Welles and others relating to property in Hampshire. fol., 1785.

122   CASSAN, (S. H.) Lives of the Bishops of Winchester, from Birinus, first Bishop of the West Saxons, to the present time (Tomline). 2 vols. Mus. B.iii. 14. 8vo., Lond. [Frome], 1827.

123   CATALOGUE of the Marquesses and Earles of Winchester. Together with their several Arms, Wives, and Issue. (From Milles' " Catalogue of Honour.")   fol., Lond., 1610.

124   —— of Works of Art, collected at Winchester in June, 1875.   Winchester, 1875.

125   CAVE, (JANE). Entertaining, Elegiac, and Religious Poems (portrait). Mus. D.viii. $\frac{24}{2}$ 12mo., Winchester, 1783.

126   Some of these Poems were reprinted (Bristol, 8vo. n.d.) under the title " Prose and Poetry, by Mrs. Rueful, with the story of her married life." It is a most curious work. Miss Cave (of Winchester), the authoress, seems to have made a most unfortunate marriage.

127   CHAFIN, (WILLIAM). Anecdotes respecting Cranborn Chase. Mus. D.ix. 3.   8vo., Lond., 1818.

CHARLES I. *See* Civil War Tracts.

128   CHILDREN of the New Forest. (From " London Society.") Mus. D.ix. $\frac{2}{15}$ 8vo., Lond., 1862.

129   CHRISTCHURCH. Historical account of Christchurch, with notices of the Seats of the Nobility, Antiquities, &c. Mus. D.ix. $\frac{9}{3}$ 8vo., Christchurch, 18 ...

CIVIL WAR.

130   An Uprore at Portsmouth : being an advertizement to all Captaines and others that are halting betweene two opinions. Shewing how Captaine *Wiles*, who was sent forth for the defence of the

kingdome, did tyrannize over his Souldiers, and
how hee did revolt to His Majestie, &ca.
> Mus. C.vii. 5.   4to., Lond., *August*, 18, 1642.

131   A Declaration Of all the passages at the taking of
Portsmouth, &ca.
> Mus. C.vii. $\frac{5}{2}$ 4to., Lond., *Septemb.* 15, 1642.

132   A True relation of the Passages which happened
at the Town of Portsmouth at the late Siege,
which began the 12th day of *August* last, and was
surrendered on the 7th day of *September* following, 1642. *Written by one that was employed in
that service.*
> Mus. C.vii. 4.   4to., Lond., *Septemb.* 21, 1642.

133   His Majesty's two proclamations to the Counties
of Southampton and Dorset, &ca.
> Mus. C.vii. $\frac{5}{3}$ 4to., Oxford, 1642.

134   Good Newes from *South Hampton* and *Basingstoke*,
in *Hampshire*, &ca.
> Mus. C.vii. $\frac{5}{4}$ 4to., Lond., 1642.

135   A True And Exact Relation Of A Great Overthrow given to the Cavalliers in *Winchester*, by
Colonel *Hurrey*, Colonel Browne, and some
others, &ca.
> Mus. C.vii. $\frac{5}{5}$ 4to., Lond., *Decemb.* 17, 1642.

136   A True Relation Of The Marchings Of The Red
Trained Bonds of *Westminster*, the Green *Auxiliaries* of *London*, and the Yellow Auxiliaries of
the *Tower* Hamlets, under the Command of Sir
William Waller. . . Briefly Delineating most
of the chiefest Passages in the Service, performed
by Sir *William Waller*, at *Basing*, *Farnham*, and
Alton, &ca. By *Elias Archer*, Lieftenant to
Captain *William Archer*.
> Mus. C.vii. $\frac{5}{6}$ 4to., Lond., 1643.

137 Mercurius Aulicus, May 11, 1644. Containing news from *Fording-Bridge, Bishops-Waltham,* and Portsmouth.

   Mus. C.vii. $\frac{5}{7}$ 4to.

138 A Coppie of Lieut. Gen. Cromwel's Letter ; Concerning the taking of Winchester Castle : &ca.

   Mus. C.vii. $\frac{5}{3}$ 4to., Lond., Octob. 9, 1645.

139 *His Majesties* Grievances Sent By a Message from His Majesty, by Mr. *John Ashburnham,* and Sir *John Barkley,* to Col. *Hammond,* Governor of the Isle of *Wyght,* &ca.

   Mus. C.vii. $\frac{5}{9}$ 4to., Lond., 1647.

140 His Majesties Gracious *Message* and Propositions From the Isle of *Wyght,* for settling of the *Church and Kingdom, and paying of the Army,* &ca. Mus.C.vii. $\frac{2}{2}$ 4to., Lond., 1647.

141 The Last Newes From The Isle Of Wight.

   Mus. C.vii. $\frac{1}{2}$ 4to., Lond., 1647.

142 A Letter Written By *John Ashburnham* Esquire, from *Carisbrook* Castle in the Isle of *Wight, Novemb.* 26, 1647, to *William Lenthall* Esquire, Speaker of the Honourable House of Commons.

   Mus. C.vii. 2.   4to., Lond., 1647.

143 His Majesties Most Gracious Message To His two Houses of Parliament, In prosecution of Peace, By A Personal Treatey.

   Mus. C.vii. $\frac{5}{10}$ 4to., Lond., 1647.

144 A Message And Declaration Sent From Colonel *Whaley.* . . Concerning The King's Majesties Royall Person. . . [in the Isle of Wight.]

   Mus. C.vii. $\frac{5}{11}$ 4to., Lond., 1647.

145 The Modest Cavallieres Advice : Together with a letter to the inhabitants of the Isle of Wight, where his Sacred Majesty is now remaining.
Mus. C.vii. 3.   4to., n.p., 1647.

146 His Majesties Most Gracious Answer To The Bils & Propositions Presented to Him at *Carisbrook Castle*, &ca.
Mus. C.vii. $\frac{5}{12}$ 4to., Lond., 1648.

147 A Declaration from the *Isle of Wyght*, and County of *Hampshire* Concerning the King : And the trials of Captain *Burley*, &ca.
Mus. C.vii. $\frac{5}{13}$ 4to., Lond., 1648.

148 Captaine *Burley* His Speech At The Place of Execution at *Winchester*, &ca.
Mus. C.vii. $\frac{3}{2}$ 4to., Lond., 1648.

149 The Independent's Loyalty. Or, The Most Barbarous Plot (to Murther his sacred Majestie) very fully Discovered, &ca.
Mus. C.vii. $\frac{5}{14}$ 4to., n.p., 1648.

150 The Votes And Proceedings In Parliament For Bringing the King out of the Isle of Wight, &ca.
Mus. C.vii. $\frac{2}{7}$ 4to., Lond., 1648.

151 Two Letters From The Isle of Wight, Being a true Relation of Mr. *Osborn's* carriage and proceedings, &ca.
Mus. C. vii. $\frac{2}{4}$ 4to., Lond., 1648.

152 A Letter Sent From the Speakers of both Houses of Parliament to his Majestie in the Isle of *Wight*. . . . Also his Majesties Answer to the said Letter, &ca.
Mus. C.vii. $\frac{5}{15}$ 4to., Lond., 1648.

153 My Lord Of Pembrokes Speech To His *Majesty* Concerning The Treaty : . . at *Newport*, in the Isle of *Wight*, &ca.
Mus. C.vii. $\frac{5}{16}$ 4to., n.p., 1648.

154 A Messenger Sent to the City of London With A Packet of Letters from the Isle of Wight, &ca.
Mus. C.vii. $\frac{2}{5}$ 4to., Lond., 1648.

155 Three New Queries Presented by the *Commissioners* To The King's Majestie at the *Treating*-house in Newport, and his Majesties most Gracious answer to the said Queries, &ca.
Mus. C.vii $\frac{2}{6}$ 4to., Lond., 1648.

156 The Soules Soliloquie . . a Sermon before the King at *Newport*, in the Isle of *Wight*, . . . by . . *Brian Duppa*, Ld. Bp. of *Salisbury*.
Mus. C.vii. $\frac{5}{17}$ 4to., Lond., 1648.

157 Two Letters containing . . . the last Newes of the King and Treaty in the *Isle of Wight*.
Mus. C.vii. $\frac{2}{8}$ 4to., Lond., 1648.

158 Packets of Letters From Severall parts of *England*. . . . A Letter from the Isle of Wight. *His Majesties Declaration to the Commissioners*, &ca.
Mus. C.vii. $\frac{2}{9}$ 4to., Lond., 1648.

159 His Majesties Declaration From the Isle of *Wight*, With The Proposals agreed on by his Excellency *Thomas* Lord *Fairfax*, &ca.
Mus. C.vii. $\frac{5}{18}$ 4to., Lond., 1648.

160 *His Majesties* Declaration *concerning* The Treaty. . . . Delivered by His Majesty to one of His Servants at His departure from the Isle of Wight, &ca.
Mus. C. vii. $\frac{5}{19}$ 4to. n.p., 1648.

161 The Independency Of England Endeavoured to be maintained by *Henry Marten* . . Against the Claim of The *Scottish Commissioners* In their late Answer Upon The Bills and Propositions Sent to the King in the Isle of *Wight*.
Mus. C.vii. $\frac{2}{3}$ 4to., Lond., 1648.

162 Certain Passages Which happened at Newport in the Isle Of Wight, Novemb. 29, 1648, Relating to King Charles I. Written by Mr. *Edward Cooke*, of *Highnam*, in *Gloucestershire*, sometime Colonel of a Regiment under *Oliver Cromwell*.
Mus. C.vii. 1.   4to., Lond., 1690.

163 A Sermon Preached Before *His Majesty* at Newport, in the Isle of Wight, *November the* 29th, 1648, &ca. By H. Ferne, D.D. [On Habak. ii. 3.]
Mus. C.vii. $\frac{1}{3}$ 4to., Lond., 1649.

164 *Pseudo Christus* : Or, a True and faithful Relation Of The *Grand Impostures, Horrid Blasphemies, Abominable Practises, Gross Deceits ;* Lately spread abroad and acted in the County of *Southhampton*, by *William Frankelin* and *Mary Gadbury*, and their Companions, &ca. By Humphry Ellis, Minister of the Word in the City of *Winton*.
Mus. C.vii. 6.   4to., Lond., 1650.

165 An Elegy Upon the Decease of the Most Incomparable Pious Lady, the Princesse Elizabeth, Who Dyed in *Carisbrook Castle* in the Isle of *Wight*, *Septemb.* 8, 1650.
Mus. C.vii. $\frac{2}{10}$ 4to., n.p., 1650.

166 The humble Petition Of The Well-affected of the County Of South-Hampton In Behalf of the Ministers of the Gospel, &ca.
Mus. C.vii. $\frac{5}{20}$ 4to., Lond., 1653.

CIVIL WAR.

167 Mercurius Politicus, 17-24th *June*, 1658, containing the list of persons to be added to the Commissioners for ejecting scandalous, ignorant, and insufficient Ministers and Schoolmasters, within the County of Southampton, &ca.
Mus. C.vii. $\frac{5}{21}$ 4to., Lond., 1658.

168 Two Declarations *From* The Town and Garrison Of Portsmouth, &ca.
Mus. C.vii. $\frac{3}{3}$ 4to., Lond., 1659.

169 The True Copys of Several Letters from Portsmouth. . . . To the Lord Fleetwood, &ca.
Mus. C.vii. $\frac{3}{3.a.}$ 4to., Lond., 1659.

170 Mercurius Publicus, *July* 24-31, 1662, containing an Account of a Murder at *Caborn* in the *Isle* of *Wight*, by a Woman who had persecuted Dr. *Sydenham*, Rector of that Parish, for his loyalty and conformity to the Church of England.
Mus. C.vii. $\frac{5}{22}$ 4to., Lond., 1662.

171 Mercurius Publicus : Decem. 4-11, 1662. Containing an account of Quakers and other Fanatics at *Southampton*.
Mus. C.vii. $\frac{5}{23}$ 4to., Lond., 1662.

172 Don Quixot Redivivus Encountring A Barns-Door Or An Exact Narrative Of The Rare Exploits Of Captain *Braines* in a Dangerious Expedition against a Certain Barn in a Town on the other side of the River Anne in the Land of *Little Ease*, and *Less Justice*, &ca.
4to., Printed for the Company of Informers.
Mus. C.vii. $\frac{3}{4}$

In the Town-chest of Andover are the original documents relating to the cases mentioned in this rare tract.

CIVIL WAR.

173   Letters Between Col: Robert Hammond, Governor of the *Isle of Wight*, and the Committee of Lords and Commons at *Derby-House.* . . Relating to King Charles I : While he was confined in *Carisbrooke Castle* in that Island. Now First Published.
Mus. B.v. 11.   8vo., Lond., 1764.

174   The Portraiture of His Sacred Majesty Charles I. in his solitude in Carisbrook Castle, 1648.
Mus. D.ix. $\frac{17}{4}$ 12mo. (Reprint), Portsea.

––––––––

175   CLARKE, (C. B.)   List of the Flowering Plants, Ferns, and Mosses, in the Neighbourhood of Andover.
Mus. D.ix. 5.   8vo., Calcutta, 1866.

176   CLARKE, (J.)   The Delineator, or a Picturesque, Historical, and Topographical Description of the Isle of Wight (Map).
Mus. D.ix. $\frac{18}{2}$ 12mo., Newport, 1812.

177   CLARKE, (W. B.)   Guide to Hayling (illustrated).
Mus. B.vi. 8.   8vo., Hayling, 1836.

178   COBBETT, (WILLIAM).   Rural rides.
Mus. B.vi. 9.   12mo., Lond., 1830.

179   COLE, (JAMES EDWIN).   Genealogy of the family of Cole.
Mus. D.ix. $\frac{3}{12}$ 8vo., Lond., 1867.

180   COLLIER, (C.)   History of Wolvesey.
Mus. D.ix. $\frac{8}{4}$ 12mo., Winchester, 1864.

181   COMYN, (HENRY).   Substance of part of the Lectures delivered in Boldre and Brockenhurst, 1817.
Mus. D.ix.   8vo., Lymington, 1818.

182 Cooke, (G. A.) Topographical and Statistical Sketch of the County of Hants.
Mus. B.v. 22.   12mo., Lond., 1819.

183 ―――― A later Edition.
Mus. B.v. 23.   12mo., Lond., n.d.

184 Cooke, (W.) New Picture of the Isle of Wight. With an introductory account of the Isle.
Mus. C.ii. 15.   4to., Lond., 1808.
―――― Reprinted.
Mus. B.v. 15.   12mo., Southampton, 1812.

185 Cooke, (W. B.) Bonchurch, Shanklin, and the Undercliff described.
Mus. D.ix. $\frac{7}{3}$ 12mo., Lond., 1849.

186 Cope, (T.) Historical Notices of the Ancient Domain of Stanbridge in Hampshire.
Mus. D.ix. $\frac{8}{2}$ 12mo., Romsey, 1865.

187 Cox, (Thomas). Topographical, Historical, Ecclesiastical, and Natural History of Hampshire. [From " *Magna Britannia.*"]
Mus. B.vi. 26.   4to., In the Savoy, 1720.

188 The Crypt or receptacle for things past : an Antiquarian and Miscellaneous Journal relating to Hampshire.
Mus. B.v. 34.   3 vols., 12mo., Ringwood, 1827-8.

189 The Crypt, and West of England Magazine, new series (1 vol., all published).
Mus. B.iv. 8.   8vo., Winchester, 1829.

Curtis, (William). *See* Thornton.

190 Dawes, (R.) Schools for the industrial classes [at King's Somborne, Abbot's Ann, &ca.]
Mus. D.ix. $\frac{10}{6}$ 12mo., Lond., 1853.
―――― *See* King's Somborne.

191   DAY, (WILLIAM).   Life and Death of Richard
      Titheridge [a native of Alresford], a Tract.
                              12mo., Alresford, 1857.

192   DOMAN, (HENRY).   Songs of Lymington.
      Mus. D.ix.   12mo., Lymington, 1867.

193   DOMESDAY Book of Hampshire, in facsimile by the
      zincographic process.
                    Mus. A. 8.   fol., Southampton, 1860.

194   DOMESDAY Book of Hampshire.   An extension of
      the Latin text, and an English translation with
      Notes by H. Moody.
                    Mus. A. 8.   fol., Winchester, 1862.

195   DOMESDAY Book of Hampshire. [From " Frazer's
      Magazine."]
                    Mus. D.ix. 11.   8vo., Lond., 1866.

      DOMESDAY Book of Hampshire. *See* Warner.

196   DOUCE, (FRANCIS).   Observations on a piece of
      Antiquity found at Selborne (Folding-plate).
                              4to., Lond., 1811.

197   DUGDALE, (JAMES).   General Description and
      History of the Isle of Wight.
                    Mus.   4to., Lond., 1819.

198   DUTHY, (JOHN).   Sketches of Hampshire, embra-
      cing the Architectural Antiquities, Topography,
      &ca., of the country adjacent to the River
      Itchen (plates).
                    Mus. B.iii. 2.   8vo., Winchester, 1839.

199   DYSON, (JOHN R.)   Methodism in the Isle of
      Wight : its Origin and Progress down to the
      present time.
                    Mus. C.ix. 3.   8vo., Ventnor, 1865.

200 ELIZABETH, the fair prisoner of Carisbrook : a Poem in nine cantos.
MN.ii. 26.   MS. 4to.

201 ELLIOT, (FRANCES). Personal recollections of the Great Duke [of Wellington].
Mus. D.ix. $\frac{1}{15}$ 8vo.

202 ENGLEFIELD, (Sir HENRY). The Isle of Wight, a description of the Beauties, and Geological Phenomena of. (Plates.)
Mus. B.ii. 2.   4to., Lond., 1816.

203 ―――――― A folio volume containing excellent impressions of the Plates of No. 202, on large paper, and proofs before letters.
Mus. H. 1.
It appears to have been the Engraver's copy.

204 ―――――― Walk through Southampton, describing its Antiquities, with an account of Clausentum. 2nd Edition, (plates).
Mus. B.iv. 18.   8vo., Southampton, 1805.

205 EYRE, (ROBERT). Assize Sermon at Winchester Cathedral : on a good conscience.
Mus. C.vii.   4to., Lond., 1693.

206 ―――――― The sinner a traitor. Assize Sermon at Winchester Cathedral.
Mus. C.vii. $\frac{3}{7}$ 4to., Lond., 1700.

207 FAITHFULL, (WILLIAM). The Late Hampshire Election [in 1790].
Mus. D.ix. $\frac{1}{8}$ 8vo., Winchester, 1791.

208 FAREHAM. Review of Facts in the litigation between Peter Barfoot, Richard Bargus and others with the Bishop of Winchester, concerning the right of Fareham quay.
Mus. D.ix.   8vo., Lond., 1788.

209 FENWICK, (GEORGE). New and original poetical historical and descriptive guide to the Isle of Wight, from a recent personal survey (illustrated).
Mus. D.ix. $\frac{13}{3}$ 8vo., Ryde, 1866.

210 FERGUSSON, (JAMES). The Peril of Portsmouth (plan).
Mus. D.ix. $\frac{4}{4}$ 8vo., Lond., 1853.

211 ———— Portsmouth protected (plates).
Mus. D.ix. $\frac{4}{5}$ 8vo., Lond., 1856.

212 FERREY, (BENJAMIN) and BRAYLEY, (A. W.) Antiquities of the Priory of Christchurch, Hants ; with particulars of the Castle and Borough (plates).
Mus. C.ii. 8.   4to., Lond., 1834.

A second edition of this work was published in 1841, consisting only of the Arthitectural history of the Church ; and omitting the Municipal history.

213 [FITZATHERLEY, ( )] Our town : or rough sketches of character, manners, &ca., by Peregrine Reedpen.
2 vols., 8vo., Lond., 1834.

This book is said to be a satire on the Inhabitants and Society of *Bishop's Waltham*. See a note inserted in this copy, in which the authorship is ascribed to Mr. FitzAtherley.

214 FORBES, (EDWARD). On the tertiary flavio-marine formation of the Isle of Wight (plates).
Mus. B.iii. 19.   8vo., Lond., 1856.

215 FREELING, (ARTHUR). London and Southampton Railway Companion.
Mus. D.ix. $\frac{16}{2}$ 16mo., Lond., 1839.

216 FREELING, (ARTHUR). Picturesque Excursions [to the Isle of Wight, Southampton, New Forest, &ca.]
Mus. D.ix.   12mo., Lond., n.d.

217 GALE, (SAMUEL). History and Antiquities of the Cathedral Church of Winchester (Plates).
Mus. B.v. 7.   8vo., Lond., 1715.

218   GAUNTLETT, (HENRY, late Curate of Botley). Farewell Address to the Inhabitants of Botley.
8vo., Southampton, 1804.

219   GIBBONS, (THOMAS). Memoirs of Isaac Watts, D.D. [a native of Southampton] (portrait).
Mus. B.iv. 16.   8vo., Lond., 1780.

220   GILPIN, (WILLIAM). Remarks on Forest Scenery Illustrated by the scenes of the New Forest (plates).
Mus. B.vi. 23. 2 vols., 8vo., Lond.. 1791.

221   ——— Observations on the Western parts of England and the Isle of Wight (plates).
Mus. B.vi. 24.   8vo., Lond., 1798.

222   ——— Observations on the Coasts of Hampshire, &ca. (plates).
Mus. B.v., 47.   4to., Lond., 1804.

223   GOSPORT. Proceedings in a dispute between Henry Lys, the Elder, Esqre., and Sarah Gainsford, Widow [both of Gosport].
Mus. C.ix. 10.   8vo., Gosport, 1789.

224   ——— Appeal of J. R. Luzuringa to the Inhabitants of Gosport, in favour of the Spanish gentleman M. Penaranda, slandered by Barnabus Rodriguez and the Revds. R. Bingham, Senr., and Junr.
Mus. D.ix. $\frac{4}{8}$ 8vo., Portsea, 1840.

225   GRACE, (HENRY, native of Basingstoke). History of the Life and Sufferings of, during several years Captivity among the savages.
H.vii. $\frac{3}{9}$ 8vo., Reading, 1765.

226   GRAVES, (Honble. H.) Designs for the Font at Binstead Church, Isle of Wight.
Mus. B.iv. 17.   8vo., 1844.

227 GREEN, (J. S.) Life of Mr. John Van, a Clergyman's Son, of Woody [East Woodhay], in Hampshire, being a series of many extraordinary events.
Mus. D.viii. 27. 2 vols., 12mo., Lond., n.d.

228 GROSE, (FRANCIS). Antiquities of the County of
Hampshire. [The part of his "Antiquities of
England, &ca.," relating to the County.] (plates.)
4to., Lond.

229 ———— Antiquities of Hampshire. (Map and
plates.)   Imp. 8vo., Lond., 1783.
Extracted from the "Antiquities of England and Wales."

230 GROVE, (R. A.) Views near Lymington.
Mus. A. 9.   4to., Lymington, 1832.

231 GUILLAUME, (G.) Architectural Account of Netley
Abbey.
Mus. C.ii. 1.   fol., Southampton, 1848.

232 GWILLIAM, (J.) Rambles in the Isle of Wight
(plates).   Mus. B.vi. 6.   8vo., Lond., 1844.

233 ———— Norris Castle, or recent Tramps in
the Isle of Wight.
Mus. B.vi. 7.   8vo., Lond., 1845.

234 HALL, (THOMAS). Poems written in the Debtor's
ward, Winchester.
Mus. D.ix. $\frac{24}{2}$ 8vo., Lond., n.d.

235 HAMPSHIRE Diocesan Church Association. Report
of Meeting at Winchester.
fol. sheet, 1870.

236 ——————— Rules.
4to.

237 HAMPSHIRE, with Map.
4to., Lond., 1793.

238 HAMPSHIRE and the Isle of Wight. Edited by
E. R. Kelly.
Mus. C.ix. 4.　　　　8vo., Lond., 1875.

239 HAMPSHIRE. Ordnance Survey. Hants. Notice of
Meeting for fixing boundaries.
fol. sheet, 1870.

240 HAMPSHIRE Repository, or an Historical, Economical and Literary Miscellany, relative to the County
and the Isle of Wight (plates).
Mus. B.iii.12.　　2 vols., 8vo., Winchester, 1798-9.

241 HAMPSHIRE and West of England Magazine (plates).
Mus. C.ix. 1.　　8vo., Winchester, 1828.

Twelve monthly numbers only were published; and it then became incorporated with " The Crypt." *See* No. 189.

242 HAMPSHIRE Volunteers : a Poem.
R.iv. $\frac{14}{21}$　　　　4to., Lond., 1794.

243 HAMPSHIRE Volunteer Battalion under Canvas.
fol., sheet, 1870.

244 HANWAY, (JONAS). Journal of eight days journey
from Portsmouth to Kingston-on-Thames (Plate).
NO.i. 8.　　　　4to., Lond., 1756.

245 ———— Second Edition (plate).
Mus. C.vii. 8.　　　2 vols., 8vo., 1757.

246 ———— Remarkable occurrences in the life of
Jonas Hanway [a native of Portsmouth] by John
Pugh.　　Mus. C.vii. 9.　　8vo., Lond., 1787.

247 HARFORD, (JOHN S.) Life of Thomas Burgess,
Bishop of Salisbury [a Native of Odiham]
(portrait).
Mus. B.iii. 11.　　8vo., Lond., 1840.

248 HARRIS, (JOHN). Sermon preached at the anni-
versary Meeting of the Natives of the County of
Southampton.
Mus. C.vii. $\frac{7}{6}$　　　4to., Lond., 1705.

249 HART, (MARY KERR). Heath Blossoms. Poems. (portrait).
Mus. D.ix. $\frac{21}{3}$ 8vo., Southampton, n.d.

250 HARTFORDBRIDGE. George, Prince of Wales, at. From Lloyd's Evening Post.
4to., Lond., Jany., 1790.

251 ——— Wooden Church at.
Mus. D.ix. $\frac{10}{10}$ 12mo. sheet, 1876.

252 HARTSHORNE, (C. H.) History and Antiquities of Porchester Castle.
YY.i. $\frac{13}{8}$ 8vo., Lond., 1846.

253 HASSELL, (J.) Tour of the Isle of Wight (Plates).
Mus. B.iv. 7.   2 vols., 8vo., Lond., 1790.

254 HAWKER, (PETER). Instructions for young sportsmen. 7th Edition (plates).
Mus. C.vii. 11.   8vo., Lond., 1833.
Contains much information as to the Natural History of the South-Western parts of the Connty.

255 HAWKINS, (E.) Notices of the Mint and Exchange of Winchester.
Mus. D.ix. $\frac{2}{8}$ 8vo., Lond., 1846.

256 HAYLING. Topographical and Historical Account of Hayling Island (coloured plates).
Mus. B.ii. 4.   4to., Havant, 1826.

257 ——— Guide to Hayling Island and Havant.
Mus. D.ix. $\frac{11}{5}$ 8vo., Hayling, 1842.

258 HEATHCOTE, (Sir WILLIAM). Catologue of his Library at Hursley Park. 2nd Edition, by James Darling.
NO.i. 29.   8vo., Romsey, 1865.
There was a Former Edition, in 4to., 1834.

259 HEWETSON, (J.) Architectural and Picturesque Views of Noble Mansions in Hampshire.
Mus. A. 6.   fol., Lond., n.d.

260 HEWETT, (General Sir GEORGE, of Freemantle). Private record of the Life of.
Mus. B.v. 46.   8vo., Newport, 1840.

261 HEYWOOD, (ABEL.) Guide to the Isle of Wight.
Mus. D.ix. $\frac{6}{6}$ 12mo., Manchester, 1869.

262 ———— Guide to Portsmouth.
Mus. D.ix. $\frac{6}{7}$ 12mo., Manchester, 1869.

263 ——— Guide to Southampton.
Mus. D.ix. $\frac{6}{8}$ 12mo., Manchester, 1869.

264 HILLIER, (GEORGE). Topography of the Isle of Wight, a useful and comprehensive Guide to its Beauties and Antiquities. (Plates and Maps.)
Mus. D.ix. $\frac{17}{3}$ 12mo., Ryde, 1855.

265 ———— Narrative of the attempted escapes of King Charles I. from Carisbrooke Castle.
Mus. B.v. 9.   8vo., Lond., 1852.

266 HISTORY of the inhuman and unparalleled murders of Mr. William Galley, Custom House Officer at Southampton, and Daniel Chater, Fordingbridge, by 14 notorious Smugglers, with the trials of 7 bloody crimnals at Chichester, and accounts of the wicked Lives and Trials of other Smugglers at East Grinstead and Poole, &ca. (Plates).
Mus. C.ix. 6.   8vo., Lond., 1779.

267 HOBHOUSE, (Bishop EDWARD). Life of Bishop Walter de Merton [of Basingstoke].
Mus. B.iii. $\frac{19}{2}$ 8vo., Oxford, 1859.

268 HOGLANDIÆ Descriptio.
Mus. D.ix. 23.   8vo., Lond., 1709.

A curious engraving of a Hog on the Title Page. The dedication is signed M.C. Gough says (British Topography) that this is by Mr. Richards, of Jesus College, Oxford (Thomas Richards, M.A., 1714?) and that it was an answer to Holdsworth's " Muscipula."
Another Edition was published in 1719, and, with an English Translation, in 1728.

269 HOLLIS, (GEORGE). Reply to "a short statement of facts," assumed by John Hancock Buckle, relative to the conduct of Mr. Hollis, as Under-Sheriff of Hants.
Mus. D.ix. $\frac{1}{10}$ 8vo., Winchester, 1816.

270 HOLLINGSWORTH, (J.) Guide to Portsmouth.
Mus. C.viii. 4.   12mo., Portsmouth, 1840.

271 HOLLOWAY, (H. R.) Walks round Ryde.
Mus. D.ix. $\frac{10}{11}$ 12mo., Lond. [Arundel], 1848.

272 HORNE, (THOMAS HARTWELL, [of Eversley].) Reminiscences Personal and Biographical.
Mus. B.vi. 14.   8vo., Lond., 1862.

273 HOWITT, (WILLIAM). Visits to Remarkable Places. 2nd Edition.
Mus. B.iv. 2.   8vo., Lond., 1840.

Contains an excellent account of Winchester.

274 HUGHES, (J. GWYNNE.) Reply to the Letter of the Rev. A. Lush, on the [Odiham] Re-Marriage Case.
Mus. D. ix. $\frac{1}{17}$ 8vo., Odiham, 1855.

275 HUMBERT, (L. M.) History and Antiquities of the Hospital of St. Cross.
Mus. C.ix.   8vo., Winchester, 1857.

276 HYDE Abbey School. Musæ Hydenses, seu Poemata quædam præmio donata, anctoribus Hydensis Scholæ Alumnis ; Prize Poems composed by Scholars of Hyde Abbey School. Two parts (Latin and English).
Mus. C.viii.8. 12mo., Winchester, 1828.

277 IBBETSON, (B.) Notes on the Geology and Chemical Composition of the various strata in the Isle of Wight.
>   Mus. B.iii. 10.   8vo., Lond., 1849.
>   Map in relief, coloured geologically.

278 ISLE of Wight. Across the Solent. From "London Society."
>   Mus. D.ix. $\frac{2}{20}$ 8vo., Lond., 1865.

279 ———— Beauties of the Isle of Wight, with account of the principal tours in the Island (plate).
>   Mus. D.ix. $\frac{18}{3}$ 12mo., Portsea, 1827.

279* ———— Beauties of the Isle of Isle of Wight, described and illustrated ; by W. H. D. Adams (plates).
>   Mus. D.ix. 19.   8vo., Lond., 1857.

280 ———— Report of the Commissioners for inquiring concerning the Charities of the Isle of Wight.
>   Mus. D.ix. $\frac{19}{3}$ 12mo., Newport, 1837.

281 ———— Circumnavigator. 17 coloured views in a case.   n.d.

282 ———— Companion to the Isle of Wight.
>   Mus. D.ix. $\frac{20}{2}$ 8vo., Southampton, n.d.

283 ———— Garland. A Ballad, in three parts. Privately reprinted by Utterson.
>   Mus. D.ix. 21.   8vo., Ryde, 1839.
>   Only twenty-five copies printed.

284 ———— Hartnall's pocket guide to the Isle of Wight.
>   Mus. D.viii., 20.   16mo., Ryde, 1843.

285 ———— Kidd's Pocket Companion to the Isle of Wight, with Engravings by Bonner.
>   Mus. D.ix. $\frac{17}{2}$ 12mo., Lond., 1838.

286 ISLE OF WIGHT. Mason's Handy Guide to the Isle of Wight.
　　　　　　Mus. D.ix. $\frac{13}{4}$　　　　8vo., Ryde, n.d.

287 ————— A Poem.
　　　　　　Mus. D.ix. $\frac{24}{6}$　　12mo., Newport, 1789.

With Plate of the Needles before the fall of the pointed rock from which the group takes its name, and two other plates.

288 ————— Poetical Excursions in the Isle of Wight (Vignette).
　　　　　　　　　　　　4to., Lond., 1777.

289 ————— From "Quarterly Review."
　　　　　　Mus. D.ix. $\frac{2}{16}$　　8vo., Lond., 1874.

290 ————— Shaw's Tourists Picturesque Guide to the Isle of Wight.
　　　　　　Mus. D.ix. 15.　　8vo., Lond., 1873.

291 ————— Tales and Legends of the Isle of Wight, with the Adventures of the Author in search of them. By Abraham Elder.
　　　　　　Mus. C.ix. 5.　　8vo., Lond., 1843.

292 ————— Visitor's Book.
　　　　　　Mus. D.ix. $\frac{13}{2}$　　8vo., Portsea, n.d.

293 ————— Wallis' Companion to the Isle of Wight.
　　　　　　Mus. D.ix. $\frac{13}{3}$　　12mo., Lond., n.d.

294 ————— In the Isle of Wight. From "Lippincott's Magazine."
　　　　　　Mus. D.ix. $\frac{2}{19}$　8vo., Philadelphia, 1873.

295 ITCHEN. A Spring Ramble on the Itchen. From the "Gentleman's Magazine."
　　　　　　Mus. D.ix. $\frac{2}{21}$　　8vo., Lond., 1875.

296 JACOB, (PHILIP). Visitation Charge to the Archdeaconry of Winchester.
　　　　　　　　8vo., Winchester, 1873.

297 JACOB, (Mrs., late Miss Kunnison of Southampton). Poems.
Mus. D.ix. $\frac{22}{2}$ 12mo., Southampton, 1821.

298 JAY, (GRANTHAM).   Mr. Percy Slipscombe's visit to the Isle of Wight.
Mus. D.ix. $\frac{8}{5}$ 8vo., Lond., 1873.

299 JEFFERSON, (JOSEPH).   History of the Holy Ghost Chapel at Basingstoke, with an account of another religious house, and curious antiquities. 2nd Edition.
Mus. D.ix. $\frac{3}{4}$ 8vo., Basingstoke, 1809.

300 ———— Ruins of a Temple : a Poem, with an Account of the Holy Ghost Chapel, at Basingstoke (Vignette).
Mus. C.ii. 12.   4to., Lond., 1793.

301 ———— Sermon on the death of Miss Sarah Glover, at Basingstoke.
8vo., Southampton, 1792.

302 ———— Memoirs of Miss Stapleton [who died at Basingstoke].
Mus. D.ix. $\frac{12}{6}$ 8vo., Basingstoke, n.d.

303 JENKINSON, (HENRY IRWIN).   Guide to the Isle of Wight.
Mus. D.ix. 14.   8vo., Lond., 1876.

304

305 JENKINSON, (HENRY T. J.)   The New Forest a matter of National Interest.
Mus. D.ix. $\frac{8}{8}$ 8vo., Lond., 1871.

306   JERVIS, (THOMAS). Refutation of an extraordinary story of a supernatural apparition related by R. Warner.

        Mus. D.ix. $\frac{1}{11}$ 8vo., Lond., 1832.

307   JOHNS, (C. A.) Inaugural Address at the Winchester and Hampshire Scientific and Literary Society.

        Mus. D.ix. $\frac{10}{8}$ 12mo., Winchester, 1869.

308   JOHNSON, (CHRISTOPHER). History of the Life and Intrigues of that celebrated Courtezan and Posture-Mistress, *Eliz. Mann,* alias *Boyle,* alias *Sample.*

        Mus. D.ix. $\frac{3}{11}$ 8vo., Lond., 1724.

She was a native of Southampton ; of which place and its inhabitants many anecdotes are given. This professes to be the *first part* only ; the second part is stated to be in the press, but, I believe, never was published.

309   JONES, (EUSTACE HINTON). Romance of Sir Bevis of Hamptoun.

        Mus. C.viii. $\frac{4}{8}$ 12mo., Southampton, 1870.

310   JONES, (HENRY). Vectis. The Isle of Wight : a Poem (Vignettes).

        4to., Lond., 1766.

311   JONES, (T. E.) Guide to Hayling.

        Mus. D.ix. $\frac{12}{3}$ 8vo., Portsea, 1866.

312   KEATE, (GEORGE). Netley Abbey : an Elegy. (Vignette).

        Mus. C.ii. 10.   4to., Lond., 1769.

A former edition was printed in 1764, under the title " The Ruins of Netley Abbey."

313   KEBLE, (JOHN). Various papers relating to, and to Hursley.

        Mus. D.ix. $\frac{12}{10.12}$

314   KELL, (E.) Letters on Mr. Hartley's bequest to the Town of Southampton.

        Mus. B.v. 24.   12mo., Southampton, 1858.

315 KELL, (E.) Description of Beaulieu Abbey.
        Mus. C.viii. $\frac{4}{5}$ 12mo., Southampton, 1870.

316 ———— Description of Netley Abbey.
        Mus. C.viii. $\frac{4}{4}$ 12mo., Southampton, 1870.

317 KINGSLEY, (CHARLES). Miscellanies.
        Mus. B.vi. 5. 2 vols., 8vo., Lond., 1859-60.
   Contain descriptions of scenery, and anecdotes of persons, in the neighbourhood of Eversley.

318 ———— Verses written for the opening of the
     Yateley Industrial Exhibition, 1867.
        Mus. C.viii. $\frac{4}{7}$ 12mo. leaf.

319 ———— Sermon preached in the Parish Church
     of Eversley, on the Sunday after the funeral of.
     By Sir William H. Cope, Bart.
                              8vo., Lond., 1875.

320 KING's Somborne. An account of King's Som-
     borne School.
        Mus. D.ix. $\frac{10}{5}$ 12mo., Lond., 1849.

321 KLITZ, (PHILIP). Sketches of Life, Character, and
     Scenery in the New Forest.
        Mus. B.vi. 4.   8vo., Lond., 1850.

322 KNIGHT, (CHARLES). Journey-book of Hampshire
     and the Isle of Wight (Woodcuts).
        Mus. C.viii. $\frac{1}{2}$ 12mo., Lond., 1841.

323 LATHAM, (JOHN). Account of ancient Sculptures
     and Inscriptions in the Abbey Church of Romsey
     (Plate).
                              4to., Lond., 1801.

     LE KEUX. See Winchester.

324 LEFROY, (Mrs., of Ashe). Poems on several
     occasions. MS.
        MN.ii. 24.   4to., transcribed, 1806.

325 LELAND's Itinerary [in Hampshire]. Transcribed
with Explanatory notes, by Henry Moody.
Mus. B.iv. $\frac{18}{7}$ 8vo., Winchester, 1868.

326 LETTERS addressed to William Garrett, Esq., relative to the state of Leigh House.
8vo., Havant Press, 1819.

327 LETTER from Thomas Haselden to Sir Peter-
Thompson, dated Portsmouth, 27th February,
1746-7.
MS. folio sheet.

328 LETTER from David Tyrie to Thomas Walker before
his removal from Winchester Gaol to the place of
execution; to which is annexed a copy of a letter
from Thomas Walker to David Tyrie, written
from London, August, 1782, during the time of
the unhappy convict's confinement, after condemnation, and to which foregoing is an answer.
MS., 12mo. size, 1783.

With a pencil drawing of David Tyrie.

329 LEWIS, (P.)   Historical Enquiries concerning
Forests and Forest Laws, with Topographical
remarks upon the ancient and modern state of
the New Forest (Plate).
Mus. C.ii. 7.   4to., Lond., 1811.

330 LINGARD. Memoir of the Rev. John Lingard,
D.D. [a native of Winchester]. From Bentley's
Miscellany (Portrait).
Mus. D.ix. $\frac{2}{9}$ 8vo., Lond., 1851.

331 LISLE, (EDWARD, of Crux-Easton). Observations
on Husbandry (Portrait).
K.iii. 2.   4to., Lond., 1757.

Contains curious information about Hampshire Agriculture, &ca., at the
beginning of the 18th Century. Another Edition, in two vols., 8vo., was
published in the same year, which contains a glossary of Hants words.

332 Lockhart, (Charles). A general Guide to the
Isle of Wight (Plates and Map).
Mus. B.vi. 2.   4to., Lond., 1870.

333 Loggon, (Samuel). History of the Brotherhood or
Guild of the Holy Ghost, near Basingstoke.
Mus. B.iv. 12.   8vo., Reading, 1742.

Horace Walpole's copy, with his Book-plate.

334 Longcroft, (Charles John). Topographical ac-
count of the Hundred of Bosmere ; including the
Parishes of Havant, Warblington, and Hayling.
(Plates and Map.)
Mus. C.ii. 17.   8vo., Lond., 1857.

335 Loudon, (Mrs. J. W.) Glimpses of Nature during
a visit to the Isle of Wight (Plates).
Mus. D.viii. 22. sq. 8vo., Lond., 1848.

336 Lowth, (Bishop Robert). The Genealogy of
Christ, as it is represented in the East window in
the College Chapel at Winchester. A Poem.
I.viii. $\frac{6}{6}$ 8vo., Lond., 1729.

337 ———— The Life of William of Wykeham,
Bishop of Winchester (Plates).
Mus. B.vi. 19.   8vo., Lond., 1758.

338 Lush, (Alfred). Letter on the Odiham Marriage
Case.
fol. sheet, Odiham, 1855.

339 ———— The Sacrament of Marriage. Four
Sermons preached at Greywell. *See* Hughes.
Mus. D.ix. $\frac{10}{13}$ 12mo., Oxford, 1855.

340 Lymington. Guide to Lymington. By a Resident.
Mus. C.viii. $\frac{5}{4}$ 8vo., Lymington, 1827.

341 LYMINGTON. Handbook for Lymington (Map and Plates).
Mus. D.ix. $\frac{14}{2}$ 8vo., Lymington, 1845.
A reprint of the " Guide," with many additions.

342 ———— Handbook for Lymington (Map).
Mus. D.ix. $\frac{14}{3}$ 8vo., Lymington, 1853.

343 ———— Pen and Pencil Sketches of Lymington, by R.O. (Plates).
Mus. B.v. 30.   sq. 8vo., Lymington, n.d.

344 ———— Views of the principal Seats, and Marine and Landscape Scenery in the neighbourhood of Lymington, drawn on stone by L. Haghe, from original pictures taken by J. M. Gilbert, with Historical and Topographical descriptions. Large Paper; Proofs on India Paper.
Mus. A. 9.   fol., Lymington, 1832.

345 MADDEN, (Sir FREDERIC). Description of the matrix of the Seal of Southwick Priory (Plates).
4to., Lond., 1831.

MANN, (ELIZABETH). See No. 308.

346 MANNING, (WILLIAM M.) Proceedings in Courts of Revision in the Isle of Wight ; and cases decided in South Hants, before the Revising Barrister.
Mus. B.v. 8.   12mo., Lond., 1836.

347 MANNINGHAM, (Bishop THOMAS). Funeral Sermon on the Lady Dorothy Norton, of Rotherfield.
Mus. C.vii. $\frac{7}{4}$ 4to., Lond., 1703.

348 MANTELL, (G. A.) Geological Excursion round the Isle of Wight (Plates).
Mus. B.vi. 10.   8vo., Lond., 1847.

349 MANWOOD, (JOHN). A treatise of the Laws of the
Forest. 2nd Edition.
Mus. D.ix. 4to., Lond., 1615.
Contains much interesting matter relating to the New Forest.

350 MARSH, (J.) Memoranda of the Parishes of
Hursley and North Baddesley (Plates).
Mus. B.iii. $\frac{3}{8}$ 8vo., Winchester, 1808.

MARTEN, (HENRY). *See* No. 161.

351 MARTIN, (G. A.) The Undercliff of the Isle of
Wight, its climate, history, and natural produc-
tions.
Mus. B.iv. 13. 8vo., Lond., 1840.

352 MARTIN, (P. I.) Observations on the Anticlinal
Line of the London and Hampshire basins.
4to., Lond., 1829.

353 MARTIN, (T.) Historica Descriptio complectens
Vitam et Res gentas Gulielmi Wicami Vintonien-
sis Episcopi. (Portrait).
Mus. B.iii. 20. 4to., Oxford, 1690.

354 MATTHEWS, (WILLIAM E.) Gems of the Isle [of
Wight].
Mus. D.ix. $\frac{21}{6}$ 12mo., Ryde, 1858.

355 MAXWELL, (ARCHIBALD). Portsmouth : a descriptive poem.
Mus. B.vi. 18. 8vo., Portsmouth, 1755.

356 MEASOM, (GEORGE). Guide to the South Western
Railway (Woodcuts).
XX.vii. $\frac{6}{5}$ 8vo., Lond., n.d.

357 MICHAELMARSH and its Antiquities, together with
notices of the New Forest.
Mus. D.ix. $\frac{3}{2}$ 8vo., Lond., 1867.

358 MIDLANE, (ALBERT). Vecta Garland.
   Mus. D.ix. $\frac{23}{3}$ 8vo., Ryde, 1860.

359 MILLARD, (JAMES ELWIN). Account of Basingstoke,
   Basing, and the neighbourhood (Woodcuts).
   4to., Basingstoke, 1874.

360 ———— Ancient English Guilds. Sermon at
   the Anniversary of the Society of Aliens.
   8vo., Winchester, 1873.

361 ———— Catalogue of Books selected from the
   Library of James Elwin Millard, D.D.
   4to., Basingstoke, [1878].

362 MILNER, (Bishop JOHN). History, Civil and Eccle-
   siastical, and Survey of the Antiquities of
   Winchester (Plates). 2nd Edition.
   Mus. B.ii. 3. 2 vols., 4to., Winchester, 1809.
   Illustrated with many additional prints, Portraits, &ca.

363 MILTON, (W., Vicar of Heckfield). The Danger
   of travelling in stage coaches.
   Mus. D.ix. $\frac{1}{16}$ 8vo., Reading, 1810.

364 MOGG, (E.) Southampton Railway and Isle of
   Wight Guide.
   Mus. D.ix. $\frac{12}{2}$ 12mo., Lond., 1845.

365 Mons Catharinæ prope Wintoniam. Poema. [by
   Thomas Warton].
   TT. ii. 9.   4to., Lond., 1760.

366 MOODY, (HENRY). Antiquarian and Topographical
   Sketches of Hampshire.
   Mus. B.v. 35. 12mo., Winchester, 1846.

367 ———— History and Description of the Hospital of St. Cross, near Winchester, with a List
   of the Masters since its foundation to the present
   time.
   Mus. B.v. 3.   8vo., Winchester.

368 MOODY, (HENRY). Notes and Essays relating to the Counties of Hants and Wilts.
Mus. B.v. 36. 8vo., Winchester, 1851.

369 ———— Our County, or Hampshire in the reign of Charles II.
Mus. B.v. 37. 8vo., Winchester, 1863.

369* MOOR, (J. F.) Guide to Hursley (Woodcuts).
Mus. C.viii. $\frac{1}{5}$ 8vo., Winchester, 1869.

370 MOSES, (H.) Account of the visit of King William IV. (when Duke of Clarence) as Lord High Admiral, to Portsmouth, in 1827, (Coloured Plates).
Mus. A. 10. fol., Lond., 1827.

371 MUDIE, (ROBERT). Hampshire, its past and present condition, and future prospects (Plates).
Mus. B.ii. 7. 3 vols., 8vo., Winchester, 1840.

372 MURRAY's Handbook for Surrey, Hampshire, and the Isle of Wight.
CR. iv. 6. 12mo., Lond., 1858.

372* NARRATIVE of the Loss of the Royal George at Spithead, including attempts and operations to raise her.
16mo., Portsea, 1841.

373 NATELEY Scures Church. From the "Gentlemen's Magazine" (Plate).
Mus. D.ix. $\frac{3}{3}$ 8vo., Lond., 1836.

374 NEW Forest. Abstract of Claims on the New Forest in 1670.
Mus. B.iv. 10. 8vo., Salisbury, 1776.

375 ———— Handbook.
Mus. D.ix. $\frac{6}{3}$ 8vo., Lyndhurst, 1875.

376 NEW Forest. Plan of the New Forest, from surveys by T. Richardson, W. King, and W. Driver. Large coloured Maps by W. Faden.
Mus. H. 2.   fol., Lond., 1789.

377 ———— Report of the Commissioners appointed to enquire into the state and condition of the Woods, Forests, and Land revenues of the Crown [on the New Forest].
Mus. H.3. Vol. 1-5.   fol., Lond., 1789.

378 ———— Report of the Honble. J. K. Howard on the New Forest.
fol., Lond, 1871.

379 ———— Report of the Select Committee on the New Forest.
Mus.   fol., Lond., 1875.

380 ———— Returns to an address of the House of Lords on Enclosures in the New Forest (Map).
fol., Lond., 1867.

381 ———— and Watering Places of the Hampshire coast. (From the "Traveller's Magazine.")
Mus. D.ix. $\frac{10}{12}$ 12mo., 1847.

382 NEWMAN, (SARAH). Poems on subjects connected with Scripture.
Mus. D.ix. 24.   8vo., Alton, 1811.

383 NEWTOWN. The case on the merits of the Election and Return for the Borough of Newtown in the Isle of Wight.
Mus. C.vii. $\frac{3}{8}$ folio sheet, n.p. or d. [1729].

384 ———— Reply to the Newtown Petitioners.
Mus. C.vii. $\frac{3}{9}$ folio sheet.

385 NOMINA Villarum of the County of Southampton.
Mus. C.viii. 1.   8vo., Romsey, 1791.

386 NUGENT, (Lord).   Ye dole of Tichborne.
Mus. B.v. 45.   Oblong, Lond., 1871.

387 NUTT, (T.)   The writings of a Person in obscurity,
and a native of the Isle of Wight.
Mus. D.ix. $\frac{23}{2}$ 12mo., Gosport, 1808.

388 ODIHAM Endowed Grammar School opening.
Mus. D.ix. $\frac{3}{16}$ 1876.

389 PAGE, (W. B.)   Prodromus, or a general nomenclature of all the Plants, indigenous and exotic,
cultivated by him in the Southampton Botanic
Garden.
Mus. B.v. 43.   8vo., Lond., 1817.

390 PARTICULARS of Estate at Aldershot Lodge. (Map).
fol., 1871.

391 PARTICULARS of the Estate of Allington Manor.
(Map).
fol., 1872.

392 PARTICULARS of Beaurepaire and Estates in Bramley,
Sherborne St. John, Pamber, and Mortimer.
(Map and Plate).
fol., 1872.

393 PARTICULARS of the Estate of Bramshaw House,
New Forest. (Map).
fol., 1872.

394 PARTICULARS of Estate at Eversley. (Parfitts).
fol., 1855.

395 PARTICULARS of Estate at Eversley.
fol., 1856.

396   PARTICULARS of the Estate of Gatcombe, Isle of Wight. (Map).

fol., 1836.

396* PARTICULARS of Hartley Row Brewery. (Map).

fol., 1876.

396**PARTICULARS of Estate of Hook-house. (Map).

fol., 1878.

397   PARTICULARS of Estate at Hurstbourne Tarrant. (Map).

fol., 1872.

398   PARTICULARS of Estates in Kingsclere and Wolverton.

fol., 1874.

399   PARTICULARS of the Estates of Northcourt and Woolverton, Isle ot Wight. (Map).

fol., 1836.

400   PARTICULARS of Properties at Ryde, Isle of Wight. (Map).

fol., 1838.

401   PARTICULARS of Leasehold Estates at Ryde, Isle of Wight. (Map).

fol., 1834.

402   PARTICULARS of the Estate of Upton Gray. (Map).
fol., 1870.

403   PARTICULARS of the Estate of Warbrook, in the Parish of Eversley. (Map).

fol., 1838.

404   PARTICULARS of the Estate of Yateley Lodge. (Map).
fol., 1862.

405   PARTICULARS of Estates at Sherfield-English, and Wellhouse farm in Bramshill. (with Charles Butler's opinion in MS.).

fol. sheet, 1783.

406 PEARCE, (WILLIAM). Hartfordbridge, or the skirts of a Camp. An operatic farce. (Frontispiece).
12mo., Lond., n.d.

407 ———— Netley Abbey. An operatic farce. (Frontispiece).
12mo., Lond., n.d.

408 PEARSALL, (J. S.) Historical memorials of a Christian fellowship [at Andover].
Mus. D.ix. $\frac{11}{6}$ 12mo., Lond., n.d.

408* ———— Outlines of Congregationalism ; with an historical sketch of its rise and progress in the Town of Andover. (Plate).
8vo., Lond., 1844.

409 PENNANT, (THOMAS). Journey from London to the Isle of Wight. (Plates).
Mus. B.ii. 8. 2 vols. in 1, 4to., Lond., 1801.

410 PIT dwellings and other early human habitations [in Hampshire]. (From the " &ca.")
Mus. D.ix. 15.   8vo., Lond., 1872.

411 POLL at the Election of Knights of the Shire.
Mus. C.vii. $\frac{7}{9}$ 4to., Lond., 1705.

412 PORCHESTER Castle. Its Origin, History, and Antiquities.
Mus. D.ix. 10.   12mo., Portsea, 1845.

413 ———— Sketches of Porchester Castle, by J. Stockman, of Portsea. [with letter-press descriptions].
Mus. C.ii. 3.   4to., Chichester, n.d.

414 PORTER, (GEORGE). Hymns and Sacred Songs.
Mus. D.ix. $\frac{16}{6}$ 12mo., Basingstoke, 1840.

415 PORTSMOUTH. Charter of the Borough of Portsmouth, 17th Nov., 3rd Charles I. [1627].
MN.ii. 27. MS.

416 ———— Answer of E. Stanyford and A. Colebrook, Churchwardens of the Parish of Portsmouth to the Printed case of William Ward, Vicar of the same.
Mus. C.vii. $\frac{5}{24}$ 4to., Lond., 1710.

417 ———— Fire in Dock Yard.
" London Chronicle," 4to., Lond., July, 1770.

418 ———— Guide.
12mo., Portsmouth (Hollingsworth), 1822-28.
Mus. D.ix. $\frac{9}{5}$

419 ———— Guide to Portsmouth, Southsea, Anglesey, and Hayling Island. (Plates and Maps).
12mo., Portsmouth (Charpentier), 1843.
Mus. D.ix..17.

420 ———— Southsea, Anglesey, and Hayling Island Guide.
12mo., Portsmouth (Charpentier), 1855.
Mus. D.ix. 25.

421 ———— Account of the Imperial and Royal visit to Portsmouth.
Mus. D.ix. $\frac{4}{3}$ 8vo., Portsmouth, 1814.

422 ———— Lewis's Hand-book of Portsmouth.
Mus. D.ix. $\frac{15}{2}$ 8vo., Portsmouth, n.d.

423 ———— Portsea, and Gosport Literary and Scientific Register of Local subjects. (a monthly Miscellany.) Vol. 1. (all published).
Mus. C.ix. 9. 8vo., Portsmouth, 1823.

424 ———— Map of.
Mus. D.ix. 4.

425 PORTSMOUTH and its neighbourhood. Nelson's Views and letter-press account.
Mus.   Lond., small oblong, n.d.

425* ———— John Charles Wallop, Earl of. Report of Proceedings of a commission to enquire into his state of mind.
8vo., Lond. [1823].

426 PRATT, (J. S.) Gleanings. Hampshire Station.
Mus. B.iv. $\frac{17}{2}$ 8vo., Lond., 1805.

427 PRESTWICH, (JOSEPH). Probable age of the London clay, and its relation to the Hampshire and Paris tertiary system.
8vo., Lond., 1847.

428 ———— On the structure of the Strata between the London clay and the chalk, in the London and Hampshire tertiary system. 2 parts.
8vo., Lond., 1852-4.

429 PROCEEDINGS of the Archæological Institute at Winchester. (Plates).
Mus. B.iii. 7.   8vo., Lond, 1846.

Containing :

Architectural History of Winchester Cathedral. By Professor Willis.
Architectural Works of William of Wykeham. By Professor Cockerell.
Notices of the Painted Glass in the Cathedral and Churches of Winchester and its neighbourhood. By C. Winston.
Architectural Notes of the Churches and other ancient Buildings in the City and Neighbourhood of Winchester. By J. H. Parker.
Notices of the Mint and Exchange of Winchester. By Edward Hawkins.
Hall of the Royal Palace & Round Table of Winchester. By Edward Smirke.
Notice of the Seals of the Earls of Winchester and Winchester City. By J. G. Nichols.
Remarks on the Common Seal of the Men of Alwarestoke (Alverstoke). By Sir Frederick Madden.
Remarks on the Monument of Sir Richard Lyster, in St. Michael's Church, Southampton. By the same.
Architecture of the Church and Hospital of the Holy Cross. By E. A. Freeman.
Observations on the Priory of Christchurch. By A. J. Beresford Hope.
Remarks on Romsey Abbey Church. By J. L. Petit.
History and Architecture of Porchester Castle. By C. H. Hartshorne.

430 PROSSER, (G. F.) Antiquities of Hampshire, illustrated in the Ruins of Ancient Buildings. (Plates).
        Mus. C.ii. $\frac{20}{2}$ 4to., Guildford, 1842.

431 ———— Thirty Illustrations of Hampshire. Picturesque views of the Seats of the Nobility and Gentry. With Descriptions.
        Mus. C.ii. 20.   4to., Lond., 1833.

432 RADCLYFFE, (C. W.) Memorials of Winchester College. (Plates).
        Mus. A. 5.   fol., Winchester, 1847.

433 RANGER, (W.) Report on the Drainage of Southampton.
        Mus. B.v. 44.   8vo., Lond., 1850.

434 RAYE, (C.) Tour through the Isle of Wight. (Coloured Plates).
        Mus. B.ii. 9. Oblong 4to., Lond., 1825.

435 REASONS for subverting the Bible Society addressed to the North-Eastern part of the County of Hants [in verse]. With notes and comments.
        8vo., Lond., 1813.

436 RECOLLECTIONS of the Vine Hunt, by a Sexagenarian [the Rev. James Edward Austen-Leigh]. (Privately printed.)
        Mus.   8vo., Lond., 1865.

437 REEVE, (MARY ANNE, of Long Sutton). Lays of the West.
        Mus. D.ix. $\frac{23}{4}$ 8vo., Odiham, 1867.

438 REPORT of the Church Congress held at Southampton, October, 1870.
        Mus. B.vi. 20. 8vo., Southampton, n.d. [1871].

438* REPORT of the Commissioners appointed to enquire into the state and condition of the Woods, Forests, and Land revenues of the Crown [on Bere Forest, Hants].

Mus. H. 3. vol. ii. 3. fol., Lond., 1792.

439 REPORT of the Proceedings of a Meeting of the County of Hants, held at Winchester 1st March, 1823.

Mus. 8vo., 1823.

440 REPORT of the Directors of the London and Southampton Railway, August, 1837.

YY.i. $\frac{19}{7}$ 4to., Lond., 1837.

Contains Map, Sections of the Line, &ca.

441 RICHMOND, (LEGH). The Dairyman's Daughter.

Mus. 12mo., Lond., 1822.

442 ROBERTS, (GEORGE). Social History of the People of the Southern Counties of England.

Mus. B.iv. 14. 8vo., Lond., 1856.

443 ROSCOE, (THOMAS). Summer Tour in the Isle of Wight, including Portsmouth, Southampton, Winchester, &ca. (Plates).

Mus. D.ix. 8vo., Lond., 1843.

444 ROTHERWICK. A true and perfect account of the free scholars appointed to be taught to write and read in the free school of Rotherwick, given by Frederick Tylney, Esq., and opened or begun on the 7th January, 17$\frac{11}{12}$. . . to 1803.

MS.

445 RUDALL, (JAMES). Memoir of the Rev. James Crabb, of Southampton.

Mus. B.v. 5. 12mo., Lond., 1854.

446 RUSSELL, (P.) Hampshire and the Isle of Wight. (From "England Displayed.") (Maps & Plates.)

Mus. fol., Lond., 1769.

447 St. Barbe, (C. I.) Records of the Corporation of the Borough of New Lymington. (Privately printed.)
Mus. C.ii. 27.   4to., Lond., 1848.

448 St. Cross. A short account of the Hospital of St. Cross.
Mus.   8pp., 4to., Birmingham, n.d.

449 ——————— A short description of St. Cross, near Winchester.
8vo., 1818.

450 St. Dionysius' Priory.
fol. sheet, 17 . .

451 Savage, (William). Guide to the ancient City of Winchester.
Mus. D.ix. 6.   8vo., Winchester, 1869.

452 Scott, (Sir G. G.) Report on the Restoration of Winchester City Cross ; with Letters, &ca., on the subject.
Mus. C.viii. $\frac{4}{3}$ 8vo., Winchester, 1866.

453 Scott, (M.) On the Defence of Spithead.
Mus. D.ix. $\frac{4}{6}$ 8vo., Lond., 1862.

454 Selborne. From the " New Monthly Magazine."
Mus. D.ix. $\frac{2}{19}$ |8vo., Lond., 1830.

455 Sewell, (Harriet). The Apple of Discord (a Winchester Play.)
Mus.   12mo., Lond., 1864.

456 Shaw, (S.) Tour to the West of England.
Mus. B.iv. 3.   8vo., Lond., 1789.

457 Sheldrake, (W.) A guide to Aldershot.
Mus. B.v. 29.   8vo., Aldershot, 1859.

458 SHERIDAN, (H. B.) St. Lawrence's Well : a fragmentary Legend of the Isle of Wight.
Mus. B.v. 2. 8vo., Lond., 1843.

459 SHERIDAN, (W. C. F. G.) Historical and Topographical account of the Isle of Wight.
Mus. B.vi. 15. 12mo., Lond., 1832.

460 SHORE, (THOMAS W.) Fragments of the Antiquity and History of Southampton.
Mus. D.ix. $\frac{4}{11}$ 10pp., 8vo., Southampton, 1874.

461 SILCHESTER. History and Antiquities of Silchester, the Vindonum of the Romans, and the Caer Segont of the Britons, with Biographical Notices of Persons connected with the place. 6th Edition.
Mus. D.ix. $\frac{3}{6}$ 8vo., Basingstoke, 1850.

462 ———— From the " Athenæum."
4to., Lond., 1867.

463 ———— From the " Building News." (Plan.)
4to., Lond., 1873.

464 ———— Excavations on the site of Roman Silchester, made in 1864-5. By James Gerald Joyce. (Plates.)
4to., Lond., 1869.

465 SLIGHT, (HENRY). History of Portsmouth, Southsea, Gosport, &ca.
Mus. B.iv. $\frac{17}{4}$ 8vo., Portsmouth, 1844.

466 ———— Metrical History of Portsmouth : with Delineations Topographical, Historical, and Descriptive.
Mus. B.iii. 15. 8vo., Portsmouth, 1820.

467 SLIGHT, (HENRY and JULIAN). Chronicles of Portsmouth.
Mus. C.viii. $\frac{3}{2}$ 12mo., Portsea, 1828.

468 SMEATON, (SAMUEL). Sermon preached at the Visitation of Ralph Bridoake, Archdeacon of Winchester.
Mus. C.vii. $\frac{7}{5}$ 4to., Lond., 1705.

469 SMIRKE, (EDWARD). The Hall of the Royal Palace, and the round table at Winchester.
8vo., Lond., 1846.

470 SMITH, (HERBERT, Curate of Stratton, and Chaplain to the New Forest Union Workhouse). The Church the appointed Guardian of the Poor.
Mus. D.ix. 8vo., Lond., 1842.

471 ———— Winchester Cathedral, &ca.
Mus. D.ix. $\frac{2}{4}$ 8vo., n.p., 1860.

472 SMITH, (THOMAS). Johannis Gravii [Colmere, prope Alresford nati] Vita.
Mus. C.viii. $\frac{7}{8}$ 4to., Lond., 1699.

Was T. Hearne's copy (with his MS. Memoranda) and by him given to Rawlinson.

473 SOUTHAMPTON Guide. An account of the Antient and Present State of that Town.
12mo., Southampton (Linden), 1768.
Mus. D.viii. 23.

Gough in a MS. note in his copy in the Bodleian says that this is written " by Mr. Letchet of Ireland, lately Curate near Salisbury."

474 ———— The Southampton Guide ; an Account of the Ancient and Present State of that Town.
12mo., Southampton (Baker), 1774.
Mus. C.viii. $\frac{5}{2}$
This, though the Title is the same, is an entirely different book from No. 473.

475 ———— The same. 3rd Edition.
12mo., Southampton (Baker), 1781.
Mus. D.viii. 25.

" To this Edition is added [prefixed] *The Southampton Rooms*, a satyrical Poem."

476　SOUTHAMPTON. The same (with *The Southampton Rooms*). 4th Edition, corrected and greatly augmented.
　　　　12mo., Southampton (Baker), 1787.
　　　　Mus. B.v. 25.

477　———— Guide. (Plates).
　　　　12mo., Southampton (Baker), 1829.
　　　　Mus. B.vi. 11.

478　———— Guide.
　　　　12mo., Lond., (Baker), 1840.
　　　　Mus. D.ix. 16.

479　———— Guide.
　　　　12mo., Lond., (Baker), n.d. [1841].
　　　　Mus. D.ix. $\frac{11}{2}$

480　———— Guide.
　　　　8vo., Southampton (Skelton), 1818.
　　　　Mus. D.ix. 11.

481　———— New Southampton Guide. By William Palin.
　　　　12mo., Southampton, n.d. [about 1830].
　　　　Mus. D.ix. $\frac{11}{4}$

482　———— Visitant's Guide to Southampton, Netley Abbey, Portsmouth, &ca.
　　　　8vo., Southampton (Scotland), 1832.
　　　　Mus. B.v. 19.

Of these guides Nos. 480, 481, 482, are reproductions, with alterations, of No. 473, and Nos. 475, 476, 477, 478, 479, are, with additions, reprints of No. 474.

483　———— Papers relating to the Meeting of the Archæological Institute at Southampton, 1872.
　　　　Mus. D.ix. $\frac{3}{14}$

484　———— Archæological Institute at Southampton, 1872.
　　　　Mus. D.ix. $\frac{2}{28}$
　　　　Extracted from the " Guardian " Newspaper.

485 SOUTHAMPTON. Ladies' College at Southampton.
fol., 1872.

486 ——— Sir John de Leon's Voyage from Southampton [in verse].
Mus. D.ix. $\frac{24}{5}$ 8vo., Southampton, n.d.

487 ——— Means of preserving life and property and of promoting European trade by the more general use of Southampton, &ca.
8vo., Lond., 1850.

488 ——— Account of a new Unitarian Chapel at Southampton.
Mus. D.ix. $\frac{4}{12}$

489 ——— Sermon preached on the occasion of the great fire at Southampton, Nov., 1837, by the Rev. W. Wilson, with a narrative of the late awful occurrence, by an Observer.
8vo., Lond. [Southampton], 1837.

490 SPECIAL Services for the Diocese of Winchester [for Missions].
Mus. D.ix. $\frac{16}{4.5.}$ 12mo., Lond., 1872-73.

491 SPEED, (JOHN, M.D., of Southampton). Commentary on Sea-Water. Translated from the Latin.
Mus. B.v. $\frac{25}{2}$ 12mo., Southampton, 1786.
See No. 62.

492 SPENCE, (C.) Essay descriptive of the Abbey Church of Romsey. (Plate).
Mus. B.iv. $\frac{18}{3}$ 8vo., Romsey, 1851.

493 ——— The same. 5th Edition. (Plates).
Mus. D.ix. $\frac{6}{2}$ 8vo., Romsey, n.d.

494 SPORTING incidents in the life of Tom Smith [of Fir Hill, Droxford], Master of Fox-hounds.
Mus. B.vi. 17. 8vo., Lond., 1867.

495 SPORTING Reminiscences of Hampshire, 1745 to 1862, by Æsop.
Mus. B.vi. 16. 8vo., Lond., 1864.

496 STEVENS, (ARCHIBALD JOHN). Charge to the Grand Jury of Winchester.
8vo., Lond., 1861.

497 STEVENS, (J.) Descriptive list of Flint Implements found at St. Mary Bourne, and Geological Features of the Upper Test Valley.
Mus. B.iv. $\frac{17}{7}$ 8vo., Lond., 1867.

STOCKMAN, (I.) *See* Porchester.

498 STURCH, (JOHN). A view of the Isle of Wight, in four letters to a friend. 3rd Edition.
Mus. D.ix. 20. 12mo., Newport, 1787.

This is the earliest History of the Island. The first edition was printed in London in 1778. The second in 1780. The Author bought a press, and printed the 3rd Edition, as above, at Newport, and a 4th in 1791.

499 SUMNER, (Bishop CHARLES RICHARD). Visitation Charges.
YY.ii. 6, and Mus. D.ix. 8vo., Lond., v.y.

These Charges contain much statistical information as to the progress of the Church and Education in Hampshire.

500 ———— Conspectus of the Diocese of Winchester.
Mus. B.iii. 3. 8vo., Westminster, 1854.

501 ———— Conspectus of the Diocese of Winchester.
Mus. B.iii. $\frac{3}{2}$ 8vo., Lond., 1864.

502 SUMNER, (GEORGE HENRY). Life of Charles Richard Sumner, Bishop of Winchester.
Mus. C.vii. 10. 8vo., Lond., 1874.

503 SYDMONTON. Correspondence with the Bishop of Winchester, and protest of the Incumbent against the Consecration of a Church at Sydmonton.
Mus. D.ix. $\frac{1}{14}$ 8vo., Lond., 1865.

504 TALBOT, (WILLIAM). Narrative of the forgeries, &ca., of Jonathan Brittain [who pretended to give information as to the fire in Portsmouth Dock-yard, 1770].
Mus. D.ix. $\frac{4}{2}$ 8vo., wants title.

505 THORNTON, (Dr.) Sketch of the life and writings of Mr. William Curtis [a native of Alton].
Mus. D.ix. $\frac{3}{10}$

506 TICHBORNE Romance. By a Barrister at Law.
Mus. C.viii. $\frac{6}{3}$ 8vo., Lond., 1872.

506* ———— Report of the case of Tichborne v. Lushington. Extracted from the " Morning Chronicle," &ca.; bound in   vols.
4to., Lond., 1871-2.

507 ———— Trial. The evidence of handwriting. Fac-similes.
Mus. D.ix. $\frac{1}{13}$ 8vo., Lond., 1874.

508 ———— Summing up of the Judges, re-printed from the " Times."
Mus. D.ix. $\frac{6}{5}$ 8vo., Lond., 1874.
[See No. 518.

509 TODD, (JOHN HENRY). Memento of the Charitable Societies of Natives and Aliens of Winchester.
Mus. D.ix. $\frac{2}{6}$ 8vo., Winchester, 1869.

510 ———— Poetical Blossoms.
MN.ii. 28.   4to., MS., 1825.

511 TOMKINS, (C.) Tour to the Isle of Wight. (Plates).
Mus. C.ii. 9.   2 vols., 8vo., Lond., 1796.

512 TOUR through some of the Southern Counties of England, by Peregrine Project and Timothy Type.
Mus. B.v. 31.   12mo., Lond., 1804.

513 TOURIST'S Guide through the Isle of Wight, describing its ancient and present state.

Mus. D.ix. $\frac{15}{3}$ 12mo., Lond., 1842.

514 ——— Guide through the Isle of Wight, with its peculiar and most interesting scenery. (Map and coloured prints).

Mus. C.viii. $\frac{1}{3.4}$.   8vo., Lond. [Southampton], 1846.

515 TOWNSEND, (C.) Winchester, and a few other compositions, in prose and verse.

Mus. B.vi. 25.   4to., Winchester, 1835.

516 TRANSACTIONS of the British Archæological Association, held at Winchester, 1845. (Plates).

Mus. B.iii. 6.   8vo., Lond., 1846.

Containing :
Municipal records of Winchester and Sonthampton. By T. Wright.
Account of John Claptone, an Alchemist of Winchester. By J. O. Halliwell.
Sales of Manors and Church Lands of the See of Winchester. By J. H. Burn.
Account of Barton Oratory, Isle of Wight. By J. A. Barton.
Notes on Monastic Estates in Hampshire. By M. de Gerville.
Reversal of a writ of Excommunication by the Bishop of Winchester. By M. F. Tupper.
Roman Roads and Stations in Hampshire. By H. Hatcher.
Antiquities of Winchester. By W. B. Bradfield.
Barrows in the Isle of Wight. By J. Dennett.
Roman remains at Bittern. By C. R. Smith.
Observations on the paintings in Winchester Cathedral. By J. G. Waller.
Mint at Winchester. By J. Y. Akerman.
Notes on an incised slab in Brading Church, Isle of Wight. By W. H. Rosser.
Winchester Cathedral. By E. Cresy.
Architectural Notes on the Church of St. Cross. By S. Jackson.
Church Notes in the neighbourhood of Winchester. By D. R. Haigh.
Abbey Church of Romsey. By A. Ashpital.
Ancient fortifications of Southampton, By W. D. Saull.

517 TREVELYAN, (FRANCES A.) Quarr Abbey, or the mistaken calling : a Poem. (Plate).

Mus. B.v. 4.   4to., Lond., 1862.

518 TRIAL of Thomas Castro, otherwise Arthur Orton, for Perjury. Extracted from " The Times," and bound in 3 vols.

NO. I. 31.   4to., Lond., 1873-4.

519 TRIAL of C. J. Heaton and others for forcible entry of a tenement at Petersfield.

Mus. D.ix. $\frac{1}{9}$ 8vo., Lond. [1820].

520 —— of James Hill, *alias* James Hind, *alias* James Aitzen (Aitken) for setting fire to the Dock-yard at Portsmouth. (Portrait inserted).

fol., Lond., 1777.

521 —— between Sir Richard Worsley, Bart., and George Maurice Bisset, for Criminal Conversation with the Plaintiff's Wife.

Mus. C.ii. 30. 4to., Lond., 1782.

With a very curious coloured folding plate inserted.

522 TUNNICLIFF, (W.) Topographical Survey of Hants, &ca.

FF.i. 3. 8vo., Salisbury, 1791.

523 TURNER, (F.) Sermon preach'd before the King (Charles II.) in Winchester.

Mus. C.vii. 7. 4to., Lond., 1683.

524 VANCOUVER, (CHARLES). View of the agriculture of Hampshire and the Isle of Wight. (Map and Plates).

Mus. B.vi. 22. 8vo., Lond., 1810.

525 VECTIS : a descriptive Poem. Printed on green paper. (Map and views).

Mus. C.viii. $\frac{4}{6}$ 12mo. size, Ryde, n.d.

526 VENABLES, (E.) Guide to the Isle of Wight.

Mus. B.v. 27. 8vo., Lond., 1860.

527 VIEWS in Hampshire.

Mus. C.ii. 28. 4to., Lond., 1799.

From " British Topography." The plates are in various states, from the first proof to the lettered impression.

528 —— Seven large volumes, containing 1458 prints and drawings of buildings, and views in Hampshire.

Mus. A.1. 7 vols. fol., v.y. and p.

529 WALCOTT, (MACKENZIE E. C.) Guide to the Coasts of Hants and Dorset.
Mus. C.viii. $\frac{7}{4}$ 8vo., Lond., 1859.

530 ———— Memorials of Christchurch Twynham.
Mus. C.viii. 6.   8vo., Christchurch, 1868.

531 ———— Memorials of Winchester.
Mus. D.ix. 2.   8vo., Winchester, 1866.

532 ———— The Priory Church of Christchurch, its Norman Keep, &ca.
Mus. D.ix. $\frac{12}{5}$ 8vo., Christchurch, 1862.

533 ———— William of Wykeham and his Colleges, containing a roll of distinguished Wykehamicts from 1454 to 1852.
Mus. B.iii. 9.   8vo., Winchester, 1852.

534 WALLER, (ESSEX). A Trip to Portsmouth, or the Wife's Election.
Mus. D.ix. $\frac{4}{9}$ 8vo., Gosport, 1822.
Reprinted from an unique copy, 1710.

535 WALPOOLE, (GEORGE AUGUSTUS). The County of Hants. (From his " New British Traveller.")
Mus.   fol., Lond., 1780.

536 WALTERS, (CHARLES). History of the Town, Church, and Episcopal Palace of Bishops Waltham, from the earliest period to the present time.
Mus. C.viii. $\frac{4}{2}$ 12mo., Winchester, 1844.

537 ———— The City Cross, Winchester, with account of similar structures, their use and design.
Mus. C.viii. $\frac{7}{5}$ 8vo., Winchester, 1856.

538 WALTHAM. The History of the Blacks of [Bishops] Waltham.
Mus. B.v. 12.   8vo., Lond., 1723.

539 WALTON, (J.) Family Walks in Hampshire.
       Mus. D.viii. 21.   12mo., Lond., 1815.

540 ———— Geography of Hampshire.
       Mus. D.ix. $\frac{10}{4}$ 8vo., Lond., n.d.

541 WANDERINGS in the Isle of Wight.
       Mus. B.v. 21. small sq. 8vo., Lond., 1846.

542 WARBURTON, (WILLIAM). Tabulated reports of Schools inspected in . . Hants.
       Mus. D.ix. $\frac{3}{13}$ 8vo., Lond., 1860.

542* WARNER, (FERDINANDO). Sermon preached at the Annual Visitation of the Bishop of Winchester at Andover.
       Mus. C.vii. $\frac{7}{7}$ 4to., Lond., 1738.

543 WARNER, (RICHARD). A companion in a Tour round Lymington.
       Mus. B.vi. 13.   12mo., Southampton, 1789.
        This was Warner's first attempt in literature.

544 ———— Attempt to ascertain the situation of the Ancient Clausentum [with proposals for compiling and publishing the History of Hampshire]. (Vignette and Plan.)
       Mus. C.ii.   4to., Lond., 1792.

545 ———— Topographical Remarks relating to the South-Western parts of Hampshire.
       Mus. B.iv. 5. 2 vols. 8vo., Lond., 1793.
   The plates intended for this work were destroyed (it is said) by an accidental fire.

546 ———— History of the Isle of Wight, Military, Ecclesiastical, Civil, and Natural.
       Mus. B.iv. 6. 8vo., Southampton, 1795.

547 ———— Collections for the History of Hampshire and the Bishoprick of Winchester, including the Isles of Wight, Jersey, Guernsey, and Sark,

by D.Y., with the original Domesday Book of the County, &c., by R. Warner, jun., of Sway, Hants. (plates).
Mus. B.ii. 5.   5 vols. 4to., Lond., [1795].

It is said in the Title-pages to be " in six volumes." That is : the 1st containing the Parochial Survey (alphabetically) is in two parts; the 2nd is a re-issue of Warner's Hampshire Domesday (published in 1789) with a different Title ; the 3rd is called the Agricultural Survey, Natural History, Honours, and Biography of Eminent Men of this County; the 4th is a reprint of Falle's History of Jersey ; the 5th contains the Islands of Guernsey and Sark.

It is a most imperfect and unsatisfactory attempt at County History. The account of the Parishes is meagre in the extreme ; sometimes reprints of articles from the " Gentleman's Magazine," sometimes the mere name and situation of the Parish, and these not always correctly given.

Warner states, in his " Literary Recollections," that this work is a most barefaced piracy ; that he did not know of its publication till he received an anonymous letter severely criticising what was supposed to be his work. He says that he then procured a copy, and on going through it was surprised to find that the compiler had incorporated into his collections not only the Domesday book, but also nearly the whole of his History of the Isle of Wight, Clausentum, and Topographical Remarks on the South-Western parts of Hampshire. But it seems incredible that respectable booksellers, whose names are on the title-page (Rivington, Cadell, and others) should have lent themselves to so gross a literary fraud ; or that Warner's Hampshire Domesday, published only six year's previously, should have been actually incorporated into the work, as the second volume, without Warner's or his publisher's knowledge and consent. And it is not a little remarkable, as throwing great doubt on Warner's story, that he himself in 1792, circulated proposals, which clearly indicate such a work as this which was subsequently published under his name ; almost the only difference being that he proposed to print it in three volumes folio. A copy of these Proposals is among Gough's Collections in the Bodleian ; and they are reprinted at the end of Warner's Clausentum. And it appears, from No. 306, that Warner was not always accurate in his statements.

I have failed to discover who D.Y. was.

It is stated on the title page, that only 250 copies were printed, 25 on large, and 225 on small paper.

My copy is illustrated by the insertion of upwards of a hundred additional prints, drawings, and maps.

548   WARNER, (RICHARD).   Literary Recollections.
Mus. B.vi. 3.   2 vols. 8vo., Lond., 1830.

This contains many interesting particulars and anecdotes about persons and places in South-Hampshire.

549   [WARTON, (THOMAS).]   Description of the City, College, and Cathedral of Winchester.
Mus. C.viii. 5.   12mo., Lond., n.d. [1760].

See Nichols' Literary Anecdotes. vi. 176.

550 WATTS. Memoirs of the Life and Writings of Isaac Watts, D.D., with extracts from his Correspondence.

8vo., Lond., 1806.

See No. 219.

551 WAYNFLEET, (WILLIAM, Bishop of Winchester). Life, by R. Chandler.

Mus. B.iii. 19. 8vo., Lond., 1811.

552 WEBSTER, (THOMAS). On the freshwater formations in the Isle of Wight. (Maps and plate.)

Mus. C.ii. 18. 4to., Lond., 1814.

553 ———— On some new variety of Fossil found in the Isle of Wight. (Plates).

Mus. C.ii. $\frac{18}{2}$ 4to., Lond., 1814.

554 ———— On the freshwater formation in Hordwell Cliff, Hants. (Plate).

Mus. C.ii. $\frac{18}{4}$ 4to., Lond., 1821.

555 WESTALL, (W.) Views of Carisbrook Castle, Isle of Wight.

Mus. 8vo., 1839.

556 WESTERN County Magazine; for Wilts, Hants, &ca.

2 vols. 8vo., Salisbury, 1789-90.

Mus. D.ix.

557 WEYHILL Ghost : a tale founded on fact, in four cantos, with some other pieces.

Mus. D.ix. 22. 8vo., Lond., 1815.

558 WEELER'S Hampshire and West of England Magazine.

Mus. C.ix. 1. 8vo., Winchester, 1828.

With this was incorporated " The Crypt," see Nos. 188, 189. Twelve Numbers (Jan. to Dec., 1828,) only were published.

559 WHITE (GILBERT). Natural History and Antiquities of Selborne. (Plates).
Mus. C.ii. 14. 4to., Lond., 1789.

The first Edition of this popular work.

560 WHITE, (WILLIAM). History and Gazetteer of Hampshire and the Isle of Wight.
Mus. B.iv. 9. 8vo., Sheffield, 1859.

561 ———— 2nd Edition [much enlarged].
8vo., Sheffield, 1878.

562 WHITAKER, (WILLIAM). List of works on the Geology of Hampshire.
Mus. D.ix. $\frac{5}{2}$ 8vo., Lond., 1873.

563 WIGRAM, (JOSEPH C.) Ministerial Watchfulness : a Sermon preached at Alton.
8vo., Lond., 1845.

564 ———— Present Aspects of Popular Education : a Charge to the Archdeaconry of Winchester.
8vo., Lond., 1849.

565 ———— Letter on the Spiritual necessities of Portsea.
Mus. D.ix. $\frac{4}{7}$ 8vo., Lond., 1851.

566 ———— Thoughts for the Christian Laity : a Charge to the Archdeaconry of Winchester.
8vo., Lond., 1857.

567 WILKINS, (ERNEST P.) Geology, Antiquities, and Topography of the Isle of Wight. (Map in relief and plates.)
Mus. C.ii. 16. 4to., Newport, n.d. [1859].

See No. 92.

568 W[ILKINSON], (A.) Brief Historical Notices of the Parishes of Harstbourne Priors, St. Mary Bourne, &ca., and of the cross-legged effigy in the Church of St. Mary Bourne.
Mus. B.iv. $\frac{17}{6}$ 8vo., Lond., 1861.

569 WILLIAM Rufus, his Tomb at Winchester. (Plates.)
Mus. D. ix. $\frac{2}{5}$ 8vo., 1870.

570 WILLMOT, (Sir JOHN E. EARDLEY). Reminiscences
of Thomas Assheton Smith, Esq. [of Tedworth].
(Plates.)
Mus. B.iii. 16.   8vo., Lond., 1860.

571 WILSON, (R. F.) Short notes of Seven years in a
Country Parish [Rownham, Hants].
Mus. B.v. 32.   8vo., Oxford, 1872.

572 WINCHESTER. History and Antiquities of Winchester. (Plates).
Mus. B.vi. 12.   2 vols., 12mo., Winton, 1773.

573 ———— Guide. A description of the Antiquities
and curiosities of that Ancient City.
Mus. D.viii. $\frac{25}{2}$ 12mo., Winton, 1780.

574 —————— or a description of the Antiquities
and curiosities of that Ancient City. (Plates).
Mus. B.v. 18.   8vo., Winton, 1796.

575 ———— History and Antiquities of Winchester,
with account of the Seats of the Gentry, Nobility,
&ca. [Extracted from Milner.] (Plates.)
Mus. B.v. 1.   8vo., Winchester, 1802.

576 ———— Historical and Descriptive Guide to the
City of Winchester, its Cathedral, &ca.
7th Edition.
Mus. D.ix. $\frac{9}{2}$ 12mo., Winchester, 1829.

577 ———— Picturesque Memorials of Winchester.
Plates by Le Keux, with descriptions.
Mus. A. 3.   fol., Winchester, 1830.

578 ———— Handbook.
Mus. B.v. 13.   8vo., Winchester, 1868.

579 WINCHESTER. Antiquities of Winchester, with an historical account of the city.
Mus. B.v. 20.　18mo., Winchester, n.d.

580 ———— Guide. Giving an account of its antiquities, and of the Hospital of St. Cross.
Mus. B.iv. $\frac{18}{4}$　8vo., Winchester, n.d.

581 ———— Guide to Winchester. 11th Edition.
Mus. D.ix. $\frac{12}{4}$　16mo., Winchester, n.d.

582 ———— Cathedral. Historical and critical account of Winchester Cathedral, extracted from the Rev. J. Milner's History.
Mus. D.ix. $\frac{2}{2}$　8vo., Winchester, 1801.

583 ———— History and Antiquities of Winchester Cathedral, with Biographical Anecdotes, by John Britton. (Plates).
Mus. A. 2.　4to., Lond., 1817.

584 ———— Observations and Correspondence occasioned by the failure and renovation of a principal pier in Winchester Cathedral. By W. Garbett.
Mus.　4to., Winchester, 1824.

585 ———— An apology for those who object to the lateral position of an organ in Winchester Cathedral.
4to., Lond., 1825.

586 ———— Ancient painted glass of Winchester Cathedral, traced from the windows by Owen B. Carter. 28 coloured plates, with descriptions.
Mus. C.ii. 25.　4to., Lond., 1845.

587 ———— Descriptive account of the Cathedral of Winchester. 8 views. Reprinted from B. Winkle's English Cathedrals.
Mus. C.ii. 21.　8vo., n.d.

588 Winchester Cathedral. Supplementary Notices to the History of Winchester Cathedral, by a Bookseller.
Mus. D.ix. $\frac{2}{3}$ 8vo., n.p. or d.

589 ———— Order for the Enthronement of Edward Harold Browne, Lord Bishop of Winchester.
fol. sheet, 1873.

589* ———— Sacrilege in Winchester Cathedral.
Mus. D.ix. $\frac{2}{22}$ extracted from Newspaper.

590 ———— College. A narrative of the Proceedings in the dispute between the Bishop of Winchester and the College of Winchester, concerning his jurisdiction.
Mus. B.iv. 19.   8vo., Lond., 1713.

591 ———— [Bridell (J.)] A short address to the Society of New College, Oxford, occasioned by a paragraph in a late dedication [of Lowth's Life of Bishop Wykeham].
Mus. B. $\frac{19}{3}$ 8vo., Lond., 1758.

592 ———— A serious and friendly admonition to the Fellows of New College in Oxford [on the Election of a Warden from Winchester College].
Mus.B. iv. $\frac{19}{2}$ Broad sheet. [1758 ?]

593 ———— A letter to the Reverend Dr. Lowth in vindication of the conduct of the Fellows of New College, Oxford, in their late election of a Warden of Winchester College. [By J. Bridell, D.D.]
Mus. B.iv. $\frac{19}{4}$ 8vo., Lond., 1759.

594 ———— A Defence of the conduct of the Warden of Winchester College, by himself [Dr. Golding].
Mus. B.iv. $\frac{19}{6}$ 8vo., Lond., 1758.

595   WINCHESTER College.   Answer to an anonymous letter to Dr. Lowth. [By Robert Lowth.]
    Mus. B.iv. $\frac{19}{5}$ 8vo., Lond., 1759.

596   ———— Reply to Dr. Golding's and Dr. Lowth's answers to the anonymous letter.
    Mus. B.iv. $\frac{19}{9}$ 8vo., Lond., 1759.

597   ———— An impartial bystander's review of the controversy concerning the Wardenship of Winchester College.
    Mus. B.iv. $\frac{19}{10}$ 8vo., Lond., 1759.

598   ———— The law and equity of the late appointment of a Warden considered. [By Mr. Pescod.]
    Mus. B.iv. $\frac{19}{7.8}$ 8vo., Lond., 1759.

599   ———— Remarks on some proceedings at the time of the late election at Winchester College, and the case of the Masters of the School fairly stated. [By Dr. Burton].
    Mus. B.iv. $\frac{20}{2}$ 8vo., Lond., 1767.

600   ———— The Wiccamical Chaplet : a Selection of Original Poetry [the Effusions of Wykehamites.] By G. Huddersford.
    Mus. C.ix. 7.   8vo., Lond., 1804.

601   ———— Report of Appeal to the Lord Bishop of Winchester, Visitor of the two St. Mary Winton Colleges, promoted by William Augustus Hare, against the Election to the vacant Scholarships at Winchester and New College in 1839 ; by Joseph Phillimore.
    Mus. B.iv. $\frac{20}{7}$ 8vo., Lond., 1839.

602   ———— The College of St. Mary Winton, by C[harles] W[ordsworth]. (Illustrations.)
    Mus. B.iii. 17.   sm. 4to., Oxford, 1848.

603 WINCHESTER College. Observations on the Public
Schools Bill, as affecting Winchester College.
By George Moberley.
  Mus. B.iv. $\frac{20}{8}$ 8vo., Winchester, 1865.

604 —————— Ups and downs of a Public School, by
a Wykehamist.
  Mus. B.v. 39.   12mo., Lond., n.d.
   Reprinted in the next article.

605 —————— The Public School Matches and those
we meet there. By a Wykehamist.
  Mus. C.viii. $\frac{6}{2}$ 12mo., Lond., 1867.

606 —————— School Life at Winchester. By R. B.
M[ansfield]. (Plates.)
  Mus. B.v. 38.   12mo., Lond., 1870.

607 —————— Winchester discipline. Extracted from
" The Times," &ca.
  Mus. B.iv. $\frac{20}{9}$ 8vo., Lond., 1872.

608 —————— Wykehamica : a History of Winchester
College and its Commoners, from the foundation
to the present day. By H. C. Adams. (Illustra-
tions.)
  Mus. D.ix.   8vo., Oxford, 1878.
   See Nos. 102, 533.

609 —————— Diocesan Calendar. Bound in volumes.
Mus. C.x. 8vo., Lond., 1865, and yearly since.

610 —————— Diocesan Inspection [of Schools] in
Religious Knowledge.
       fol. sheet, 1875.

611 —————— Christening of Prince Arthur, at Winchester [from Monthly Magazine].
  Mus. D.ix. $\frac{2}{27}$ 8vo., 1812.

612 WINCHESTER. Abstract of the Report of the Commissioners concerning Charities in the management of the Corporation of Winchester.
Mus. D.ix. $\frac{2}{7}$ 8vo., Winchester, n.d.

613 ———— Scientific and Literary Society. Report for 1870.
Mus. D.ix. $\frac{5}{3}$ 8vo., Winchester, 1870.

614 ———— Scientific and Literary Society. Proceedings. Vol. I.
Mus. D.ix. $\frac{5}{4}$ 8vo., Winchester, 1875.

615 ———— New Guildhall.
4to. sheet, Lond., 1873.

616 ———— Prize Ode, and five other nuptial odes [on the Marriage of the Prince of Wales].
Mus. D.ix. $\frac{23}{8}$ Winchester, 1863.

617 ———— Tanner's Winchester Quarterly Record of Public Events.
Mus. D.ix. $\frac{8}{6}$ 8vo., Winchester, v.y.

617* WINDOVER, (NICHOLAS). The Englishman's Guide to Plenty, containing the observations of an old Hampshire farmer on the national produce, &ca.
Mus. B.vi. 21.   8vo., Lond., 1807.

617**WISE, (J. R.) The New Forest, its History and its Scenery. (Illustrations).
Mus. B.iii. 8.   8vo., Lond., 1867.

618 WITHER, (LOVELACE). Cottage Allotments in some Parishes of North Hampshire.
Mus. D.ix. 1.   8vo., Lond., 1832.

619 ———— Letter to the farmers of some Parishes in North Hampshire on the means of reducing Poor-rates.
Mus. D.ix. $\frac{1}{2}$ 8vo., Lond., 1832.

620 WITHER Family. Private case before the House of Lords, between Andrew Wither and others and Dr. William King, relating to Lands and Estates in the County of Southampton.
Mus.   fol., privately printed, 1735.

621 WODEHOUSE, (ALGERNON). A few words to the Parishioners of Odiham.
Mus.   12mo., 1858.

622 ———— Letters to the Masters, Mistresses, Teachers, and Children of the Odiham National and Sunday Schools.
12mo., 1858.

623 ———— Letter to the Parishioners of Odiham.
12mo., 1858.

624 WOOD, (C.) Reminiscences of Winchester. (Plates).
Mus. C.ii. 19.   4to., Winchester, n.d.

625 WOODWARD, (B. B.), WILKS, (T. C.), and LOCKHART, (C.) General History of Hampshire and the Isle of Wight. (Plates.)
Mus. B.ii. 6.   3 vols., 4to., Lond., n.d.

626 WOOLL, (JOHN). The King's House at Winchester: a Poem in two parts.
MN.ii. 25.   4to., Lond., 1793.

627 ———— Biographical Memoirs of the Reverend Joseph Warton, D.D.
Mus. C.ii. 24.   4to., Lond., 1806.

628 WOOLMER Forest. Report of the Commissioners appointed to enquire into the state and condition of the Woods, Forests, and Land Revenues of the Crown [on Aliceholt and Woolmer Forest].
Mus. H. 3.   Vol. I. 6. fol., Lond., 1790.

629 WORSLEY, (Sir RICHARD). History of the Isle of Wight. Mus. D.ii. 13. 4to., Lond., 1781.

Bound in 3 vols.; interleaved, and illustrated with additional plates, portraits, and drawings.

———— *See* No. 521.

630 ———— Museum Worsleyanum ; or a collection of Antique Basso-relievos, Bustos, Statues, and Gems ; with Views of Places in the Levant. Taken on the spot in the years 1785-6 and 7. Mus. B.ii. 1. 2 vols., 4to., Lond., 1824.

The original Edition was in folio, 1794—1803.

631 WRIGHT, (HENRY PRESS). Story of the Domus Dei at Portsmouth. (Plates). Mus. B.v. 14. 8vo., Lond., 1873.

632 WYATT, (THOMAS HENRY). Report on repairs of Basing Church. (Plates). Mus. fol., Lond., 1873.

633 ———— On the old Hall and New Assize Courts at Winchester. (Plate and Plan.) 4to., Lond., 1874.

634 WYNDHAM, (H. P.) Picture of the Isle of Wight. Mus. B.iv. 4. 8vo., Lond., 1794.

635 YATELEY. Description of Monumental Brasses in Yateley Church, by W. M. Wylie. Mus. D.ix. $\frac{2}{26}$ 3pp. 8vo., Lond., 1870.

636 ———— Account of opening of Yateley Industrial Exhibition, 1875. Mus. D.ix. $\frac{2}{29}$

637 YOUNG, (E.) Discourse at the Winchester Assizes, 11th July, 1695. Mus. C.vii. $\frac{7}{4}$ 4to., Lond., 1695.

638 YOUNG, (Mrs.) Aldershot and all about it. Mus. B.v. 28. 8vo., Lond., 1858.

ADDENDA.

639 ACCOUNT of the principal Church Organs in Hampshire.   4to. MS.

640 ADKINS, (THOMAS.) Sermon on the death of Mr. Bullar [of Southampton].
        8vo., Southampton, 1859.

641 ANDOVER. Papers relating to a contested Election for Andover, 1702, including Copies of the Charters, &ca., of that Borough and many original documents.
    Mus. H. 4.   fol. MS.

642 BASING. Account of Basing Castle and Manor, formerly belonging to the ancient family of De Port.   4to. MS.

643 BASINGSTOKE. Pedestrian feats and humorous adventures of the late Mr. Charles Spier, upwards of forty years Clerk of Basingstoke Church. 9th Edition.
        Basingstoke, 1871.

644 BISSE, (THOMAS). Sermon preached at the opening of the Church of St. Marie, Southampton.
        8vo., Lond., 1712.

645 BRANNON, (GEORGE). The Landscape Beauties of the Isle of Wight, as described by the Rev. Leigh Richmond. (Plates.)
        8vo., Wootton, I. of W., n.d.
This is a different book from No. 86.

646 BRANNON, (PHILIP). Picture of Southampton. (Plates.)
        8vo., Southampton, n.d.

647 CHRISTCHURCH. Case of Mr. Richard Holoway, one of the Burgesses inhabiting the Town of Christchurch. With a Poll-list of the Voters at the Election, 1727.

8vo., n.p., or d.

648 COLLECTION of Reports and Statements of the Royal Hants County Hospital ; the Hampshire Friendly Society; and other Religious, Educational and Charitable Associations in Hampshire : consisting of 25 articles.

8vo., v.p. and y.

649 COLLECTION of Sermons preached in Churches in Hampshire on special occasions : consisting of 18 articles.   8vo., v.p., and y.

650 CRONDALL. Proposed Plan for building a new Church in the tythings of Crookham and Ewshot. (Plate and Map).

8vo., Lond., 1839.

651 FORBES, (EDWARD). On the pluvio-marine tertiaries of the Isle of Wight. [From the " Journal of the Geological Society."]

8vo., [Lond.,] 1853.

652 GARROW, (DAVID). History of Lymington.

8vo., Lond., 1825.

652* HAMPSHIRE. From Kendall's Picture of England.

8vo., Lond., 1831.

653 HOARE, (C. J.) Educational statistics. A charge delivered on visitation [to the Arch-deaconry of Winchester.]

8vo., Winchester, 1847.

653* ———— Parochial Statistics. A charge delivered on visitation.

8vo., Winchester, 1844.

654 HOARE, (S.) Correspondence and Ex-Communion of the Rev. Edmund Dewdney, Minister of St. John's Chapel, Portsea.
12mo., Portsmouth, 1837.

655 HOGLANDIÆ Descriptio.
Mus. D.ix. $\frac{23}{2}$ 8vo., Lond., 1709.

This is a different edition from No. 268 (the type and the cut of the Hog on the title-page being entirely dissimilar), though published the same year.

656 ———— The (Latin) Description of Hogland, with its Dedication : Imitated in English.
Mus. D.ix. $\frac{23}{3}$ 8vo., Lond., 1711.

The cut of the Hog on the title-page different from either of the preceding.

657 ISLE OF WIGHT. Evidence in the House of Lords on the Isle of Wight Railway.
8vo., Lond., 1860.

658 ———— Sir John Oglander's account of the Isle of Wight.
Mus. C.ii. 5. fol. MS., Transcribed, 1794.

659 ITCHEN River. Address of Mr. Wade and Mr. Goldfinch, in refutation of a pamphlet by Mr. Hollis.
8vo., Winchester, n.d.

660 JEFFERSON, (JOSEPH). Horæ Poeticæ. Poems Sacred, Moral, and Descriptive.

This is said to be the first book printed at Basingstoke.

661 KELL, (EDMUND). Tribute to the Memory of Alderman Richard Andrews [of Southampton], with a Memoir.
8vo., Southampton, 1859.

662 KING, (Bishop HENRY). Sermon at the Funeral of Bryan [Duppa], Lord Bishop of Winchester.
Mus. C.viii. 7.   4to., Lond., 1662.

663　KING, (JAMES).　Sermon at the Anniversary of the Natives of the County of Southampton.

8vo., Lond., 1708.

663*　KING, (THOMAS).　Poems.　[Privately printed.]
Mus. D. $\frac{24}{9}$　　Basingstoke, 1849.

664　LAKE, (OSMUND, Minister of the Word of God at Ringwood.)　A Probe Theologicall : or . . . The Christian Pastor's proofe of his Parishioners *Faith.*

Mus. D.ix.　　4to., Lond., 1612.

" A very curious and uncommon book, and unnoticed by our etymologists " and commentators on the old English dramatists."—MS. note in this copy.

665　LOWTH, (WILLIAM).　Sermon preached at Petersfield.

8vo., Lond., 1723.

666　————　Answer to remarks of Mr. John Norman on the above Sermon.

8vo., Lond., 1723.

See No. 680.

667　MANNINGHAM, (Bishop THOMAS).　Sermon at the Hampshire Feast, on Shrove Tuesday, 1686.
Mus. C.vii. $\frac{7}{5}$　　4to., Lond., 1686.

668　—————　Sermon at the Funeral of Sir John Norton, Bart.
Mus. C.vii. $\frac{7}{6}$　　4to., Lond., 1687.

See No. 347.

669　MAP of the Environs of Andover.　(By Burgiss Brown).　　　　1873.

670　MAP of Hampshire, with Views of the Needles, Netley Abbey, Calshot, Carisbrooke, and Porchester Castles, two views of Silchester walls, a view of the Amphitheatre, and a plan of Silchester, by Isaac Taylor.　　1759.

671 MAP of Hampshire, by Thomas Kitchen.

672 ——————————— by John Cary. 1828.

673 ——————————— shewing all the Railways and Stations. (G. F. Cruchley.)

674 —— of the London and Southampton Railway.
(James Wyld), 1839.

675 —— of the London and Southampton Railway, with the Stations to Basingstoke.

676 —— of Southampton, by George Doswell.
With Views.

677 PLAN of the Town and Borough of Southampton.
(James Wyld), 1844.
Other Maps and Plans are bound up with Nos. 527 and 547.

678 NEW FOREST. Berkeley, (the Honble. Grantley F.) Letter to the Viscount Palmerston [on hunting in the New Forest].
8vo., Lond., 1855.

679 NORMAN, (JOHN). God to be worshipped in spirit and in truth. Sermon at Portsmouth. With remarks on a Sermon preached by the Rev. William Ward, Vicar of Portsmouth, at the Opening of the Organ there.
8vo., Lond., 1718.

680 ——————— Remarks on a Sermon preached at Petersfield, by the Rev. William Lowth.
8vo., Lond., 1723.
See Nos. 662, 663.

681 NORRIS, (WILLIAM). Letter to the Inhabitants of the Parish of Warblington, on the new Poor Law.
8vo., Winchester, 1834.

682 PORTSEA. Address to the Members of the Portsea
Institution for Educating the Infant poor.
8vo., Lond., 1813.

683 ROMSEY. Companion to the Abbey Church of
Romsey. (Plates).
8vo., Romsey, 1827.

684 SOTHEBY, (W.) Poems : The Priory in the Isle
of Wight, Farewell to Bevis Mount, and Netley
Abbey. 4to., Bath., 1790.

685 SOUTHAMPTON. Bye-Laws of the Local Board, under
the Local Government Act, 1858 ; and Reports
(6) on the Paving and Drainage of Southampton,
by James Lemon.
Mus. C.ix. 11. 8vo., Southampton, 1866-72.

686 ———— Sermon preached in the Church of
All Saints, Southampton, at the rebuilding of
the ancient Church of St. Lawrence ; by Henry
William Wilberforce.
8vo., Southampton, 1839.

687 ———— Statement and Depositions relative to
the origin of the Fire at Springfield House, Southampton. (Plate with Plan.)
8vo., Lond., 1842.

688 STORY of a Sailor's life, as related by Francis
Bergh [living at Gosport].
12mo., Gosport, 1834.

689 STRAY'D Lamb (from Gosport) ; or, the Baptist no
Seducer. [In verse.]
Mus. D.ix. $\frac{24}{8}$ 8vo., Lond., 1812.

690 TICHBORNE Trial. The summing up of the Lord
Chief Justice, &ca. (verbatim report), with a
History of the Case, &ca.
8vo., Lond., 1874.
A different report from No. 508.

691 THE TOPOGRAPHER.
Mus. B.iv. 15. 4 vols., 8vo., Lond., 1789-91.

Contains the following articles relating to Hampshire :--
History of the Parish of Dummer.
———— Kempshot.
———— Ewhurst.
———— and Description of the Vine.
———— of Mottisfont.
———— of Rotherwick.
———— Stratfield-Say.
Basingstoke.
Account of Malsanger.
Historical list of Hampshire families.
Additions to "Hampshire," in Gough's Camden.
Notes from Egham to Stratfield-Say.
History of Winchester College (with plate).
Account of Ellingham.
———— the family of Brocas, of Beaurepaire.
———— Winslade.
History of Ash and Deane.

692 TRIAL of Jonathan Britain for Forgery, capitally
convicted [and executed] at Bristol.
4to., Lond., 1772.
See No. 504.

693 WINCHESTER. Views of Winchester.
8vo. size, n.p. or d.

694 ———— Sermon before the Governors of the
County Hospital, at its opening. By Alured
Clarke. . To which is added a collection of
Papers, &ca., relating to the rise, progress, and
government of this Charity.
8vo., Lond., 1737.

695 ———— College. Account of the Supervision
held at the College, by the Warden and Supervisors of New College, 3rd September, 1766.
Mus. B.iv. 20. 8vo., Lond, 1767.

696 ———— Letter to Sir Samuel Romilly from
Henry Brougham, upon the abuse of Charities.
XX.i. 4. 8vo., Lond., 1818.

697 WINCHESTER College. Letter to H. Brougham, Esq., in reply to the Strictures on Winchester College, contained in his letter to Sir Samuel Romilly. From the Rev. Liscombe Clarke. Mus. B.iv. $\frac{20}{4}$ 8vo., Winchester, 1818.

698 ———— Some account of the system of Fagging at Winchester School. By Sir Alexander Malet, Bart. Mus. B.iv. $\frac{20}{5}$ 8vo., Lond., 1828.

699 ———— Letter to Sir Alexander Malet, in reference to his pamphlet touching the late Expulsions from Winchester School. By an old Etonian. Mus. B.iv. $\frac{20}{6}$ 8vo., Lond., 1829.

700 ———— Marquis of. Life and Death of William Pawlet, 1st Marquis of Winchester [in verse]. By Rowland Broughton. (Portrait.) 8vo., Lee Priory Press, 1818.
Reprint ; originally printed in 1572.

701 WINCHFIELD. Copies of Monumental Inscriptions in Winchfield Church. 4to. MS.

W. J. GOTELEE, PRINTER AND BOOKSELLER, MARKET PLACE, WOKINGHAM.

HISTORICA DESCRIPTIO

COMPLECTENS

VITAM, ac RES GESTAS

BEATISSIMI VIRI

Gulielmi Wicami

QUONDAM

VINTONIENSIS Epifcopi, & ANGLIÆ
Cancellarii, & FUNDATORIS
duorum Collegiorum
OXONIÆ & VINTONIÆ.

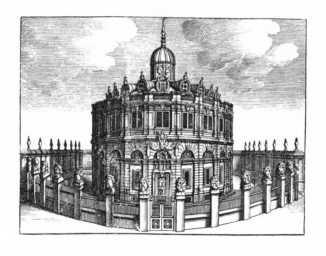

OXONIÆ,

E THEATRO SHELDONIANO, *An. Dom.* MDCXC.

[Figure 6; 17.7 x 22.9 cm]

THE
HISTORY OF HAMPSHIRE,

BY THE

Rev. Theodore C. Wilks.

Hurst Castle.

LONDON.

JAMES S. VIRTUE. CITY ROAD.

[Figure 7; 26.9 x 35.5 cm]

Bibliotheca Hantoniensis

A

List of Books relating to Hampshire

INCLUDING

MAGAZINE REFERENCES

&c. &c.

BY

H. M. GILBERT

AND

G. N. GODWIN

With an Additional List of Hampshire Newspapers

BY

F. E. EDWARDS

TO BE HAD AT

YE OLDE BOKE SHOPPE

26, ABOVE BAR, SOUTHAMPTON

[83]

ERRATA.

Page 94

Benham (Rev. Wm., F. S. A.) History of Diocese of Winchester.
Note should read—"A Biography of the Wife and Son of
the late Archbishop Tait."

Berry (W.) History of the Island of Guernsey.
Read—'4to.' instead of '8vo.'

Bowles (Rev. Wm. Lisle) Life of Thomas Ken.
Note should read—Sir 'Peter' Lely, not 'Walter.'

Page 153

List of Articles relating to Hampshire refers to 'The Topographer,
4 vols., 8vo., 1789-91,' not to 'Tomkins.'

CONTENTS.

PREFACE.

———◆———

IN sending forth this volume, the Compilers are desirous herewith to acknowledge the kind help received from SIR WM. COPE, Bart., LADY HEATHCOTE, Rev. G. W. MINNS, T. W. SHORE, Esq., O. T. HOPWOOD, Esq., W. WHITAKER, ESQ., MR. KIDDLE, and many other friends.

This work, from its nature, must necessarily be incomplete, but no pains have been spared to make it as accurate as possible. If anyone interested in the subject meets with Books, &c., relating to Hampshire not entered in this List, the Compilers will be glad to receive information of the same, that they may be included in a future edition.

H. M. GILBERT,
26, ABOVE BAR, SOUTHAMPTON.

G. N. GODWIN,
THE VICARAGE, EAST BOLDRE, HANTS.

May, 1891.

Bibliotheca Hantoniensis.

Abbot's Ann. See Dawes

Acts of Parliament for exchange of Lands at Portsmouth between the Ordnance Office and Thomas Missing, Esq. (1723); for repair of roads between Petersfield and Portsmouth (1726); between Reading and Basingstoke (1726); between the Golden Farmer and Hartford Bridge (1757); Odiham (1819); between Winchester, Whitchurch, and Andover (1823); between Stockbridge, Winchester, and Southampton (1822); for enclosure of Common Lands at Abbot's Ann (1774); Andover (1781); Upper Clatford (1785); King Somborne (1783); Fratton, Southsea (1789); Dibden (1790); Odiham, North Warnborough, Hillside, Rye, Stapely (1789); Shipton (1790); Monk Sherbourne, (1792); to Elvetham (1813); Also for making a railway from London to Southampton (1831); and for an exchange of lands at Whippingham (I. of W.) between Winchester College and R. Blackford, Esq. (N.D.); for enlarging the Market Place in Basingstoke (1829); for the Increase and better Preservation of Salmon and other Fish in Southampton Rivers (1835); for making a Canal from Andover to Redbridge (1789); for a Canal from Basingstoke to the River Wey (1793); for enclosing Common Lands at Carlstone in the Parish of Burghcleare and at Barton Stacey, for the better paving, etc., of Gosport (1763); for the sale of the Estates of Henry Grey (Itchingwell Grange).

Adams (H. G.) Wykehamica: A History of Winchester College and its Commoners, from the foundation to the present day. Illustrations. 8vo. 1878.

Adams (W. H. Davenport) The Beauties of the Isle of Wight, described and illustrated. Post 8vo. 1857.

Adams (W. H. Davenport) The Garden Isle ; or the History Topography, and Antiquities of the Isle of Wight. 4to. 1856.

Adams (W. H. Davenport) Handbook of the Isle of Wight, (Map and Illustrations) New edition. 8vo. 1862-1866.

Adkins (Rev. T.) Brief Records of the Church of Christ of the Independent Denomination at Southampton, from its establishment to the present time. 12mo. 1836.

Adkins (Thomas) Jubilee of the Rev. T. Adkins ; Proceedings of Public Meetings, Edited by John Bullar. 12mo. 1860,

"Æsop" Sporting Reminiscences of Hampshire from 1745-1862. Post 8vo. 1864.

Agriculture. Rules of the N.E. Hants Agricultural Association. 8vo. 1849.

Agricultural Riots. Charge to the Grand Jury at Winchester by the Hon. Mr. Baron Vaughan. 8vo. 1830.

Agricultural Riots, 1830. Report of the Proceedings at the Special Commission held at Winchester, 1830. 8vo. 1831.

Agricultural Riots. An Address to the Labouring Classes on the subject of destroying Machinery. 8vo. N.D.

Aitken (T. J.) Visitors' Guide to Bournemouth. 2nd Edition, with appendix. 8vo. 1842.

Akerman (J. Y.) Description of some Merovingian and other gold coins discovered in the parish of Crondall, Hampshire. Reprint from No. 23, *Numismatic Chronicle.*

Akermann (John Yonge) Excursions to the Isle of Wight. 12mo. N.D.

Akermann (John Yonge) Account of Excavations on the site of some ancient Potteries in the New Forest. 4to. 1853.

Akermann (R.) History of Winchester College. 4to. 1816.

Albin (J.) Vectiana or a Companion to the Isle of Wight. 12mo. (1808), 1813, 1819, 1826, 1829, Twelfth Edition. 1813.

Albin (J.) History of the Isle of Wight. 8vo. 1795.

Albin's Map of Isle of Wight. 1802.

Albin. *Isle of Wight Magazine,* (The)—From January 1799 to December, with Supplement; edited by J. Albin. 12mo. 1800

Aldershot, Sketches of the Camp at Aldershot, also Farnham, Waverley Abbey, Moor Park. &c. 12mo. 1858.

Aldershot. A Record of Mrs Daniell's Work among Soldiers and its Sequel. By her Daughter. 8vo. 1879.

Aldershot. See Cope : Ewing : Hervé : Sheldrake, (Postans).

Algæ Cæsareæ or Dried specimens of Marine Plants collected in Jersey, classified according to Professor Harvey. post 8vo. 1851.

Allotments of Land. See Lefroy.

Alresford. See L'Estrange : Symonds.

Alton. See Curtis.

Andrews (Charles) A Guide to Southampton, Netley Abbey, the Isle of Wight, Portsmouth, Gosport, Winchester and Basingstoke. 8vo. 1831.

Allen (Luke) History of Portsmouth, with the Towns of Portsea and Gosport, Portchester Castle, and the Isle of Wight. 12mo. 1817.

The Appendix contains many of the Charters granted to the Town.

Alresford (or Cheriton Fight) See Barnard : Civil War Pamphlets: Day : Heylyn.

Alresford. A fuller relation of the great victory obtained through God's Providence, at Alsford, on Friday, March 28th, 1644, by the Parliament's forces, under the command of Sir William Waller and Sir William Balfore against Lord Hopton. small 4to. 1644.

Also see Cheriton Fight.

Alton (and Farnham) See Archer : Civil War Pamphlets : Thornton.

Alverstoke. See Gosport.

Andover. Account of frightful Destitution in the Andover Union. 8vo.

Andover. *The Andover Weekly Oracle, or Magazine of Literature, Instruction and Local Intelligence.* 12mo. 1830-31.

Andover. Don Quixote Redivivus encountering a Barns-door, or an exact Narrative of the rare Exploits of Capt. Braines in a dangerous Expedition against a certain Barn in a town on the other side of the River Anne in the land of Little Ease and Less Justice, under the command of Tom Coxcomb, Signifer, an overgrown Tapster and principal member of the Disloyal Society at Visios, and of the corruption of the said Town, and sometime a Justler of the Peace there. small 4to. 18 leaves. Mus. C. vii., ¾. Printed for the Company of Informers.

This rare and curious Tract relates to Andover and the Prosecutions of Non-Conformists therein 1673. S. Shaw, Esq. of that Town, writes me : " I have found the original convictions relating to the same cases in the Town Chest of the Borough, and the book is quite correct and truthfull ; drawn up, I suppose by one of the Ministers."

Andover. See Civil War : Clarke : Kell : Merewether : Parker : Pearsall : Poor Law : Symonds.

Andrewes (Lancelot, Lord Bishop of Winton) The form of Consecration of a Church, or Chappel, and of the place of Christian Buriall. 24mo. 1659.

The Service of Consecration of Jesus Chapel, Pear Tree Green, Southampton. It contains some very curious information as to the dangers attending the passage over from one side of the River Itchen to the other at this date. The water sometimes being so tempestuous as to prevent Ministers crossing to attend the sick and dying.

Andrews (W., Attorney of Southampton) Poems. 12mo. 1793.

Andwell (or Endwell) Priory. See Gunner.

Anglesea. See Gosport.

Anglo-Saxon Charters (See Cartularium Saxonicum) Roy. 8vo.

" The Anglo-Saxon Charters are among the earliest documents of English Literature. The earliest which are known to me connected with Hampshire are the grant by Cynewald, King of Wessex, A.D. 672, of land at Dunton to Winchester Cathedral, and the grant by King Ine in A.D. 701, to the Cathedral at Winchester, of land at Alresford in this county. Another early charter is " The grant of privileges by King Ine to the Churches of Wessex," of which kingdom this county was the home country and seat of government. This charter is dated 26th May, A.D. 704."

Annales Monastici. Edited by Henry Richards Luard, M.A. 1864-69.

Vol. ii. contains Annales Monasterii de Wintonia, A.D. 519-1277.

Ansted (D. T.) and Latham (R. G.) The Channel Islands. 8vo. 1862.

Archæological Institute of Great Britain and Ireland. Catalogue of the Museum of Antiquities, exhibited . . . at the 2nd Annual Meeting, September, 1845, at Winchester. Sewed, 8vo. 1845. 20 pp.

Archæological Institute. See Winchester.

Argyle (F. B.) Account of the Altar Screen in the Priory Church, Christchurch, as it existed up to A.D. 1520. 8vo. 1879.

Ashe. See Thoyts.

Ashley (Hon. Evelyn) Life of Lord Palmerston from 1846 to 1855. 2 vols. 8vo. 1876.

Born and resided at Broadlands, near Romsey.

Ashley (John) Mr. Moberly and the letter which appeared at Mr. Pearce's Bank, at Southampton. A short answer of the matter. 12mo. 1857.

Atcheson (R. S.) History of Churcher's College at Petersfield, Hants, with Life of Churcher. 8vo. 1823.

Atkins (Henry) The Isle of Wight; a Poem, with other pieces in verse. 12mo. 1837.

Another Edition in 1832.

Austen-Leigh (Rev. J. E.) Recollections of the Vyne Hunt, by a Sexagenarian. Privately Printed. 8vo. 1865.

Avery (Robert) Reflections on the untimely end of, condemned and executed at Winchester, 23rd March, 1805. 12mo.

Avery (Robert) Life of. 8vo. 1805.

Ayloffe (Sir Joseph) Historical description of the Ancient Painting representing the Encampment at Portsmouth in 1545, at Cowdray, Sussex. 4to. 1778.

Baddesley. See Hospitallers : Larking : Marsh.

Baigent (F. J.) Winchester Stained Glass at South Kensington. Leaflet, 1880.

Baigent (F. J.) Family of De Lymerston and its Heiress, the Foundress of the Tichbourne Dole. 8vo. N. P. or D.

Baigent (F. J.) Locks on Pews [in Elvetham Church]. 8vo Broadsheet.

Baigent (F. J.) Sheriff's seals in Hampshire. 8vo. N.D.

Baigent (F. J.) Unlearned Clerks [in Hants]. 8vo. Broadsheet.

Baigent (F. J.) Winchester in 1852 and 1865. 3 pp. 8vo. 1865.

Baigent (F. J.) On the Martyrdom of St. Thomas of Canterbury, and other paintings, discovered at St. John's Church, Winchester. 8vo. N.D.

Baigent (F. J.) History and Antiquities of the Parish Church of Wyke, near Winchester (with plate of a remarkable Monumental Brass). 8vo. 1865.

Bailey (C.) Transcripts from the Municipal Archives of Winchester, and other documents, elucidating the Government, Manners, and Customs of the same City, from the 13th century to the present period. Post 8vo. 1856.

Bailey (Samuel) Life and Death of, of Hale Common, commonly known as Old Sam Bailey. 8vo. 1821.

Hale is near Fordingbridge.

Ball (Chas.) Historical account of Winchester, with descriptive Walks. Roy. 8vo. 1818.

Banking. Deed of Settlement of the Hampshire Banking Company, executed, July 2nd, 1834. Small 16mo. 1834.

Barber (F.) Picturesque Illustrations of the Isle of Wight (Steel Engravings and descriptive Letterpress) Roy. 8vo. 1845, &c.

Baring (William Bingham) Letter to the Inhabitants of Winchester, on his conduct as a Magistrate, in the arrest of Mr. and Mrs. Deacle. 8vo. 1831.

Baring (W. B.) Answer to Mr. Bingham Baring's letter to the Inhabitants of Winchester, on his conduct as a Magistrate, etc. 8vo. 1831.

Baring. Reply to a letter of justification of the arrest of Mr. and Mrs. Deacle, by the Rev. D. Williams. 8vo. 1832.

Baring. Letter to Hon. W. B. Baring, being a defence of his more active friends at the late election for Winchester, and a protest on their behalf against some of the views contained in his published "Vindication." By a Conservative Reformer. 8vo. 1835.

Baring. Correspondence between the Hon. W. B. Baring and his Election Committee, upon their requisition, that agreeably to the tenor of a written pledge he should resign his seat as one of the representatives of Winchester. 8vo. 1837.

Barnard (Dr.) See Heylyn.

Barnes (John, of Winchester) An Essay on Fate, and other Poems, by John Barnes, 14 years of age. 12mo, 1807.

Barrey (H. G.) Pre-Historic Lymington. 8vo. 1885.

Bartlett (J. Pemberton) Ancient Potteries in the New Forest (plates.) 6 pp. 8vo.

Barton (John Alfred) Descriptive account of the Convent or Oratory of Barton in the Isle of Wight. Sewed, 4to. 8 pp. 1845.

Barton Stacey. Writ in Error Ryder *v.* Bailey of Barton Stacey, respecting monetary and other transactions. Folio. 1709.

Basing House in Hampshire, the History of containing an interesting account of the Siege it sustained during the Civil War. 8vo. 1815.
10th Edition. 8vo. 1858.

Basing House. History of the Siege during the Civil War, with notices of celebrated persons concerned in its transactions. 8vo. 1839.

Basing and Basing House. See Archer, Asser, Burton, Carlyle, Civil War Pamphlets, Cromwell, Deane, Gage, Godwin, Goodman, Heath, History of Basing House (vide Basingstoke), Holme (vide Odiham), Johnson, Millard. Planché, Prosser, Rawdon, Symonds, Wyatt.

Basingstoke. History of the Ancient Town and Manor of Basingstoke in the County of Southampton, with a brief account of the Siege of Basing House, A.D. 1643-5, by Francis Thomas Baigent and James Elwin Millard (plates). Thick 8vo. 1889.

Basingstoke. Memoirs of Miss Stapleton (who died at Basingstoke), by J. Jefferson. Basingstoke, N.D.

Basingstoke. News from Basingstoke of one Mrs. Blunden, a Maltster's Wife, who was twice buried alive, for which neglect several persons were indicted at the last Assizes held at Winchester, and the Town of Basingstoke compelled to pay a great fine. Small 4to. N.D.

Basingstoke. History of the supposed Death of Madame Blunden, who was buried alive in the Chapel Liten, Basingstoke 8vo. 18—

Basingstoke. History of Holy Ghost Chapel at Basingstoke, in Hants, with an account of another Religious House, and curious Antiquities. 8vo. 1819.

Basingstoke. The Book of the Accounts of the Wardens of the Fraternity of the Holy Ghost in Basingstoke, A.D. 1551 to 1654. 4to (wrappers). 1882.
Edited by Rev. J. E. Millard, D.D., only a few copies printed.

Basingstoke. Pedestrian feats and humourous adventures of the late Mr. Charles Spicer, upwards of forty years Clerk of Basingstoke Church. 9th edition. 8vo. 1871.

Basingstoke. Sermon (J. Jefferson) on the death of Miss Sarah Glover at Basingstoke. 8vo. 1792.

Basingstoke. See Andrews, Baigent, Millard, Civil War Pamphlets, Grace, Hobhouse, Jefferson, Loggan Minns.

Baskett (Herbert) Island Minstrel, by H. Fitzherbert. 12mo. London, 1842.
The writer of this poem was Herbert Baskett, a journeyman gardener, son of Thomas Baskett, for many years a resident and owner of a lodging-house and garden on the West side of George Street, Ryde.

Batt upon Batt ; a poem on the parts, patience, and pains of Barth : Kempster, Clerk, Poet, Cutler, of Holy-Rood parish, Southampton, by a person of quality, &c. 5th edition. 8vo. 1706.

Batten (Edmund Chisholm) The Register of Richard Fox, while Bishop of Bath and Wells, 1492-1494, with a Life of Bishop Fox, Bishop of Winchester, 1501-1528. 100 copies privately printed. 4to. 1889.

Beal (Samuel Benoni) Church of St. Thomas, Newport, Isle of Wight ; Elizabeth Stuart, the prisoner of Carisbrooke (plates). 8vo. 1856.

Beardmore (J.) Catalogue, with Illustrations of the Collection of Ancient Arms and Armour, at Uplands, near Fareham, Hants (plates). Folio. 1844.

Beaulieu. See Edward IV., Grey Abbey, Kell, Vergil, Walford.

Beauworth. See Hawkins.

Bell (Anthony) Land Agent, Winchester ; Letter to John Fitzgerald, Esq. 8vo. Privately printed, 1808.

Benham (Rev. Wm., F.S.A.) History of the Diocese of Winchester. 12mo. London, 1884.
"A literary clergyman who was born in Hampshire is the Rev.
William Benham, F.S.A., a native of West Meon. Mr. Benham is
the author of "Memorials of Catherine and Crauford Tait," a
biography of the late Archbishop Tait."

Bennett (W. B. G.) Southampton Sewage Clarification. 8vo.
1887.

Bentworth. See Wither.

Bere Forest. Report of the Commissioners appointed to enquire into the state and condition of the Woods, Forests,
and Land Revenues of the Crown. folio. London, 1792.

Berry (W.) History of the Island of Guernsey. 8vo. 1814.

Berry (W.) County Genealogies: Pedigrees of the Families in the
Counties of Hants. Folio. 1833.

Bevan (G. Phillips) Tourists' Guide to Hampshire, including the
Isle of Wight. 12mo. 1881.

Bible Society. Reasons for subverting the Bible Society,
addressed to the North-Eastern part of the County of
Hants, (in verse). With notes and comments. 8vo. 1813.

Bingham (C. W.) Private Memoirs of John Pottinger, 1647-1733.
12mo. 1841.
A Native of Winchester.

Bingley (Rev. W.) Explanatory Address relative to the History
of Hampshire. 8vo. 1817.

Bingley (Rev. William) Topographical account of the Hundred
of Bosmere, comprising the parishes of Havant,
Warblington and Hayling (plates). 4to. 1817.
A note at the introduction states that his work was compiled for the
use of an intended History of Hampshire, undertaken by the Rev.
W. Bingley, under the patronage of the Right Hon. G. Rose, but
as that work was laid aside, a few copies only were printed for the
author's friends.

Bishopstoke. See Kell.

Bishops' Waltham.—The History of the Blacks of [Bishops']
Waltham. 8vo. 1723.

Bishops' Waltham. See Civil War : Companion in a Tour
round Southampton : Fitzatherley, Garneray, Walters.

Bitterne. See Clausentum, Roach, Smith, Wright,

Black (A. and C.) Tourist Guide to Hampshire and Dorsetshire.
8vo. Edinburgh, 1855.

Black (A. and C.) Guide to Hampshire, new edition. 8vo.
Edinburgh, 1872.

Black (A. and C.) Guide to the South Eastern Counties of
England, Hampshire and the Isle of Wight. 8vo. Edinburgh,
1861.

Blanchard (E. L. Adams) Descriptive Guide to the Channel Islands, the Isle of Wight, and the Isle of Man (with maps). 12mo. 1859.

Blore (Edward). A Report addressed to the Dean of Winchester on the proposed removal of the organ from the side to the centre of the Cathedral. 4to. See Winchester Cathedral.

Bloxam (J.C.) Meteorology of Newport,Isle of Wight. 4to. 1860.

Boldre. See Gilpin, Southey.

Bonner (G.W.) Picturesque Views in the Isle of Wight, Hampshire etc., Letterpress by Mackenzie. Oblong 4to. N.D.

Bosmere, Hundred of. See Bingley, Longcroft,

Botley. Botley and South Hants Farmer's Club, Annual Report of. 8vo. 1855 &c.,

Botley. See Cobbett.

Bournemouth.—Complete and Descriptive Guide to, and its vicinity, embracing Christchurch, Wimborne, and Corfe Castle. 8vo. N.D.

Bournemouth. The Visitors' Guide to Bournemouth and its neighbourhood. Third edition. 1850.

Bournemouth. From Bournemouth to Bridgenorth in a Yellow Cart. 8vo. 1878.

Bournemouth Society of Natural Science, Annual Reports. 8vo. N.D.

Bournemouth Illustrated. Folio. 1886.

Bournemouth. See Aitken, Brannon, Curtis, Dobell, Lee, Spindler.

Bowles (W. L.) Vindiciæ Wykhamicae ; a Vindication of Winchester College, in a letter to H. Brougham, Esq. 8vo. 1818.

Bowles (Rev. Wm. Lisle). The Life of Thomas Ken, D.D., Deprived Bishop of Bath and Wells. Including some account of the fortunes of Morley, Bishop of Winchester chaps. v. and vi. Containing much matter respecting Isaak Walton ; brother-in.law of Bishop Ken. 8vo. 1830.

" Isaac Walton, the well-known author of the Complete Angler, was buried in Winchester Cathedral. He married a sister of Bishop Ken, a man closely connected with this county. Ken was the Prebend of Winchester who refused Charles II his house when it was wanted for Nell Gwynne. Subsequently to this, when the Bishopric of Bath and Wells had to be filled up, and there were plenty of would-be Bishops, the King said " Let the little parson at Winchester have it who refused to give Nelly a night's lodging." Isaac Walton wrote several well-known books in addition to the Complete Angler. Nell Gwynne's country mansion was at Avington Park, the present seat of Mr. Shelley, which still contains some of Sir Walter Lely's portraits of that period."

Bowtell (John). Excursion Guide to the Isle of Wight. 8vo. London. 1859.

Bradbury (John). Isle of Wight : how to see it for six guineas. 8vo. 1876.

Brading, The Troubles of, by the Vicar. 8vo. 1847.

Bramdean. See Duthy, Portsmouth Literary Society.

Bramshill. Recollections of a visit to Bramshill. 8vo. London. N.D.
> Reprinted for private circulation from Sir Bernard Burke's " Visita tion of the seats of Noblemen and Gentlemen in Great Britain.

Bramshill.—Pictures in the Reredos of the Chapel of Bramshill House.

Bramshill. See Burke, Cope, Hall, Holme (under Odiham).

Bramston (A. R.) and Leroy (A. C.) Historic Winchester. Post 8vo. 1882.

Brand (Rev. J.) Explanation of a Seal of Netley Abbey. 4to. 1797.

Brannon (George) Graphic delineations of the most prominen objects in the Isle of Wight. Oblong. N.D.

Brannon (George) The Landscape Beauties of the Isle of Wight as described by the Rev. Leigh Richmond (plates). 8vo N.D.

Brannon (George). Sketches of the scenes in the Isle of Wight illustrative of Leigh Richmond's "Annals of the Poor," etc. 8vo. 1832.

Brannon (George) Picture of the Isle of Wight (map and plates). 8vo. 1843.

Brannon (George) Pleasure visitors' companion in surveying the Isle of Wight. 12mo. 1883. Other Editions, 1834, 1836, 1838, (1842) (1843) (1845) (1846) 1856.

Brannon (George) Views of Isle of Wight. Oblong fol. 1822-25

Brannon (George. Vectis Scenery; views of the Picturesque Beauties of the Isle of Wight with typographical description of the Island. Folio. Southampton. 1825.

Brannon (George). Vectis Scenery ; views of the Picturesque Beauties of the Isle of Wight with descriptive letter-press. 4to. Other editions, 1843, 1849, 1862.

Brannon (George) Pictorial Sketches of Remarkable Objects in the Isle of Wight with descriptive letter-press. 8vo. N.D.

Brannon (Philip) Strangers' Guide to Netley Abbey. 8vo.
> Frequently reprinted.

Brannon (Philip). The Picture of Southampton and Strangers' Handbook to the town and neighbourhood, with engravings 8vo.
> Frequently reprinted.

Brannon (Philip) The Strangers' Guide to Southampton, &c. 12mo. 1851.

Brannon (Philip) Two Hundred and Five Memorials of Southampton, Steel Engravings with Descriptive Letterpress. 12mo. 1866.

Brannon (Philip.) Illustrated Historical and Picturesque Guide to Bournemouth 12mo. 1861.

Brayley (E. W.) & Britton (J.) Beauties of England and Wales, topographical, historical and descriptive of each county. Vol. vi. Hampshire and Isle of Wight. 8vo. 1805.

Brayley (E. Wedlake.) See Christchurch, and also Ferrey (B.)

Brettell (T.) Handbook to the Isle of Wight composing its history, topography etc., Third edition. 1840, 1844.

Brettell (T.) Historical recollections of Carisbrooke Castle, &c. 12mo. 1844.

Briddon (J.) Illustrated Handbook to the Isle of Wight. 12mo. 1865.

Brierly (J.) On New Forest Water. Hants Field Club Papers, iv. 71.

Brion and Wilkin. Geology, Topography, and Antiquities of the Isle of Wight. Imp. 8vo. 1859.

British Archæological Association, Transactions of, at Winchester, 1845. 8vo. 1846.

British Association, Report, 1882.

Britton (J.) History and Antiquities of the See and Cathedral Church of Winchester, with Biographies of Bishops and Persons connected with the Cathedral. 4to, (plates) 1817.

Britton and Brayley. Topographical and Historical description of Hampshire and the Isle of Wight. 8vo. 1805.

Broadlands. See Clifford.

Bromfield (W. A.) Hampshire Botany; Papers from the Phytologist. 8vo. 1849.
  "Dr. William Arnold Bromfield, the botanist, and author of Flora Vectensis, was a native of Boldre, near Lymington. He died in Damascus. A lady who assisted Dr. Bromfield in his Isle of Wight Flora was Miss G. Kilderbee, who herself formed a herbarium, and who is often mentioned in Bromfield's work. Bromfield's herbarium went to Ryde Museum; and Miss Kilderbee's herbarium was after her death given to the Hartley Institution, where it is now preserved."

Bromfield (W. A.) List of flowering plants likely to be found growing wild in the Isle of Wight, 8vo. 1850.

Bromfield (W. A.) Flora Vectensis; a description of the flowering plants of the Isle of Wight, edited by Hooker and Bell (with map in case). 8vo. 1856.

Bromley (S.) Southampton and the Isle of Wight: a Poem in four books. 12mo. 1849.

Broughton (Rowlande, Gent.) Discourse of the Lyfe and Death of W. Powlett, Marquis of Winchester. 8vo. 1572. Reprinted, Lee Priory Press; a Poetical tract. 8vo. 1818.

Broughton. See Steele.

Browne (Samuel, of Tadley) Travels of Seektruth. 12mo. 1805.

Browne (John, of Whitchurch) Poetical translations from various authors. 4to. 1786.

Buckell (E.) List of Rarer Plants in Test Valley, especially Mottisfont District. Hants Field Club Papers, iv. 52.

Buckholt. See Kell.

Bullar (J.) Historical particulars relating to Southampton. 8vo. 1820.

Bullar (J.) Companion in a visit to Netley Abbey, to which is annexed Mr. Keat's Elegy. 12mo. 1812-1844.

Bullar (J.) Companion in a Tour round Southampton, comprehending particulars of New Forest, Lymington, Christchurch, 12mo. 179—, 1801, 1809, 1819.

Bullar (J.) Historical and Picturesque Guide to the Isle of Wight. 12mo. 1806. Other editions 1823, 1824, 1826, 1840.

Bullar (J.) and Drew (John) Hints to assist Visitors to Southampton and the Isle of Wight. 8vo. 1846.

Bunyon (C. J.) Memoirs of Bishop Francis Thomas McDougall, and of Harriet, his Wife. 8vo. 1889.
    Vicar of Shorwell, I. W., and Canon of Winchester.

Burgess (Thomas) Bishop of Salisbury (a native of Odiham), Life of, by J. S. Harford. 8vo. 1840.

Burke (Sir B.) Visit to Bramshill. 8vo. N.D.
    Reprinted, for private circulation, from Sir B. Burke's "Visitation of the Seats of Noblemen and Gentlemen in Great Britain."

Burley. See New Forest.

Burrard (S.) The Annals of Walhampton. 8vo. 1874.

Burrows (M.) Brocas of Beaurepaire and Roche Court, the Family of. Large 8vo. 1886.
    A very ancient Hampshire family.

Burt (Charles H.) Caxton's Gift, A Retrospect, An Invocation, An Ode. 12mo. Winchester. 1877.

Burton (Dr.) Remarks on some proceedings at the time of the late election at Winchester College, and the case of the Masters plainly stated. 8vo. 1767.

Butcher's Borough of Portsmouth Directory, including Gosport, Fareham and Havant, for 1874-75. 8vo. 1874.

Byles (G., of Southampton) Reveries in Contentment: a Poem. 4to.

Byng (Admiral) The Genuine Tryal of, at Portsmouth (with portrait). 12mo. 1757.

Calvert (F.) The Isle of Wight, pictorially illustrated, and accompanied by Topographical and Historical descriptions (coloured plates). 4to. 1846.

Camden (W) History of Hampshire and the Isle of Wight, with additions by R. Gough. Folio. 1805.
Taken from Camden's Britannia.

Canals. Observations on the proposed Junction Canal, between Winchester and the Basingstoke Canal. 8vo. 1808.

Canals. See Priestley.

Carey (H.) Memorials of the Great Civil War in England, from 1646 to 1652. 2 vols. 1842.

Carnarvon (Earl of) Speech at the Hampshire Meeting of Lay Members of the Church of England on the Claims put forth by Dissenters. 8vo. 1834.

Carnarvon (Henry, Earl of) Hampshire, its early and later history: being two lectures delivered at the Basingstoke Literary Institute. 12mo. 1857.

Carr (R.) Portsmouth Guide, to which is added some account of the Isle of Wight. 12mo. 1775.
The earliest known Portsmouth Guide.

Carter (Rev. Isaac) "Minister of God's Word at Portsmouth." A Broad Hint to Nobody, or the Child whipt with its own Rod, with Poem entitled "Minister's puzzle for religious drones, old maids, and rickety children." 8vo. 1794.

Carter (O. B.) Headbourn Worthy Church. 4to. N.D.

Carter (O. B.) Ancient Painted Glass of Winchester Cathedral traced from the windows (28 coloured plates, with descriptions). 4to. 1845.

Cassan (Rev. S. H.) Lives of the Bishops of Winchester, from Birinus, first Bishop of the West Saxons, to the present time. 2 vols, 8vo. 1827.
This also contains a reprint of Gale's Antiquities of Winchester Cathedral.

Cave (Jane) Entertaining, Elegiac and Religious poems (portrait). 12mo. 1783.
Some of these poems were reprinted (Bristol, 8vo, N.D.) under the title "Prose and Poetry," by Mrs. Ruetul, with the story of her married life. It is a most curious work, Miss Cave (of Winchester), the authoress, seems to have made a most unfortunate marriage.

Channel Islands. First Report of the Commissioners appointed to enquire into the state of the Criminal Law in the Channel Islands. 2 vols in 1. Part 1, Jersey; part 2, Guernsey. Folio. 1847.

Channel Islands. Report of the Commissioners appointed to enquire into the Civil, Municipal and Ecclesiastical Laws of the Island of Jersey, together with the Minutes of Evidence and Appendix by Sir John W. Awdry, the Earl of Devon and Richard Jebb. Folio. 1861.

Channel Islands. See Ansted, Berry, Blanchard, Chamberlain, Clayton, Coghlan, Connolly, Cooke, Corbière, Duncan, Egerton, Evans, Falle, Heylyn, Hoskins, Inglis, Jacob, Jersey, Jewitt, Le Cras, Le Quesse, Pitts, Plees Rooke, Stevens, Sullivan, Syvret, Timbs, Thomson, Topographical Description of Hampshire, Tupper, Warner, Williams.

Charities. Abstract of the Returns made to Parliament in 1780-8, of Charitable Donations in the County of Hants. Folio. 1788.

Charles I. Works of that great Monarch and Martyr, containing Letters, Speeches, c. Folio. 1687.
References to Isle of Wight and Hurst Castle.

Chevalier (Rev. W. A. C.) Boyhood of William Longe of Wykeham. 8vo. 1883.

Christchurch. Case of Mr. Richard Holloway, one of the Burgesses inhabiting the Town of Christchurch, with a Poll List of the Voters at the Election, 1727. 8vo. N.P. or D.

Christchurch, Historical Account of, with notices of the Nobility, Antiquities, &c. 12mo. 18—

Christchurch. See Argyle, Bournemouth, Clarke, Companion in a Tour round Southampton, Dowden, Emmet, Ferrey and Brayley, Freeman, Hilliard, Malmesbury (Earl of), Merewether, Pickersgill-Cunliffe, Roberts, Rose, Shooting, Walcott.

Church (Prof. A. J.) The Count of the Saxon Shore, a story of the Villa in Vectis, and the Departure of the Romans from Britain. 8vo. 1890.

Church Congress, Report of, held at Southampton, October, 1870. 8vo. N.D. (1871).

Church Congress. See Portsmouth and Southampton.

Chute (C. W.) History of the Vyne in Hampshire, (plates). 4to. London 1888.

Clarke (A.) Sermon preached at the Cathedral at Winchester before the Governors of the County Hospital, with a Collection of Papers relating to the Rise, Progress, and Government of the said Charity. 8vo. 1737.

Clarke (C. B.) List of the Flowering Plants, Ferns, and Mosses in the Neighbourhood of Andover, Hants. 8vo. 1866.

Clarke (J.) Description of the Isle of Wight. 8vo. 1819.

Clarke (J.) The Delineator, or a Picturesque, Historical, and Topographical Description of the Isle of Wight. 12mo. 1812. 2nd edition, 1814. 6th edition, 1824.

Clarke (Rev. Liscombe) Letters to H. Brougham, Esq., in reply to the Strictures on Winchester College, contained in his letter to Sir Samuel Romilly. 8vo. 1818.

Clarke (W. B.) Guide to Hayling (Illustrated). Post 8vo. 1836.

Clausentum. See Kell.

Clifford (Sir A. W. J.) Description of Westfield, Ryde, Isle of Wight. 4to. 1862. Privately Printed.

Clifford (E.) Broadlands as it was. 8vo. 1890. Privately Printed.

Clutterbuck (Rev. R. H.) Silchester, by the Rev. R. H. Clutterbuck. pp. 4., sewed 8vo, with map. Read before the Archæological Association, August 16th, 1883.

Cobbett (W.) Life of William Cobbett. By Himself. 8vo. 1809.
Resided at Botley.

Coghlan (Francis) Hand-book to the Channel Islands, (with maps). 16mo. 1843.

Cole (James Edwin) Genealogy of the Family of Cole. 8vo. 1867.

Coleridge (Sir J. T.) Memoirs of Rev. John Keble, of Hursley. 8vo. 1870.

Collier (Rev. C.) History of Wolvesey. 12mo. 1864.

Collingwood (C. E. S.) Notes on Ventnor and the Undercliff. 8vo. London, 1879.

Colmer (Near Alresford). See Hervey, Smith.

Comyn (Henry) Substance of part of the Lectures delivered in Boldre and Brockenhurst, 1817. 8vo. 1818.

Cook (Thomas) Hand-book to International Tours : Combining the Coast Towns of England and France, with the Channel Islands of Guernsey, Jersey, and the Isle of Wight. 8vo. (1865).

Cooke (G. A.) Topographical and Statistical Description of the County of Hants. 16mo. 1819

Cooke (W.) New Picture of the Isle of Wight, with an Introductory Account of the Isle of Wight. 4to. 1808.

Cooke (W. B.) Bonchurch, Shanklin, and the Undercliff described. 12mo. 1849.

Cooke (W. B.) Views in Isle of Wight. 6 parts. 4to. 1843-52.

Cope (T.) Historical Notices of the Ancient Domain of Stanbridge in Hampshire. 12mo. 1865.

Cope (Sir W. H. Bart.) Bramshill, its History and Antiquities. London, 4to. N.D.

Cope (Sir W. H. Bart.) A Glossary of Hampshire Words and Phrases. 8vo. 1883.

Cope (Sir W. H. Bart.) List of Books relating to Hampshire in the Library at Bramshill. 8vo. 1879. (Not Published).

Cope (Sir W. H. Bart.) Sermon preached in the Parish Church of Eversley, on the Sunday after the funeral of Rev. C. Kingsley. 8vo. 1875.

Corn Laws. Report of a Discussion after Vestry in a rural Parish of Hampshire. 12mo. 1846.

Cowper (Capt. Cowper) The Spithead Forts. 8vo. 1862.

Cowper (Frank) Caedwalla, or the Saxons in the Isle of Wight. 8vo. 1888.

Cowper (Frank) The Captain of the Wight, a Romance of Carisbrooke Castle in 1488. 8vo. 1889.

Creswick (T). See Bartlett.

Cox's History of Hampshire. 4to. Cir. 1710.

Cox (Thomas). Topographical, Historical, Ecclesiastical and Natural History of Hampshire, (From Magna Britannia). 4to. 1726.

Crabb (J.) The Mournful Remembrancer, being a brief account of the loss of lives, etc., by the late destructive fire at Southampton. 8vo. 1837.

Crabb. See Rudall, Southampton.

Criminals. Chaplain's Report to the Magistrates of the County of Southampton. 8vo. 1847.

Cromwell. See Carlyle, Civil War, Duthy, Guizot, Hursley.

Crondall. See Akermann, Hoare, Jefferson, Warren.

Crouch (W.) Posthuma Christiana, or a Collection of some papers of William Crouch. 1712.

A native of Penton, near Weyhill, and a persecuted Quaker.

Crux Easton. See Lisle.

Cundy (N. W.) Reports on the Grand Ship Canal from London to Arundel Bay and Portsmouth. 8vo. 1827.

Curtis (C. H. Octavius, F.S.A.) Bright's Illustrated Guide to Bournemouth. 182 pp. 8vo. cloth. 1886.

CIVIL WAR PAMPHLETS.

Alton. A Narrative of the great victory obtained by the Parliament Forces, under Sir William Waller, at Alton, in Hants, December 13th, 1643. Small 4to. 1643.

Alton. See Archer.

Archer (Lieut. Elias) A True Relation of the Marchings of the Red Trained Bands of Westminster, the Green Auxiliaries of London, and the Yellow Auxiliaries of the Tower Hamlets, under the command of Sir William Waller. . . . . briefly delineating most of the chiefest Passages in the Service performed by Sir William Waller at Basing, Farnham, and Alton, &c., by Elias Archer, Lieutenant to Captain William Archer. 4to. 1643.

Balfore (Sir William) Letter of March 30th, 1644, to His Excellency the Earl of Essex, Lord General. 6 pp., 8vo. 1882. Privately printed for the Clarendon Historical Society.

Describes Cheriton Fight.

Basing House. The Soldier's Report concerning Sir William Waller's Fight against Basing House, on Sunday, November 12th. Small 4to. 1643.

Basing House. Mercurius Rusticus ; or, a Country Messenger informing divers things worthy to be taken notice of. Small 4to. 1463.

This tract gives a good account of the fortifying of Basing House.

Basing House. A Diary; or, an exact Journall of true Intelligence. Small 4to. 1644.

Gives Items of News of the Siege of Basing and the march to Andover.

Basing. See Civil War Pamphlets, Odiham.

Basing House. Gage (Colonel Sir Henry) Official Report of the Relief of. Small 4to. 1644.

Basing. A description of the Siege of Basing Castle, kept by the Lord Marquisse of Winchester for the service of His Majesty, against the forces of the Rebells under the Command of Col. Norton. Oxford : Printed by Leonard Lichfield, Printer to the University. Small 4to. 1644. Reprinted, 8vo, 1880.

Basing House. Beech (W., Minister of the Army before Basing House) More Sulphur for Basing, or God will fearfully annoy and make quick riddance of his implaccable enemies, surely, sorely, suddenly, shewed in a Sermon, at the Siege of Basing, on last Lord's Day, with a word of advice, full of love, to the Club Men of Hampshire. Small 4to. Motto, Rev. xiv. 11. Text, Psalm. lxxxiii. 9. 1645.

Basing House. Cromwell's letter to the Speaker, telling of the taking of Basing House, &c. Small 4to. 1645.

Basing House. Mercurius Aulicus : communicating the affairs of the times (containing particulars relative to the taking of Basing House). Small 4to. 1645.

Basing House. Peters (Rev. Hugh) "A Relation to the House of Commons" of the Taking of Basing House, October 15th, 1645. Small 4to.

Basing House. A Looking Glasse for the Popish Garrisons as held forth in the Life and Death of Basing House. Small 4to. October 24th, 1645.

Basing House, the History of, with an account of the Siege, &c. 8vo. (Frequently reprinted). 1844.

Basing House. Gage (Sir Henry) Life of. 1645.
Relief of Basing House

Basing House. Life of Marmaduke Rawdon of York Camden Society, 1863.

Bishops Waltham. See Portsmouth.
Governor of Basing House.

Cheriton Fight. Case (Master Thomas, Preacher at Milk Street, and one of the Assembly of Divines) Thanksgiving Sermon, on April 9th, 1644 (afternoon) before the House of Commons, at St. Margaret's Church, Westminster, for the Victory at Cheriton. Small 4to. Motto, Psalm ix. 10. Text, Daniel xi. 32. See Sedgwick.

Cheriton Fight. Sedgwick (Rev. Obadiah, B.D., Pastor of Coggeshall, Essex) Thanksgiving Sermon on April 9th, 1644 (forenoon) before the House of Commons, at St. Margaret's Church, Westminster, for the Victory at Cheriton. Small 4to. Motto, 1 Samuel vii. 12. Text, Psalm iii. 8 See Case.

Cheriton Fight. See Alresford.

Farnham Castle (in Surrey) See Milford.

Fordingbridge. See Portsmouth.

Hampshire, The humble Petition of, to the Right Honourable the House of Peers, assembled in Parliament, and also to the Honourable the House of Commons, now assembled in Parliament, The humble Petition of the High Sheriffs, Knights, Esquires, and Gentlemen of the Grand Inquest, Ministers, Freeholders and Inhabitants of the County of Southampton at the General Assizes, March 11th. London. Printed for Joseph Hunscott, 1641. The Petition to the House of Lords was read on the 10th of March. Broadside, March 11th, 1642.

Hampshire, Humble Petition of, to the Right Honourable the House of Peers, assembled in Parliament, praying that the Popish Lords' Votes may be taken away, and all Papists confined, and to beseech His Majesty to reside near his Parliament. With a similar Petition to the House of Commons. March 11th. London. Printed for Joseph Hunscott. Broadside, March 11th, 1642.

Hampshire. Collection of all Remonstrances, Declarations, Orders, Ordinances, Proclamations, etc., between the King's most excellent Majesty and his High Court of Parliament, 1641-3. 4to. 1643.
Interesting to Hampshire Collectors from the fact that it contains the Proclamation of Pardon to the Inhabitants of Southampton, November, 1642.

Hampshire. His Majesty's two Proclamations to the Counties of Southampton and Dorset, &c. 4to. Oxford, 1642.

Hampshire. Calendar of the proceedings of the Committee for Compounding, 1643-1660. Large 8vo. 1889. List of persons Sequestered in Hants, pp. 104-106, &c.

Hampshire Pseudo Christus; or, a true and faithful Relation of the Grand Impostures, Horrid Blasphemies, Abominable Practices, Gross Deceits, lately spread abroad and acted in the County of Southampton, by William Frankelin and Mary Gadbury, and their companions, &c., by Humphry Ellis, Minister of the Word in the City of Winton. 4to. 1650.

Hampshire. The humble Petition of the well-affected of the County of Southampton, in behalf of the Ministers of the Gospel, &c. 4to. 1653.

Hampshire. Special Passages from several places, relating to the Civil War in Hampshire, &c. Small 4to. 1642.

Hampshire. Perfect Diurnal of some Passages and Proceedings of and in relation to the Armies in England, &c. 4to. 1653, etc.

Hampshire. Mercurius Politicus, 17th-24th June, 1658, containing the list of persons to be added to the Commissioners for ejecting scandalous, ignorant, and insufficient Ministers and Schoolmasters, within the County of Southampton, &c. 4to. 1658.

Isle of Wight. His Majesty's Grievances, sent by a message from His Majesty, by Mr John Ashburnham and Sir John Barkley, to Col. Hammond, Governor of the Isle of Wyght, &c. 4to. 1647.

Isle of Wight. Col. Whaley's Message and Declaration concerning the King's Majesties Royale Person, also touching Mr. John Ashburnham, now attending his Royal Person in the Isle of Wight. 4to. 1647.

Isle of Wight. Hammond (Colonel) Letter from Carisbrook to the Speaker of the House of Lords. 1647.

Isle of Wight. A Letter written by John Ashburnham, Esquire, from Carisbrook Castle in the Isle of Wight, November 26th, 1647, to William Lenthall, Esquire, Speaker of the Honourable House of Commons. 4to. 1647,

Isle of Wight. The Modest Cavalliere's Advice ; together with a letter to the Inhabitants of the Isle of Wight, where his Sacred Majesty is now remaining. 4to. 1647.

Isle of Wight. Duppa (Brian) Bishop of Salisbury, The Soule's Soliloquie. . . . A Sermon before the King at Newport, in the Isle of Wight. 4to. 1648.

Isle of Wight. Ferne (Rev. H., D.D.) A Sermon preached before His Majesty, at Newport, in the Isle of Wight (on Habbakuk ii. 3), November the 29th, 1648. 4to. 1649.

Isle of Wight. The last Newes from the Isle of Wight. 4to. 1647.

Isle of Wight. His Majestie's Gracious Message and Propositions from the Isle of Wyght for settling of the Church and Kingdom, and Paying of the Army, &c. 4to. 1647.

Isle of Wight. His Majestie's Most Gracious Message to his two Houses of Parliament in Prosecution of Peace by a Personal Treaty. 4to. 1647.

Isle of Wight. A Letter sent from the Speakers of both Houses of Parliament to His Majestie in the Isle of Wight . . . Also His Majestie's answer to the said Letter, &c. 4to. 1648.

Isle of Wight. Copy of an Intercepted Letter from His Majesty to the Lords and Gentlemen, Committees of the Scots' Parliament, together with the Officers of that Army. Dated at Carisbrook, Monday, 31st July 1648. Broadside, July 31st, 1648.

Isle of Wight. New Declaration and Message presented to the King's Majesty in the Isle of Wight, for a present Peace and Agreement. 4to. 1648.

Isle of Wight (Newport). The commencement of the Treaty between the King's Majesty and the Commissioners of Parliament at Newport. A Prayer, drawn by His Majestie's Speciall direction and dictates, for a blessing on the Treaty at Newport. Newport, in Insula Vectis. September 6th, 1648. Broadside, September 16th, 1648.

Isle of Wight. My Lord of Pembroke's Speech to His Majesty Concerning the Treaty. . . . at Newport, in the Isle of Wight, &c. 4to. 1648.

Isle of Wight. A Messenger sent to the City of London with a Packet of Letters from the Isle of Wight, &c. 4to. 1648.

Isle of Wight. Three New Queries presented by the Commissioners to the King's Majestie at the Treating-house in Newport and his Majestie's most Gracious Answer to the said queries, &c., 4to. 1648.

Isle of Wight. Two letters containing . . . . the last newes of the King and Treaty in the Isle of Wight. 4to. 1648.

Isle of Wight. Packets of Letters from severall parts of England . . . A letter from the Isle of Wight. His Majestie's Declaration to the Commissioners, &c. 4to. 1648.

Isle of Wight. His Majestie's Declaration from the Isle of Wight, with the proposals agreed on by his Excellency Thomas Lord Fairfax, &c. 4to. 1648.

Isle of Wight. His Majestie's Declaration concerning the Treaty . . . . Delivered by his Majesty to one of his Servants at his departure from the Isle of Wight, &c. 4to. 1648.

Isle of Wight. The Independency of England endeavoured to be maintained by Henry Marten . . . . Against the claim of the Scottish Commissioners in their late answer upon the Bills and Propositions sent to the King in the Isle of Wight. 4to. 1648.

Isle of Wight. Certain Passages which happened at Newport in the Isle of Wight, November 29, 1648, relating to King Charles I., Writtten by Mr. Edward Cooke, of Highnam, in Gloucestershire, sometime Colonel of a Regiment under Oliver Cromwell. 4to. 1690.

Isle of Wight. Packets of Letters, with a Message from Col. Hammond of his refusing to let Col. Ewers secure the King and carry him to Carisbrook Castle. 4to. 1648.

Isle of Wight. Joyful News from the King, and His Majestie's Remonstrance and Resolution touching the Army, delivered to Captain Hatfield, on Saturday last, in the Isle of Wight. Also a Fleet at Sea near the Isle of Wight to Rescue His Majesty. Small 4to. 1648.

Isle of Wight. The Portraiture of His Sacred Majesty, Charles I., in his solitude at Carisbrooke Castle. 12mo. 1648.

Isle of Wight. King Charles ye First. Majesty in Misery. An Imploration to the King of Kings, wrote by his Majesty during his Captivity in Carisbrooke Castle, Anno Domini 1648. T. Cobb, Sculp., Bow Churchyard, London. Broadside, 1648.

Isle of Wight. Letters between Col. Robert Hammond, Governor of the Isle of Wight, and the Committee of Lords and Commons, at Derby House. . . . relating to King Charles I., while he was confined in Carisbrooke Castle in that Island. Now First Published. 8vo. 1764.

Isle of Wight. Bibliotheca Regia ; a Collection of Papers of Charles I. 12mo. 1659.
Isle of Wight Treaty, pp. 517-524.

Isle of Wight. His Majestie's Most Gracious Answer to the Bills and Propositions presented to him at Carisbrook Castle, &c. 4to. 1648.

Isle of Wight. The Votes and Proceedings in Parliament for bringing the King out of the Isle of Wight. 4to. 1648.

Isle of Wight. Declaration from the Isle of Wight and County of Hampshire concerning the King and the tryall of Captain Burley upon High Treason about the late meeting in the said Isle, with the burning of the gates of Canterbury and delivering up Dover Castle. 4to. 1648.

Isle of Wight. Two Letters from the Isle of Wight, being a true relation of Mr. Osborn's carriage and proceedings, &c. 4to. 1648.

Isle of Wight. The Independent's Loyalty ; or, The most Barbarous Plot (to murther his sacred Majestie), at Carisbrooke Castle, Isle of Wight, very fully Discovered, &c. Small 4to. 1648.

Isle of Wight. An Elegy upon the Decease of the most incomparable, pious Lady, the Princesse Elizabeth, who dyed in Carisbrook Castle, in the Isle of Wight, September 8, 1650. 4to. 1650.

Isle of Wight. Six Original Letters addressed from Persons high in the State, in the years 1647 and 1648, to Colonel Hammond, Governor of the Isle of Wight, chiefly relating to the intended escape of King Charles the First from the Castle of Carisbrooke. Archæologia, pp. 149-155. vol. xix. 1821.

Isle of Wight. Answer to a scandalous letter written by Hammond, the Head Gaoler in the Isle of Wight, to Mr. Lenthall, Speaker of the House of Commons, by a Friend of Master Osborne's and a Lover of Truth. 4to. 1645.

Isle of Wight. Mercurius Publicus, July 24-31, 1662 : containing an Account of a Murder at Caborn, in the Isle of Wight, by a Woman who had persecuted Dr. Sydenham, Rector of that Parish, for his loyalty and conformity to the Church of England. 4to. London, 1662.

Odiham. A Victory obtained by Colonel Norton and Colonel Jones. Small 4to. 1644.

Portsmouth. The apprehension of Captain Butler at Porch-mouth, in the county of Southampton, and his followers, who were bound with ammunition for Ireland. 4to. 1641.

Portsmouth. An Uprore at Portsmouth, being an advertize-ment to all Captaines and others that are halting betweene two opinions. Shewing how Captain Wiles, who was sent forth for the defence of the kingdome, did tyrannize over his souldiers, and how hee did revolt to his Majestie, &c. 4to. August 18th, 1642.

Portsmouth. A Relation from Portsmouth, wherein is declared the manner how the Castle (Southsea) was taken on Saturday night last, as it was sent in a letter by one there present, September 6th, 1642. Small 4to. 1642.

Portsmouth. A true Relation of the passages which happened at the town of Portsmouth at the late Siege, which began the 12th day of August last, and was surrendered on the 9th day of September following, written by one that was employed in the service. 4to. September 21st, 1642.

Portsmouth. A Declaration of all the Passages of the taking of Portsmouth, shewing the reasons why it was surrendered up to the Committee of both Houses of Parliament, to-gether with a true Copy of the articles ageed upon between the Committee and Col. Goring. 4to. 1642.

Portsmouth. Mercurius Aulicus, May 11th, 1644. Containing news from Fording-Bridge, Bishops-Waltham, and Ports-mouth. 4to. 1644.

Portsmouth. A Letter from Sir Arthur Haselrigge in Ports-mouth to an Hon. Member of the late Parliament. 4to (sewed). 1659.

Portsmouth. Two Declarations from the Town and Garrison of Portsmouth, &c. 4to. 1659.

Portsmouth. The True Copys of several Letters from Ports-mouth. . . . To the Lord Fleetwood, &c. 4to. London, 1659.

Southampton. Good Newes from South Hampton and Basing-stoke, in Hampshire, &c. 4to. 1642

Southampton. Mercurius Publicus, December 4-11, 1662. Containing an account of Quakers and other Fanatics at Southampton. 4to. 1662.

Wickham. Letters from a gentleman to his father upon occasion of the Armie's Retreat to Wickham in Hampshire. Small 4to. 1647.

Winchester, Cromwell (Lieut. Gen.) Letter to the Right Sir Thomas Fairfax, General of the Parliament's Army (describ-ing his entry into Winchester). Small 4to. October, 1645.

Winchester. A true relation of the putting to death one Master Boys (who went to see his father in Hampshire), on his return, by Col. Aston, a known and professed Papist; an account of the Battle of Winchester, with a list of the Gentlemen of Hampshire that came to assist the Cavaliers and were taken prisoners by the Parliamentary Forces. Small 4to. 1642.

Winchester. A True and Exact Relation of a Great Overthrow given to the Cavalliers in Winchester, by Colonel Hurrey, Colonel Browne, and some others, &c. 4to. London, December 17th, 1642.

Winchester, Its History, &c. Sixteen Pamphlets, some very rare. 4to. 1642-1792.

Includes : Captain Corbets' Discourse and the Sermon before King Charles II., at Winchester, after the Rye House Plot.

Winchester. Letter to Mr. William Longland, Maior of Winchester, demanding the surrender of the City, and the reply of Mr. Longland. Small 4to. October, 1645.

Winchester. Peters (Rev. Hugh) Report to the House of Commons of the Taking of Winchester. Small 4to. October, 1645.

Winchester. Cromwell (Lieut. Gen.) Letter concerning the taking of Winchester Castle, with the report of the House of Commons. 4to. October 9, 1645.

Winchester. Captaine Burley, His Speech at the Place of Execution, at Winchester, &c. 4to. 1648.

Winchester. Burleigh (Capt. Jno.) True and brief relation of the arraignment, condemnation and suffering of Captain John Burleigh, who was hanged, drawn, and quartered at Winton. Small 4to. 1648.

For further Civil War details see Birch, Carey, Carlyle, Clarendon, Cromwell, Devereux, Dugdale, Ellis, England's Black Tribunal, Fuller, Gardiner, Godwin, Guizot, Hammond, Haselrigge, Heylyn, Howell, Johnson, Journals of Houses of Lords and Commons, Ludlow, Milford, Money, Sprigge, St. Barbe, Trial of Charles I., &c., Vernon, Vicars, Waller, Whitelocke.

See also the various News Letters of the Period, such as :— Mercurius Aulicus, or Court Mercurie (Cavalier), Mercurius Britannicus (Parliamentarian), Mercurius Civicus (Parliamentarian), Mercurius Rusticus (Parliamentarian), Certain Information (Parliamentarian), City Scout (Parliamentarian), Diary or Exact Journal (Parliamentarian), The Kingdom's Weekly Intelligencer (Parliamentarian), The Kingdom's Weekly Post (Parliamentarian), Moderaet

Intelligencer (Parliamentarian), Parliament's Scout (Parliamentarian), Parliament's Post (Parliamentarian), Perfect Diurnall (Parliamentarian), Perfect Passages (Parliamentarian), Scottish Dove (Parliamentarian), True Informer (Parliamentarian), Weekly Accompt (Parliamentarian).
Copies of most of these will be found in the King's Pamphlets, British Museum.

Daniell (Mrs.) See Aldershot.

Darling (J.) Catalogue of Books belonging to Sir W. Heathcote, at Hursley Park. Roy 8vo. 186—

Davies (Rev. J. S.) History of Southampton, partly from the MS. of Dr. Speed in the Southampton Archives. Roy. 8vo. 1883.
Also 50 copies on Large Paper in 4to.

Davies (W. H.) of Meonstoke. The Bride of Albion, and other Poems. 12mo. 1880.

Dawes (Rev. Richard) An Account of the King's Somborne School. Extracted from the Minutes of the Committee of Council on Education, 1847-48. 18mo. 1849.

Day (William) Life and Death of Richard Titheridge [a native of Alresford], a Tract. 12mo. 1857.

Dayman (H.) Memoir of the late Joseph Bullar. 8vo. 1869.

De Crespigny (Mrs.) Legend of the New Forest, an Operetta. 8vo. 1889.

Deverell (J.) St. John's Hospital and other Charities in Winchester. 8vo. 1879.

Dibdin (Charles) [Native of Southampton]. The Songs of, chronologically arranged, with notes . . . . and the Music of the Best and Most Popular of the Melodies. Memoir of the Author by George Hogarth. 2 vols, roy 8vo. 1842. (See Thorn).

Directory (Post Office) of Hampshire, Dorsetshire, Wiltshire, &c. 8vo. (1848) and seq.

Dobell (H.) The Medical Aspects of Bournemouth and its Surroundings. 8vo. 1885.

Doddridge (Dr.) See Jennings (Rev. Dr.)

Doman (Henry) Songs of Lymington. Mus. D. IX. 12mo. 1867.

Domesday Book.—Hampshire — Extracted from Domesday Book, with an . . . . English Translation, a Preface, and an Introduction . . . . to which is added a Glossary by R. Warner. 4to. 1789.

Domesday Book of Hampshire in fac-simile by the zincographic process. Folio. 1861.
" With the Literary history of *Domesday Book* Hampshire has some connection. This work was, for a long time, preserved at Winchester—and it was just on the border of the county, at Norman Court, that William I. stayed for some time, while the great Gemot was held near Salisbury, in August, 1086. It was at or near Norman Court that the Chief Barons of England swore fealty to William.

Domesday Book of Hampshire (The) An Extension of the Latin Text and an English Translation, with Notes by H. Moody. Folio. 1862.

Douce (Francis) Observations on a Piece of Antiquity found at Selbourne (folding plate). 4to. Archæologia, 1811.
Reprinted.

Douce (Francis) Ancient Purse found at Selbourne (plate). 4to. Archæologia, 1811.
Reprinted.

Drew (John) and Bullar (J.) Hints to Assist Visitors to Southampton and the Isle of Wight. 8vo. Southampton, N.D.

Driver (A. and W.) General View of the Agriculture of the County of Hants, with View of the Isle of Wight Agriculture, by Rev. R. Warner, and a Postscript by A. Young. 4to. 1794.

Droxford. See Smith and " Sporting."

Dudley (H.) Juvenile Researches, or a Description of some of the Principal Towns in the West of Sussex and the Borders of Hants. 16mo. 1835.
Printed and composed by H. Dudley, aged 15.

Dugdale (James) General Description and History of the Isle of Wight. 4to. 1819.

Duncan (J.) History of Guernsey, with Occasional Notices of Jersey, Alderney and Sark. 8vo. 1841.

Duthy (John) Sketches of Hampshire, embracing the Architectural Antiquities, Topography, &c., and of the Country adjacent to the River Itchen (plates). Royal 8vo. 1839.

Dyson (John R.) Methodism in the Isle of Wight, its Origin and Progress down to the Present Time. 8vo. 1865.

Earle (Rev. John) Legends of St. Swidhun and Sancta Maria Egyptiaca (with Photozincographic Examples). Folio. London, 1861.
Gives a good account of Anglo-Saxon Times.

East (R.) See Murrell.

East Woodhay. See Green.

Edwards (F. A.) The Early Newspaper Press of Hampshire. 12mo. 1889.

Elder (Abraham) Tales and Legends of the Isle of Wight, with the Adventures of the Author in search of them (plates by Cruikshank). 12mo. 1839. 2nd edition, 1843.

Eling. See Pauperism.

Ellingham. See Hall.

Ellis (Sir Henry). See Brand.

Ellis (Humphry) Minister of the Word in the City of Winton ; Pseudo-Christus, or a True and Faithful Relation of the Grand Impostures, Horrid Blasphemies, Abominable Practices, Gross Deceits, lately spread abroad and acted in the County of Southampton, by William Frankelin, Mary Gadbury, and their Companions, &c. Mus. C. vii., 6. 4to. 1650.

Elvetham. The Honourable Entertainment given to the Queen's Majestie in progress, at Elvetham, in Hampshire, by the Right Honorable the Earle of Hartford. Small 4to. 1591.
Reprinted in " Gentleman's Magazine," February and March, 1779.

Elvetham. See Baigent Holme (under Odiham).

Ems, Valley of the. See Longcroft.

Emmett (M.) The Legend of the Priory of Christchurch. 8vo. 1864.

Empson (C. W.) Index to the Registers of Baptisms, Marriages and Burials of the Parish of Wellow. 8vo. 1889.

Enclosures of Common Lands. See Acts of Parliament.

Englefield (Sir H.) Walk through Southampton, describing its Antiquities, with an Account of Clausentum. 8vo. 1801. 2nd edition, 4to, 1805.
Also edited by John Bullar, small 4to, 1850 (?)

Englefield (Sir H. C.) The Isle of Wight, a Description of the Beauties, Antiquities, and Geological Phenomena of (maps and numerous engravings by W. and G. Cooke, from original drawings by Sir H. C. Englefield). 4to. 1816.

Englefield (Sir H. C.) Account of an Ancient Building at Southampton (3 plates). 4to. Archæologia, 1811.
Reprinted.

Eversley. See Kingsley.

Exchange of Hampshire Lands. See Acts of Parliament.

Faden. Map of Hampshire, including the Isle of Wight. 8vo. 1796.

Faithfull (William) The Late Hampshire Election [in 1790]. 8vo. 1791.

Falle (P.) An Account of Jersey. 8vo. 1734.

Falvey (Timothy) [In Memoriam], Reprinted from the *Hampshire Independent*, of Oct. 12th, 1889. 16 pp. sewed, 8vo.

Fareham, Review of Facts in the litigation between Peter Barfoot, Richard Bargus and others, with the Bishop of Winchester, concerning the Right of Fareham Quay. 8vo. 1788.

Fareham. (Uplands near). See Beardmore.

Faunthorpe (J P.) The Geography of Hampshire for Use in Schools (with a map). 8vo. 1872.

Fearon (Rev. W. A.) The Life and Times of Henry of Blois, a Lecture Delivered in the Hall of the Winchester Mechanics' Institute, on Wednesday, March 20th, 1878. 12mo. sewed, 32 pp. 1878.

Fenwick (--) New and Original Poetical, Historical, and Descriptive Guide to the Isle of Wight, from a Recent Personal Survey. Illustrated. 8vo. 1866.

Fergusson (James) The Peril of Portsmouth, or French Fleets and English Forts (with a plan.) 8vo. 1852.

Ferrey (B.) and BRAYLEY (E. W.) Antiquities of the Priory of Christchurch, Hants ; with Particulars of the Castle and Borough (plates) 4to. 1834. 2nd edition, 4to. 1841.
> Revised by Britton.

Fiddes (Richard, D.D.) 1671-1725. The Life of Cardinal Wolsey. Fol. 1724.
> Cardinal Wolsey was Bishop of Winchester.

Field Club. See Hampshire.

Fitt (J. N.) Covertside Sketches. Post 8vo. 1879.
> Mr. J. N. Fitt, the author of "Covertside Sketches," and well known from his connection with one or more of the highest class of sporting papers, is a Hampshire man—of the Westley family of that name—and formely lived at Nether Wallop.

Fitt (J. N.) Hearths and Homesteads, a Series of Papers on Subjects connected with Agriculture. 8vo. N.D.
> Contains references to Hampshire.

[Fitzatherly, (—)] Our Town ; or, Rough Sketches of Character, Manners, etc., by Peregrine Reedpen. 2 vols. 8vo. 1834.
> This book is said to be a satire on the Inhabitants and Society of *Bishops Waltham.*

Fitzherbert (H.) The Island Minstrel. 12mo. 1842.
> The writer of the volume of Poems was Herbert Baskett, a journeyman gardener.

Fordingbridge. History of the Murders committed on the Bodies of Mr. D. Chater, of Fordingbridge, and Mr. W. Galley of Southampton. (Relates particulars of smuggling.) 4to. 1749.

Fordingbridge. See Civil War Pamphlets, Hall, Hannan.

Forests. See Brown.

Franks (Augustus W., F.S.A.) In a Letter to Sir Henry Ellis, K.H., F.R.S.,Director. Notes on Bronze Weapons, found on Arreton Down, Isle of Wight (Illustrated). From the Archæologia, vol. xxxvi. Sewed, 4to, p. 6. 1856.

Freeling (Arthur) Picturesque Excursions [To the Isle of Wight Southampton, New Forest, etc.] 12mo. (1839).

Freeling(Arthur) London and Southampton Railway Companion, with Guides to Southampton and the Isle of Wight. 12mo. 1840.

Freeman (E. A.) Architecture of the Church and Hospital of the Holy Cross, Winchester. 8vo. 1846.

Freeman (Dr. E. A.) The Reign of William Rufus and the Accession of Henry the First. 2 vols. Large 8vo. 1882.
Refers to Sparsholt, Romsey, New Forest, Winchester, &c.,

Gale (S.) History and Antiquities of the Cathedral Church of Winchester. 8vo. 1715. See Hyde.
Contains contributions from B. Willis.
This was afterwards reprinted in Casson's " Lives of the Bishops of Winchester."
The Earl of Clarendon,author of the "History of the Great Rebellion," was a Hampshire man, the family of Hyde having an estate at Catherington. The Earl of Clarendon began a History of Winchester, which was left unfinished, and completed by S. Gale in 1715.

Gaol (County). Report of the Committee Appointed to Examine into the State of the Hampshire County Gaol and Bridewells. 8vo. 1817.

Garbett (W.) Observations and Correspondence, occasioned by the Failure and Restoration of a Principal Pier in Winchester Cathedral. 4to. 1824.

Garneray (Louis Ambrose) Captivité de Louis Garneray, neuf Années en Angleterre. Mes Poutons Illustrés par l'Auteur et Janet-Lange. Royal 8vo. N.D.
The author was eight years (1806-1814) a prisoner of war in the hulks at Porchester and at Bishops Waltham.

Garrow (D.) History of Lymington and its Vicinity. 8vo. 1825.

Gibbons (Thomas) Memoirs of Isaac Watts, D.D. [Native of Southampton]. 8vo. 1780.

Gilbert (H. M.) Bibliotheca Hantoniensis, an Attempt at a Bibliography of Hampshire (printed for subscribers). Large paper. 4to. N.D.

Gilbert (J. M.) See Haghe (L.)

Gilpin (Rev. W.) Remarks on Forest Scenery, &c., illustrated by the Scenes of New Forest in Hampshire. 2 vols. 8vo. 1791, 1794, 1808.
Addenda to the first edition by a friend of the author. 8vo. 1794. Edited by Sir T. D. Lauder. 2 vols. Post 8vo. 1834. Another edition by Heath. Post 8vo. 1887.

Gilpin (Rev. W.) Regulations of Boldre School. 4to sheet. N.D.

Gilpin (Rev. W.) Account of the New Poor House, erected at Boldre. 12mo. 1798.

Gilpin (Rev. W.) Observations on Western parts of England, to which are added a few remarks on the Picturesque Beauties of the Isle of Wight. 8vo. 1798. Second edition. 8vo. 1808.

Gilpin (Rev. W.) Observations on the Coasts of Hampshire, Sussex and Kent (with plates). 8vo. 1804.

Gilpin (Rev. W.) Explanation of the Duties of Religion for the use of Boldre School. 12mo. 1798.

Gipsies. Report of the Southampton Committee for the Amelioration of the State of the Gypsies. 8vo. 1832.
Farewell Address to, by James Crabb on the occasion of the 19th Anniversary. 8vo.

Glenie (James) Short Enquiry into the Nature of the Titles conferred at Portsmouth and the Camps by George III., shewing the Origin and Ancient Privileges of Knights Banneret. 8vo. 1779.

Godesfield. See Hospitallers and Larking.

Godwin (George) Ancient Structures in Winchester and Romsey. 8vo. N.D.

Godwin (Rev. G. N.) The Civil War in Hampshire, 1642-45, and the Story of Basing House. Small 4to. 1882.

Godwin (Rev. G. N.) The Civil War in South-West Hampshire. 24 pp. Small 4to. 1886.

Godwin (Rev. G. N.) Civil War in and around Winchester. Small 4to. 1886

Godwin (Rev. G. N.) Portsmouth to London by "The Rocket," the Coach Route between Portsmouth and London. Post 8vo. 1877.

Godwin (Rev. G. N.) Green Lanes of Hampshire, Surrey, and Sussex. 8vo. 1884.

Golding (Dr.) A Defence of the Warden of Winchester College, by himself. 8vo. 1759.

Golding (Dr.) Warden of Winchester College. Answer to an Anonymous Letter to Dr. Lowth. 8vo. 1759.

Goodyeare (Wm., Merchant of Southampton) Voyage of the "Wandering Knight," from the French. 4to. 1581.
Dedicated to Sir Francis Drake, and is said to have been much used by Bunyan in the writing of his "Pilgrim's Progress." (See Bunyan).

Gosport. Answers to Several Objections made to the Bill for better paving Gosport. Folio. 1763.

Gosport. The Whole Proceedings in a Dispute between Henry Lys the Elder, Esq., and Sarah Gainsford, Widow, which was referred to Arbitration. 8vo. 1789.
(A curious case of reputed marriage).

Gosport. The Strayed Lamb (from Gosport) or the Baptist no Seducer, by Philo Oves. 8vo. 1812.

Gosport. Appeal of J. R. Luzuringa to the Inhabitants of Gosport, in favour of the Spanish Gentleman, M. Penarauda, slandered by Barnabus Rodriguez and the Revs. R. Bingham, Senr. and Junr. 8vo. 1840.

Gosport Tragedy (The) A Poetical Chap Book. 12mo. N.D.

Gosport. See Alverstoke, Anglesea, Portsea, Portsmouth.

Grace (Henry, native of Basingstoke, Hants) History of the Life and Sufferings of, during several years captivity among the Savages. 8vo. 1765.

Graves (Hon. H.) Designs for the Font at Binstead Church, Isle of Wight. 8vo. 1844.

Green (J. S.) Life of Mr. John Van, a Clergyman's Son, of Woody [East Woodhay], in Hampshire, being a Series of many Extraordinary Events. 2 vols. 12mo. N.D.

Greenfield (B. W.) The Heraldry and Exterior Decorations of the Bar Gate, Southampton. 8vo. 1875.

Greenfield (B. W.) The Wrothesby Tomb, Titchfield, Hants. 8vo. 1889.
Reprinted from Proceedings of the Hampshire Field Club (with illustrations).

Greenville (W.) Description of the City, College and Cathedral of Winchester, their Antiquities and Present State. 8vo. N.D.

Greywell. See Holme (under Odiham).

Grose (F.) Antiquities of the County of Hampshire (illustrated). Extracted from the Antiquities of England, etc. 4to. 1783.

Grove (R. A.) Views of the Principal Seats and Marine and Landscape Scenery in Lymington (26 plates). Folio. 1832

Gubbins (E.) Ancient Inscriptions in Winchester Cathedral and other places. 12mo. 1884.

Gudgeon (R. H.) Souvenir of the Opening of the George Hotel, Winchester, on St. George's Day, April 25th, 1889.
History of this Ancient Hostelry from the Reign of Edward I.

Guillaume (George) Architectural Views and Details of Netley Abbey, partly shown as it originally existed. Folio. 1848.

Gunn (Alexander). See Timbs.

Guise (Gen.) and HERVOT (Mr.) Plain Narrative, or True State of the Case between. 4to. 1751.
Respecting a Marriage Settlement. The Tract dedicated to Matthew Woodford, Esq., of Southampton.

Gunner (Rev. W.) An Account of the Alien Priory of Andwell, or Endwell, in Hampshire, etc. 8vo.

Gwilliam (J.) Norris Castle, or Recent Tramps in the Isle of Wight. Post 8vo. 1845.

Gwilliam (J.) Rambles in the Isle of Wight during the Summers of 1841 and 1842. 8vo. 1843. Second edition. 8vo. 1844.

Hackwood Park (near Basingstoke). See Carew, Mitchell, Holme (under Odiham).

Haghe (L.) Views of principal Seats and Marine and Landscape Scenery in the Neighbourhood of Lymington, drawn on Stone by, from Original Pictures taken by J. M. Gilbert, with Historical and Typographical Descriptions. Large Paper ; Proofs on India Paper. Folio. 1832.

Hale Common. See Bailey.

Hall (Rev. P.) A Few Topographical Remarks relative to the Parishes of Ringwood, Ellingham, Ibbesley, Harbridge, Fordingbridge and the New Forest. Post 8vo. 1869.

Hall (Thomas) Poems written in the Debtor's Ward, Winchester. Mus. D. ix. 24-2. 8vo. N.D.

Hambledon. See Hughes.

Hammond (Colonel Robert) of Carisbrooke Castle. See Civil War Pamphlets (I. of W.)

Hampden (Rev. James) Remarks on some Proceedings at the time of the late Election at Winchester College, in the Case of the Masters and the School fairly stated. 8vo. 1767.

Hampshire Field Club Papers and Proceedings, edited by Rev G. W. Minns, LL.B. 1st Series, 1887. 2nd Series, 1888 3rd Series, 1889. 4th Series, 1890. 8vo.

Hampshire Notes and Queries. Vols. I. and II. 8vo. 1834.

Hampshire Notes and Queries. Reprinted from the *Winchester Observer*. 4 vols. 4to. 1883-1889.
A rich mine of Hampshire information.

Hampshire. Old Pocket Book, with much information relating to Hampshire. 12mo. 1785.

Hampshire. Report of Proceedings of a Meeting of the County of Hants, held at Winchester, 1st March, 1823, etc. 8vo. 1823.

Hampshire. Survey of the County, with Arms of the Nobility, etc. 8vo. 1791.

Hannan (R.) Notes on the Town and Neighbourhood of Fordingbridge. 12mo. 1883,

Hanway (Jonas) Journal of Eight Days' Journey from Portsmouth to Kingston-on-Thames (Plate). 4to. 1756.
Jonas Hanway, a merchant, philanthropist, and author, was born at Portsmouth in 1712. Several of his works are in the Hartley Library, Southampton. He first introduced umbrellas into England.

Harbridge. See Hall.

Harding (J. D.) See Bartlett.

Harrison (G. Y.) Vectis Poetice, Descriptive Sonnets on Isle of Wight Scenery. 8vo. 1827.

Hartfordbridge. George Prince of Wales at. From *Lloyd's Evening Post.* 4to. January, 1790

Hartfordbridge. See Pearce.

Hartnall (E.) Pocket Guide to the Isle of Wight. 16mo. 1843.

Hartshorne (C. H.) History and Antiquities of Porchester Castle, Read before the Archæological Institute of Great Britain and Ireland, at Winchester, September, 1845. 8vo. 1846.

Haselden (Thomas) Letter from, to Sir Peter Thompson, dated Portsmouth, 27th February, 1746-7. M.S. folio sheet.

Haselrigge (Sir Arthur) Letter from, in Portsmouth, to an Hon. Member of the late Parliament. 4to, sewed. 1659.

Hassell (J.) Tour of the Isle of Wight. 2 vols. 8vo. 1790.

Havant. Letters addressed to William Garrett, Esq., Relative to the State of Leigh House. 8vo. 1819.

Havant. See Bingly, Longcroft.

Hawkins (E.) Notices of the Mint and Exchange of Winchester. 8vo. 1846.

Hawkins (E.) Account of a large Collection of Coins found at Beaworth, Hants. 4to. 1834.

Hayling Island. See Bingly, Clarke, Jones, Longcroft, Portsmouth Guide, Scott.

Hayling Island. Topographical and Historical Account of Hayling Island, Appendix on Smuggling. (By Richard Scott). Post 8vo. 1826.

Hayling. Guide to Hayling Island and Havant, in the County of Hants (Wood Engravings from sketches by W. B. Clarke.) 12mo. 1836. Another edition. (1843.)

Headbourne Worthy. See Carter Slessor.

Hearne (Thomas). See Spelman.

Heathcote (Sir W.) Catalogue of Books belonging to, at Hursley Park. 4to. 1834. Another by J. Darling. Royal 8vo. 186—

Heckfield. See Milton.

Herve (C. S.) Traditions about Aldershot. 8vo. 1881.

Hervey (Rev. T.) a History of the United Parishes of Colmer and Prior's Dean (with Photographs). 4to. 1880.

Hervot (Mr.) and Guise (Gen.) Plain Narrative, or True State of the Case between, Respecting a Marriage Settlement. The tract dedicated to Matthew Woodford, Esq., of Southamton. 4to. 1751.

Hewett (Gen. Sir G., of Freemantle, Hants) Private record. of the Life of. 8vo. 1840.

Hewetson (J.) Architectural and Picturesque Views of Noble Mansions in Hampshire. Large 4to. N.D.

Heywood (Abel) Guide to the Isle of Wight, Cowes, Newport, Ryde, etc 8vo. (1867).

Heywood (Abel) Guide to Portsmouth and the adjoining Towns of Southsea, Portsea, and Landport, etc. 8vo. 1868.

Heywood (Abel) A Guide to Southampton, its River and Docks, Ancient Boundary Walls, etc. 8vo. 1868.

Highclere. See Lisle, Milles.

Hill (Du Boulay) The Church Bells of Winchester. 8vo. 1877.

Hilliard (J.) Fire from Heaven burning the Body of one John Hitchell, of Holmeshurst, within the Parish of Christchurch. Small 4to. 1613.

Hillier (G.) The Topography of the Isle of Wight. 12mo. Ryde, 1850.

Hillier (G.) A Voyage round the Isle of Wight. 12mo. 1850.

Hillier (G.) History and Antiquities of the Isle of Wight (Illustrated). 4to. London. N.D.
Printed for Subscribers only, and not published.

Hillier (G.) Narrative of the Attempted Escapes of King Charles I. from Carisbrooke Castle. Post 8vo. (See Civil War Pamphlets.) 1852.

Hillier (G.) Result of the Excavations on Brightstone and Bowcombe Downs, Isle of Wight, August, 1854 (with illustrations). Sewed, p. 7. 4to. London. 1854.

Hindhead. See Dickens and Pepys.

Hoare (Sir R. Colt) Observations on Mosaic Pavements Discovered at Thraxton, Bramdean, and Crondall. 4to. Archæologia (Reprinted). 1811.

Hobhouse (Bishop E.) Life of Bishop Walter de Merton (of Basingstoke). 8vo. 1859.

Hogarth (G.) See Dibdin.

Holdsworth (Edward) 1688-1747. Muscipula, a Latin Poem. (for which see Richards).
Gough says that " Hoglandiæ Descriptio " is an answer to this Poem.

Hollingsworth (—) Guide to Portsmouth. 12mo. 1840.

Holloway (H. R.) Walks round Ryde. Second edition. 16mo. 1848.

Holme (Rev. C.) A Topographical Account of Odiham and its Vicinity. Post 8vo. N.D. (about 1880).

Hollis (George) Reply to " A Short Statement of Facts " assumed by John Hancock Buckle relative to the conduct of Mr. Hollis as Under Sheriff of Hants. 8vo. 1816.

Hordle Cliff. See Brander-Webster.

Hoskins (S. Elliot, M.D.) Charles II. in the Channel Islands. 2 vols. 8vo. 1854.

Hospitallers (Knights) in England. Small 4to. Camden Society, 1857.
Enumerates their possessions at Godesfield and Baddesley.

Howard (Henry) On the Tomb of King Alfred at Hyde Abbey, near Winchester. 4to. Soc. Ant., 1798.

Huddersfield (G.) The Wiccamical Chaplet : a Selection of Original Poetry [the Effusions of Wykehamites]. 8vo. 1804.

Hughes (J. Gwynne) Reply to the Letter of the Rev. A. Lush, on the [Odiham] Marriage Case. 8vo. 1855.

Huguenot. See Serres.

Humbert (Rev. L. M.) Memorials of the Hospital of St. Cross and Almshouse of Noble Poverty (illustrated with photographs). 4to. 1868.

Hursley. Portfolio containing Plans and Elevations of All Saints' Church, Hursley.

Hursley Magazine. Selections from the " Hursley Magazine " for 1848 and 1849. 30 copies only, privately printed by Ladies at Hursley Park (" Illustrations copied from the originals by the same hands "). Royal 8vo. 1861.

Hursley. See Carlyle, Coleridge, Cromwell, Darling, Duthy, Guizot, Heathcote, Imber, Keble, Marsden, Marsh, Moor, Noble, Settle.

Hurstborne Priors. See St. Mary Bourne.

Hurst Castle. See Bartlett, Charles I.

Huxford (Alfred Lear) History of Portchester Castle. N.D.

Hyde (Henry, Earl of Clarendon). The History and Antiquities of the Cathedral Church at Winchester, etc. 8vo. 1715.
See Gale (who completed this work).

Hyda, Liber Monisteria de Hyda. A Chronicle and Cartulary of Hyde Abbey, Winchester, 455-1023 A.D. (Rolls Publications). Roy. 8vo. 1866.

Hyde Abbey. See Howard.

Ibbesley. See Hall.

Imber (M.) The Case, or an abstract of the Customs of the Manor of Merdon, in the Parish of Hursely in the County of Southampton. 8vo. 1707.

Inglis (H. D.) The Channel Islands. 2 vols. 1834.

Inglis (H. D.) The Channel Islands. 2 vols. 8vo. 1835.

Isle of Wight. The true description of a monstrous chylde borne in the Isle of Wight in the yeare 1564. Folio-sheet. 1564

Isle of Wight (Saltmakers of). A True Remonstrance of the state of the Salt Business, undertaken (for the furnishment thereof between Barwick & Pool, they with the Isle of Wight and members inclusive), by the Societie of Salt-makers of South and North Shields and of Scotland. Broadside. December, 1638,

Isle of Wight. Report of the Commissioners for inquiring concerning the Charities of the Isle of Wight. Mus. D. ix. 19. 3. 12mo. 1837.

Isle of Wight System of Roads and System of Guardians of the Poor: not a Model, but a Warning, to the Legislature. 8vo. 1845.

Isle of Wight. Case on the merits of the Election and Return for the Borough of Newtown in the Isle of Wight. [1729]

Isle of Wight. Newtown. See Merewether.

Isle of Wight. Reply to the Newtown Petitioners. Folio-sheet.

Isle of Wight. Part of Poll Book. Folio. December, 1832.

Isle of Wight. Poetical Excursions in. 4to. 1777.

Isle of Wight. A Poem, with Plate of Needle Rocks before the fall of the pointed rock from which the group takes its name. 12mo. 1782.

Isle of Wight. Vectis, a descriptive Poem. 12mo. N.D.

Isle of Wight, Vectigalia, or Gleanings from the. Oblong Folio.

Isle of Wight. Garland. A Ballad, in three parts. Privately reprinted by Utterson. 8vo. 1839.
Only twenty-five copies printed.

Isle of Wight. Sabrina, or the Pilgrims of the Isle, a Poem founded on Scenery in the Isle of Wight. 8vo. 1842.

Isle of Wight. A New, Correct, and much Improved History of the Isle of Wight. 8vo. 1795.

Isle of Wight. A Companion to the Isle of Wight. 2nd. edition 12mo. 1800. 3rd edition, 12mo. 1802. See Albin.

Isle of Wight, New Picture of the. (26 Plates). 8vo. 1813.

Isle of Wight. Tour in the, in the autumn of 1820. 8vo. 1822.

Isle of Wight. Beauties of the Isle of Wight, with an account of the principal Towns. 12mo. 1826. 2nd edition, 12mo. 1827. 3rd edition, 12mo. 1828.

Isle of Wight, A Visit to the. 12mo. 1828.

Isle of Wight, Picturesque Scenery of the. 8vo. 1829.

Isle of Wight, Vectis Directory ; or general guide to the, 8vo. 1839.

Isle of Wight, Miniature Road Book of the. 8vo. 1842.

Isle of Wight, A new pocket guide to the, giving a concise and rapid sketch of the line from London to Southampton. 18mo. 1844.

Isle of Wight, Wanderings in the. 8vo. (1846).

Isle of Wight. The Tourist's Guide through the, with its peculiar and most interesting scenery. (Illustrated.) 8vo. 1846.

Isle of Wight. A Remembrance of Bonchurch, Isle of Wight. The Burial Place of the Rev. W. Adams. 8vo. (1849).

Isle of Wight. Account of Bonchurch, by J. W. 8vo. 1849

Isle of Wight, Views of, engraved by Cousen, Godfrey, and others. Royal 8vo. 1856.

Isle of Wight, Rough notes and rambling reminiscences of a visit to the, August, 1858, by L. W. S. 12mo. (1858 ?)

Isle of Wight, Views in the, with descriptive letter-press. 12mo. (1859).

Isle of Wight, Concise exposition of the geology, antiquities, and topography of the, (Favourite localities of the tourist, No. 1.) 4to. (1861).

Isle of Wight. A Trip round the Southern side of the Island. Second Series. 12mo. 1862.

Isle of Wight. Fenwick (R. G.) Home Thoughts, or the Lapidary of Ventnor, being Reminiscences of a Tour in the, Isle of Wight. 8vo. 1866.

Isle of Wight, The Tourists . . . Guide to the. 8vo. (1872).

Isle of Wight. Visitors' Book. 8vo. N.D.

Isle of Wight. Miscellany (The). By various contributors· From Jan. 6, 1844 to —— 1844.

Isle of Wight. Carisbrooke Magazine, Newport. 2 vols. 8vo. 1880-81. All published.

Isle of Wight. Binstead. See Withers.

Isle of Wight. Carisbrooke Castle : a Poem in seven Parts historical and descriptive, with Notes. sewed, 12mo. pp 28. N.D.

Isle of Wight. Carisbrooke. Case of Breeks against Woolfrey [relating to the setting up a monument in Carisbrooke churchyard], with the judgment of Sir Herbert Jenner thereon added in MS. 8vo. 1838.

Isle of Wight. Carisbrooke. See Beattie, Brettell, Freeman, Civil War, Sharp, Varring, Westall.

Isle of Wight. Chale. See Lempriere.

Isle of Wight. Cowes. See Bartlett, Hook, Newport, Sharp.

Isle of Wight, (Freshwater). Proceedings of a Court of Inquiry upon Lieut. Josiah Dornford, and 7 of the Crew of the Coast Guard Station at Freshwater for conniving at Smuggling. 8vo. 1836.

Isle of Wight. Catalogue of Books of the Isle of Wight Institution. 8vo. 1848.

Isle of Wight. Church of St. Thomas, Newport. Elizabeth Stuart, the captive of Carisbrooke. 4to. Privately Printed, 1856.

Isle of Wight. Newport, sketches of. Description taken on sailing from, to Lymington, with a return by Southampton to Cowes. 8vo. 1792.

Isle of Wight. Newport. Cutts (Lord), Speech to the Mayor and Aldermen of Newport at Carisbrooke Castle, upon the Swearing of Mr. Leigh, the New Mayor. Folio. 1693.

Isle of Wight. Newport, the Ladies Poetical Petition for a Winter Assembly at. 4to. 1806.

Isle of Wight. Newport. See Brettell, Civil War, Nicholls, Sharp, Tarnbull.

Isle of White. Quarr Abbey. See Trevelyan.

Isle of Wight. Shanklin. See Walford.

Isle of Wight. (St. Lawrence Well). See Sheridan.

Isle of Wight. Ventor. See Spindler.

Isle of Wight. Yarmouth. See Merewether.

Isle of Wight. See Adams, Akerman, Albin, Andrews, Ashburnham, Atkins, Barber, Barton, Baskett, Beal, Bevan, Black, Blanchard, Bloxham, Bonner, Boutell, Bradbury, Brannon, Brettell, Bridden, Brion and Wilkin, Britton and Brayley, Bromfield, Bromley, Bullar, Bunyon, Calvert, Camden, Chamberlain, Charles I., Churoh, Civil War, Clarke, Clifford, Cook, Cooke, Collingwood

Cowper, Drew, Dugdale, Dyson, Edgar, Elder, Englefield,
English History, Faden, Fenwick, Ferne, Fitzherbert, Forster,
Franks, Freeling, Gilpin, Granville, Graves, Gwilliam,
Hampshire Repository, Harrison, Hartnall, Hassell,
Heywood, Hillier, Holloway, Hook, James, Jay,
Jenkinson, Jones, Kell, Kelly, Kidd, Knight, Land
We Live In, Lee, Le Feitt, Lockhart, Long, Loudon,
Manning, Marshall, Martin, Mason, May, Metaxa,
Midland, Mogg, Moor, Mudie, Murray, Nelson,
New Guide to Portsmouth, Nutt, Pennant, Price,
Raine, Raye, Richmond, Roscoe, Russell, Rye, Sharp,
Shaw, Sheridan, Sotheby, Spickernell, Sturch, Sturge,
Taylor, Tennyson, Tomkins, Topographical Description,
Trevelyan, Vancouver, Venables, Vergil, Wallis, Ware,
Warner, Wayland, Webster, Westall, White, Wilks, Wood-
ward, Worsley, Wyndham, Young.

Keate (George) Netley Abbey, an Elegy. 4to. 1769.
The first edition was published in 1764, and called " The Ruins of
Netley Abbey." Reprinted in *Bullar's Companion* in a Visit to
Netley Abbey.

Keble (Rev. John) Various Papers relating to, and to Hursley.

Keble (Rev. John) Memoirs of, by Sir J. T. Coleridge. 8vo.
1870.

Keble. See Moor.

Kell (Rev. E.) The Founders of our Town ; Three Lectures
delivered at the Athenæum, Newport. See *Hampshire
Independent*, December 18th, 1852, January 1st, 1853.
March 26th, 1853.

Kell (Rev. E.) Brief Notice of Clausentum. 8vo. 1858.

Kell (Rev. E.) Mr. Hartley's Intentions Respecting the Application of his Munificent Bequest. Sewed, 16mo. 1858.

Kell (Rev. E.) Additional Correspondence in favour of the
Foundation of a Collegiate Institution on the Hartley
Bequest. Sewed, 16mo. 1858.

Kell (Rev. E.) Tribute to the Memory of Alderman Richard
Andrews [of Southampton] with a Memoir. 8vo. 1859.

Kell (Rev. E.) Lecture on Dr. Watts, July 21st, 1861, after the
Inauguration of Dr. Watts' Statue in the Park at Southampton, by the Earl of Shaftesbury, July 17th, 1861.

Kell (Rev. E.) Description of Beaulieu Abbey. 12mo. 1870.

Kell (Rev. E.) Description of Netley Abbey. 12mo. 1870.

Kell (Rev. E.) Account of Coins, etc., found in a Marsh con-
tiguous to Newport, Isle of Wight, pp. 8. Sewed, 8vo.
Journ. Arch. Assoc., N.D.

Kell (Rev. E.) Hampshire Archæology. 8vo. N.D.
Contents.
The Discovery of a Roman Building at Castlefield, near Andover.
The Castle and other Ancient Remains at Southampton.
The Saxon Bone Pits near St. Mary's Road, Southampton, and on a
Coin of Offa, King of Mercia.
On Leaden Seals from Gurnard Bay and elsewhere.
The Discovery of a Roman Building at Gurnard Bay.
On Roman Coins found in the Isle of Wight.
On the Ancient Site of Southampton.
Excavations on Brightstone and Bowcombe Downs, Isle of Wight.
The Discovery of Two Cemeteries in the Isle of Wight.
A Terminal Statue found at Bevis Mount, Southampton.
The Discovery of a Glass Factory at Buckholt.
On the Site of Mediæval Cemetery at Shirley.
Greek Vessels found near Rowland's Castle, Hants.
An Urn found on Bembridge Down, near Sandown, Isle of Wight.
A Romano-British Pottery at Barnes, near Brixton, Isle of Wight.
On the Largest Barrow in the Anglo-Saxon Cemetery on Bowcombe
Down, Isle of Wight.
On a Leaden Coffin found at Bishopstoke.

Kell (Rev. E. and Mrs.) of Southampton, Memorials of. 8vo.
1875.

Kelly (E. R.) County Topographies; Hampshire and the Isle of
Wight, edited by E. R. Kelly. 8vo. 1875.

Kemble. See Larking.

Kempster (Bartholomew) The Parts, Patience and Pains of.
4to. London, 1680.
Frequently reprinted. See "Batt upon Batt" under the heading
Southampton.

Ken (Thomas, Bishop of Bath and Wells, previously Prebend of
Winchester) Life of, by a Layman. 8vo. 1851. 2 vols.
8vo. 1854.

Ken (Thomas) Life, by W. Hawkins. 4 vols. London, 1721.

Ken (Thomas) Life, by Dean Plumptre. 1890.

Ken (Thomas) Life. *Lond. Gent. Mag.*, vol. 84.

Ken (Thomas) Life. *Lond. Gent. Mag.*, February, 1845, pp.
175, 176.

Ken (Thomas) Life. *Fraser's Magazine*, vol. iv., 387.

Ken (Bishop). See Bowles.

Kidd's Pocket Companion to the Isle of Wight (with engravings
by Bonner). 12mo. 1838.

King (Edward) Old Times re-visited in the Borough and Parish
of Lymington, Hants. 8vo. 1879.

King (James) Poem on Leigh Park. 8vo. 1829.

Kingsley (Rev. C.) Death and Funeral of, at Eversley. See
Professor F. Max Muller's Preface to "The Roman and the
Teuton." 8vo. 1884. Macmillan.

Kingsley (Rev. C.) Verses written for the opening of the Yateley Exhibition. A 12mo sheet. 1867.

Kingsley (Rev. C.) His Letters and Memories of his Life. Edited by his Wife. 2 vols. 1877.

Kingsley (Rev. C.) Sermon preached in the Parish Church of Eversley, on the Sunday after the funeral of, by the Rev. Sir William H. Cope, Bart. 8vo. 1875.

King's Somborne. See Dawes.

Kitchin (Very Rev. G. W.,D.D., Dean of Winchester) Winchester Cathedral Records: No. 1. A Consuetudinary of the 14th Century for the Refectory of the House of St. Swithun in Winchester. 4to. 1886.

Kitchin (Very Rev. G. W., D.D., Dean of Winchester) Winchester Cathedral Records: No. 2. A Charter of Edward III., Confirming and Enlarging the Privileges of St. Giles' Fair, Winchester, A.D., 1349. 4to. 1886.

Kitchin (Very Rev. G. W., D.D., Dean of Winchester) and Madge (Rev. F. T.) Documents relating to the Foundation of the Chapter of Winchester. A.D., 1541-1547. 8vo. 1889. *Hampshire Record Society's Publications.*

Kitchin (Very Rev. G. W., D.D., Dean of Winchester) Historic Towns : Winchester. 8vo. 1890.

Klitz (Philip) Sketches of Life, Character and Scenery in the New Forest. Post 8vo. 1850.

Lainston near Winchester. See Chudleigh.

Langston Harbour, and the Proposed Docks and Railway. 8vo. 1855.

Latham (Dr.) Account of the Ancient Sculptures and Inscriptions in the Abbey Church, Romsey. 4to. 1801.

Latham (R. G.) See Ansted.

Le Brocq (Philip) Outlines of a plan for making the tract of land called the New Forest, a Real Forest. 8vo. 1794.

Le Cras (A. J.) The Laws, Customs, and Privileges of the Island of Jersey. 12mo. 1839.

Lee (E.) The Undercliff (Isle of Wight) and Bournemouth. 8vo. 1856.

Lee (Sir J. T., of the Elms, Hants.) Memoirs of his Life, etc. 4to. 1836.

Lefevre (Lt. Col. C. S.) Standing Orders of the Hants Yeomanry. Small 8vo. London. 1848.

Legge (Rt. Hon. Henry Bilson) Account of the character of, (with letters and particulars relating to the Hampshire Election, 1759.) 4to. 1764.

Le Gros (Augustus Apsley) Mont Orgueil Castle, its History and its Ruins. Post 8vo. N.D.

Leigh House and Park. See Havant, King, Staunton.

Leigh Park Estate, Notices of the. 8vo. 1836.
Printed for private circulation.

Le Keux. Picturesque Memorials of Winchester (plates with descriptions). 4to. 1830.

Leland (John) Hampshire, 300 years ago, transcribed from the Itinerary of John Leland. With explanatory notes by H. Moody. 8vo. 1868.

Leon (Sir John De) Voyage from Southampton (in verse). 8vo. N.D.

Leroy (A. C. and Bramston, A. R.) Historic Winchester. Cr. 8vo. 1882.

L'Estrange (Rev. A. G.) Royal Winchester. 8vo. 1889.

Lefroy (Charles Edward) Letter to Sir Thomas Baring, on the Subject of allotments of Land to the Poor at West Ham, Basingstoke. 8vo. 1834.

Lempriere (W.) Report on Medicinal Effects of the Chalybeate Waters of Chale, Isle of Wight. 8vo. N.D.

Le Quesne (C.) A Constitutional History of Jersey. 8vo. 1856.

Letchiot (Mr., " of Ireland, lately Curate near Salisbury,") Southampton Guide. 12mo. 1768.
Gough in a MS. note says that Mr. Letchiot was the author of this book.

Lewis (H.) Illustrated Hand-book of Portsmouth, and Guide to the Royal Dockyard, Harbour and Haslar Hospital, Gosport, &c. 8vo. 1860.

Lewis (P.) Historical Enquiries concerning Forests and Forest Laws, with Topographical Remarks upon the Ancient and Modern State of the New Forest, in the County of Southampton. 4to. 1811.

Lisle (Edward, of Crux-Easton) Observations on Husbandry (Portrait). 4to. 1757.
Contains curious information about Hampshire Agriculture, &c., at the beginning of the 18th Century. Another Edition, in two vols., 8vo, was published in the same year, which contains a glossary of Hants words.

Lisle, Lady. See Western Martyrology.

Littlehale's (H.) Romsey Abbey or a history of the Benedictine Nunnery founded in the 10th Century at Romsey in Hampshire. (Front.) 12mo. 1866.

Lockerley. See Titherley (East).

Lockhart (Charles) A General Guide to the Isle of Wight, (Illustrated). Small 4to. 1870.

Loggon (S.) History of the Brotherhood, or Guild of the Holy Ghost, in the Chapel of the Holy Ghost, near Basingstoke, Hampshire. 8vo. 1742.

London and South Western Railway, Official Guide to (with maps and illustrations). Small 12mo. 1887.

London and South Western Railway. See Acts of Parliament, Freeling, Isle of Wight, Meason, Mogg, Wylde.

London and Southampton Railway. Report of the Directors, August, 1837 (contains map, Sections of the Line, etc.). 4to. 1837.

Long (W. H.) Dictionary of the Isle of Wight Dialect. Post 8vo 1886.

Long (W. H.) Oglander Memoirs, Extracts from the MSS. of Sir J. Oglander (Kt.), Isle of Wight. 4to. 1888.

Longcroft (Charles John) Topographical Account of the Hundred of Bosmere, in the County of Southampton, including the Parishes of Havant, Warblington and Hayling (plates, etc.). Imp. 8vo. 1857.

Longcroft (Charles John) The Valley of the Ems. 8vo. 1863

Long Sutton. See Reeve.

Loudon (Mrs. J. W.) Glimpses of Nature during a Visit to the Isle of Wight (plates). Square 8vo. London, 1848.

Lowth (Bishop Robert) The Life of William of Wykeham, Bishop of Winchester. 8vo. 1758. Second edition, 1759. Third edition, 1777.
> Dr. Robert Lowth, an eminent divine, Bishop of London, son of Dr. William Lowth, was author of a number of theological works and of the Life of William of Wykeham. He was born at Buriton in 1710. He was rector of Ovington, near Winchester, and subsequently of East Woodhay, previously to his episcopal promotion.

Lowth (Bishop Robert) The Genealogy of Christ, as it is represented in the East Window in the College Chapel at Winchester : a Poem. 8vo. 1729.

Lowth (Rev. Dr.) Answer to an Anonymous Letter concerning the late election of a Warden of Winchester College. 8vo. 1759.

Lucas (R. C., Sculptor) Hetty Lothe and Palmerstoniana. (Part I., Autobiography of the Author between the ages of 60 and 74 years). Small 4to. 1875.

Lyford (H. G.) Address to the Members of Winchester Mechanics Institute on the Opening of the Second Session, 1836. 12mo. 1836. With List of Members.

Lymington, Pen and Pencil Sketches of, and Ten Miles round. 12mo. N.D

Lymington, A New Guide to, by a Resident. 12mo. 1828.

Lymington, Handbook for (map and plates). 8vo. Lymington, 1845.
A reprint of the *Guide*, with many additions. Another edition, 8vo, 1853.

Lymington, Round, and Through the New Forest. 12mo.

Lymington. See Barrey, Companion in a Tour round Southampton, Doman, Garrow, Gilbert, Grove, Haghe, King, Merewether, Newport, St. Barbe, Warner, Wilson.

McFadden (Frank) Vestiges of Old Southampton, a series of 12 etchings, with Letterpress Descriptions by T. W. Shore, F.G.S., etc. Folio. 1891.

Madden (Sir Frederick) Description of the Matrix of the Seal of Southwick Priory (plates). 4to. 1831.

Madge (Rev. F. T.) and Kitchin (Rev. Dr., Dean of Winchester) Documents relating to the Foundation of the Chapter of Winchester, A.D. 1541-1547. 8vo. 1889.

Magazines. "Western County Magazine," particularly dedicated to the inhabitants of Wilts, Hants, etc. 8vo. 1787, *te seq.*

Magazines. "The Hampshire Repository"; or an Historical, Economical and Literary Miscellany, relative to the County and the Isle of Wight (plates). 2 vols. 8vo. 1798-9.

Magazines. "The Hampshire Miscellany" 1819.

Magazines. "The Crypt," or a Receptacle for Things Past ; an Antiquarian and Miscellaneous Journal [relating to Hampshire and adjoining counties]. 3 vols and vol. I. New Series. 12mo. and 8vo. 1827-9.

Magazines. "Hampshire and West of England Magazine." Plates. 8vo. 1828.
Twelve monthly numbers only were published, and it then became incorporated with " The Crypt," which see.

Magazines. "Hampshire Magazine," 'The Hawk,' 'A Year's Experiment.' N.D.

Malet (Sir Alexander) Some account of the system of Fagging at Winchester School. 1828.

[**Malet** (Sir Alexander)] Letter in reference to his late pamphlet, by an old Etonian. 8vo. 1828.

Malmesbury (Earl of) Memoirs of an Ex-Minister. 2 vols. 8vo. 1884.
Born, and resided at "Heron Court, an old manor house near Christchurch."

Manning (Wm. M.)—Proceedings in Courts of Revision in the Isle of Wight ; and cases decided in South Hants before Revising Barrister. 12mo. 1836.

M[ansfield] (R. B.). School Life at Winchester, (coloured plates) 12mo. 1870.

Manwood (John). A Treatise of the Laws of the Forest, including most interesting matter relating to the New Forest. Small 4to. 1598. 2nd edition. 1615. 3rd. edition. 4to. 1655. 4th. edition. 4to. 1665. 5th. edition. 8vo. 1717. Revised, with new title. 1744.

Maps of Hampshire. Cary (John). Map of Hampshire. 1810, and 1825.

> Hampshire in Unions (Poor Law Unions in colours) (Greenwood, C. and J.) 1834. Walker's Map of London and Southampton Railway. N.D. Map of New Forest (Faden). 1789. Map Winchester Division "Part of Kentish's Great Map of Hampshire" Otterbourne, St. Cross, etc., N.D. Travelling Chart :—Basingstoke, Winchester, Gosport, etc., N.D.

Marsh (J.) Memoranda of the Parishes of Hursley and North Baddesley, in the County of Southampton. (Coloured Plates). 8vo. 1808.

Marshall (William)The Rural Economy of the Southern Counties, comprising Kent, Surrey, Sussex, the Isle of Wight, the Chalk Hills of Wiltshire, &c., 2 vols. 8vo. 1798.

Martin (G. A.) The Undercliff of the Isle of Wight, its climate, history and natural productions. 12mo. 1849.

Martin (T.). Historica Descriptio complectens Vitam et Res Gestas Gulielmi Wicami Vintoniensis Episcopi. 4to. 1597, and 4to. 1690.

Mason's Poetical Excursions in the Isle of Wight. (Vignette). 4to. 1777.

Mason's Handy Guide to the Isle of Wight. 8vo. (1868).

Mason (James), Tourist's Guide to the Isle of Wight. 8vo. 1878.

Masters (F. M.) A Guide to The County Hall and the Assize Courts at Winchester, together with a Brief History of the Hall and a Full Description of the Heraldic Decorations, respectfully dedicated to Melville Portal, Esq., sewed 24. pp. 8vo. N.D.

Maxwell (Archibald). Portsmouth, a Descriptive Poem, in two Books. 8vo. 1755.

May (N.) Guide to the Isle of Wight. 8vo. N.D.

Measom (George). Guide to the South Western Railway (woodcuts). 8vo. N.D.

Meason (G.) Illustrated Isle of Wight Railway Guide. 8vo. 1864.

Meeson (F.R.) Genealogical Records of the Families of Muddle, Dun, Soffe and Tucker. Royal 8vo. 1888.
The Millbrook branches of the family of Soffe, of Hampshire.

Merton (Bishop Walter de), Life of, by Bishop E. Hobhouse 8vo. 1859.
A native of Basingstoke.

Meonstoke. See Davis.

Metaxa (Count A. R. N.) Round " the Wight " and across " the Solent " in an Open Canoe. 8vo. sewed, pp. 14.

Metaxa (Count A. R. N.) Walking Tour Through the Isle of Wight in the Year 1870. 8vo. sewed. pp. 10. 1870.

Michaelmarsh and Its Antiquities, together with Notices of the New Forest. 8vo. 1867.

Michell (R.) Hackwood Park : a poem. 4to. 1765.

Midland (Albert). Vecta Garland. 8vo. Ryde, 1860.

Midland (Albert). Lays of Carisbrooke Castle. sewed. 12mo. N.D.

Milbrook. See Meeson.

Millard (James Elwin), Account of Basingstoke Basing, and the neighbourhood. (Woodcuts). 4to. 1874.

Millard (James Elwin., D.D.) Catalogue of Books selected from the Library of, 4to. [1878]

Milles (Rev. Issac), Account of the Life and Conversation of, Rector of High Cleer, Hants ; with Funeral Sermon, 9th, July, 1720. 8vo. 1721.

Milner (Rev. Dr, Bishop of Castabald, Born 1752, died 1826.) The History, Civil and Ecclesiastical, and survey of the Antiquities of Winchester. 2 vols. 4to. 1798-1801. 3rd edition. 4to. 1809. 4th Edition. Imp. 8vo. 1839.

Milner (Rev. Dr.) Short view of the History and Antiquities of Winchester, with an account of the seats of the neighbouring nobility. 8vo. 1799. 2nd edition,1802. Another, 1815.

Milner (Rev. Dr.) Historical and Critical Account of Winchester Cathedral, extracted from his history &c., of Winchester. 148 pp. 8vo. 1801. 2nd edition, 8vo. Winchester. 1807. 7th edition. 8vo. Winchester. 1809. 8th. edition. 8vo. Winchester. 1815. 9th edition. 12mo. Winchester. 1830.

Milner (Rev. Dr.) Historical and Descriptive Guide to the City of Winchester, its Cathedral, &c. 12mo. Winchester. 1825. Seventh Edition. 12mo. 1829. Eleventh Edition. London. 8vo. 1850.

Milner (Rev. Dr.) A short Description of the Hospital of St. Cross, near Winchester. 12mo. (1840.) Twenty-Second Edition. 8vo. (1850).

Milner (Rev. Thomas) The Life, Times, and Correspondence of the Rev. Isaac Watts, D.D. 8vo. 1834.
A native of Southampton.

Milton (W., Vicar of Heckfield). The Danger of Travelling in Stage Coaches. 8vo. 1810.

Missing (J.) Titchfield, a Poetical Essay. 4to. 1749.

Mitford (Miss.) See L'Estrange, Murch.

Moberley (Rev. George, D.C.L.) Sermons preached at Winchester College, with a Preface on "Fagging." 12mo. 1844-48.

Moberley (Rev. George, D.C.L.) Five Short Letters to S William Heathcote, Bart., M.P., for the University of Oxford, on the Studies and Discipline of Public Schools. 8vo. 1861.

Moberley (Rev. George) Observations on the Public School Bill as affecting Winchester College. 8vo. 1865.

Moberley (Rev. G. H.) Life of William of Wykeham. Royal 8vo. 1887.

Mogg (E.) Southampton Railway and Isle of Wight Guide (maps of the Line, Isle of Wight, etc.). 12mo. 1845.

Monk (Cuthbert) Churches in and around Southampton. 4to. 1886.

Monk (Cuthbert) A Descriptive and Historical Sketch of the Cistercian Monastery of Netley. 12mo. 1886.

Montagu Family. See Sandford and Meredith.

Moody (H.) Hampshire in 1086. Alphabetical List of such of the present Parishes, Tythings and Manors, with the exception of those in the Isle of Wight as are mentioned in the Domesday Book. p. 8. Sewed. 1845.

Moody (H.) Antiquarian and Topographical Sketches of Hampshire. 12mo. 1846.

Moody (H.) The Hampshire Mirror of Things Past and Present, edited by H. Moody. 8vo. 1846.

Moody (H.) Notes and Essays relating to the Counties of Hants and Wilts. 8vo. 1851.

Moody (H.) Our County, or Hampshire in the Reign of Charles II. Crown 8vo. 1863

Moody (H.) History and Description of the Hospital of St.. Cross, near Winchester, with a List of the Masters from its Foundation to the Present Time. 8vo. (1840.)

Moody (H.) See Leland.

Moor (F.) Guide to the Scenery in the environs of Ventnor, and Description of the Undercliff &c., with a Delineation of Appuldurcombe House and environs, and of the Antiquities of the Museum Wersleyanum. Small 4to. N.D.

Moor (Rev. J. F.) Keble (Rev. J.) The Birthplace, Home, Churches, and Memorials of. 4to. 1867.

Moor (Rev. J. F.) Guide to Hursley. 8vo. 1869.

Moses (H.) Account of the Visit of King William IV. (when Duke of Clarence), as Lord High Admiral to Portsmouth in 1827. Folio. 1827.

Mudie (Robert) Hampshire, its Past and Present Condition, and Future Prospects. 3 vols. Imp. 8vo. 1840.

Mudie (R.) The Isle of Wight ; its Past and Present Condition, and Future Prospects. Royal 8vo. (1841).

Mudie (R.) The New Forest, its Towns, Villages, etc. Royal 8vo. N.D.

Muller (Prof. Max). See Kingsley.

Murray (J.) Handbook for Travellers in Surrey, Hampshire and the Isle of Wight. Post 8vo. 1858. Second edition, 12mo, 1865. Third edition, 12mo, 1876.

Murrell (R. J.) and East (R.) Extracts from the Records in the Procession of the Municipal Corporation of the Borough of Portsmouth 4to. 1884.

Nelson (T.) The Isle of Wight, with a description of the Geology of the Island. 8vo. 1859. Another edition. 1869.

Nelson (T.) Portsmouth and Its Neighbourhood. Oblong 16mo. (1870).

Netley Abbey. The Ruins of, a Poem ; to which is prefixed a short account of that Monastery. 4to. 1765.
<small>Printed by Mr. Dummer, the proprietor, for the use of his friends; this is an entirely different poem from Keate's, by the same title.</small>

Netley Abbey, A companion in a visit to. 12mo. 1800.

Netley Abbey. Visitant's Guide to, also Southampton, Portsmouth &c., &c., 12mo. 1832.

Netley Abbey. See Adams, Andrewes, Barham, Beattie, Brand, Brannon, Bullar, Guillaume, Jones, Keate, Kell, Monk, Pearce, Sotheby, Warner, Westall.

Netley. Royal Victoria Hospital. See Macaulay.

New Forest. Abstract of Claims preferred at a Justice Seat for the New Forest, Hants . . . A.D. 1670. With a return made by Commissioners acting under the Acts of the 39 and 40 and 41, George III., cap. 108, as to encroachments in the said Forest. 8vo. 1853.

New Forest. An Abstract of all the claims on the New Forest . . . . entered at the Chief Justice in Eyre's Court . . . . held at Lyndhurst, June 27th, 22nd Year of Charles II. 8vo. 1776.

New Forest. 2. P. The Hampshire Wonder, or the Groaning Tree. 8vo. 1742.

New Forest, Two Historical Accounts of the making of, by King William the Conqueror, and Richmond New Park in Surrey by King Charles I. 8vo. 1751.

New Forest, Report of the Commissioners appointed to enquire into the state and conditions of the Woods, Forests and Land Revenues of the Crown on the. Vols. 1-5. Folio. 1789.

New Forest, Plan of the, from surveys by T. Richardson, W. King, and W. Driver. Large coloured Maps by W. Faden. Folio. 1789

New Forest, Proceedings in a bill entitled an act for the better Preservation of Timber in the. 8vo. 1800.

New Forest. Berkeley (the Honble. Grantley F.) Letter to the Viscount Palmerston [on hunting in the New Forest]. 8vo. 1855.

New Forest. Register of Decisions on Claims to Forest Rights. 8vo. 1858.

New Forest, Returns on Enclosures in the, &c., with Map. Folio. 1867.

New Forest, Report of the Honble. J. K. Howard on the. Folio. 1871.

New Forest, Report of the Select Committee on the. Folio. 1875.

New Forest, Account of the Burley Meeting House in the, six miles from Ringwood. 12mo. 1823.

New Forest. Statement of the case of the office of the Judge Promoted by Farnall *v.* Rev. J. K. Craig in the Arches Court at Canterbury, with remarks by the Rev. E. Craig. 8vo. 1848.
Refers to affairs at Burley.

New Forest. See Akermann, Bartlett, Berkeley, Blackmore, Braddon, Brand, Brown, Clarke, Companion in a Tour Round Southampton, Comyn, Cooper, De Crespigny, Edgar, Forests, Freeling, Freeman, Gilpin, Hall, Heath, Jenkinson, Jewitt, Johns, Klitz, Le Brocq, Lewis, Manwood, Marryat, Michelmersh, Mudie, Nichols, Ordericus Vitalis, Phillips, Pococke, Roberts, Rose, Scott, Smith, Warner, Wise, Wood.

Nichols (J. G.) Examples of Inlaid Gothic Tiles. 24 facsimiles size of the Originals in Winchester Cathedral. 4to. N.D.

Nichols (T.) Observations on the Propagation and Management of Oak Trees in general, more particularly applying to the New Forest. 8vo. (1791).

Nicholls (F.) Burning Shame, or Punishment for Bad Lawyers, a Custom peculiar to Newport, Isle of Wight, a Poem. 8vo. 1812.

Noble (T. C.) See Spanish Armada.

Nomina Villarum of the County of Southampton. 8vo. 1791.

Norris (William), Letter to the Inhabitants of the Parish of Warblington on the new Poor Law 8vo. 1834.

Norris (Rev. W.) An Address . . . . to the Emsworth Natural History Society, on July 19th, 1881. 12mo, sewed, 16 pp. 1881. History of Warblington Church and Castle.

    Mr. Norris was Curate of Warblington from 1818 till 1827, and Rector from 1827 till 1878.

Notes and Queries. See Hampshire.

Nugent (Lord). Ye Dole of Tichborne. 1871.

Nunnaminster, The Book of, an ancient manuscript of the 8th or 9th Century, formerly belonging to St. Mary's Abbey, or Nunnaminster, Winchester, edited by Walter de Gray Birch, F.S.A., of the British Museum. Published by the Hampshire Record Society. 8vo. 1889.

Nursling. See Wake.

Nutt (T.) The Writings of a Person in Obscurity, and a Native of the Isle of Wight. 12mo. 1808.

Odiham. See Burgess, Clark, Creighton, Harford, Holme, Hughes, Webb, Wodehouse.

Osborn (H.) Convenient and Simple Mode of Detecting the Presence of Lead in Water by means of a single test, also a Paper on the Injurious Action of Water on Lead, in the suburbs of Southampton. 12mo. 1848.

Otterbourne. Remarks on the Speeches of William Paul Clerk and John Hall, of Otterbourne, executed for Rebellion at Tyburn, July 13th, 1716. 8vo. 1716.

Otterbourne. See Yonge.

Overton (Rev. J. H.) and Wordsworth (Elizabeth) Christopher Wordsworth, Bishop of Lincoln (1867-1885). Winchester College. Chap. 1. 8vo.

Owen (—.) New Book of Fairs and Roads. 8vo. 1827. Hampshire Fairs. pp. 28-31.

Page (W. B.) Prodromus, or a General Nomenclature of all the Plants, indigenous and exotic, cultivated by him in the Southampton Botanic Gardens. 8vo. 1817.

Palin (William) New Southampton Guide. 12mo. N.D. [About 1830].

Palmerston. See Ashley, Trollope.

Parker (H. W.) Two Letters to the Right Hon. Sir George Gray, Bart., concerning the Andover Union. 8vo. 1847.

Parker (J. H.) See Turner.

Parliamentary Elections. A Letter of Congratulation to the Friends of J. C. Jervoise, Esq. Folio. 1779.

Parliamentary Elections. Collection of all the hand-bills and squibs published during the late Election for the County of Hants, between Sir Rd. Worsley, Bart., and J. Clarke Jervoise, Esq., with Poll of each Division. 8vo. 1780.

Parliamentary Elections. Poll Book for Hampshire. 4to. 1790.

Parliamentary Elections. Poll Book for the County Candidates : Chute, Mildmay, Herbert and Thistlethwayte. 8vo. 1807.

Parliamentary Elections. Report on the Proposed Division of the County of Hants, for the Purposes of the Reform Act, with statistical information. Folio. N.D.

Parliamentary Elections. Polls at the election of Knights of the Shire. 1705, 4to, 1705. 1710, 8vo, 1714. 1712. 1713, 4to, 1714. 1779, 8vo, 1780.

Pauperism. Statements of Kirriemuir, Forfarshire, and Eling, Hants. 8vo. 1825.

Pearce (William) Hartfordbridge, or the Skirts of a Camp, an Operatic Farce (Frontispiece). 12mo. N.D.

Pearce (William) Netley Abbey, an operatic farce (Frontispiece). 12mo. N.D.

Pearsall (J. S.) Historical Memorials of a Christian Fellowship [At Andover]. 12mo. N.D.

Pearsall (J. S.) Outlines of Congregationalism, with an historical sketch of its rise and progress in the Town of Andover. (Plate). 8vo. 1844.

Pennant (T.) Journey from London to the Isle of Wight. 2 vols. 4to. 1801.

Petersfield, History of Churcher's College at, with a life of Richard Churcher, the Founder, and a report of the case between the Trustees and the Inhabitants of Petersfield. 8vo, Boards. 1823.

Petersfield, Report of the Case of the Borough of. Royal 8vo. 1831.

Petersfield. See Atcheson, Merewether, Rober, "Trial," Williams.

Phillimore (Joseph) Report of Appeal to the Lord Bishop of Winchester, Visitor of the two Mary Winton Colleges, promoted by William Augustus Hare, against the Elections to the vacant Scholarships at Winchester and New College in 1839, by Joseph Phillimore. 8vo. 1839.

Phillips (C. J.) The New Forest Hand-book, Historical and Descriptive (with a map and itinerary). 8vo. 1875. Second edition, 8vo, 1876.

Pickersgill-Cunliffe (Mary) Dead and Buried, a Romance of Christchurch. 8vo. 1890.

Pinnock (William) The History and Topography of Hampshire (Vol. II. of Pinnock's County Histories). 12mo. N.D.

Pitts (J. L.) The Patois Poems of the Channel Islands. 8vo. 1883.

Plees (W.) Account of the Island of Jersey. 8vo. 1824.

Pond (Henry) Fifty Years' Temperance Work and Temperance Workers in Southampton, 1835-1885. Sewed, 12mo, 16 pp. 1885.

Poor Law. Newnham (H.) Letter to Mr. W. J. Barton, Overseer of the Poor of the Parish of Silchester. (For private circulation). 8vo. 1845.

Poor Law. Andover Union. Parker (H. W.) Letters to Sir James Graham on the Recent Proceedings. London, 1845. Two Letters to Sir George Grey, Bart., and William Day, Esq. London, 1847. Letter to Lord Courtenay, Chairman of the Andover Committee. 8vo. 1847.

Popham (Sir Gilbert de) A Legend of Hampshire in the Time of King John. Sewed, small 4to. N.D. 16 pp.

Portchester Castle, its Origin, History and Antiquities, with Anecdotes of its Occupation during the French Wars (plate). 12mo. 1849.

Portchester Castle, its Origin, History and Antiquities. 12mo. 1845.

Portchester Church, Copy of an Old Account in. 8vo. N.D.

Portchester and Wykor, Customs of the Manors of. 8vo. N.D.

Portchester. See Besant, Carew, Clark, Garneray, Hartshorne, Huxford, Jack Ashore, Teonge, Wright.

Portsea. Logic by Question and Answer, for the use of Portsea Academy. 12mo. 1774.

Portsmouth. A Narrative of the Disputation between some Ministers of the Presbyterian, and others of the Baptist Persuasion, concerning the Subjects and Manner of Baptism. Post 8vo. 1699.

Portsmouth. An Impartial Account of the Portsmouth Disputation, &c. 12mo. 1699.
Curious Details as to Religious Dissensions in Portsmouth.

Portsmouth, An historical description of an ancient painting at, Cowdry, &c. (representing the encampment of the English forces near). 4to. 1778.

Portsmouth, The Encampment of the English Forces near, from a coeval painting at Cowdray in Sussex. Engraved by J. Basire. Folio. 1778.

Portsmouth, A short sketch of the conduct of administration to the Borough of. 4to. 1780.
Relates to a contested election for Mayor of Portsmouth.

Portsmouth, Private case in the House of Lords between James Middleton and Richard Willes and Catherine Wilson, with pedigree of the Wilsons of Portsmouth. 1785.
Privately Printed.

Portsmouth, Charter of King Charles I. to the Corporation of 8vo. N.D.

Portsmouth, History of, with an account of the towns of Portsea, Gosport and Isle of Wight. 12mo. 1809.

Portsmouth. John the Painter's Ghost how he appeared on the night of his execution to Lord Temple (and circumstances relating to it), in verse. 4to. 1777.

Portsmouth. Fire in Dock Yard. " London Chronicle, " 4to. July, 1770.

Portsmouth, Life of Jonathan Britain, containing amongst other things a history of the conflagration at, 8vo. 1772.

Portsmouth, Copy of a letter from Lord Sydney to the Duke of Richmond on the Plans for better securing His Majesty's Dockyard at, etc. Folio. 1786.

Portsmouth, St. Thomas Church at, Churchwardens' accounts of 1564, by W. H. Saunders, Esq. (British Archæological Society's Transactions, 1888). 8vo.

Portsmouth. The Accounts and Disbursements of Eli Stanniford and Anthony Colebrooke, Churchwardens of Portsmouth for 1709-10. Published for the edification of the Churchwardens of Hampshire. 8vo. 1708.

Portsmouth, Answer to E. Stanyford and A. Colebrooke, Churchwardens of the parish of, to the printed case of William Ward, Vicar of the same. 4to. 1710.

Portsmouth, The case of the Churchwardens of, in relation to their several Law-suits and disputes with their Vicar. 4to. 1711.

Portsmouth. " Mary Rose," Narrative of the Loss of, at Spithead, July 20th, 1545, from the original MSS. bound in wood of the wreck. 8vo. 1844.
For account of the loss of the " Mary Rose " see Kingsley's "Westward Ho. "

Portsmouth. " Royal George " Narrative of the Loss of, at Spithead, August 1782, (bound in oak from the timbers of the ship), including attempts and operations to raise her 18mo. 1841.

Portsmouth. Short Essay on the Modes of Defence best adapted to the situation and circumstances of this Island. 8vo. 1785.
Fortification of Portsmouth and Plymouth.

Portsmouth. Answer to the Short Essay. 8vo. 1785. Fortifications of Portsmouth and Plymouth.

Portsmouth, Visitors' Guide to, also to Southampton, Netley Abbey, &c., &c. 12mo. 1832.

Portsmouth. The New Portsmouth, Southsea, Anglesey, and Hayling Island Guide. 1836. 2nd edition, 16mo, 1837. 3rd edition (plates and maps), 12mo, 1841. 4th edition, 12mo, 1846. 6th edition, 12mo, 1850. 10th edition, 12mo, 1859. Another edition, 8vo, 1863.

Portsmouth, The New Guide to, and Handbook to the Isle of Wight. 8vo. 1863.

Portsmouth. The People's Guide to Portsmouth and its Neighbourhood. Sewed, 8vo, 30 pp. 1877.

Portsmouth, A Descriptive Account of. 8vo. N. D.

Portsmouth and its Neighbourhood, Views and Letterpress Account. Small oblong. N. D.

Portsmouth, Portsea, and Gosport Literary and Scientific Register ; a Monthly Miscellany. 8vo. 1823.

Portsmouth and Portsea Literary and Philosophical Society. Report of the Proceedings, 1833-4, &c. Sewed, 8vo, 1834. pp. 48-57, Roman Villa at Bramdean.

Portsmouth, Account of the Imperial and Royal Visit to, in 1814. N. D.

Portsmouth, The Royal Visit to, 28th February, 1842. 12mo. 1842.

Portsmouth. Proceedings at the Ceremony of Presenting a New Stand of Colours to the Portsmouth Division of the Royal Marines, on October 27th, 1827. 8vo. 1827.

Portsmouth. Miss Robinson, "The Soldiers' Friend." 8vo. 1877.

Portsmouth, Corporation of, Descriptive and Historical Account of the Silver Plate belonging to. 8vo. 1885.

Portsmouth, Report of the Church Congress at. 8vo. 1885.

Portsmouth, Earl of, Account of the Wallop Family. 8vo. N.D.

Portsmouth, John Charles Wallop, Earl of. Report of Proceedings of a Commission to enquire into his state of mind. 8vo. [1823].

Portsmouth Common, Laws and Regulations of the Beneficial Society of the, 12mo. 1788.

Portsmouth Ghost. A Poetical chap book. 12mo. N.D.

Portsmouth Guide. 12mo. 1775. Curious Folding View.

Portsmouth Guide. Corrected to 1828. Post 8vo. (Front.) 1828.

Portsmouth Harbour, Proposed Improvements of. 8vo. 1823. (Plan). Privately Printed.

Portsmouth, Portsea, and Gosport. The Ancient and Modern History of, and their Environs. 12mo. (1800).

Portsmouth Tracts, No. 1. Richard and Alice, a Tale, founded on facts, which occurred in Portsmouth in the Reign of Queen Elizabeth. Sewed, 16mo. 1840.

Portsmouth. See Ackland-Troyte, Adams, Allen, Andrews, Annals of England, Austen, Ayloffe, Bartlett, Besant, Bourne, Butcher, Byng, Carr, Carter, Chamier, Church Congress, Civil War, Cobbe, Connolly, Cope, Cowper, Cundy, Fairholt, Fergusson, Forster, Galloway, Glascock, Glenie, Gosport, Hall, Hanway, Haselden, Haselrigge, Heylyn, Heywood, Hollingsworth, Huntingdon (Henry of), Jack Ashore, Land we live in, Lewis, Marryat, Maxwell, Merewether, Moses, Murrell, Napier, Neale, Nelson, Plumpton, Pounds, Rennie, Rice, Rimmer, Rober, Roscoe, Saunders, Scott, Shipwrecks, Slight, Southampton Guide, Stirling, Talbot, Teonge, Tracey, Trial, Vanderstegen, Vicars, Waller, Wayland, Wilkins, Wright.

Portswood. See Merewether.

Pounds (Mr. John) of Portsmouth, Memoir of. 12mo. 1839.

Pratt (H.) Annual Hampshire Repository. 2 vols. 8vo. 1799-1801.

Pratt (J. S.) Supplementary Gleanings, Hampshire Station. 8vo. 1805.
Refers to Southampton and the New Forest.

Price (John E.) and Price (F. G. Hilton) Guide to the Roman Villa recently discovered at Morton, between Sandown and Brading, Isle of Wight. Fifth edition. 12mo. 1881.

Priors' Dean. See Hervey.

Project (Peregrine) and Timothy Type. Tour through some of the Southern counties of England. 12mo. 1804.

Prosser (G. F.) Antiquities of Hampshire, illustrated in the Ruins of Ancient Buildings. Royal 4to. 1842.

Prosser (G. F.) Thirty illustrations of Hampshire, Picturesque Views of the Seats of the Nobility and Gentry, with Descriptions. 4to. 1833.

Prouten (T.) Winchester Guide. Sewed, 8vo. N. D.

Pye (Henry James Poet Laureate).—Naucratia, or Naval Dominion : a Poem, containing lines on " Millbrook." Second edition. 1798.

For some of his poems see Pratt's " Harvest Home." He is believed to be the author of the satirical lines :—
" Southampton's wise sons had a river so large,
' 'Twould carry a ship, 'twould not carry a barge."

Radcliffe (C. W.) Memorials of Winchester College, etc. Folio. (1847 ?)

Raine (Robert) The Queen's Isle : Chapters on the Isle of Wight. 16mo. 1849. Second edition, 1861.

Ranger (W.) Report on the Drainage of Southampton. 8vo. 1850.

Raye (C.) Tour through the Isle of Wight (coloured plates). Oblong 4to 1825.

Rennie (John) Report and Estimate of the Grand Southern Canal, proposed to be made between Tunbridge and Portsmouth. 4to. 1810.

Richards (F. W., M.D.) William Rufus, his tomb in Winchester Cathedral : Account of the Opening and Removal (plates), paper covers. 8vo. 1868.

Richards (T.) Hoglandiæ Descriptio, or Description of Hampshire, a mock heroic poem. 8vo. 1719. A curious large etching of a Hog on the Title Page. The dedication signed " M.G.C." With an English translation. 8vo 1728.

Gough says (Brit. Topog.) that this is by Mr. Richards, of Jesus College, Oxford (Tho. Richards, M.A., 1714 ?,) and that it is in answer to [Holdsworth's] Muscipula. See Holdsworth.

Richmond (Rev. Legh) Landscape Beauties of the Isle of Wight. 8vo. (1843).

Richmond (Rev. Legh) Annals of the Poor. 8vo. N.D.
Many descriptions of Isle of Wight Persons and Places.

Richmond (Rev. Legh) Isle of Wight Scenery of, Richmond's Annals of the Poor, with descriptive letter-press. 16mo, (1860).

Ringwood. Notes on Ringwood History from the Ringwood Illustrated Almanack. 8vo. 1890.

Ringwood. See Hall, Merewether, Roberts.

Roach Smith (C.) Remarks on an unpublished inscription to the Emperor Tetricus found at Bitterne. 8vo. 1842.

Roads. Miniature Road Book for Hampshire, with a map, a population table, &c 32mo. 1842.

Rober (W.) Scapin Triumphant, or a Journey to Petersfield and Portsmouth. 4to. 1757.

Rogers (W. H.) Guide to the New Forest. 12mo. N.D.

Rogers (John) Sketch of the Life and Reminiscences of (written by himself), with etched portraits by Frank McFadden. Post 8vo. 1889.

Romsey. Account of the Barbarous and Bloody Murder by Esther Ives on the body of her husband, at Romsey. 4to 1686.

Romsey. Historical and Descriptive Companion to the Abbey Church of Romsey. (Plates) 12mo. 1827. 2nd ed. 12mo. 1827.

Romsey. Historical and Descriptive Account of the Abbey Church, Romsey, also of the Town, its Charities, etc. Post 8vo. 1848.

Romsey. See Ashley, Capgrave, Companion in a Tour round Southampton, Davidson, Freeman, Godwin, Latham, Little-holes, Spence, Trollope, Winter.

Rooke (O.) The Channel Islands. 8vo. 1856.

Rookely (near Stockbridge). See Poole.

Roscoe (Thomas) Summer Tour to the Isle of Wight, including Portsmouth, Southampton, Winchester, &c. (Illustrated) 8vo. 1843.

Rose (William Stewart) Rhymes. 12mo. 1837. "Gundimore" is a description of Mr. Rose's Italian villa near Mudiford.
William Stewart Rose, who lived at Gundimore, near Mudiford, was a poetical writer of his day. He wrote the poem of " The Red King," and refers to Lyndhurst—
> And still in merry Lyndhurst's hall
> Red William's stirrup decks the wall.

His poem on Gundimore is especially interesting to Hampshire—
> Here Walter Scott has woo'd the northern muse,
> Here he with me has joyed to walk or cruise ;
> And hence has pricked through Ytene's holt, where we
> Have called to mind how, under greenwood tree,
> Pierced by the partner of his woodland craft,
> King Rufus fell by Tyrell's random shaft ;
> Hence have we ranged by Celtic camps and barrows,
> Or climed the expectant bark to thread the narrows
> Of Hurst, bound eastward to the gloomy bower
> Where Charles was prisoned in yon island tower.

Rowlands Castle. See Kell.

Rownhams (near Romsey). See Wilson.

Rudall (John) Memoir of the Rev. James Crabb, late of Southampton. 8vo. 1854.

Rudborne (Thomas, Monk of Winchester) Historia Major de Fundatione and Successione Ecclesia Wintoniensis, 633-1277 A.D. Published in Vol. I. of Warton's Anglia Sacra. p. 177. 2 vols., folio. 1691.

Russell (P.) Hampshire and the Isle of Wight (from " England Displayed "), maps and plates. Folio. 1769.

Saltmakers. See Isle of Wight.

Satchell (T.) See Westwood.

Saunders (W. H.) Annals of Portsmouth, Historical, Biographical, Statistical, &c. 8vo. 1880.

Saunders (W. H.) History of the Parish Church of Portsmouth 8vo. 1886.

Saunders (W. H.) Churchwarden's Account of St. Thomas, Portsmouth, A.D. 1564. Brit. Archæological Society's Transactions. 8vo. 1888.

Saunders (W. H.) Descriptive and Historical Account of the Silver Plate belonging to the Corporation of Portsmouth 8vo. 1885.

Saunders (W. H.) Who Stole the Painter? a Portsmouth and Gosport Story of the Last Century, 1777-82. 12mo. N. D.
Describes the execution, &c., of " Jack the Painter."

Savage (William) Guide to the Ancient City of Winchester. 8vo. 1869.

Scott (G. C.) A Report of the Proceedings at a Meeting of the City Cross Restoration Building Committee, held at the Guildhall, Winchester, 20th December, 1865, with the Report of Mr. G. Scott. Sewed, 12mo. (1866)

Scott (M.) On the Defence of Spithead. 8vo. 1862.

Scott (Richard) A Topographical and Historical Account of Hayling Island, Hants. 4to. 1826.

Sea-marks. See Edwards.

Selborne. See Douce, White.

Settle (Elkanah) 1648-1724 ("At one time the rival of Dryden ") Thalia Triumphans, a Congratulatory Poem to the Honoured William Heathcote, Esq. (afterwards Sir William Heathcote, of Hursley, Bart.), on his happy marriage. Folio. 1720.

Sewell (Harriet) The Apple of Discord (a Winchester Play). 12mo. 1864.

Russell (Rev. A.) Memoirs of the Life and Works of . . . Lancelot Andrewes, D.D., Lord Bishop of Winchester. Large 8vo. 1863.

Sharp (Wm., of Newport, Isle of Wight) Sincerity, a Poem. 4to. 1763.

Sharp (W.) A Ramble from Newport to Cowes, in the Isle of Wight. 4to. 1782.

Sharwood (Albert), Penny Guide to Bournemouth. 18mo.

Sharwood (Albert), Penny Guide to Christchurch, Corfe Castle, Wimborne Minster, Swanage, and Poole. 18mo.

Shaw, Tourists' Picturesque Guide to the Isle of Wight. 8vo. 1873.

Sheldrake (W.) A Guide to Aldershot, Hants and its Neighbourhood. Post 8vo. 1859.

Sheridan (H. B.) St. Lawrence Well, a Fragmentary Legend of the Isle of Wight. 8vo 1845.

Sheridan (W. C. F. G.) Historical and Topographical Account of the Isle of Wight. (Illustrated). 12mo. 1832.

Shore (T. W.) Fragments of the Antiquity and History of Southampton. 8vo. 1874.

Shore (T. W.) Guide to Southampton and Neighbourhood. 12mo. 1882.

Shore (T. W.) The Proposed National School of Forestry considered as a Hampshire Commercial Question. A Paper read before the Southampton Chamber of Commerce, Dec. 3, 1888. Sewed, 8vo, pp. 13.

Shaw (T. W.) Distribution and Density of the Old British Population of Hampshire. Reprinted from Journ. Anthrop. Inst., May, 1889. (2 plates) Sewed 8vo, pp. 14.

Silchester, The History and Antiquities of, in Hants, the Vindonum of the Romans and the Caer Sejont of the Ancient Britons : with Biographical Notices of Persons connected with the place. 8vo. 1792. Other Editions. 8vo. 1821, 1823, 1837.

Silchester. See Clutterbuck, Freeman, Godwin and Plummer, Joyce, L'Estrange, Poor Law.

Slessor (Rev. J. H.) Notes on the Church of S. Swithun, Headbourne Worthy. 4to. 1888.

Slight (H.) A Metrical History of Portsmouth, with delineations Topographical, Historical, and Descriptive of the Port and Arsenal. 8vo. 1820.

Slight (H.) The Royal Port, Garrison, Dockyard, and Borough of Portsmouth. 8vo. 18—

Slight (H.) History of Portsmouth, Southsea, Gosport, &c. Post 8vo. 1836. Another edition. 8vo. 1844.

Slight (H.) The Prior's Picture, a narrative illustrative of the Broad Seal of the Ecclesiastical and Manorial Borough of Gosport and Alverstoke. N.D. 24mo. See Archælogical Society at Winchester. 1845,

Slight (H.) Thomas Thistlethwayte, his Ancestors, and others, each Lord of the Manor of the Priory of Southwick from 1539 to 1850. 24mo. N.D.

Slight (Henry and Julian) Chronicles of Portsmouth. 12mo. 1828.

Smirke (E.) Winchester in the Thirteenth Century. From No. 28, Archælogical Journal. 1846.

Smirke (E.) On the Hall of the Royal Palace and Round Table at Winchester. 8vo. 1846.

Smith (Horace) The New Forest, a Novel. 3 vols, 8vo. 1829.

Smith (Thomas) Johannis Gravii [Colmere, prope Alresford nati] vita. 4to. 1699.

Smith (Thomas, of Foxhill, Droxford, Master of Foxhounds) Sporting Incidents in the Life of. 8vo. 1867.

Sopley. Account of the Restoration of St. Michael's Church, Sopley (1868-70). 12mo, 1871.

Sotheby (W.) Poems : The Priory in the Isle of Wight, Farewell to Bevis Mount and Netley Abbey. 4to. 1790.

Southampton. History of the Murders committed on the Bodies of Mr. W. Galley, of Southampton, and Mr. D. Chater, of Fordingbridge. 8vo. 1749. Relates Particulars of Smuggling. See Fordingbridge.

Southampton and the Polygon, Plan of. 4to. 1771.

Southampton. The Hampshire Pocket Companion . . . . for 1788. 8vo. (1787)

Southampton Guide (The). 12mo. Cunningham, 1790.

Southampton, Directory for the Town of. 12mo. 1803. Continued periodically.

Southampton. Acts of Parliament. 1768-1825.

Southampton. Act for Taking Down and Rebuilding the Parish Church of All Saints, Folio. 1791.

Southampton. The Civil Wars of Southampton, containing Copies of all the Handbills, &c., relative to a controversy respecting a bill to be brought into Parliament for the better regulation of the Poor, &c. ; also New Wars respecting a navigable cut to Salisbury, extension of the quay, dry docks, &c. 12mo. 1794.
In this occurs: "Southampton's wise sons &c."

Southampton. Strictures and Observations on the Intended Canal from Southampton to Salisbury. 8vo. 1793.

Southampton. Strictures upon Strictures respecting the Intended Canal from the Town of Southampton to the City of Salisbury. 8vo. 1793.

Southampton. Cemetery Act. Folio. 1848.

Southampton. The Southampton Cemetery, fees, rules, &c. Sewed, 8vo. 1865.

Southampton. Local Reports, Bye-laws, etc. 2 vols. Folio· N.D.

Southampton. Poll Books for 1774, 1779, 1790, 1794, 1802, 1806, 1812, 1818, 1820, 1831, 1832, 1835, 1841, 1842, 1865.

Southampton. *Argus (The)* A Review of Southampton News and Politics. 8vo. 1831.

Southampton. Town Election Petitions, Minutes of Pro ceedings and Evidence. 2 vols. Folio. 1842.

Southampton. Extracts from Plays adapted to Southampton Characters. 4to. About 1790.

Southampton. Companion in a Tour round Southampton, containing particulars relative to the New Forest, Lymington, Christchurch, Romsey Waltham, Titchfield, etc. Post 8vo. 1799. Second edition, 1801.

Southampton. List of the Voters who polled at the Election of two Members of Parliament for Southampton, on July, 12th, 1865. 8vo. 1865.

Southampton. Account of the Ancient and Present State of Southampton, and the most remarkable relics of Antiquity in the neighbourhood. 12mo. 1768, 1774, 1781, etc.
The third edition contains a Satirical Poem on the Southampton Rooms.

Southampton. Visitants' Guide to Southampton,Netley Abbey, Portsmouth, etc. 8vo. 1832, etc.

Southampton Past and Present. being a Condensed History of the Town, etc. 12mo. 1839.

Southampton. Complete Narrative of the Calamitous Fire, which took place at Southampton, Nov. 7, 1837 . . . . Report of the Inquest held upon the Deceased, &c. 12mo. 1837.

Southampton. A Summer Excursion to Southampton and its Neighbourhood. 16mo. (1840).

Southampton. Royal Agricultural Society of England, Southampton Meeting, Handbook for the week with a diary of appointments, &c. 12mo. 1844.

Southampton. Bye Laws for regulating Hackney Coaches, &c. 12mo. 1845.

Southampton. Waterworks, Duplicate MSS. proceedings of Revision Committee. Folio. 1848.

Southampton. Means of preserving life and of promoting European trade by the more general use of Southampton, &c. 8vo. 1850.

Southampton to Calcutta. The Route of the Overland Mail to India (with Illustrations). 8vo. 1850.

Southampton. Artesian Well, Report of Town Committee. 12mo. 1852.

Southampton. Report of Church Congress held at, in October, 1870. 8vo. (1871).

Southampton. Papers relating to the Meeting of the Archæological Institute at. 1872.

Southampton. Last Charter of the County of the Town of Southampton, dated June 27th, 1641. 12mo. 1826.

Southampton. List of Charters, Letters Patent, and other Muniments of the Corporation of Southampton, by John Cordy Jeafferson. 8vo. 1886.

Southampton. Manuscripts of the Corporations of Southampton and King's Lynn. Eleventh Report Appendix, Part iii. Hist. MSS. Commission. Lond. 8vo. 1887.

Southampton. Vestiges of Old Southampton. 12 etchings by Frank McFadden, with letterpress descriptions by T. W. Shore, F.G.S., F.C.S. Folio. 1891.

Southampton. British Association Report. 1882

Southampton. See Acts of Parliament, Adkins, Ainsworth, Andrews, Annals of England, Ashley, Bartlett, "Batt upon Batt" (vide Kempster and Speed) Bennett, Brannon, Brit. Assoc., Bromley, Brooke, Bullar, Bunyan, Butler, Byles, Capgrave, Carlyle, Carter, Crabb, Civil War, Church Congress, Clark, Cobbe, Collier, Connolly, Cummerbund, Davies, Drew, Englefield, English History, Eyton, Fordingbridge, Freeling, Gibbons, Gomme, Goodman, Goodyeare, Granville, Greenfield, Guise, Hart, Henty, Hervot, Hewett, Heylyn, Heywood, Hoveden, Jacob, Jeaffreson, Johnson, Jones, Kell, Knight, Land we live in, Leon, Letchiot, Linden, Lyall, McFadden, Marryat, Milner, Minot, Monasteries, Mogg, Monk, Newport, Noailles, O'Keeffe, Osborn, Page, Palin, Plumpton, Pococke, Pond, Poole, Pye, Queen, Ramble, Ranger, Rivers, Rogers, Roscoe, Rudall, Shakespeare, Shooting, Shore, Sotheby, Speed, Tanner, Thompson, Thorn, Virgil, Warburton, Warner, Watts, Weiss, Wilson, Wing, Wright, Wylde.

Sir Beves of Hamtoun ; a Metrical Romance, edited by W. H· D. D. Turnbull, from the Auchinleck MS. for the Maitland Club. 4to. 1838.

Sir Bevis of Hamptoun, the Adventures of, rendered with his torical preface, etc., by E. H. Jones. 12mo. 1870. See Macaulay's " Biographies," and Smile's " Character."

This work was a very favourite book of Bunyan's, and was suggestive to him of many parts of his " Pilgrims' Progress."

Sir Bevis of Hampton, the son of Guy, Erle of Southampton, his Life and Adventures. Small 4to. Pynson (N.D.) and frequently reprinted. See Shakespeare's " Henry VI," Act ii, Scene 3.

Of Bevois, who gave his name to the Mount, it may be mentioned that his history is a legend of the age of the Troubadours, and about the date of the Crusades. The earliest ballads now extant relating to Bevois and his deeds are in French. A copy of this romance in French was part of the literary possessions of the Abbey of Leicester early in the 16th century. Henry V., a king much connected with Southampton, had tapestries made representing the achievements of Sir Bevois. In the time of Henry VIII., these tapestries still existed, as " the arras of Sir Bevois' " was a tapestry at Richmond at that time. Chaucer alludes to Bevois, so the romance must be older than the 14th century. Scott brings him up in the introduction to Marmion Canto I. last few lines. The romance has been translated under various European languages. In the Red Book of Hergest is an " Ystore Boun o Hamtun," and in the Sports of Vedice of the Riva dei Schiavoni, some survival of the legend of Sir Bevis remain in the shows corresponding to our Punch and Judy shows at the present day.

Southern Coast of England, a Handbook of Travel Round the. 8vo. 1849. Hampshire, pp. 223-296.

South Tedworth. See Willmott.

Southwick Park. Copy of an Extraordinary Will of Richard Norton, Esq., of Southwick Park. 8vo. 1727.

Southwick. See Madden, Slight.

Speed (John, M.D., of Southampton) Commentary on Sea Water, translated from the Latin. 12mo. 1786.

Speed (Dr.) Batt upon Batt ; a Poem upon the Parts, Patience and Pains of Bartholomew Kempster, Clerk, Poet, Cutler of the Holy Rood Parish in Southamptom (to which is annexed the Vision, wherein is described Batt's person and ingenuity), with an Account of the Ancient and Present State and Glory of Southampton, by a Person of Quality (Dr. Speed). [Dedicated to the Gentry of Hampshire for their Diversion, but more especially to the Inhabitants of Southampton]. 4to. 1680, 1690, 1694. 8vo. 1706, 1708, 1711 and 1764. First edition, 6 leaves.

Gough says this work has been ascribed to Mr. John Rooke, of Southampton, who was said to have broken Batt's head. Captain Johnston, in his life of Mrs. Elizabeth Nash, says Batt printed it under the title of " Jack upon Jack." The Doctor's enemies asserted that he bought up Batt's impression, and its author's silence, with a suit of black. Batt's wit turned chiefly in playing upon the Doctor's verses. The printer's preface to the first edition is signed " T. A. Gough " (in a MS. note), and says there was an earlier edition in *folio* of eight pages. John Speed, M.O., of Southampton, the reputed author, was grandson of the Historian.

Spence (C.) Essay, descriptive of the Abbey Church of Romsey, in Hampshire. 8vo. 1841, etc.

Spickernell (W.) The Roman Villa, Carisbrooke, Isle of Wight. 12mo. 1859.

Spindler (W.) A Few Remarks about Ventnor, Bournemouth, etc. 8vo. 1877.

Sporting Reminiscences of Hampshire from 1745-1862, by Æsop. Post 8vo. 1864. See " Æsop."

Sporting. See Fitt, Smith (T.) also Willmott.

Stanbridge. See Cope.

Staunton (Sir George) Speeches to the Electors of South Hampshire. 8vo. 1835.

Staunton (Sir George T., Bart.) Memoirs of the Chief Incidents in the Public Life of, Leigh Park Estate, pp. 169-173. 8vo. 1856.

St. Barbe (C.) Records of the Corporation of the Borough of New Lymington, in the County of Southampton. 4to. Privately Printed. 1848.

St. Cross, A short account of the Hospital of, 8pp. 4to. N.D.

St. Cross, History of, near Winchester. 8vo. 1822.

St. Cross, near Winchester. See Freeman, Humbert, Milner, Moody, Robinson, Winchester Guides.

St. Deny's Priory. Encaustic Tiles, Patterns of, found at the ruins of the Priory dedicated to St. Dyonisius, near Southampton, drawn and engraved from the original tiles in the collection of T. A. Skelton. 38 plates coloured like the originals. 1857.

According to the preface only four copies were privately printed and one of them was priced 30/- by a bookseller in 1871.

Steele (Anne), "Theodosia" of Broughton, 1716-1778. Poems on Subjects Chiefly Devotional (with memoir by Caleb Evans). 3 vols. 8vo. 1780.

A poem on Danbury Hill, near Stockbridge, was written by Anne Steele'e sister, Mrs. Dunscombe, The tomb of the Steele family is in Broughton Churchyard, to the south of the church. The epitaph on her tomb is—

Silent the lyre and dumb the tuneful tongue
That sung on earth her great Redeemer's praise ;
But now in heaven she joins the angelic song,
In more harmonious, more exalted lays.

Steele (Anne) ["Theodosia" of Broughton] Hymns, Psalms and Poems by (with Memoir by John Sheppard). 8vo. 1863.

Stevens (J.) Brief Historical Notices of the Parishes of Hurstbourne Priors, and St. Mary Bourne, Hampshire. 8vo. 1861.

Stevens (J.) St. Mary Bourne, Past and Present, containing an Account of the Hamlets, Geology, and Antiquities of the Parish. 8vo. 1863.

Stevens (J.) Descriptive List of Flint Implements found at St. Mary Bourne (with illustratio̤s of the principal types). 8vo. 1867.

Stevens (J.) Parochial History of St. Mary Bourne and Hurst bourne Priors. Royal 8vo. 1888.

St. Mary Bourne. See Stevens, Wilkinson.

Stockbridge. The Importance of the "Guardian" in a second letter to the Bailiff of Stockbridge, by a friend of Mr. St—le. 8vo. 1713.

Stockbridge. See Rice.

Stockman (J., of Portsea) Sketches of Portchester Castle, with letterpress descriptions. 4to. N.D.

Stratton, near Winchester. See Cobbett, Russell.

Sturch (John) A view of the Isle of Wight, in four letters to a friend. 3rd Edition, 12mo, Newport, 1787. 5th Edition, corrected and enlarged, 12mo, 1794. 7th Edition, corrected and enlarged, 12mo, 1803.
This is the earliest History of the Island. The first edition was printed in London in 1778. The second in 1780. The Author bought a press, and printed the third edition, as above, at Newport, and the fourth in 1791.

Sturch (Johann) Nachricht von der Insel Wight. 8vo. 1781.

Sturges (John, LL.D.) Reflections on the Principles and Institutions of Popery, occasioned by the Rev. John Milner's History of Winchester. 4to. 1799.

Sullivan (John) L'Hermitage de Saint Helier, La Chapelle de Saint Magloirè, La Foret de Scissy et l'Introduction du Christianisme à Jersey. 2nd edition. Sewed, 8vo. 1866.

Sullivan (John) Le Guide du Touriste à Jersey. 1867.

Sullivan (John) Un Mot sur l'Ile de Jersey. 1867. Sewed. pp. 8.

Sullivan (John) Elégee sur la Mort de Lord Palmerston, also Biography, and English Translation by Martin Tupper, D.C.L., etc. 1867.

Sullivan (John) Histoire Illustré de l'Ile de Jersey, et des îles adjacentes (Map of Jersey and other illustrations). Large 4to. 1868

Sumner (George Henry) Life of Charles Richard Sumner, Bishop of Winchester. 8vo. 1874.

Sumner (Heywood) The Itchen Valley from Tichborne to Southampton (twenty-two etchings by Heywood Sumner, with descriptive letterpress). Folio. 1881.

Sumner (Dr. Charles Richard, Bishop of Winchester) Conspectus of the Diocese of Winchester. Royal 8vo. 1854. (Not published).

Sumner (Dr. Charles Richard, Bishop of Winchester) Charges delivered to the Clergy of the Diocese of Winchester in 1833, 1837, 1841, 1845, 1850. 1850.
Much information respecting Hampshire.

Sydmonton.—Correspondence with the Bishop of Winchester, and Protest of the Incumbent against the Consecration of a Church at Sydmonton, Hants. 8vo. 1865.

Syvret (G. S.) Chroniques des Iles de Jersey, Guernsey, Auregny, and Sark. 8vo. 1832.

Tadley, Some account of the village of, and of the Independent Church. 8vo. 1862.

Tadley. See Browne.

Talbot (William) Narrative of the Forgeries, &c., of Jonathan Brittain [who pretended to give information as to the fire in Portsmouth Dock-yard, 1770]. 8vo. Wants title.

Tanner. Winchester Quarterly Record of Public Events. 8vo.

Taylor (John, the Water Poet). Travels from London to the Isle of Wight, with his return and occasion of his journey. 4to. 1648.
The occasion was to see Charles I. This rare tract was privately printed, but has been reprinted for sale.

Tennyson Land, In, Particulars of Lord Tennyson's Residence in the Isle of Wight. 8vo. 1889.

Thorn (Henry G.) Charles Dibdin, one of Southampton's Sons, what he did for the Nation, and what the Nation has done for him. (See Dibdin). 12mo. 1888.

Thorn (H. G.) John O'Keeffe; a Few Particulars relating to One of The Illustrious Dead in Southampton. Reprinted (with additions), from the *Hampshire Independent*, of January 26th, 1889. 12mo. 12pp. sewed.
Resided in Southampton, 1828-1833.

Thornton (Dr.) Sketch of the Life and Writings of Mr. William Curtis [a native of Alton].

Thoyts (F. W.) History of Esse or Ashe, Hampshire. 8vo. 1888·

Tichborne Romance, The. By a Barrister at Law. 8vo. 1872.

Tichborne. See Dole (Baigent, Nugent) also "Trial."

Titchfield. See Ashburnham, Companion in a Tour round Southampton. Greenfield Missing.

Tetherley (East) and Lockerley, Account of the Foundation of the Public School at. 8vo. 1839. Not printed for sale.

Todd (John Henry). Memento of the Charitable Societies of Natives and Aliens of Winchester. 8vo. 1869.

Tomkins (C.) Tour to the Isle of Wight (Illustrated with 80 views) 2 vols. Royal 8vo. 1796.
Contains the following articles relating to Hampshire:—
History of the Parish of Dummer.
History of Kempshot.
History of Ewhurst.
History and Description of the Vyne.
History of Mottisfont.
History of Rotherwick.
History of Stratfield-Say.
History of Basingstoke.
Account of Malsanger.
Historical List of Hampshire Families.
Additions to Hampshire in Gough's Camden.
Notes from Egham in Stratfield-Say.
History of Winchester College (with plate).
Account of Ellingham.
Account of the Family of Brocas, of Beaurepaire.
Account of Winslade.
History of Ash and Deane.

Topographical Description of Hampshire, with Description of the Isle of Wight and Channel Islands. 4to. 169-.

Topographical Miscellanies, containing Ancient Histories and Modern Descriptions of that portion relating to Hampshire. 4to. 1792.

Townsend (Fredk.) Flora of Hampshire. 8vo. 1883.

Townshend (C.) Winchester and a few other Compositions in prose and verse. 4to. 1835.

Tracey (Wm.) A Candid and Accurate Narrative of the operations used in endeavouring to raise H.M.S. " Royal George " at Spithead. 8vo. 1812.

Trevelyan (Francis A.) Quarr Abbey, or, the Mistaken Calling. A Poem. 4to. 1862.

Trial of James Hill, alias James Hind, alias James Aitzen (Aitken) for setting fire to the Dockyard at Portsmouth. Folio. London. 1777.

Trial of David Tyrie for High Treason, at the Assizes at Winchester, August 10th, 1782. 8vo. sewed. pp. 29.

Trial, with the whole of the evidence between Rt. Hon. Sir R. Worsley, Bart., and G. M. Bissell, Esq., for criminal conversation with the Plaintiff's wife. 4to. 1782.

Trial. Case of Appellants and Respondents before the House of Lords, between James Middleton and others, and Richard Welles and others, relating to property in Hampshire. Folio. 1785.

Trial of C. J. Heaton and others for forcible entry of a tenement at Petersfield. 8vo. [1820.]

Trial of the Mutineers of H.M.S. "Temeraire" in Portsmouth Harbour.

Trial, Tichborne. Tichborne *v.* Lushington before Lord Chief Justice Bovill, and a Special Jury, from June 8th, 1871 to March 6th, 1872, (with Photographs of Letters and Documents.) 11 vols. 8vo. 1871-2.

Trial, Tichborne. Who's Your Fat Friend. A Few notes of Our Trial, contributed by Master Brummell, Middle Class School Boy, Imprinted in the Holidays by desire of the School, and now modestly offered to the Public Gaze. Sewed, pp. 24. 8vo. 1871.

Trial, Tichborne. Trial of Thomas Castro, otherwise Arthur Orton, for Perjury. Extracted from "The Times," and bound in 3 vols. 4to. 1873-4.

Trial, Tichborne. The evidence of hand-writing. Facsimiles. 8vo. 1874.

Trial, Tichborne. Summing up by the Lord Chief Justice of England, Addresses of the Judges, the Verdict, and the Sentence. 8vo. 1874.

Trial, Tichborne. Edited by Dr. Kenealy. 8 vols. Folio. 1875-79.

Trial, Tichborne ; Many other Publications relating to. See also Tichborne.

Trollope (Anthony). Life of Lord Palmerston. 8vo. 1882. Born, and resided at Broadlands, near Romsey.

Tunnicliff (W.) Topographical Survey of Hants, Wilts, &c., with Maps. 8vo. 1791.

Tupper (F. B.) History of Guernsey and the Bailiwick, with occasional notices of Jersey. Large 8vo. 1854.

Turnbull (—) On the Parochial Condition of Newport, in the Isle of Wight. 8vo. 1844.

Type (Timothy) and Peregrine Project. Tour through some of the Southern Counties of England. 12mo. 1804.

Vancouver (C.) General View of the Agriculture of Hampshire and the Isle of Wight. (Maps, Plates, and Tables). 8vo. 1810.

Vanderstegen (W.) A Reply to a Pamphlet entitled " A Refutation of the charges brought by W. Vanderstegen, Esq., against Mr. T. Walton and others, &c.,
These three pamphlets relate to the salt works at Portsea, and to Mrs. Amelia Stewart, the proprietor of them.

Vanderstegen (W.) Observations on Frauds practised in collection of the Salt duties, &c. 8vo. 1794.

Vanderstegen (W.) Refutation of the charges brought by W. Vanderstegen Esq., against Mr. T. Walton and others, &c. 8vo. 1794.

Varney (W.F.) Historic and descriptive Handbook of Carisbrooke Castle in the Isle of Wight. 8vo. 1876.

Venables (E.) A Guide to the Isle of Wight, &c. 8vo. 1860.

Venables (E.) Guide to the Undercliff of the Isle of Wight, Shanklin, and Blackgang. 12mo. (1867).

Vernon (Rev. George) The Life of the Learned and Rev. Dr. Peter Heylyn, Chaplain to Charles I., and Charles II. 12mo. 1682.
Dr. Heylyn was Rector of Alresford.

Views in Hampshire. 4to. 1799.

Volunteers, The Hampshire. A Poem. 4to. 1794.

Vyne, (The) near Basingstoke. See Austen-Leigh, Chute, Walpole.

Wake (G. A.) Ancient Bronze Figure of a Stag, found at Nursling 4to. 1839.

Wake (Rev. H.) Statement of Facts and Trial between the Rev. H. Wake, and the Churchwardens and Overseers of Over Wallop. 8vo. 1819.

Walcott (M. E. C.) William of Wykeham and his colleges, containing a Roll of distinguished Wykehamists from 1434 to 1851. 8vo. 1852.

Walcott (M. E. C.) A Handbook for Winchester Cathedral. 8vo. 1854.

Walcott (M. E. C.) Guide to the coasts of Hants and Dorset. 8vo. 1859.

Walcott (M. E. C.) Memorials of Winchester. 8vo. 1866.

Walcott (M. E. C.) Memorials of Christchurch, Twynham. 8vo. 1868.

Walcott (M. E. C.) The Priory Church of Christchurch, the Norman Keep of Christchurch-Twyneham. 8vo. 1862.

Walhampton. See Burrard.

Wallace (N. W.) Chronicle and List of Officers of the 60th Reg. (Depot at Winchester). Royal 8vo. 1879.

Waller (E. Gent), A Trip to Portsmouth, or the Wife's Election. Reprinted from an unique copy. 8vo. 1710, 1822.

Wallis. Companion to the Isle of Wight. 12mo. N.D.

Wallop, Over. See Carlyle, Wake.

Walters (Rev. C.) The City Cross, Winchester, with account of similar structures, their use and design. 8vo. 1856.

Walters (Rev. C.) History of the Town, Church and Episcopal Palace of Bishops Waltham from the earliest period to the present time. 12mo. 1844.

Walton (Izaak). See Bowles, Waltoniana.

Walton (J.) Family Walks in Hampshire. 12mo. 1815.

Walton (J.) Geography of Hampshire. 8vo. N.D.

Warblington. See Bingly, Longcroft, Norris.

Ware (J. R.) The Isle of Wight, illustrated by photography by R. Sedgfield and F. M. Good. 4to. 1869.

Warner (R.) Hampshire Domesday Book, with English Translation, Preface, and Introduction, and an account of this Record, with Glossary. 4to. 1789.

Warner (R.) A Companion in a Tour round Lymington, Hants. 12mo. 1789. Refers also to New Forest, Isle of Wight, &c.
This was Mr. Warner's maiden effort.

Warner (R.) A Southampton Guide. 12mo. 1790.

Warner (R.) Attempt to ascertain the situation of the Ancient Clausentum, with proposals for publishing the History of Hampshire (Map and Vignette). 4to. 1792.

Warner (R.) Topographical Remarks relating to the South-Western parts of Hampshire. 2 vols. 8vo. 1793.
The plates intended for this work were destroyed by an accidental fire.

Warner (R.) History of the Isle of Wight, Military, Ecclesiastical, Civil and Natural. 8vo. 1795.

Warner (R.) View of the Isle of Wight Agriculture (See Driver). 4to. 1794.

Warner (R.) Collections for the History of Hampshire and the Bishoprick of Winchester, including the Isles of Wight, Jersey, Guernsey and Sark, by D. Y., with the original Domesday Book of the County, &c., by R. Warner, Jun., of Sway, Hants. 5 vols in 6. 4to. (1795).
Warner states, in his " Literary Recollections," that this work is a barefaced piracy ; that he did not know of its publication till he received an anonymous letter, severely criticising what was supposed to be his work. He says that he then procured a copy, and on going through it, was astonished to find that the compiler had incorporated into his " Collections," not only the Domesday Book, but also nearly the whole of his " History of the Isle of Wight," " Clausentum," and Topographical Remarks on the South-Western parts of Hampshire. But it seems incredible that respectable booksellers, whose names are on the title-page (Rivington, Cadell, and others) should have lent themselves to so gross a literary fraud ; or that Warner's " Hampshire Domesday," published six years previously, should have been actually incorporated into the work as the second volume, without Warner's knowledge and consent. And it is not a little remarkable, as contradicting Warner's story that he himself, in 1792, circulated " Proposals," which clearly indicates such a work as was subsequently published under his name, almost the only difference being that he proposed to print it in 3 vols., folio. A copy of these " Proposals " is among Gough's collections in the Bodleian, and they are reprinted in Warner's " Clausentum."

Warner (R.) Netley Abbey, a Gothic Story. 2 vols. 1794.

Warner (R.) Literary Recollections. 2 vols. 8vo. 1830.
This contains some interesting particulars, both about the people and places of Hampshire

Warren (Rev. T. A.) Poem on the New Church at Gally Hill, Crondal. 4to. 1841.

Warren (W. T.) History of Winchester (with illustrations). Royal 4to. N. D.

Warren (W. T.) Sixpenny Guide to Winchester. Small 8vo. N. D.

Warren (W. T.) Handbook to Winchester and St. Cross. 8vo. N. D.

Warton (Rev. Thomas). Mons. Catharinæ, Prope Winton, a Poem. 4to. 1760.

Warton (Rev. Thomas). Description of the City, College and Cathedral of Winchester (illustrated). 12mo. (1750-1857) The Notes, &c., were printed in 1857.

Watcombe. See Dixon.

Watts (Dr. J.) See Milner and Gibbons.

Watts (Isaac). Proceedings at the Inauguration of Memorial Statue at Southampton, July 17th, 1861. 12mo. 1861. Sewed. pp. 35.

Watts (Dr. J.) See Jenner and Doddridge, Jennings, Jones, Kell.

Wayland (Henry). Wayland's Voyage round the Isle of Wight. 8vo. 1876.

Wayland (H.) Tours through the Isle of Wight, Guide to Ryde and Portsmouth. 16mo. (1878). Another edition, 8vo, 1882.

Waynfilete (W., Bishop of Winchester) Life of, by R. Chandler. Royal 8vo. 1811.

Waynflete (Bishop). See Birch.

Webb (B., of Odiham) Essay on Education (dedicated to the gentlemen educated there). 8vo. 1782.

Wellow. See Empson.

Westall (W.) A History of Carisbrooke Castle, with an Account of the Imprisonment of King Charles I. (plates). 8vo. N.D.

Westall (W.) Views of Carisbrooke Castle, Isle of Wight. 8vo. 1839.

Westall (W.) Ten Views of Netley Abbey. Folio cloth. 1828.

West Ham (near Basingstoke). See Lefroy.

Weyhill Fair. See Piers the Plowman.

Weyhill Fair, The Humours of, by Maurice Mushroom, Esq. 8vo. 1790.

Weyhill Ghost (The) A Tale founded on fact, in four cantos. with some other pieces. 8vo. 1815.

Wherwell (near Andover). Wevill.—A Journey, with Description of Wevill, with the Accomodations and Conveniences thereof exprest, etc. 1716.

Wherwell. See Huntingdon (Henry of), Vergil.

Whitchurch. See Browne.

White (Rev. Gilbert) Natural History and Antiquities of Selborne, in the County of Southampton. 4to. 1789. Many subsequent editions.

White (Rev. Gilbert) Works of, in Natural History. 3 vols. 8vo. 1802.

White (Rev. Gilbert) Naturalist's Calendar (kept at Selborne). 8vo. 1795.

White (W.) History. Gazetteer and Directory of Hampshire and the Isle of Wight. 8vo. 1859. Second edition. 8vo. 1878.

Whitehead (A.) A pocket guide to the Isle of Wight. 8vo. 1844.

Wickham. See Civil War Phamphlets, Lowth.

Wilkins (R.) Portsmouth. The Borough, being a faithful, tho' humorous description of one of the strongest garrisons and seaport towns in Great Britain. 8vo. 1748.

W[ilkinson] (A.) Brief Historical Notices of the Parishes of Hurstbourne Priors, St. Mary Bourne, etc., in Hampshire, and of the cross-legged effigy in the Church of St. Mary Bourne. 8vo. 1861.

Williams (Rev. David, D.C.L) Sermons preached before the University of Oxford and in Winchester Cathedral, with a brief memoir of the Author. 8vo. 1862.
Dr. Williams was Head Master of Winchester College, 1824-36, Canon of Winchester Cathedral, 1833-60, Warden of New College, Oxford, 1840-60.

Williams (Rev. J.) History of Petersfield. 8vo. N.D.

Williams (T.) Jersey Legends in verse. 8vo. 1865.

Willis (Rev. R.) Architectural History of Canterbury, Winchester and York Cathedrals. 8vo. 1845.

Wilson (E.) A few observations of the practicability of improving the port of Lymington. 8vo 1855.

Wilson (R. F.) Short notes of seven years in a Country Parish. [Rownham's Hants.] 8vo. 1872.

Bibliotheca Hantoniensis.

Wilson (Rev. W.) A Sermon preached on the event, (Fire in Southampton in 1837), and a narrative of the late awful conflagration appended by an observer. 8vo, 1837.

Winchester. Petition of the Citizens of Winchester 1450, concerning the Ruinous State of the City. 4to. 1755.

Winchester. Copy of a Letter written from Master T. M. neere Salisbury, concerning the proceedings at Winchester, where Lords Cobham, etc., and Sir Griffith Markham were all attainted of High Treason, and ready to be executed, with his Majesty's warrant to suspend the execution at Winchester. Small 4to. 1603.

Winchester. History of Local Follies, or Comments upon the Times, Addressed to the Inhabitants of the City of Winchester. 8vo. Second edition. 1785.

Winchester. The Antiquities of, with an historical account of the City. 12mo. 1829.

Winchester. History and Antiquities of Winchester (plates). 2 vols. 12mo. 1773.

Winchester, Two Acts for the Better Paving, etc. the City of, (1771 and 1808). 8vo. 1817.
Contains names of leading citizens with their occupations.

Winchester, Picturesque Memorials of, with Descriptive Letterpress. 4to. 1830.

"Winchester." A Poem, by a Native of Winchester, 1831. Sewed, 8vo. 12 pp. 1831.

Winchester. Transactions of the British Archæological Association, held at Winchester in 1845 (plates). 8vo. 1846.
Containing :—
Municipal Records of Winchester and Southampton, by T. Wright.
Account of John Claptone, an Alchemist of Winchester, by J. O. Halliwell.
Sales of Manors and Church Lands of the See of Winchester, by J. H. Burn.
Account of Barton Oratory, Isle of Wight, by J. A. Barton.
Notes on Monastic Estates in Hampshire, by M. de Gerville.
Reversal of a Writ of Excommunication by the Bishop of Winchester, by M. F. Tupper.
Roman Roads and Stations in Hampshire, by H. Hatcher.
Antiquities of Winchester, by W. B. Bradfield.
Barrows in the Isle of Wight, by J. Dennett.
Roman Remains at Bitterne, by C. R. Smith.
Observations on the Paintings in Winchester Cathedral, by J. G. Waller.
Mint at Winchester, by J. Y. Ackerman.
Notes on the Incised Slab in Brading Church, Isle of Wight, by W. H. Rosser.
Winchester Cathedral, by E. Cresy.
Architectural Notes on the Church of St. Cross, by S. Jackson.
Church Notes in the Neighbourhood of Winchester, by D. R. Haigh.
Abbey Church of Romsey, by A. Ashpital.
Ancient Fortifications of Southampton, by W. D. Saull.

Winchester. Hyde Abbey School, Musae Hydeneses, sen Poemata queadam praemio donata, anctoribus Hydensis Scholae Alumnis ; Prize Poems composed by Scholars of Hyde Abbey School. Two parts (Latin and English). 12mo. 1828.

Winchester, Proceedings of the Archæological Institution at, (plates). 8vo. 1846.

Containing :—

Architectural History of Winchester Cathedral, by Professor Willis.

Architectural Works of William of Wykeham, by Professor Cockerell.

Notices of the Painted Glass in the Cathedral and Churches of Winchester and its neighbourhood, by C. Winston.

Architectural Notes of the Churches and other Ancient Buildings in the City and Neighbourhood of Winchester, by J. H. Parker.

Notices of the Mint and Exchange of Winchester, by Edward Hawkins.

Hail of the Royal Palace and Round Table of Winchester, by Edward Smirke.

Notices of the Seals of the Earls of Winchester and Winchester City, by J. G. Nichols.

Remarks on the Common Seal of the Men of Alwarestoke (Alverstoke), by Sir Frederick Madden.

Remarks on the Monument of Sir Richard Lyster, in St. Michael's Church, Southampton, by the same.

Architecture of the Church and Hospital of the Holy Cross, by E. A. Freeman.

Observations on the Priory of Christchurch, by A. J. Beresford Hope.

Remarks on Romsey Abbey Church, by J. L. Petit.

History and Architecture of Porchester Castle, by C. H. Hartshorne.

Winchester Scientific and Literary Society, Reports and Proceedings. Eight parts and other pamphlets. 8vo. N.D.

Winchester, Miniature Memorials of. (Plates). 12mo. 1834.

Winchester Quarterly Record (The), of Public Events, Meetings, &c. 1848-9-50.

Winchester, A new Historical and Descriptive Guide to. 3rd. edition. (1850).

Winchester. New Winchester Handbook. 8vo. 1868.

Winchester, Penny Illustrated History of. 12mo. N.D.

Winchester. Political Economy Papers on Ecclesiastical, Military and Social Reform. 1 vol. 8vo. Commencing June 1st, 1855.

Contents.—

Winchester, the Most Celebrated of all the Cities of England.

A Concise account of the Barracks.

A Visit to the Hospital of St. Cross, and several other Hampshire Pamphlets.

Winchester. Catalogue of Charters and other Objects exhibited at St. John's Rooms during the Celebration of the 700th Anniversary of the Mayoralty. 8vo. 1884.

Winchester, The Voice of William of Wykeham from, (Edited by Mr. Herbert Smith). 8vo. (No. 1). June. 1855.

Winchester. Handbills &c., chiefly relating to the Proceedings at the Celebration of the 700th Anniversary of the Mayoralty. Folio 8vo. 1885.

Winchester, Warren's Illustrated History of. Folio. 1885.

Winchester. Abstract of the Report of the Commissioners concerning Charities in the management of the Corporation of Winchester. 8vo. N.D.

Winchester. See Report of Proceedings of a Meeting of the County of Hants, held at Winchester, March 1823, etc. 8vo. 1823.

Winchester (County Hall). See Smirke, Wyatt.

Winchester, State of the County Hospital at. 8vo. 1746. Statutes and Constitutions for the use of. See Clarke. 4to. 1772.

Winchester, City Cross. Restoration of, by Mr. G. G. Scott, Architect, the Statue of William of Wykeham. Sewed 12mo. (1866).

Winchester (City Cross). See Walters.

Winchester (Wolvesey). See Collier.

Winchester. Royal and others Proclamations, 1571-1719. Folio.

Winchester. Proceedings in Borough Mote, Sept. 22nd, 1552, to Feb. 7th, 1660. Folio.

Winchester. Proceedings of the Corporation, Nov. 7th, 1589, to Sept. 7th, 1598. Folio.

Winchester, City of, Proceedings in the Town Court. October 1st, 1651 to August 13th, 1661. Folio.

Winchester, City of, Proceedings of Court of Quarter Sessions September 25th, 1666 to August 9th, 1716. Folio.

Winchester, A memento of the Natives' Society. 8vo. 1859.

Winchester, City of, Two copies of Tarrage Book, May 24th, 1686 to August 10th, 1726. Folio.

The MSS. Tarrages of Winchester in the Addit. MSS. of the British Museum, and the Liber de Winton are works of the middle ages relating to that city.

Trussel's Annales Wintoniensis were written in MSS., dated 1644 ; Rudborne's Historia Major Wintoniensis, is a work of the middle ages and another work more or less historical, was written a hundred years before Rudborne, by another ecclesiastic—Henry Knighton.

Another *Annales Wintoniensis* appear to have been written before Trussell's time, who was an Alderman of Winchester in the 17th century, a fifteenth century Annales Wintoniensis, I believe, also exists.

Winchester, City of, Proceedings of the Corporation, July 6th, 1597 to April 3rd, 1605. Large 4to.

Winchester. See Ainsworth, Akermann, Ancient Laws, Andrews, Annals of England, Annales Monastici, Arch. Inst. Assoc., Baigent, Bailey, Ball, Baring, Barnes, Bell, Benham, Bingham, Braddon, Bramston, Brand, Brit. Arch Assoc., Brome, Brooke, Bunyon, Capgrave, Carlyle, Carter, Cave, Chamberlain, Churton, Clapton, Clark, Cobbe, Collier, Civil War, Cope, Deane, Deverell, Dixon, Dunstan, Earle, Edgar, Edward (King), Edwards, Egerton, Ellis, English History, Eyton, Freeman, Gardiner, Godwin, Gomme, Goodman, Greenville, Gudgeon, Hall, Hawkins, Hill, Hoveden, Howitt, Huntingdon (Henry of), Inett, Johns, Judges, Ken, Kingsley, Kitchin, Land We Live In, Le Keux, Leroy, L'Estrange, Lingard, Lyford, Malmesbury (William of), Marryat, Masters, Mereweather, Merridew, Milner, Monasteries, Novum Testamentum, Nunnaminster, Paris (Matthew), Pauli, Piers the Plowman, Plasse, Plumpton, Prousten, Queen, Reformation, Rimmer, Rispanger, Roscoe, Savage, Scott, Sewell, Shakespeare, Spelman, St. John, Stuart, Todd, Townshend, Trial, Trollope, Tutler, Vergil, Vetusta Monumenta, Walcott, Wallace, Walton, Worcester (Florence of), Wood, Wright, Wriothesley, Young.

Winchester Assizes. Report of the Proceedings at, for Rioting at Fordingbridge and other places. 8vo. 1831.

Winchester (Bishop of), Conduct of as Visitor of Magdalen College fully stated. 8vo. 1770.

Winchester, Bishops of. See Winchester Cathedral.

Winchester Cathedral, Statutes of, as revised by King Charles I, MS. 144 pages of vellum, 24th October, 1638. Signed by the King on title page, and by Archbishop Laud on every page.

Winchester Cathedral. Three Letters concerning the non-ejection of the Monks from the Church at Winchester. Succession of the Priors of the Church at Winchester. Eulogium of William of Waynflete (Bishop of Winchester) p. 320-326, of Wharton's Anglia Sacra. 2 vols. Folio. 1691.

Winchester. Descriptive account of the Cathedral of Winchester, 8 views. Reprinted from B. Winkle's English Cathedrals. 8vo. N.D.

Winchester Cathedral. Supplementary notices to the History of Winchester Cathedral, by a Bookseller. 8vo. N.D.

Winchester Cathedral. Leaflets relating to. 8vo. V.D.

Winchester Cathedral. An Apology for those who object to the lateral position of an organ in Winchester Cathedral. 4to. 1825.

Winchester Cathedral. See First Report of H. M. Commissioners, appointed Nov. 10th, 1852, to enquire into the State and condition of Cathedral and Collegiate Churches in England and Wales. Small folio. 1854.

Winchester Cathedral. Handbook to the Cathedrals of England, (Southern Division). 6 vols. 8vo. 1861.

Winchester Cathedral. William Rufus, his tomb in, (see Richards). 8vo. 1870.

Winchester Cathedral. See Batten, Blore, Britton, Carter, Cassan, Chandler, Clarke, Dixon, Fearon, Fiddes, Gale, Garbett, Gibbon, Godwin, Gubbins, Hook, Kitchin, Lowth, Madge, Mercarius Rusticus, Milner, Nichols, Organs, Perry, Political Songs, Pontoys, Richards, Rudborne, Russell, Serres, Sumner, Waagen, Walcott, Warton, Wilberforce, Willis, Wriothesley.

Winchester Diocesan Calendar. Bound in volumes. 8vo. London. 1865. And yearly since.

Winchester College. Account of the Supervision held at the College, near Winchester, by the Warden and Supervisors of St. Mary Winton College, in Oxford, on 3rd Sept., 1766. and some Proceedings consequent thereupon. 8vo. 1767.

Winchester College. Ups and Downs of a Public School, by a Wykehamist. 12mo. N.D.

Winchester College. Account of Mr. Harris's Election at Winchester last May, in a Letter to a Person of Quality in London, dated January, 1704-5. 4to.

Winchester College, The Plea of the Fellows of, against the Bishop of Winchester's Local and Final Visitatorial Powers over the said College. 4to. 1711

Winchester College. A Narrative of the Proceedings in the Dispute between the Bishop of Winchester and the College of Winchester, concerning his Jurisdiction. 8vo. 1713.

Winchester College. A Letter to the Rev. Dr. Lowth, in Vindication of the Conduct of the Fellows of New College, Oxford, in their late Election of a Warden of Winchester College. 8vo. 1758.

Winchester College. The Law and Equity of the Late Appointment of a Warden considered. 8vo. 1759.

Winchester College. A Defence of the Conduct of the Warden of Winchester College in Accepting that Wardenship. 8vo. 1759.

Winchester College. An Impartial Bystander's Review of the Controversy concerning the Wardenship of Winchester College. 8vo. 1759.

Winchester College. A Reply to Dr. Golding and Dr. Lowth's Answers to the Anonymous Letter. 8vo. 1759.

Winchester College. A Letter to H. Brougham, Esq., in reply to the Strictures on Winchester College contained in his letter to Sir Samuel Romilly from Rev. L. Clarke. 8vo, 1818.

Winchester College. Wordsworth (Bishop Charles) The College of St. Mary Winton, near Winchester. 4to. 1848.

Winchester College. Natural History Society's Reports. 5 vols. 8vo. 1871-82.

Winchester College. Wykehamica: A History of Winchester College and Commoners. Crown 8vo. 1878.

Winchester College. Inscriptions Wykehamicæ. Crown 8vo. 1885.
Copies of the epitaphs in the Cloister at Winchester College.

Winchester College. See Acts of Parliament, Adams, Akermann, Bompas, Bowles, Buckland, Burton, Clarke, Golding, Hampden, Huddersfield, Ken, Lowth, Malet, Mansfield, Moberley, Organs, Overton, Phillimore, Radclyffe, Rye, Staunton, Stephens, Trollope, Waagen, Walcott, Warton, Williams, Wooll, Wordsworth.

Winchester Discipline. Extracted from " The Times," etc. 8vo. 1872.

Winchester Guide. A description of the Antiquities and Curiosities of that Ancient City. 12mo, 1780.

Winchester Guide. Giving an account of its Antiquities and of the Hospital of St. Cross. N.D.

Winchester Guide, or a Description of the Antiquities and Curiosities of that Ancient City (plates). 8vo. 1796.

Winchester School. The public school matches, and those who met there, by a Wykehamist. 12mo. 1867.

Windover (Nichs.) The Englishman's Guide to Plenty, containing the observations of an old Hampshire Farmer on the national produce, etc. 8vo. 1807.

Wing (Dr. Edwin), Southampton considered as a Resort for Invalids, with a notice of its Chalybeate Spa. 12mo. 1848.

Winter (Rev. R). Parental Retrospect : a very brief Memoir of Rebecca Beddome of Romsey. 12mo. Only a very few printed. 1821.

Wise (J. R.) The New Forest, its History and its Scenery. (63 illustrations by W. Crane). First Edition, 4to, 1863. 8vo. 1880. Artist edition, 1883.

Wither Family. Private case before the House of Lords, between Andrew Wither and others and Dr. William King, relating to Lands and Estates in the Countyof Southampton. Folio. Privately Printed, 1735.

Wither (Lovelace) Cottage Allotments in some Parishes of North Hampshire, or the Means of Reducing Poor-rates. 8vo. 1832.

Wither (L. B.) Letter to the Farmers of North Hampshire on reducing the Poor Rates. 8vo. N.D.

Withers (R. T.) Church of the Holy Cross, Brinstead, Isle of Wight. 4to. N.D.

Wood (Christopher), Reminiscences of Winchester in verse (Plates). 4to. (1860).

Wood (J.) The King's House at Winchester, a poem in two parts. 4to. 1793.

Woodward (B. B.) Wilks (T. C.), and Lockhart (C.) General History of Hampshire and the Isle of Wight. (Plates). 3 vols. 4to. N.D

Woolmer Forest. Report of the Commisioners appointed to Enquire into the State and Condition of the Woods, Forests, and Land Revenues of the Crown [on Aliceholt and Woolmer Forest]. Vol. I., 6. Folio. 1790.

Woolmer Forest in Hampshire, a Topographical Account of. 4to. 1821.

Worsley (Sir R., Bart.) History of the Isle of Wight (illustrated) 4to. 1781.

Worsley (Sir R.) See Trial.

Wright (Henry Press) Story of the Domus Dei, Portsmouth, commonly called the Royal Garrison Church (plates). 8vo. 1873.

Wright (Thomas) Remarks on the Municipal Privileges and Legislation of the Middle Ages. Read at the Second Congress of the Brit. Arch., Assoc. Winchester, August 4 1845. as illustrated from the Archives Sewed 8vo. pp. 13, 1845.

Wyatt (Thomas Henry) Report on Repairs of Basing Church (plates). Folio. 1873.

Wyatt (Thomas Henry) On the old Hall and New Assize Courts at Winchester (Plate and Plan). 4to. 1874.

Wyke (near Winchester). See Baigent.

Wykeham (William of) by Bishop Robert Lowth. 8vo. 1758. Second edition, 1759. Third edition, 1777.

Wykeham (William of). See Birch, Chevallier, Lucas, Martin Wallcott.

Wykor. See Portchester.

Wyndham (Henry Penruddocke), Picture of the Isle of Wight, Delineated upon the Spot, in the Year 1793. 8vo. 1794.

Wylde's London and Southampton Railway Guide, Topographical, Antiquarian and Geological Account of the Country, within ten miles, and a guide to the environs of Southampton. 18mo. 1839.

Yateley. See Kingsley.

Young (A.) Postscript to General View of the Agriculture of Hants, with View of the Isle of Wight Agriculture. 4to. 1794. (See Driver and Warner.)

Young (Mrs.) Aldershot and all about it (illustrations). 8vo. 1857.

Yonge (C. M.) Old Times at Otterbourne. 8vo. N.D.

THE LIFE OF

WILLIAM OF WYKEHAM,

BISHOP OF WINCHESTER.

Collected from Records, Regifters, Manufcripts,
and other Authentic Evidences:

By ROBERT LOWTH, D.D.
PREBENDARY of DURHAM,
And Chaplain in Ordinary to HIS MAJESTY.

Quique fui memores alios fecere merendo. VIRG.

LONDON,
Printed for A. MILLAR, in the Strand; and
R. and J. DODSLEY, in Pall-Mall.
MDCCLVIII.

[Figure 8; 12.0 x 20.0 cm]

BRANNON'S

PICTURE

OF

The Isle of Wight;

OR,

The Expeditious Traveller's

INDEX

To its prominent Beauties & Objects of Interest.

The Pulpit-Rock, Bonchurch, looking towards Ventnor.

Compiled especially with Reference to those numerous Visitors who can spare but two or three Days TO MAKE THE

Tour of the Island.

Printed and Published by George Brannon, Wootton,
ISLE OF WIGHT.

[Figure 9; 13.4 x 20.9 cm]

BOOKS & PERIODICALS

CONTAINING

𝕽eferences to 𝕳ampshire.

—▸═▪▪▪═▸—

Acland-Troyte (J. E.) Through the Ranks to a Commission, 8vo. 1881. Soldier Life at Portsmouth, pp. 1-214.

Adams (W. H. D.) Famous Ships, post 8vo. London, 1872. Contains History of H.M.S. Victory, now at Portsmouth.

Agriculture, Employment of Women and Children in, 8vo. 1843. Refers to Hampshire.

Agriculture, General View of the, of the various Counties, (including Hampshire), 4to. v. y., 1794.

Aikin (Dr. John) England Described, (including Hampshire), 8vo. 1818.

Ainsworth (W. H.) Cardinal Pole, 3 vols, post 8vo. London, 1863. Contains references to Southampton and Winchester.

Alderney Cows. *Saturday Magazine*, p. 47, vol. vii. 1835.

Aldershot, Down at. *Sunday at Home*, p. 248, vol. xi. 1864.

——— the Camp at. *All the Year Round*, p. 58, vol xxxii. 1883.

——— in Camp at. *Once a Week*, p. 658. 1874.

——— Town and Camp. *All the Year Round*, p. 401, vol. i. 1859.

——— in 1863 ; *Sunday at Home,* July 11th, 1884.

——— Mission House and Soldiers' Institute at. *Cassell's Illustrated Family Paper*, p. 413, vol xi. 1863.

——— Mrs. Daniell at. *Girls' Own Annual*, p. 51. 1880.

——— Revisited. *All the Year Round*, p. 224, vol. xxiii. 1879.

——— Women at. *Household Words.* April 19th, 1856.

Alton, Some Local Celebrities of, Rev. John Vaughan, M.A., *Hampshire Chronicle*, January, 1890.

Ancient Laws and Institutes of England, and Monumenta Ecclesiastica Anglicana, 2 vols, 8vo. 1840. Winchester : Ath. I. 14 ; Edg. II. 8. C. E., I. ; C. S., 30.

Anderson (John P.) The Book of British Topography, a Classified Catalogue of the Topographical Works in the Library of the British Museum, relating to Great Britain and Ireland, (*Hampshire Topography*, pp. 114-125), 4to. London, 1881.

Bibliotheca Hantoniensis.

Andrewes (Lancelot, Bishop of Winchester) *Saturday Magazine*, vol. xxiv. p. 221. 1844.

Antiquarian and Topographical Cabinet, 10 vols, 12mo. 1811. Plates and Letterpress Descriptions. Carisbrooke Castle, vol. ii., plate 1 ; Godshill Church, Isle of Wight, vol. iii., plate 49 ; Netley Abbey, vol. v., plate 37, 39, 41, 43, 45 ; St. Cross, vol. v., plate 1, 3, 5, 7, 9 ; St. Denys' Priory, vol. x., plate 29 ; Shalfleet Church, vol., x., plate 95 ; Southwick Priory, vol. vii., plate 37 ; Southampton, vol. v., plate 31 ; Winchester, vols. i and ii., plate 63 ; Winchester, vol. iv., plate 1 ; Winchester, vol. ix., plate 61.

Annals of England ; an Epitome of English History, 3 vols, 8vo. 1862. Mention made of Winchester, Southampton, Portsmouth, &c.

Arcachon to Bournemouth. *Gentleman's Magazine*, p. 566, vol. 258. 1885.

Archæological Album, or Museum of National Antiquities ; Romsey, pp. 228-231. Silchester, pp. 150-154 ; Winchester, pp. 218-223 ; Southampton, pp. 223-228 ; illustrated, 4to. 1845.

Armada (Spanish) The names of those persons who subscribed towards theDefence of this Country at the Time of the Spanish Armada, 1588, and the amount each contributed, with Historical Introduction and Index by T. C. Noble, 8vo. 1886. Hampshire, pp. 24-26.

Around and About, Scenes in the Highways and Byways of Life. Reprinted from *The Hampshire Independent* and *The Southern Echo*, crown 4to. 84 pp. 1890.

Arreton Church (Isle of Wight), p. 321, vol. xx. (See Brading.) *Church of England Magazine*.

―――― Down, Isle of Wight. Notes on Bronze Weapons found on ; Archæologia, pp. 326-331, vol, xxxvi. ii.

―――― See Brading.

Ashburnham (J.) Narrative of his Attendance on King Charles I., 2 vols, 8vo. 1880. Events at Titchfield and in the Isle of Wight, 1647.

Ashey Down, (Isle of Wight), Notes on the opening of the Tumuli on Ashey Down, p. 162. *Journ. Brit. Arch. Assoc.*, vol. x. 1854.

Ashton (John) Romances of Chivalry, told and illustrated in fac-simile, royal 8vo. 1887. Sir Bevis of Hampton, pp. 121-171.

Asser (Bp.) died A.D. 910, Aelfredi Regis Res Gestae. (Published by Abp. Parker, 1574, folio.) Refers to Basing, Winchester, and the West Saxons.

Austen (Jane) Mansfield Park, 8vo. 1814. Portsmouth is graphically described in a few words.

―――― (Jane) Letters of. Edited by Lord Brabourne, 2 vols, 8vo. London, 1884. A very large number of these letters relate to Hampshire scenes and persons nearly a century ago.

―――― (Jane). *Time*, p. 193, vol. i. 1889.

―――― (Jane). *Cornhill Magazine*, p. 158, vol. xxiv. 1871.

―――― (Jane). *Temple Bar*, p. 350, vol. lxiv. 1882.

―――― (Jane) At Home. *Fortnightly Review*, p. 262, vol. xxxvii. 1885.

―――― (Jane), More Views of. *Gent. Mag.*, p. 26, vol. cclviii. 1885.

―――― (Jane). See Elwood, Murch.

Avon, a Day's Fishing on the. *Once a Week*, p. 628, vol. x. 1864.

Baddesley, Hampshire, Groaning Tree of. *Mirror*, p. 419, vol. xix. 1832.

Barham (Rev. R. H.) *Ingoldsby Legends*, 8vo. 1879. Contains : Netley Abbey, A Legend of Hampshire.

Bibliotheca Hantoniensis.

Barnes, near Brixton (Isle of Wight), a Romano-British Pottery at. *Journ. Brit. Arch. Assoc.*, vol. xii, p. 141. 1856.

Bartlett (W. H.) Harding (J. D.) and Creswick (T.) Ports, Harbours and Watering Places of Great Britain, 2 vols, 4to. N.D. Vol. ii, Hurst Castle, Cowes, Southampton, Portsmouth, &c.

Basing. —Will of Luke de Poynings, Lord St. John, 1376. From a Copy in the Register of William of Wykeham, p. 45. *Arch. Journ.*, vol. xi. 1854.

—— Day at. *Sharpe's Journal*, p. 222.

—— House, Sieges of. *All the Year Round*, p. 542, vol. ii. 1874.

Basingstoke.—Description of an Æolipile, discovered in digging the Basin of the Canal. *Archæologia*, p. 410, vol. xiii.

Beattie (Dr. Wm.) Castles and Abbeys of England, illustrated, roy. 8vo, N.D. Carisbrook Castle, pp. 281-304, 349-51; Netley Abbey. pp. 305-330, 352.

Beaulieu Abbey and Witch of Beaulieu. *All the Year Round*, pp. 449-471, vol. xi. 1874.

—— Abbey, A Winter's Drive to, *Sharpes Journal*, 1850, pp. 266.

—— Abbey. See Grey Abbey, Walford.

Bede (Venerable) Historiæ Ecclesiasticae Gentis Anglorum,Libri, V. folio, 1644. Records Ecclesiastical affairs in Wessex.

Berkeley (Hon. Grantley F.) My Life and Recollections. (The Author lived near Christchurch) 2 vols. la. 8vo. 1865. New Forest Deer, vol. ii. chap. i.; New Forest, Sport in, vol. ii. chap. xi; Fishing in the Avon, chap. xiv.

Bertram (C.) Description of Britain translated from Richard of Cirencester, and a Commentary on the Itinerary, Illustrated with maps, 8vo. London, 1809.

Besant (Walter), The Holy Rose, (Christmas Number of *All the Year Round*), 4to. London, 1886, The scene is partly laid at Portchester.

Besant (Walter) and Rice (J.) By Celia's Arbour, 3 vols. post 8vo. London. A Story of Portsmouth.

Betham (Rev. Wm.) The Baronetage of England, 4to, London, 1801-5

Birch (Colonel John) Military Memoir of. Camden Society, 1873, sm. 4to. Contains much interesting Civil War Information.

Birch (Thomas) Heads of Illustrious Persons of Great Britain engraved by Mr, Houbraken and Mr. Vertue with their lives and characters by Thomas Birch, A.M, F.R.S. folio, 1743. Contains lives of William of Wykeham,William Waynflete and others.

—— (Rev. Thomas) Life of Henry, Prince of Wales, eldest son of James I. 8vo. 1760. Bramshill House was built for this Prince.

Bishop (Rev. H. H.) Pictorial Architecture of the British Isles. Many Hampshire illustrations, folio. 1887.

Bishopstoke, Roman leaden coffin found at, p. 227. vol. 4, Second Series Proc. Soc. Antiq. London.

Bitterne near Southampton, Remarks on an unpublished Inscription to the Emperor Tetricus found at. *Archæologia* pp. 257-261. vol. xxix.

Black Gang Chine. *Saturday Magazine*,vol. v. p. 109. 1834.

Blakey (Robert) Angler's complete guide to the rivers and lakes of England. Printed at Winchester, 8vo. 1859.

Blackmore (R.D.) Cradock Nowell. 8vo. 1884. Largely concerned with the New Forest.

Blank Book (The),of a Small Colleger. Contains a story "Mr. Reuben Pottle" relating to Hampshire. 12mo. 1824.

Bloody Assizes (The), *Gentleman's Magazine.* p. 381. vol. 256. 1884. (Trial and Execution of Alice Lisle).

Blount (T.) Fragmenta Antiquitatis or ancient Tenures of Land and Jocular Customs of some Manors, 8vo. 1784. Several Hampshire references.

Boldre Church and School. *Penny Magazine.* vol. iv. p. 92. 1835.

Bompas (G.C.) Life of Frank Buckland. 8vo. 1889. Winchester College. pp. 10-37.

Bones of our Sovereigns. *Leisure Hour,* April 8th, 1858.

Bossington, Discovery of a Roman Sword at, p. 374. *Journ. Brit. Arch. Soc.* vol. xviii. 1887.

Botley, The Discovery of an Ancient War Ship near. *Journ. Brit. Arch. Assoc.* p.70, vol. xxxii. 1876.

Bourne (H.R.F.) English Seaman under the Tudors. 2 vols. 8vo. 1865. Spithead, Victory at, 1545. vol. i., 78-79,

Bournemouth, *London Society,* p. 497, vol xl. 1881. *See* Arcachon.

—— See Progress of Watering Places, *London Society,* p. 607, vol. xxxix., 1881.

—— A Sketch from. *Blackwood's Magazine,* p. 740, vol. cxxxiv, 1883,

—— In Winter. *All the Year Round,* p. 259, vol. xl. 1887.

Bowles (Caroline). *See* Southey.

Braddon (M. E. now Mrs. Maxwell). Henry Dunbar, a Novel, 3 vols, crown 8vo. London, 1864. Refers to Winchester and its Neighbourhood.

—— Vixen, a Novel, 3 vols, crown 8vo. London, 1879. Much Mention of the New Forest.

Brading, (Isle of Wight). A Passage from the Oglander MSS. relating to the Arrival of Charles I. in the Isle of Wight. *Arch. Journ.,* p. 308, vol. xxxi. 1874.

Brading and Arreton, A Visit to, (Isle of Wight). *Sunday at Home,* August 30th, 1855.

Brading, (Isle of Wight), Bones found in a Roman Villa, at Morton, near. *Journ. Anthrop. Inst.,* vol. xxi., p. 116. 1882.

—— Hoard of Bronze Bracelets at. *Journ. Brit. Arch. Assoc.,* p. 423, vol. xxxviii. 1882.

—— Remarks on the Roman Mosaic Pavements at. *Journ. Brit. Arch. Assoc.,* p. 361, vol. xxxix. 1883.

Bramshill, In Hampshire. *Saturday Magazine,* vol. xvii., p. 2. 1840.

Bramshill House. From *The Antiquary.* 1873.

Brading, (Isle of Wight), Roman Villa lately discovered at. *Journ. Brit. Arch. Assoc.,* p. 363, vol. xxxvi. 1880.

Brand (John) F. S. A. and Ellis (Sir Henry). Observations on the Popular Antiquities of Great Britain, 3 vols, 8vo. 1855. Hampshire, vol. ii., p. 512. Winchester, vol. i., p. 452, ii., 162-456. New Forest, ii., p. 260.

Bridger (C.) An Index to Printed Pedigrees contained in County and Local Histories, the Herald's Visitations, &c., 8vo. 1867. Many Hampshire References.

—— (J.) A Book of Fairs, 8vo. 1800.

Brightstone and Bowcombe, (Isle of Wight), Excavations at Brightstone and Bowcombe Downs, p. 34 ; The Antiquities of the Isle of Wight, p. 177 ; The Lords of the Isle of Wight, p. 213. *Journ. Brit. Arch. Assoc.*, vol. xi., 1855.

Britain, Early, 5 vols ; Celtic Britain, 5 vols ; Roman Britain, 5 vols ; Anglo-Saxon Britain, 5 vols ; Norman Britain, 5 vols ; Post Norman Britain, 5 vols, sm. 12mo. 1884-86. All contain references to Hampshire.

Britain, Greek Trade Routes to. Folk Lore, March 1890. Tends to prove the identity of the Isle with Ictis (Diod. Sic.) and Mictis (Pliny).

British Coins found in Hants, Sussex, Surrey, Dorset. *Collectanea Antiqua.* vol. I.

Brocas of Beaurepaire, and Roche Court, Family of. *Edin. Rev.*, p. 225, vol. clxvi. 1887.

Brome (Rev. James) Travels over England, Scotland and Wales, 8vo. 1707. Hampshire, p.p. 264-271. Winchester, p. p. 49-53.

Brooke (Ralph) A Catalogue and Succession of the Kings and Nobles of this Realm of England from 1066 till 1622. 4to. 1622. Southampton p. 323. Winchester p. 342.

Brown (Dr. J. C.) The Forests of England and the Management of them in Bye-gone Times. 8vo. 1883. New Forest, pp. 51-74. Aliceholt and Woolmer Forests, pp. 113-116. Bere, Buckholt, Char, New Forest, West Forest, Wutmer, etc., etc., p. 134.

Browne (Willis) Notitia Parliamentaria, or an History of the Counties, Cities, and Boroughs in England and Wales. 8vo. 1730. Hampshire pp. 35-37, and appendix.

Bunyan (John) Works of, 2 vols. folio, London, 1692. " John Bunyan's Pilgrim's Progress has some indirect connexion with Southampton. His conception of the wandering Pilgrim was probably derived from the many romantic histories of wandering knights and pilgrims of the Middle ages. He is believed, in particular, to have used in this respect a book by John Cartheny, written originally in French, and named " The Wandering Knight." This book was translated in a 4to form into English in 1581 by William Goodyeare, a merchant of Southampton. This was probably the edition Bunyan used. [See Goodyeare] The idea of the two lions guarding the gate in Bunyan's work is probably borrowed from the legend of Sir Bevis and the lions guarding the cave. The lions at the Southampton Bar perpetuate this same idea."

Burn (J.S.) The History of Parish Registers in England. 8vo. 1862. Some Hampshire References.

Burroughs (John) Fresh Fields. 12mo. cloth. Much reference to Hampshire.

Burton (R.) Wars in England. 12mo. 1681. Describes Relief of Basing House, &c.,

Burton (William) L.L.B. Antoninus, his Itinerary or Journeys of the Roman Empire so far as it concerns Britain. A Commentary on. London, 1658. Describes the position of Roman Towns in Hampshire.

Butler (Samuel) Hudibras. 2 vols. post 8vo. London, 1859.

> There was an ancient sage philosopher
> That had read Alexander Ross over.
> Part II, Canto II : also in Part II. Canto II, line 670).

Twice refers to Rev. Alexander Ross, author of " Mystagogus Poeticus " 8vo. 1675. A former Master of Southampton Grammar School.

Calamy (Rev. Edmund D.D.) Ejected or Silenced Hampshire Ministers, Vol. II. pp. 333-352. Account of The Ministers, Lectures, Masters, and Fellows of Colleges, and Schoolmasters who were ejected or silenced after the Restoration in 1660, by or before the Act for Uniformity, 2 vols. 8vo. 1713.

Calendarium Rotulorum Patentium in Turri Londinensi, folio, 1802. References to Hampshire.

Calendarium Rotularum Chartarum et Inquisitionum ad Quod Damnum. folio, 1803. Numerous Hampshire references.

Calendarium Inquisitionium post Mortem sive Exactarum. 4 vols. folio, 1806. Many Hampshire References.

Camps, News from the. *All the Year Round*, Sept. 30th. 1871.

Capgrave (J.) The Book of the Illustrious Henries. 8vo. 1858. Notices of Winchester, Southampton, &c.,

——The Chronicle of England (From the Creation to the year 1417.) Edited by Rev. F. C. Hingeston. roy 8vo. 1858. Capgrave's " Legende of Englonde" contains the Legends of Morwenna and Elfleda, the Founders or first Abbesses of Romsey Abbey.

Carew (Bamfylde Moore) The History of, (King of The Beggars). 8vo. N.D. This celebrated character was a visitor at Portchester and Hackwood Park.

Carisbrooke Castle and its ancient Lords. p. 193. *Journ. Brit. Arch. Assoc.* Vol. xi. 1855. Isle of Wight.

Carisbrooke Castle, Description of, *Saturday Magazine*, Vol. iv. p. 191. 1834.

——(with Illustrations). *Mirror*, p. 41. vol. xxviii. 1836.

——*Penny Magazine.* vol i. p. 356. 1832.

——*Penny Magazine.* 1836.

Carisbrooke. Roman Villa at, *Collectanea Antiqua*, Vol. vi. p. 121.

Carlisle (N.) Endowed Grammar Schools of England and Wales. 2 vols. 8vo. 1818. Hampshire, pp. 433-471.

Carlyle (Thos.) Cromwell's Letters and Speeches, 5 vols. post 8vo, London. 1871 Vol 1. gives details of operations at Winchester and Basing, and refers to Hursley, Wallop, and Southampton.

Carter (John) The Ancient Architecture ot England, including the Orders during the British, Saxon, and Norman Eras, and under the Reigns of Henry III., and Edward III., 109 engravings, folio. 1887. Refers to Winchester, Southampton, &c.

Carter (John) Specimens of the Ancient Sculpture and Painting now remaining in England, from the Earliest Period to the Reign of Henry VIII., 120 plates, folio. 1887. Several references to Hampshire.

Cartularium Saxonicum, a Collection of Charters relating to Anglo-Saxon History, vol. i., 4to. 1885. vol. ii., 4to. 1887 *(Rolls Publications)*. Many Grants of Land in Hampshire.

Cary (John) New Itinerary, a correct Delineation of the Great Roads, both Direct and Cross, throughout England and Wales, 8vo. 1821. Describes Coach Routes in Hampshire.

Catalogue of the MSS. in the Cottonian Library deposited in the British Museum, folio. 1802. Many of these MSS. relate to Hampshire Persons and Places.

Chamberlain (John) Letters of, during the Reign of Queen Elizabeth, sm. 4to. Camden Society, 1861. Mentions Jersey, Isle of Wight, Winchester, &c.

Bibliotheca Hantoniensis.

Chambers' Book of Days. roy. 8vo, 2 vols. N.D. Many references to Hampshire Persons and Places.

Chamier (Capt.) Ben Brace, or the Last of the Agammemnons, post 8vo, new edition. 1867. Amusing Stories of Portsmouth.

Champlin (J. D.) Chronicle of the Coach, (Charing Cross to Ilfracombe), 8vo. 1886. Hampshire, pp. 52-94.

Channel Islands, Primeval Antiquities of the, pp. 142-222, *Arch. Journal*, vol. i. 1846.

—— (The). *Argosy*, vols. xxxvii-xxxviii. 1884. See Holiday Making in Mid Channel.

—— History and Description of. *Penny Magazine*, vol. vi., pp. 329-336, 377-384. 1837

—— (The). *Saturday Magazine*, vol. xvi., pp. 105-137. 1840.

—— a Packet from the. *Good Words*, 1890.

Christchurch, Description of an Ancient Fortification near. *Archæologia*, pp. 237-240, vol. v.

—— *Mirror*, p. 441, vol. xv. 1830.

——*Saturday Magazine*, vol. xvii., p. 145. 1840.

—— Archæological Association, *Gentleman's Magazine*, p. 308, vol. x. N.S., 1861.

Christchurch on Avon. *Sunday at Home*, July, 1890.

——Priory, Singular Discovery of a quantity of Bird's Bones buried in. *Archæologia*, pp. 117-118, vol. iv. Remarks upon this Discovery, pp. 414-418, vol. iv.

—— Priory, Observations on the Stone Coffins discovered at. *Archæologia*, pp. 224-229, vol. v.

—— Priory, The Rood Screen in. p. 142, vol. v. *Arch. Journal*, 1848.

Chronicles and Memorials of Great Britain and Ireland during the Middle Ages, published under the Direction of the Master of the Rolls, large 8vo. V. D. Many references to Hampshire Persons and Places.

Chudleigh (Elizabeth, Duchess of Kingston, tried for Bigamy before the House of Lords), Life and Memoirs of, 4to. 18th Cent. Married at Lainston Church, near Winchester.

—— (Miss, Duchess of Kingston). *All the Year Round*, p. 88, vol. xxi. 1878.

Churton (E.) The Early English Church, 8vo. 1878. References to Winchester and Hampshire.

Cirencester (Richard of) Speculum Historicale de Gestis Regum Angliæ. Edited by J. E. Mayor, 2 vols, 8vo. 1863. Describes Roman Roads and Stations in Hampshire.

Clarendon (Edward, Earl of) History of the Rebellion and Civil Wars in England, 3 vols, folio. 1702-1704. Describes Cheriton Fight, Siege of Basing House, &c.

Clark (G. F.) Mediæval Military Architecture in England. Christchurch Castle, vol. i., p. 385; Odiham Castle, vol. ii., 336; Portchester Castle, p. 338. Southampton Defences, vol. iv., 472.

Clarke (S. R.) Vestigia Anglicana, 2 vols, 8vo. 1826. King Edgar near Andover, vol. i., pp. 139-140; Death of Rufus, vol. i., 232-234.

Clayton (J. W.) Personal Memoirs of Charles II., 2 vols, 8vo. 1859. Jersey, vol. i., p. 148; Hampshire, vol. i., pp. 161-175, 318, 319; vol. ii., pp. 201, 345, &c.

[173]

Cobbe (T.) History of the Norman Kings of England, 8vo. 1869. References to Winchester, Southampton, Portsmouth, &c.

Cobbett (W.) History of the Protestant Reformation, 2 vols, 8vo. 1829. Stratton, Micheldever, p. 186, Monasteries in Hampshire, vol. ii.

——— Rural Rides in the Counties of Surrey, Kent, Sussex, Hampshire, &c., 12mo. 1830. Another edition, edited by Rev. Pitt Cobbett, 2 vols, 8vo. 1885. Cobbett's "Rural Rides" are perhaps more connected with Hampshire and its borders than any other county.

——— *Household Words*, December 3rd, 1853.

Collier (Jeremy) An Ecclesiastical History of Great Britain, 9 vols, 8vo. 1840-41. Refers to Winchester, Southampton, &c.

Connolly (T. W. J.) History of the Royal Sappers and Miners, 1772-1856, 2 vols, large 8vo. 1857. Refers to Southampton, Portsmouth, Jersey, &c.,

Cooke (William) Southern Coast of England, Hand-book of Travel round the. 35 engravings. 8vo. 1849.

Cooper (E. E.) Hide and Seek, a Story of the New Forest in 1647, 8vo. 1881. The Scene is laid at Grove Place House, Nursling.

Cope (Sir William) History of the Rifle Brigade, 8vo. 1877. Many references to Winchester, Aldershot, Portsmouth, &c.

Coppin (Captain) *Chambers' Journal*, April 20th, 1878. Describes remarkable salvage operations at Bembridge, Isle of Wight.

Corbière (J. E.) Scarlet and Buff, 8vo. 1890. A story of the Civil War in Hants.

——— Mont Orgueil Castle, 8vo. 1890. "A well told tale of Jersey during the Wars of the Roses."

Courthope (W.) Baronetage of England, Synopsis of, 8vo. 1835. Hampshire, pp. 5, 12, 36, 39, 63, 115, 134, 148, 172, 190, 220, 230, 240, 245, 247, 250, 252, 254.

Cowes Regatta. *Mirror*, p. 389, vol. xiii. 1829.

Creighton (M.) Life of Simon de Montfort, 12mo. 1876. The Montfort Family lived at Odiham Castle.

Cricket, History of. *English Illustrated Magazine*. September 1884, References to Hampshire cricketers.

Cromwell (Oliver). Quarrel between the Earl of Manchester and Oliver Cromwell: An Episode of the English Civil War. *Camden Society*, sm. 4to. 1875. Important, with reference to the Siege of Basing House, &c.

Cromwell (Richard) and his Wife. *Penny Magazine*, vol. viii., pp. 461,476, 486,490. 1839. Richard Cromwell resided at Hursley.

Cruttwell (Rev. C.) Tour through the whole Island of Great Britain. Hampshire vol. ii., pp. 139, 211, 6 vols, 8vo. 1801.

Cummerbund (C.) From Southampton to Calcutta, 8vo. 1860. Southampton, pp. 1-4.

Curfew Bell, (The). *The Mirror*, April 28th, 1832.

Curtis (William) Life of. Memoirs, Historical and Illustrative of the Botanick Garden at Chelsea belonging to the Society of Apothecaries of London, pp. 80,85, 8vo. 1820. A Native of Alton, Author of Flora Londiniensis.

Dacre (Lady) Tales of Peerage and Peasantry, 3 vols, second edition, 8vo. 1835. The Hampshire Cottage, vol. ii., pp. 161,336.

Dallas (Rev. A. R. C.) Life and Ministry of. By his Widow. 3rd edition. post 8vo. 1872-3. Mr. Dallas was a well known Rector of Wonston.

Danebury, (near Stockbridge) Or the Power of Friendship, a tale with two Odes by a Young Lady. 4to. N.D.

——— See Day.

Dashwood (J. B.) The Thames to the Solent by Canal and Sea, or the Log of the Una Boat " Caprice." sm. 8vo. 1868. Hampshire pp. 65-91.

Day (William, of Danebury) Reminiscences of The Turf. 8vo. 1886. Contains much relating to Hampshire.

Deane (J. B.) Life of Richard Deane, one of the Judges of Charles I. 8vo. London, 1870. Taking of Winchester and Basing House.

Debrett (John) The Baronetage of England. 18mo. London, 1808. 8vo. London, 1840. Contains references to many Hampshire Families.

Defoe (Daniel), Tour Through the whole Island of Great Britain, &c., by a Gentleman. 8vo. 1724. Hampshire pp. 71-82.

De Gray-Birch (Walter) Fasti Monastici Aevi-Saxonici, An Alphabetical List of the Heads of Religious Houses in England previous to the Norman Conquest. 8vo. 1873. Many References to Hampshire Religious Houses.

Devereux (W. B.) Lives and Letters of the Earls of Essex. 2 vols. 8vo. 1853. References to Civil War in Hampshire. vol. ii., pp. 365-441.

Dibden, Ancient Yew Tree at. *Saturday Magazine.* vol. x., p. 47. 1837.

Dibdin (Charles), The Songs of. *Penny Magazine*, vol. x., p. 372. 1841.

Dibdin (Charles). *Mirror*, p. 376, vol. xxxii. 1838.

——— and his Songs. *Cornhill Magazine*, p. 578, vol. xvii. 1868.

——— At Sea. *Temple Bar*, p. 341, vol. lxxviii. 1886.

Dickens (Charles) Nicholas Nickleby, 8vo. N.D. Contains reference to Hindhead. Nicholas Nickleby's introduction to Mr. Crummles, the theatrical manager, took place in Hampshire, the scene being at the Bottom Inn, formerly the Horse and Groom, but now disestablished, between Butser Hill and Horndean, on the road to Portsmouth from Petersfield.

Dixon (Hepworth M.) John Howard and the Prison World of Europe, 12mo. 1849. Watcombe, pp. 92-94.

——— Her Majesty's Tower, 4 vols, 8vo. 1869. Trials at Winchester, vol. ii., pp. 75-82.

——— History of Two Queens, 4 vols, 8vo. 1874. Refers to Cardinal Wolsey, Bishops Fox and Gardiner, &c.

——— Royal Windsor, 4 vols, 8vo. 1879. Many references to William of Wykeham, and other Bishops of Winchester.

Dodd (Anna Bowman) Cathedral Days, a Tour through Southern England, illustrated by E. Eldon Deane, 8vo. 1887. Hampshire, pp. 110-213.

Domesday Book. *Leisure Hour*, p. 766, vol. xv. 1866.

——— of Hampshire. *Frazer's Magazine*, 1866.

——— *Walford's Antiquarian*, pp. 189, 269, vol. i. 1887.

Domus Dei at Portsmouth. *Leisure Hour*, pp. 117, 364, vol. xvi. 1867.

Dowden (Prof. Edw.) Percy Bysshe Shelley, 2 vols, 8vo. 1887. pp. 529-538. Refers to Boscombe and Christchurch.

Down Channel. p. 110, vol. xiv. *Argosy*, 1872.

Drayton (Michael). *Poly-Olbion*, folio. London, 1613. Drayton's Poly-Olbion refers to Hampshire, its forests, rivers, and scenery (about 1610).

Dryden (John), Works of, edited by Sir Walter Scott, 18 vols, 8vo. 1808.
" Annus Mirabilis, The Year of Wonders," (1666). Dryden's " Annus
Mirabilis " contains a reference to Sir Robert Holmes, who lived at
Yarmouth, and was subsequently governor of the Isle of Wight.
" Holmes the Achates of the General's Fight," " Who first bewitched
our eyes with Guinea gold." (*Stanza* 173.) Dryden also wrote an
epitaph, contained in his published works, on John Paulet, fifth
Marquis of Winchester, the defender of Basing—

> He, who in impious times undaunted stood,
> And midst rebellion durst be just and good.

Milton also wrote the epitaph on the first wife of the marquis, and
this is included among his works. This lady is credited with the
authorship of " The Siege of Basing," the MSS. of which is now in
Bodleian Library. Ben Jonson wrote an elegy on the first wife of
the Marquis of Winchester, daughter of Lord Savage—found p. 354,
vol. iii. of his works, published by Hotten.

Dugdale (Sir William) 1605-1686. Monasticon Anglicanum, or the History
of the Ancient Abbeys, Monasteries, &c., in England and Wales,
(continuation by Stevens), 3 vols, folio. 1655, 1667, 1673. Much
information respecting Hampshire Monasteries.

——A Short View of the Late Troubles in England,folio. 1861. Records
the Taking of Winchester, Basing House, &c.

Dunstan (St., Archbishop of Canterbury) Memorials of, large 8vo. 1874.
(Rolls Publications). References to Winchester.

Ecton (John) Liber Valorum et Decimarum. Diocese of Winchester, pp.
334-342. 8vo. 1811.

Edgar (G.) Danes, Saxons, and Normans, or Stories of our Ancestors, 8vo.
1863. Winchester, pp. 35,170,172,230. Isle of Wight, p. 187.
New Forest, pp. 227-230.

Edward (King, The Confessor) Lives of, large 8vo. *Rolls Publications.*
1858. Winchester, C. C. 472,587. L. 667.

Edward I. in Hampshire. *Collectanea Archæologica*, vol. ii. pp. 115,316, &c.

Edward II. in Hampshire. *Collectanea Archæologica*, vol. i. pp. 136,144.

Edward IV., History of the Arrivall of Edward IV. in England, sm. 4to.
1471. *Camden Society*, 1838. Beaulieu, pp. 22-44.

Edwards (E.) Liber Monasterii de Hyda. Edited by E. Edwards, 8vo.
1866.

Edwards (E. Price) Our Seamarks, 8vo. 1884. Needles, p. 32 ; Owers,
p. 100.

Egerton Papers, The (Temp. Elizabeth and James I.), sm. 4to. *Camden
Society.* 1840. Refers to Wichester, Jersey, &c.

Elliot, (Frances). Personal recollections of the Great Duke [of Wellington]
giving accounts of Strathfieldsaye, Hants. 8vo.

Elvetham, Queen Elizabeth's Visit to. *All the Year Round*, p. 467., vol. xi.
1874.

Elwood. Memoirs of Literary Ladies of England, 2 vols, 8vo. 1843.
Life of Jane Austen, vol. ii., pp. 174-186.

England, History of the South Western Portion of. *Arch. Journ.*, vol. xxix.
p. 212. 1872.

England's Black Tribunal, Trial of Charles I. 8vo. 1737. Cheriton Fight
pp. 259, 263, 271. Basing, p. 273.

English Baronets, The. 18mo. 1727. 8vo. 1741.

English History, Political Songs and Poems relating. 2 vols, large 8vo. 1859. *Rolls Publications.* Southampton, vol. i. p. 64 ; Winchester, vol. ii. p. 255 ; Isle of Wight, vol. i. p. 457 ; vol. ii. p. 199.

English Place Names. *Cornhill Magazine.* November 1881. References to Hampshire.

Ethelwerd (Fabius). Chronicle From the Beginning of the World, to the Year of Our Lord, 975. Mention made of Hampshire and the West Saxons.

Evans (John). The Ancient Stone Implements, Weapons, and Ornaments of Great Britain, large 8vo. 1872. References to Hampshire and Guernsey.

Evelyn (J.), Diary and Correspondence of. 4 vols, 8vo. 1852. References to Hampshire, including mention of a large yew tree at Bishop's Sutton. vol. i., p. 375.

Ewing (Julia H.), Story of a Short Life. 8vo. N.D. A Tale of Aldershot Camp.

Eyton (R.W.). Court, Household, and Itinerary of Henry II. 4to. 1878. Refers to Hampshire, Winchester, and Southampton.

Fairholt(F.W.) (Editor) Poems & Songs relating to George Villiers, Duke of Buckingham, and his Assassination (at Portsmouth) by John Felton, August 23rd 1628

Farnham Castle (in Surrey), See Mitford.

Finkley, near Andover. Roman and Saxon Remains at. *Journ, Brit. Arch. Assoc.* vol. xxvii. p. 327. 1872.

Forest Deer, *Once a Week.* p. 155. 1865. Refers to the New Forest.

Forests, English, and Forest Trees. 8vo. 1853. New Forest, pp. 152-176.

Forster (John) Life of Charles Dickens. 3 vols. 8vo. 1874. Undercliff (I.of W.) vol. 11 pp. 396,400-402; Dickens born at Portsea, Vol i.,1-3.

Francis (Francis) and Cooper (Alfred W.) Sporting sketches with pen and pencil. 1878. London, 4to. (Contains Sketches of Hampshire Anglers).

———A Cruise in Hampshire Waters, (in 8 nos.) *Field,* 1860.

———Round Southsea, (in 13 nos.) *Field,* 1865.

Freeman (E A.) English Towns and Districts. 8vo. 1883. Silchester, p. 157 ; Christchurch, p. 165 ; Carisbrooke, p. 172.

———Norman Conquest, 6 vols, 8vo, N.D. Numerous References to Hampshire, Winchester, Romsey, &c.,

French Exiles, Story of The. *Dublin Review,* January, 1887.

Froxfield, Roman Pavement at, p. 191. Vol. iii. *Proc. Soc. Antiq. Lond.*

Fuller (T. A.) Church History of England, 3 vols, 1827. Various references to Hampshire,

Fuller (Dr. Thomas) History of the Worthies of England. folio, 1662. " Thomas Fuller, the Church historian, took refuge at Basing during the Civil War in Hampshire. Here in 1644 he wrote the greater part of his work on the " Worthies of England." While living at Basing during the siege he went on quietly with his work, and merely stated that the noise of the cannon was an inconvenience to him in his literary avocations."

———*Cornhill Magazine,* p. 28. vol. xxiv. 1872.

Gale (Rev. Thomas) D.D. Antonini Iter Britanniarum, 4to. 1709. Describes Roman stations in Hampshire.

Bibliotheca Hantoniensis.

Gale (Frederick) The Game of Cricket. 8vo. 1888. Hampshire Cricket. pp. 27-38.

Gardiner (Linda) "His Heritage" crown 8vo. 1888. Contains descriptions of Winchester and Hampshire.

Gardiner (Samuel R.) History of the Great Civil War (1642-1649) 2 vols. large 8vo. 1866. Describes Cheriton Fight, Siege of Basing, &c.,

Gasquet (Rev. F. A., O.S.B.) Henry VIII. and the English Monasteries (Catholic Standard Library,) 2 vols, 8vo. 1888-9. Contains several references to Hampshire Monasteries.

Gay (John) Beggar's Opera, London, Nov. 1727. "John Gay, the poet and writer, seems to have been about Hampshire a great deal : he wrote his fables at Amesbury, just over the border in Wiltshire. Gay's summer-house is still there. Gay's well-known dramatic work "The Beggar's Opera" is connected closely with Hackwood Park. The original representative of "Polly Peacham" in this was Lavinia Fenton, who ultimately became Duchess of Bolton. The theatre, a "Salon de Musique" still stands in the French garden at Hackwood. Gay's journey to Exeter contains an account of Stockbridge, and an account of the election bribery carried on there."

Gilpin (Rev. W.) Lives of the Reformers, 2 vols 8vo. 1809. Account of Gardiner, Bishop of Winchester, vol ii. pp. 50-84.

Glascock (William Nugent) Naval Sketch Book or Service Afloat and Ashore, 2 vols, post 8vo. 1826. Vol i. Leaves from the Private Log of a Captain (Portsmouth) pp. 34-40; vol ii. A Galley Story. pp. 27-39.

Godwin (Earl) Life and Death of. *Arch. Journ.* pp. 236-330, vol. xi. 1851, p. 47, vol. xii. 1855.

Godwin (F. A.) A Catalogue of the Bishops of England. 8vo. 1615 Bishops of Winchester, pp. 207-267 ; Mitred Abbot of Hyde, p. 699.

Godwin (Rev. G. N.) Buckler's Hard. A Deserted Ship Yard. *Hampshire Observer*, August 30th, 1890.

Gomme (G.L.) Primitive Folk Moots, or Open Air Assemblies in Britain. Hampshire pp. 122, 243, 301 ; Southampton, p. 155, Winchester, pp. 57, 120.

Goodman (Dr. G.) The Court of James I, edited by J. S. Brewer, 2 vols, 8vo, 1839. Queen Elizabeth at Basing, vol. ii. p. 20. ; Executions at Winchester, vol. ii. 87 ; Southampton, vol. ii, 145.

Gough (John) Some Account of the the Alien Priories, and of such lands as they are known to have possessed in England and Wales. 1779. 2 vols, 8vo; second edition, 2 vols, 8vo. 1786. Some of these Priories were in Hampshire.

Granville (Dr. A. B.) The Spas of England and principal Bathing Places. Southern Division, Bournemouth p. 512 ; Isle of Wight—Southampton, pp. 537-558. 8vo. 1841

Great Catastrophe, Centenary of a. *Good Words*, p. 641. 1882. Loss of the *Royal George*.

Great Thinkers and Workers. Lives of Rev. Charles Kingsley and Lord Tennyson.

Grey Abbey by Old Calabar, 2 vols, post 8vo. Relates to Beaulieu and Southampton.

Grose (Francis) Antiquities of England and Wales. 4 vols, super 4to. Supplement 1786-87. 2 vols, sup. r. to. Includes Hampshire.

Bibliotheca Hantoniensis.

Guernsey, Sepulchral Caves in the Isle of. p. 306. *Journ. Brit. Arch. Assoc.*
Vol. i. 1846.

Guizot (M.) History of Richard Cromwell, and the Restoration of Charles
II. translated by A. R. Scoble. 2 vols. 8vo, 1856. See Cromwell and
Hursley

Gurnard Bay, (Isle of Wight) Roman Building in. *Journ. Brit. Arch. Assoc-*
Vol. xxi. p. 351. 1866.

Haggard (H. Rider) Mr. Meeson's Will. 8vo. 1888. Refers to Southampton.

Haines (Rev. Herbert) A Manual of Monumental Brasses. 2 vols, 8vo.
1861. List of Brasses in Hampshire, Vol. ii. pp. 71-76,

Hall (E. Garnett) A Tribute to England's Heroes. Many of these poems
refer to events at Portsmouth and its neighbourhood.

Hall (Mrs. Matthew) Queens before the Conquest. 2 vols, 8vo. London,
1854. Contains lives of Queens Emma and Edith, &c.,

Hall (S.C.) Baronial Halls and Ancient Picturesque Edifices of England.
(many illustrations) 2 vols, 4to. 1858. Bramshill House, vol. ii.

Hamble, Alien Priory of St. Andrew and its Transfer to Winchester
College in 1391. *Archæologia*, pp. 251-262. Vol. L. part II.

Hampshire, An old Family (Tichborne). *All the Year Round.* p. 583. vol.
vi. 1871.

————Arboriculture in. *Trans. of Royal Scottish Arbor. Soc.* Vol. xi. part 3
and vol. xii. part 2.

————Ghost Story A. *Gentlemen's Magazine.* pp. 547, 666, vol. ix. 1872.

————Gilds of. *Antiquarian Magazine and Bibliographer.* p. 302. 1883. vol.
II.

————Hamlet A. *English Illustrated Magazine*, p. 673. July 1888.

————Health Hunting In. *Tourist and Traveller*, pp. 138-185, Aug. Sept.,
1887. Liphook Lanes, (Illustrated).

————Pit dwellings and other early human habitations in. From the
" Etcetera." 8vo. 1872.

————Legends and Traditions of, (The New Forest, Elvetham, Beaulieu
and Winchester, Sir Bevis of Hampton, The Site of Old Southampton.) *All the Year Round*, March and June. 1874.

Hanway (Jonas) *Gentleman's Magazine*, p. 296. vol. 254. 1883. A Native of
Portsmouth.

Hardy (Thomas Duffus) A Description of the Patent Rolls in the Tower
of London, to which is added an Itinerary of King John. 8vo. 1835.
Records visits of King John to various places in Hampshire.

Harford (J.S.) Life of Thomas Burgess, Bishop of Salisbury, (A Native of
Odiham), 8vo, 1840.

Harmony Hall, Notes of a Journey to Harmony Hall, A Socialist Community. 8vo. 1842.

————See Rambles, &c.,

Hawke, Lord. *Army and Navy Magazine*, June 1883.

Hawker (Peter) Instructions for young Sportsmen, 7th. Edition. (Plates),
8vo. 1833 Colonel Hawker, who wrote "Instructions for young
sportsmen" lived at Keyhaven, and was a noted character in his day.
Contains much Information about the Natural History of the South
Western parts of the County.

Hayling Island, Churches of. *Church of England Magazine*, August 5th.
1843.

Bibliotheca Hantoniensis.

Hayling (South), Church. *Church of England Magazine*, January 27th. 1844.

Hayling Island, Tunorbury ; p. 420. *Journ. Brit. Arch. Assoc.* vol. xv. 1884.

—— -Saxon Font in South Hayling Church, p. 65, *Journ. Brit. Arch. Assoc.* vol. xlii. 1886.

Heath (Francis George) Our Woodland Trees, 3rd edition, 8vo. 1878. (The New Forest, pp. 111-192).

——Autumnal Leaves, (Illustrated) 8vo, 1885. The New Forest, pp. 33-180.

——Sylvan Winter, 8vo. 1886. 20 Landscape Drawings of New Forest Scenery.

Heath (James) 1629-1664. A brief Chronicle of the late Intestine War, in the Three Kingdoms of England, Scotland and Ireland. 8vo, 1661. Events in Civil War in Hampshire.

Henty (G.A.) Under Drake's Flag. A Tale of the Spanish Main. Post 8vo. 1882. Refers to Southampton.

Herbert (Sir Thomas) Memoirs of the Two Last Years of Charles I. (with Portrait), 8vo. 1813. Hampshire pp. 54-142.

Herm, Night's Conger Fishing off, *London Society*, p. 334, vol. xlii. 1882.

Heylyn (Peter, D.D) The Two Journeys of. The 2nd. Journey, pp. 277-424 is "A Survey of the estate of the two islands, Guernzey and Jarsey " 8vo. 1656.

——A Help to English History, 12mo, 1709. Winchester, pp. 539-541, Southampton, pp. 496-498, Portsmouth, p. 456. 12mo. 1709.

—— Ecclesia Restaurata or the History of the Reformation of the Church of England (with the Life of the Author by John Barnard, D.D.) 2 vols. crown octavo. 1849.

Highclere Castle, A glimpse of. *English Illustrated Magazine*, April, 1890.

Hissey (James John) On the Box Seat from London to Land's End, 8vo. 1866. Hampshire, pp, 51-109. 8vo. 1866.

Hofland (T .C.) British Angler's Manual. New edition revised and enlarged by C. Jesse, Esq., (Illustrated) 8vo. 1845. Hampshire Rivers, pp. 282-287.

Holiday Making in Mid-Channel. *Belgravia*, p. 183, vol. lx. 1886. See Channel Islands, Herm, Jersey, Sark, &c.,

Hook (Theodore) Jack Brag, 8vo, London, 1839. Refers to Cowes and yachting in the Solent.

Hook (Dr. W.F, Dean of Chichester,) Ecclesiastical Biography, 8vo. 1845-52. Contains lives of Beaufort, Boniface, Waynflete, Wykeham, Andrewes, Fox, Gardiner, Heylyn, Ken, &c.

Horsley (John) Britannia Romana, folio, London, 1753. (Much information as to Roman Stations in Hampshire).

Hoveden (Roger de) Annales. (A.D. 731-1202.) In "Scriptores post Bedam" folio, 1595. Mentions Winchester and Southampton.

Howell (James) 1524-1666, England's Fears for the Present Wars ; curious frontispiece, 4to. 1644.

Howitt (William) Rural Life of England, 2 vols, 8vo. 1838. New Forest vol. ii. pp. 83, 99.

——Visits to Remarkable Places, (Containing an excellent account of Winchester and the New Forest.) 2nd edition. 8vo. 1840.

——See New Forest.

Huntingdon (Henry, Archdeacon of), died after 1154. History of England in eight books from the earlier accounts until 1154. In "Scriptores post Bedam." 1596. folio. Siege of Winchester, Wherwell, Portsmouth, &c.

Hursley, Cromwell (Richard), and {Major (Richard) p. 190. Vol. i. *Second Series. Proc. Soc. Antiq. Lond.*

———A Forgotten Cromwellian Tomb, *Walford's Antiquarian*, p. 91. Vol. 1. 1887.

———Vicarage, Recollections of, *Monthly Packet.*

Hughes (J.) The Boscobel Tracts, Relating to the Escape of Charles the Second after the Battle of Worcester, &c. Much connected with Hambledon and its Neighbourhood. 8vo. 1857.

Inett (J.) Origines Anglicanæ, History of the English Church, 3 vols, 8vo. 1855. Many references to Winchester &c.

Isle of Wight, The. *Mirror*, pp. 178, 231, vol. xxiv. 1834.

Isle of Wight, The. *Saturday Magazine*, vol. iv. pp. 160-191. 1834.

——— *Penny Magazine*, vol. v. pp. 337, 377, 395. 1836.

——— (With pictures of Wilke's Cottage, Sandown). *Mirror*, vol. xx. 1832.

——— In the. *Lippincott's Magazine*. Philadelphia, 1873.

——— Through the. *The Fireside*, 1888.

——— Tunnel. *Chambers' Journal*, p. 751. 1883.

——— Notes on an Unique Implement of Flint found in, (as stated) p. 28. *Arch. Journ.*, vol, xxx. 1873.

——— Investigation into the rude Pit Habitations of the Ancient Britons in Gallibury and Rowborough. *Journ. Brit. Arch. Assoc*, p. 305. vol. xi. 1855.

——— Scratchell's Bay, In. *Penny Magazine*, vol. iii. p. 135. 1834.

——— See Out-door Tuition.

——— Alien Priories in, and their Seizure by Edward the First. *Arch. Journ.* vol. xxix. p. 230. 1872.

Isle of Wight and Southampton. Proceedings of Congress held in the Isle of Wight and at Southampton. *Journ. Brit. Arch. Assoc.* vol. xi. pp. 267, 314. 1855.

Isle of Wight, Discovery of an Ancient British Barrow in the. *Journ. Brit. Arch. Assoc.* vol. xxxviii. p. 109. 1882.

Itchen, A Spring Ramble on the. *Gentleman's Magazine*, 1875.

Jack Ashore. 8vo. 1823. Stories of Portsmouth and Portchester.

Jacob (John) Annals of some of the British Norman Isles constituting the Bailiwick of Guernsey. Large 8vo. 1830.

———(Mrs.) Late Miss Kunnison of Southampton, Poems. 12mo. 1821.

James (Henry) Portraits of Places, 8vo. 1883. Hampshire, pp. 292-297.

Jay (Grantham) Mr. Percy Slipscombe's visit to the Isle of Wight. 8vo. 1873.

Jeaffreson (John Cordy) List of Charters, Letters Patent, and Muniments of the Corporation of Southampton. 8vo. 1886.

Jefferson (Rev. J.) Account of the Roman Mosaic Pavement discovered at Badley Pound Farm, Crondall, in Hampshire, 26th May, 1817. 8vo. 18—

——History of the Holy Ghost Chapel at Basingstoke, with an account of another religious house, and curious antiquities, (2nd edition.) 8vo. 1819.

——Horæ Poeticae. Poems Sacred, Moral, and Descriptive. This is said to be the first book printed at Basingstoke.

——Memoirs of Miss Stapleton [who died at Basingstoke]. 8vo. N.D.

——Ruins of a Temple, a Poem, with an Account of the Holy Ghost Chapel at Basingstoke (vignette.) 4to. 1793.

——Sermon on the death of Miss Sarah Glover, at Basingstoke. 8vo. 1792.

Jenkinson (Henry T. J.) The New Forest, &c., a matter of National Interest. 8vo. 1871.

Jennings (Rev. Dr.) and Doddridge (Dr.) Works of Dr. Isaac Watts with Memoir of his Life. 6 vols., 4to. 1753

Jenkinson (Henry Irwin) Practical Guide to the Isle of Wight. 2nd edition. 8vo. 1879.

Jersey Illustrated, A Holiday Ground, A Health Resort. 4to. N.D. A Fund of Useful Information.

——Post Office Directory of Jersey. . . with Hampshire. 8vo. 1852.

——Guide Pratique de Jersey. 12mo. 1886.

——See Algæ, Le Gros, Sullivan.

—— *Macmillan's Magazine*, p. 474, vol. lix. 1889.

—— *London Society*, p. 57, vol. xlix. 1886.

—— A Week in. *Argosy*, p. 497, vol. xlviii. 1889.

—— Discovery of 400 Roman Coins in. p. 272, *Journ. Brit. Arch. Assoc.* 1849.

—— Castle of Mont. Orgueil. *Once a Week*, p. 713, vol. ix. 1863.

—— Elizabeth Castle. *Penny Magazine*, vol. v., p. 76. 1836.

—— Jottings in. *Once a Week*, p. 216, vol. iii. 1860.

—— My Escape from. *Once a Week*, p. 681, vol. iv. 1861.

—— Recent Tour in. *Mirror*, pp. 260, 278, vol. xiv. 1829.

——— Seaweed Harvest in. *Leisure Hour*, August 1st, 1861. See Algæ.

Jervis, (Thomas) Refutation of an extraordinary Story of a supernatural apparition related by R. Warner. 8vo. 1832.

Jesse (Edward) An Angler's Rambles, 8vo. 1836. Two Days Fly-fishing on the Banks of the Test, pp. 110-125; The Village Cricket Club, pp. 292-311.

—— (J. H.) Memoirs of the Court of England from 1688, 3 vols, 8vo, 1843. Life of the Duchess of Kingston, and other references to Hampshire.

Jewitt (Llewellyn, F.S.A.) Grave Mounds and their Contents, 8vo. 1870. Channel Islands, p. 63; New Forest, pp. 119-165.

Johns (Rev. C. A.) Forest Trees of Britain, 8vo. London, N.D. Refers to the New Forest, pp. 37, 55, &c

Johns (C. A.) Inaugural Address at the Winchester and Hampshire Scientific and Literary Society. 12mo. 1869.

Johnson (Christopher) History of the Life and Intrigues of that celebrated Courtezan and Posture-Mistress, Eliz. Mann, alias Boyle, alias Sample. 8vo. 1724. She was a native of Southampton, of which place and its inhabitants many anecdotes are given. This professes to be the first part only ; the second part is stated to be in the press but, I believe, never was published.

——(Thomas, M.D. (Killed at Basing, 1644.) Mercurius Botanicus sive plantarum gratiâ suscepti itineris, anno 1634 descriptio. 8vo. 1634. This book was the result of a journey with some associates of the Company of Apothecaries through Oxford, to Bath and Bristol, and back by Southampton, the Isle of Wight and Guildford, with the professed design to investigate rare plants.

Jones (Eustace H.) Verses (bearing the Motto " Pergite Pierides ") on the erection of a monument to Isaac Watts at Southampton. 1861.

——The Sir Bevis Guide to Southampton and Netley. 12mo. 1861. Another Edition. 1870.

——(H.) Vectis, or the Isle of Wight, a Poem in three cantos. 4to. 1766.

——(T.E.) Guide to Hayling. 8vo.

Jones (Sir William). *Penny Magazine*, vol. viii., p. 121. 1839. Much connected with Chilbolton.

Journey Book of England, The. sq. post 8vo, sewed. 1841. Includes Hampshire.

Joyce (Rev. J. G.) Excavations on the site of Roman Silchester, made in 1864-5. 4to. 1869.

Judges of Assizes, Riding the Western and Oxford Circuits, Expenses of 1596-1601. *Camden Society*, 1859. Details gifts received and expenses paid at Winchester. sm. 4to.

Keble, A Visit to. *Macmillan's Magazine*, p. 132, vol. xx. 1869.

Kemble (J. M.) The Saxons in England, a History of the English Commonwealth till the Norman Conquest. 2 vols. 8vo. 1849. References to Hampshire.

Ken (Bp.)—Manual of Prayers for use of the Scholars of Winchester College. 12mo. 1679. Frequently Reprinted.

——Life of. *Sharp's London Magazine*, vol. v., p. 192.

Kendall's Picture of England, includes Hampshire. 8vo. 1831.

Kidd (William) Picturesque Companion in a Tour round the Southern Coast of England. (More than 400 engravings by G. W. Bonner). 2 vol. 12mo. N.D.Isle of Wight, vol. i. pp. 1-144.

King Arthur. *Saturday Magazine*. October 31st 1840.

——The Round Table. *Leisure Hour*. December 13th, 1860.

——*Saturday Magazine*, p. 188. vol. ii. 1833.

King's Palace in the Thirteenth Century. *Household Words*. November 1st, 1851. Several References to Hampshire Royal Residences.

Kingsley (Henry). Hetty, and other Stories. 8vo. 1871. Southampton. p. 342.

——(C.) Hereward the Wake. 8vo. 1883. Contains a fine description of Hampshire and Norman Winchester.

——Prose Idylls. post 8vo. 1884. (Refers to Hampshire Angling.)

——Miscellanies. 2 vols. 8vo. 1859-60. Contains descriptions of scenery, and anecdotes of persons, in the neighbourhood of Eversley.

Kingsley (C.) *Belgravia*, p. 71. vol. xxvi. 1875.

———*Macmillan's Magazine*, p. 337. vol. xxxv. 1877.

———*Good Words.* 1882.

———As a Fisherman. *Gentleman's Magazine*, p. 671. vol. 249. 1880.

———In the Saddle. *Gentleman's Magazine*, p. 318, vol. xiv. 1875.

———and Eversley. *Eng. Illust. Mag.*, July 1886.

———Fragments of Teaching in Eversley Church. *Good Words*, 1883. pp. 36, 189, 396, 545, 561, 764.

———Letter from. *Macmillan's Magazine*, p. 71, vol. xxiii., 1871. Concerning Hampshire.

———Miscellanies. *Frazer's Magazine*, 1859.

———The Two Breaths. *Good Words*, July 1st, 1869.

Kingston (Duchess of). *Cornhill Magazine*, p. 151, vol. viii. 1887. See Chudleigh, Scandalous Romance, Trials.

Kitchen Midden at Ventnor, by Mr. Hodder M. Westropp. *Journ. Anthrop. Inst.*, vol. vii., p. 83. 1877.

Knight (E. F.) Cruise of the "Falcon," 8vo. 1884. Southampton, pp. 1-13.

Kohl (K. G.) Travels in England and Wales, 12mo. N.D. Hampshire, pp. 380-420.

Labouring Population, Reports on Sanitary Condition of. 4 vols. 8vo. 1842-3. Hampshire References.

Land, Owners of, in England and Wales. 2 vols. large 4to. 1873. Hampshire References.

Land we live in. 4 vols in 2. Imp. 8vo. (Charles Knight) Lond., N.D. Vol. 1, Description of Portsmouth ; Vol. 2, Isle of Wight ; Vol. 4, Winchester and Southampton.

Langton (Benet) *Cornhill Magazine*, p. 728, vol. xxx. 1874. Friend of Dr. Johnson, buried in St. Michael's Church, Southampton.

Larking (Rev. L.) The Knights Hospitallers in England (with an introduction by J. M. Kemble). sm. 4to. *Camden Society*, 1855. Godesfield, pp. 21-23, also Baddesley.

Le Feuvre (J. E.) Masonic Calendar for Hampshire and the Isle of Wight. 18mo. 1884.

L'Estrange (Rev. A. G.) The Friendships of Mary Russell Mitford. 2 vols. 8vo. 1882. Miss Mitford lived at Alresford. Description of Silchester, vol. ii., p. 67.

Leslie (Robert C.) A Sea Painter's Log. 8vo. 1886. Much reference to the Hampshire Coast.

Light Vessels. *Cornhill Magazine*, p. 33, vol. iii. 1861. Describes Light-Ships on the Hampshire Coast.

Lingard (Rev. John, D.D., a native of Winchester) Memoirs, with Portrait. *Bentley's Miscellany*, 1873.

Lipscomb (G.) A Journey into Cornwall, through the Counties of Southampton, Wilts, Dorset, Somerset and Devon. 8vo. 1799.

Lisle (Dr. Thomas) "Porsenna," and other pieces in Dodsley's Collection. vol. vi., p.p 161, 162-177. 8vo. 1770. References to beautiful scenery about Highclere.

London and South Western Railway. *Murray's Magazine*, p. 802, vol. iii. 1888.

" Longstone " The, and other Pre-Historic Remains in the Isle of Wight. By A. L. Lewis, F.C.A., M.A.J. *Journ. Anthrop. Inst.*, vol. xiv., p. 45. 1885. See also vol. xviii., p. 192. 1889.

Lucas (R. C.) of Chilworth, An Essay on Ancient Glass Painting. sm. 4to. *Spring Time*, 1877. Contains notices of William of Wykeham.

Ludlow (Edmund, Lieut.-Gen.) Memoirs. 3 vols. 8vo. Gives details of the Civil War in Hampshire.

Lyall (Edna) Derrick Vaughan, Novelist. 8vo. 1889. Speaks of Southampton, pp. 20-41.

Lymington. See Winchester.

Lyndhurst. *Gent. Mag.*, p. 353, vol. 256. 1884. See New Forest.

Longparish. Romano—British Interment found at Fir-Grove, near, p. 123. *Journ. Brit. Arch. Assoc.*, vol. xxxvi. 1880.

Macaulay (Dr.) Victoria R. I. Her Life and Reign. (Portraits and illustrations.) small 4to. 1887. Visits to Netley Hospital, pp. 222-224.

Malmesbury (William of) De Gestis Pontificum Anglorum Libri Quinque. roy, 8vo. *Rolls Publications.* 1870. Many references to Winchester, &c.

Malmesbury (Lord), *Temple Bar.* p. 60, vol. 73. 1885.

Marryat (Capt.) Peter Simple. 3 vols. London, 12mo. 1834. Relates to Portsmouth,

——Percival Keene. 8vo. N.D. The Story opens near Southampton.

——Children of The New Forest. 2 vols. 12mo. London. 1847.

——Midshipman Easy. 3 vols. 12mo. London. 1836. Relates to Portsmouth

——(Florence), " Nelly Brooke " London, 8vo. Describes Winchester under the name of " Hilstone."

Marsden (J. B.) History of the Early Puritans, from the Reformation to 1642. 8vo. 1850.

——History of the Later Puritans, from the 1642 to 1662. 8vo. 1852. Stephen Marshall, Minister of Hursley. pp. 112-115.

Mason (Charlotte M.) The Forty Shires, their Scenery, History, Art and Legends. 8vo. 1881. Hampshire, p.p. 354-372.

Meon (East) Description of the Old Font in the Church there in 1789, with some observation on Fonts. *Archæologia*, pp. 183-209, vol. x.

Meon Stoke, Notes on the British Oppidum called " Old Winchester." *Journ. Brit. Arch. Assoc.*, p. 227. vol. xii. 1884.

Mercurius Rusticus or the Countries Complaint of the Barbarous Outrages Committed by the Sectaries of this late flourishing Kingdom. 12mo. 1685. See Civil War Pamphlets, p. 144. Gives an account of damage done at Winchester Cathedral.

Mere Shakings. *Tinsley's Magazine*, p. 463. vol xxxix. 1886. Partly a Southampton Story.

Merewether(H. A) and Stephen (A. J.) History of Boroughs and Municipal Corporations. Andover, p. 338. Christchurch, p. 109. Lymington, p. 1368. Newtown, p. 1367. Petersfield, p. 308, Portsmouth, p. 372. Portswood, p. 751. Ringwood, p 589. Winchester, p. 39. Yarmouth, p. 386. 3 vols. 8vo. 1835.

Merridew (John) The Noble and Renowned History of Guy, Earl of Warwick. 12mo. 1821. Winchester, pp. 124-132.

Middleton (Lieut. E., Late H.M.S.) Cruise of the "Kate," Being a Single-handed voyage in a small Yacht, around England, made in the year 1869. 8vo. 1871. Hampshire, pp. 62-72. New Edition, much altered. 1888.

Milford (Rev. R. N.) History of Farnham Castle, (in Surrey.) References to Civil War in Hants. 12mo. 1874.

Military and Militia Camps in 1778. *All The Year Round*, p. 414. vol. vi. 1871. Interesting details of Hampshire encampments.

Minot (Laurence) Fourteenth Century Poems, Edited by Joseph Ritson. crown 8vo. London, 1795. Second Edition. crown 8vo. London, 1825. In the political poems I. 64 of the Rolls' series are the lines by Minot on the French at Southampton n 1338.

Mitford, Mary Russell. *Argosy*, vol. 38. p. 110. 1884.

Mitford, Mary Russell. *Macmillan's Magazine*, p. 346. vol. xxi. 1870.

Monasteries, Suppression of, Three Chapters of Letters Relating to. small 4to. 1843. Southampton, pp. 202, 213. Winchester, pp. 71, 195, 198, 202, 216, 219.

Money (Walter) The First and Second Battles of Newbury. 8vo. 1884. (Maps, Plans, and Portraits.) Much valuable information concerning the Civil War in Hampshire.

Monks Sherbourn, on Wrought Metal Work at. *Journ. Brit. Arch. Assoc.* p. 264. vol. xxxii. 1876

Montagu (James, Bishop of Winchester,) Will, Inventories, and Funeral Expenses of. vol. xliv. ii. *Archæologia*, pp. 393-421.

——(Lord) of Beaulieu, Letter on Oyster Culture. *Jour. Marine Biol. Assoc.* New Series, vol. i., no. 3., pp. 282-285. April 1890. Deals with Hampshire Oyster Beds.

Morgan (——) Romano-British Mosaic Pavements. Disputes the claims of Bitterne to be on the site of the Roman Clausentum.

Moore (James) A List of the Principal Castles and Monasteries in Great Britain. Hampshire, pp. 15-16.

Murch (Jerome) Mrs. Barbauld and Contemporaries, A Paper read before the Bath Literary and Philosophical Association, Oct. 20th 1876. sewed, 8vo. pp. 36. 1876. Jane Austen, p. 7. Miss Mitford, p. 10.

Napier (Major General Elers) Life and Correspondence of Admiral Sir Charles Napier, K.C.B. 2 vols, large 8vo. 1862. References to Portsmouth, &c.

Neale (J.) The Mutiny at the Nore, and the Mutiny at Spithead. 12mo. N.D. 1797.

Needle Rocks, The. *Saturday Magazine.* Vol. v., p. 172. 1834.

Netley, Roman Coins found at. *Journ. Brit. Arch. Assoc.* Vol. xxiii., pp. 168, 396. 1867.

——Abbey, an Account of an Engraved Brass Plate, by John Latham, M.D., F.R.S. *Archæologia.* p. 302., vol. xv. 1806.

——Abbey, Explanation of a Seal of, by Rev. John Brand. *Archæologia.* pp. 193, 195, vol. xiii. 1807.

——Abbey. *Church of England Magazine*, September 14th, 1844.

——Abbey. Old Humphrey's Country Strolls. London, N.D.

——Abbey. *Gentleman's Magazine.* pp. 172, 657, 684, vol. x., N.S. 1861.

——Abbey, Historical Notice of. *Penny Magazine.* Vol. ii., p. 137. 1833.

——Hospital, Queen's Gift to. *Sunday at Home*, April 7th, 1883.

——Hospital. *Gentleman's Magazine.* p. 71, vol. 249. 1880.

Netley and Haslar Hospitals, " Her Majesty's Nursing Sisters " by Honor Morton. *Illustrated Naval and Military Magazine*, May, 1890.

———Royal Victoria Hospital. *Leisure Hour*, April, 1883.

———See Roman Coins.

New Forest, The. *All the Year Round.* p. 445, vol., xi. 1874. See Lyndhurst.

———Forest, The, In Hampshire. *Saturday Magazine.* Vol. xxv., p. 229. 1844

———Forest. *Leisure Hour.* p. 492. 1882.

———Forest. *Journal of Forestry.* Vols. iii and v. (Several references.)

———Forest, Hogs in the. *Saturday Magazine.* Vol. ix., p. 22. 1836.

———Forest, The, and its Swineherds. *Leisure Hour*, October 14th. 1852.

———Forest and Watering Places of the Hampshire Coast. *Traveller's Magazine.* 1847.

———Forest, The, as a National School, by Francis H. Candy. *Gentleman's Magazine*, March, 1890.

———Forest, Notes on the. *Penny Magazine.* Vol. viii., pp. 357, 367, 460, 475, 498. 1839.

———Forest, In the. *English Illustrated Magazine*, June and July. 1885.

———Forest, Autumn in the. *Once a Week.* p. 537, vol. x. 1863.

———Forest, Autumn from Bramble Hill. *Journal of Forestry.* Vol. vi., p. 404. 1883.

———Forest, Howitt's Walk in the. *Mirror.* p. 39., vol. xxxii. 1838.

———Forest, Cadenham Oak, The, (with Illustration.) *Saturday Magazine*, December 21st. 1833.

———Forest, The Cadnam Oak. *Leisure Hour*, December 20th. 1862.

Noailles (Ambrose de), Ambassades de. Ambrose de Noailles, a writer of the 16th Cent., and French Ambassador, gives an account of Philip IV. at Southampton, where he first tasted English beer.

Noble (Rev. Mark) Memoirs of the Protectorate House. 2 vols., 8vo. 1784 Richard Cromwell and his Family at Hursley. Vol. i., pp. 202-269 Richard Major and his Family at Hursley. Vol. ii., pp. 427-432.

Nonarum Inquisitiones in Curia Scaccarii, folio. 1807. *Hampshire*, pp. 106-127, 459.

Norris Castle, Isle of Wight. *Saturday Magazine.* p. 21. 1835.

Novum Testamentum, Vulgatæ Editionis juxta exemplum Parisiis editum apud fratres Barbon, sumptibus Academiae Oxoniensis in usum Cleri Gallicani in Anglia exulantis. Cura et studio quorundam ex eodem clero Wintonia commorantium Oxonii,e typographio Clarendoniano 1796. There were many refugee French Priests at Winchester in 1796, and they aided in the work.

Nursling, Roman Steel-Yard Weight Found at. *Collectanea Antiqua.* Vol. iv., p. 57.

———Roman Remains found at Nursling. p. 296. *Journ Brit. Arch. Soc.* Vol. xxxvii. 1881.

———Further Notes on, and on other Roman Roads in the New Forest. p. 182. *Journ. Brit. Arch. Assoc.* Vol. xli. 1885.

Odiham, Gold Fibula, found at. p. 46, vol. ii. *Arch. Journ.*, 1846.

Odiham Castle, p. 331. *Arch. Journ.*, vol., xxix. 1872.

Bibliotheca Hantoniensis.

O'Keeffe (John) Recollections of the Life of, written by himself, 2 vols, large
8vo. 1826. Actor and Poet; Resident in Southampton from 1828
till 1833.

Old English Clans. *Cornhill Magazine*, September, 1881.

Oliver (Captain S. P.) On Board a Union Steamer, 8vo. 1881. Hampshire,
pp. 1-5.

Ordericus (Vitalis) The Ecclesiastical History of England and Normandy,
translated by Thomas Forrester, M.A., 3 vols, 8vo. 1854. New
Forest, vol. iii., pp. 259, 260-265.

Organs. A Short Account of Organs built in England from the reign of
King Charles the Second to the Present Time, 12mo. 1847.
Winchester Cathedral, pp. 54, 89, 105; Winchester College, p. 63.

Out-door Tuition. A Visit to the Isle of Wight. *Chambers' Journal*, Oct.
11th, 1845.

Palgrave (Mary E.) Pictorial Geography of the British Isles, folio. 1888.
Contains some Hampshire views and descriptions.

Palmer (S.) Nonconformists' Memorial of the Ministers Ejected in 1662.
Ministers Ejected in Hampshire, vol. ii., pp. 1-29.

Palmerston (Lord). *Once a Week*, p. 548. 1865.

Paris (Matthew) Historia Major, folio. 1640. Bishopric of Winchester,
pp. 11, 17, 23, 35, 37, 50, 187, 216, 217.

Parkinson (A.) Collectanea Anglo-Minoritica, or a Collection of the Antiquities of the English Franciscans or Friers Minors, commonly
called Grey Friers, 4to. 1726. Accounts of Hampshire Monasteries.

Parliament, Members of, from the Earliest Times till 1879. Hampshire
references.

Pauli (Dr. R.) King Alfred, Life of. 8vo. 1853. King Alfred was much
connected with Winchester, &c.

Peacock (M. G.) Index of Royalists whose Estates were confiscated, 4to.
1879. Hampshire, see pp. 26-28, 47.

Pepys (Samuel) Memoirs of, edited by Lord Braybrooke, 2 vols, roy 4to.
1825. Often re-printed. "Samuel Pepys, the author of the well
known Diary, alludes to places in Hampshire in his writings. Being
Secretary to the Admiralty, Pepys had occasionally to travel between
London and Portsmouth. He also took a tour through the county,
and was pleased with Southampton High-street as it was in the 17th
century. He describes his journey over Hindhead, late at night,
and to Liphook, "So to coach and got to Liphook late over Hindhead,
having an old man a guide in the coach with us; but got thither with
a great fear of being out of our way, it being 10 at night. Here good
honest people, and after supper to bed." Pepys must have put up
at the Royal Anchor at Liphook, one of the most noted of Hampshire
Inns, now kept by Mr. J. Peake, and deserving its character of 200
years ago. The Pepys bequest to Magdalene College, Cambridge,
called the Pepsian Library, contains some rare 16th century books
on ships, beautifully illustrated, among which are large engravings
of the ships called Dromons, built at Southampton up the river Itchen.

Perrinchiefe (Richard) Life and Death of Charles I., 8vo. 1676, 1727.
Residence in Isle of Wight, pp. 68-71.

Perry (Rev. George) The Life of St. Hugh of Avalon, Bishop of Lincoln,
8vo. 1879. pp. 188-191, an interesting account of the magnificent
MS. Bible at Winchester. See also the "Magna Vita," p. 92.

Petty (Sir William). *Penny Magazine*, vol. i., p. 61. 1832. A Native of
Romsey.

Piers the Plowman, the Vision of William Concerning, by William Langland, edited by Rev. W. Skeat, M.A. "To Wy and to Winchestre I went to the faire." Winchester Fair is mentioned, Passus v., 205, &c., temp. Edw. I., see Liber Albus, p. 201.

Pitts (Thomas) Western Martyrology, or the Bloody Assizes. . . . together with the Life and Death of George L. Jeffreys. Lady Lisle 156-158.

Placita de Quo Warranto, in Curia Receptae Scaccarii Westm. Asservata, folio. 1818. Hampshire, pp. 763-776.

Placitorum in Domo Capitulari Westmonasteriensi Asservatorum Abbreviatio, folio. 1811. References to Hampshire.

Planché (J. R.) The Conqueror and his Companions, 2 vols, large 8vo. 1874. Hugh de Port of Basing held 55 Hampshire Manors, vol. ii., pp. 249-251.

Plasse (Rev. F. A.) Le Clergé Française refugié en Angleterre, 2 vols, 8vo. 1886. Interesting accounts of Winchester and other places in Hampshire.

Plumpton Correspondence, A Series of Letters, chiefly domestic, written between the Reigns of of Edward IV. and Henry VIII. *Camden Society*, 1839. sm. 4to. Mentions Winchester, Southampton, Portsmouth, &c.

Pococke (Richard) D.D., L.L.D., Bishop of Ossory, A Description of the East, and some other Countries. fol. vol. i., 1743. fol. vol. ii., parts 1 and 2, 1745. Richard Pococke, Bishop of Ossory, a great traveller of his day, was born in Southampton. His writings contain reference to his travels through this county and some details of the New Forest.

Political Songs of England, from the Reign of John to that of Edward II. *Camden Society*, 1839. sm. 4to. (Songs upon Bishops of Winchester).

Pontoys (John de) Successio Episcoporum Wintoniensium, from 1277 to the Reformation. In *Wharton's Anglia Sacra*, pp. 315-319. 2 vols. folio. 1696.

Poole (R. L.) A History of the Huguenots of the Dispersion. 8vo. 1880. Southampton and Rookley, p. 87-88.

Pope (Alexander) Works of, edited by Rossetti. Lond. 8vo. N.D. "Alexander Pope went to school at Twyford, near Winchester. His first poetical performance was a lampoon on his schoolmaster there, which out of a care for his reputation he has not sent down to us. He wrote an inscription on the Crux Easton grotto of the nine sisters Lisle. Pope visited Lord Peterborough at Bevois Mount."

Portal (F. Baron de) Les descendants des Albegios et des Huguenots, ou Memoires de la famille de Portal. 8vo. 1860. This work contains genealogical and historical matter relating to a family that have occupied a considerable position in Hants for the last two centuries

Portchester Castle. vol. xx., 121. *Church of England Magazine.*

Portsdown Fair. *Mirror*, p. 121-3, vol. xx. 1832.

Portsea Sailors' Welcome. *Sunday at Home*, June 3rd, 1882.

Portsmouth Dockyard. *Sharpe's London Magazine*, March-June, 1848, p. 209.

——Dockyard. *Once a Week*, pp. 653, 683, vol. vii. 1862.

——Dockyard, a Day in. *Good Words*, December, 1874.

——How the Bell Ringers Mutinied, and Old Mark rang his own Knell. A Christmas Story of the Reign of Queen Anne. sewed, 6 pp. 8vo By W. H. Saunders.

Bibliotheca Hantoniensis.

Portsmouth (Illustrated) by an East Anglian Bluejacket. *Illustrated Naval and Military Magazine*, May, 1890.

——Old and New, (Soldiers Institute at). *All the Year Round*, p. 202, vol. xx. 1878.

——Our Soldiers and Sailors at Home. A Narrative of Sarah Robinson's Work for them, by Ellice Hopkins. *Good Words*, 1883, p. 170.

——Road, The. *English Illustrated Magazine*, p. 359. Feb. 1888.

——Shoemender of (John Pounds) *Chambers' Journal*, Dec. 20th, 1845. See Pounds.

——See Seaport and Seaside. *Gentleman's Magazine*, p. 220, vol. xiii, 1874. Wightmouth. *Household Words*, April 5th, 1856.

Poste (Beale) *Britannia Antiqua*. 8vo. 1857. Allusions to Hampshire, pp. 312-318.

Pounds (Mr. John) The Gratuitous Instructor of Poor Children. *Penny Magazine*, vol. viii, p. 67. 1839. A Shoemender of Portsmouth.

Pounds (John) The Cobbler. *Sharpe's London Magazine*, vol. x., p. 146. See Portsmouth.

Pratt (J. S.) Harvest Home, consisting of Supplementary Gleanings, Original Dramas and Poems, &c. 3 vols. 8vo. 1805. Several Poems relating to Hampshire.

Pre-Reformation Shrines and Pilgrimages in England. *Cornhill Magazine*. p. 81, vol. xx. 1869. Refers to a famous Crucifix at Winchester.

Priestley (Joseph) Historical Account of the Navigable Rivers, Canals and Railways of Great Britain. 8vo. 1831. Andover Canal, p. 23. Avon River, p. 37. Basingstoke Canal, p. 55. Itchen Navigation, p. 347. Portsmouth and Arundel Canal, p. 527. Salisbury and Southampton Canal, p. 557.

Queen Elizabeth, Processions and Progresses of, *Saturday Magazine*. vol xii. pp. 2, 17, 57, 97, 145. 1838.

——Jane and Queen Mary, *Camden Society*, sm 4to. 1850. Queen Mary's Marriage at Winchester, pp. 77, 78, 134, 144.

——Margaret of Anjou, Letters of Bishop Beckington, and others. *Camden Society*, sm. 4to. 1863. Southampton pp. 111-112, 113, 145, Winchester, p. 93.

——Victoria, The Progresses of Her Majesty Queen Victoria, and H.R.H. Prince Albert, in France, Belgium, and England (Illustrated). 4to. 1844. Hampshire, pp. 2-6.

Rambles from Sidney to Southampton, Recollections of. 1851. Mentions Robert Owen of Harmony Hall. 8vo. p. 337.

Reclus (Elisée) The Universal Geography (European Section), Division VII., Royal 8vo. N.D. Hampshire, pp. 136-141.

Redenham, near Andover, Discoveries at, p. 97. *Jour. Brit. Arch. Assoc.*, Vol. xxxviii. 1882.

Reformation, Narratives of the Days of the. *Camden Society*, sm. 4to. 1859. Winchester pp, 47-57, 168-170.

ice (J.) History of the British Turf, 2 vols. 8vo. 1879. vol. 1. Reference to Stockbridge, etc.,

——and Besant (W.) By Celia's Arbour. 3 vols, cr. 8vo. London. 1878. A story of Portsmouth.

Rimmer (Alfred) Ancient Stone Crosses of England. (73 illustrations on Wood). 8vo. 1875. Winchester " Butter " Cross, pp, 1-5

——About England with Dickens (Illustrated) 8vo. 1883. Describes Portsmouth, p, 121-125,

Ringwood, Monumental Brass at, p. 171. *Antiquary*, Vol. ii. 1889.

Rishanger (William De) Chronicles of the Barons Wars etc., *Camden Society*, 1840. sm 4to, Winchester, pp. 8, 48, 49, 64, 134.

Rivers, Industrial,of the United Kingdom. By various well-known Experts. 8vo. 1888. (Southampton pp. 158-174.)

Rivers, Navigable. See Priestley.

Rivers, Pollution of, Reports of the Commissioners on, 8vols. N.D. References to Hampshire.

Roberts (G.) Life of James, Duke of Monmouth, 2 vols, 8vo. 1844. Capture near Ringwood, pp. 104-121.

——Social History of the People of the Southern Counties of England, 8vo. 1856. Hancock (of Christchurch), pp. 218-223.

——(Mary) Ruins and Old Trees associated with Memorable Events in English History, 8vo. N.D. New Forest, pp. 151-172.

Robinson (F. W.) As Long as She Lived, 3 vols, crown 8vo. 1876. Gives a graphic description of St. Cross.

Roman Roads in the South of Britain. *Gent. Mag.*, pp. 289-305, vol. vii., N.S. 1837.

Romsey Abbey. *Church of England Magazine*, Dec. 6th, 1845.

——Observations on the Sculptures and Inscriptions. *Archælogia*, pp. 141-142, vol. xiv.

——Conjectures respecting the Ancient Sculptures and Inscriptions on Two Pillars at, by William Latham. *Archæologia*, pp. 304-310, vol. xv. 1806.

Romsey, On a bronze stirrup of the Scandinavian Period found near. *Archæologia*, pp. 530-533, vol. l., part ii.

Rotuli Hundredorum, Temp. Hen. III. and Edw. I., In Turr " Lond " et in Curià Scaccarii Westmr Asservati, 2 vols, folio. 1818. Hampshire, pp. 220-224.

Rotulorum Originalorum in Curià Scaccarii Abbreviatio, 2 vols, folio. 1805. Many Hampshire references.

Royal George, Loss of (at Spithead), Stories relating to, Cowper's Poem upon. *Leisure Hour*, Oct. 21st, 1858.

——Loss of the. *Penny Magazine*, vol. i., p. 127. 1832.

——Narrative of the Loss of. *Penny Magazine*, vol. iii., p. 174. 1834.

Rufus (William) Death of. *Leisure Hour*, p. 743, vol. xv. 1866.

Rushworth (John) 1607-1690. Historical Collections from 1618 to 1648. A Storehouse of Civil War Information.

Russell (Lady Rachel) Letters of. 4to. "London, 1773. The neighbourhood of Stratton and Micheldever appears in English literature in the well-known letters of Lady Rachel Russell to her husband and friends, some of which were written there. " Lady Russell's walk " is a local name still known at Stratton."

Russell (Lady Rachel Wrothesley) Some account of the Life of; followed by a Series of Letters from Lady Russell to her husband, William, Lord Russell, from 1672-1682, 8vo. 1819. Many allusions to Stratton.

Rutland Papers, The Original Documents Illustrative of the Courts and Times of Henry VII. and Henry VIII., sm. 4to. Camden Society, 1842. Visit of Charles V. to England, p. 100.

Ryde, Regatta Week at. *London Society*, p. 282, vol. xvi. 1889.

Rye (William Brenchley) England as seen by Foreigners in the days of Elizabeth and James the First, sm. 4to. 1865. Isle of Wight, p. 48 ; Winchester College, p. 25.

Salmon (Nathaniel) New Survey of England. 2 vols., 8vo. 1731. (Includes Hampshire.)

Sammes (Aylett.) *Britannia Antiqua Illustrated.* Folio. 1676. Kingdom of the West Saxons, pp. 561-582.

Sandford (——) and Meredith (——). *The Great Governing Families of England.* 8vo. 1865. The Montagus. p. 303.

Sark, A Reminiscence. *Time.* p. 121, vol. vii. 1882.

——A Tradition of. *Chambers' Journal,* August 8th. 1846.

——A Week's Imprisonment in. *Cornhill Magazine.* p. 537, vol. iv. 1862.

——Just a Peep at. *London Society.* p. 470, vol. xxxvii. 1880

——Caves and Rocks of. *Good Words.* 1885.

Saull (W. D.) Notitia Britanniæ or Observations Illustrative of the Early History of the Aborigines of Britain. St. Catherine's Hill, p. 13. Roman Road, p. 32. 8vo. 1845.

Scandalous Romance, A, (Duchess of Kingston). *Temple Bar.* p. 531, vol. lix. 1880. See Chudleigh, also Duchess of Kingston.

Schools Inquiry Commission. 12 vols., 8vo. 1868. Refers to Hampshire.

Scott (Sir Walter) Poetical Works of. Edited by Rossetti. 8vo. N.D. "Sir Walter Scott resided with Mr. Rose during the summer of 1807, and he wrote part of ' Marmion '· while living in Hampshire. The introduction to Canto I of ' Marmion ' is dedicated to William Stewart Rose, Esq., and the last eighteen lines of this introduction relate entirely to the New Forest and to the hero of Southampton's legendary history—

> Well has thy fair achievements shown
> A worthy meed may thus be won.
> Ytene's oaks, beneath whose shades
> Their theme the merry minstrels made,
> Of Ascupart, and Bevois bold,
> And that Red King, who while of old
> Through Boldrewood the chase he lead,
> By his loved huntsman's arrow bled."

Scudamore (Charles) A Chemical and Medical Report on the properties of the Mineral Waters of Buxton, Matlock, Tunbridge Wells, Harrogate, Bath, Cheltenham, Leamington, Malvern, and the Isle of Wight. 8vo. 1820.

Seaport and Sea-Side (Portsmouth) *Gentleman's Magazine,* p. 220. vol. xiii. 1874. See Wightmouth.

Sea-Side Watering Places, Giving accounts of Hampshire Watering Places, etc.. 8vo. sewed. London, N.D.

Selborne, A day at. *Once a Week,* p. 25. vol. viii. 1862-3.

——Description of. *Saturday Magazine,* Vol x., p. 8. 1837.

——White's Natural History of. *Penny Magazine,* Vol ii., p. 36. 1833.

——a Pilgrimage to. *Chambers' Journal,* August 22nd. 1846.

——Gilbert White's Residence at, (with illustrations) *Mirror,* p. 313, vol. xvi. 1830.

——Past and Present, Rev. J. Vaughan M.A. *Murray's Magazine,* March, 1890.

——The Centenary of White's. *National Review,* March, 1890.

Bibliotheca Hantoniensis.

Serres (Jean) of Montauban, Huguenot Galley Slave, Memorials of, afterwards a resident in England. Buried in Winchester Cathedral. sm. 4to, p. 4. 1889.

Shakespeare (William) Chronicle History of Henry the Fifth. 4to. 1608. Refers to Southampton. Act ii. Chorus. Scene ii. (" Southampton " also Hampton) Act iii. Chorus.

——The Contention of the Two Famous Houses of York and Lancaster in 2 parts. 4to. 1600. Act ii., Scene iii. "As Bevis of Southampton fell on Ascapart." Refers to Winchester Part 1. (13) (14) (iii. i.) (v. i4.) Part ii. (1. i.)

——Enterlude of King Henry VIII. 4to. 1604. Allusions to Winchester (iii. 2.) (iv. 1.) (v. 2.)

——The History of Troilus and Cressida. 4to. 1609. Refers to Winchester (v. 11.)

Shalfield Church (Isle of Wight), Sculptured slab in. p. 302. *Journ. Brit. Arch. Assoc.* vol. xi. 1855.

Shanklin. *Once a Week*, p. 551. vol. iv. 1861. See also Walford.

Shaw (S.) A Tour to the West of England in 1788. 8vo. 1789. Hampshire, pp. 479-526.

Ship Biscuit made by Machinery, (Royal Clarence Yard, Gosport,) *Saturday Magazine*, Vol. x., p. 154. 1837.

Shipwrecks, Great; A Record of Perils and Disasters at Sea, 1544-1877. Loss of the *Mary Rose*, p. 9, of the *Royal George*, p. 88.

Shirefield, Copy of the Original Letters Patent of the 44th year of King Edward III. relative to the Manor of. *Archæologia*, pp. 398-399. vol. xv.

Shooting and Fishing Trips in England, France, Alsace, Belgium, Holland and Bavaria. Solent and Southampton Water Vol i., p. 80. Vol. ii., p. 165, Christchurch Bay and Harbour, Vol. 1., p. 111.

Shore (T. W.) F.G.S.,F.C.S. (some of the numerous papers contributed by) The Manor of Odiham, *Hampshire Antiquary*, vol. i. The Meon Country, *Hampshire Antiquary*, vol. i. Old Hampshire Industries, *Hampshire Antiquary*, vol. i. The Basis of Hampshire History, *Hampshire Antiquary*, vol. i.

——Characteristic Survivals of the Celts in Hampshire. *Journ. Anthrop. Inst.* 1890. Early Boroughs in Hampshire. *Archæological Review*, Nov. 1889. The Ancient Water Gate of Southampton Castle. *Antiquary*, April, 1887. A List of Ancient Camps and other Earthworks in Hampshire, and remarks on their present condition. *Hampshire Field Club Papers and Proceedings.* 1889.

——Vestiges of Old Southampton. Description of the Plates and Etchings by F. McFadden. Gilbert, 1890. Traces of Ancient Sun Worship in Hampshire and Wiltshire. *Report Brit. Assoc.*, 1886. Birmingham Meeting.

——Orientation of Hampshire Churches. *Walford's Antiquarian*, Sept. 1886. The Ancient Venetian Trade with Southampton. *Southampton Times*, Dec. 24th and 31st, 1886.

——Old Roads and Fords of Hampshire. *Archæological Review*, April, 1882. Old Iron Works in Hampshire. *Antiquary*, May, 1887. Traces of Old Agricultural Communities in Hampshire. *Antiquary*, Feb. 1888. Titchfield and its Associations, a Paper read at the Meeting of the Hampshire Field Club. *Hampshire Independent*, Jan. 2nd, 1888.

[193]

Shore (T. W.) Ellingham, Moyles Court, and Ancient Hampshire Courts. *Hampshire Independent*, Aug. 1888. Stoke Charity and Micheldever. *Hampshire Antiquary*, vol. i. The Manor of Woodcote and the Geology of Bramdean Valley. *Hampshire Independent*, July 7th, 1888. Some Hampshire Persons and Places in connection with English Literature. *Hampshire Independent*, December, 1885, to January, 1886.

——The Clays of Hampshire and their Economic Uses, Hants Field Club Papers, iv. 23.

Shorwell (Isle of Wight) Discovery of Rural Paintings at. *Journ. Brit. Arch. Assoc.*, vol. iii. 1848.

Silchester, p. 227. *Arch. Journ.*, vol. viii. 1851.

——The Excavations at, with plan of the Basilica and Forum. p. 10, *Arch. Journ.* vol. xxx. 1873.

——Roman Eagle found at. p. 183. *Journ. Brit. Arch. Assoc.*, June, 1873.

——Description of a Gold Ring of a singular formation discovered at. *Archæologia*, p. 449. vol. viii.

——Account of a curious Roman Eagle in steel, discovered at. *Archæologia*, p. 370. vol. ix.

——On the Excavations at. Three Notices. *Archæologia*, pp. 403-416, vol. 40, part 2 ; pp. 329-343, vol. 46, part 2 ; pp. 344-365, vol. 46, part 2.

——Survey of that part of the Roman Road called the Imperial Way, which lies between Silchester and Staines. *Gentleman's Magazine*, p. 535. vol. v, N.S. 1836.

Six Weeks Tour through the Southern Counties of England and Wales. 8vo. London. 1768.

Smith (C. Roach, F.S.A.) Retrospections. 8vo. Discusses the claims of Bitterne to be on the site of the Roman Clausentum.

Soames (H.) History and Revenues of the Anglo-Saxon Church. 8vo. 1838. Hampshire, *Chaps*, iii. and iv.

Solent, Across the. *London Society*. 1865.

Southampton, Account of. *Saturday Magazine*. vol. xi., p. 2. 1837.

——Some Notices of Records preserved among the Corporation Archives at. p. 229, vol. iii. *Arch. Journ.* 1846.

——On the Building called the King's House, and other Architectural Remains in the Town of Southampton. p. 7, vol. iv. *Arch. Journ.*, 1847.

——Artesian Well at. *Chambers' Journal*, p. 474. 1883.

——Archæological Institute at. 1872. Extract from the " Guardian " Newspaper.

——Bar-Gate, Notice of. *Penny Magazine*, vol. ii. p. 185. 1833.

——Coffee Room, or Bound for the Brazils. *Household Words*. October 13th, 1855. Embarkation at Southampton.

——Overland Mail at. *Household Words*. May 1st, 1852.

——Railway. *Mirror*, p. 424. vol. 31. 1838.

——Saxon Remains Found at. *Collectanea Antiqua*, vol. iv., p. 58.

——See Isle of Wight.

Southey (C. A.) Poetical Works. New Edition. 1876. 12mo. " The Broken Bridge," refers to Boldre.

——(Robert) His Second Wife. *Cornhill Magazine*, p. 217. vol. xxx. 1874.

Southwick, Priory of, Notices of, in the County of Southampton. p. 214 vol. iii. *Arch Journ.* 1846.

Speed (John) 1555-1629. The History of Great Britain. Folio. 1614. Many references to Hampshire.

Spelman (Sir John) and Hearne (Thomas). Alfred the Great. 8vo. 1709. King Alfred resided at Winchester. Many other " Lives " published.

Sportsmen, Young, Instructions for. See Hawker.

Sprigge (Joshua) Anglia Rediviva, England's Recovery, being the History of the Army under Sir Thomas Fairfax. 1645. folio. 1647. Records Military Events in Hampshire.

Staunton (Howard) Great Schools of England, (Winchester College &c.) 8vo. London, 1869.

St. Cross, Hospital and Church of. *Penny Magazine,* vol. viii. pp. 425-446. 1839.

――――Hospital of. *Church of England Magazine.* August 19th, 1843.

――――A Pilgrimage to. *Once a Week,* p. 18. 1869.

――――Church, Winchester. *Once a Week,* p. 445. 1872.

――――Winchester, Famous Abbeys and Castles. *Pictorial World,* February 6th, 1890.

Stephens (A. J.) See Merewether.

――――(M. R. W.) Life and Letters of Walter Farquhar Hook (Dean of Chichester). 2 vols., 8vo. 1879. p. 24, Describes Rebellion at Winchester College in 1818.

Sternhold and Hopkins' Psalms. *Quiver.* p. 341. 1889. Sternhold who composed 53 Psalms, owned Slackstead Manor, near Hursley.

Stevens (Dr. Abel) History of Methodism. 2 vols., roy 8vo. N.D. Channel Islands. Vol. ii., 80, 250.

Stillingfleet (E., Bishop) Origines Britannicae : or the Antiquities of the British Churches. Folio. 1685. Hampshire, pp. 323, 340, &c.

Stirling (Edward) John Felton, A Play, In Three Acts. No. 30 of The British Drama. Dicks, London. Relates to Murder of Duke of Buckingham at Portsmouth, temp. Charles I., post 8vo.

St. John (J. A.) The Life of Sir Walter Raleigh. 2 vols., 8vo. 1868. Trial and Sentence at Winchester. Vol. ii., pp. 119, 171.

St. Mary Bourne, The Font at. *Journ. Brit. Arch. Assoc.* Vol. xxxvi., p. 30. 1880.

Stoke Charity. See Winchfield.

Strathfieldsaye. *Penny Magazine.* Vol. viii., p. 369. 1839. The residence of the Duke of Wellington.

Tedworth, The Drummer of. *All the Year Round.* p. 462., vol. vi. 1871. A Tale of 1661 on the borders of Wilts and Hants.

Stuart Esmé, The Prisoner's Daughter, A Story of 1758. 8vo., N.D. A Story of French Refugees in Winchester.

Stukeley (William, D.D.) Itinerarium Curiosum . . . . . Travels through Great Britain illustrated with Copper Prints. Folio. 1724. Hampshire. pp. 183-187. Some curious Hampshire Prints.

――――An Account of Richard of Cirencester, Monk of Westminster, and of his Work. . . . . and the Itinerary of Roman Britain. 4to. 1757. (Map).

Symonds (Richard) Diary of the Marches of the Royal Army, during the Great Civil War. *Camden Society.* sm. 4to. 1859. Alresford, Andover, Basing, &c.

Tanner (Thomas) Notitia Monastica, or a Short History of Religious Houses in England and Wales. 12mo. 1695. (Hampshire Monasteries. pp. 75, 83.)

Taxatio Ecclesiastica Angliæ et Walliæ auctoritate P. Nicolai IV. circa. 1291. Folio. 1802. Hampshire Parishes. pp. 210-215.

Taylor (Rev. Isaac) Scenes in England for Tarry-at-Home Travellers. 12mo. 1822.

——(John) A Catalogue of Tavernes in tenne Shires about London. 12mo. 1636.

——(John) The Water Poet, All the Works of, being 63 in number. 4to. 1630. Hampshire. pp. 25, 33.

Temple, The Family of. *Cornhill Magazine.* p. 749, vol. xii. 1865.

Tennyson (Lord) Poems. 8vo. London, 1889. His poems contain allusions to Isle of Wight. See Invitation to Rev. F. D. Maurice, and the sonnet written in the garden at Swainston.

Teonge (Rev. Henry) The Diary of, Chaplain on Board H.M.S. *Assistance, Bristol* and *Royal Oak,* Anno, 167-5, now first published from the original MS. 8vo. London, 1823. Gives accounts of Portsmouth and Portchester.

Test (River). See Jesse.

Testa De Nevill sive Liber Feodorum in Curia Scaccarii. Folio. 1807. Hampshire. pp. 230-242.

Thiselton-Dyer (T. F.) *English Folk-Lore.* 8vo. 1880. Isle of Wight. p. 134.

Thompson (James) Works of. 4 vols., 12mo. London, 1750. " James Thompson, the poet, was the friend and guest of the Stanley family, at Paulton's Park. He alludes to Miss Stanley in " Summer," beginning at line 546—
    And art thou Stanley, of that sacred band ?
His epitaph on Miss Stanley, in Holy Rood Church, Southampton, is well-known, and included in all editions of his works."

——(Dr. Spencer) Health Resorts of Britain and How to Profit by them. 8vo. 1860. Hampshire and the Channel Islands. pp. 117-148.

Thorpe (Benjamin) edited by, The Anglo-Saxon Chronicle according to the Several Original Authorities, with a Translation, 2 vols, 8vo. 1861.

Timbs (John) and Gunn (Alexander) Abbeys, Castles, and Ancient Halls of England and Wales, 3 vols, 8vo. 1873. Hampshire, vol. ii., pp. 384-439 ; Channel Islands, pp. 533-539.

Towns, Health of, Commission Reports, 8 vols, 8vo. 1844-5. References to Hampshire.

——Large, Report of Commissioners for enquiring into the State of. 4 vols. 8vo. 1844-5. Hampshire References.

Trial of Charles I. and of some of the Regicides, &c., with Biographies of Bradshaw, Ireton, Harrison, and others, with notes, 8vo. 1832. Refers to Isle of Wight, Hurst Castle, and Winchester.

Trials. An exact Abridgement of all the. . . . in the Reigns of King William III. and of. . . . Queen Anne, 12mo. 1703. Last Speech of Madam Lisle, beheaded at Winchester in Sept. 1685, p. 407.

——State, Complete Collection of, from the Eleventh Year of King Richard II., till the 16th Year of King George III., 11 vols, folio. 1781. Dowager Duchess of Kingston, vol. xi., pp. 198-264 ; Trials of Sir Walter Raleigh at Winchester, vols i., vii., viii.

Trollope (Anthony) The Warden, post 8vo. 1855. Often said to be based upon the history of the Hospital of St. Cross.

——Barchester Towers, 3 vols, post 8vo. 1857 "I was struck with the resemblance which Trollope's Cathedral City bears to our own." *Hampshire Notes and Queries,* vol. i., 19.

——An Autobiography, 3 vols, 8vo. 1889. Winchester College, vol. i., pp. 8-14.

Tucker (Colonel J. M.) The Life of the Duke of Wellington, numerous engravings, large 8vo. N.D. The "Iron Duke" resided for many years at Strathfieldsaye. Many other "Memoirs" by various authors.

Turner (T. H.) and Parker (J. H.) Some Account of Domestic Architecture in England, from Richard II. to Henry VIII., 4 vols, 8vo. 1851-9. Hampshire, vol. i., p. 32, vol. ii. pp. 293, 295, vol. iii., p. 322.

Tyler (Rev. J. E.) Henry of Monmouth, or Memoirs of the Life and Character of Henry V., 2 vols, 8vo. 1839. Hampshire, vol. ii., 105-144.

Tytler (P. F.) The Life of Sir Walter Raleigh, 8vo. 1832. Trial and Sentence at Winchester, pp. 263-310.

Undercliff, Isle of Wight. *Chambers' Journal,* July 29th, 1848. (See Ventnor).

Valor Ecclesiasticus, Temp. Henry VIII., 6 vols, folio. 1810. Hampshire and Channel Islands, vol. ii., 1-27.

Ventnor and the Undercliff in Summer and Winter. *London Society,* p. 546, vol. xxxvii. 1880.

——National Hospital, p. 270. *London Society,* vol. xvi. 1889.

Vergil (Polydore) English History, (1422-1485), sm. 4to. Camden Society, 1844. Southampton, vol. i., p. 16; Winchester, vol. i., pp. 35, 180, 244; Wherwell Abbey, vol. i., p. 241; Isle of Wight, 17, 112, 149, 179, 181; Beaulieu, vol. iii., p. 148.

Vetusta Monumenta; published by Soc. Antiq., 6 vols, folio. 1747. Description of the Hospital of St. Mary Magdalen near Winchester, (2 plates) &c.

Vicars (John) 1582-1652; Magnalia Dei Anglicani, or England's Parliamentary Chronicle, 4to. 1646. Describes the Siege of Portsmouth, 1642.

Victory (H.M.S.) *Chambers' Journal,* February, 1888.

Vyne in Hampshire, History of the. *Edin. Review,* vol. clxix., p. 44. 1889.

Waagen. Treasures of Art in Great Britain. 3 vols. 8vo. 1854 Winchester Cathedral and College. vol. iii., pp. 135-6.

Wakefield (Priscilla) Family Tour through the British Empire. 8vo. 1840. (Hampshire, pp. 443-464).

Walcott (Mackenzie E. C.) Guide to the South Coast of England, from the Reculvers to the Land End, &c. Thick 12mo. Cloth. Folding maps. 1859.

Walford (Edward) Pleasant Days in Pleasant Places. 8vo. 1878. A Day at Shanklin, p. 16. A Summer Day at Beaulieu, p. 234.

Walker (Rev. John) An Attempt towards recovering an account of the Numbers and Sufferings of the Church of England . . . in the late times of the Grand Rebellion. folio. 1714. Gives accounts of many deprived Hampshire Clergymen.

Waller (Sir William) Parliamentary General. Vindication of his Character &c. 8vo. 1793. "Valuable and Interesting." Refers to Civil War

Walpole (Right Hon. Horace) Letters of, (Edited by Peter Cunningham) 9 vols. 8vo. 1858-9. " Horace Walpole, in his celebrated letters, has many references to the Vyne, near Basingstoke, one of the most famous country houses. This was the seat of his friend Mr. Chute. Walpole's letters also contain a description of Netley, and what he wrote concerning Ælia Lœlia Chudleigh is wholly connected with a Hampshire event, viz., Miss Chudleigh's marriage at Lainston, &c." See Chute.

——(G. A.) The New British Traveller, or a complete . . . display of Great Britain and Ireland, being a New Tour through England, Wales, Scotland, Ireland, the Isles of Man, Wight, &c. folio. (1784).

Walsingham (Sir Francis) Journal of (1570-1583.) *Camden Miscellany.* small 4to. vol. vi. 1871. Gives information about Queen Elizabeth's Progresses in Hampshire.

Walton (Isaak) Waltoniana, Inedited Remains in Prose and Verse of. with Notes and Preface by Richard Herne Shepherd. 8vo. London. 1878. Contains Isaak Walton's Will, made at Winchester, August 9th, 1683.

Warblington Castle. *Church of England Magazine*, February 15th, 1845.

Warburton (George) Memoir of Charles Mordaunt, Earl of Peterborough and Monmouth. 2 vols. 8vo. 1853. Lord Peterborough resided at Bevois Mount.

Warnford. Observations on an Ancient Building at Warnford. *Archæologia*, pp. 357, 366. vol. v.

Warton (Rev. Joseph) D.D. Odes on various Subjects. London. 4to. 1746. p. 47. 8vo. 1794. Many of his poems relate to Hampshire, such as : Ode to a Friend on leaving Winslade ; A Sonnet written at Winslade ; Prologue on the old Winchester Play-House,

——(Thomas). *Cornhill Magazine*, p. 733. vol. xi. 1865.

——(Thomas). Poet Laureate, Letter of. *Walford's Antiquarian*, p. 62. vol. ii. 1887.

Wartons, The. *Cornhill Magazine*, p. 534. vol. xxx. 1874.

Watts (Isaac) The Father of modern English Hymn Writers. *Quiver*, 1881.

Watts (Rev. T.) D.D. 1674-1748. " Horae Lyricæ " (Lyric Poems) 1706. 12mo. Contains an Elegant Latin Ode to the Rev. John Pinhorne, Master of the Free School, Southampton.

——(Isaac) D.D. *Sunday at Home*, May 1st. 1869.

Wass (Charles) History of the French Protestant Refugees. Translated by Frederick Hardman. large 8vo. 1854. Southampton, pp. 210, 217.

Wellington (Duke of), See Tucker.

Wedgewerth (Julia) John Wesley and his Evangelical Reaction of the 18th Century. 8vo. 1870. Refers to Hampshire.

Wendover (Roger De) Flowers of History, the Latin Edition by the Rev. H. O. Cox of the Bodleian Library, published by the English Historical Society. Bohn, 8vo, 1849. Many references to Hampshire.

Westwood(T). and Satchell (T).Bibliotheca Piscatoria,a Catalogue of Books on Angling, the Fisheries and Fish Culture. 8vo. 1883. References to Hampshire Streams, p. 99.

Whippingham Church (Isle of Wight). *Sunday at Home*, p. 535. vol. xi. 1864.

White, Gilbert. See Selborne.

White, Gilbert and Selborne. *Leisure Hour*, December 8th. 1853,

Whitelock (Sir Bulstrode) 1605-1676. Memorials of the English Affairs from the beginning of the Reign of King Charles I. to King Charles II. his Happy Restoration. folio. 1682. (Civil War occurrences in Hampshire.)

Wightmouth, *Household Words*, April 5th. 1856. Graphic Description of Portsmouth.

Wilberforce (R.G.) and Ashwell (Rev. Canon) Life of Samuel Wilberforce D.D., Bishop of Oxford and Winchester. 3 vols, 8vo. 1879.

———(Bishop), *Blackwoods' Magazine*, p. 291, vol. 133. 1883.

Willis (B.) Parochiale Anglicanum, or the names of all the Churches and Chapels within the Dioceses of Canterbury, Rochester, London, Winchester, etc., 4to. 1733.

———A survey of the Cathedrals of York, Durham, Carlisle, &c. 3 vols, 4to, 1742. Contains list of Hampshire Parishes in the annexed Parochiale Anglicanum.

——— 1682 - 1760. Notitia Parliamentaria, containing an account of the First Returns and Incorporations of the Cities, Towns, and Boroughs of England and Wales. 8vo. 1750.

Wilmot (Sir John E. Eardley, Bart.) Reminiscences of the late Thomas Assheton Smith, Esq., of Tedworth, Hants, (Illustrations and Portrait). 8vo. 1860. Another Edition. 1862.

Winchester, A Sketch of Fallen Greatness, *A*1. *Magazine*, Sept. and Oct 1889.

———In and About. *Cassell's Family Magazine*, Dec. 1881.

———Altar Inscribed to the Deæ Matres, found at. *Collectanea Antiqua*, vol. iv. p. 41.

———in the 13th. Century, Original Documents. *Arch. Journal*, No. 23.

———Ancient Consuetudinary of. p. 69. *Arch. Journ.* Vol. ix. 1852.

———Observations on the Wait Service mentioned in the Liber Winton, and on the supposed monastery of Sapalanda. p. 339, vol. iii. *Arch. Journ.* 1846.

———Trial of Sir Walter Raleigh, Sheriff's Expenses at. pp. 58-63, vol i Second Series. *Proc. Soc. Antiq. Lond.*

———Mediæval Mill at. p. 291. *Walford's Antiquarian*. Vol. ii. 1885.

———Early Hanoverian Quarter Sessions at. p. 71. *Antiquary*. Vol. ii. 1889.

———Archæological Meeting at. *Chambers' Edinburgh Journal*, November 8th. 1845.

———Bishop of, (Bp. Sumner). *Sunday at Home*. p. 792, vol. xi. 1864.

———(Bishops of) Arms at Esher. *Gentleman's Magazine*. p. 238, vol. viii. N.S. 1837.

———Butter Cross at. *Saturday Magazine*. Vol. xxiii, p. 201. 1843.

———Market Cross. *Penny Magazine*. Vol. v., p. 295. 1836.

———Market Place. *Mirror*. p. 266, vol. 32. 1838.

———Christening of Prince Arthur at. *Monthly Magazine*. 1812.

——— History of the Round Table at. *Sharpe's London Magazine*. vol. ii. p. 90.

———Wall Paintings and Roman Altar at. *Collectanea Antiqua*. vol. iii. p. 271.

Bibliotheca Hantoniensis.

Winchester to Lymington as the crow flies, Due South. *All the Year Round*, October, 9th. 1869.

——Cathedral, Historical Notice of. *Penny Magazine.* vol. ii. p. 332. 1833.

——Cathedral. *Saturday Magazine.* p. 201. vol. vi. 1835.

——Cathedral. *Sunday at Home.* December 23rd, 1871.

——Cathedral. *Century.* p. 323. vol. 38. 1888.

——Cathedral. *Century Magazine.* July. 1889.

——Cathedral. Observations on an effigy called that of William of Foix. *Journ. Brit. Arch. Assoc.* p. 216. vol. i. 1846.

——Cathedral. Remarks on the effigy of a Knight in. p. 125. *Arch. Journ.* vol. xv. 1858.

——Cathedral. Opening and Removal of a Tomb reputed to be that of King William Rufus. *Arch.* pp. 309-321. vol. 42, ii.

——Cathedral, Izaak Walton's Tomb in. p. 246. *Antiquary.* vol. ii. 1889.

——Cathedral, Colouring in the Norman Arches of. p. 92. vol. i *Proc. Soc Antiq.* London.

——Cathedral, Discoveries in. pp. 140, 187. *Walford's Antiquarian.* 1886. vol. i.

——Cathedral, Report on the recent discoveries at. p. 300. *Journ. Brit. Arch. Assoc.* vol. xlii. 1886.

——Cathedral. See Waagen.

——Fagging at. *Mirror.* p. 365. vol. xii. 1828.

——College and its Library. *Penny Magazine.* Vol. ix., pp. 41, 54, 63. 1840.

——College, Catalogue of Books belonging to. p. 59. *Arch. Journ.* Vol. xv. 1858.

——College. " Dulce Domum," Historical Notice of. *Saturday Magazine.* Vol. xxi., p. 205. 1842.

——College (St. Mary's.) *Church of England Magazine,* June 3rd. 1843.

——College, Reminiscences of. *Temple Bar.* 1873.

——College (with Illustrations). *Art Journal,* May. 1890.

——College, some Ornaments discovered in. p. 159. *Journ. Brit. Arch. Assoc.* Vol. x. 1854.

——College. See Waagen.

——Palace. *Mirror.* p. 274, vol. 36. 1840. See King's Palace.

——Sonnet on Leaving. Mirror. p. 259, vol. xiv. 1829.

Winchfield and Stoke Charity, Discoveries of Mediæval Paintings, &c. *Journ. Brit. Arch. Assoc.* Vol. vi., p. 76. 1851. See also vol. v., p. 265.

Wither George, Abuses Stript and Whipt. sm. 8vo. London, 1613. " Of other poets we must not omit George Wither, the Puritan poet, born at Bentworth, 1588. In his " Abuses stript and whipt " he alludes to " the beechy shadows " of " our Bentworth." He sold his paternal estate at Bentworth to raise a troop of horse for the Parliament. Wither alludes to the legend of Bevis in terms of contempt—
> Bevis of Hampton or such trumpery.

Butler alludes to George Wither, in Hudibras—Part I, Canto II, line 645—
> Thou that with ale or viler liquors
> Didst inspire Wither, Pryn, and Vicars

Wither (George) *Sunday at Home*, Nov. 2nd, 1854.

――*Macmillan*, May, 1890.

――(with portrait). See English Lyrics under the First Charles. *Harper's Monthly Magazine*, May, 1890.

――(Honest George). *Day of Rest*, July, 1875.

Wood (Anthony) Athenæ and Fasti Oxoniensis, 2 vols, folio. 1691-2. Gives accounts of several Hampshire persons.

――(Rev. J. G.) The Brook and its Banks, sm. 4to. N.D. Refers to New Forest.

Wooll (Rev. John) Biographical Memoirs of the late Joseph Warton, D.D., (with portrait), 4to. 1806. Head Master of Winchester College, &c.

Worboise (Emma Jane) Maude Bolingbroke, 8vo. 1882. A Hampshire story.

Worcester (Florence of) Chronicon from the Creation till 1118, with anonymous continuation till 1141. 4to. London, 1592. Many references to Winchester.

Wordsworth (Elizabeth) See Overton.

Worsley (Sir A.) Museum Worsleyanum. 2 vols, folio. 1824. Relates to the Isle of Wight.

Wright (Thomas) Three Chapters of Letters relating to the Suppression of the Monasteries. *Camden Society*, 1843. sm. 4to. Gives details concerning Hampshire Monasteries.

――Biographia Brittannica Literaria, Anglo-Saxon Period. 8vo. 1842. Lives of St. Boniface, Asser, Alfred the Great, etc.,

――The Celt, Roman, and Saxon, History of the early inhabitants of Britain. 8vo. 1852. References to Bitterne, Portchester, etc.,

Wriothesley (Charles) A Chronicle of England, during the Reigns of the Tudors (1485-1559) 2 vols. *Camden Society*. small 4to. 1877. Queen Mary's Marriage at Winchester. pp. 118-121.

――Earl of Southampton. *All the Year Round*. p. 181, vol. vi. 1871. Interred at Titchfield Church under a stately monument.

Wykeham, William of. *Saturday Magazine*. March 29th. 1834.

――William of. *Church of England Magazine*. January 13th. February 10th. 1844.

――William of, His Architecture. *Gentleman's Magazine*. vol. i., N.S 1834.

Yateley, Crystal Cup at. p. 396. vol. iii. Second Series. *Proc. Soc. Antiq.* London.

A LIST

OF

Hampshire Newspapers,

COMPILED BY F. A. EDWARDS.

Beyond the lists of papers in Mitchell's, May's, Sell's and other newspaper press guides—which necessarily exclude defunct papers—I am not aware of any attempt to make an approximately complete list of those connected with the county. The following is by no means perfect, but it will serve as a nucleus, any additions to which—or corrections—will be welcome. I have included the names of some newspapers, not actually printed in the county, which make a practice of publishing correspondence from the parts of Hampshire adjacent to their own counties. The papers marked with an asterisk (*) are still published.

F. A. EDWARDS.

Hampshire Independent Office.

ALDERSHOT AND FARNHAM OBSERVER. 1872. Lasted about a year.

*ALDERSHOT CAMP GAZETTE. Established 1879. Became *May's Aldershot Camp Gazette*, 1886. Wednesday 1d.

ALDERSHOT CAMP TIMES. 1869. Lived about 9 months.

*ALDERSHOT GAZETTE. Established 1859. A localized issue of *Surrey and Hants News* (Farnham). Friday 1d.

*ALTON AND PETERSFIELD OBSERVER (Winchester). Established 1877. A localized edition of the *Hampshire Observer* (q.v.). Saturday 1d.

*ANDOVER ADVERTISER AND NORTH HANTS GAZETTE. Established 1837 [Sell], 1857 [Mitchell], or 1858 [May]. Friday 1d.

ANDOVER CHRONICLE. Established 1870. *North Hants Telegraph* incorporated with it,——? Incorporated with the *Andover Standard* (q.v.) 1879.

*ANDOVER STANDARD AND NORTH HANTS CHRONICLE. Established 1858. *Andover Chronicle* (q.v.) incorporated with it, 1879. Friday 1d. Conservative.

Bibliotheca Hantoniensis.

THE ARGUS ; OR RECORD OF POLITICS, LITERATURE, AND THE ARTS AND SCIENCES (Southampton). No. 1—1831 Feb. 5. No. 8 (and last)—1831 May 21. 8vo. "Published every other Saturday morning." 6d. This is not strictly a newspaper, but as it deals largely with politics of the time it can hardly be excluded from this list.

BASINGSTOKE OBSERVER. Established 1883, August 11. Incorporated with the *Winchester Observer*, 1884.

BASINGSTOKE STANDARD AND NORTH WILTS GAZETTE. Ceased several years ago.

BOURNEMOUTH GAZETTE AND HANTS AND DORSET CONSERVATIVE JOURNAL. Established 1889. No. 43—1890 February 1, the last number published. Friday, 1d.

*THE BOURNEMOUTH GUARDIAN. Established 1883 August. Saturday. 1d. Liberal. A localized issue of the *Southern Guardian* (*q.v.*)

*THE BOURNEMOUTH OBSERVER AND GENERAL VISITORS' LIST. Established, 1875 March 31, Wednesday. 1d.

*BOURNEMOUTH VISITORS' DIRECTORY, AND POOLE, CHRISTCHURCH AND EAST DORSET ADVERTISER. Established 1858 as a fortnightly publication. Soon became a weekly. and about 1879 a bi-weekly. Wednesday and Saturday. 1d.

*CHAT (Portsmouth). Established 1884. Friday. 1d.

CHRISTCHURCH CHRONICLE. Incorporated with the *Observer and Chronicle for Hants*, 1879.

CHRISTCHURCH GUARDIAN. Established 1883. Incorporated with the *Southern Guardian*, 1887, or with the *Bournemouth Guardian*.

*CHRISTCHURCH TIMES. Established 1855, June 30. Saturday. 1d.

*THE CHRISTIAN CITIZEN : AN ADVOCATE OF RIGHTEOUSNESS IN RELIGION, POLITICS AND SOCIAL LIFE (Portsmouth). No. 1—1890 May 1. royal 8vo. 52 pages and wrappers, 1d.

COUNTY CHRONICLE. Established 1787. This paper is spoken of as having made "many profitable tours one hundred miles round London." For various editions the title at one time was preceded by *Middlesex, Hertfordshire, Bedfordshire, Berkshire, Buckinghamshire, Surrey, Hampshire*, or *Essex*. [May's Press Guide (1889), pp. 208, 210.]

CRESCENT (Portsmouth). No. 17—1888 March 16. Friday. 8 pages of 4 columns. 1d.

DIAL (Portsmouth). 1880 Aug. 3 numbers only published.

EVENING ECHO (Portsmouth). No. 1—1888 July 7. Saturday. Last number—1888 July 12. Daily. Liberal. 4 pages. ½d.

*EVENING MAIL FOR HAMPSHIRE, ISLE OF WIGHT AND SUSSEX (Portsmouth). Established 1884, Jan. Daily. ½d. Conservative. [See *Printers' &c., Effective Advertiser* (1889, Feb.) p. 41.]

*EVENING NEWS (Portsmouth). Established 1877, April. *Southern Standard* incorporated with it, 1883? Daily ½d. Liberal.

EVENING STAR (Southsea). Commenced, 1882 Sept 6. Stopped 1883 Nov. 17.

FUN AND GOSSIP : RADICAL-POLITICAL, QUIZZICAL AND SATIRICAL, COMICAL AND FARCICAL, SPORTING AND THEATRICAL, AND IN NO SENSE DULL, HEAVY AND LACKADAISICAL (Landport). No. 3—1887 Sept. 29. Saturday. 16 pages 4to. 1d.

THE GNAT (Ventnor). Wednesday ½d. See *Ventnor Post*.

Bibliotheca Hantoniensis.

THE GOSPORT TIMES AND PORTSMOUTH, ISLE OF WIGHT, AND SUSSEX WEEKLY NEWS. No. 1—1886 January 5, Friday. A localized issue of the *Hampshire Independent*. No. 54 (the last)—1867 January 11.

HAMPSHIRE ADVERTISER (Southampton).—See *Southampton Herald*.

*HAMPSHIRE CHRONICLE. Established at Southampton, 1772, as the *Hampshire Chronicle or Southampton, Winchester, and Portsmouth Mercury*. No. 3—Monday 1772 September 7. 2½d. Sub-title dropped, 1775 August 15. Office removed to Winchester and first number printed there, 1778 June 1. Monday, 3d. Title became *Salisbury and Winchester Journal and Hampshire Chronicle*, 1784 January 5, and for a few weeks the second title was *Hampshire and Wiltshire Chronicle* but *Wiltshire* was dropped 1784 August 16. There were thus two *Salisbury and Winchester Journals* in the field at one time. With No. 690, Monday, 1785 December 5, name changed to *The Hampshire Chronicle and Portsmouth and Chichester Journal*. Price raised to 3½d., 1789 August 8. Enlarged to 20 columns, 4d., 1795 September 29. Price increased to 6d., 1797. Sub-title altered to *Winchester, Southampton, Portsmouth and Chichester Journal*, 1800 March. Became the *Hampshire Chronicle and Weekly Advertiser for the Counties of Southampton, Sussex, Surrey, Berks and Dorset*, 1806. Price raised to 6½d., 1809 May 29. Enlarged, 1813 September 27, and name *Hampshire Chronicle and South and West of England Pilot*. In September 1814 it was called the *Hampshire Courier* for a few weeks. Price raised to 7d., 1836 September. Name became *Hampshire Chronicle and Courier*, 1816 July. No. 2283—Monday, 1818 February 9, *The Hampshire Chronicle and Courier; Portsmouth, Portsea, Gosport, Chichester, Salisbury, Winchester, Southampton and Isle of Wight Gazette; and South of England Pilot; Or Naval, Military, Commercial and Agricultural Register for the Counties of Hants, Sussex, Surrey, Berks, Wilts and Dorset*. 7d. In 1823 it became the *Hampshire Chronicle and Southampton Courier*. Reduced to 5d., 1836 September 19. Enlarged 1837 May. Day of publication altered to Saturday, 1844 January 6. Enlarged to 8 pages (40 columns), 1849 May, price 2d.; and to 48 columns, 1881. Present title: *Hampshire Chronicle, Basingstoke, Andover, Alton, Alresford, Southampton, and Isle of Wight Courier, and General Advertiser for the South and West of England*.

HAMPSHIRE CHRONICLE, OR PORTSMOUTH, WINCHESTER AND SOUTHAMPTON GAZETTE. Established 1778 September, at Southampton, in opposition to the *Hampshire Chronicle* published at Winchester. Saturday. 3d. Removed to Portsmouth, 1780. Office destroyed by fire and publication ceased, about 1785-6.

HAMPSHIRE COUNTY TIMES (Portsmouth). Established 1873 January [Mitchell's Directory and Sell's Dictionary], or 1885 [May's Press Guide (1889)]. A Wednesday edition of the *Portsmouth Times (q.v.)*. Discontinued 1889 Dec. 25.

HAMPSHIRE COURIER (Portsmouth). Published from 1809 to 1815 (or later). Monday. 7½d.

HAMPSHIRE COURIER (Winchester). The *Hampshire Chronicle (q.v.)* was for a few weeks published under this title (1814 September).

*THE HAMPSHIRE HERALD AND ALDERSHOT ARMY REVIEW (Alton). Established 1885. Friday. 1d. Conservative.

*THE HAMPSHIRE INDEPENDENT, ISLE OF WIGHT AND SOUTH OF ENGLAND ADVERTISER (Southampton). No. 1—Saturday, 1835 March 28. 4 pages, 7d. Price reduced to 4½d., 1836 September 17, and time of publication altered from Saturday afternoon to Saturday morning. Price raised to 5d., 1837 July 1. Increased to 8 pages, price 6d., 1846 March 21. Reduced to 3d. unstamped, 4d.

stamped, 1858 April 3. Extra issue on Wednesdays, price 1d., commenced 1861 October 1, and price of Saturday issue reduced to 2d. [This was the first penny newspaper in the county.] Saturday issue reduced to 1d., 1870 January 1. Daily issue commenced, 1870, January 3; discontinued, 1872 March 31. The Wednesday issue merged in *The Southern Echo (q.v.)*, 1888 August 22. Enlarged to 64 columns, 1889 Feb. 9. Saturday. 1d. Liberal. [See *Gosport Times.*]

*Hampshire Observer (Winchester). *Winchester Observer (q.v.)* became *Hampshire Observer*, 1886 [Willing's Press Guide] or 1887 [Sell's Dictionary]. Saturday. 1d. Liberal Unionist.

*Hampshire Post (Portsmouth). Established 1874 as *Southsea Observer (q.v.)*. Friday. 1d.

*Hampshire Telegraph and Sussex Chronicle, and General Advertiser for Hants, Sussex, Surrey, Dorset and Wilts (Portsmouth). Liberal. Established 1799 Oct. 14. 4 pages. 6d. *The Sussex Chronicle* amalgamated with it, and the paper enlarged, 1803. Price raised to 6½d., 1815 ; reduced to 4d., 1860. A Wednesday issue at 1d. started, 1865 July 5, the Saturday issue being reduced to 2d. The Wednesday issue discontinued, 1883 October.

*Hants and Berks Gazette and Middlesex and Surrey Journal (Basingstoke). Established 1878. Saturday. 1d.

The Hants and Dorset Journal, and Bournemouth, Poole and Christchurch Conservative Gazette (Bournemouth). No 11 —1889 June 22. Saturday.

*Hants and Surrey Times (Aldershot). *May's Aldershot Advertiser (q.v.)* became *Hants and Surrey Times*, 1880. Friday. 1d.

*The Herald and Southampton Free Press. No. 132—1890 June 20 4 pages weekly. Gratis.

*Island Standard (Sandown). Established 1887. Saturday 1d.

*Isle of Wight Advertiser and Ryde and Ventnor Times (Ventnor). Established 1859 August 27. *Ryde and Ventnor Times (q.v.)* incorporated with it,——? Saturday. 1d. Conservative.

*Isle of Wight Chronicle (Sandown). Established 1866 May. Thursday. 1d. Conservative.

*Isle of Wight County Press (Newport, I.W.) Established 1884 November 29. Saturday. 1d.

*Isle of Wight Express, Island Liberal Newspaper. Established at Ventnor, 1870 April. *Shanklin and Sandown Weekly News* incorporated with it, 1887. Removed to Newport, 1890 January 25.

*The Isle of Wight Herald and Cowes Visitors' Directory (Cowes). Established 1864. Saturday. 1d. Conservative.

Isle of Wight Journal, Newport Times amd General County News (Portsmouth). Established 1870. An Island edition of the *Portsmouth Times*. Saturday. 1d. Discontinued 1890.

*Isle of Wight Mercury. Established 1855. Ceased 1863. Restarted 1868 ? Became *Ventnor Gazette*, 1884. Became *Isle of Wight Mercury and Ventnor Gazette*, 1890. Wednesday. 1d.

*Isle of Wight Observer (Ryde). Established 1852 September 4. The oldest newspaper printed in the Isle of Wight. Saturday. 1½d. Conservative.

*Isle of Wight Times and Hampshire Gazette (Ryde). Established 1862 April. Thursday. 1½d. Liberal.

Lantern (Portsmouth). After 1880. August. 1d.

*LYMINGTON AND SOUTH HANTS CHRONICLE. Established 1857 Nov 13. Thursday. 1d. Liberal. A localized edition of the *Poole and Bournemouth Herald* (*q.v.*). [See *The World's Printers' &c. Effective Advertiser* (1888 July), p. 25.]

LYMINGTON OBSERVER. Established 1867. Incorporated with the *Observer and Chronicle for Hants*, 1879.

MAY'S ALDERSHOT ADVERTISER. *May's Monthly Circular* (*q.v.*) became *May's Aldershot Advertiser*, 1879. Became *Hants and Surrey Times* (*q.v.*) 1880.

MAY'S MONTHLY CIRCULAR (Aldershot). Established 1879. Became *May's Aldershot Advertiser* (*q.v.*), 1879.

MAY'S ALDERSHOT CAMP GAZETTE. See *Aldershot Camp Gazette.*

THE MONITOR (Portsmouth). No. 1.—1878 June 22. Ceased 1880. July 17. Saturday. 12 pages demy 4to. 1d.

*THE NEWBURY EXPRESS. A CONSTITUTIONAL JOURNAL FOR BERKS, HANTS AND WILTS. Establ. 1886. Thursday. 1d.

*THE NEWBURY WEEKLY NEWS AND GENERAL ADVERTISER FOR SOUTH BERKS, WEST HANTS AND EAST WILTS (Newbury). Establ. 1867. Thursday. 1d.

NEW FOREST GUARDIAN (Bournemouth). *Ringwood Guardian* became *New Forest Guardian*, 1885. An edition of the *Bournemouth Guardian.* Iucorporated with the *Southern Guardian*, 1887.

NEWPORT ECHO. [Brown's Advertiser's A.B.C. (1890) p. 567.]

NEWPORT TIMES. A local edition of the *Portsmouth Times.* Establ.—? Ceased —?

NORTH HANTS TELEGRAPH. Incorporated with *Andover Chronicle,*—?

*THE OBSERVER AND CHRONICLE FOR HANTS AND DORSET (Bournemouth). Establ. 1872 April. *Christchurch Chronicle, Poole Sun, and Lymington Observer* incorporated with it, 1879. Saturday. 1d. Conservative.

*THE PARROT (Portsmouth). 1890. 1d.

*PETERSFIELD EXPRESS AND EAST HANTS JOURNAL (Lewes, Sussex). Establ. 1864. A localized issue of the *Sussex Agricultural Express* (Lewes). Tuesday. 1d. Conservative.

*PETERSFIELD WEEKLY NEWS. Establ, 1883. Wednesday. 1d.

*POOLE AND BOURNEMOUTH HERALD (Poole). Establ. 1846 April 9, as the *Poole and Dorsetshire Herald*, which became *Poole and Southwestern Herald*, 1849, and became *Poole and Bournemouth Herald*, 1877 June. Thursday. 1d. Liberal. [See *Lymington and South Hants Chronicle.*]

PORTSEA AND GOSPORT JOURNAL (Portsea). Establ. 1802. Ceased——? Sunday morning. 6½d.

THE PORTSMOUTH AND GOSPORT GAZETTE AND SALISBURY JOURNAL (Salisbury). Establ. 1736-8? No. 736—1752 February 24. This was evidently a localized edition of the *Salisbury Journal.*

*PORTSMOUTH TIMES AND NAVAL GAZETTE. No. 1—1850, March 30, 4 pages, price 5d. Increased to 8 pages, 1850 June 22. Enlarged 1853 July 2, price 6d. Price reduced to 5d., 1853 July 7; 3d., 1857 November 28; and 2d., 1861 April 4. Wednesday issue, price 1d., commenced, 1872 April 3. Enlarged to 56 columns 1873. Price reduced to 1d., 1880 Jan. 30, and Wednesday paper enlarged to 8 pages. *West Sussex County Chronicle* (establ. 1877) incorporated with it, 1880. Enlarged, 1889 Dec. 28, on the discontinuance of the Wednesday edition—the *Hampshire County Times.* Saturday. Conservative. [See *The World's Printers', &c., Effective Advertiser* (1889 Feb. 1) p. 41.]

Bibliotheca Hantoniensis.

THE PORTSMOUTH PIONEER: A CHRONICLE OF THE PRINCIPAL LOCAL EVENTS AND HAMPSHIRE FREE PRESS. No. 8—1883 February 24. Saturday. 8 pages of 3 columns, demy folio. 1d.

THE PORTSMOUTH, PORTSEA AND GOSPORT HERALD. Establ. 1829 August. Ceased 1835. Sunday. 7d. 4 pages.

RINGWOOD GUARDIAN. Establ. 1883. Became *New Forest Guardian (q.v.)*, 1885.

ROMSEY CHRONICLE. Establ. 1854. Ceased——?

*ROMSEY REGISTER. Establ. 1861. Alternate Thursdays. 1d.

ROMSEY STANDARD. Incorporated with *Andover Standard*.

THE ROMSEY WEEKLY REGISTER. No. {3—1816 December 16. Monday. 1½d. 4 pages, 8¾in. x 10½in.

*RYDE AND ISLE OF WIGHT NEWS. Establ. 1869. Friday. 1d.

RYDE AND VENTNOR TIMES. Establ. 1857. Incorporated with the *Isle of Wight Advertiser*.

*THE SALISBURY AND WINCHESTER JOURNAL (Salisbury). Establ. 1729 as the *Salisbury Journal*. Became the *Salisbury and Winchester Journal*, 1772 December 7. At present, Saturday, 8 pages, 2d. Contains correspondence from Winchester and western parts of the county. [See *Portsmouth and Gosport Gazette*.]

SALISBURY AND WINCHESTER JOURNAL (Winchester). This title was adopted by the *Hampshire Chronicle* for a short time (1784 January 5 to 1785 Dec. 5), doubtless to combat the already existing *Salisbury and Winchester Journal*.

SANDOWN FREE PRESS. Establ. 1883. Incorporated with the *Shanklin and Sandown Weekly News*, 1886.

SHANKLIN AND SANDOWN WEEKLY NEWS. *Shanklin Weekly News* became *Shanklin and Sandown Weekly News*, 1886. *Sandown Free Press* incorporated with it, 1886. Incorporated with the *Isle of Wight Express*, 1887.

SHANKLIN FREE PRESS. Establ. ——? Incorporated with the *Shanklin Weekly News*, —— ?

SHANKLIN WEEKLY NEWS. Establ. 1878. *Shanklin Free Press* incorporated with it, —— ? Became *Shanklin and Sandown Weekly News*, 1886.

*SHELDRAKE'S ALDERSHOT AND SANDHURST MILITARY GAZETTE AND FARNHAM CHRONICLE (Aldershot). Establ. 1859 August 6. Saturday. 1d. Conservative.

*THE SOUTHAMPTON HERALD AND ISLE OF WIGHT GAZETTE. No. 1— Monday, 1823 July 28. Price 7d. Name changed to *Southampton Town and County Herald, Isle of Wight Gazette, and General Advertiser*, 1825 ; and again to *Hampshire Advertiser and Royal Yacht Club Gazette*, 1831 September 29. A Wednesday issue, 1d., started, 1869 March 31, the Saturday issue being reduced from 4d. to 2d. Conservative.

THE SOUTHAMPTON LUMINARY AND COUNTY CHRONICLE, ISLE OF WIGHT, PORTSMOUTH, WINCHESTER AND LYMINGTON GAZETTE (Southampton). No. 3—Sunday, 1822 April 28. Price 7d. No. 16—Monday, 1822 July 29. Ceased —— ?

*SOUTHAMPTON OBSERVER AND WINCHESTER NEWS (Southampton). Establ. 1867. Saturday. 1d. Conservative.

SOUTHAMPTON STANDARD. About 1870 ? Only lasted about a fortnight ?

*SOUTHAMPTON TIMES AND HAMPSHIRE EXPRESS. Establ. 1860. Saturday. 1d. Liberal.

*Southern Counties Review (Basingstoke). No. 2—1890 April 19. Saturday. 1d. 8 pages demy folio, illustrated.

*The Southern Echo (Southampton). Established 1888 August 20. Daily. ½d. 4 pages.

Southern Gazette (Alton). About 1875. Became *Winchester Observer.*

Southern Guardian (Wimborne). Established 1887. *New Forest Guardian* and *Christchurch Guardian* incorporated with it, 1887. Saturday. 1d. Liberal. [Same as *Bournemouth Guardian ?*]

Southern Post (Bournemouth). Established 1885.

The Southern Reformer, a Political, Social and Critical Review for the Southern Counties (Southampton). No. 1—1880 May 29. 45th and last No., 1881 May. Saturday. 1d.

The Southern Standard and Hampshire Evening Telegraph (Portsmouth). No. 3—1883 September 26. Wednesday. Daily. 4 pages ½d. Incorporated with the *Evening News,*—?

South Hants Daily Press (Southsea). No. 55—1880 March 4. 4 pages, ½d.

South Hants Evening Star (Southampton). No. 1—1888 August 20 ½d. Ceased, 1888 August 27.

Southsea Observer. Established 1874. Became *Hampshire Post,* 1874.

*Surrey and Hants News (Farnham). Established 1859. Saturday. 1d

Ventnor Gazette. See *Isle of Wight Mercury.*

Weekly Illustrated Isle of Wight Guardian (Shanklin). Established 1882 October. Saturday. 1d.

*Western Chronicle (Yeovil). *Sherborne, Dorchester, and Taunton Journal* became *Western Chronicle,* 1886. Friday. 1d. Liberal.

*The Western Gazette (Yeovil). Established 1863. Friday, 1d.

*West Sussex Gazette (Arundel, Sussex). Established 1853. Thursday. 1d.

Wide Awake : a Journal for Gosport, Portsmouth, and Isle of Wight (Southsea). No. 5—1881 April 2. 12 pages demy 4to. Saturday. 1d. [A successor to *The Monitor ?*]

Winchester Herald. Established 1869. Saturday. 1d. Conservative Ceased——?

Winchester Journal or Weekly Review (Reading and Winchester). Established 1743 ; No. 84—1745 May—. 4 folio pages, 2d. Ceased ——?

Winchester Observer and County News. Established 1877 August. Liberal. *Basingstoke Observer (q.v.)* incorporated with it, 1884. Became *Hampshire Observer* 1886 or 1887.

*Wykehamist (Winchester). Winchester School Magazine. Established ——? About monthly, except during vacation. 4d.

FOSSILIA HANTONIENSIA

COLLECTA,

ET IN MUSÆO BRITANNICO

DEPOSITA,

A

GUSTAVO BRANDER

R. S. & S. A. S. Muf. Brit. Cur.

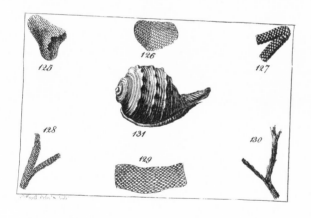

L O N D I N I.   1766.

[Figure 10; 19.5 x 25.6 cm]

GEOLOGICAL EXCURSIONS

ROUND

THE ISLE OF WIGHT,

AND ALONG THE

ADJACENT COAST OF DORSETSHIRE;

ILLUSTRATIVE OF THE MOST

INTERESTING GEOLOGICAL PHENOMENA, AND ORGANIC REMAINS.

BY

GIDEON ALGERNON MANTELL, ESQ. LL.D. F.R.S.

AUTHOR OF " THE MEDALS OF CREATION ;"
" THOUGHTS ON ANIMALCULES ;"
ETC.

FOSSIL LOBSTER FROM ATHERFIELD.

" That beautiful Island, which he who once sees never forgets, through whatever part of the wide world his future path may lead him."
SIR WALTER SCOTT's *Surgeon's Daughter.*

LONDON:

HENRY G. BOHN, YORK STREET, COVENT GARDEN.

M DCCC XLVII.

[Figure 11; 11.5 x 18.3 cm]

WORKS

ON THE

Natural History & Geololgy of Hampshire.

Angell (A.) Notes on a Collection of Foraminifera from the Chalk in the neighbourhood (Winchester). *Rep. Winchester and Hants Sci. & Lit. Soc. for* 1870-71, p. 20.

——— Notes on the Probable Origin of Flints. *Journ. Winchester Sci. & Lit. Soc.*, vol. i, part 3, pp. 146-151. 1874.

Animal Remains. (Bones at Northwood, Isle of Wight). (Anon). *Phil. Mag.*, vol lii,, p. 68, 1818.

Austin (Rev. J. H.) A Guide to the Geology of Purbeck and the S.W. Coast of Hampshire. 8vo. Blandford, 1852.

Barrington (Hon. D.) Some account of a Fossil lately found near Christchurch in Hampshire. *Phil. Trans.*, vol. lxiii., part i.. p. 171. 1773

Barrois (Ch.) Sur la Craie de l'Ile de Wight. (On the chalk of the Isle of Wight). *Ann. Soc. Geol. Nord.* t. i., pp. 74-81 ; *Bull. Soc. Geol. France*, ser. 3, t. ii., pp. 428-433. 1874.

——— Ondulations de la Craie dans le Sud de l'Angleterre. (Undulations of the Chalk in the South of England). *Ann. Soc. Geol. Nord.* t. ii. pp. 85-111. 1874.

——— Description Géologique de la Craie de l'Ile de Wight. (Of the Chalk of the Isle of Wight). *Ann. Soc. Geol.* ser. 4, t. vi. livr. 2, p. 30. 1874.

——— L'Age des debouches, Blackdowny, Devonshire. *Ann. Soc. Geol. Nord.*, t. iii., p. 1-8. 1875. Describes the U. Greensand of the Isle of Wight and Dorsetshire.

Bell (Professor T.) See Owen.

Berger (Dr. J. F.) Sketch of the Geology of some parts of Hampshire and Dorsetshire. *Tran. Geol. Soc.*, vol. i., p. 249. 1811.

Beyrich (Prof.) On the Demarcation of the Oligocene Division of the Tertiary Period. *Quart. Journ. Geol. Soc.*, vol. xx., part 2, p. 5. 1864

Birds (J. A.) Geology of the Channel Islands. *Geol. Mag. dec.* 2, vol. v., pp. 79-86. Woodcut (Geol. section)., pp. 111-115. 1878.

Birds (J. A.) Beekite in the Channel Islands.Records occurrence in Triassic conglomerate, Bouley Bay, Jersey. *Geol. Mag. dec.* 2, vol. vi., p. 334. 1879.

Black (Dr. J.) On the Submerged Forests of Great Britain. *Geologist.* p. 174. (In 1869). *Trans. Manchester, Geol. Soc.*, vol. viii., p. 39. 1843.

Bonney (Prof. T. G.) On the Occurrence of a Variety of Picrite (Scyelite) in Sark. *Geol. Mag.*, p. 109. 1889.

Bowerbank (J.) Lower Freshwater formation in the Isle of Wight. *Mag. Nat. Hist., ser.* 2, vol. ii, p. 674. 1838.

—— On the London and Plastic Clay Formations of the Isle of Wight. *Trans. Geol. Soc.*, ser. 2, vol. vi., p. 169. 1841

Brander (Gustavus) Fossilia Hantoniensa Collecta et in Mussæo Britannico deposita. 4to. 1776. This collection was of the class of Fossils called Hordle.Cliff Fossils, the products of the blue alluvial clay on the coast between Lymington and Christchurch.

Brannon (Philip) Illustrated, Historical and Descriptive Guide to Bournemouth. 10th edition, 8vo. 1869. Geology referred to pp. 2, 3, 18, 19, 55-60, 63-66, 70, 71, 75, 76, 85-88. 96-98.

Brion (R. F.) Isle of Wight, Relievo Map of. The Geology from the Geological Survey Map. Scale (of Map) 3 miles to an inch. 1874.

Bristow (H. W.) For Hampshire Basin see Map of the Geological Survey of England. Sheet 17 (N.E. corner), 18 (S.E. corner), 19 (Part of Horizontal Section), 20 (Horizontal Section), 22 (Horizontal Section) 16 (the greater part), 10 (the greater part), 14 (nearly the whole), 14 (S.E. corner), 11 (nearly the whole), 47 (Horizontal Section), description published in 1859, revised in 1870, 25 (Vertical Section and description of), 56 (Horizontal Section)

—— Sheet 12 (Southern part), 5 (S.W. corner),9 (Southern part, 2 sheets) 75-78 (part of Horizontal Section), 73 (Horizonial Section).

—— The Geology of the Isle of Wight. Lists of Fossils revised by R. Etheridge. Notes on the Eocene Flora of Alum Bay, by Dr. de la Harpe and J. W. Salter. Geological Survey Memoir, 8vo, Lond. 1862. 2nd edition revised and enlarged by Clement Reid and Aubrey Strahan, 8vo, Lond. 1889.

—— See Whitaker.

Brodie (Rev. P. B.) Note on the Occurrence of Plants in the Plastic Clay of the Hampshire Coast. *Proc. Geol. Soc.*, vol. iii., p. 592. 1842

—— On the Discovery of a large and varied series of Fossil Insects and other associated fossils in the Eocene (Tertiary) Strata of the Isle of Wight. *Proc. Warwick Field Club*, pp. 3-12. 1878.

—— Fossil Birds (Isle of Wight). *Geological Magazine.* New Series, Dec. 3, vol. ii., p. 384. 1885.

Browne (A. J.) The Valley of the.Yar, Isle of Wight. *Geological Magazine*, vol. viii., p. 561. 1871.

Buchanan (Dr. G.) Report on the Distribution of Phthisis as affected by Dampness of Soil (with Geological Map of S.E. England.) The prefatory account of the Geological formations (of Hants Basin) and the materials for the accounts of local Geology, by W. Whitaker. Report of Medical Officer of Privy Council, p. 57, 8vo. London.

Buckland (Rev. Prof. W.) On the Discovery of the Anoplotherium Commune in the Isle of Wight. *Ann. of Phil.*, ser. 2, vol. x., p. 360. 1825.

―― On the Formation of the Valley of Kingsclere and other Valleys by the Elevation of the Strata that enclose them, and on the Evidences of the Original Continuity of the Basins of London and Hampshire. *Trans. Geol. Soc.*, ser. 2, vol. v., p. 118. 1826.

―― Address to the Mayor and Members of the Artesian Well Committee of Southampton. 8vo. Southampton, 1844.

Carruthers (William) On the Flora of the London Clay of Sheppey. *Proc. Geol. Assoc.*, vol. 4, No. 5, pp. 318-319. 1876 Speaks of deposits in Isle of Wight and at Bournemouth.

Carus-Wilson (C.) On some Decomposed Flints from Southbourne-on-Sea. *Nature*, vol. 42, p. 7. 1890.

Chambers (R.) Ancient Sea Margins, as Memorials of Changes in the Relative Level of Sea and Land (pp. 240-3), 8vo. Edinburgh and London, 1848. (Hants, pp. 240-243).

Charlesworth (E.) Record of the Discovery of an Alligator, with several new Mammalia, in the Freshwater Strata at Hardwell, by S. V. Wood. *Ann. and Mag. Nat. Hist.*, ser. 1, vol. xiv., p. 349. 1844

―― On some New Species of Testacea from the Hampshire Tertiary Beds. *Rep. Brit. Assoc.* for 1849. Trans. of Sections, p. 52.

―― Fossil Exploration of Suffolk Crag (Oxford Castle). Hampshire Eocene Cliffs. Extract from Brander's *Fossilia Hantoniensia*. Notes on Hampshire Fossils, and Notes on English Crag History. 8vo. London, 1878, p. 8.

Clark (J. E.) Christchurch Ledge. *Nat. Hist. Journ.*, vol. iii., p. 27. 1879

Clarke (Rev. W. B.) on the Peat Bogs and Submarine Forests of Bournemouth, Hampshire, and in the neighbourhood of Poole, Dorsetshire. *Proc. Geol. Soc.*, vol ii., No. 54, p. 599. 1838.

Codrington (T.) Notes to Accompany a Section of the Strata, from the Chalk to the Bembridge Limestone at Whitecliff Bay, I. of W. *Quart. Journ. Geol. Soc.*, vol. xxiv., p. 519. 1868.

―― On the Superficial Deposits of the South of Hants and of the Isle of Wight. *Quart. Journ. Geol. Soc.*, vol. xxvi., p. 528. 1870.

―― The Geology in W. C. Spooner's paper, "On the Agricultural Capabilities of the New Forest" (with Map). *Journ. Roy. Agric. Soc.*, ser. 2, vol. vii., 220. 1871.

Colenutt (G. W.) Discovery of Fossil Fish in the Eocene Strata of Ryde, Isle of Wight. *Sci. Goss.*, 1880, p. 141.

―― On the Osborne Beds of the Isle of Wight. *Geol. Mag.*, p. 358 1888.

Colson (Charles) On Portsmouth Dockyard Extension Works. (Paper read at the Inst. Civil Engineers, Feb. 1, 1881). *Engineer*, vol. li., p. 100. 1881.

Conybeare (Rev. W. D.) and W. Phillips. Outlines of the Geology of England and Wales. London, 8vo. 1822.

Conybeare (Rev. J. J.) On the Substances contained in the Interior of Chalk Flints. *Trans. Geol. Soc.*, ser. 2, vol. i., p. 422. 1824. Refers to Broughton.

Cooke (B.) An Observation of an Extraordinary Damp in a Well in the Isle of Wight. *Phil. Trans.*, vol. xl., No. 450, p. 379. 1738.

Crane (Agnes) The Underground Geology of the South-East of England. *Leisure Hour,* April 17, pp. 248-253, 10 woodcuts (section and fossils). 1880.

Croll (J.) On the South of England Ice Sheet. *Geol. Mag.,* Dec. 2, vol. i., p. 257. 1874.

Curtis (C. H.) Notes on the Geology of Bournemouth. 8vo. 1877.

Danby (T. W.) Elevation and Subsidence of Land in Jersey. *Geol. Mag.* Dec. 2, vol. iii., pp. 143-144. 1876.

Davidson (T.) a Monograph of British Cretaceous Brachiopoda. *Paleontograph Soc.* 4to. London, 1852. Only one note (Isle of Wight).

Davies (Rev. J. S.) A History of Southampton. 8vo. Southampton and London, 1883. Refers to the flint implement period and the deep well.

Dawkins (W. B.) Early Man in Britain and His Place in the Tertiary Period. 8vo. 1880.

Decken (H. von.) Palaeozoic Rocks of S.E. England. *Verh. Nat. Ver. Preuss Rheinl.-Bd.,* 37. Sitz, pp. 32-39. 1880.

De Luc (J. A.) Geological Travels (vols ii. and iii., Travels in England). Translated from the French MS. 8vo. London, 1811. See vol. ii., pp. 114-24, 128-35, 175-7, 187-201.

Duncan (Prof. P. M.) First Report on the British Fossil Corals. *Rep. Brit. Assoc.* for 1868, p. 70.

—— British Fossil Corals, a Monograph of. 2nd series (Tertiary)

—— British Fossil Corals, a Monograph of. 2nd series, (Cretaceous). 4to. *Paleontograph Soc. London,* 1866-1869.

—— British Fossil Corals, First Report on the. *Rep. Brit. Assoc.* for 1868, p. 75.

—— On Asterosmilia Reeds; a new species of Coral from the Oligocene of Brockenhurst, Hants. *Rep. Brit. Assoc. for* 1881, pp. 618-619. 1882.

Earle (B. N.) Remarks on the Excavations being made for the foundations of the New Town Hall (Winchester). *Rep. Winchester and Hants. Sci. and Lit. Soc. for* 1870-71, p. 34.

Edwards (F. E.) A Monograph of the species of the genus Tellina, occurring in the Eocene deposits at Bracklesham Bay and Barton. *Lond. Geol. Journ.,* pp. 44, 100, 1847.

—— A Monograph of the Eocene Mollusca, Part 1, Cephalopoda. Part 2, Pulmonata. *Paleontograph Soc.* 4to. Lond. 1849 & 1852.

—— A Monograph of the Eocene Mollusca. Part 3, Prosobranchiata, No 1, 1855. Prosobranchiata, No. 2, 1857. Prosobranchiata, No. 3, 1861, *Paleontograph Soc.* 4to, Lond. Descriptions of some new Eocene Species of Cypræa and Marginella. *Geol. Mag.,* vol ii, p. 536. 1865

Elwes (J. W.) On the classification of Oligocene Strata in the Hampshire Basin. *Rep. Brit. Assoc. for* 1882, pp. 539-540. 1883.

—— The Middle Headon Marine Bed at Hordwell, *Geol. Mag.,* dec. ii, vol. x, pp. 527, 528. 1883.

—— London Clay in the vicinity of Southampton. *Geol. Mag.,* dec. iii, vol. i. pp. 548-551. 1884.

—— See Shore.

Englefield (Sir H. C.) Observations on some remarkable Strata of Flint in a Chalk pit in the Isle of Wight. *Trans. Lin. Soc.*, vol. vi., pp. 103, 303. 1802.

——A Description of the Principal Picturesque Beauties, Antiquities and Geological Phenomena of the Isle of Wight. With additional Observations on the Strata of the Island, and their continuation in the adjacent parts of Dorsetshire, by T. Webster. (Chap. ii. *Coast Chines*, pp. 83-86. *Undercliff*, pp. 129, &c., London, 8vo. 1816.

Etheridge (R.) Tertiary Beds of Hampshire Basin. Opening address of Section C., British Association. *Nature*, vol. xxvi., pp. 422-434. 1882 *Rep. Brit. Assoc. for* 1882, pp. 502-529. 1883.

Ettingshausen (C. von.) Report on Phyto-Paleontological Investigations of the Fossil Flora of Alum Bay. *Proc. Roy. Soc.*, vol. xxx., pp. 228-236, and *Journ. Bot.*, 1880, pp. 156-158. 1880.

——See Gardner.

Evans (E.) Christchurch Bar. *Nat. Hist. Jour.*, vol. vi., No. 46, p. 16. See also No. 49. p. 82. 1882.

——(C.) On the Geology of the Neighbourhood of Portsmouth and Ryde. Part I.

——On the Geology of the Neighbourhood of Portsmouth and Ryde. Part II. *Proc. Geol. Assoc.*, vol. ii., No. 3. p. 61. 1871. and *Proc. Geol. Assoc.*, vol. ii., No. 4, p. 149. 1872.

——(J.) On some recent Discoveries of Flint Implements in Drift Deposits in Hants and Wilts. *Quart. Journ. Geol. Soc.*, vol. xx., p. 188. 1864.

——The Ancient Stone Implements, Weapons, and Ornaments of Great Britain. (Flint Implements from the Drift, Hants Basin, pp. 543-559). 8vo. London. 1872.

Fairholme (G.) New and Conclusive Physical Demonstrations, both of the Fact and Period of the Mosaic Deluge, &c. (Chap. vii., " Description of the Isle of Wight and its Coasts, " &c.) London. 8vo. 1837.

Fisher (Rev. O.) On the Brackesham Beds of the Isle of Wight Basin. *Quart. Journ. Geol. Soc.*, vol. xviii., p. 65. 1862.

Futton (William H.) A Stratigraphical Account of the Section from Atherfield to Rocken End, on the S.W. of the Isle of Wight. 8vo. p. 289. 1847. *Quart. Journ. Geol. Soc.*, vol. iii.

Flight (Dr. Walter) a Native of Winchester, Obituary of. *Geol. Mag.*, N.S., dec. iii., vol. ii., p. 575. 1885.

Forbes (Prof. E.) and Captain L. L. B. Ibbetson, On the Tertiary and Cretaceous Formations of the Isle of Wight. *Rep. Brit. Assoc. for* 1844. Trans. of Sections, p. 43.

——Monograph of the Echinodermata of the British Tertiaries. *Paleontograph Soc.*, 4to. London. 1852.

——On the Fluvio-Marine Tertiaries of the Isle of Wight. *Quart. Journ. Geol. Soc.*, vol. ix., p. 259. 1853.

——On some New Points in British Geology. *Edin. New Phil. Journ.*, vol. lv., p. 263. 1853.

——On the Tertiary Fluvio-Marine Formation of the Isle of Wight. Edited by R. A. C. Godwin-Austen. With notes by H. W. Bristow, and Descriptions of Fossils by Prof. J. Morris, J. W. Salter, T. R. Jones. *Geological Survey Memoir.* 8vo. London. 1856.

Fox (Rev. W.) When and How was the Isle of Wight severed from the Mainland ? *Geologist*, vol. v. p. 452. 1862.

Gardner (J. S.) On the Lower Bagshot Beds of the Hampshire Basin. *Proc. Geol. Assoc.*, vol. v., No. 2. pp. 51-68, plate and woodcuts. *Nature*, vol, xv., pp. 279-280. *Geol. Mag.*, dec. ii., vol. iv., pp. 129-135. 1877.

——On the Tropical Forests of Hampshire. *Nature*, vol. xv., pp. 229-232, 258-260, woodcuts. *Geol. Mag.*, dec. ii., vol. iv., pp. 23-26. Also *Geol. Mag.*, dec. ii., vol. iv., pp. 137-138, Reply to S. V. Wood, Junr. (See, Wood). 1877.

——The Red Clay of the Deep Sea and the Gault Deposits. *Geol. Mag.* dec. ii. vol. iv., p. 377. 1877.

——Fossil Hunting at Bournemouth. *Nature*, vol xvii., p. 369. 1878

——On the British Eocenes and their Deposition. *Proc. Geol. Assoc.*, vol. vi., No. 2, pp. 83-106, pl 1., 2 woodcuts. 1879. (Chart of Atlantic Soundings).

——Description and Correlation of the Bournemouth Beds. Part I.—Upper Marine Series—Coast Erosion, Bournemouth and Hengistbury Head, pp. 219, 220. *Quart. Journ. Geol. Soc.*, vol. xxxv., p. 209. 1879.

——Description and Correlation of the Bournemouth Beds. Part II.—Lower or Freshwater Series. *Quart. Journ. Geol. Soc.*, vol. xxxviii.,pp. 1-15 .,3 woodcuts. 1882.

——On the Extent of the Gap between Chalk and Eocene in England, and on the so-called Upper Cretaceous Floras. *Pop. Sci. Rev.*, N.S., vol. iii., p. 55-60. 1879.

——On the Correlation of the Bournemouth Marine Series, with the Bracklesham Beds,the Upper and Middle Bagshot Beds of the London Basin, and the Bovey Tracey Beds. *Geol. Mag.*, dec. ii., vol. vi., pp. 148-154. 1879.

——Report of Excursion to the Hampshire Coast. *Proc. Geol. Assoc.* vol. vi. pt. 7, pp. 316-320. 1881.

——Suggestions for a Revised Classification of the British Eocenes. *Geol. Mag.*, dec. ii., vol. ix., pp. 466-472. And *Rep. Brit. Assoc.* for 1882, p. 539. 1882.

——Observations sur la formation Eocene de l'Angleterre. *Bull. Soc. Geol.*, France, ser. 3, t. xi. p. 195. 1883.

——On the Relative Ages of the American and the English Cretaceous and Eocene Series. *Geol. Mag.*, dec. iii, vol. i., pp. 492-506. 1884

——On the Eocene Flora at Bournemouth. *Nature*, vol. xxi. pp. 181-183. 1879.

——On the Alum Bay Flora. *Nature*, vol. xxi. p. 588. 1880.

——On the Eocene Flora of Bournemouth. *Nature*, vol. xxi. p. 181. 1880.

——and Ettingshausen (C. von) A Monograph of the British Eocene Flora. Vol. I., pt. 2. *Pal. Soc.*, vol. xxxiv., pp. 39-58. 1880. Vol. I. pt. 3. *Pal. Soc.*, vol. xxxvi., pp. 59-85, 2 plates. 1886.

——On the Eocene Flora of Bournemouth. *Nature*, vol. xvii. pp. 47-48 1877.

——A Monograph of the British Eocene Flora. Vol. ii. pt. 1. Gymnospermæ. *Pal. Soc.*, vol. xxxvii., pp. 1-60, plates i-ix. 1883. Vol. ii. pt. 2. *Pal. Soc.*, vol. xxxviii. pp. 61-92, plates x.-xx. 1883.

——Oscillations of Level along our Southern Coast since the human period. *Geol. Mag.*, N.S., dec. iii. vol. ii. p. 145. 1885.

——On the Land Mollusca of the Eocenes. *Geol. Mag.*, N.S., dec. iii., vol. ii., p. 241. 1885.

Gardner(J.S.)Distribution of Teredo-Bored Wood. *Geol. Mag.*, p. 161. 1886.

——Fossil Flowering Phanerogamous Plants. *Geol. Mag.*, p. 495. 1886.

——Report on the Fossil Plants of the Secondary and Tertiary Beds of the United Kingdom. *Geol. Mag.*, p. 564. 1887.

——Report on the Higher Eocene Beds of the Isle of Wight. *Memoir—Brit. Assoc. Meeting.* 1887. *Geol. Mag.*, p. 461. 1887.

——The Upper Eocene, comprising the Barton and Upper Bagshot Formations. *Geol. Mag.*, p. 232. 1888.

——Report on the Eocene Plants of the Isle of Wight. *Trans. Brit. Assoc.* 1889.

Geological Bibliography of the Isle of Wight. See Geology of the Isle of Wight. Appendix iv., 2nd Edition. *Geological Survey Memoir.* 8vo. Lond. 1889.

——Holidays, No. 2. The Hampshire Coast. *Nat. His. Notes*, vol. ii.. pp, 126-128. 1882.

——Holidays, No. 3. Freshwater, Isle of Wight. *Nat. His. Notes*, vol. iii., pp. 40, 41. 1883.

Geologists' Association, Easter Excursion to the Hampshire Coast. *Nature*, vol. xxi., p. 590. 1880.

Gervais (Prof. F.) On some Teeth of the Anchitherium recently discovered in the Isle of Wight. *Geologist*, vol. i., p. 153. 1858,

Gilpin (Rev. W.) Observations on the Coasts of Hampshire, Sussex and Kent, relative chiefly to Picturesque Beauty. (Retirement of Sea, Work of Sea on Coast, pp. 60-65). 8vo. London. 1804.

Godwin-Austen (R. A. C.) On Land surfaces Beneath the Drift Gravel. *Quart. Journ. Geol Soc.*, vol. xi., p. 112. 1855.

——On the Newer Tertiary Deposits of the Sussex Coast. *Quart. Journ. Geol. Soc.* vol. xiii., p. 40. 1857.

Goss (Herbert). Insects from Bournemouth (in Eocene) Leaf Beds. *Proc. Entom. Soc.*, London. p. 8. 1878. Notes the Genera.

Greenwood (Col. G.) Our Springs, Streams and Wells. *Hampshire Chronicle*, November, 1864. Reprinted in "River Terraces," pp. 69-71. 8vo. London. 1864.

——Rain and Rivers. 8vo. 1876. Geology of Hampshire, &c.

G[riffith] (C.) Geological List, 3rd Rep. Winchester College. *Nat. Hist. Society*, pp. 132-135. 1875.

——The Chalk Formation. *Journ. Winchester Sci. Soc.*, vol. i., pt. 4. pp. 246-258. 1875.

——Geological List, 4th. Rep. *Winchester Coll. Nat. Hist. Soc.*, pp. 86-90. 1877.

——List of the Principal Pits and Geographical Sections in Winchester and the Neighbourhood, with list of Fossils. *Rep. Winchester Coll. Nat. Hist. Society*, 1881. pp. 107-110. 1881.

Grimshaw (H.) On a Peculiar Feature in the Water of the Well in Carisbrooke Castle, Isle of Wight. *Chem. News.*, vol. xl., pp. 310, 311. 1879.

Harris (T.) and Davies (W.) Note on a Section and a Jaw-Bone of Deer from No Man's Land Shoal. *Geol. Mag.*, vol. ii., p. 46. 1865.

Harrison (W. J.) A Sketch of the Geology of Hampshire. *In White's History, Gazetteer, &c.*, of the County, p. 12. 8vo. Sheffield. 1877.

——On the Deep Borings in the S.E. of England. *Mid. Nat.*, vol. iii., pp. 188-190. plate ii. 1880.

Hastings (Marchioness of) On the Freshwater Eocene Beds of the Hordle Cliff, Hants. *Rep. Brit. Assoc.* for 1847. Trans. of Sections, p. 63.

——Description Géologique des falaises d'Hordle, sur la côte du Hampshire, en Angleterre. *Bull. Soc. Géol.*, France, 2 ser., t. ix., p. 91. 1852.

——On the Tertiary Beds of Hordwell, Hampshire. *Phil. Mag.*, ser. 4, vol. vi., p. 1. 1853.

Hérbert (Prof.) Comparison des couches tertiares inférieures de la France de l'Angleterre (with Discussion, by Lyell). *Bull. Soc. Géol.*, France, 2 ser., t. ix., p. 350. 1852.

Heer (Dr. O.) On Certain Fossil Plants from the Hempstead Beds of the Isle of Wight (with an Introduction by W. Pengelly). *Quart. Journ. Geol. Soc.*, vol. xviii., p. 369. 1862.

Helmer (O.) New Analysis of the Sandrock (I. of W.) *Mineral Water Analyst.* vol. vii. p. 109. 1882.

Hicks (Henry) Classification of the Eozoic and Lower Palaeozoic Rocks of the British Isles. *Pop. Sc. Rev.*, N.S., vol. v., pp. 289-309, plates vii, viii, and plate of sections. 1881.

Higgins (W. M.) The Harbours of the South Eastern Coast. *Weale's Quart. Papers on Eng.*, vol. ii. part 3. 1844.

Hill (Edwin) Problems in the Geology of the Channel Islands. *Rep. Brit. Assoc.* for 1882, pp. 550, 551. 1883.

——On a Continuous succession in part of the Guernsey Gneiss. *Proc. Camb. Phil. Soc.*, vol. v. pp. 154-156. 1884.

——The Rocks of Guernsey. With an Appendix on the Rocks referred to by T. G. Bonney. *Quart. Journ. Geol. Soc.*, vol. xl., pp. 404-430. Sketch map and section. 1884.

——the Rocks of Sark, Herm and Jethon. *Rep. Geol. Soc.* London. March 23rd, 1887.

Hill (Rev. E.) On the Rocks of Alderney and the Casquets. *Rep. Geol. Soc.* London, May 8, 1889.

Hinde (G. J.) On Beds of Sponge-Remains in the Upper and Lower Greensands of the South of England. *Rep. Roy. Soc.* London. 1885.

Holgate (B.) On " Notes on the Geology of Bournemouth " (Abstract)' *Trans. Leeds. Geol. Assoc.*, pt. ii., pp. 61-62. 1886.

Holmes (T. V.) Geology and Scenery of the South-East of England—(Abstract of Lecture). *5th, Annual Rep. and Proc.*, 1883, *Lewisham and Blackheath Sci. Assoc.*, pp. 31-37. 1884.

Hulke (J. W.) Polacanthus Foxii, a large undescribed Dinosaur from the Wealden Formation in the Isle of Wight. *Proc. Roy. Soc.*, vol. xxxi. p. 336, *and Phil. Trans.*, vol. 172. pt. iii. pp. 653-662. 7 plates. 1881.

Huxley (Prof.) On the Dermal Armour of Crocodilus Hastingiæ. *Quart. Journ. Geol. Soc.*, vol. xv. p. 678. 1859.

Ibbetson (Capt L. L. B.) Notes on the Geology and Chemical Composition of the various strata in the Isle of Wight, &c. (With a small relief map). 8vo. London. 1849.

Irving (A.) On the Bagshot Sands as a Source of Water Supply. *Geol. Mag.*, dec. ii., vol. x., pp. 404-412. 1883.

—— (Rev. A.) General Series of the Bagshot Beds from Aldershot to Wokingham (Deep-Well Sections, pp. 493-496). *Quart. Journ. Geol. Soc.*, vol xli., p. 492. Water Supply from the Bagshot and other strata (No. 2). *Geol. Mag.*, dec. iii., vol. ii., pp. 17-25. 1885.

Irving (Rev. A.) A General Section of the Bagshot Strata from Aldershot to Wokingham. *Geol. Soc. London Proc.* April 15th, 1885.

—— Bagshot Beds of London Clay. *Geol. Mag.*, p. 402. 1886.

—— Tertiary Outliers on the North Downs. *Geol. Mag.*, p. 123. 1888.

Isle of Wight, Stanford's Relief Map of, modelled by J. Brion, coloured geologically. London, 1858. See Geological Bibliography.

James (Major-Gen. Sir H.) On a section exposed by the excavation at the New Steam Basin in Portsmouth Dockyard. *Quart. Journ. Geol. Soc.*, vol iii., p. 249. 1847.

—— (Capt. H.) [Major-Gen. Sir H.] Description of the Steam Basin,&c., recently executed in Portsmouth Dockyard, Geological Notice of the Foundation Papers of the Corps of Royal Engineers. Ser. 2,vol. iii., p. 79. 1853.

Jenkinson (H. J.) Practical Guide to the Isle of Wight. 8vo. London, 1876.

Jones (Prof. T. R.) A Monograph of the Tertiary Entomostraca of England. *Paleontograph Soc.* 4to. London, 1857.

—— On the Microscopical Examination of some Bracklesham Beds. *Geologist*, vol. v., p. 59. 1862.

—— (Prof. T. Rupert) and Sherborne (C. Davies) Further Notes on the Tertiary Entomostraca of England, with special reference to those from the London Clay. *Geol. Mag.*, pp. 385, 450. 1887.

——(Prof. T. R.) Ostracoda from the Weald Clay of the Isle of Wight. *Geol. Mag.*, p. 534. 1888.

Judd (J. W.) The Classification of the Tertiary Deposits. *Pop. Sci. Rev.*, N.S., vol. iv., pp. 122-136. 1880.

—— On the Oligocene Strata of the Hampshire Basin. *Quart. Journ, Geol. Soc.*, vol. xxxvi., pp. 137-177, pl. vii. (woodcut sections). 1880.

—— On the Occurrence of the Remains of a Cetacean in the Lower Oligocene Strata of the Hampshire Basin, with an appendix by H. G. Seeley. *Quart. Journ. Geol. Soc.*, vol. xxxvii., pp. 708-712, 3 wood. cuts. 1881.

—— The Headon Hill Section. *Geol. Mag.*, dec. ii., vol. ix., pp. 189, 190. 1882.

—— On the Relations of the Eocene and the Oligocene Strata in the Hampshire Basin. *Quart. Journ. Geol. Soc.*, vol. xxxviii., pp. 461-489, woodcut. 1882.

Keele (J. R.) On the Artesian Well on the Southampton Common. *Rep. Brit. Assoc. for* 1846. Trans. of Sections, p. 52.

—— On the Artesian Well on the Southampton Common. *Rep Brit. Assoc.*, 1846, Sections, p. 52. 1847.

Keeping (H.) and Tawney (E. B.) On the Beds at Headon Hill and Colwell Bay in the Isle of Wight. *Quart. Journ. Geol. Soc.*, xxxvii., pp. 85-127, pl. v. 1881.

Köenen (A. Von.) On the Correlation of the Oligocene Deposits of Belgium, Northern Germany and the South of England. *Quart. Journ. Geol. Soc.*, vol. xx. 1864.

L'Apparent (A. de) Note sur la Pegmatete de Luchon. *Bull. Soc. Geol. France, ser* 3, t. viii., No. 1, pp. 11-13. 1880.

——Note sur les éroches ruptives de l'ile de Jerseu, *Bull. Soc. Geol. France, ser* 3, t. xii. pp. 284-289. 1884.

Leighton (W. H.) On an Excursion to the Isle of Wight. *Proc. Geol. Assoc.* p. 28, (*Geol. and Nat. Hist. Repertory*). 1866.

Lemon (W. G.) Deep Borings in S.E. of England. *Rep. West. Kent. Nat. His. Soc.* for 1881-82, pp. 9-20. 1882.

Liveing (G. D.) On the Rocks of the Channel Islands. No. 2. *Proc. Camb. Phil. Soc.*, vol. iv., pp. 122-129. 1882.

Lovett (E.) Notes on the Natural History of Jersey (Geology). *Sci. Gossip.*, 1881. pp. 269-271. 1882, pp. 35-38. 1881-82.

Lucus (J.) The Hydrogeology of the Lower Greensands of Surrey and Hampshire. *Proc. Inst. Civ. Eng.*, vol. lxi., pp. 200-227, pl. 7. (Geol. map). 1880.

——(A. H. S.) On the Headon Beds of the Western Extremity of the Isle of Wight. *Geol. Mag.*, dec. ii., vol. ix., pp. 97-103. 1882.

Lydekker (R.) Note on the Anthracotheriidæ of the Isle of Wight. *Geol. Mag.*, dec. iii., vol. i., pp. 547, 548. 1884.

——Notes on the Hordwell and other Crocodilians. *Geol. Mag.*, p. 307, 1887.

——Notes on Tertiary Lacertilia and Ophidia. *Geol. Mag.*, p. 110. 1888.

——On a Coeluroid Dinosaur from the Wealden. *Geol. Mag.*, p. 119. 1889.

——On a Peculiar Horn-like Dinosaurian Bone from the Wealden, Isle of Wight. *Quart. Journ. Geol. Soc.*, vol. xlvi., p. 185. 1890.

——On Remains of Small Sauropodus Dinosaurus from the Wealden, Isle of Wight. *Quart. Journ. Geol., Soc.*, vol. xlvi., p. 182., pl. ix. 1890.

Lyell (Sir C.) On a Recent Formation of Freshwater Limestone in Forfarshire, and on some recent deposits of Freshwater Marl. (Romsey, p. 88). *Trans. Geol. Soc.*, ser. 2., vol. ii., p. 73. 1826.

——On the Strata of the Olastic Clay Formation exhibited in the Cliffs between Christchurch Head, Hampshire, and Studland Bay, Dorsetshire. *Trans. Geol. Soc.*, ser. 2, vol. ii., p. 279. 1827.

——On the Freshwater Strata of Hordwell Cliff, Beacon Cliff, and Barton Cliff, Hampshire. *Trans. Geol. Soc.*, ser 2, vol. ii., p. 287. 1827.

Lyons (H. G.) On the LondonClay and Bagshot Beds of Aldershot. (Refers to Wells, pp. 434, 436, 437, 439-441). *Quart. Journ. Geol. Soc.*, vol. xliii. p. 431. 1887.

——In the London Clay and Bagshot Beds of Aldershot. *Rep. Geol. Soc* London, April 27th. 1887.

Mantell (Dr. G. A.) Geological Excursions round the Isle of Wight and along the adjacent coast of Dorsetshire. 8vo. London. 1847. (Ed. 2, in 1851). (Wells, Southampton, pp. 87, 88).

Marshall (W.) Rural Economy of the Southern Counties. Vol. ii.. 8vo. London ,1798. 2nd edition. London, 8vo, 1799.

Martin (P. J.) On the Relative Connection of the Eastern and Western Denudations. *Proc. Geol. Soc.*, vol. iii., p. 349. 1841.

—— On the Anticlinal Line of the London and Hampshire Basin. *Phil. Mag.*, ser. 4, vol. ii., pp. 41, 126, 189, 278. 1851.

—— On the Anticlinal Line of the London and Hampshire Basins. *Phil. Mag.*, ser. 4, vol. xii., p. 447. 1856. Also, *Phil. Mag.*, ser. 4, vol. xiii., p. 33. 1857.

Matthews (W.) The Wells and Borings of the Southampton Water-works. *Proc. Inst. C. E.*, vol. xc., pp. 33-39, pl. i. Discussion, p. 40, &c. 1884.

—— Report upon the Proposed New Source of Water Supply from Otterbourne, &c. Fol. 1884.

Maw (G.) On the Sources of the Materials composing the White Clays of the Lower Tertiaries. *Quart. Journ. Geol. Soc.*, vol. xxiii., p. 387. 1867.

Meyer (C. J. A.) On Lower Tertiary Deposits recently exposed at Portsmouth. *Quart. Journ. Geol. Soc.*, vol. xxvii., p. 74. 1871.

―― (C. H.) Temporary Work and Plant at the Portsmouth Dockyard Extension. *Proc. Inst. C. E.*, vol. lxiii., pp. 174-201, pl. 8. 1880.

Middleton (J.) Outlines of the Mineral Strata of Great Britain. *Monthly Mag.*, vol. xxxiv., No. 232, p. 198. 1812.

Mitchell (W. S.) On some hitherto Unrecorded Leaf-forms from the Pipe Clay of Alum Bay. *Geol. Mag.*, vol. ii., p. 515.

―― Report of the Committee appointed to investigate the Alum Bay Leaf-Bed. *Rep. Brit. Assoc: for* 1866, p. 146.

Noury (Le P. Ch.) Géologiè de Jersey. (Coloured map), p. 173. 8vo. 1887.

Moore (J. C.) Notes on the Occurrence of Eocene Freshwater Shells at Beaulieu, Langley, &c., in Hampshire. *Quart. Journ. Geol. Soc.*, vol. v., p. 315. 1849.

Morris (John) The Chalk, its Distribution and Subdivisions. *Proc. Geol. Assoc.*, vol. viii., No. 4, pp. 208-226, tables. 1883,

―― (Prof. J.) Fact and Situation of the Occurrence of Seeds and certain Species of Shells in the Lower Formation of the Isle of Wight. *Mag. Nat. Hist.*, vol. viii., p. 391. 1835.

Mudie (R.) Hampshire, its Past and Present Condition and Future Prospects. 3 vols. 8vo. Winchester, 1839. Geological remarks throughout chap. 4, vol. ii., mostly Geological ; chap. 3, vol. iii., Geology of the Isle of Wight.

Murchison (Sir. R. T.) Geological Sketch of the North Western Extremity of Sussex, and the Adjoining Parts of Hants and Surrey. *Trans. Geol. Soc.*, ser. 2, vol. 2., p. 97. 1826.

―― On the Distribution of the Flint Drift of S.E. England, on the Flanks of the Weald, and over the Surface of the South and North Downs. *Quart. Journ. Geol. Soc.*, vol vii., p. 349. 1851.

Nelson (T.) The Isle of Wight, with a Description of the Geology of the Island. 8vo. 1859. Another edition. 8vo. 1869.

Newton (E. T.) A Contribution to the History of Eocene Siluroid Fishes. *Proc. Zool. Soc.*, pp. 201-207, pl. xxi. Refers largely to Barton, &c.

Nicolls (Lt.-Col. W. T.) Mammalian Remains in the Hampshire Gravel. *Geologist*, vol. vi., pp. 110, 154. 1863.

――Remarks on some Sarsens or *Eratic* Blocks of Stone found in the Gravel in the Neighbourhood of Southampton. *Geol. Mag.*, vol. iii., p. 296. 1866.

Norman (M. W.) Notes on the Geology of Whitecliff Bay, Isle of Wight. *Proc. Geol. Assoc.*, vol. i., p. 38. 1860.

――(Mark)A Popular Guide to the Geology of the Isle of Wight,with a note on its Relation to that of the Isle of Purbeck. 8vo, p. 240, with Map Sections and 15 plates of Fossils. 1887.

O'Meara (Rev. E.) On the Occurrence of Recent Diatomaceæ in the Lower Tertiaries of Hampshire. *Journ. Geol. Soc., Dublin*, pp. 105, 185. 1859.

Owen (Prof. R.) Description of some Fossil Remains of Chæropotamus, Palaeotherium, Amplotherium, and Dichobunes, from the Eocene Formation, Isle of Wight. *Trans. Geol. Soc.*, ser 2, vol vi., p. 41. 1841.

Owen (Prof. R.) Report on the British Fossil Mammalia. *Rep. Brit. Assoc. for* 1843, p. 208.

――Description of an Upper Molar Tooth of Dichobune Cervinum from the Eocene Marl at Binsted, Isle of Wight. *Quart. Jour. Geol. Soc.,* vol. ii., p. 91. 1846.

――On the Dichodon cuspatus. *Quart Journ. Geol. Soc.,* vol. xiii, p. 190. 1857.

――Description of the lower Jaw and Teeth of an Anoplotheroid Quadruped (Dichobune ovina) from Upper Eocene Marl, Isle of Wight. *Quart. Journ. Geol. Soc.,* vol. xiii. p. 254. 1857.

――On the Fossils obtained by the Marchioness of Hastings from the Freshwater Eocene Beds of the Hordle Cliffs. *Rep. Brit. Assoc. for* 1847. Trans. of Sections, p. 65.

――Descriptions of Teeth and portions of Jaws of two Extinct Anthracotheroid Quadruped (Hyopotamus Vectianus and H. Bovenus), discovered in the Eocene Deposits on the N.W. Coast of the Isle of Wight. *Quart. Journ. Geol. Soc.,* vol. iv., p. 103. 1848.

――On the fossil remains of Mammalia, referable to the genus Palæotherium and to two genera : Paloplotherium and Dichodon, hitherto undefined from the Eocene Sand at Hordle, Hampshire. *Quart. Journ. Geol. Soc.,* vol. iv., p. 17. 1848.

――On new Fossil Mammalia from the Eocene Freshwater Formation at Hordwell, Hants. *Rep. Brit. Assoc. for* 1851. Trans. of Sections, p. 67,

――Report on British Fossil Reptiles, Part II. *Rep. Brit. Assoc. for* 1841. p. 60. (pp. 67, 181). 1842.

――and Bell (Prof. T.) Monograph on the Fossil Reptilia of the London Clay. Part I. Chelonia (pp. 30, 46-76). *Paleontograph Soc.* 4to. London. 1849.

――Monograph on the Fossil Reptilia of the London Clay, Part ii. Crocodilia, Ophidia. *Palaeontograph Soc.* 4to. London. 1850.

Parkinson (C.) The Cephalopoda of the Chalk Marl and Upper Greensand, Isle of Wight. *Sci. Goss.* No. 177, pp. 204, 205, with 12 illustrations. 1879.

――Upper Greensand and Chloritic Marl, Isle of Wight. *Quart. Journ. Geol. Soc.,* vol. xxxvii., pp. 370-375. 1881.

――The Peetens of the Upper Greensand and Chloritic Marl of the Isle of Wight. *Sci. Goss.,* 1884. pp. 52-54. 1884.

Pengelly (W.) On the Correlation of the Lignite Formation of Bovey Tracey, Devonshire, with the Hempstead Beds of the Isle of Wight. *Trans. Devon. Assoc. of Sci. and Art.* part IV., p. 90. 1865.

Phillips (Prof. J.) Oxford Fossils, No. 1 (Fossil Wood from the Chalk, Winchester). *Geol. Mag.,* vol. ii , p. 292. 1865.

Phillip's (W.) See Conybeare,

Pilbrow (J.) On a Well Section near Gosport. *Quart. Journ. Geol. Soc.,* vol. xvi., p. 447. 1860.

Pilkington (W.) Description of some Fossil Shells found in Hampshire. *Trans. Lin. Soc.,* vol. vii. p. 116. 1804.

Portlock (Lt.-Col.) On Apparent Changes in the Level of the Coast near Portsmouth. *Rep. Brit. Assoc.* for 1848. Trans. of Section, p. 72.

――On the Inequalities of the Sea-Bottom during the Tertiary Epoch (Well at Portsmonth). *Journ. Geol. Soc.,* Dublin, vol. iv., p. 245. 1850

Pratt (S P.) Remarks on the Existence of the Anaplotherium and Palæotherium in the Lower Freshwater Formation at Binstead, near Ryde, in the Isle of Wight. *Trans. Geol. Soc.*, ser. 2, vol. iii., p. 451. 1835.

Prestwich (J.) On the Occurrence of Cypris in a part of the Tertiary Freshwater Strata of the Isle of Wight. *Rep. Brit. Assoc. for* 1846. Trans. of Sections, p. 56.

——On the Tertiary or Supracretaceous Formations of the Isle of Wight, as exhibited in the Sections at Alum Bay and White Cliff Bay. *Quart. Journ. Geol. Soc.*, vol. ii. p. 223. 1846.

——On the Main Points of Structure, and on the Probable Age of the Bagshot Sands, and on their Presumed Equivalents in Hampshire and France. *Quart. Journ, Geol. Soc.*, vol. iii. p. 378. 1847.

——On the Probable Age of the London Clay, and its Relations to the Hampshire and Paris Tertiary Systems. *Quart. Journ. Geol. Soc.*, vol. iii., p. 354. 1847.

——On the Position and General Characters of the Strata exhibited in the Coast Section, from Christchurch Harbour to Poole Harbour. *Quart. Journ. Geol. Soc.*, vol. v. p. 43. 1849.

——On the Structure of the Strata between the London Clay and the Chalk. Part I. The Basement Bed of the London Clay. *Quart. Journ. Geol. Soc.*, vol. vi., p. 252. 1850.

——On the Structure of the Strata between the London Clay and the Chalk. Part II. The Woolwich and Reading Series. *Quart. Journ. Geol. Soc.*, vol. x., p. 75. 1854.

——On the Thickness of the London Clay, on the relative position of the Fossiliferous Bed of Sheppey, Highgate, &c. *Quart. Journ. Geol. Soc.*, vol. x. p. 401. 1854.

——On the Distinctive, Physical and Palæontological Features of the London Clay and the Bracklesham Sands, and on the independence of these two groups of Strata. *Quart. Journ. Geol. Soc.*, vol. xi., p. 439. 1854.

——On the Correlation of the Eocene Tertiaries of England, France, and Belguim. Part II. The Paris Group. *Quart. Journ. Geol. Soc.*, vol. xiii., p. 89. 1857.

——On the Presence of a Raised Beach on Portsdown Hill, near Portsmouth, and on the occurrence of a Flint Implement on a high level at Downton. *Quart. Journ. Geol. Soc.*, vol. xxviii., p. 38. 1872.

——Notes Relating to some of the Drift Phenomena of Hampshire. *Rep. Brit. Assoc. for* 1882, pp. 529, 530. 1883.

——On the Relation of the Westleton Shingle to other Pre-glacial Drifts . . . &c., Part III. *Hants*, p. 161. *Quart. Journ. Geol. Soc.*, vol. xlvi., p. 155. 1890.

Prévost (C.) Coupe d'Alum Bay et d'Headen Hill, dans l'île de Wight. *Bull. Soc. Geol.*, France, t. viii. p. 76. 1837.

Price (F. G. H.) The Gault, being the substance of a Lecture delivered in the Woodwardian Museum, Cambridge, 1878, and before the Geologists' Association, 1880. pp. 80. 8vo. London, price 3s 6d. analysis by Dr. C. Barrois. *Ann. Soc. Geol. Nord.*, t. vi. pp. 225, 226.

Ranger (W.) Report to the General Board of Health on a Preliminary Inquiry into the . . . supply of water . . . . of the Borough of Southampton. (Note of Wells, &c., p. 5) 8vo. London. 1850.

—— Report to the Local Board of Health, Southampton, on the Various Sources of Water Supply (Well Sections). 8vo. Southampton. 1851.

Bibliotheca Hantoniensis.

Ranger (W.) Report and Letters of (on Water Supply), in the Report of the Town Committee,appointed at the Public Meeting held at the Guildhall, Southampton, Feb. 11th, 1852, comprising . . . . an Appendix on the Artesian Well. 8vo. Southampton. 1852.

Reclus (Elisée) The Universal Geography (European Section,Division vii.). Royal 8vo. N.D. Geology of Hampshire, pp. 125-129.

Redman (J B.) On the Alluvial Formations and Local Changes of the South Coast of England. *Proc. Inst. C. E.*, vol. xi., p. 162. 1854.

Reid (Clement) The Extent of the Hempstead Beds in the Isle of Wight. *Geol. Mag.*, p. 510. 1887.

Ricketts (Dr. C.) On the Oscillations of Level on the Coast of Hampshire during the Eocene Period. *Proc. Liverpool Geol Soc.*, Session 8, p. 11. 1867.

Rickman (W.) Earth Falls at the Undercliff in the Isle of Wight. *Proc. Inst. C. E.*, vol. i., p. 35. 1840.

Robson (J. H.) Analysis of the Water of the Artesian Well, Southampton. *Quart. Journ. Chem. Soc.,* vol. iv., pp. 7-12. 1852.

Rogers (W. H.) Guide to the New Forest. Southampton. N.D. Geology, pp. 26, 27. (1880-84?).

Ryle (T.) On Cretaceous Fossils from the Isle of Wight. Papers Eastbourne. *Nat. Hist. Soc.*, 1873-4, pp. 11-13.

Sandberger (Prof. F.) On Upper Eocene Fossils from the Isle of Wight. *Quart. Journ. Geol. Soc.*, vol xviii., p. 330. 1862.

Sedgwick (Rev. Prof. A.) On the Geology of the Isle of Wight. *Ann. Phil.*, ser. 2, vol. iii., p. 329. 1822.

Seeley (H.) Note on Some New Genera of Fossil Birds in the Woodwardian Museum. *Ann. and Mag. Nat. Hist.*, ser. 3, vol. xviii., p. 109. 1866.

—————— (H. G.) Notice of the Occurrence of Remains of a British Fossil, Zeuglodon (Z. Wanklyni, Seeley), in the Barton Clay of the Hampshire Coast. *Quart. Journ. Geol. Soc.*, vol. xxxii., pp. 429-432. 1876.

—————— On Remains of Emys Hordwellensis (Seeley) from the Lower Hordwell Beds, in the Hordwell Cliff, contained in the Woodwardian Museum, &c. *Quart. Journ. Geol. Soc.*, vol. xxxii., pp. 445-45c, 2 woodcuts. 1876.

—————— On a Remarkable Dinosaurian Coracoid from the Wealden of Brook, in the Isle of Wight, preserved in the Woodwardian Museum of the University of Cambridge, probably referable to Ornithopsis. *Quart. Journ. Geol. Soc.*, vol. xxxviii., pp. 367-371, 4 woodcuts. 1882.

—————— On the Dorsal Region of the Vertebral Column of a Dinosaur (indicating a new genus, Sphenospondylus) from the Wealden of Brook in the Isle of Wight, preserved in the Woodwardian Museum of the University of Cambridge. *Quart. Journ. Geol. Soc.*, vol. xxxix., pp. 55-61, 5 woodcuts. 1883.

—————— See Judd.

Sharpe (D.) Description of the Fossil Remains of Mollusca found in the Chalk of England. Cephalopoda, part I., *Paleontograph Soc.* 4to. London. 1853. Cephalopoda, part II., *Paleontograph Soc.* 4to. London. 1855. (Isle of Wight).

Sherborne. See Jones (T. Rupert).

Sheridan (W. C.) A Historical and Topographical Guide to the Isle of Wight. (*Geology*, pp. 230-265). 8vo. London. (1832 ?).

Shore (T. W., *F.G.S.*) and Westlake (E., *F.G.S.*) The Southampton Artesian Well. *Report of the Brit. Assoc.* 1882. Southampton Meeting.

Shore (T. W., *F.G.S.*) Guide to Southampton and Neighbourhood. 8vo. pp. 126. Southampton. Price, 8d. 1882.

——Well Sections at the S.W.R. Terminus, Southampton, and at the Southampton Docks. The Circulation of Underground Waters. *Report of the Brit. Assoc. Committee*, 1883. Southampton Meeting.

——and Thomas (J. B.) Underground Temperature in the Artesian Wel at Southampton. *Rep. of the Committee, Brit. Assoc. Report*, 1883. Southport Meeting.

——and Westlake (E.) On the Southampton Artesian Well. *Hampshire Independent.* Aug. 30, 1882, *and Rep. Brit. Assoc. for* 1882. pp. 547-549. 1883.

——Springs and Streams of Hampshire. *Hampshire Independent*, Nov., 1886.

——The Geology of Hampshire in connection with some of the Industries of the County. *Hampshire Independent*, Nov. 26th, 1887, and following weeks.

——Horn Corls and Part of Skull of Bos Primigenius found in the Dock Excavation at Southampton. *Geological Magazine*, Nov, 1887.

——Remains of *Bos Primigenius* recently found at Southampton. *Geol. Mag.* p. 519. 1887.

——Beds exposed in the Southampton New Dock Excavation. *Report Brit. Assoc.*, 1888. Bath Meeting.

——Ancient Hampshire Forest, and the Geological Conditions of their Growth. *Hampshire Field Club Papers and Proceedings.* Part II. 1888.

——Southampton Town Geology. *Hampshire Independent*, October, 1888.

——(F.G.S., F.C.S.) The Geology of Bramdean Valley and the Manor of Woodcote. *Hampshire Independent*, July, 7 1888.

——and Elwes (J. W.) The New Dock Excavation at Southampton. *Hampshire Club Papers and Proceedings.* Part III. 1889.

——(F.G.S., F.C.S.) The Clays of Hampshire and their Economic Uses. *Hampshire Field Club Papers and Proceedings.* Part IV. 1890.

Sorby (H. C.) On the Microscopical Structure of some British Tertiary and Post-Tertiary Freshwater Marls and Limestones. *Quart. Journ. Geol. Soc.* vol. ix., p. 344. 1853.

——On the Physical Geography of the Tertiary Estuary of the Isle of Wight. *Edin. New. Phil. Journ.*, ser 2, vol. v., p. 275. 1857.

Sowerby (J.) The Mineral Conchology of Great Britain. 5 vols. London. 8vo. 1812-25.

——(G. B.) On the Geological Formations of Headen Hill in the Isle of Wight. *Ann. of Phil.*, ser. 2, vol. ii., p. 216. 1821.

Stevens (J.) St. Mary Bourne, past and present, containing an account of the . . . Geology . . . . of the Parish. 8vo. London. 1863.

——A Descriptive List of Flint Implements found at St. Mary Bourne . . . with a sketch of the Geological Features of Upper Test Valley, and a list of Fossils from the Upper and Lower Chalk of St. Mary Bourne, Hants. 8vo. London. 1867.

——Flint Chips, a Guide to Pre-historic Archæology, as illustrated by the collection in the Blackmore Museum, Salisbury (Drift Series, p. 12.) by Dr. H. P. Blackmore, 8vo. London and Salisbury. 1870.

Stevens (J.) Sarsens, Greywethers, or Druid Stones. *Journ. Winchester Sci. Soc.*vol. i., part IV., pp. 224-236. 1875.

Tawney (E. B.) Excursion to the East End of the Isle of Wight. *Proc. Geol. Assoc.*, vol. vii., No. 3, pp. 185-189. 2 sections by W. Topley. 1881.

——On the Upper Bagshot Sands of Hordwell Cliffs, Hampshire. *Proc· Camb. Phil. Soc.*, vol. iv. pp. 140- 155. (1881), *and Rep. Brit. Assoc.* for 1881, p. 633. 1882.

——On the Outcrop of the Brockenhurst Bed, near Lyndhurst. *Rep. Brit. Assoc.* for 1882, p. 540, and *Geol. Mag.*, dec. ii., vol. x., pp. 157-160. 1883.

——See Keeping.

Test Valley, Report on the Drainage of. Large 8vo, sewed, 16 pp. 1846.

Thomas (J. B.) See Shore.

Topley (William) The Geology of the Weald, parts of the Counties of Kent, Surrey, Sussex and Hants. *Geological Memoir.* 8vo. London. 1875.

——See Tawney.

Townsend (Fredk.) Flora of Hampshire. 8vo. London. pp. 24, 524. 1883. (Soil and Geology Mentioned.)

Townshend (Rev. J.) The Character of Moses established for veracity as an Historian, recording Events from the Creation to the Deluge. 4to. Bath and London. 1813. Almost wholly a Geological work.

Trimmer (J.) On the Agricultural Geology of England and Wales. *Journ. Roy. Agric. Soc.*, vol. xii., p. 445. 1851.

——On the Superficial Deposits of the Isle of Wight. *Quart. Journ. Geol. Soc.*, vol. x. p. 51. 1854.

——On the Agricultural Relations of the Western Portions of the Hampshire Tertiary District, and on the Agricultural Importance of the Marls of the New Forest. *Journ. Roy. Agric. Soc.*, vol. xvi., p. 125. 1855.

——Notes on the Geology of the New Forest, in relation to its capabilities for the growth of Oak and for cultivation, with illustrative maps. In the Appendix to the 1st Report of the Select Committee of the House of Commons on Woods and Forests. 4to. 1849.

Transon (A.) Note sur l'île de Jersey. *Bull. Soc. Géol.*, France, ser. 3, vol. ix., pp. 82-85. 1882.

Tylor (A.) On the Occurrence of Productive Iron Ore in the Eocene Formations of Hampshire. *Quart. Journ. Geol. Soc.*, vol. vi. p. 133. 1850.

——On Quaternary Gravels. *Quart. Journ. Geol. Soc.*, vol. xxv. p. 57. (pp. 77, 78, 81, 97, 99.) 1869

Vancouver (C.) General View of the Agriculture of Hampshire, including the Isle of Wight (Map and Account of Soils and Minerals). London. 8vo. 1808 ? Another edition in 1813.

Venables (Rev. E.) A Guide to the Isle of Wight. Part III. chap. i., *Topography* (chap. 6, *Geology*). 8vo. London. 1860.

Wanklyn (A.) Description of some new species of Fossil Forms from the Bournemouth Leaf Bed. *Ann. and Mag. Nat. Hist.* ser 4, vol. iii., p. 10. 1869.

Ward (Dr. Ogier). On the Sinking of the South Coast of England. *Papers Eastbourne Nat. Hist. Society.* 1876.

Warner (F. T.) On a Specimen of Fossil Wood from the Winchester Chalk. *Journ. Winchester. Sci. Soc.*, vol. i., part III., pp. 152-155. 1875.

———(Rev. R.) The History of the Isle of Wight, Military, Ecclesiastical Civil and Natural. 8vo. Southampton. 1795.

Watts (W. W.) A Week's Rambling with a Hammer in the Isle of Wight. *Sci. Goss.*, 1882, pp. 30, 31, 57-59. 1882.

Webster (T.) On some New Variety of Fossil found in the Isle of Wight. 4to. 1814.

———On the Freshwater Formations of the Isle of Wight with some observations on the Strata over the Chalk in the South East of England. *Trans. Geol. Soc.*, vol. ii., p. 161. 1814. (See Englefield)

———On a Freshwater Formation in Hordwell Cliff, Hampshire, and on the subjacent beds from Hordwell to Muddiford. *Trans. Geol. Soc.*, ser 2, vol. i., p. 90. 1822.

Westlake (E.) The Early History of the Neighbourhood (of Fordingbridge) as written in its rocks (chap. vii. of Hannen's " Fordingbridge and its Neighbourhood, " in Mitchell's Fordingbridge Almanack for 1884) 8vo. 1883.

———See Shore.

Whitaker (W.) and Bristow (H. W.) Geology of Parts of Berks and Hants, 8vo. 1862.

———On some evidence of there being a reversal of the Beds near White-cliff Bay, Isle of Wight. *Geol. Mag.*, vol. i., p. 69. 1864.

———On the Chalk of the Isle of Wight. *Quart. Journ. Geol. Soc.*, vol. xxi. p. 400. 1865.

———On Sub-aerial denudation and on Cliffs and Escarpements of the Chalk and the Lower Tertiary Beds (Part II). *Geol. Mag.*, vol. iv., p. 483. (Corrections, vol. v., p. 47). Reprinted with further corrections, &c., for private distribution. 1867.

———On the Connection of the Geological Structure and the Physical Features of the South-East Coast of England, with the Consumption Death-Rate. *Geol. Mag.*, vol. vi., p. 499. 1869.

———Memoirs of the Geological Survey of England and Wales. Vol. iv. The Geology of the London Basin. Part I. The Chalk and the Eocene Beds of the Southern and Western Tracts. (Springs, pp. 391-392; Well Sections, pp. 422-563). 8vo. London. 1872.

———Report (to the Corporation) upon the Water-Supply of Southampton. Privately printed (lithographed). Fol. Southampton. p. 7, plate, (section). 1884.

———On the Area of Chalk as a Source of Water Supply. *Journ. Soc. Arts*, vol. xxxii., p. 847, and *The Health Exhibition Literature*, vol. viii., pp. 364, 373, 596, 597. 1884.

White (Rev. Gilbert) The Natural History and Antiquities of Selborne, in the County of Southampton. Ed. by Prof. Thos. Bell. 2 vols. 8vo. London. (1877). New Ed. of a work first published in 1789. Contains a note on the Geology of Selbourne by William Curtis.

Whitley (N.) The Physical Geography of the South-Western Counties of England. *Journ. Bath and W. Eng. Soc.*, ser. 2. vol. iv. p. 227. 1856

Wilkins (Dr. E. P.) Mammalian Remains (I. of Wight,) *Geologist*, vol. i., p. 444. 1858.

———A Concise Exposition of the Geology . . . of the Isle Wight. 8vo. 1859.

———Sand Pipes near Swainstone, Isle of Wight. *Geologist*, vol. ii., p. 175. 1859

Wilkins (D. E. P.) On a Newly Discovered Outlier of the Hempstead Strata on the Osborne Estate, Isle of Wight. *Proc. Geol. Assoc.*, vol. i. ,p. 194. 1862.

Wilkinson (Rev. J.) The Farming of Hampshire (Account of Soils). *Journ. Roy. Agric. Soc.*, vol. xxii., p. 329. 1861.

Wise (J. R.) The New Forest, its History and Scenery (Geology, pp. 234-249). 4to. London. 1863. Ed. 2, 4to. London. 1867.

Wood (S. V.) On the Discovery of an Alligator and of several new Mammalia in the Hordwell Cliff, with Observations upon the Geological Phenomena of that Locality. *Lond. Geol. Journ.*, pp. 1, 117. 1846.

—— (S. V., Jun.) On the Formation of River and other Valleys in the East of England. *Phil. Mag.*, ser. 4, vol. xxvii., p. 180. 1864.

—— Physical Geology of East Anglia in the Glacial Epoch. *Geol. Mag.*, dec. ii., vol. iii., pp. 284-288. 1876. Refers to Portsdown Hill.

—— The Tropical Forests of Hampshire. *Geol. Mag.*, dec. ii., vol. iv., pp. 95, 96, 141, 187, 188. 1877. (See Gardner.)

—— A Monograph of the Eocene Mollusca. Part IV.,Bivalves No. 1, *Paleontograph Soc.* 4to. London. 1861. No. 2, *Paleontograph Soc.* 4to. London. 1864. Part III.,Bivalves,*Paleontograph Society.* 4to. London. 1871.

—— The Raised Beach on Portsdown Hill. *Geol. Mag.*, vol. ix., p. 92. 1872.

—— On the Climate of the Post Glacial Period. *Geol. Mag.*, vol. ix., p. 153. 1872.

Woods (H.) On the Occurrence of Phosphatic Nodules in the Lower Greensand, East of Sandown, Isle of Wight. *Geol. Mag.*, p. 46. 1887.

Woodward (H.) On a New Genus of Shore-crab, Goniocypoda Edwardoi, from the lower Eocene of Hampshire. *Geol. Mag.*, vol. iv., p. 529. 1867.

—— Notes on Some New Crustaceans from the Lower Eocene of Portsmouth. *Quart. Journ. Geol. Soc.*, vol. xxvii., p. 90. 1871.

—— Further Notes on Eocene Crustacea from Portsmouth. *Quart. Journ. Geol. Soc.*, vol. xxix. p. 25. 1873.

—— (Dr. Henry) On the Occurrence of Branchipus or Chirocephalus in a Fossil State in the upper part of the Fluvio-Marine (Middle Eocene) at Garnet and Thorness Bays, near Cowes, Isle of Wight, in a thin band of freshwater limestone in the Bembridge series. *Rep. Brit. Assoc. for* 1877. Sections, p. 78.

——On the Occurrence of Branchipus (or Chirocephalus) in a fossil state associated with Eosphœroma and with numerous Insect remains in the Eocene Freshwater (Bembridge) Limestone of Gurnet Bay, Isle of Wight. *Quart. Journ. Geol. Soc.*, vol. xxxv. pp. 342-350. plate xiv. 1879. Abstract (with fuller list of insects) in *Geol. Mag.*, dec. ii., vol. v., pp. 88, 89. 1878.

——(H. B.) Mammoth not Pre-Glacial in Britain. (Letter) *Geol. Mag.*, dec. ii., vol. vi., p. 235. 1879.

Wright (Dr. T.) A Stratigraphical Account of the Section from Round Tower Point to Alum Bay, on the N.W. Coast of the Isle of Wight. *Ann. and Mag. Nat. Hist.*, ser. 2. vol. vii. p. 14. and *Proc. Cotteswold Nat. Club*, vol. i., p. 87. 1851.

Bibliotheca Hantoniensis.

Wright (Dr.T.) A Stratigraphical Account of the Section at Hordwell, Beacon and Barton Cliffs, on the Coast of Hampshire. *Ann. and Mag. Nat. Hist.*, ser. 2, vol. vii., p. 433. and *Proc. Cotteswold Nat. Club*, vol. i., p. 120. 1851.

——Contributions to the Paleontology of the Isle of Wight. *Ann. and Mag. Nat. Hist.*, ser. 2. vols. x. p. 87, and *Proc. Cotteswold Nat. Club*, vol. i., p. 229. 1852.

——A Monograph of the British Fossil Echinodermata from the Cretaceous Formation. Vol. i. part III. On the Diademedæ (Sussex Chalk), p. 129. Part. IV. On the Diademedæ and Salenidæ. *Paleontograph Soc.* 4to. London. 1864, 1870, 1871.

ADDENDA.

Beaulieu. See *Cornhill Magazine*, 1891.

Birch (W. de Gray, F.S.A.) The Hyde Register. 8vo. 1891. (Hampshire Record Society).

Doman (Henry) Songs in the Shade. 8vo. 1881. Refers to Beaulieu Abbey, &c.

Doman (Henry) The Cathedral and other Poems. 8vo. 1864 References to Hurst Castle, Walhampton, &c.

Eyre (Rev. W. L. W.) A Brief History of the Parishes of Swarraton and Northington, with Notices of the Owners of the Grange, in the County of Southampton. London : Simpkin and Co. ; Winchester : Warren and Son. N.D. (1890).

Godwin (Rev. G. N.) A Deserted Shipyard, or The Beaulieu River a Hundred Years Ago. *Adams' Southampton Almanack*, 1891.

Hampshire. Summer Tour to the Isle of Wight, including Portsmouth, Southampton, Winchester, &c., by T. Roscoe. (Numerous Fine Engravings). 8vo. 1843.

Hampshire Antiquary and Naturalist. Being the Local Notes and Queries, Reports of Meetings of the Hampshire Field Club and other Archæological and Natural History Matters. Reprinted from *The Hampshire Independent*. 100 pp. crown 4to. 1891.

Hope (W. H. St. John) Excavations at Silchester. *Antiquary*, 1890.

Kitchin (Very Rev. G. W., D.D., Dean of Winchester) The Great Screen of Winchester Cathedral. 8vo. 1891.

Pilgrims' Way from Winchester to Canterbury. *Art Journal*, 1891.

Silchester, Excavations at. See *Sunday Magazine*, March, 1891.

Stooks (Rev. C. D.) and Baigent (F. J.) The Records of the Manor of Crondal. 8vo. 1891. (Hampshire Record Society).

Warren (W.) New Handbook to Winchester Illustrated. (Three Maps). 8vo. 1890.

Winchester. Description of the Frescoes in Holy Trinity Church, by E. M. P. 8vo. 1890.

THE

HISTORY AND ANTIQUITIES

OF

SILCHESTER,

In Hampshire,

THE VINDONUM OF THE ROMANS,

AND THE

CAER SEGONT

OF THE

ANCIENT BRITONS.

WITH

BIOGRAPHICAL NOTICES OF PERSONS CONNECTED
With the Place.

COMPILED FROM AUTHENTIC SOURCES.

" Is this your joyous city, whose antiquity is of ancient
date ? "   ISAIAH.
" Seges ubi Troja fuit. "

BASINGSTOKE :

PRINTED AND SOLD BY SAMUEL CHANDLER.
SOLD ALSO BY J. RUSHER, READING, AND W. JACOB,
WINCHESTER.

1821.

[Figure 12; 11.9 x 19.9 cm]

THE
NATURAL HISTORY
OF
SELBORNE.

— where the Hermit hangs his straw-clad cell.

Τρηχει, αλλ' αγαθη κυροτροφος. υτι εγωγε
'Ης γαιης δυναμαι γλυκερωτερον αλλο ιδεσθαι.   Homeri Odyff.

Tota denique noſtra illa aſpera, & montuoſa, & fidelis, & ſimplex, & fautrix ſuorum regio.
Cicero Orat. pro Cn. Plancio.

[Figure 13; 18.8 x 24.9 cm]

ARCHITECTURAL VIEWS

AND

DETAILS

OF

𝕹etley 𝕬bbey,

PARTLY SHOWN AS IT ORIGINALLY EXISTED,

WITH

BRIEF HISTORICAL ASSOCIATIONS OF THAT ANCIENT RUIN, AND
DESCRIPTION OF LATE DISCOVERIES.

BY

GEORGE GUILLAUME,

ARCHITECT.

SOUTHAMPTON:
PRINTED BY FORBES AND KNIBB, 143, HIGH STREET.
LITHOGRAPHED BY DAY AND HAGHE, LONDON.
———
M.DCCC.XLVIII.

[Figure 14; 24.2 x 37.3 cm]

[229]

PAPERS

AND PROCEEDINGS

OF THE

Hampshire · Field · Club,

ESTABLISHED 1885,

For the Study of the Natural History and Antiquities of
the County.

VOL III.   1894-1897.

EDITED BY

THE REV. G. W. MINNS, LL.B., F.S.A.

SOUTHAMPTON:

PRINTED AT THE "HAMPSHIRE INDEPENDENT" AND "SOUTHERN ECHO" OFFICE.
1898.

SUPPLEMENTARY HAMPSHIRE

BIBLIOGRAPHY.

By the Rev. Sumner Wilson, M.A.

Being a List of Hampshire Topograhy not included in the
" Bibliotheca Hantoaensis."

The following selection from my own library has been
deemed worthy of publication as a supplement in part of the
very full list contained in *Bibliotheca Hantoniensis*,[1] and contains, I believe, only books, &c., published up to the date of
the publication of that work in 1891. Such a selection is
not very easy to make. Doubtless exception may be made
to some works or tracts here given, as of small general or
even local interest, but as these, from their very nature, are
likely to be quickly forgotten it is well to record their existence.
There are many other books, Acts of Parliament, Poll Books,
Archæological, Controversial, and other tracts, which reflect
more or less the thoughts, customs and opinions of the past,
and may well find a place, as one may hope, in a second
edition of the above-named useful work. Since 1891 many
very valuable books have been published which, together
with MSS. in public institutions and private libraries or
muniment rooms, may well be indexed for the use and com-
fort of students of local history. It may be permitted perhaps
for me to point out a few accessible MSS. which are perhaps

---

[1] Bibliotheca Hantoniensis, a list of books relating to Hampshire, includ-
ing Magazine references, &c., &c., by H. M. Gilbert and the Rev.
G. N. Godwin, with a List of Hants Newspapers, by F. E. Edwards,
Southampton, 1891.

not well known to those who would be much interested in their perusal. I quote from my own rough notes, which were intended for my own use, and which I am unable at the present moment to verify by reference to the originals. I believe them to be however substantially correct.

Suckling's MSS., Add. MSS., British Museum, contains many interesting notices of Hampshire Churches, with sketches, coats of arms, &c.

My list contains Herriard, Ellisfield, Basingstoke, Nateley, Sherborne St. John, Silchester, Old Basing, Alton, Scures, Bramley, Binsted (Hants), Chilton Candover, Church Oakley, Cliddesden, Hackwood House, Odiham Castle, Tunworth. Pamber Priory, Abp. Warham, Selborne, Sherfield, Stratfield Mortimer, Wield.

Madden's (Sir Fk.) MSS. contains many notes of the whole county, references to other sources of information in the British Museum and elsewhere, and especially full extracts and copies of deeds and charters connected with St. Mary Southwick from the muniment room of Mr. Thistlethwaite, which will be found of very great service to one who is interested in the early history of any parish formerly connected with that Priory.

The Journal of Mr. Skinner in many volumes, also in the B. Museum, contains numerous drawings of Hampshire antiquities. There is a very copious index in two volumes, and it is well worth more close study than I have been able to give it.

Mr. Luke Allen MS. in the same place is very valuable; and the *Latham MSS.* are also very interesting to those who seek information of Romsey History.

Of printed books, not in my collection, I will only add a note which may be of service.

Collectanea Topographica. Vols. VII. and VIII. contains church notes of Aldershot, Crondal, Farnborough, Long Sutton, Yateley, Bentley, Binsted (Hants), Dogmersfield, Elvetham, Eversley, South Warnboro', Froyle, Winchfield, Odiham, Basing, Cliddesden, Farley Wallop, Sherborne St. John [Signed C.E.L. (? Chs. Ed. Long)].

Articles from the *Gentleman's Magazine* I have not inserted in my selection as they have been lately republished in the volumes of Topographical articles taken from each county,[1] but as this reprint does not contain the engraving so often accompanying the articles in the magazine itself, it is manifest that the originals are still of very great interest.

The *Anastatic Society*, a publication in several volumes, contains many interesting sketches of Hampshire Antiquities with descriptions.

The above is, of course, only a very small indication of sources of information with regard to Hampshire Topography, but may be of some service to those interested in the subject.

[1] The Gentleman's Magazine Library, edited by G. L. Gomme, F.S.A.

Supplementary Hampshire Bibliography.

ALFRED THE GREAT. Annals of, Edited by Stevenson. Church Historians of England. 8vo. Lond. 1854.

ALLINGHAM (Wm.), alias Patricius Walker, Rambles. New Forest Gilpin, Winchester, &c. Lond. 1872.

ALETHPHILOS, Letter to Dr. Addams, D.C.L., shewing Purgatory inseparately connected with prayers to the dead. *re* Widow Woolfrey and Parson Breeks. 8vo. I. of Wight, Newport. 1840.

ANDERSON (H.), Vicar of King's Sombourne. A loyal tear dropt on the vault of K. Charles II. Lond. 4to. 1685.

ANDOVER MUSEUM, by an Honorary Curator (Dr. Stevens). 12mo Andover. 1873.

—— Members of Parliament for, from 1295 to 1880, by F. W. Buxton, M.P., Andover. Broadsheet. 1881.

ASHBURNER (E.), Sermon at ordination of Rev. Sir H. Trelawney, Bart., at Southampton. 1777. Southampton.

ASHE (Rt. Hoadley), Letter to Rev. J. Milner, *re* Bishop Hoadley. Lond. 8vo. B. Long, Winchester. 1799. pp. 96.

ANDREWS (Lt. Bishop of Winchester), Life of, by H. Isaacson.

ANNALS of the Church of Winchester. Edited by Stevenson. Church Historians of England. 8vo. Lond. 1856.

ATTWOOD (J. S.) Manors in Hampshire formerly part of the possessions of the Duchy of Lancaster. n. d.

AUSTEN (Jane), Memoirs of, by Austen Leigh. Pls. 8vo. 1870.

ARGYLE (F. B.), Cymri in, Hants. 12mo. Ch. Church. N. D. pp. 50. sewed.

BAIGENT (F. J.), Prelates of the Courtenay family, especially Peter Courtenay, Bishop of Winchester. Collec. Archæol.4to. Vol. 1.

BAKER (J.), King Charles and his murderers. Winchester. 1875.

BAKER (F. W.), Notes and Plans of Netley Abbey. 1857.

BARING (W. B.) Letters to the Reformers of Winchester on the magisterial conduct of W. B. Baring (defending him), pamphlet not mentioned with others in the Bibla. Hants. 8vo. Lond. 1831.

—— Letter to the Electors of Winchester in vindication of his conduct in Parliament. 8vo. Lond. 1835.

BARNES (H.), of Southgate, Winchester. Acct. of discovery of Anglo-Saxon Seal. 4to. Lond. Archæologia, vol. xxiv. Plate.

BARTON (P.), Vicar of Portsea. Sermon at Consecration of St. George's Chapel, Portsea. Oxford. 1755.

BATTS, A(nthony). The Wreckers, Needles, Hurst, &c. 12mo. Lymington. 1849.

BINSTEAD CHURCH, I. of Wight. Weale's Quarterly Papers. Plates and letterpress.

BUONAPARTE (Prince Lucien). Dialects of the Southern and South-Western Counties. English Dialect Society. 8vo. 1877.

BONCHURCH, Reminiscences of, by Ht. Sewell. Lond. 1849.

BROUGH (W.), Eight views of St. Cross, Winchester, with description. obl. 4to. 1858. Cheltenham.

BULLAR (J.), Memoirs of Rev. W. Kingsbury, of Southampton. Lond. 1819.

BURNETT (Bishop) Sermon on death of Lady Brooke, of Breamore. Lond. 4to. 1691.

BURNS (J. S.), History of the foreign Refugees, description and plate of God's House Chapel, Southampton. 8vo. Lond. 1846.

BUTLER (C.), Master of Holy Ghost Chapel, Basingstoke, Feminine Monarchy, concerning Bees. 24mo. 1704.

CARISBROOKE AND CHARLES I. Portraiture of his sacred Majesty in his solitude, at Carisbrooke Castle, Portsea (reprint of edition of 1685, Norton).

CARTER (O. B.), Penton Mewsey Church. Plates and letterpress. 4to. Lond. 1845. Weale's Quarterly Papers

————Beaulieu Abbey. Plates and letterpress. 4to, Lond. 1845. Weale's Quarterly Papers.

CATALOGUE of the Earls of Northampton and Southampton, together with their several armes, wives, and issue. From Mille's Catalogue of Honours. Fol. Lond. 1610.

CAYLEY AND SALTER, Architectural Memoir of Old Basing Church, armorials, &c. in ditto. 8vo. Basingstoke. 1891.

CHRIST CHURCH, Choice carving at, (by James Garside). Ryl. 8vo. Lond. n.d. phots.

CLAYTON (Wm.), Tales and recollections of the Southern Coast. 12mo. Lond. 1861.

COLE (H. D.), Heraldic Bearings of Winchester, in 4 numbers. 4to. 1885.

COLLIER (Mary), Washerwoman at Petersfield. Woman's labour, a Poem. Lond. 1739.

COLLIER (C., Vicar of Andover), Roman pavement at Itchen Abbas, plate and letterpress. Archl. Assn. 1878.

——— Account of some skeletons found near Portsmouth. Archl. Assn. 1888.

——— Two historic legends of Winchester. Winchester Literary Society. 8vo. 1874.

COLLINGRIDGE (Ignatius), Sermon at St. Peter's Winchester, cause of discontinuance of attendance of troops. Lond. 1850.

CIVIL WAR PAMPHLETS, Exceeding good news from the Isle of Wight, being a true relation of a great quantity of ammunition, &c. sm, 4to. 1641.

——— Isle of Wight, Scots Commissioners. Declaration of the Lords and Commons concerning the papers of, and concerning the proceedings of the said Commissioners in the Isle of Wight. sm. 4to. 1647.

——— The notes and proceedings in Parliament for bringing the King out of the Isle of Wight—also the proceeding against Major Rolfe. sm. 4to. 1648.

————His Majesties declaration upon his departure from the Isle of Wight, &c. sm. 4to. 1648.

CROOKHAM, Two photographs of flint axes, with description found at Banks farm. Newbury Field Club Proceedings, vol. 1. 1871.

CUNDY (N.W.), Imperial Ship Canal. Reply to author of abuse, &c., with plan. 8vo. 1828.

—— Prospectus for making the Canal. fol. 1827.

COPE (Sir A. T.), Meditations on XX. select Psalms. Reprint of edition 1547, with Biographical notice of Sir A. T. Cope, by Sir W. H. Cope. 8vo. 1848.

DAVIS (J.), of Winchester, Bookseller and Schoolmaster. St. Cross, a poem, with the execution of the Duke of Kent before the Castle Gate at Winchester. 24mo. Winchester. 1836.

DAVIDSON (G.), St. Swithin. Legend of, Poem, with plates by J. Faed, R.S.A. 4to. Aberdeen. 1869,

DAVIDSON (A.), Academy, Lymington. Sermons in blank verse. List of Subscribers. 8vo. Romsey. n.d.

DALLAS (A.) My churchyard—Reminiscences of deceased parishioners at Wonston. 12mo. Lond. 2nd Ed. 1848. Plate of church.

—— (A.) Incidents in the life of, by his Widow. 8vo. Lond. 1871.

DENMAN (Jos., Admiral), pressing necessity for increased docks and basins at Portsmouth. 3rd Edn. 8vo. Lond. 1863,

DUMMER and the Dummer Family, by Thos. Bond. Plate. Somersetshire Arch. Soc. 1871.

DUMMER, Early British Cemetery at, by J. Stevens. Plate. 8vo. Arch. Assn. 1889.

ELECTION PETITION, SOUTHAMPTON, Blue Book. Fol. 1842.

ELVETHAM. Antiquaries Museum, Schnebbelie (J). 2 Plates with Letterpress. 4to.

EXAMINATIONS before Secretary of State, and 2 letters. re Philip Caryl of North, nr. Petersfield, and Dr. Caryl of Clanfield. Lond. 1723.

EX-CHAPLAIN. Address to Lord Lieutenant, &c,, of co. of Southampton, on treatment of prisoners. 2 parts. 8vo. 1845,

EAST (Rt.) Extracts from Records, &c., of Portsmouth. New and enlarged edition. Ryl. 8vo. 1891. Portsmouth.

ELLIS (W. S.). Notices of the Ellises, derived from W. Ellis, of Ellaton, now Allington, in Mansbridge hundred, co. Hants. Papers with Supplements, separately paged, also pedigrees. 8vo. 1857 to 1875.

EYRE (W. L. W.) Brass formerly in Brown Candover Church. Sy. of Autiquaries. 8vo. 1889. Plate.

EYRE (Ths.) & CAKE (D.). Remarks on Holy Scriptures with very rough portraits of authors, 2 views of Burley Chapel New Forest, and Inscriptions in. Ringwood. 1827. 24mo.

FEARON (W. A,). Cardinal Beaufort, a lecture. Winchester. 1880.

FERRY (B. E.). Notes on St. Catherine's Church, Catherington. Sy. of Antiquaries. 1884.

GARBETT. Letter to Rev. T. Milner, on certain erroneous statements. 8vo. Lond. 1826.

GIBBON (E), Historian, of Buriton, Autobiography of, Edited by Lord Sheffield. 2 vols. 18mo. 1827.

GARNIER (T., Dean of Winchester). Death bed of John Duffin, Bishopstoke, carrier. 8vo. Winchester. 1836,

GILPIN (W.). Catalogue of Drawings, &c., to be sold for the endowment of Boldre school—priced throughout—together with the Author's acct, of the drawings contained in it. 8vo. Lond. 1802.

GOUNTERS (Colonel) Escape of Charles II., now first printed, Hants places mentioned, Hinton Daubeney, Hambledon, Warnford, Winchester. Lond. 1846.

GRIFFIN (J). Independent Minister at Portsea, memories of, by his sons. 8vo. Lond. 1840.

GRYLL GRANGE. New Forest scenes, by the author of Headlong Hall, (Peacock). Lond. 1861. 1st edition.

GUIDOTT (W.), of Preston Candover, M.P. for Andover), Respondent. Duchess of Marlborough, Appellant. His case. Fol. 1727. To be read at bar of House of Commons.

GUNNER (W. H.). Remarks on one of the great seals of Edward III. Plates. 8vo. Archl. Journal.

——— Notices of the Priory of Southwick. 8vo. Archl. Inst. 1845.

——— Inventory of plate given to Winchester College, by Wm. of Wykeham. No. 39 Archl. Journal.

HALL (E. & T.) Series of original etchings of ancient buildings, to illustrate Englefield's walk through Southampton, six in number. 4to. 1817.

HAMPSHIRE from Britannia Curiosa. 12mo. 74 pp. 1777.

——— Catalogue of Harefield Library. 8vo. Lond. 1887. Hampshire books, 74 lots.

——— Catalogue of Tracts, Pamphlets, and Prints. J. Russell Smith. 8vo. Lond. 1878.

HANNAN (Regd.). Tales of the Hundred of Fordingbridge. 12mo. 1890.
——— History of Fordingbridge. 2nd edition, with additions of his " Notes on the Town of Fordingbridge." 12mo. 1889.

HARTLEY ROW. Curious sermon by Rev. Mr. Hyberdin, made at the request of certain thieves, that robbed him on a hill, near Hartley Row. 8vo. New Lond. Magazine. 1788.

HERVEY (Rev. T.). History of Colmer and Priors Dean, with additions 2nd edition. 4to. 1891. Colmer. Printed for private circulation.

——— Colmer and Priors Dean. Parish Registers of. 4to. Colmer. 1886. Privately printed.

——— Bishops of Winchester. 12mo. Colmer. 1877. Privately printed,

HENLEY (Rt.) E. of Northington, Lord Chancellor, Life of. 8vo. Lond. 1831. Plates.

HEYLIN (Peter, Rector of Alresford), Life of, by J. Barnard. 18mo. Lond. 1683.

HOARE (Sir R. Colt), Letter in Gent. Mag., signed by R.C.H., on the Thruxton Roman Pavement. 1823.

HOPE (W. H. St. John), Seals of English Bishops—Bishops Winchester. Illustrated. Journal Socy. of Antiquaries. 1887.

—— Maces and Swords of State, including many in Hants. Illustrated. June, 1888.

—— Maces of Newtown, I. of Wight, &c. Illustrated. 1889.

HOTTEN (J. Camden) Handbook to Topography of Hants. 8vo. Lond. n.d.

HYDE, Book of, Edited by J. Stevenson. Church Historians. 8vo. Lond. 1854.

HUMBERT (L. M.), Histy. and Antiqs. of St. Cross. 24mo. 3rd Ed. 1864.

INSCRIPTIONS in Winchester Cathedral and other places, by E. G. 12mo. 1884.
Printed for funds towards an organ in Upham Church.

ISLE OF WIGHT. Article upon, in Quarterly Review. 1874

——————————— ——————— Edinburgh Review. 1892.

ISLAND QUARTERLY. Containing Articles on Churches, by Stratton.

JONES (E. H. J. on title page), Legend of Netlie, or Three Christmas Eves. Southampton.

JACKSON (Canon J. E.), Notes on the Borders of Wilts and Hants. Reprinted from the Wiltshire Arch. and Nat. Histy. Mag. 4to. Devizes. 1884.

JARVIS (Sir Raymond), Plain statement of facts relating to the proceedings of the Hampshire Friendly Society. 8vo. Lond. 1837.

JENKINSON (H. T. J.), New Forest, Preservation of the Old Timber, &c. 8vo. Lond. 1871.

JONES (Rupert), Geology of the Kingsclere Valley. Newbury Field Club Proceedings. Vol. I. 1871.

KELL (Rev. E.), Remarks on Longstone and the Barrows on Wroxall Down.

—— Notices of Sites of Roman Villas at Brixton and Clatterford, in the Isle of Wight.

—— Netley Abbey with an account of recent excavations. Col. Arch. Vol. II. 4to.

—— Address delivered by, before the Hartley Committee, at a meeting of the Hartley Bequest. 16mo. 1858.

KINGSBURY (W.), Sermon for Southampton Hospital. Southampton. 8vo. 1800.

LAKE (Osmund) Minister of the Word of God, at Ringwood. Probe Theological, or first part of the Christians Pastors proof of his learned Parishioner's faith. 4to. Lond. 1612.

LEACH (Isaac, Master of the Grammar School at Alton). New enquiry of the earth's motion. Diagrams and Poem. 24mo. Lond. 1731. Subscribers' names, probably consisting mostly of Scholars at Eggar's School.

LEVIEN (E.), Documents relating to captivity of Charles I. at Carisbooke. 8vo. Archl. Assn. 1863.

LLOYD (John), Vicar of Holy Roods (sic), Southampton. Song of Songs. Paraphraze on the Chronicles of Solomon. Lond. 1682.

LOWTH (Bishop Robert), Supplement to 1st Ed. of Life of Wm. Wykeham. 8vo. 1759.

LOWTH (G. T.) High Places, a Winchester Story. 3 vols. Post 8vo. 1861.

—— Memoirs of Colonel J. G. Lowth. Winchester. 12mo. 1855.

LUSH (A.), Curate of Greywell. Letter on the Odiham marriage case. Fol. sheet. Odiham. 1855.

MACLAUCLAN (H.) and WAY (Albert). Silchester. Archl. Journal. No. 31. Plan and 2 plates.

MADDEN (Sir F.) Creation of Lewis de Bruges, as Earl of Southampton. 4to. Soc. of Antiq. 1835.

MADDOCK (S.), Vicar of Ropley. Statement of difference about Alresford Union Chaplaincy.

MAN (Ths.) Bible Society. Remonstrance addressed to Rev. W. F. Hook. 8vo. Southampton. 1826.

MANNINGHAM (Ths., Rector of East Tistead, afterwards Bishop). Funeral Sermon on the Lady Dorothy Norton, of Rotherfield. 4to. Lond. 1703.

—— Sermon at the Funeral of Sir John Norton, Bart. 4to. Lond. 1687.

—— Sermon at Hampshire Feast. 4to. Lond. 1686.

MANORS IN HAMPSHIRE, formerly part of the possessions of the Duchy of Lancaster. J. T. Attwood. n. d.

MARSHALL (Emma). Winchester Meads in the days of Bishop Ken. 8vo, Lond. 1890. Plates.

MAP OF MANOR and Haven of Beaulieu, with description. Large 4to. n.d.

MILNER (J.) Letters to a Prebendary. 24mo. Derby. 1843.

—— Dissertation on the modern style of altering Cathedrals. 4to. Lond. 1798.

—— Essays on Gothic Architecture by Milner and Warton. Plates, including details of Winchester Cathedral. 8vo. Lond. 1804.

—— Account of some painting discovered in Winchester Cathedral. Archa. 1788.

MILLS (Isaac), Rector of Burghclere, Life of. 12mo. Lond. 1721.

MOLESWORTH (J. E. N.), Curate of Millbrook. Sermon at funeral of F. Proudley, executed at Winchester. 12mo. Southampton. 1827.

MONEY (Walter). Reprint of description of the siege of Basing Castle, kept by the Marquis of Winchester. 8vo. Oxford. 1880.

MOSES (H.), Sketches of Shipping Views in Portsmouth Harbour· Obl. 4to. Southsea. 1817.

NEALE'S Views of Seats in Hampshire, extracted from his work on English Seats generally. 12 engravings with letterpress. 4to. Lond.

NEW FOREST, by the author of Brambletye House. 2 vols. New York. 1829.

—— Sketches. Many plates. British Architect. 1886.

NORTON (Richard). Notes on Sermon, intituled "Cabinet of Hell unlocked," addressed to. 4to. 1698.

NORTON (A. W.) Carisbrooke and other Poems, also author of "Spithead." n.d. Lond. 12mo.

NORRIS (W.) Description of an ancient Yew Tree in Warblington Churchyard. Remarks upon Yew Trees generally. Mirror, 1835. 8vo. Lond. pp. 98-100 and 119-121. Plates.

ODIHAM. Account of the Odiham Society for the encouragement of Agriculture and Industry. 8vo. Lond. c. 1786. List of Subscribers, Premium, Candidates, &c. 88 pp.

ORIENTALIS. The Umbrella, an o'er true and Regal Romaunt, or Legend of Osborne House. 12mo. Cowes. 1844. Plates.

P (J. H.) On some arrangements for the Hanging of Bells in Churches without towers. Woodcuts. Among others Corhampton, Littleton, Ashley, King's Sombourne, Penton Mewsey, Godshill. 8vo. Lond. Arch. Inste. 1845.

PADDON v. DENMARK. Law v. Physic. 8vo. Portsmouth. 1812.

PAGE (W. B.) Southampton Botanic Gardens. List of Subscribers, Rules, &c. 12mo. 1821.

PALEY (F. A.) Remarks on the Architecture of Christ Church Priory. New Ed. Plates. n.d.

PEARCE (L.), Dean of Winchester. Translation of a Latin Sermon by, before Convocation, with dedication to the author, by a member of the Lower House of Convocation. 18mo. Lond. 1742.

PEARCE (Wm.) Arrived at Portsmouth. Operatic farce. Lond. 1794.

PENTON MEWSEY. Description of, with plates. Weale's Quarterly Papers. 4to.

PLANCHÉ (J. R.), Earls of Devon and Lords of I. of Wight. Coll. Arch. Brit. Archl. Assn. 22 pp. 4to. Lond.

PORTCHESTER. From Braley's Graphic and Historical Illustrator. Plates.

PORTSMOUTH. List of Plates, Maps, &c., in British Museum, relating to Portsmouth, &c. 8vo.

PORTSMOUTH. Charles Dickens, a tribute to his memory. Presentation of his portrait to the Inhabitants of Portsmouth, by Aldn. Whitcombe. Plates. 4to. 1891. Portsmouth.

PRESBYTER (Rev. E. Thoyts, of Ashe). Buried Church at Silchester. Paper read at a meeting of Clergy. 12mo. Reading. 1892.

PRICE (John E.) and Price, (F. G. Hilton), Excavations of Tumuli on Brading Down. 1882. Plate.

—— Remains of Roman building near Brading. 4to. Lond. 1880. Inste. of Brit. Architects, Plate.

PROSSER (G. F.) Illustrations of Hampshire. Number of Plates, 63. Bibliotheca Hants. gives number as 30.

REEKS (H.) List of flowering plants, ferns, and mosses, observed in the parish of East Woodhay. Transactions of Newbury Field Club. Vol. I.

QUEENWOOD COLLEGE. Notes of the Summer Term 1889. 6 photos. Queenwood four, East Dean Ch., Cottages at West Tytherley.

RALEIGH (Sir Walter), Life of, with his trial at Winchester. 12mo. Lond. 1677.

ROMSEY CHARITIES. Committee of Education of the lower orders. Blue book. Fol. 1818.

RUSSELL (Lord Wm.) The last speech and behaviour of. 1683. **Fol.**

—— The late Lord Russell's case by H. P. Lord de la Mere. Fol. **1679.**

—— Defence of, by Sir Rt. Atkins. Fol. 1689.

—— Antidote agst poison, Remarks upon paper printed by direction of Lady Russell. Fol. 1683.

—— Animadversions upon a paper intituled Speech of the late Lord **Wm.** Russell. fol. 1683.

—— Answer to a late paper intituled " A True Copy of a paper written by Captain Thos. Walcott," by Robert West. fol. Lond. 1683.

SEYMOUR (S. F.) & Trower (C. F.), Winchfield, Hants. Past and Present. Winchester. 1891. Photos.

SHERLOCK (Wm.), Dean of St. Paul's, Sermon at the funeral of Richard Meggot, Dean of Winchester. 4to. Lond. 1693.

SLIGHT (H.) Henville Window in St. Thomas Church, Portsmouth. 24mo. Portsmouth. n.d.

—— Matin of St. Thomas, Some facts in the life of the Worshipful the Mayor of Portsmouth—Wm. Brandon. 24mo. Portsmouth. 1847.

SHENTON (F. K. G.), Winchester Records. Gents. Mag. 1872.

SHORE (T. W.), Old roads and fords of Hampshire. Archl. Review. 1889.

—— Early Boroughs in Hampshire. Do. 1889.

SMIRKE (E.) Ancient Ordinances of Guild Merchants, Southampton, 2 papers. Archl. Journal. 1869.

——Ancient Consuetudinary of the City of Winchester. Archl. Journal. 1882.

SMART (W. W.), Roman remains found at Nursling. Archl. Assn. 1881.

—— Further notes at Nursling, and on other Roman stations and roads in the New Forest. Pl. Archl. Assn. 1885.

SMITH (Major H.), Glossary of words in use in the Isle of Wight, with additions by C. Roach Smith. 8vo. 1881. English Dialect Society.

SOTHEBY (W.), Memorial of Sir H. Englefield, Bart. Lond. 1882.

SOUTHAMPTON Literary and Philosophical Institution. Introductory lecture by Rev. J. Davis. 1828.

—— Richard Andrews. Narrative of the life of.

—— Register of the French Church at Southampton, edited by H. M. Godfrey. Huguenot Society of London. 4to. Lymington, 1890.

SOUTHEY (Caroline), Chapters on Churchyards, with etchings of Boldre Church. new edition. 12mo. 1841.

STEVENS (J), Hampshire Inn Signs. 8vo. Winchester. 1879.

—— Discoveries at Finkley, vol. 1. Newbury Field Club. 1871.

—— Roman Remains at Finkley. Not duplicate of above.

—— Brank or Scold's Bridle. 1877.

—— Scold's Bridle at Vernham Deans. 1877.

—— Roman Remains found on the Loddon. 1880.

—— Relics of early races found in the Upper Test Valley. 1879.

—— Geological notices of North Hampshire. Reprint from Newbury Field Club. 1872.

ST. CROSS, Hospital of, Scheme for the interim management of, approved by Court of Chancery.

——On the Vale of Itchin, a descriptive Poem, also the Brothers Garden, and Verses on St. Cross, &c. 12mo. 1830. Romsey.

—— Indenture of the Patronage of. 1185. Coll. Heraldica & Geologica.

STOKE CHARITY, from Carter's Vetusta Monumenta. Fol. Letterpress, with engravings.

SUMNER (C. R., Bishop). Conspectus of the Diocese. 1864. Royal 8vo., not published. Biba. Hants., only mentions the earlier edition of. 1854.

SWITZER (Stephen), Gardener—native of Stratton. Ichnographia Rustica. 3 vols. Plates. 1742. And other similar works.

SYKES (A. A.), Sermon preached at Winchester Cathedral. General Thanksgiving for suppression of rebellion. 4to. Lond. 1746.

TADLEY Acct. of, by (B)enham (D)aniel. Large paper copy. 4to. Not given in Bibla. Hants., with two plates.

TICHBORNE, A letter formerly written to Mr. Titchborne in the Tower, to remind him of death. Lond. 4to. 1661.

—— (Sir R.), Cluster of Canaan's Grapes. 4to. Lond. 1657.

—— (Chidiock), Story of the brave but unfortunate, by Isaac Disræli. 12mo. Lond. 1873.

TALON (Nichs.) Holy living, translated by the Marquess of Winchester. 4to. Lond. 1753.

TITCHFIELD ABBEY REGISTER, Taxation of the 10th and 15th in Hampshire. Abbots of Titchfield. Colla., Top. and Mis. Vol. 1.

—— Acct. of Monastic, Library of, New Monthly Magazine.

TOPOGRAPHER. Vol. 5 for the year 179c. Addl. vol. by Sir T. Phillips. Salisbury. 8vo. 1821. 60 pp. All published. Contains—
Hants Ch. Notes, by W. H. (Hamper?)

> Winston (Wonston)
> Stoke Charity
> Hunton
> Weyhill   Inscriptions in churches many now
> Abbots Ann   probably not to be found.
> Monxton
> Quarley

Pedigree of Wm. Lenche, of Southampton.

TOPOGRAPHICAL Miscellanies, 1792. Vol. 1. 4to.
Note in Brit. Museum, copy " no more of this work published, it is a continuation of the Topographer. Impt. copy, pages missing." 15 pp. refer to Hampshire. Crondal 2 pp. Avington 4 pp. Easton. Worthy. The Grange. Popham 2 pp. Stratton. Steventon. **Deane**. Ash. Extracted from the above work.

TRIGG (H. R.) Guide to Hayling Island. Photographs. 1878.

VECTIS MAGAZINE, 6 Nos. ; ? all published March to August. 8vo. 1822.

VENABLES (E), Passage from the Oglander MS.S. relating to arrival of Charles I. in the Isle of Wight. Archæol. Inst. 1874.

———— Alien Priories in the Isle of Wight. Archl. Journal. 1872.

WALTERS (Alfred), Plates of Hampshire fonts, with description. 4 pp. n.d.

WALKER (Sir E.) Perfect copies of all the votes, letters, &c., relating unto the treaty of Newport in the Isle of Wight. 1648. Reprint. Lond. 1705.

WARD (G. R. M.), Foundation Statutes of Bishop Fox for Corpus Christi College, Oxford, with a life of the Founder. 8vo. Lond. 1843. Portrait and 3 plates.

WARNER (R.) Miscellanies including sketch of R. Gilpin, &c. Distinct from " Recollections." 2 vols. 12mo. Bath. 1819.

———— Antiquitates Culinariæ. Plates. 4to. Lond. 1791. Including enthonization of Abp. Warham, native of Hants. Scarce, in consequence of its issue being ¦withdrawn because of dispute with Grose, the Antiquary. See Recollections by R. Warner.

WARTON (Anthony) of Breamore. Refinement of Zion. 4to. Lond. 1647.

WELLOW EAST. Plate and short description of Mural painting in church. From drawing of Mr. F. Baigent. Archl. Journal. 1852.

WHITAKER (W.) List of works on Geology of Hampshire. 8vo. Lond. 1873.

WHITCHURCH, Tales by a Young Lady of. Plates. 8vo. Lond. 1810.

WILLMOTT (Sir J. E. Eard.ey, Bart.) Reminiscenses of Thomas Assheton Smith. New Ed. 1862.

WINCHESTER COLLEGE. Education. Evidence. Rev. D. Williams, James Ralfe, Phil. Williams, Rev. Liscombe, Clerk. Blue book. Fol. 1813.

———- Charities. Charity Commission. Report.

———— City Cross. Judgment of the Architect and building proceedings. Fol. broad sheet. 1866.

———— and Hampshire Literary Society. Including Papers (local) by F. G. Warner, W. Whitaker, C. Collier, Canon Kingsley, &c. 8vo. 1874.

———— Review. 8vo. 1880. ? Four numbers published.

———— St. Maurice Ch. $\left\{\begin{array}{l}\text{Ceremony of Laying Foundation Stone}\\\text{Order of } \quad,, \quad ,,\\\text{Form of Service.}\end{array}\right.$ 3 sheets. 1840.

—— Magdalen Chapel. 3 plates with description, seal of Chapel. Fol. 1790. Carter's Vetusta Monumenta.

—— Montagu Bishop. Will and Inventories of. Archæologia. 4to 1876.

—— Cathedral. Plates and descriptions. Storer's Cathedrals.

—— ——— Opening of the tomb of Bishop Fox. Account of by Dr. Nott, Canon of Winchester. MS.

—— Chapter. Church Commission. 8vo. Lond. 1838

—— ——— Assignment by Eccl. Comrs. of Estates, &c. London Gazette. Fol. 1861.

—— College. Letter by H. Brougham, Lord Brougham, to Sir S. Romilly, upon the abuse of Charities. 8vo. Lond. 1818.

—— ——— Case of the Subwarden and Bursars of. Large 4to sheet. 1710.

—— ——— Recollections of the two St. Mary Colleges. 1883.

WITHERS (H. J.) Beaulieu Abbey, Encaustic Tiles from. Weale's Quarterly Papers. 4to. Plates.

WITHER (G.), of Bentworth, Poet. Poems with portrait. Privately printed. 1827. J. B. Pulham, Gower St., nr. London.

—— A single Si quis, reprinted 1840. Private press, J. B. P., as above.

—— Shepherds hunting. Reprint 100 copies only. Preface containing an account of Author's family. Portrait. Lond. 1814.

WITTWOR (L. O.), Geological Sketch of the I. of Wight. 12mo. Manchester. 1814.

WRENCH (G. K.), Winchester College Word Book. Winchester 4to. 1891.

YATELEY. Description of Monumental Brasses in, by Wm. M. Wylie. 3 pp. 8vo. Lond.

YOUNG (C. M.) Picturesque Architecture. Contains 10 Hampshire Plates. 4to. Birmingham. 1869.

THE LIVES

OF THE

Bishops of Winchester,

FROM

BIRINUS,

THE FIRST BISHOP OF THE WEST SAXONS,
TO THE PRESENT TIME.

BY

THE REV. STEPHEN HYDE CASSAN, A.M.

Curate of Mere and West Knoyle, Wilts; Chaplain to the Earl of
Caledon, K. P. Author of the Lives of the Bishops of
Salisbury, and Sermons on various subjects.

IN TWO VOLUMES.

VOL. I.

CONTAINING THE LIVES OF

THE ROMAN CATHOLIC BISHOPS.

LONDON:

PUBLISHED BY C. AND J. RIVINGTON;

JACOB AND JOHNSON, WINCHESTER; BRODIE AND DOWDING, SALISBURY;
PARKER, OXFORD; AND DEIGHTON, CAMBRIDGE.

Crockers, Printers, Frome.

1827.

[Figure 15; 13.6 x 21.6 cm]

THE

DIRECTORY.

FOR THE

Town of Southampton,

IN 1811;

TO WHICH ARE APPENDED.

THE

Southampton Register;

WITH

The Assessed Taxes and other Duties;

CONCLUDING WITH

The exact Distances from Southampton to the
Principal Towns in England and Scotland.

[Figure 16; 10.0 x 16.7 cm]

HISTORY,

GAZETTEER, AND DIRECTORY

OF

HAMPSHIRE

AND

THE ISLE OF WIGHT,

COMPRISING

GENERAL HISTORICAL SURVEYS OF THE COUNTY & ISLAND,

AND OF THE

DIOCESE OF WINCHESTER;

AND SEPARATE

HISTORICAL, STATISTICAL, AND TOPOGRAPHICAL DESCRIPTIONS

OF THE

TOWN AND COUNTY OF THE TOWN OF SOUTHAMPTON,

THE CITY OF WINCHESTER,

THE POPULOUS

PORT, BOROUGH, & SUBURBS OF PORTSMOUTH,

AND OF ALL THE

Towns, Boroughs, Ports, Bathing Places,

UNIONS, PARISHES, TITHINGS, VILLAGES, HAMLETS, SEATS, &c.,
IN THIS INTERESTING COUNTY AND ITS BEAUTIFUL CHANNEL ISLE;

SHEWING THEIR EXTENT AND POPULATION;

THEIR TRADE, COMMERCE, MANUFACTURES, MARKETS, FAIRS, FISHERIES, AND AGRICULTURAL
AND MINERAL PRODUCTIONS; THEIR CHURCHES, CHAPELS, CHARITIES, AND PUBLIC
INSTITUTIONS; THEIR EMINENT MEN; THE PATRONS, INCUMBENTS, AND VALUE OF THE
BENEFICES; THE TITHE COMMUTATIONS; THE LORDS OF THE MANORS AND PRINCIPAL
OWNERS OF THE SOIL; THE CIVIL AND ECCLESIASTICAL JURISDICTIONS; THE ADDRESSES
OF THE PRINCIPAL INHABITANTS; THE POST-OFFICE REGULATIONS; THE

Seats of the Nobility and Gentry;

THE MAGISTRATES AND PUBLIC OFFICERS;

AND A GREAT VARIETY OF OTHER USEFUL INFORMATION:
IN ONE VOLUME, WITH A LARGE NEW

MAP OF HAMPSHIRE AND THE ISLE OF WIGHT.

BY WILLIAM WHITE,

AUTHOR OF SIMILAR WORKS FOR YORKSHIRE, DEVONSHIRE, NORFOLK, SUFFOLK,
ESSEX, AND MANY OTHER COUNTIES.

PRINTED FOR THE AUTHOR, BY ROBT. LEADER, SHEFFIELD,
AND SOLD BY
WM. WHITE, BROOM HALL PARK, SHEFFIELD,
BY HIS AGENTS, AND SIMPKIN, MARSHALL, AND Co., LONDON.

1859.

[Figure 17; 13.6 x 21.2 cm]

[245]

PAPERS
AND PROCEEDINGS

OF THE

𝕳𝖆𝖒𝖕𝖘𝖍𝖎𝖗𝖊 𝕱𝖎𝖊𝖑𝖉 𝕮𝖑𝖚𝖇

AND

𝕬𝖗𝖈𝖍𝖆𝖊𝖔𝖑𝖔𝖌𝖎𝖈𝖆𝖑 𝕾𝖔𝖈𝖎𝖊𝖙𝖞,

ESTABLISHED 1885,

For the Study of the Natural History and Antiquities of the County.

VOL. V.   1904-6.

EDITED BY

THE REV. G. W. MINNS, LL.B., F.S.A.

AND

F. J. C. HEARNSHAW, M.A., LL.M.

SOUTHAMPTON :

H. M. GILBERT & SON, 24, ABOVE BAR, AND AT WINCHESTER.

PRINTED AT THE "HAMPSHIRE INDEPENDENT" AND "SOUTHERN DAILY ECHO" OFFICE.

1906.

A SECOND SUPPLEMENT

TO

HAMPSHIRE BIBLIOGRAPHY.

By Rev. R. G. Davis.

The Bibliography of Hampshire was first attempted by the Rev. Sir W. H. Cope, Bart., who compiled and printed " A List of Books Relating to Hampshire, in the Library at Bramshill." 8vo. 1879. (Not Published.)

The entire collection, with many volumes of Hampshire Views and Illustrations, was bequeathed by Sir W. Cope to the Hartley Institution, mainly through the influence of the late Mr. T. W. Shore, and on the death of the donor in 1892 was removed to Southampton. The List compiled by the original owner being " privately printed " became very rare, and was necessarily incomplete. In 1891 a much fuller and more accurate Bibliography was published with the following title :—" Bibliotheca Hantoniensis, a List of Books relating to Hampshire, including Magazine References, &c., &c., by H. M. Gilbert and the Rev. G. N. Godwin, with a List of Hampshire Newspapers, by F. E. Edwards. Southampton. 1891.

The List given in the above publication was considerably augmented by a Supplementary Hampshire Bibliography, compiled by the Rev. Sumner Wilson, Rector of Preston Candover, printed in the Papers and Proceedings of the Hampshire Field Club. Vol. III., p. 303. A further addition to the subject is here offered with a view to rendering the Bibliography of Hants as complete as possible. Publications referring to the Isle of Wight are not comprised in this List.

[247]

FIRST PORTION.—Letters A to K.

ACT for widening the roads from the end of Stanbridge Lane, near a barn in the Parish of Romsey. 1764.

ACT ; another relating to same. 1785.

ACT for enclosing lands in the Parish of Portchester, in the County of Southampton. 1808.

ACT for making navigable Canal from the Town of Basingstoke, to communicate with the River Wey in the Parish of Chertsey, 1777.

ACT. Repairing High Way from Sheet Bridge, Petersfield to Portsmouth. 1726. Ditto. 1742. Act relating to the Will of Richard Norton, of Southwick, about the Manor of Old Alresford, and Lands in the County of Southampton.

ACTS OF THE STATES, General Orders, &c., connected with the Militia. Government House, Jersey. 1816.

ADAIR (R. A. S.) The Militia of the United Kingdom, &c. Defences of Portsmouth. 1870.

AHIER (John). Tableaux de la Civilization à Jersey. 8vo. Jersey. 1852.

ALDERSHOTTANA, or Chinks in my Hut. 1859.

ANASTATIC Drawing Society. Plates of Views in Monmouth, Hants, &c. 1860.

ANDERSON (H.), Vicar of Kings Somborne. A loyal Tear dropt on the Vault of the High and Mighty Prince Charles II. 1685.

ANDREWES (Lancelot), Bishop of Winchester. Private Devotions, translated from the Greek and Latin by Rev. P. Hall. 1830.

—————— The Pattern of Catechistical Doctrine, or a learned and pious exposition of the Ten Commandments. 1650.

ANDREWS (Wm.) Bygone Hampshire. London. 1899.

ANSTED'S GUIDE to the Channel Islands. 1878.

ANTIENT and Modern History of Portsmouth, Portsea, and Gosport.

AUSTEN (Jane), born Steventon. 1775, died Winchester, 1817. Persuasion. Northanger Abbey. Pride and Prejudice.

BAIGENT (F. J.) and Millard (J. E.) History of the Antient Town of Basingstoke. 8vo. 1889.

BALE (John). Admoniton to the Bishoppes of Winchester, London, and others. From Roane, by Michael Wood, Anno MDLIII., the 1st of October.

BAKER. Southampton Guide. 1774, 1781, &c.

BATTS (A.) The Wreckers, and other Poems. 1850.

BECHER (A. B.) Views in Fareham. Circa, 1830.

BECHERVAISE (John). A Farewell to my old Shipmates and Messmates, by the Old Quarter Master. Portsea. 1847.

BENHAM (D.) Some Account of the Village of Tadley, and of the Independent Church there. Printed for the Compiler. 1862.

BILSON (Thomas), Bishop of Winchester. True Difference between Christian Subjection and Unchristian Rebellion. 8vo. 1586.

—————— The Perpetual Government of Christes Church. 4to. Imprinted at London by the Deputies of Christopher Barker. 1593.

BILSON (Thomas). Bishop of Winchester. Christ's Descent into Hell. Folio. 1604.

BINFIELD (J. Bilson). The Order of Daily Service according to the Antient Winton Use. 8vo. 1846.

BINGHAM (Joseph), Rector of Headborn-Worthy. Scholastical History of the Practise of the Church in Reference to Baptism by Laymen. 1712.

—— Works edited by his lineal descendant, Richard Bingham, Jun. 8vo. Univ. Press. Oxford. 1855.

—— Origines Ecclesiasticae, or the Antiquities of the Christian Church, giving an Account of the Festivals and of the Marriage Rites. 1722.

BIRCH (Walter de Gray). Liber Vitae. Register and Martyrology of New Minster and Hyde Abbey, Winchester. 8vo. 1892.

BITTERN (Hants). The Antient Clausentum. 1792.

BLACKMORE (R. D.) Cradock Nowell, Tale of the New Forest. 1883·

BLANCHARD (W.) Trial of the Hon. Augustus Keppel by Court Martial at Portsmouth. Fo. F. Almon. 1779.

BLORE. Monumental Remains of Noble and Eminent Persons of Great Britain. 1824. Some Engravings of Monuments in Winchester Cathedral.

BOLAND (H.) Les Iles de la Manche. Paris, 1904.

BOYNE and ATKINS. Tradesmen's Tokens of the 17th Century, issued in Hampshire. 1889.

—— Tradesmen's Tokens of the 17th and 18th Centuries. Hants and Wilts. 1892.

BRACKENBURY (Rev. E. B.) Advent and Lent Lectures. Bournemouth. 1883.

BRAMSTON (A. R.) and Le Roy (A. C.) A City of Memories Winchester. 4to. 1893.

BRAMSTON (Rev. J. T.) Sermons to Boys in Winchester College Chapel. 1890.

BRANDER (G.) Fossilia Hantoniensia Collecta, et in Musaeo Britannico Deposita. 1766.

BRASSEY (T. A.) Naval Annual. Portsmouth. 1893.

BROMLEY (Rev. S.) Verses occasioned by being told that Rev. Mr. Knibb was dead. 12mo. Southampton. 1840.

BROOME (Samuel). The Travels of Seektruth. Basingstoke. 1805.

BROWN (S.), of Portsmouth. Real Christian or Sincere Good Man described. 1714.

BROWNE (Simon). A Sermon at Portsmouth for the Accession of George I., with two hymns. 1715.

BULKELEY (J.) La Hougue Bie de Hambie. A tradition of Jersey, with historical, genealogical, and topographical notes. 1837.

BULLAR (John). An Account of the Character and Peaceful Death o Peter Whitty. April 14, 1811. Southampton.

—— Questions on the Scriptures to be Answered in Writing, as Exercises in School, or in the course of Private Instruction. Southampton. 1808.

[249]

BULLAR (John). Pretor and Thomas Whitty, of Sherborne, Dorset. A brief narrative of their characters and death. Southampton. 1821.

BULLAR (Dr. W.), of Southampton. Thoughts of a Physician. 1868.

———— Letters from Abroad. From a Physician in search of health. 1861.

BURLINGTON. Universal British Traveller. Old English Views of Hants, &c. 17—.

BURN (John S.) The History of the French, Walloon, Dutch, and other Foreign Protestant Refugees settled in England from the Reign of Henry VIII. to the Revocation of the Edict of Nantes. 1846.

BURROWS (Montagu). History of the Foreign Policy of Great Britain. 1895.

B.R. Account of the Trial and Execution of John Slade, Schoolmaster, and John Body, M.A. Printed at London by Richard Jones, 1583. Written by an eye witness, and signed R. B. Executions took place at Winchester and Andover.

CADELL (Gen. Sir Rob., K.C.B.) Sir John Cope and the Rebellion of 1745, 1898.

CAESAREA. The Island of Jersey, its History, Customs, &c., also its Antiquities and the Biography of eminent Natives. 1840.

CARTER (O. B.) Account of Penton Mewsey Church. n.d.

CARTWRIGHT (Julia). The Pilgrim's Way from Winchester to Canterbury.

CARUS (Rev. W. Canon of Winchester). Memorials of the Rt. Rev. Chas. Pettit, D.D., late Bishop of Ohio, 1882.

CHANDLER (R.) Life of William Waynflete Bishop of Winchester, and Founder of Magdalene College, Oxford.

CHEKI (Joannis Angli). Graecæ Linguae Disputationes cum Stephano (Gardiner) Wintoniensi Episcopo. Basil. 1555.

CHURCH PSALMODY; a selection from different Authors. 12mo. Wonston, Hants. 1837.

CLARENDON AND GALE. History and Antiquities of the Cathedral Church of Winchester. 1715.

CLAYTON (J.) A Memoir of the Rev. R. R. Dolling. 1902.

COLLECTION of Psalm Tunes for the use of Gosport in Hampshire, Hymns for the Festivals. (Portsmouth Printed.) 1758.

COLLECTS prepared by a Clergyman. 8vo. Privately printed. (Whitchurch, Hants.) 1855.

COOKSON (J.) Thoughts on Polygamy, &c. Winchester. 1782.

———— Book of Common Prayer, with Psalms, &c., elucidated on an entire new plan. Winchester. 1789.

COOPER (Rev. Mark). Death and its Consequences ; nine sermons. Southampton. 1865.

COOPER (Thomas). Bishop of Winchester. Admonition to the People of England, wherein are answered not onely the slanderous untruethes, reproachfully uttered by Martin the libeller, but also many other crimes by some of his broode. 1589.

COPE (Sir W. H.) History of the Rifle Brigade, formerly the 25th. 8vo. 1877.

COPE (Sir W. H.) List of Works written and edited by Card. Newman in the Library at Bramshill.

―――― Ancient Ecclesiastical Stained Glass. Privately printed. 1897.

COPE AND STRETTON. Visitatio Infirmorum, or Offices for the Clergy in praying with the Sick and Inflicted. 8vo. 1850.

CORNE (Thomas). Singular Adventures, &c. Portsmouth, 1833.

CORNISH (C.J.) The New Forest. Bournemouth. 1899.

CORRY (A. C.) Executive Officer's Orders, &c., with regard to the Internal Economy of a Man-of-War. Portsmouth. 1888.

COTGREAVE (A.) Encyclopaedic Catalogue of the Library and Museum of Guernsey. 1891.

COX (R.) Miscellaneous Works, consisting of Fables, Essays, Poems, and Letters. Southampton. 1809.

CRABB (Rev. James), of Southampton. The Gipsies' Advocate, or Observations on the Origin, Character, Manners, and Habits of the English Gipsies. 1832.

CRADOCK (Lieut. C.) Wrinkles in Seamanship. Portsmouth. 1894.

CUTHELL (Lt.-Col. T. G.) Sailing Guide to the Solent and Poole Harbour, s.a.

DAVIDSON (Rev. A.), of Lymington. Sermons in blank verse. Romsey. n.d.

DAVIDSON (Archbishop). A Charge delivered to the Clergy of Winchester. 8vo. 1899.

DE CRESPIGNY AND HUTCHINSON. The New Forest, its Traditions, Inhabitants and Customs. Murray. 1895.

DESCRIPTIVE Account of the Cathedral Church of Winchester. Winchester. 1840.

DEWDNEY (Rev. Edmund). A Selection of Psalms and Hymns for St. John's Chapel. 12mo. Portsea. 1845.

DICEY. Historical Account of Guernsey, from its first settlement before the Norman Conquest, to the present time. London. 1751.

DOLLING (Rev. R. R.) Ten years in a Portsmouth Slum. 8vo. 1896.

EAST (Robert). Extracts from Records in the possession of the Municipal Corporation of the Borough of Portsmouth. 1891.

EDWARDS (Peter). The White's Row Lectures (a little enlarged) delivered on Portsmouth Common. 1790.

ELLIS (Hon. Charlotte). The True and Romantic History of William Pegg. Esq., M.P. for Ham(p)shire, or Life's Burlesque in Black and White, 1879.

FAWCETT (B.) Extracts from the Diary of Joseph Williams of Kidderminster. 8vo. Romsey. 1816.

FENTON (T.), M.A. Assize Sermons at Winchester. 1729.

FINCHAM (John). Directions for laying off Ships on the Mould-loft Floor. Portsea. 1822.

―――― History of Naval Architecture. 1851.

―――― A Treatise on Masting Ships and Mast-making. 1854.

―――― An Outline of Shipbuilding.

[251]

FOX, G. E. AND ST. JOHN HOPE, W.H.   Excavations on the Site of the Roman City at Silchester.   4to.   1891.

FULLER (Nicholas), born Southampton, 1557, died 1622.   Miscellanea Theologica.

GAGE (J.)   Benedictionale S. Ethelwaldi Episcopi Wintoniensis.   1832.

GALLIENNE (Richard le).   Travels in England.   (Selborne, Winchester, &c.)   1900.

GARDINER (Steven). Bishop of Winchester.   A Declaration of suche true articles as George Joye hath gone about to confute as false.   London.   1546.

GARDINER (Frederick), D.D.   A Harmony of the Four Gospels in Greek, according to the text of Tischendorf, with a collation of the Textus Receptus.   Andover.   1880.

GARNIER (A. E.)   The Chronicles of the Garniers of Hampshire, during four centuries.   1730 1900.   Norwich.   1900.

GARRETT (W.)   Anthems. Psalms, and Hymns as sung in Winchester Cathedral.   Winchester.   1843.

GASQUET (F. A.)   Hampshire Recusants.   A story of their troubles in the time of Queen Elizabeth.   1890.

GASTINEAU (E. T.)   A Hobble through the Channel Islands.   1860.

GATES (W. G.)   History of Portsmouth.   1900.

GAY (John).   Fables.   Havant.   1816.

GEARING (W), of Lymington, Hants.   The Arraingment of Pride, its causes, kind, &c.   1660.

——— A Prospect of Heaven, or a Treatise of the Happiness of the Saints in Glory.   1673.

——— The Eye and Wheel of Providence, &c.   1662.

——— Sacred Diary, or Select Meditations, &c.   1688.

GEREE (J.)   Sermons at Winchester Cathedral at the Assizes.   1706.

GEYT (Phillippe Le).   Les Manuscrits de, Ecuyer, Lieutenant Bailli de l'Ile de Jersey, sur la Constitution, les Lois, et les Usages, de cette Ile.   St. Helier.   1846.

GILBERT.   Series of Drawings illustrating H. Majesty's Visit to Spithead.   Lymington.   1845.

GILMOUR (D. E.)   Historical and Descriptive Guide to Winchester.   (Eleven Editions).   Winchester.   n.d.

GILPIN (W.), Vicar of Boldre.   Essay on Prints, 1781.

——— Memoirs of Josias Rogers, Commander of H.M.S. Quebec.   1808.

——— Sermons preached to a Country Congregation.   4 vols. 8vo.   1803.

——— Observations relative chiefly to Picturesque Beauty made in 1774.   8vo.   1786.

GODFREY (H. M.)   Registre de l'Eglise Wallonne de Southampton.   1889.

GODWIN (Rev. G.)   English Church History, 1625-1649.   1895.

GRIFFIN (John).   A Selection of Hymns.   Portsea.   1814.

GRIFFITH (Rev. C. H.)   A History of Strathfield Saye.   1892.

GRIFFITH (W. P.) Flags National and Mercantile, &c. Portsmouth. 1891.

—— Antient Gothic Churches. Winchester, Romsey, &c. 1847.

GRIFFITHS (Capt. A. N.), R.N. Observations on some points of Seamanship, with practical hints on Naval Economy. Portsmouth. 1828.

GUERNSEY. Chapel of St. Apolline. Transactions of Cambridge Camden Society. 1841.

HALES (Steph.), D.D., F.R.S., Rector of Farringdon, Hants. Statical Essays, or an account of some experiments on the Sap in Vegetables, &c. 1738.

HAMILTON (Lady). Memoirs with Anecdotes of her friends and contemporaries. Annotated by W. H. Long. 1892.

HAMPSHIRE, 1622 and 1686. Middle Hill Press.

HAMPSHIRE COUNTY COUNCIL. Proceedings from 1899 to 1902. Portsmouth.

HAMPSHIRE DOWN FLOCK BOOK. 1890-91.

HAMPSHIRE RECORD SOCIETY. Sixteen Volumes. 1889 to 1904.

HAMPSHIRE REPOSITORY. Historical, Literary, and Antiquarian. 1799—1801.

HAMPSHIRE SERMONS. Rev. J. Langley, of West Tudderly. 1644. Rev. C. Tesdale of Hurstborne Tarrant. 1644.

HANKINSON'S GUIDE to Bournemouth. 1878.

HARVEY (Thomas), M.A. The Parish Registers of Priors Dean, 1538—1812 ; Colmer, 1563—1812, with index. Colmer, Printed for the Subscribers, 1886.

HAWKER (Peter. Col.). Diary of, from 1802 to 1853. with an introduction by Sir Ralf Payne-Gallway, Bart., 1893. Refers to Southampton, Lymington, and other parts of Hampshire.

HAYLING ISLAND, Topographical and Historical Account of. Havant. 1826.

HELE (Arthur), Master of Free School, Basingstoke. The Four Gospels Harmonised. Reading. 1750.

HERSCHELL (R. H.) Reasons why I a Jew, have become a Catholic ; a letter in reply to R. W. Sibthorp, of Ryde. London. 1842.

HOLGATE (C.W.) Winchester Long Rolls. 1653—1721, 8vo. 1890.

—— Winchester Commoners, 1836—1890. 8vo. 1891.

HORNE (R.) Bishop of Winchester. Answere to a book entituled :—The Declaration of such Scruples and Stores of Conscience, touching the Oathe of Supremacy. as M. John Fekeham, by wrytinge did deliver unto the Bishop of Winchester, with his Resolutions made thereunto. 1566.

HUDDESFORD (Rev. G.) Salmagundi : a Miscellaneous Combination of Original Poetry, &c. 1791.

—— The Wiccamical Chaplet. 1804.

HUGUENOT SOCIETY PUBLICATIONS. Vol. IV. Registre des Baptismes, Marriages, &c., et des Isles de Jersey, Guernsey, Serq, Origny, &c., etablie a Southampton par patente du Roy Edouard Sixe, et de la Reine Elizabeth. Lymington. 1890.

HUMFREY (Lawrence). Presidente of Magdaleine Coll. in Oxforde ; Dean of Winton ; Puritan. The Nobles or of Nobilitye. The original nature, dutyes, right, and Christian Institution thereof, three Bookes. Fyrste eloquentlye written in Latine ; late englished. Whereto is coupled the small treatyse of Philo a Jewe englished. Thomas Marshe, 1563. Printed in black letter.

INGRAM. Haunted Houses of Great Britain. Warblington Parsonage.

INMAN (James). Introduction to Naval Gunnery. Portsea. 1878.

IRVINE (J. T.) Description of the Saxon Church of Boarhunt. 1877.

JACOB (John). Annals of some of the British Norman Isles constituting the Bailiwick of Guernsey, &c. Part 1, all published. 1830.

JAMES (Col. Sir H.) Notes on the Great Pyramid of Egypt. 4to. Southampton. 1869.

JAMES (Sir H.) Plans and Photographs of Stonehenge, and of Turusachan in the Island of Lewis, with Notes on the Druids and Cromlechs in Ireland. Southampton. 1867.

JEFFERY (W.) The King's Yard. A Story of Old Portsmouth. 8vo. 1903.

JENNER (Thomas). Directory for the English Traviller, by which he shal be inabled to Coast about all England, &c. London. 1643.

JENNINGS (Henry). Heavenly Melodies : original and select poems. Tadley, near Basingstoke. 1865.

JERSEY, ILE DE. Lois et Reglements passés par les Etats de Jersey revetus de la Sanction Royale, et non compris dans le Code de 1771. Jersey. 1878.

JERSEY, ISLAND OF : Its History, Government, &c., with Biography of Eminent Men, 1840.

JERSEY, ISLAND OF. New Description of the Queen of the Isles, by a twenty years resident, &c. London, 1841.

JONES (J. D.) The Model Prayer, expositions on the Lord's Prayer. Bournemouth. 1903.

———— The Glorious Company of the Apostles, studies in the character of the Twelve. Bournemouth. 1904.

KEBLE (Rev. John), Rector of Hursley, 1836—1866. Contributions to Lyra Apostolica. 1836.

———— The Psalter in English Verse. (Anon). 1839.

———— The Case of Catholic Subscription to the Thirty Nine Articles. (Private Print). 1841.

———— An Horology. (Under Initials J. K.) 1842.

———— Heads of Consideration in the case of Mr. Ward. 1845.

———— Lyra Innocentium. (Anon). 1846.

———— Sermons, Academical and Occasional. 1847.

———— Against Profane Dealing with Holy Matrimony. 1849.

———— Pastoral Tracts on the Gorham Question. 1850.

———— Church Matters in 1850. 1850.

———— On the Representation of the University of Oxford. 1852.

KEBLE (Rev. John). A very few Plain Thoughts on the Proposed Addition of Dissenters to the University of Oxford. 1854.

—— An Argument for not Proceeding immediately to Repeal the Laws which treat the Nuptial Bond as Indissoluble. 1857.

—— On Eucharistical Adoration. 1857.

—— The Life of Thomas Wilson, Bishop of Sodor and Man. 1863.

—— A Litany of our Lord's Warning. Some separate Sermons. 1864.

KENT, Organist of Winchester Cathedral. Musical Compositions. 1780.

KIDD (W.) Picturesque Companion to Southampton, &c.

KING (J. W.) The Warships of Europe. Portsmouth. 1878.

KINSEY-MORGAN (Dr. A.) Climate of Bournemouth in relation to Disease, especially Phthisis. Bristol. 1897.

KITCHIN (Dean A.) A Memoir of Bishop Harold Browne. 8vo. 1895.

KITCHIN (Rev. G. W.) Prayers for the use of Twyford School, sm. 8vo. 1857.

—— Compotus Rolls of St. Swithin's Priory, Winchester. 1892.

—— The Great Screen of Winchester Cathedral. 1891.

KNIGHT. The Land we live in. Portsmouth, &c. Circa. 1843.

KINGSLEY (Rev. Charles), Rector of Eversley, 1844—1875. The Saints' Tragedy. 1848.

—— Twenty-five Village Sermons. 1849.

—— Alton Locke. (anon). 1850.

—— Cheap Clothes, and Nasty. 1850.

—— The Application of Associative—Principles to Agriculture. 1851.

—— Yeast. (Anon from Fraser's Magazine). 1851.

—— The Message of the Church to labouring Men. 1851.

—— Phæton. 1852.

—— Sermons on National Subjects. 1852—4.

—— Hypatia. (From Fraser's Magazine). 1853.

—— Alexandria and Her Schools. 1854.

—— Who Causes Pestilence? 1854.

—— Sermons for the Times. 1855.

—— Westward Ho! 1855.

—— Glaucus. 1855.

—— The Heroes. 1856.

—— Two Years Ago. 1857.

—— Andromeda. 1858.

—— The Good News of God. 1859.

—— Miscellanies. 1859.

—— The Limits of exact Sciences as applied to History. 1860.

—— Why should we pray for Fair Weather? 1860.

—— Town and Country Sermons. 1861.

—— A Sermon on the death of the Prince Consort. 1862.

KINGSLEY (Rev. Charles).   Speech of Lord Dundreary—on the great
    Hippocampus Question.   (Anon).   1862.

—— The Gospel of the Pentateuch.   1863.

—— The Water Babies.   1863.

—— What, then, does Dr. Newman mean ?   1864.

—— The Roman and the Teuton.   1864.

—— Hints to Stammerers.   (Anon).   1864.

—— David.   1865.

—— Hereward the Wake.   1866.

—— The Temple of Wisdom.   1866.

—— Three Lectures on the " Ancien Regime."   1867.

—— The Water of Life.   1867.

—— The Hermits.   1868.

—— Discipline.   1868.

—— God's Feast.   1869.

—— Madame How and Lady Why.   1870.

—— At Last.   1871.

—— Town Geology.   1872.

—— Prose Idylls.   1873.

—— Plays and Puritans.   1873.

—— Health and Education.   1874.

—— Westminster Sermons.   1874.

—— Lectures delivered in America.   1875.

A SECOND SUPPLEMENT

TO

HAMPSHIRE BIBLIOGRAPHY.

By Rev. R. G. Davis.

SECOND PORTION.—Letters L to Z.

LANCASTER (Rev. Daniel). A Discourse occasioned by the Death of the late Walter Taylor. Preached at South Stoneham Church, on the 8th of May, 1803. Winchester.

—— Two Sermons preached at the Assizes at Winchester, for the year 1800. Robbins, Winchester. 1800.

LANGLEY (John of West Tiderly, Southampton), Gemitus Columbae, the Mournful Note of the Dove. A Sermon before the House of Commons. 1644.

LATHAM (John, M. D.). General History of Birds. 11 vols. 4to. 200 Coloured Plates. Winchester. 1821-28.

LAW (Rev. W.). Serious Call to a Devout and Holy Life, with sketch of Author, Letters, etc. 8vo. Romsey. 1816.

LEACH (A. F.). History of Winchester College. Plates. 8vo. 1899.

LESTER-GARLAND (L. V.). Flora of the Island of Jersey. Map. 8vo. 1903.

LEIGH (Rev. J. E.). Sermon at Sherborne St. John, on the death of Mrs. Chute of the Vine. 8vo. Basingstoke. 1842.

LEIGHTON (W. A.). Lichen-Flora of Great Britain, Ireland and the Channel Islands. 8vo. 1879.

LEWES (G. H.). Seaside Studies at Ilfracombe, Tenby, the Scilly Isles and Jersey. 8vo. 1860.

LE LIEVRE (F.). Guide to Guernsey, containing the Topography, History, Antiquities, &c., of the Island. Map. 8vo. Guernsey. 1863.

——Guide to Jersey, with some Account of its Government, Laws, &c. Map and Plates. 8vo. Jersey. 1861.

LIARDET (Capt. F., N.R.). Professional Recollections on Points of Seamanship, Discipline, xc. 8vo. Portsea. 1849.

[257]

LITURGIE ANGLOISE, ou le Livre des Prières Publiques, de l'Administration des Sacrements et autres orders et Cérémonies de l'Eglise d'Angleterre. 4to. à Londres par Jehan Bill. 1616. Prepared for the Use of the Channel Islands.

LA LITURGIE ou Formulaire des Prières Publiques. a Jersey, de l'Imprimerie de M. Alexandre. 1785.

LA LITURGIE ou Formulaire des Prières Publiques, selon l'Usage de l'Eglise Unie d'Angleterre et d'Irlande avec le Psautier ou les Psaumes de David. 8vo. Guernesey. 1833.

LA LITURGIE des Prières Publiques, selon l'Usage de l'Eglise Anglicane. 8vo. a Guerneset. 1802.

LLOYD-VERNEY (Col.). Records of the Infantry Militia Battalions of the County of Southampton, 1757 to 1894. Portraits. 4to. 1894.

LONG (W. H.). Medals of the British Navy, and how won. Coloured illuminated facsimiles. 8vo. 1895.

LONG (W. H.). Memoirs of Lady Hamilton, edited and annotated by. Portraits. 8vo. 1899.

LORDAN (C. L.). Colloquies, chiefly upon Poetry and Poets. 8vo. Romsey. 1844.

LORDAN (C. L.). The Unwritten Book, Colloquies Desultory, but chiefly upon Poetry and Poets, between an Elder Enthusiastic and an Apostle of the Law. 8vo. Romsey.

LOUTH (W., Prebendary of Winchester). Commentary upon Ezechiel. 4to. 1723.

LOWELL (Alex.). History of Various Lodges of Freemasonry, from 1786 to 1893. Portsmouth. Privately printed. 1894.

LOVELL (Langford). A letter to a Friend, relative to the State of the Island of Dominica. 8vo. Winchester. 1818.

MADDOCK (Rev. S.). A Sermon at Bishop's Sutton Church, on occasion of a very sudden death in that Parish. 8vo. 1838.

MANLEY (Mrs. Mary de la Riviere of Guernsey). The Lost Lover, or The Jealous Husband : a Comedy. 4to. Printed for R. Bentley, London. 1696.

MANSFIELD (R. B.). School Life at Winchester College : or The Reminiscences of a Winchester Junior, 1835—40. Illustrations. n.d.

MANT (Richard, Master of the Grammar School, Southampton.). The First and Second Books of Phaedrus. 8vo. So'ton. 1791.

MARSHALL (Mrs.). Winchester Meads. 8vo. 1895.

Map of the London and Southampton Railway, from London to Basingstoke. Six Views. 8vo. 1838.

MARRYAT (Captain). The Children of the New Forest. Illustrated by Sir John Gilbert. 8vo.

MARTIN (C. Wykeham). An attempt to establish the Descent of William of Wykeham, from the Family of Wykeham, of Swalcliffe, Oxfordshire. 8vo. Privately Printed. 1852.

MARTIN (Thomas). The Manger, or the Birth of Christ. A Poem. 12mo. Portsea. 1816.

———The Sunday School. An Essay. 12mo. Portsea. 1818.

MASQUERADE (The). A Collection of new Enigmas, &c. 2 vols. T. Baker, Southampton. 12mo. n.d.

MATCHLESS VILLANY, or a Full and Authentic Narrative of the Robbery and Murder of John Penny. 8vo. 1741.

MATE (C. H.). The Evergreen Valley, Bournemouth.

MAURICE (Rev. F. D.). The Reformation of Society. A Lecture. 12mo. Southampton. 1851.

Memoir of the Life and Family of the late Sir George Leonard Staunton, Bart. Views and other Plates. 8vo. Havant Press, for Private Circulation only. 1823.

MERCURIUS AULICUS, for the week ending Dec. 16, 1643. Refers to Affairs at Basing and elsewhere in Hampshire. 4to. 1643.

METCALF (C. J.). The Channel Islands. Historical and Legendary Sketches in Verse. 8vo. 1852.

METIVIER (G.). Dictionnaire Franco-Normand ou Recueil des Mots Particuliers au Dialect de Guernsey. 8vo. 1870.

———Poesies Guernesiaises et Francaises avec Glossaire. 8vo. Guernsey, 1883.

MILLARD (Rev. J. E.). Book of Accounts of the Wardens of the Fraternity of the Holy Ghost in Basingstoke. 1557-1654. 4to. Southampton. 1882.

MILTON (Rev. J.). Presbuteros to the Reader, and a Loyal Voice to the Queen. Southampton. 1842.

MINNS (Rev. G. W.). The Ancient Christian Church at Silchester. Plates. 8vo. 1892.

MITCHELL (W. F.). Ships of the Royal Navy. Series of coloured Plates from original Drawings, with descriptive text. 2 vols. 8vo. Portsmouth. 1875.

MOBERLEY (Mr.), and the Letter which appeared at Mr. Pearce's Bank. Southampton. 1857.

MOENS (W. J. C.). The Walloons and their Church at Norwich. 1565-1832. 4to. Lymington. 1888.

MOENS (W. J. C.). Allegations for Marriage Licenses granted by the Bishop of Winchester, 1689-1837, 2 vols. 8vo. Harleian Society. 1893.

MONSELL (Rev. J. S. B.). The Winton Church Catechist. 12mo. 1872.

MOODY (H.). An Extension of the Latin Text and an English Translation of the Domesday Book as far as it relates to Hampshire. 4to. Winchester. 1862.

MOON (Rev. J. F.). The Birthplace, Home, Churches and other Places connected with the Author of The Christian Year. 4to. Illustrations. Winchester. 1866.

MOORSOM (Rev. R. M.). The Writers of Hymns Ancient and Modern. 8vo. R.M. Cottage, N. Valence, Alton.

MORANT (P.). Caesarea or An Account of Jersey, the greatest of the Islands remaining to the Crown of England. Map. 8vo. 1734.

MORLEY (H.. Bishop of Winton). Several Treatises written upon several occasions both before and since the King's Restoration. 4to. London. 1683.

MORLEY (H., Bishop of Winton). Vindication of Himself against Mr. Richard Baxter. 4to. London. 1683.

MOSES (Henry). Sketches of Shipping ; Views in Portsmouth Harbour. 36 Plates. 4to. 1824.

Movements for Cavalry : provisionally approved for Cavalry at Aldershot. 1874.

MUDIE (Robert). The Historical and Topographical Description of the Channel Islands. Map and Plates. 8vo. Winchester. 1850.

Narrative of the Loss of the " Mary Rose," at Spithead, July 20, 1545, from original Mss. 18mo. Portsea. 1842.

Narrative of the loss of the " Royal George," at Spithead, Aug. 1782. 18mo. Portsea. 1842.

NEALE (Thos., of Warneford, Southampton). Treatise of Direction how to Travell safely and profitably into Forraigne Countries. 12mo. 1643.

New British Traveller, being a Complete Tour through England, &c,. Sark, Jersey, Guernsey, Alderney, &c. Numerous Plates. London. G. A. Walpoole. Fol. 1784.

NICHOLS (J. G.). On the Seals of the Earls of Winchester, and the City. 8vo. 1846.

NICOLLE (Eliza). The Martyr Religious and Political. Life of. Winchester. 8vo. For the Author. 1869.

NOMINA VILLARUM. A List of Boroughs, Hundreds, Parishes and Tythings, with their Quotus to the County Rate. 8vo. Romsey. 1791.

Observations upon the Evidence adduced before the Committee of the H. of C. upon the Application for a Bill for making a Navigable Canal, from the River Kennet, at Midgham to join the Basingstoke Canal, to be called the Hants and Berks Canal. 8vo. Maidenhead. 1825.

OLD QUARTER-MASTER, An. Thirty-six Years of Sea-Faring Life. by. 8vo. Portsea. 1839.

OSBORNE (Rev. C. E.). Life of the Rev. R. R. Dolling. Portrait. 8vo. 1903.

OULESS (P. J.). Scenic Beauties of the Island of Jersey, with Descriptions by Rev. E. Durell. 24 lithos. fol. St. Heliers. 1840.

OLD CALABAR. Grey Abbey. A Novel. 2 vols. 8vo. 1877.

OUVRY (M. H.). A Lady's Diary before and during the Indian Mutiny. 8vo. Lymington. 1892.

OVERBURY (Sir T.). The Arraignment and Conviction of Sir Walter Rawleigh, at the King's Bench-Barre at Winchester, Nov., 1603. Coppied by. 1648.

Owners of Land in the County of Hants. fol. 1873.

PARK (Thomas). Sonnets and other small Poems. Plates. 12mo. 1803. Amongst plates view of Twyford Church.

PATTON (P., Admiral). The Natural Defence of an Insular Empire, earnestly recommended, with a sketch of a Plan, to attach real seamen to the Service of their Country. 4to. Southampton. 1810.

PAYNE (J. B.). Armorial of Jersey, an Account of all the principal Families. Plates. 4to. 1870.

PEEP AT OUR NEIGHBOURS, A. Channel Islands. 1847.

PHILLIMORE (W. P. W.). Hampshire Parish Registers. Marriages. 6 vols. 1899-1904.

PIKE (S. & S. Hayward). Religious Cases of Conscience. 8vo. 1755. Reprinted, Romsey. 1817.

Pilgrimage to the Monastery of La Trappe. 8vo. Havant. 1815.

Plan of His Majesty's Forest called the New Forest. Large coloured Map. 1789.

PORTAL (W. W.). Some Account of the Settlement of Refugees at Southampton and the Hospital of God's House, also notes on the Paper Making Industry as practised by the Southampton Refugees. Plates. 4to. 1902.

PORTER (J.) Kingsclere. Edited by Byron Webber. Portraits and illustrations. 8vo. 1896.

POWLETT FAMILY. Catalogue of the Marquesses and Earles of Winchester. 30 cuts of arms. fol. 1610.

PRYNNE (William) Mount-Orgueil : or Divine and Profitable Meditations, &c., to which is Prefixed a Poeticall Description of Mount-Orgueil Castle, in the Isle of Jersey. 4to. 1641.

Psalms and Hymns for the Church. 12mo. Lymington. (?1830).

Psalms and Hymns for Public Worship in the Church of England. 18mo. Bishop's Waltham. 1843.

QUEEN'S VISIT TO JERSEY, The, Sept. 3, 1846. 25 large views. fol. Pub : by P. Falle, Jersey. 1847.

RAGG (Alban E.). History of Jersey, from the Earliest Times down to the Year 1895. 8vo. Plates. Jersey. 1896.

Railway Chronicle Travelling Chart, or Iron Road Book. London to Basingstoke, Winchester and Southampton. Woodcuts, Panoramic Sheet. 1840.

RANDOLPH (Vice-Admiral). Problems in Naval Tactics. Plans. 8vo. Portsmouth. 1879.

RANKER, A. Life in the Royal Navy by. Plates. 8vo. Portsmouth. 1891.

RAVIGLIO ROSSO (G.). Historia delle cose accorse nel Regno d'Inghilterra in Materia del Duca di Notomberlan dopo la Morte di Odoardo vl. 8vo. Nell' Academia Venetiana. 1558. Account of the landing of Philip of Spain at Southampton, his journey to Winchester and marriage.

Recollections of a Ramble from Sydney to Southampton, via S. America, Panama, West Indies, Niagara, &c. 8vo. 1851.

Recollections of the early Days of the Vine Hunt, and of its Founder, W. J. Chute. 8vo. 1865.

Recollections of the two St. Mary Winton Colleges. 8vo. 1883.

REDSTONE. Guernsey and Jersey Guide. 1844.

Report from Select Committee of the H. of C. on Andover Union, together with the Minutes of Evidence, etc. 2 vols. Fol. 1846.

Report from Select Committee on the New Forest, with Proceedings, Minutes of Evidence, Appendix and Index. Fol. 1875.

Report on the Hampshire County Goal (Winchester) and Bridewells. 8vo. 1817.

RICH (W. P.). The authentic and interesting History of Miss Moreton and the Faithful Cottager. 8vo. Portsea. 1798.

ROBARTS (Rev. Rich.). An Answer to the Question, Why are you a Methodist ? Guernsey. 1816.

ROBINSON (Dr. H.). Scholae Wintoniensis Phrasae Latinae. The Latin Phrases of Winchester School, &c. 8vo. 1685.

———Roll Call of Winchester College, 1867-70. 18mo.

Roman Pavement discovered in a field at Thruxton, near Weyhill, Hants, 1823. Plate. fol.

ROSS (Alexander, Master of the Free School, Southampton). God's House made a Den of Thieves. Southampton. 1638.

———God's House, or the House of Prayer, vindicated from Sacrilege and Profaneness. Southampton. 1641.

———Philosophicall Touch Stone. 4to. 1645.

———An Abridgement of Christian Divinity, by J. Wollebius, D.D. Translated by. 12mo. 1656.

ROSS (Sir J.). Memoirs and Correspondence of Admiral Lord de Saumarez, from the family papers. Plates. 8vo. 1838.

ROWE'S (Mrs. Eliz.). Letter from the Dead to the Living, with Thoughts on Death, etc., and Life of Author. 8vo. Romsey. 1815.

ROWLANDSON (James, Pastor). God's Blessing in Blasting, and His Mercy in Mildew, two Sermons at East Tysted. 4to. 1623.

ROYAL NAVY, The. Coloured Lithographs. Portsmouth. 1873.

Rules, Orders, etc., for the Goal and Bridewell at Winchester. 8vo. 1818.

RUSSELL (Dr. W.). True Narrative of the Portsmouth Disputation between the Presbyterians and the Baptists, revised. 8vo. 1699.

RYLE (H. E.), Bishop of Winchester. On Holy Scripture and Criticism, Address and Sermons. 8vo. 1904.

———On the Church of England. 8vo. 1904.

RIDOUTT, (F.). The Early Baptist History of Portsmouth, and the Formation of the Churches in the Town. 8vo. Privately printed Landport. 1888.

RIMMER (A.). Antient Streets and Homesteads of England. Includes Winchester. 8vo. 1877.

SILCHESTER (The Sack of). A.D., 493, by the Author of " Proverbial Folk Lore." 8vo. Reading. Circa 1890.

SAVAGE (W.). Guide to the Antiquities of Winchester. Plates. 12mo. n.d. School Life at Winchester College, or Reminiscences of a Winchester Junior. 8vo. 1870.

SCLATER (W.). Civil Magistracy by Divine Authority, asserted and laid forth in a Sermon at Winchester Assizes. 1653.

SELBORNE (Roundell Palmer). Earl of. Book of Praise, from the best English Hymn Writers. 12mo. 1863.

———Notes on some Passages in the Liturgical History of the Reformed English Church. 8vo. 1878.

———A Defence of the Church of England against Disestablishment. 8vo 1887.

———Antient Facts and Fictions concerning Churches and Tithes. 8vo. 1888.

———Hymns : their History and Developement, in the Greek and Latin Churches. 12mo. 1892.

———Memorials : Family, Personal and Political. 1766—1895. 4 vols. 8vo. 1896.

———The Catholic and Apostolic Church. Letters to his Son. 8vo. 1899.

THOROLD (Bishop). Selections from the Works of. Portrait and Preface by the Bishop of Winchester. 8vo. 1897.

SERGEANT (P. W.). Winchester Cathedral, in Bell's Cathedral Series.

SHAW (Rev. T.). Tour to the West of England, in 1788. 8vo. 1789.

SHAW (S.). The Topographer, containing a Variety of Original Articles relating to Sussex and Hampshire. 4to. Plates. 1791.

SHAW (W. A.). English Government and the Relief of Protestant Refugees. 8vo. Lymington. 1896.

SHEBBEARE (Dr., attributed to). An Authentic Narrative of the Oppressions of the Islanders of Jersey, with a History of that Island. 2 vols 8vo. 1771.

SHEDD (W. G. T., D.D.). Discourses and Essays. 8vo. Andover. 1856.

———Sermons to the Natural Man. 8vo. Andover. 1879.

———The Doctrine of Endless Punishment. 8vo. Andover. 1886.

SHELLEY FAMILY Pedigree of, of Hampshire. 4to. 1880.

SIMCOX (Rev. W. H.). The Beginnings of the Christian Church. 8vo. 1881. (Lectures delivered in the Chapter Room of Winchester Cathedral).

SIMPKINSON (C. H.). Life and work of Antony Wilson Thorold, 79th Bp. of Winton. 8vo. 1896.

SLEEMAN (C. W). Torpedoes and Torpedo Warfare. Plates and Plans. Portsmouth. 1880.

SLIGHT (H.) A Looking Glass for Portsmouth and its Environs. 8vo. n.d.

S. (male) (H). Serio-Comico-(Canino)-Polyglottos : by an Old Wykemist. 24mo.

SMITH (T.). The Original Ordinances of more than One Hundred English Gilds, together with ye Olde Usages of ye Cite of Wynchestre &c. 8vo. E.E.T.S. 1870.

SMYTH (J. C.). Jail Distemper, as it appeared amongst the Spanish Prisoners at Winchester. 8vo. 1795.

Southsea and Hayling Guide. 12mo. Portsmouth 1850.

SOUTHAMPTON DRAWING BOOK, The, or Graphic Views of the Town and Neighbourhood. Plates. 8vo. n.d.

SOUTH WESTERN, The, or London, Southampton and Portsmouth Railway Guide. 12mo. Wyld. 1839.

SPENCE (C.). The Abbey Church of Romsey, founded by King Edward the Elder. Plates. 8vo. Romsey. 1862.

Squibs, Songs, Essays, Handbills, &c., during the late Election between Worsley and Jervoise. 8vo. John Wilkes, Winchester. 1780.

SQUIRE (John Traviss). Mount Nod, a Burial Place of the Huguenots, at Wandsworth, Surrey. 8vo. Lymington. 1887.

The Registers of the Parish of Wandsworth, Surrey. 1603-1787. 8vo. Privately printed. Lymington. 1889.

STEPHENS (E. L.). Statement of the Local and National Benefits which will be produced by the Southampton and London Railway. 8vo. Maps. 1831.

STEPHENS (W. R. W.). Documents relating to the History of the Cathedral Church of .Winchester in the 17th Century. 8vo. Winchester. 1897.

STORER. History of Winchester Cathedral. Plates. 4to. 1814.

SUMNER (Charles, Bishop of Winton). Ministerial Character of Christ. practically considered. 8vo. 1824.

TORRIGIANO (Pietro), the Sculptor. The Reformation Period as delineated in the Priory Church of Christchurch. 8vo. 188—

TAYLOR (Henry), vicar of Portsmouth. The Apology of Benjamin Ben Mordecai to his Friends for embracing Christianity. 2 vols. 8vo. 1784.

TAYLOR (H). Rector of Crawley, Hants. Considerations upon Antient and Modern Creeds, compared with a Treatise on the Soul. 8vo. 1788.

THEATRIC TOURIST, The, with accounts of the Principal Provincial Theatres in the United Kingdom. 24 Plates. 4to. 1805.

THORNTON (John). The English Herd Book of Jersey Cattle. 14 vols. 1879—1902.

——--Supplements or Registers of Births. 10 vols. 1881—94.

——--Jersey Cattle. Their Feeding and Management. 8vo. 1898.

THORN (W.), of Winchester. The Union of Church and State Anti-Scriptural and Indefensible. 12mo. n.d.

TIERNEY (Rev., M.A.). A Sermon at the Opening of the Catholic Chapel, Southampton. 8vo. Southampton. 1830.

TOASE (W.). Memoir of the Rev. Richard Roberts. Portrait. Guernsey. 1820.

——--Funeral Sermon occasioned by the Death of Frederick Warner, House Surgeon to the Hampshire County Hospital. 8vo. 1838.

Topographical Account of the Hundred of Bosmere in Hampshire. Plates. 4to. 1817.

Topographical and Descriptive Account of Hayling Island, Hants. 8vo. Havant. 1826.

Tradesmen's Tokens of the Seventeenth and Eighteenth Centuries, issued in the Counties of Hampshire and Wiltshire. 8vo. 1892.

TRENCH (R. C., Archbishop of Dublin). A Sermon with reference to the late calamitous Fire at Southampton. 12mo. 1837.

Tres Hymni ad usum Scholarium Wiccamicorum olim anglice compositi nunc latine redditi. Dies Oriens et Occidens Christianus ; sive duo Carmina, libro, qui "Christianus Annus" conscribitur, praemissa latine reddita. 8vo. Wintoniae. 1815.

TRUE BLEW. The Humours of Portsmouth, or "All is well that ends well." Farce by. n.d.

TRUPP (H.). Reminiscences of old times, at Winchester College. 8vo. Winton. 1888.

TIBB (R.). A Calm Dispassionate Reply to the Rev. H. Wake. 8vo. Andover. 1818.

TUCKWELL (W). The Antient Ways : Winchester Fifty Years Ago. Plates. 8vo. 1893.

TUPPER (F. B.). The Chronicles of Castle Cornet, Guernsey, with details of its nine years' siege. Plates. 8vo. Guernsey. 1851.

VARLO (C.). New System of Husbandry from a Variety of Experiments never before made public. 3 vols. 8vo. Winchester, 1772.

VYVYAN (Rev. V. F.) and Lyne (Rev. C., of Cornwall). Psalms and Hymns. 12mo. Southampton. 1831.

WALCOTT (M. E. C.), William of Wykeham and his Colleges. Plates. 8vo. 1852.

——--Historical and Descriptive Guide to Winchester, including the Hospital of St. Cross. 8vo. Winchester. 1870.

WALL (J. C.)., Alfred the Great, His Abbeys of Hyde, Athelney, and Shaftesbury. 8vo. 1900.

WARNER (John, Pastor of the Church at Christ Church in Hantshire). A Discourse of the Object and Office of Faith as justifying. 8vo. Oxford. 1657.

WARNER (R. T.), Winchester. Great Public Schools. Plates. 1900. Winchester College, or the Reminiscences of a Winchester Junior Plates. 8vo. Hotten. 1866.

WHITE (Richard, of Basingstoke). (Richard II.). Viti Basinstochii Comitis Palatini Historiarum Libri V., cum notis Antiquitatum Britannicarum. 8vo. 1597.

——Richardi Viti Basinstochii Comitis Palatini Historiarum Britanniae Insulae, libri novem priores. 8vo. 2 vols. C. Boscard. Douay. 1602. A second edition was printed in 1606.

——Richardi Viti Basinstochii Oratio Septima de Religione legum romanarum, ad Reverendum Dominum, Dominum Nicolaum Mainfroy, electum Abbatem Bertinianum. 8vo. C. Boscard. Douay. 1604.

——Brevis Explicatio privilegiorum juris et consuetudinis circa Sacramentum Eucharistiae, per Ricardum Vitum Basinstochii. 12mo. C. Boscard. Douay. 1609.

——Brevis Explicatio Martyrii S. Ursulae et Undecim Millium Virginum Britannicarum ; 12mo. P. Auray. Douay 1610.

——Of the Author and Substance of the Protestant Church and Religion. Two Bookes. Written first in Latin by R.S. Doctour of Divinity, and now reviewed by the Author and translated into English by W. Bas. Permissu Superiorum. 1621.

WHITE (Rev. Thomas, of Winchester). Sermons for the different Sundays and Festivals of the Year, arranged by John Lingard, D.D. 2 vols. 8vo. 1828.

WHITE (Walter). Sailor-Boy's Log Book from Portsmouth to the Peiho. Edited by. Portrait. 8vo. 1852.

WHITLOCK (Rev. J. Aston). Brief and Popular History of The Hospital of God's House, Southampton. Plates. 8vo. n.d.

WILBERFORCE (Samuel, Bishop of Winchester). Essays contributed to the Quarterly Review. 2 vols. 8vo. 1874.

WILCOCKS (J. C.). The Sea Fisherman, comprising the chief methods of Hook and Line Fishing in the British and other Seas. Plates. Guernsey. 1865.

WINCHESTER COLLEGE, 1393-1893, by old Wykhamists. (Published in commemoration of the 500th anniversary). 4to. 1893.

Winchester Diocesan Chronicle, a monthly record of Church Work in the Diocese. Winchester. 1893.

Winchester and a few other Compositions in Prose and Verse. 4to. Winchester. 1835.

WITHERS (R. J.). Encaustic Tiles from St. Mary's Abbey, Beaulieu. 4to. 1844.

WITTS (Rev. F. W., Vicar of Ringwood), Parish Sermons. 12mo. For private circulation. 1885.

WOOL (Rev. J.). Biographical Memoirs of the Rev. Joseph Warton, D.D., Master of St. Mary Winton College, to which is added a selection of his works. 4to. 1806.

WOOD (W.). Hampshire Fossils, collected and deposited in the British Museum by Gustaves Brander, 1776. Plates. 4to. 1829.

WOODFORD (Bp. J. R.), Ordination Sermons preached in the Diocese of Winchester. 1860-72. 8vo. 1872.

WYKEHAMICAL CRICKET SCORES, from the Year 1825. 8vo. Winchester. 1838.

WYKEMIST. Ups and Downs of a Public School. 8vo. n.d.

YONGE (C. M.). John Keble's Parishes; a History of Hursley and Otterbourne. Map and Plates. 8vo. London. 1898.

YOUNG (Rev. H. Lindsay) and Good (Rev. P. H.), The Hymnal Supplement. 18mo. Portsmouth. 1881.

RICARDI VITI
BASINSTOCHII
COMITIS PALA-
TINI HISTORIARVM
LIBRI,

1. *Ab Origine ad Brotum.*
2. *Ab illo ad Mulmutium.*
3. *Ab hoc ad Helium.*
4. *Ab isto ad Lucium.*
5. *Ab eo ad Constantium.*

CVM NOTIS ANTI.
quitatum Britannicarum.

ATREBATI,
Ex Officina Gulielmi Riuerij,
M. D. XCVII.

[Figure 18; 9.1 x 15.1 cm]

Andw Crawford - 1828

THE ANNUAL

HAMPSHIRE REPOSITORY;

OR,

HISTORICAL, ECONOMICAL, AND LITERARY

MISCELLANY;

A Provincial Work, of entirely original Material

Comprising all Matters relative to

THE COUNTY, including THE ISLE OF WIGHT, &c.

UNDER THE FOLLOWING HEADS :—

COUNTY HISTORY	CIVIL AND MUNICIPAL	CHARITIES	ARTS AND SCIENCES
CHRONICLE	AFFAIRS	AGRICULTURE	LETTERS
REGISTRY	PUBLIC WORKS	NATURAL HISTORY,	BIOGRAPHY
NAVY	COMMERCE	PHILOSOPHY, AND	PROJECTS
ARMY	SCHOOLS	CURIOSITIES	MISCELLANIES
CHURCH	STATE OF THE POOR	ANTIQUITIES, AND	NOTICES TO
LAW	ECONOMY	TOPOGRAPHY	CORRESPONDENTS

&c. &c.

PUBLICA MATERIES PRIVATI JURIS ERIT. HOR.

VOL. I.

TO BE CONTINUED ANNUALLY.

The whole Work under the Direction of a Conductor, with the Assistance of regular Contributors and occasional Communicators.

Communications on any of the above Subjects, in future Aid of this Work, (for which general Arrangements are already made) and any Suggestions towards its Improvement, are respectfully requested ; the Expence incurred in furnishing which, will, if required, be repaid.

☞ All Letters or Packets, Post and Carriage free, are desired to be addressed to

Mr. ROBBINS, WINCHESTER.

Subscribers, who are willing to encourage this Work, will do so in a most essential Manner, by favouring Mr. ROBBINS with their Names ; Payment only successiv e on each annual Delivery.

Printed by ROBBINS;

Sold also by him and Burdon, Winchester ; Messrs. White, London ; and to be had at all Booksellers in the County.

[Figure 19; 12.7 x 21.7 cm]

THE

H I S T O R Y

OF THE

I S L E   O F   W I G H T.

St. Catharines Tower.

L O N D O N,

PRINTED BY A. HAMILTON;

And Sold by R. DODSLEY, T. CADELL, G. ROBINSON, R. FAULDER, and
G. NICOL: COLLINS and Co. Salisbury; and BURDON, at Winchester.

MDCCLXXXI.

[Figure 20; 22.3 x 28.4 cm]

[268]

A

BIBLIOGRAPHICAL ACCOUNT

OF

THE PRINCIPAL WORKS

RELATING TO

𝔈𝔫𝔤𝔩𝔦𝔰𝔥 𝔗𝔬𝔭𝔬𝔤𝔯𝔞𝔭𝔥𝔶:

BY

WILLIAM UPCOTT,

OF THE LONDON INSTITUTION.

IN THREE VOLUMES.
VOL. I.

" A painfull work it is I'll assure you, and more than difficult; wherein
what toyle hath been taken, as no man thinketh, so no man believeth,
but he that hath made the triall."

ANT. à WOOD's Preface to his Hist. of Oxford.

LONDON:

PRINTED BY RICHARD AND ARTHUR TAYLOR.

M DCCC XVIII.

[269]

HAMPSHIRE.

I.

COLLECTIONS for the HISTORY of HAMPSHIRE and the Bishopric of Winchester; including the Isles of Wight, Jersey, Guernsey, and Sarke, by D.Y. with the original *Domesday* of the County, and an accurate English Translation, Preface, and Introduction: containing an Account of this curious Record, a View of the Anglo-Saxon History and Form of Government, from the Reign of Alfred : together with a slight Sketch of the most material Alterations which the latter underwent at the Period of the Conquest. To which is added a Glossary, explanatory of the obsolete Words. By RICHARD WARNER of Sway, in the County of Southampton, and of St. Mary Hall, Oxford.—Illustrated with upwards of Sixty Plates, elegantly engraved; Views of remarkable Places, or Portraits of eminent Men, taking Honours from this County, or being Natives.—In SIX VoLUMES.

LONDON : Printed for the Authour, and sold by Messrs. Rivington, St. Paul's Church-yard; Messrs. Cadell and Davies, Strand; Law, Ave-Maria Lane; Sewel, Cornhill; the Booksellers of Salisbury, Oxford, Winchester, and Southampton. *Quarto.*

VOL. I.

SECT. I.—Containing the first Part of the *Topographical* Description alphabetically arranged.

Title-page as above.

Dedication to the Right Honourable the Marquis of Hertford, signed D. Y. and dated May 26, 1795, [b] p. iii–x.

Preface, [b] dated July 20, 1795, 4 pages.

Table of the Plates in the Six Volumes, and Contents, 2 pages.

(History of) Hampshire, [A–Ll 3] 270 pages; concluding thus : " END OF SECTION I."

HAMPSHIRE.

PLATES.

SECTION II.

Containing the last Part of the *Topographical* Description alphabetically arranged.

Title-page as before.

[271]

The Topographical Description continued. The first leaf beginning with signature A, *⁎* then follow signature A–ss 3, 318 pages.

Errata of paging :—From p. 99 to 158 (the signatures being N to X inclusive) are omitted, but the error is accounted for ;— pp. 162, 3, 4 are repeated ;—p. 210, 211 are omitted.

PLATES.

1. Merden Castle, (*from Grose's Antiq.*) Sparrow sc. p. 27.
2. Netley Abbey, Plate I. (*from Grose's Antiq.*) p. 32.
3. Netley Abbey, Plate II. (*from Grose's Antiq.*) p. 33.
4. Abbot's Kitchen at Netley Abbey, (*from Grose's Antiq.*) Sparrow sc. p. 34.
5. Odiam Castle, (*from Grose's Antiq.*) Sparrow sc. p. 80.
6. Porchester Church, (*from Grose's Antiq.*) Sparrow sc. p. 86.
7. Porchester Castle, (*from Grose's Antiq.*) Sparrow sc. p. 88.
8. The Gate to Porchester Priory, (*from Grose's Antiq.*) J. Newton sc. p. 88.
9. Somerford Grange, (*from Grose's Antiq.*) Sparrow sc. 1784. p. 171.
10. Water-Gate, Southampton, (*from Grose's Antiq.*) D. L. sc. p. 175.
11. East Gate, Southampton, (*from Grose's Antiq.*) p. 176.
12. The South-Gate and Tower, Southampton, (*from Grose's Antiq.*) p. 176.
13. South-sea Castle, (*from Grose's Antiq.*) J. Newton sc. p. 180.
14. Titchfield House, (*from Grose's Antiq.*) Godfrey sc. p. 198.
15. Titchfield House Chapel, (*from Grose's Antiq.*) T. Bonnor sc. p. 200.
16. Warblington Castle, (*from Grose's Antiq.*) Sparrow sc. p. 216.
17. King John's House (at Warnford,) (*from Grose's Antiq.*) p. 219.
18. Cathedral Church of Winchester, (*from Grose's Antiq.*) J. Newton sc. p. 254.
19. The Castle or County Hall, Winchester, (*from Grose's Antiq.*) J. Newton sc. p. 264.
20. Bp. of Winchester's House at Waltham, (*from Grose's Antiq.*) Plate I. L. D. sc. p. 267.
21. (Interior View of the) Bp. of Winchester's House at Waltham, (*from Grose's Antiq.*) Plate II. L. D. sc. p. 269.

22. Wolvesley Castle, (*from Grose's Antiq.*) Sparrow sc. p. 270.
23. The Chapel of Wolvesley Castle, (*from Grose's Antiq.*) D. L. sc. p. 271.
24. The Hospital of St. Cross, near Winchester, (*from Grose's Antiq.*) D. L. sc. p. 278.
25. The Church of St. Cross, near Winchester, (*from Grose's Antiq.*) T. Bonnor sc. p. 281.

VOL. II.

Containing the original Domesday, with Mr. Warner's Introduction and Glossary*.

Title-page as before.
Preface, [a–b 3] p. v–xvii.
The Introduction, [b 4–f 3] 32 pages.
Names of the Hundreds, Manors, Towns, Vills, &c. in the County of Hants at the time of the general Survey, with the modern ones adapted to them, p. xxxiii–xliii.
Names of the Land-holders in Hampshire, xliv–xlvi.
Extract from Domesday, with Translation, [b–ss 4] 319 pages.
The Glossary, 8 pages.

VOL. III.

Containing the Agricultural Survey, Natural History, Honours, and Biography of eminent Men of this County, [b–ii 4] 248 pages.

N. B. A Title-page to the " General View of the Agriculture of the Isle of Wight," forms pages 41 and 42.

PLATES.

A Vine Plantation in the Isle of Wight, on the letter-press of page 54.

---

* This volume was published separately with the following Title-page: " HAMPSHIRE extracted from Domesday Book ; with an accurate English Translation, a Preface, and an Introduction, containing an Account of this curious Record, a View of the Anglo-Saxon History, and Form of Government, from the Reign of Alfred : together with a slight Sketch of the most material Alterations which the latter underwent at the Period of the Conquest. To which is added a GLOSSARY, explanatory of the obscure and obsolete Words. By RICHARD WARNER, jun. of Sway, in the County of Southampton, and of St. Mary Hall, Oxford.
" LONDON : Sold by Faulder, Bond-street ; Robinsons, Paternoster-row ; Law, Ave-Mary-Lane ; Sewel, Cornhill ; Flexney, Holborn ; Hookham, Bond-street ; White and Son, Fleet-street ; Richardson, Royal Exchange ; Bliss, Oxford ; and Metrill, Cambridge. MDCCLXXXIX."

1. Henry Wriothesley, 3rd Earl of Southampton, ob. Nov'r 10th, 1624. T. S. Seed sc. p. 95.
2. Thomas Wriothesley, Earl of Southampton, Lord High Treasurer to Charles 2nd, p. 96.
3. W'm Paulet, 1st Marquis of Winchester. p. 98.
4. Louise, Duchess of Portsmouth. Sir Peter Lely pinx. T. S. Seed sc. p. 102.
5. Philip Earl of Pembroke, numbered 51. p. 102.
6. Sir W'm Petty. p. 146.

VOL. IV.

Containing the Island of Jersey by Mr. Fall, a new Edition, with great Additions, [B–H h 3] 238 pages.

PLATES.

1. Elizabeth Castle, Jersey, (*from Grose's Antiq.*) D. L. sc. p. 55.
2. Mont Orgueil Castle, Jersey, (*from Grose's Antiq.*) D. L. sc. p. 64.
3. Plan of the Form of Jersey.
    N. B. This is mentioned in the printed list of plates, but is not to be found in any of the copies which the Editor has had the opportunity to examine.
4. Druids' Temple found in the Island of Jersey, (*from Grose's Antiq.*) Plate I. J. Newton sc. p. 143.
5. Another View of the Druids' Temple found in the Island of Jersey, (*from Grose's Antiq.*) Plate II. S. Sparrow sc. p. 144.
6. Notre Dame.—[N. B. The Inscription under the plate says *Guernsey*, but it should be *Jersey*.] (*from Grose's Antiq.*) Sparrow sc. p. 151.

VOL. V.

Containing the Islands of Guernsey and Sarke, [B–N 3] 94 pages.

PLATES.

1. St. Michael's, or the Vale Castle, Guernsey, (*from Grose's Antiq.*) Sparrow sc. 1777. p. 53.
2. The Vale Church, Guernsey, (*from Grose's Antiq.*) Sparrow sc. 1776. p. 54.
3. St. Sampson's Church, Guernsey, (*from Grose's Antiq.*) Sparrow sc. 1777. p. 56.
4. Castle Cornet, Guernsey, Plate I. (*from Grose's Antiq.*) D. L. sc. p. 64.

5. Castle Cornet, Guernsey, Plate II. (*from Grose's Antiq.*) D. L. sc. p. 64.

6. Marsh Castle, (*from Grose's Antiq.*) Sparrow sc. p. 58.

N.B. *Two hundred and fifty* copies of this work were printed; viz. 225 on small, and TWENTY-FIVE on LARGE PAPER.

II.

TOPOGRAPHICAL REMARKS relating to the South-Western Parts of HAMPSHIRE: To which is added, a Descriptive Poem. By the Rev. RICHARD WARNER of Fawley, near Southampton. In Two Volumes. LONDON: Printed for R. Blamire, Strand. MDCCXCIII. *Octavo.*

VOL. I.

Half Title, " Topographical Remarks."

Title-page as above.

Dedication to Sir Harry Burrard, Bart. of Walhampton, near Lymington, signed Richard Warner, jun. and dated Fawley Parsonage, March 15th, 1793, 3 pages.

Contents of both volumes, 4 pages.

Topographical Remarks, [B-x] 299 pages.

VOL. II.

Half Title and Title-page as in Vol. I.

Topographical Remarks continued, [B-o 4] 200 pages.

HENGISTBURY HEAD: a Descriptive Elegiac Poem, p. 201–215.

Contents of the Appendix, 3 pages.

Appendix, [a-e 3] 70 pages.

Errata in Vol. I and II. with Directions to the Binder for placing the Engravings, 2 pages; and the Volume concludes with the following Notice:

" The Author of the Topographical Remarks respectfully informs the Public, that the *Engravings* intended to accompany his Work, were consumed, together with the Copper-plates, &c. in a Fire which happened on Sunday, the 28th of April, 1793, at the House of the Copper-plate Printer, Mr. Pushee, in Tottenham-street. As, however, he had advertized the Work for publication previous to the Accident, he deemed it more consistent to present it to the World at a *greatly reduced price*, than to with-hold it altogether.—London, May 13th, 1793."

III.

The ANNUAL HAMPSHIRE REPOSITORY: or, Historical, Economical, and Literary Miscellany: a provincial Work of entirely original Materials, comprising all Matters relative to the County, including the Isle of Wight, &c. under the following Heads:—County History, Chronicle, Registry, Navy, Army, Church, Law, Civil and Municipal Affairs, Public Works, Commerce, Schools, State of the Poor, Economy, Charities, Agriculture, Natural History, Philosophy, and Curiosities; Antiquities and Topography; Arts and Sciences; Letters, Biography, Projects, Miscellanies, Notices to Correspondents, &c. &c. In Two Volumes.

" *Publica Materies privati juris erit."* HOR.

(WINCHESTER:) Printed by Robbins: sold also by him and Burdon, Winchester; Messrs. White, London; and to be had at all Booksellers in the County. *Octavo.* No date.

VOL. I.

Title-page as above.
Advertisement, dated March 31, 1799.
Preface.—To the Public, dated Winchester, May 1, 1798, p. iii–xxii.
Civil and Political History of Hampshire, or the Public Conduct of it as a County, &c. [A–Q 4] 128 pages.
State of the Poor, Population, Economy, Charities, Agriculture, Antiquities, [2 A–2 T 3] p. 1–150.*
Notice to Correspondents, 1 page, concluding thus: " End of Vol. I."
Appendix, or Part II.—Contents and Errata, 2 pages.
Biography, [*2 A–2 D 2] 28 pages.
Poetry, Essays, and Criticisms, [3 A–3 U 5] 161 pages.

---

* There is an apparent omission in this part of the work from the signatures not following in regular and alphabetical order: the Editor has been very anxious to ascertain the fact positively; but as the book was published in the country, and is little known, he has been unable to procure the inspection of more than two copies besides that in the library of the London Institution, which are precisely the same as the one above described.

PLATES.

1. Plate of the Pitch of a Wheel Plough. p. 91, of Agriculture.
2. A Balance on the Principle of the Steel-yard, to show the Draft of a Plough. p. 91, of Agriculture.
3. Plan of the ancient Clausentum, a Roman Station, now Bittern, with the new Bridge and Road making there. Folded. p. 92, of Antiquities.
4. Two Plants, coloured; viz. Ophrys apifera and Ophrys nondescript. Folded. Sowerby del. p. 122, of Botany.
   Also a folded Statistical Table, (No. 4.) p. 46, of the Supplement to County History.

VOL. II.

Title-page as in Volume I.
Contents, and List of Plates, p. 3–6.
Preface, dated Winchester, April 15, 1801, p. vii–xii.
Civil and Political History of Hampshire, [A–2 Q] 296 pages.
   Between pages 82–3 are two leaves containing a List of Magistrates for the County, *not* paged.
Miscellanies.—Survey of Hampshire, &c. [4 A–4 K 3] 78 pages.
Letters, beginning with "Prize Exercises," [3 A–3 P 3] 116 pages.
Criticisms, and Supplement to Poetry, [3 P 4–3 D d] p. 117–207.
   Erratum :—p. 29 of the Chronicle for p. 26.

PLATES.

1–2. Mechanism of a fraudulent E O Table detected at Winchester.
3. Mr. Taylor's Patent Machines for raising Water. Folded. T. Younge del. Southampton. p. 94, of Civil and Political History.
4. A Chinese Dwarf Tree. Coloured. W. Fitzhugh, Esq. del. T. Medland aq. fort. fec. p. 301.
5–9. Antiquities of Ancient Clausentum, now Bittern. Five Plates. Sir H. C. Englefield del. J. Basire sc. p. 300.
10. A View of the New Bridge at Northam. Folded. Moneypenny, Architect. Drawn by T. Younge, engraved by T. S. Seed. p. 301.
11. Bursledon Bridge, and View. Engraved by Tho. Scott Seed, Southⁿ. p. 301.

IV.

The History and Antiquities of the Cathedral Church of Winchester: containing all the Inscriptions upon the Tombs and Monuments; with an Account of the Bishops, Priors, Deans, and Prebendaries: also the History of Hyde Abbey.—Begun by the Right Honourable Henry, late Earl of Clarendon, and continued to this time by Samuel Gale, Gent. Adorned with Sculptures.

London: Printed for E. Curll, at the Dial and Bible against St. Dunstan's Church in Fleet-street. mdccxv. *Octavo**.

Title-page as above.

Dedication to the Rt. Rev. Father in God Jonathan (Trelawney), Lord Bishop of Winton, signed S. Gale, 6 pages.

Preface, dated Sep. 8, 1715, signed S. G. 7 pages.

The History and Antiquities of the Cathedral Church of the Holy Trinity in Winton. By Samuel Gale, Gent.

> " Delicta, *majorum inmeritus lues,*
>   *Romane, donec templa refèceris."*   Hor. Edit. Bent.

London: Printed in the year mdccxv."

The History of the Cathedral Church, [a 2–c 2] p. 3–35.

Donationes Terrarum Ecclesiæ Winton, 4 pages.

Charters and Records in the Tower of London relating to the Church of Winton; several Religious Houses, Chapels, Colleges, and Hospitals in and about that City, 24 pages.

The Antiquities of the Cathedral, beginning with its Dimensions, [b 5–f 6] 91 pages.

Index to the Antiquities, 2 pages.

Some Account of the Bishops, Priors, Deans, and Prebendaries of the See of Winchester, [f 6–i 4] p. 91–136.

Addenda, Errata, and Corrigenda, [k] p. 137–144.

Index, 4 pages.

Pages 90 and 91 are repeated, with an *, containing the Inscription from the Monument of the Rev. Thomas Fletcher.

---

* Some copies have a reprinted Title-page, with the following imprint:
" London: Printed for W. Mears, at the Lamb without Temple Bar; and J. Hooke, at the Flower-de-luce against St. Dunstan's Church in Fleet Street. mdccxxiii."

PLATES.

1. View of Winchester Cathedral. Dedicated to Jonathan (Trelawney), Lord Bishop of Winchester, and Prelate of the Most Noble Order of the Garter. Folded. M. V. d^r Gucht sc. p. 1, of the Hist. of the Cathedral.

2. An ancient square Font in Winchester Cathedral: this and the four following Plates are dedicated to Samuel Gale. Folded. C. Woodfield del. M. V. d^r Gucht sc. p. 23.

3, 4, 5, 6. Bas reliefs on each side of the Font. p. 24.

7. The Entrance to the Choir, the Work of Inigo Jones. Dedicated to the Dean and Chapter of the Cath^l Church of Winton. C. Woodfield del. M. V. d^r Gucht sc. p. 25.

8. The Chests of the West Saxon Kings, &c. on the North Wall of the Presbytery, and the Tomb of William Rufus before ye Altar. Folded. Dedicated to Mr. William Lock, of London, Merchant. C. Woodfield del. M. V. d^r Gucht sc. p. 27.

9. South View of the Chantry of Bishop Fox. Dedicated to the Rev. the President and Fellows of Corpus Christi College, Oxon. C. Woodfield del. M. V. d^r Gucht sc. p. 29.

10. Monument of William Wainfleet, Bp. of Winton. Dedicated to the Rev. the President and Fellows of Magdalen College, Oxon. C. Woodfield del. M. V. d^r Gucht sc. p. 30.

11. Monument of Richard, Son of William the Conqueror. Dedicated to Ralph Throsby, of Leeds, Esq. p. 30.

12. Monument of Richard Weston, Earl of Portland. Folded. Inscribed to Roger Gale, Esq. C. Woodfield del. M. V. d^r Gucht sc. p. 35.

13. Monument of W^m of Wyckham, Bishop of Winchester. Inscribed to the Rev. the Warden and Fellows of New College, Oxon. H. Hulsbergh sc. p. 39.

14. Monument of Baptista Levinz, Bishop of Sodor and Man, and inscribed to the Lady Levinz. p. 42.

15. Monument and Statue of Sir John Clobery, and inscribed to his Co-heirs. H. Hulsbergh sc. p. 45.

16. Monument of the Rev. John Nicholas, Prebendary of Winchester. Dedicated to Edward Nicholas, Esq. H. Hulsbergh sc. p. 59.

17. Monument of the Rev. William Harris, Prebendary of Winchester. Inscribed to Charles Savage, Esq. H. Hulsbergh sc. p. 84.

18. Seals of Winchester Cathedral, and, of Stephen Gardiner, Bishop of Winchester. Folded. Inscribed to Peter Le Neve, Esq. M. V. d͏ʳ Gucht sc. p. 136.

N. B. There are copies of this work upon LARGE PAPER.

V.

A DESCRIPTION of the CITY, COLLEGE, and CA-THEDRAL of WINCHESTER: exhibiting a complete and comprehensive Detail of their Antiquities and present State. Illustrated with several curious and authentic Particulars, collected from a Manuscript of Anthony Wood, preserved in the Ashmolean Museum at Oxford; the College and Cathedral Registers, and other original Authorities. To which is added an authentic Account of the most remarkable Events and memorable Occurrences from its earliest State to the present Time. (By the Rev. THOMAS WARTON.)

WINCHESTER: Printed and sold by W. Greenville. *Duodecimo,* 84 pages.

VI.

The HISTORY and ANTIQUITIES of WINCHESTER, setting forth its original Constitution, Government, Manufactories, Trade, Commerce, and Navigation: its several Wards, Parishes, Precincts, Districts, Churches, Religious and Charitable Fonndations, and other public Edifices. Together with the Char-ters, Laws, Customs, Rights, Liberties, and Privileges of that ancient City.—Illustrated with a variety of Plates.—In Two Volumes.

WINTON: Printed and sold by J. Wilkes: sold also by S. Crow-der and R. Baldwin in Paternoster-row, London; and by J. Hodson and Co. in Salisbury. MDCCLXXIII.

VOL. I.

Title-page as above.

Dedication to the Worshipful Sir Paulet St. John, Bart. Mayor, and to the Corporation and Citizens of Winchester, dated Winton, Sep. 2, 1772.
Preface, 6 pages.
Directions for placing the Cuts to both volumes, 1 page.
The History and Antiquities of Winchester, [B–L 11] 237 pages.

PLATES.

1. Frontispiece: Justice resting on a Shield bearing the Arms of Winchester. W. Cave del. Winton. I. Taylor sc.
2. A View of the Ruins of the King's Palace at Winchester. W. Cave del. Dent & Innes sc. p. 6.
3. A View of the Cathedral Church of Winchester. W. Cave del. I. Taylor sc. p. 32.
4. A View of the Episcopal Palace of Winchester. W. Cave del. I. Taylor sc. p. 86.
5. A View of St. Mary's College in Winchester. Folded. W. Cave del. I. Taylor sc. p. 90.
6. The Trusty Servant. W. Cave del. p. 92.
7. A View of the College of Clergymen's Widows at Winchester. W. Cave del. I. Taylor sc. p. 224.
8. Winchester Cross. W. Cave del. I. Taylor sc. p. 227.

VOL. II.

Title-page as in Volume I.
Errata to both Volumes, 1 page.
Historical Part continued, [B–O 4] 299 pages.

Errata:—page 340 for 240 ;—p. 225 for 252 ;—pages 265 to 269 are omitted ;—p. 266 for 296.

PLATES.

1. Florence de Lunn, Esq. first Mayor of Winchester A.D. 1184. I. Taylor sc. as a Frontispiece.
2. The County Hospital at Winchester. W. Cave del. I. Taylor sc. p. 149.
3. A View of the original State of the Magdalen Hospital. W. Cave del. I. Taylor sc. p. 155.
4. A View of the Ruins of Magdalen Hospital. W. Cave del. Dent & Innes sc. p. 201.
5. A View of the Hospital of St. Cross. Folded. W. Cave del. I. Taylor sc. p. 230.

VII.

The HISTORY CIVIL and ECCLESIASTICAL, and SUR-
VEY of the ANTIQUITIES of WINCHESTER. By the
Rev. JOHN MILNER, M.A. F.S.A. In Two Volumes.

> " *Guintoniam titulis claram gazisque repletam*
> *Noverunt veterum tempora prisca patrum.*
> *Sed jam sacra fames auri jam cæcus habendi*
> *Urbibus egregiis parcere nescit amor.*"
> ALEX. NECHAM. Poeta Sæc. 12.

WINCHESTER: Printed and sold by Jas. Robbins: and sold in
London by Cadell and Davies, in the Strand; Robson, New
Bond-street; Leigh and Sotheby, York-street, Covent-gar-
den; Wilkie, Paternoster-row; and Coghlan, Duke-street,
Grosvenor-square. *Quarto.*

VOL. I.
Being the Historical Part.

An engraved Title-page as above, representing the Altar Screen
of the Cathedral, with a View of the City from Oliver's Bat-
tery. T. H. Turner del. J. Pass sc.

Dedication to the Right Honourable the Countess Chandos
Temple, signed John Milner, and dated Winchester, Ap. 6,
1798, 4 pages.

Preface, p. 5–19.

Contents, 5 pages.

The History, Ecclesiastical and Civil, of Winchester, Part I.
[A–3 L 2] 451 pages.

Errata on the reverse of page 451.

PLATES.

1. North East View of Winchester Cathedral. Folded. James
   Cave, Winton. del. J. Pass sc. p. 41.
2. North East View of St. Mary's College, Winton.—North
   View of the Middle Tower, and part of the West end of
   the Library. Folded. J. Cave del. J. Pass sc. p. 303.
3. East View of the King's House and the adjoining Offices, as
   intended to have been finish'd by Sir Christopher Wren.
   J. Cave del. ex autographo C. Wren, Equ.; with a West
   and East View of the ancient Castle of Winchester. Folded.
   J. Cave del. ad mentem J. Milner. J. Pass sc. p. 433.
4. West View of the City Cross in its original State; and
   various Antiquities discovered near Winchester. Folded.
   J. Cave del. J. Pass sc. p. 449.

HAMPSHIRE.

VOL. II.

Being the Survey of the Antiquities.

Engraved Title-page, with a representation of the "Side in-
closure of (the) Cathedral Sanctuary, with the Mortuary
Chests.—North View of the City from the Monk's Walk.—
Part of Wolvesey Ruins.—Stone Coffins from Hyde Abbey,
and Druidical Altar near St. Peter's Chapel. J. Cave del.
J. Pass sc.

"._____ Sic omnia verti
Cernimus, atque alias assumere robora gentes;
Concidere has. Sic magna fuit censuque virisque.
Nunc humilis veteres tantummodo (Venta) ruinas,
Et, pro divitiis, tumulos ostendit avorum."—OVID. Metam. l. xv.

Preface, 6 pages.   Contents, 4 pages.

The Survey of Winchester, and Supplement, Part II. [A–2I 2]
248 pages.

Explanation of the Plans of Winchester, between pp. 248–249.

Appendix, [2K–2N] p. 249–270.

Index and Errata, 8 pages.

Erratum:—p. 208 for 218.

PLATES.

1. South View of the Outside of William of Wykeham's
Chantry.—South View of the Chantry of Bishop Fox.—
North View of William of Wykeham's Tomb, with part
of the Inside of his Chantry. James Cave del. J. Pass
sc. p. 23.

2. North East View of Cardinal Beaufort's Chantry, and a
South East View of Bishop Waynflete's Chantry in Winchester Cathedral. J. Cave del. J. Pass sc. p. 59.

3. South West View of the Church and Hospital of St. Cross,
with curious Specimens of Architecture in the Church.
J. Cave del. J. Pass sc. p. 147.

4. East View of West Gate, and North West View of the Cathedral. J. Carter del. 1789. Basire sc. p. 177.

5. Interior and exterior Views of St. Peter's Chapel, Winton;
with a Norman Door-way leading to the Chapel from
St. Peter's Street. Folded. J. Cave del. J. Pass sc. p. 229.

6. Ancient Ichnography of the City and Environs of Winchester, folded; with the Ichnography of the Cathedral
Church. J. Cave del. ad mentem J. Milner. To face
p. 249, and to front the Explanatory Tables.

N. B. TWELVE COPIES only of this edition were taken off on
LARGE PAPER.

VIII.

The HISTORY CIVIL and ECCLESIASTICAL, and SURVEY of the ANTIQUITIES of WINCHESTER. By the Rev. JOHN MILNER, D.D. F.S.A. In Two Volumes.—The Second Edition, corrected and enlarged *.

WINCHESTER: Printed and sold by Jas. Robbins; and sold in London by Cadell and Davies, in the Strand; J. Richardson, Royal Exchange; Keating, Brown, and Keating, Duke-street, Grosvenor-square; and Joseph Booker, New Bond-street. 1809.

VOL. I.

Engraved Title-page, as in the preceding Edition.

Dedication to the Rt. Hon. the Countess Chandos Temple, as before, 4 pages.

Advertisement concerning the Second Edition, and Directions for placing the Plates, 2 pages.

Preface, [B–C 4] 15 pages.

Contents, 5 pages.

Description of the Plans of Winchester, 1 page.

The History of Winchester, [D 3–3 o 4] 451 pages.

PLATES.

1. Ichnography of Winchester, &c.   p. 24.

---

* The following extract from the advertisement will explain the difference between the two editions, though the first must claim the preference both in paper and in the superior impressions of the plates.

"A copious postscript is annexed to the present edition, in which the several strictures contained in the reviews and other works that have been published on the subject of the History are detailed and discussed. Several considerable additions are interspersed throughout the work, and particularly amongst the notes: one of these contains observations upon a work lately published, in two octavo volumes, called *British Monachism.* Another addition consists of a whole new chapter; being a Survey of the most remarkable modern Monuments in Winchester Cathedral.

"Certain notes, which seemed to be of little importance, are abridged or omitted in this edition: and the whole preface to the second volume is left out, as the substance of it is contained in the Postscript.

"The style of the whole work has been carefully revised and (it is hoped) considerably improved.

"Lastly, the plates have not only been re-touched, but also corrected and improved. Three new plates are also given in this edition."

2. Winchester Cathedral. p. 41.
3. St. Mary's College. p. 303.
4. Miscellaneous Plate. p. 374.
5. The King's House. p. 433.

VOL. II.

Title-page as before.
The Survey of Winchester, Supplement, Postscript, Appendix, and Index, [A–R R 4] 312 pages.

Errata:—pages 137 to 144 are repeated, and follow;—p. 174 for 172.

PLATES.

1. An interior View of Winchester Cathedral, to the West. Jas. Cave del. 1808. Jas. Basire sc. p. 23.
2. Chantries of Bishops Wykeham and Fox. Jas. Cave del. J. Pass sc. p. 25.
3 View of the Choir, Winchester Cathedral. Jas. Cave del. 1808. Jas. Basire sc. p. 35.
4. Chantries of Beaufort and Waynflete. James Cave del. J. Pass sc. p. 60.
5. Monuments of Bishop Hoadley and Dr. Joseph Warton in Winchester Cathedral. Jas. Cave del. 1809. Jas. Basire sc. p. 91.
6. The South West View of the Church and Hospital of St. Cross. J. Cave del. J. Pass sc. p. 152.
7. East View of West Gate, and North West View of the Cathedral. J. Carter del. 1789. Basire sc. p. 180.
8. Inside and Outside View of St. Peter's Chapel, &c. Folded. James Cave del. J. Pass sc. p. 240.

N. B. There are Large Paper copies of this edition.

IX.

An HISTORICAL and CRITICAL ACCOUNT of WINCHESTER CATHEDRAL, with an engraved View and ichnographical Plan of that Fabric. Extracted from the Rev. Mr. Milner's History and Antiquities of Winchester. To which is added a Review of its Monuments.

" *Redditus his primum terris tibi,* Christe, *sacravit*
Sedem hanc Birinus, posuitque immania templa." ÆNEID. l. vi.

WINCHESTER : Printed and sold by Ja. Robbins, 1801. *Octavo,*
150 pages.

PLATES.

North West View of the Cathedral. J. Carter del. 1789.
J. Basire sc.
Ichnography of the Cathedral. Folded.

X.

HISTORICA DESCRIPTIO complectens Vitam ac Res
Gestas Beatissimi Viri Gulielmi Wicami quondam
VINTONIENSIS Episcopi, & Angliæ Cancellarii, &
Fundatoris duorum Collegiorum Oxoniæ & Vintoniæ.

OXONIÆ, e Theatro Sheldoniano, An. Dom. MDCXC. *Quarto,*
137 pages.

With the Arms of William of Wykeham, to front the Title-page.

N. B. The author of this Memoir was Dr. Thomas Martin,
Chancellor of this Diocese under Bishop Gardiner, and it was first
printed in quarto in 1597.—GOUGH.

XI.

The LIFE of WILLIAM of WYKEHAM, Bishop of
WINCHESTER. Collected from Records, Registers,
Manuscripts, and other authentic Evidences. By
ROBERT LOWTH, D.D. now Lord Bishop of Ox-
ford.

" *Quique sui memores alios fecere merendo,*" VIRG.

The Third Edition corrected.

OXFORD: at the Clarendon Press, MDCCLXXVII, Sold by
D. Prince: and by J. Dodsley and T. Cadell, London. *Octavo* *.

Title-page as above, with the Tomb of William of Wykeham,
as a Vignette.

---

* The first edition appeared in 1758, the second in the following year,
with additions, from which this edition of 1777 is printed,

Dedication to the Right Rev. Benjamin (Hoadley), Lord Bishop of Winchester, dated 1758, 4 pages.
The Preface, p. vii–xxvii.
Lines addressed to the Author by W. Whitehead, Poet Laureat, 2 pages.
The Contents, 2 pages.
The Life, [B–Y] 321 pages.
Appendix, [a–g 2] 52 pages.

PLATES.

1. Cantaria et Monumentum Will'mi de Wykeham Ep'i Wint. in Ecclesia Cathedrali Winton. J. Taylor, Surveyor, del. F. Patton sc. To face the Title.
2. Baculus Pastoralis Will'mi de Wykeham Ep'i Winton in Thesauro Coll. Nov. Oxon. asservatus : ex argento deaurato et pictura encaustica ornato. J. Green del. & sc. Oxon. p. 263.
3. Tabula Genealogica exhibens cognatos & affines W^{mi} de Wykeham quorum in antiquis monumentis mentio habetur. Folded. To face the last page of the Appendix.

XII.

The LIFE of WILLIAM WAYNFLETE, BISHOP of WINCHESTER, Lord High Chancellor of England in the Reign of Henry VI., and Founder of Magdalen College, Oxford : Collected from Records, Registers, Manuscripts, and other authentic Evidences, by RICHARD CHANDLER, D.D. formerly Fellow of that College.

LONDON: Printed for White and Cochrane, Horace's Head, Fleet-street, by Richard Taylor and Co. Shoe-lane. MDCCCXI. *Royal octavo.*

Half Title.
Title-page as above, with the Bishop's Tomb as a Vignette.
Engraved Dedication to the Revd Dr Routh, President; and the Fellows of St. Mary Magdalen College, Oxford; with the Arms of Magdalen College as a head piece. J. Girtin sc.
Advertisement, signed Charles Lambert, Inner Temple, May 7, 1811.

The Author's Preface, p. v–xii.

Contents, and List of Plates, p. xiii–xvi.

Half Title: "The Life of William Waynflete, Bishop of Winchester."

The Life, and Appendix, [B–2 D 4] 408 pages.

Corrections and additional Notes by the Editor, p. 409–410.

Index, 18 pages.

PLATES.

  i. Portrait of William Waynflete, Bishop of Winchester. Ex dono Collegii Sæ Mæ Magdalenæ Oxoniensis. W. Bromley sc. To face the Title.

  ii. The Chapel and School-house at Wayneflete in Lincolnshire, erected by William Wayneflete, Founder of Magdalen College, Oxford. Engraved by B. Pouncy. p. 112.

  iii. Magdalen College, Oxford. J. C. Buckler, jun. del. J. C. Bromley, jun. sc. p. 186.

  iv. Monument of Bishop Waynflete in the Cathedral Church of Winchester. Ex dono Collegii Sæ Mæ Magdalenæ Oxoniensis. p. 234.

  v. Monument of Richd Patten in the Church of Waynflete, Lincolnshire. p. 242.

    The Seal of Magdalen College, Oxford, on the letter-press of p. 296.

N. B. Fifty copies were printed on LARGE PAPER.

XIII.

The HISTORY of the BROTHERHOOD or GUILD of the HOLY GHOST, in the Chapel of the Holy Ghost near Basingstoke, in Hampshire, dissolved by King Edward VI. and re-established by K. Philip and Q. Mary: wherein is contain'd the History and Antiquities of Holy Ghost Chapel near Basingstoke, and an Inquiry into the Patronage of that Chapel: with an Account of another religious House founded at the same place by King Henry III. (By SAMUEL LOGGON.)

READING: Printed for the Author, by J. Newbery and C. Micklewright: and sold by R. Ware, in Amen Corner, and T. Cooper, in Paternoster-row. 1742. *Octavo.*

Title-page as before.

Dedication to the Rt. Hon. Philip, Earl of Hardwick, signed Samuel Loggon, and dated Basingstoke, 1742, 4 pages.

Preface, p. v–viii.

The Contents, and Addenda and Corrigenda, 2 pages.

Historical Part, and Appendix, [B–G 2] 43 pages.

N. B. This Tract was again reprinted in 1808.

XIV.

The CASE, or an ABSTRACT of the CUSTOMS of the MANNOR of MERDON, in the Parish of HURSELY (*Hursley*), in the County of SOUTHAMPTON, which are to be observed and performed by the Lord and the Customary Tenants of the said Mannor, their Heirs and Successors for ever. As they were taken out of a Decree made and inrolled in the Honourable Court of Chancery, for ratifying and confirming the same Customs. Together with some remarkable passages, Suits at Law and in Equity, and the great differences and expences therein. By MATTHEW IMBER, Gent.

LONDON: Printed Anno Dom. 1707. *Small octavo*, 93 pages *.

Erratum :—page 92 for p. 90.

XV.

The NATURAL HISTORY and ANTIQUITIES of SELBORNE, in the County of SOUTHAMPTON : with Engravings, and an Appendix. (By the Rev. GILBERT WHITE.)

---

* Printed for private use. The suit about the Manor of Merdon began in 1691, when O. Cromwell, Esq. was lord, (who died with about twenty of the tenants during the interval,) and the decree was made in 1698, ratifying certain articles made in 1650 between Richard Major, then lord, and the tenants: and an authenticated copy of it is preserved in Hursley Church. The suit cost 1074*l*. which was to have been paid by the tenants according to the values of their estates. They empowered Mr. John White to carry on the suit, but had not reimbursed him at the time of his death, 1699.—GOUGH.

"————— *Ego Apis Matinæ*
More modoque
Grata carpentis—per laborem
Plurimum."   HOR.

" *Omnia benè describere, quæ in hoc mundo, a Deo facta, aut Naturæ creatæ*
viribus elaborata fuerunt, opus est non unius hominis, nec unius ævi.
Hinc Faunæ & Floræ *utilissimæ: hinc* Monographi *præstantissimi.*"
        SCOPOLI Ann. Hist. Nat.

LONDON: Printed by T. Bensley, for B. White and Son, at Horace's Head, Fleet-street. MDCCLXXXIX. *Quarto.*

Title-page as above.
Advertisement, signed Gil. White, and dated Selborne, Jany. I, 1788, 3 pages.
Title-page: " The Natural History of Selborne," &c. with a Vignette of the Hermitage.
The Natural History of Selborne, in 65 Letters addressed to Thomas Pennant, Esq. [B–Rr] 305 pages.
Title-page: " The Antiquities of Selborne, in the County of Southampton," with a Vignette representing the Seal of the Priory, and two lines from Virgil.
The Antiquities of Selborne, with Appendix, [Rr 3–ooo] page 309–468.
Index, List of Plates, and Errata, 13 pages.

For the List of Plates, see the next article.

XVI.

The NATURAL HISTORY and ANTIQUITIES of SELBORNE, in the County of SOUTHAMPTON: to which are added the Naturalists' Calendar; Observations on various parts of Nature; and Poems. By the late Rev. GILBERT WHITE, formerly Fellow of Oriel College, Oxford.—A new Edition, with Engravings.

LONDON: Printed for White, Cochrane, and Co.; Longman, Hurst, Rees, Orme, and Brown; J. Mawman; S. Bagster; J. and A. Arch; J. Hatchard; R. Baldwin; and T. Hamilton. 1813. *Quarto.*

Title-page as above.

Advertisement; Biographical Records of the Author; and Advertisement to the new Edition, signed J. W. and dated Selborne, May 10, 1813, 6 pages.

Title-page: " The Natural History of Selborne," with Vignette of the Hermitage, as in the first edition.

The Natural History of Selborne, [B–2 Q 3] 301 pages.

Title-page: " The Antiquities of Selborne, in the County of Southampton," with the Seal of the Priory as a Vignette.

The Antiquities of Selborne, [2 R–3 H 2] p. 305–419.

Appendix, [3 H 3–3 M 4] p. 421–456.

Half Title: " A comparative View of the Naturalists' Calendar, as kept at Selborne in Hampshire, by the late Rev. Gilbert White, M.A. and at Catsfield, near Battle, in Sussex, by William Markwick, Esq. F.L.S. from the year 1768 to the year 1793."

Naturalists' Calendar, [3 N 2–3 P] p. 459–474.

Half Title: " Observations on various parts of Nature, from Mr. White's MSS. with Remarks by Mr. Markwick."

Observations, beginning with " Birds in general," [3 Q 3–4 A 2] p. 477–548.

Half Title: " Summary of the Weather," with " Measure of Rain in Inches and Hundreds" on the reverse.

Summary of the Weather, [4 A 4–4 B 4] p. 551–559.

Half Title: " Poems."

The Poems, [4 C 2–4 D 2] p. 563–571.

Index, and List of the Plates, [4 D 3–4 F 2] p. 573–587.

Erratum :—page 257 for 527.

PLATES.

1. North East View of Selborne, from the Short Lythe. Folded. To front the Title.
2. The Hermitage; a Vignette in the Title-page to the Natural History of Selborne. S. H. Grimm del. D. Lerpiniere sc.
3. View of the Residence at Selborne of the late Rev. Gilbert White. J. Harris del. W. Angus sc. Tail-piece to the Biographical Sketch. p. ix. [*Not in the first edit.*]
4. Mytilus, Crista Galli; a Fossil. p. 7. [p. 7, *first edit.*]
5. Charadrius, Himantopus; a rare Bird. Folded. p. 258. [p. 259, *first edit.*]
6. Seal of the Priory; a Vignette in the Title-page to the Antiquities of Selborne. P. Mazell sc.
7. South View of Selborne Church. S. H. Grimm del. P. Mazell sc. p. 311. [p. 315, *first edit.*]

8. Copy of a Picture presented to the Church of Selborne, (supposed to be painted by John de Maubeuge,) the Gift of the late Benjⁿ White, Esq. Drawn and etched by T. Harris. [*Not in the first edit.*] p. 314.

9. North View of Selborne Church. S. H. Grimm del. P. Mazell sc. p. 318. [p. 323, *first edit.*]

10. Temple, in the Parish of Selborne. S. H. Grimm del. D. Lerpiniere sc. p. 338. [p. 343, *first edit.*]

11. The Pleystow, vulg. the Plestor. S. H. Grimm del. P. Mazell sc. p. 340. [p. 345, *first edit.*]

12. A Hybrid Bird (Pheasant). Coloured. Elmer pinx. J. F. Miller sc. p. 485. [*Not in the first edit.*]

N. B. FIFTY COPIES of this work were printed on LARGE PAPER, divided into Two Volumes, the Natural History forming the First, and the Antiquities the Second; with the outline of the Painting presented to the Church, at page 314, beautifully coloured in imitation of the original Picture.

XVII.

The NATURAL HISTORY of SELBORNE, by the late GILBERT WHITE, A.M. Fellow of Oriel College, Oxford. To which are added, the Naturalists' Calendar, Miscellaneous Observations, and Poems. A new Edition, with Engravings. In Two Volumes.

LONDON: Printed for White, Cochrane, and Co.; Longman, Hurst, Rees, Orme, and Brown; J. Mawman; S. Bagster; J. and A. Arch; J. Hatchard; R. Baldwin; and T. Hamilton. 1813. *Octavo.*

VOL. I.

Half Title.   Title-page as above.
Advertisement and Biographical Memoir, 4 pages.
The Natural History of Selborne, [B–z 8] 351 pages.

PLATES,
The same as in the preceding Articles; viz.

1. The Hermitage. To front the Title.
2. Mytilus, Crista Galli. p. 13.

VOL. II.
Half Title and Title-page as in Vol. I.

The Natural History of Selborne continued, with the Natu-
ralists' Calendar, and Observations on various parts of Nature,
[B-Y 7] 333 pages.
Poems, and Index, [Y 8–2A 6] p. 335–364.

PLATES.

1. Charadrius, Himantopus. To front the Title.
2. A Hybrid Bird (Pheasant). Coloured. Elmer pinx. J. F.
   Miller sc. p. 214.

N. B. Of the edition printed in 1802, in Two Volumes, there
are LARGE PAPER copies.

XVIII.

The ANCIENT and MODERN HISTORY of PORTES-
MOUTH, PORTSEA, GOSPORT, and their Environs.

> " ISLAND of bliss, amidst the subject seas,
>   That thunder round thy rocky coast, set up;
>   At once the wonder, terror, and delight
>   Of distant nations: whose remotest shores
>   Can soon be shaken by thy naval arm:
>   Not to be shook thyself, but all assaults
>   Baffling: as thy hoar cliffs the loud sea wave." THOMSON.

GOSPORT: Printed and sold by J. Watts. *Duodecimo,* 132
pages.

XIX.

A COMPANION in a TOUR round LYMINGTON : comprehending a brief Account of that Place and its
Environs, the New Forest, Isle of Wight, and Towns
of Southampton, Christchurch, &c. &c. By RICHARD
WARNER, jun. of Sway, near Lymington.

SOUTHAMPTON : Printed and sold by T. Baker. MDCCLXXXIX.
Duodecimo, 274 pages.

XX.

A WALK through SOUTHAMPTON. By Sir HENRY C.
ENGLEFIELD, Bart. F.R.S. and F.A.S. Second
Edition, considerably augmented : To which is added

some Account of the Roman Station, Clausentum. [First Edit. 1801.]

SOUTHAMPTON : Printed and sold by Baker and Fletcher : sold also in London by J. Stockdale, Piccadilly, and by T. Ostell, Ave-Maria-lane. MDCCCV. *Octavo.*

Title-page as above.

To the Reader, dated Dec. 1, 1801, 2 pages.

Advertisement to the Second Edition, dated Oct. 1, 1805, 2 pages.

Contents, 4 pages.

List of Plates and Wood Cuts, 1 page.

The Walk through Southampton, [A–M 2] 91 pages.

Half Title : " Appendix."

Another Half Title : " Account of an ancient Building in Southampton. By Sir H. C. Englefield, Bart. F.R.S. and V.P.A S. &c."

The Account of an ancient Building in Southampton, &c. [N] p. 97–104.

Half Title : " Account of Antiquities discovered at the ancient Roman Station *Clausentum* (now Bittern) near Southampton, &c."

The Account of Antiquities discovered at Bittern, and additional Discoveries made in 1804–5, [O 2–Q 4] p. 107–128.

Half Title : " Addenda."

Notes, &c. [R 2–S 2] p. 131–140.

Description of the Plates, and Errata, p. 141–148.

PLATES.

i. Engraved Title-page, preceding the printed one, composed from Fragments extant in the Town. H. C. Englefield del. & sc. 1801.

ii. Five southernmost Arches in the Town Wall near West Quay. Sir H. Englefield, Bart. del. J. Basire sc. p. 21.

iii*. Another part of the Arches in the same Wall near Bridle Gate. Sir H. C. Englefield, Bart. del. & sc. 1804. p. 23.

iv. The Regalia of the Corporation. Sir H. C. Englefield, Bart. del. & sc. 1801. p. 38.

v.* Two ancient Seals, one of Edw. I. for Recognizances ; the other, the Seal of the Staple. Basire sc. 1805. p. 42.

vi.* View in Porter's Lane, looking West. Sir H. C. Englefield del. & sc. 1804. p. 50.

vii. Inside View of St. Michael's Church, taken from the South Door looking North. Sir H. C. Englefield, Bart. del. & sc. p. 63.

viii. Font in St. Michael's Church. Sir H. C. Englefield, Bart. del. Basire sc. p. 65.

ix. View up Blue Anchor Lane. Sir H. C. Englefield, Bart. del. & fec. 1801. p. 68.

x.* Elevation of the central Part of the Building in Porter's Lane. Folded. Sir H. C. Englefield, Bart. del. & sc. 1804. p. 97.

xi.* Plan of the Roman Station at Bittern. Sir H. C. Englefield, Bart. del. & sc. 1804. p. 107.

xii.* Antiquities found at Bittern. Sir H. C. Englefield, Bart. del. & sc. 1804. p. 108.

WOOD CUTS ON THE LETTER PRESS.

i.* Altar dedicated to the Goddess Ancasta. p. 123.

ii.* Fragment of a Military Column. p. 124.

iii.* Inscription to the Emperor Gordian. p. 125.

iv.* Inscription to the Emperors Gallius and Volusianus. p. 126.

v.* Inscription to Tetricus. p. 127.

The plates marked thus * were added to the Second Edition.

N. B. Some copies of this work were printed in SMALL QUARTO.

XXI.

An ATTEMPT to ascertain the SITUATION of the ancient CLAUSENTUM. By the Rev. RICHARD WARNER, of Vicar's Hill, near Lymington, Hants.

> " .———Our narrow ken
> Reaches too far, when all that we discern,
> Is but the havock of wide wasting Time,
> Or what he soon shall spoil."

> " ———*Si quid novisti rectius istis*
> *Candidus imperti; si non, his utere mecum.*"

LONDON: Printed for R. Blamire, Strand, 1792. *Quarto,* 40 pages; including "Observations on the Utility of Provincial History: and Proposals for compiling and publishing the History of Hampshire."

It has an engraved Title-page with a vignette View of a Building in ruins, in aqua tinta, and a Plan of Bittern, the ancient Clausentum. Engraved by Neele.

XXII.

NETLEY ABBEY: an Elegy. (With a prefatory History of the Abbey, and other Additions.) By GEORGE KEATE, Esq. The SECOND EDITION, corrected and enlarged.

> "*Horrendum Sylvis et Relligione parentum.*" VIRG.

LONDON: Printed for J. Dodsley, in Pall Mall. MDCCLXIX. *Quarto*, 31 pages.

With a View of the East Front of Netley Abbey, as a Vignette in the Title-page. G. S. (George Stevens) del. C. Grignion sc. The first edition was printed in 1764, and was intituled " The Ruins of Netley Abbey." There has likewise been published,

" The Ruins of Netley Abbey: a Poem in blank Verse: to which is prefixed a short Account of that Monastery, from its first Foundation, collected from the best Authority. Lond. 1765." 4to. Printed by Mr. Dummer, the Proprietor, for the use of his Friends.

XXIII.

REMARKS on FOREST SCENERY and other Woodland Views, (relative chiefly to picturesque Beauty,) illustrated by the SCENES of NEW FOREST in HAMPSHIRE. In Three Books. By WILLIAM GILPIN, A.M. Prebendary of Salisbury, and Vicar of Boldre in New Forest, near Lymington. (In Two Volumes.) The SECOND EDITION.

> " ————————Happy he,
> Whom what he views of beautiful, or grand,
> In nature, from the broad, majestic oak
> To the green blade, that twinkles in the sun,
> Prompt with remembrance of a present God."
> COWPER's Poems.

LONDON: Printed for R. Blamire, in the Strand, 1794.

VOL. I.

Half Title.   Title-page as above.

Dedication to William Mitford, Esq. Lieut. Col. of the Southern Battalion of Hampshire Militia, dated Vicar's Hill, March 4, 1791, 7 pages.

Observations on Forest Scenery, [B–z 2] 340 pages.
Translation of Quotations in the First Volume, 4 pages.
With *Seventeen* Plates.

VOL. II.

Half Title and Title-page as above.
Observations on Forest Scenery, Book III. [B–x 3] 310 pages.
Translation of Quotations in the Second Volume, and Errata in
both Volumes, 4 pages.
A Catalogue of the Prints, 3 pages.
Addenda, [a–b 7] 30 pages.
Index, 20 pages.
With *Fifteen* Plates.

N.B. The first edition of this publication appeared in 1791,
of which some copies were printed in QUARTO; the second in
1794, the one above noticed; and the third, in 1808, with the
same number of plates: printed for Messrs. Cadell and Davies,
in the Strand, London.

XXIV.

HISTORICAL ENQUIRIES concerning Forests and Forest Laws, with topographical Remarks upon the
ancient and modern State of the NEW FOREST, in
the COUNTY of SOUTHAMPTON. By PERCIVAL
LEWIS, Esq. F.A.S.
    " *Non mea quidem spe, sed diligentia*
    Solummodo."

LONDON: Printed for T. Payne, Pall Mall, by J. McCreery,
        Black-horse-court. 1811. *Quarto.*

Half Title: " Ancient and modern State of the New Forest."
Title-page as above.
Table of Contents, 3 pages.
Dedication to Sir Edward Hulse, Bart. of Breamore House, in
the County of Southampton.
Preface, 6 pages.
The Historical Enquiries, beginning " Of the Antiquity of Fo-
rests," and Appendixes and Errata, [B–2 G 2] 228 pages.

PLATES.

Frontispiece. Engraved by C. Sheringham for the Author.
Map of the New Forest and adjacent Country. Folded and
    Coloured. Engraved by C. Smith for the Author. p. 1.

XXV.

Fossilia Hantoniensia collecta, et in Musæo Britannico deposita, a Gustavo Brander, R.S. et S.A.S. Mus. Brit. Cur.

Londini, 1766. *Quarto.*

Half Title: "Fossilia Hantoniensia.—Hampshire Fossils."
Title-page as above.
Preface in Latin and English, 4 pages.
Descriptive Part in Latin, [B-M 2] 43 pages.
With eight Plates, and a Vignette, containing 131 specimens.
Green del. & sc.

XXVI.

General View of the Agriculture of the County of Hants: with Observations on the Means of its Improvement. By Abraham and William Driver, of Kent Road, Surrey: to which is added a View of the Agriculture of the Isle of Wight, (forming a part of Hampshire,) by the Rev. Mr. Warner. Drawn up for the Consideration of the Board of Agriculture and internal Improvement; with a Postscript to the Survey of Hampshire by Arthur Young.

London: Printed by Colin Macrae, 1794. *Quarto,* 78 pages.

XXVII.

General View of the Agriculture of Hampshire, including the Isle of Wight. Drawn up for the Board of Agriculture and internal Improvement. By Charles Vancouver.

" Experientia præstantior Arte."

London: Printed for Richard Phillips, Bridge-street, in 1810; and for Messrs. Sherwood, Neely, and Jones, 1813. *Octavo.* 532 pages.

With a Map, exhibiting the leading Character of Soil and Substrata of the eight Districts comprised within the County of Hants. Engraved by Neele; folded and coloured.—Thirteen miscellaneous Plates, and ten folded Tables of the Population of Hampshire, with the amount of parochial Levies and Disbursements.

ISLE OF WIGHT.

I.

The HISTORY of the ISLE of WIGHT. (By Sir RI-
CHARD WORSLEY, Bart.)

LONDON: Printed by A. Hamilton: and sold by R. Dodsley,
T. Cadell, G. Robinson, R. Faulder, and G. Nicol; Collins
and Co., Salisbury; and Burdon, at Winchester. MDCCLXXXI.
Royal quarto.

Title-page as above, with St. Catherine's Tower as a Vignette.
Godfrey sc.
Dedication to the King, (George III.) dated June 4, 1781.
Preface, 4 pages.
Contents, 3 pages.
The History of the Island, [B–N n] 274 pages.
Table of Contents of the Appendix, [* a] 8 pages.
Appendix, [a–x] 162 pages.
Postscript, containing the List of Errata, 1 page.

PLATES.

1. A Sheet Map of the Isle of Wight. Drawn and engraved by
   John Haywood, June 4th, 1781. Folded and coloured.
   p. 1.
2. View of the Needles and White Cliffs from Allum Bay.
   Folded. Ant. Devis del. T. Vivares sc. p. 6.
3. View of the Village of St. Lawrence, the Church, and the
   Rocks. Folded Ant. Devis del. Tho. Vivares sc. p. 9.
   The Needles in 1762. Godfrey sc. On the letter-press of
   p. 25.
4. Carisbrook Castle. Folded. Ant. Devis del. Tho. Vivares sc. p. 41.
5. Plan of Carisbrook Castle in the Isle of Wight. Folded. p. 43.
6. Plan of Sandown Fort. P. Mazell sc. p. 46.
   Cowes Castle. Godfrey sc. On the letter-press of p. 47.
7. Plate of Seals, marked plate I. p. 50.
8, 9, 10, 11. Plate of Seals, marked plates II. III. IV. V. p. 52,
   54, 56, 58.

12. Henry Duke of Warwick, as King of the Isle of Wight, and
    Eleanor Dutchess of Somerset, sister to the same. p. 68.
    Seal of the Knights' Court. On the letter-press of p. 84.
    The Land-mark on Ashey Down. On the letter-press of
    p. 145.
13. Seals of the Boroughs of the Isle of Wight. p. 146.
    Yarmouth Castle. Godfrey sc. On the letter-press of p. 162.
14. The Remains of Quarr Abbey, the Property of John Fle-
    ming, Esq. Folded. Rich. Godfrey del. & sc. p. 172.
15. Ancient View of Appuldurcombe. Drawn by Robert Wors-
    ley, 1720. p. 181.
    The Church at St. Lawrence. Godfrey sc. On the letter-
    press of p. 183.
16. Nunwell, the Seat of Sir William Oglander, Bart. Folded.
    Godfrey del. & sc. p. 198.
17. Priory near St. Hellens, in the possession of Nash Grose,
    Esq. Folded. J. Bretherton del. Godfrey sc. p. 200.
18. St. John's, the Seat of Lieutenant-General Amherst. Folded.
    Godfrey del. & sc. p. 200.
19. St. Boniface Cottage, belonging to Col. Hill. Godfrey del.
    & sc. p. 203.
20. View from Ventnor Cove, toward Steephill and Niton.
    Godfrey sc. p. 204.
21. Knighton, the Seat of George M. Bisset, Esq. Rich. God-
    frey sc. p. 206.
22. Appuldurcombe Park, the Seat of the Right Honourable Sir
    Rich. Worsley, Bart. Governor and Vice-Admiral of the
    Isle of Wight. A. Devis del. Peter Mazell sc. p. 218.
23. The Cottage at Steephill, belonging to the Rt. Hon. Hans
    Stanley, Governor of the Isle of Wight. Godfrey del.
    & sc. p. 221.
24. A North View of Osborne, the Seat of Robert Pope Blach-
    ford, Esq. Folded. Godfrey del. & sc. p. 229.
25. Fairlee, the Seat of John White, Esq. Folded. Godfrey
    del. & sc. p. 230.
26. Gatcomb, the Seat of Edwd Meux Worsley, Esq. Folded.
    Godfrey del. & sc. p. 240.
27. Black-Gang Chine, near Chale. Godfrey sc. p. 248.
28. Swainston, the Seat of Sir Fitz Williams Barrington, Bart.
    G. B. Fisher del. W. Watts sc. p. 257.
29. Westover Lodge, a Hunting Box, belonging to Leon^d
    Troughear Holmes, Esq. Folded. G. B. Fisher del.
    Godfrey sc. p. 258.

30. View from Freshwater Gate.   Godfrey sc.   p. 269.
31. The Cave under Freshwater Cliff.   Godfrey sc.   p. 272.
32. The Needles, Hurst Castle, and Mouth of Lymington River.
      Godfrey sc.   p. 274.
      Godshill Church.   Godfrey sc.   On the letter-press of
      p. 274.

II.

A VIEW of the ISLE of WIGHT, in Four Letters to a
Friend, containing not only a Description of its Form
and principal Productions, but the most authentic
and material Articles of its natural, political, and
commercial History.   By JOHN STURCH.   (Fourth
Edition, corrected and enlarged.)

> " ————The roving sight
> Pursues its pleasing course o'er neighbouring hills,
> Of many a different form and different hue,
> Bright with ripe corn, or green with grass, or dark
> With clover's purple bloom."   SCOTT's Amwell.

Printed for and sold by the Author in Newport, Isle of Wight.
        MDCCXCI.   *Duodecimo*, 84 pages.
With a folded Map of the Island, drawn from Surveys, and en-
        graved expressly for this publication.

III.

A new, correct, and much-improved HISTORY of the
ISLE of WIGHT, from the earliest Times of authentic
Information to the present Period : comprehending
whatever is curious or worthy of attention in Natural
History, with its Civil, Ecclesiastical, and Military
State in the various Ages, both ancient and modern.

> The modern History, in a more especial manner, from the
> topographical arrangement under which it is related,
> and from the liberal Communications of Gentlemen of
> the Island, has peculiar claims to public notice, and
> demands, from its interesting and important tendency,
> the most particular regard; so as to render the Work
> every way far superior to any thing yet published relative
> to this favourite Spot.   To which is annexed a very co-

pious Index of the Subjects contained in it: and to the whole is prefixed a new and very elegant Map of the Island, dedicated by permission to the Right Honorable THOMAS ORDE POWLETT, Governor of the Island, purposely engraved for this Work, Table of Contents, &c. (By J. ALBIN.)

NEWPORT: Printed by and for J. Albin; and sold in London by Scatcherd and Whitaker, Booksellers, Ave-Maria-lane; and all the Booksellers. 1795. *Octavo.*

Title-page as above.
Preface, dated Newport, July 14, 1795, 2 pages.
Contents, 2 pages.
Subscribers' Names, 4 pages.
Introduction, 8 pages.
Historical Part, [B 5–xx] 666 pages.
Conclusion and Appendix, 4 pages.
Index, 8 pages.

Errata: — p. 450 for 550; — 571 not paged; — p. 658 for 598.

A Sheet Map of the Isle of Wight, folded, and dedicated to the Governor, as specified in the Title-page, with a Plan of Newport at the left corner, drawn by J. Malham, and engraved by S. Neele, is prefixed.

IV.

The HISTORY of the ISLE of WIGHT; Military, Ecclesiastical, Civil, and Natural. To which is added a View of its Agriculture. By the Rev. RICHARD WARNER, Editor of "Hampshire extracted from Domesday Book," and of the "Antiquitates Culinariæ;" and Author of "Topographical Remarks relating to Hampshire," and "An Attempt to ascertain the Situation of the ancient Clausentum."

> " *Tu nimio nec stricta gelu, nec sidere fervens,*
>   *Clementi cælo, temperieque places.*
> *Cum pareret Natura parens varioque favore*
>   *Divideret dotes omnibus una locis,*
> *Seposuit potiora tibi, matremque professa,*
>   ' *Insula sis felix, plenaque pacis,' ait.*
> ' *Quicquid amat luxus, quicquid desiderat usus,*
>   ' *Ex te proveniet, vel aliundè tibi.'*"

SOUTHAMPTON: Printed for T. Cadell, jun. and W. Davies, (Successors to Mr. Cadell,) in the Strand, London; and T. Baker, Southampton. MDCCXCV. *Octavo.*

Title-page as before.

Dedication to Sir William Heathcote, Bart. and William Chute, Esq. Members for the County of Hants; Sir Harry Burrard, Bart. George Rose, Esq. James Mowbray, Esq. and the Rev. William Gilpin, dated Bath, Feb. 1, 1795.

Advertisement, 4 pages.

Contents, 5 pages.

The Historical Part, beginning with " the Military History of the Isle of Wight," [B–R r 4] 311 pages.

Appendix, 14 pages.

Errata, 1 page.

Index, 17 pages.

PLATES.

1. A new and accurate Map of the Isle of Wight, with a Plan of Newport at the bottom corner. Folded. Tho. Bowles sc.

2. View of the Needle Rocks in the year 1760. Hixon sc. p. 200.

3. Six Roman Coins found in the Isle of Wight. Folded. Hixon sc. p. 1, of the Appendix.

V.

A PICTURE of the ISLE of WIGHT, delineated upon the Spot in the Year 1793. By H. P. W. (WYNDHAM.)

> " ———All is here that the whole earth yields,
> Variety without end:——— Sweet interchange
> Of hill and valley, rivers, woods, and plains,
> Now land, now sea, and shores with forest crown'd,
> Rocks, dens, and caves!"
> MILTON. Par. Lost, book vii. l. 541. and book ix. l. 115.

LONDON: Printed by C. Roworth, for J. Egerton, Military Library, Whitehall. MDCCXCIV. *Octavo.*

Title-page as above.   Preface, v–xii.

Descriptive Part, [A–T] 146 pages.

Index, 6 pages.

With a sheet Map of the Island, dedicated to the Rt. Hon. Thomas Orde Powlett, Governor (*the same as in Albin's History*).

[303]

VI.

TOUR of the ISLE of WIGHT. The Drawings taken and engraved by J. HASSELL. Dedicated, by permission, to His Royal Highness the Duke of Clarence. In Two Volumes.

" *I wish I had been with you to see the Isle of Wight.*"—JOHNSON.

LONDON: Printed by John Jarvis, for Thomas Hookham, in New Bond-street. MDCCXC. *Octavo.*

VOL. I.

An engraved Title-page, with the Arms of the D. of Clarence as a Vignette.

The printed Title-page as above.

Dedication, signed T. Hookham, and dated New Bond-street, May 1, 1790, 2 pages.

Introduction and Errata, 4 pages.

List of Subscribers, 12 pages.

Contents of the First Volume, 4 pages.

The Tour, [B–P 8] 224 pages, and *seventeen* Plates, neither numbered nor described.

VOL. II.

Engraved and printed Title-pages as in Vol. I.

Table of Contents, 6 pages.

Continuation of the Tour, [B–R 4] 248 pages, and *thirteen* plates.

N. B. There are copies of this work on LARGE PAPER.

VII.

A TOUR to the ISLE of WIGHT (in 1793), illustrated with EIGHTY VIEWS drawn and engraved in Aqua Tinta. By CHARLES TOMKINS. In Two Volumes.

LONDON: Printed for G. Kearsley, Fleet-street. 1796. *Royal octavo.*

VOL. I.

Title-page as above.

HAMPSHIRE (*Isle of Wight*).

Dedication to Sir John Barrington, Bart. signed Charles Tomkins.

Preface, 2 pages.

Directions for placing the Prints, 1 page.

The Tour, [without signatures after B] 186 pages.

PLATES.

1. Plan of the Isle of Wight, surveyed and engraved by Charles Tomkins. Folded. To face p. 1.
2. West View of Netley Abbey. p. 43.
3. Inside View of Netley Abbey. p. 45.
4. Netley Abbey Fort. p. 51.
5. Calshot Castle. p. 52.
6. Cowes Harbour. p. 54.
7. Cowes Castle. p. 56.
8. Norton Lodge, the Seat of Mr. Binstead. p. 120.
9. Hurst Castle. p. 121.
10. Allum Bay and the Needles. p. 122.
11. West End of the Isle of Wight. p. 123.
12. Black Gang Chine. p. 128.
13. Northwood Church. p. 142.
14. Entrance into Newport. p. 154.
15. Coffin of Elizabeth, 2nd Daughter of King Charles I. p. 167.
16. Medina River. p. 181.
17. Another View of Medina River. p. 182.
18. Fairlee, the Seat of John White, Esq. p. 182.
19. Newport from Fairlee. p. 183.

VOL. II.

Title-page as in Vol. I.

List of Plates, 2 pages.

A Continuation of the Tour, beginning with "Carisbrook Castle," [without signatures] 133 pages.

Errata in both volumes, on the reverse of p. 133.

Index to Vol. I. and II. 8 pages.

PLATES.

1. Entrance of Carisbrook Castle. p. 6.
2. The Keep at Carisbrook Castle. p. 12.
3. (Interior of) Carisbrook Castle. p. 16.
4. (Distant View of) Carisbrook Castle. p. 41.
5. Ancient Monument at (in) Carisbrook (Church.) p. 43.

48. Mirables, from Cripple Path.   p. 115.
49. Wolverton Undercliff.   p. 117.
50. (W. View of) St. Laurence's (Church).   p. 118.
51. Steep Hill.   p. 119.
52. (View of) Western Lines.   p. 120.
53. Ventnor Mill.   p. 121.
54. Bon Church Village (looking westward).   p. 122.
55. (S.West View of) Bon Church.   p. 122.
56. Dunnose (a Promontory).   p. 126.
57. Bon Church Shute.   p. 127.
58. Luccombe Chine.   p. 127.
59. (S.W. View of) Shanklin Church.   p. 128.
60. Antique Chest at Shanklin.   p. 128.
61. Shanklin Chine.   p. 129.
62. Horse Ledge.   p. 129.

N. B. There are copies of this work on LARGE PAPER, in Two Volumes QUARTO.

VIII.

A JOURNEY from LONDON to the ISLE of WIGHT. By THOMAS PENNANT, Esq.   In Two Volumes.

LONDON: Printed at the Oriental Press, by Wilson and Co. for Edward Harding, No. 98, Pall Mall; and sold by West and Hughes, No. 40, Paternoster-row. 1801.   *Quarto.*

VOL. I.
From London to Dover.

Half Title.   Title-page as above.
Preface and Advertisement, 5 pages.
List of Plates in Volume I. 1 page.
The Journey from London to Dover, [B–D d 3] 205 pages.

PLATES.

Map of the Road from London to Dover.   Folded and coloured.   To face the Title.
1. The Temple Stairs.   Tomkins del. Harding sc.   p. 1.
2. Trinity Hospital, Deptford.   Tomkins del. Angus sc.   p. 10.
3. Whole-length Portrait of Sir John Packington, from an original Drawing in the Collection of R. Bull, Esq.   Harding sc.   p. 12.
4. Marie la Duchesse de Chevreuse, from a scarce Print in the Collection of R. Bull, Esq.   Harding sc.   p. 13.

VOL. II.

From Dover to the Isle of Wight.

Half Title.   Title-page as before.
Advertisement, 1 page.
List of Plates in the Second Volume, 1 page.
The Tour continued, from Dover to the Land's End, [B–Dd 4] 207 pages.
Index to both Volumes, p. 209–217.

PLATES.

1. Map from Dover to the Isle of Wight. Folded and coloured. To front the Title.
2. Portrait of W. Harvey, M.D. but is called William Chillingworth on the Plate. Harding sc. p. 5. [*Not in the printed List of Plates.*]
3. Sandgate Castle and Town. J. Nixon del. Comte sc. p. 7.
4. Winchelsea Church. J. Nixon del. Harding sc. p. 26.
5. Battle Abbey. J. Nixon del. Newton sc. p. 36.
6. Sir Ant^y Brown on Horseback. R. H. Cromek sc. p. 41.
7. Pevensey Castle. J. Nixon, Esq. del. Comte sc. p. 48.
8. Newhaven, Sussex. J. Nixon del. Sparrow sc. p. 65.
9. Pavilion at Brighton. Folded. Gardiner del. Newton sc. p. 68.
10. New Shoreham Church. J. Nixon, Esq. del. Newton sc. p. 86.
11. Inside View of Arundel Castle. J. Nixon del. Newton sc. p. 98.
12. View of Chichester. J. Nixon, Esq. del. Comte sc. p. 105.
13. View of Emsworth. J. Nixon, Esq. del. Comte sc. p. 118.
14. Warblington. J. Nixon, Esq. del. Sparrow sc. p. 130.
15. Cowes Castle. J. Nixon, Esq. del. Sparrow sc. p. 157.
16. Carisbrook Castle, from the Newport Road. J. Nixon, Esq. del. Comte sc. p. 162.
17. The Coffin of Elizabeth, 2nd Daughter of K. Charles 1st. p. 167.
18. St. Catherine's Tower, Isle of Wight. Turner del. Sparrow sc. p. 186.
19. St. Catherine's Light-house Point, Isle of Wight. J. Nixon, Esq. del. Comte sc. p. 188.
20. Yarmouth. F. Grose, Esq. del. Angus sc. p. 200.

N. B. Some copies were printed on LARGE PAPER.

IX.

VECTIANA; or a COMPANION to the ISLE of WIGHT, comprising the History of the Island, and the Description of its local Scenery, as well as all Objects of Curiosity. By JOHN ALBIN.

Printed for and sold by J. Albin, Newport, Isle of Wight, containing an engraved Title-page, with a vignette View of Carisbrook Castle.—*Duodecimo,* 106 pages, no date, and a poetical Dedication to the Rt. Honble Lord Fitzharris.

With a Map of the Island, the same as in the Author's History of the Isle of Wight in octavo.

X.

A NEW PICTURE of the ISLE of WIGHT, illustrated with Thirty-six Plates of the most beautiful and interesting Views throughout the Island, in imitation of the original Sketches, drawn and engraved by WILLIAM COOKE. To which are prefixed an introductory Account of the Island, and a Voyage round its Coast. SECOND EDITION, with Improvements.

" A precious stone set in the silver sea."

SOUTHAMPTON : Printed by and for T. Baker; and for Sherwood, Neely, and Jones, Paternoster-row, London; sold also by J. Fletcher, Southampton, and neighbouring Booksellers. 1813.* *Octavo.*

Title-page as above.
Prefaces to both Editions, 6 pages.
Contents, 4 pages.
List of Plates, 2 pages.
Introductory account of the Isle of Wight, signed J. E. and dated Islington, Sept. 4, 1808, 28 pages.
Half Title : " The Plates ; with Descriptions."
Description of the Plates, [C 8–K 4] p. 31–136.
Half Title : " Voyage round the Island."

---

* This publication appeared for the first time in 1808 in *quarto* and *octavo;* but the preface of the second edition states " that the Editors have rejected some of the plates the least worthy of notice, and have added new ones of the most interesting views. In the descriptive part such alterations have been made as time and circumstances required ; and some additional information given :" they add likewise, " that the plates are executed in a far more finished style than before."

An edition has also been printed in *duodecimo* in 1813, with *twenty-six* of the plates only, and a reduced coloured map of the island engraved by W. Jeffreys: which plates are as follow :

1. Norris.—2. Carisbrook Castle.—3. Gateway to Carisbrook Castle.—4. Rocks in Freshwater Bay.—5. Freshwater Bay and Cliffs.—6. Needles.—7. Light-house on Freshwater Cliffs.— 8. Yarmouth.—9. Fernhill.—10. Binstead Cottage and Church.—11. St. John's.—12. Lodge, or Cottage Entrance to St. John's.—13. The Priory.—14. Rock Cottage.—15. Undercliff.—16. Mirables.—17. Steephill Cottage.—18. St. Boniface.—19. Bon-Church Village.—20. Shanklin Chine.—21. Black Gang Chine.—22. Appuldurcombe.—23. Godshill.—24. Cowes Castle and Harbour.—25. Westhill Cottage.— 26. Cottage at East Cowes.

The Account of the Voyage, p. 139–150.
Half Title: " Routes of the Island."
The Routes, p. 153–158.
Index and Directions to the Binder, 4 pages.

PLATES.

Map of the Isle of Wight. Coloured and folded. To pre-
cede the Frontispiece.

1. Norris, the Seat of Ld Henry Seymour, at East Cowes, Isle
of Wight, as a Frontispiece. [p. 143, *first edit.*]
2. Carisbrook Castle. p. 31. [p. 45, *first edit.*]
3. Gateway to Carisbrook Castle. p. 34. [p. 48, *first edit.*]
4. Village of Carisbrook. p. 39. [p. 54, *first edit.*]
5. Rocks in Freshwater Bay. p. 41. [p. 56, *first edit.*]
6. Arched Rock in Freshwater Bay. p. 42. [p. 57, *first
edit.*]
7. Freshwater Cliffs. p. 43. [p. 58, *first edit.*]
8. Needles, from Scratchell's Bay. p. 52. [p. 67, *first edit.*]
9. Light-house on Freshwater Cliff. p. 54. [p. 69, *first edit.*]
10. Farringford Hill, the Seat of Ed. Rushworth, Esq. [p. 70,
first edit.]
11.* Yarmouth, Isle of Wight. G. Cooke sc. p. 57. [*Not in
the first edit.*]
12. Shalfleet Church. p. 61. [p. 74, *first edit.*]
13. Swainston, the Seat of Sir John Barrington, Bart. p. 63.
[p. 75, *first edit.*]
14. Fernhill, the Seat of Mrs. Shute. *New plate.* p. 64.
[p. 77, *first edit.*]
15. Binstead Cottage and Church. p. 67. [p. 80, *first edit.*]
16. Appley near Ryde, the Seat of Captain Hutt. p. 83.
[p. 72, *first edit.*]
17. St. John's, the Seat of Edward Simeon, Esq. p. 74. [p. 86,
first edit.]
18. Lodge, or Cottage Entrance to St. John's. p. 77. [p. 90,
first edit.]
19. The Priory, the Seat of Sir Nash Grose, Knt. p. 80.
[p. 93, *first edit.*]
20. Niton. p. 83. [p. 96, *first edit.*]
21*. Sandrock Hotel, near Niton. G. Cooke sc. p. 85. [*Not
in the first edit.*]
22. Undercliff, taken near Mirables. p. 90. [p. 98, *first edit.*]
23. Mirables, the Villa of Mrs. Arnold. p. 94. [p. 102, *first
edit.*]

24. Marine Villa of the late Sir Richard Worsley, Bart. and now of the Hon, C. A. Pelham. p. 96. [p. 104, *first edit.*]

25. Steep Hill, Cottage Villa of the Earl of Dysart. p. 98. [p. 106, *first edit.*]

26. St. Boniface, formerly the Villa of Thomas Bowdler, Esq. and late of Lieut. Col. Hill. p. 101. [p. 109, *first edit.*]

27. Bon-Church Village. p. 105. [p. 113, *first edit.*]

28. Shanklin Chine, looking outwards. p. 107. [p. 121, *first edit.*]

29. Gatcombe House, the Seat of Col. Campbell. p. 115. [p. 126, *first edit.*]

30. Black Gang Chine. (*A new plate.*) G. Cooke sc. p. 117.

31. Appuldurcombe, the Seat of the late Sir Richd Worsley, Bart. and now of the Hon. C. A. Pelham. p. 121. [p. 132, *first edit.*]

32.* Godshill, taken in the Road to Newport. p. 123. [*Not in the first edit.*]

33. Cowes Castle and Harbour. p. 126. [p. 134, *first edit.*]

34. Westhill Cottage near Cowes, the Residence of Lord Fitz-harris, late of General Whitelock. p. 129. [p. 137, *first edit.*]

35. Mrs. Lambert's Cottage at East Cowes. p. 131. [p. 139, *first edit.*]

36. East Cowes Castle, the Villa of J. Nash, Esq. p. 132. [p. 140, *first edit.*]

The plates marked with an asterisk are *not* in the first edition; and the following, which are there given, are *omitted* in the present one:

The Marina, near Ryde. p. 89, but serving as a Frontispiece.
Shanklin Chine, looking inwards. p. 116.
Black Gang Chine, looking outwards. p. 127.
Black Gang Chine, from the Beach. p. 130.

XI.

POETICAL EXCURSIONS in the ISLE of WIGHT.

" ———— *Casiá, atque aliis intexens suavibus herbis,*
Mollia luteolá pingit vaccinia calthá.
Et vos, O Lauri, carpam: et Te, proxima, myrte;
Sic positæ quoniam suaves miscetis odores."—VIRG. Eclog. ii. 49.

LONDON: Printed for N. Conant (Successor to Mr. Whiston), in Fleet-street. MDCCLXXVII. *Quarto*, 42 pages; and are dedicated to Lord Camden.

With a large vignette View of Carisbrook Castle in the Title-page, under which is this motto:

" An awful Pharos to each British king !"

There has likewise been published

VECTIS; or The ISLE of WIGHT, a Poem in Three Cantos, by HENRY JONES. Lond. 1766. *Quarto.*

XII.

The DELINEATOR: or a Picturesque, Historical, and Topographichal DESCRIPTION of the ISLE of WIGHT. By JAMES CLARKE, (Land Surveyor, Newport.)

Printed and sold by Tayler and Co. Newport. (1812.) *Duodecimo*, 99 pages.

Illustrated with a Sheet Map, coloured, entituled, " A Military, Marine, and Topographical Survey of the Isle of Wight, by James Clarke, Land Surveyor, Newport. 1812."

XIII.

The ISLE of WIGHT MAGAZINE, from January 1799 to December, and Supplement.

NEWPORT, Isle of Wight: Printed by and for John Albin, *Duodecimo*, containing 650 pages, four pages of Index, and four of Preface.

XIV.

TWELVE VIEWS in the ISLE of WIGHT. 22 Inches by 17. Drawn and etched by J. KING and S. BARTH.

LONDON: Published by W. Cribb, Tavistock-street, 1813, (*in colours.*)

1. Carisbrook Castle.—2. Carisbrook.—3. Wooton Bridge.—4. St. Helen's Sea Mark.—5. Brading.—6. Sandown Bay.—7. Newport.—8. Yarmouth.—9. Ashey Down.—10. Nighton House.—11. St. Laurence.—12. Steep Hill.

[313]

XV.

TWELVE SELECT VIEWS in the ISLE of WIGHT, from Drawings by T. WALMESLEY. 27 Inches by 21.

LONDON : Published by James Daniell and Co. Strand, 1810–15, both plain and in colours.

1. Brixton Church. Cartwright sc.
2. View of Mirables. Hassell sc.
3. Carisbrook Castle. Cartwright sc.
4. View of St. Catherine's Head. Chesham sc.
5. View of Ryde, opposite Portsmouth. Cartwright sc.
6. View of Steephill. Cartwright sc.
7. Entrance to the Village of Carisbrook. Bluck sc.
8. Carisbrook Castle near the Village. Bluck sc.
9. View of a Cottage near Ryde. Cartwright sc.
10. View of the Mirables among the Rocks. Cartwright sc.
11. Distant View of Freshwater Cliff from Staples Heath. Bluck sc.
12. View of the Needles. Cartwright sc.

N. B. The same set of plates were published in a smaller size in 1813 ; viz. 15¼ inches by 12¼, both plain and in colours.

XVI.

SIX VIEWS in the ISLE of WIGHT and of NETLEY ABBEY. Drawn and published by R. B. HARRADEN of Cambridge, and aquatinted by J. B. HARRADEN. 1814. Size 17 Inches by 11¾.

1. Shanklin Chine.—2. Black Gang Chine.—3. Bon-Church Village.—4. Carisbrook Castle.—5. Netley Abbey.—6. Another View of Netley Abbey.

HAMPSHIRE.

I.

A Short View of the History and Antiquities of Winchester; with a brief Account of the Seats of the neighbouring Nobility, Gentry, &c. Being chiefly extracted from the Rev. Mr. Milner's History and Survey of Winchester.

> " Non indignemur mortalia corpora solvi
> Dum patet exemplis oppida posse mori."

Winchester : Printed and sold by Robins. 1799. *Octavo,* 50 pages.

II.

An Historical and Critical Account of Winchester Cathedral; with an engraved View and Ichnographical Plan of that Fabric. Extracted from the Rev. Dr. Milner's History and Antiquities of Winchester. To which is added a Review of its modern Monuments.

> " Redditus his primum terris tibi, Christe, sacravit
> Sedem hanc Birinus, posuitque immania templa."—ÆNEID. vi. 18.

Third Edition.

Winchester : Printed and sold by James Robbins, College Street. 1809. *Octavo,* 144 pages, exclusive of an Advertisement and Explanation of the Plan.

With a North West View of the Cathedral. J. Carter del. 1789. Basire sc. and a folded Plan.

III.

Memoranda of the Parishes of Hursley and North Baddesley, in the County of Southampton. (By John Marsh.)

Winchester : Printed by James Robbins, College Street. 1808. *Royal octavo.*

Title-page as above.

Half Title to the Parish of Hursley.

Dedication to Sir William Heathcote, Bart. dated Hursley, Aug. 10, 1808.

Advertisement and Contents, 2 leaves.

Memoranda of the Parish of Hursley, [B–I 4] 63 pages.

Half Title to the Parish of North Baddesley.

Dedication to Sir Nathaniel Holland, Bart.

Memoranda of the Parish of North Baddesley, [K 3–O 2] 32 pages.

PLATES

Drawn and etched by J. Powell.

1. Front of the Old Lodge in Hursley Park.   p. 1.
2. Plan of the Encampment on Cranbury Common.   p. 36.
3. The Tower of Hursley Church.   p. 41.
4. North Baddesley Church.   p. 21 of the Description.

IV.

A COMPANION in a TOUR round SOUTHAMPTON; comprehending various Particulars, Ancient and Modern, of New Forest, Lymington, Christchurch, Romsey, Bishop's Waltham, Titchfield, &c.; with Notices of the Villages, Gentlemen's Seats, Curiosities, Antiquities, &c. occurring in the different Roads described. By JOHN BULLER.

> " *Ille terrarum mihi præter omnes*
> *Angulus ridet.*"

The Third Edition, improved and enlarged.

SOUTHAMPTON : Printed and sold by Baker and Fletcher. 1809. *Duodecimo,* [A–A a 6] 281 pages, and 4 pages of Index.

V.

The RUINS of a TEMPLE; a Poem. By the Rev. JOSEPH JEFFERSON. To which is prefixed an Account of the Antiquity and History of Holy Ghost Chapel, Basingstoke, Hants; with an Appendix, containing historical and explanatory Notes.

> " *Omnium rerum, heus!* VICISSITUDO *est.*"—TERENCE.

> " While oft some temple's MOULD'RING top between
> With venerable grandeur marks the scene."
> GOLDSMITH'S Traveller.

SUPPLEMENT (*Isle of Wight*).

LONDON : Printed for the Author by T. North, Little Tower
  Street. MDCCXCIII. *Quarto*, 24 pages.

With a View of the Chapel, drawn by Terrell as a Vignette.

VI.

The HISTORY of the BLACKS of WALTHAM in Hampshire; and those under the like Denomination in
Berkshire.

LONDON : Printed for A. Moore, near St. Paul's. 1723. *Octavo,*
  32 pages, exclusive of the Title.

ISLE OF WIGHT.

I.

A Description of the principal Picturesque Beauties,
Antiquities, and Geological Phænomena of the ISLE
of WIGHT. By Sir HENRY C. ENGLEFIELD, Bart.
With additional Observations on the Strata of the
Island, and their Continuation in the adjacent Parts
of Dorsetshire, by Thomas Webster, Esq. Illustrated
by Maps and numerous Engravings by W. and G.
Cooke, from original Drawings by Sir H. Englefield
and T. Webster.

LONDON : Printed by William Bulmer and Co. Cleveland Row,
  St. James's, for Payne and Foss, Pall Mail. 1816. *Royal
  quarto.*

Half Title, and Title-page as above.
Dedication to Mrs. Spencer.
Contents, 1 page.
Preface, [a 1–3] p. i–vi.
Explanation of the Plates, [a 4–d 2] p. vii–xxvii.
Description of the Isle of Wight, beginning with an Half Title,
  [B–H h 3] 238 pages.
Index, 4 pages.

SUPPLEMENT (*Isle of Wight*).

PLATES.

Portrait of Sir Henry Englefield in a Circle within a border. E. Scott del. W. Evans sc. To face the Title.—1. Clay Cliffs, White Cliff Bay. p. 23.—2. Chalk Cliffs, White Cliff Bay. p. 78.—3. Dunnose Cliffs. p. 72.—4. Black Gang Chine. p. 85.—5. Freshwater Cliff. p. 27 or 79.—6. Freshwater Cave. p. 27.—7. Knighton House. p. 105.—8. Chale Farm. p. 109.—9. Yaverland Church. p. 102.—10. The Ivy House. On the letter-press of p. 113.—11. Long Stone. On the letter-press of p. 89.—12. Quarr Abbey. p. 93.—13. Ancient Chapel at Swainston. p. 104.—14. Yaverland Church, South Door, and Shalfleet Church, North Door. W. Alexander del. p. 101.—15. Vertical and Curved Strata, White Cliff Bay. p. 119.—16. Vertical Clay Cliffs, White Cliff Bay. p. 120.—17. No. 1. White Cliff Bay from Culver Cliff.—No. 2. Colwell Bay.—No. 3. Allum Bay and the Needles. Folded. p. 120 or 160.—18. Culver Cliff from the Sea. p. 120.—19. No. 1. Sandown Bay and Culver Cliff from the South side near Shanklin.—No. 2. Sandown Bay and Dunnose Head from the Fort.—No. 3. Allum Bay and Headen Hill from the Needles. *Coloured.* p. 123, or 211, 212.—20. Chalk Pit on Brading Down. p. 123.—21. Binnel Bay, below Wolverton. p. 136.—22. Compton Bay. p. 152.—23. Curved Strata and Sand Pit in Headen Hill, Allum Bay, as it appeared in 1811. p. 159.—24. Curved Stratum, Headen Hill. p.   .—25. Scratchell's Bay and the Needles. Folded. p. 80.—26. No. 1. Handfast Point, one Mile off.—No. 2. Swanwich Bay from Peverel Point.—No. 3. Studland Bay, South side. Folded. p. 169.—27. Handfast Point in Dorsetshire. Folded. p. 166.—28. Insulated Chalk Rocks, Handfast Point. p. 165.—29. No. 1. Swanwich Bay, from the North side.—No. 2. Durlstone Bay. Folded. p. 169, or 171.—30. Contorted Strata, Durlstone Bay. p. 172.—31. Breccia at Durlstone Head. p. 173.—32. No. 1. Durlstone Head.—No. 2. Windspit Quarries. Folded. p. 173, or 191.—33. Tilly Whim Quarry. p. 174.—34. No. 1. Clay Pit near Newport.—No. 2. Chalk Pit, Mount Joy. p. 24, or 208.—35. Coast of Dorsetshire and Portland Island from Worthbarrow. p. 183.—36. No. 1. Durdle Cove, with Barn Door.—No. 2. Arish Mell, in Worthbarrow Bay. p. 194.—37. No. 1. The Coast of Dorsetshire from Flowerbarrow to St. Adhelm's Head.—No. 2. Worthbarrow Bay, looking East.—No. 3. View from St. Adhelm's Head, looking West. Folded. p. 186.—38. West Lulworth and Cove. p. 185.—39. Nos. 1, 2. Lulworth Cove, West and East sides. p. 185.—40. St. Adhelm's Head. **p. 188.** —41. St. Adhelm's Chapel. p. 189.—42. St. Adhelm's Chapel, Plan, &c. p. 191.—43. Interior of St. Adhelm's Chapel. p. 189.—14. Stare Cove. p. 193.—45. Durdle Cove. p. 195. —46. No. 1. Coast of Dorsetshire from Bat's Corner to Weymouth.—No. 2. Bat's Corner.—No. 3. White Nore, Dorsetshire. Folded. p. 196.—47. Theoretical Sections. p. 201, 204, or 219.—48. Map of the Isle of Wight. Folded. T. Webster del. J. Walker sc. p. 1.—49. Map of the Coast of Dorsetshire from Handfast Point to the Isle of Portland. Folded. T. Webster del. J. Walker sc. p. 1.—50. Geological Map of the Isle of Wight, and the adjacent Parts of Hampshire and Dorsetshire. Folded, and *coloured.* T. Webster del. J. Walker sc. p. 1.

*** There are copies of this volume in Folio, with proof impressions of the Plates.

II.

A Catalogue Raisonné of the principal Paintings, Sculptures, Drawings, &c. &c. at APPULDURCOMBE HOUSE, the Seat of the Right Hon. Sir Richard Worsley, Bart. taken June 1, 1804.

" The practice of Architecture is directed by a few general and even mechanical rules. But Sculpture, *and above all,* Painting, propose to themselves the imitation not only of the forms of nature but of the characters and passions of the human soul. In those sublime arts the dexterity of the hand is of little avail unless it is animated by fancy, and guided by the most correct taste and observation."—GIBBON.

LONDON : Printed by William Bulmer and Co. Cleveland Row, St. James's. 1804. *Folio.* (Not published.)

Half Title.   Title-page as above.

The Select Catalogue ; List of Painters whose Pictures are described ; List of Pictures, Drawings, Gems, and other Curiosities ; and Addenda, [B–Q 2] 55 pages.

With a View of Appuldurcombe House. Davis del. Fittler sc. as a Frontispiece.

N. B. Pages 33–36 are repeated, and follow.

*** An ample analysis and collation of the "*Museum Worsleyanum*" is given in Savage's Librarian, vol. i. 1808.

A COMPANION

IN A TOUR

ROUND LYMINGTON:

COMPREHENDING A BRIEF

Account of that Place & its Environs,

THE

NEW FOREST,

ISLE OF WIGHT,

AND TOWNS OF

SOUTHAMPTON,

CHRISTCHURCH, &c. &c.

By RICHARD WARNER, Junr.

Of SWAY, near LYMINGTON.

SOUTHAMPTON:

PRINTED AND SOLD BY T. BAKER; SOLD ALSO
BY R. JONES, LYMINGTON; R. FAULDER,
NEW BOND STREET; AND B. LAW,
AVE MARY LANE, LONDON.

[Figure 21; 9.9 x 17.7 cm]

VIEWS OF THE PRINCIPAL SEATS,

AND

Marine & Landscape Scenery,

in the Neighbourhood of

LYMINGTON:

Drawn on Stone by

L. HAGHE,

from Original Pictures taken on the Spot by J. M. Gilbert,

and dedicated with permission, to

ADMIRAL SIR HARRY NEALE, Bart G.C.B.

by

R. A. GROVE.

Accompanied by

HISTORICAL AND TOPOGRAPHICAL DESCRIPTIONS.

Painted by J. M. Gilbert.

On Stone by L. Haghe.

HURST CASTLE and the NEEDLES from FILEWELL.

Pub.d by R. A. Grove Lymington. Hants. March 1832.

Pur.& Haghe Lith.rs to the King 17 Gate St

[Figure 22; 25.4 x 34.5 cm]

The Illustrated

HISTORICAL & PICTURESQUE GUIDE TO

BOURNEMOUTH.

THE SANDS. BOURNEMOUTH

BY PHILIP BRANNON.

POOLE. PUBLISHED BY R. SYDENHAM.

LONDON. LONGMAN & Cº

[Figure 23; 11.7 x 17.9 cm]

[320]

A CATALOGUE

OF

TRACTS, PAMPHLETS, PRINTS,

AND

DRAWINGS,

ILLUSTRATING

Hampshire, Isle of Wight, & Channel Islands

On Sale for Ready Money by

ALFRED RUSSELL SMITH,

36, SOHO SQUARE, LONDON, W.

1878.

Price Sixpence each County, also Wales, Scotland, and Ireland, Sixpence each, or the entire Catalogue of 1200 pages 10s. 6d. half-bound in morocco, which will be allowed in a £5 purchase.

Editor's note: the Channel Islands section
of this list has been omitted

Hampshire.

2016 WORTHIES of Hampshire (cut out of Fuller's Worthies of England.) Folio, 2s

2017 ACCOUNT of Hampshire, the Isles of Alderney, Guernesy, Jersey, and Sarke (from Cox's Magna Britannia, 1726.) 4to, 1s 6d

2018 HISTORY of Hampshire and the Isle of Wight (from the Beauties of England and Wales). 400 pages, 8vo, 2s   1810

2019 HAMPSHIRE (from Salmon's Survey of England). 8vo, 6d   1728

2020 KNIGHT'S Journey-Book of Hampshire. Sq. 12mo, 33 *engravings*, 2s   1841

2021 MANNYNGHAM'S (Tho., of East Tysted) Sermon at the Hampshire Feast. 4to, 1s   1686

2022 KING'S (I.) Sermon before the Natives of the County of Southampton. 8vo, 1s   1708

2023 HOGLANDIÆ Descriptio (*a Latin Poem on Hampshire.*) 8vo, 1s 6d   1709

2024 COLLECTION of all the Hand-bills, squibs, &c. published during the late Election for the County of Hants between Sir Rd. Worsley Bart., and J. Clarke Jervoise, Esq., with the Poll of each division. 8vo, 4s 6d   *Winchester*, 1780

2025 POLL Book for Hampshire. 4to, 2s 6d   1790

2026 EXPLANATORY Address of the Rev. W. Bingley relative to the History of Hampshire. 8vo, *privately printed, 2s*   1817

2027 REPORT of the Committee appointed to Examine into the state of the Hampshire County Gaol and Bridewells. 8vo, *Plates*, 1s   1817

2028 SPEECHES of Sir George Staunton to the Electors of South Hampshire. 8vo, 1s   1835

2029 NORTH Hampshire Cottage allotments. By the Rev. Lovelace B. Wither. 8vo, 1s   1832

2030 REPORT on the Proposed Division of the County of Hants for the Reform Act with statistical Information. Folio, *map*, 1s

2031 ABSTRACT of the Returns made to Parliament in 1786-8 of Charitable Donations in the County of Hants. Folio, 1s 6d

2032 DEALTEY'S (Dr.) Visitation charge in Hampshire. 8vo, 1s   1831

2033 SUMNER'S (Bishop) Conspectus of the Diocese of Winchester. Royal 8vo, *not printed for sale*, 3s   *Winchester*, 1854

2034 A BUNDLE of 25 Ancient and Modern Pamphlets relating to Hampshire. 2s 6d

2035 A BUNDLE of 16 Pamphlets relating to Hampshire. 2s

2036 NARRATION of the great Victory by the Parliament Forces under Sir Wm. Waller at Alton against the Cavaliers. 4to, 5s   1643

2037 CHANDLER'S (S. *Minister at Andover*,) Sermon at Andover and at Portsmouth on the death of William III. 4to, 2s   1702

2038 BURD'S (R. *of Over Wallop*) Visitation Sermon at Andover. 4to, 1s   1703

2039 SMEATON'S (Sam. *Vicar of Nether Wallop*,) Visitation Sermon at Andover. 4to, 1s   1705

2040 EYRE'S (Canon) Visitation Sermon at Andover. 8vo, 1s   1717

2041 MILLAR (David) Sermon at the Funeral of Mrs. Martha Bunny of Andover. 8vo, 1s 6d   1727

2042 ACT for making a Canal from Andover to Redbridge. Folio, 1s 6d   1789

2043 WRIT in Error Ryder *v.* Baylie of Barton Stacy respecting Monetary and other transactions. Folio, 1*s* 6*d*   1709

2044 HISTORY of Basing House with an interesting account of the Siege it sustained during the Civil War. 8vo, 1*s* 6*d*   *Basingstoke,* 1827

2045 HISTORY of Basing House, the Siege during the Civil War, with notices of celebrated persons concerned in its transactions. 8vo, *frontispiece,* 1*s* 6*d*   1839

2046 NEWS from *Basing Stoak* of one Mrs. Blunden, a Malster's Wife, who was buried alive, but was overheard by some school boys, for which that town was fined. 4to, *curious and rare,* 4*s,*
John Millet, (1650)

2047 ACT for a Canal from Basingstoke to the River Wey. Folio, 1*s* 6*d*
1793

2048 THE History of the Brotherhood or Guild of the Holy Ghost in the Chapel of the Holy Ghost, near Basingstoke, dissolved by King Edward VI, with its antiquities, &c. 8vo, *original edition* 5*s,*
Reading, 1742

2049 TOLL'S (E., *of Dogmersfield*) Visitation Sermon at Basingstoke. 8vo, 1*s*   1751

2050 JEFFERSON (Revd. Jos.) Ruins of a Temple, a Poem and Account of the Antiquity and history of Holy Ghost Chapel, Basingstoke. 4to, *vignette,* 2*s*   1793

2051 HISTORY of the Holy Ghost Chapel, Basingstoke, and of the Brotherhood or Guild of the Holy Ghost in the said Chapel. 8vo, *Plates,* 1*s* 6*d.*   *Basingstoke,* 1819

2052 EASTMAN'S Discourse at Basingstoke before the Ministers of the Hampshire Association. 8vo, 1*s*   *Portsea,* 1825

2053 GILPIN'S Funeral Sermon at Boldre on W. Baker, with account of his Life. 12mo, 1*s*   1791

2054 GILPIN'S Account of the new Poor House erected at Boldre. 12mo, 1*s*   1798

2055 GAUNTLETT (Revd. Henry) Farewell address to the Inhabitants of Botley. 8vo, 1*s*   *Southampton,* 1804

2056 BURNET (Bishop), Sermon preached at the Funeral of the Rt. Hon. Anne Lady-Dowager Brooke, buried at Breamor. 4to, 2*s*   1691

2057 ACTS for enclosing grounds in Earlstone in the parish of Burghcleare. 1*s.*—Ditto for enclosing lands at Barton Stacy. 1*s*

2058 CAPELL (Dowager Lady Elizabeth), Sermon at her Funeral, with memorials of her most holy life and death. By Edw. Barker, Rector of Buriton. 4to, 3*s* 6*d*   1661

2059 ACCOUNT of the Burley Meeting House in the New Forest, six miles from Ringwood. 12mo, *curious,* 1*s* 6*d*   *Ringwood,* 1823

2060 STATEMENT of the case of the office of the Judge Promoted by Farnall *v.* Rev. J. K. Craig in the Arches Court of Canterbury, with remarks, by the Rev. E. Craig, (*relating to affairs at Burley in the New Forest.*) 8vo, 1*s* 6*d*   1848

2061 SLEIGH (S.), Sermon at Christchurch before the Meeting of the Associated Independent Churches of Hampshire. 8vo, 1*s*   1818

2062 ACCOUNT of the Roman Mosaic Pavement discovered at Badley Pound Farm, Crondal, in Hampshire. 12mo, 1*s* 6*d*
Basingstoke, 1817

2063 WARREN'S (Rev. T. A.) Poem on the New Church at Gally Hill, Crondal. 4to, 1*s* 6*d*   *Basingstoke,* 1841

2064 LEFROY'S Description of Coins discovered at Crondall. 8vo, 2 *plates,* 1*s* 6*d*   1844

2065 DANEBURY, or the power of Friendship, a Tale with two Odes. By a young Lady. 4to, 1*s* 6*d*   *Bristol,* ——

2066 WARREN'S (Ed.) Sermon at Fordingbridge at the Funeral of the Rev. R. Whitaker. 8vo, 1s 6d 1718

2067 REPORT of the Proceedings at Winchester Assizes for Rioting, at Fordingbridge and other places. 8vo, 2s 1831

2068 ACT for the better Paving &c. of Gosport. Folio, 2s 1763

2069 ANSWERS to several objections made to the bill for better paving Gosport. Folio, 1s

2070 THE Stray'd Lamb (from Gosport) or the Baptist no Seducer. By Philo Oves. 8vo, 1s 1812

2071 THE whole proceedings in a dispute between Henry Lys the Elder, Esq., and Sarah Gainsford, Widow, which was referred to Arbitration. 8vo, (*a curious case of reputed marriage*), 3s. *Gosport,* 1789

2072 BOGUE'S Sermon on the death of Mr. Thos. Hayter of Gosport. 8vo, 1s *Newport,* 1809

2073 BENNETT'S Sermon at Gosport before the Associated churches of Hampshire. 12mo, 1s 1814

2074 BOGUE'S (D.) Sermon at Gosport on the Death of his Son James. 8vo, 1s 1823

2075 BINGHAM (Revd. Richd.) Two Sermons at Gosport on the Birth of the Prince of Wales. 8vo, 1s 1841

2076 HARTFORD Bridge or the Skirts of the Camp, a Farce by W. Pearce. 8vo, 1s 1793

2077 ACCOUNT of the Life and Conversation of the Rev. Isaac Milles, Rector of Highcleer, Hants, with Funeral Sermon, 9th July, 1720. 8vo, 3s 1721

2078 HOWARD (Henry) on the Tomb of King Alfred at Hyde Abbey near Winchester. 4to, *plates.* 1s *Soc. Antiq.* 1798

2079 DODS (Robert Boyce, *of Haslar Hospital*) Sermon on his death. By David Bogue. 8vo, 1s 1818

2080 BROCKETT'S (I., *Minister of Elsfield*) Sermon at the Funerall of the most religious lady, the Lady Lucie Jervoise, sometime wife of Sir Thos. Jervoise at Herriot. 4to, 5s 1642

2081 WILKINSON'S (A.) Historical Notices of the Parishes of Hurstbourn Priors and St. Mary Bourn. 8vo, 2s 6d 1861

2082 ACT for the sale of the Estates of Henry Grey (Itchingswell Grange, Kingscleer). Folio 1s 6d

Isle of Wight.

2083 DECLARATION from the Isle of Wyght and County of Hampshire concerning the King and the tryall of Capt. Burley upon high treason about the late Meeting in the said Isle with the burning of the gates of Canterbury and delivering up Dover Castle. 4to, 5s 1648

2084 ANSWER to a Scandalous Letter written by Hammond, the Head Gaoler in the Isle of Wight to Mr. Lenthall, Speaker of the House of Commons. By a Friend of Master Osborne's and a Lover of Truth. 4to, 2s 1648

2085 FERNE'S (Dr. H.) Sermon at Newport before Charles I. 4to 1s 1649

2086 CUTTS (Lord) Speech to the Mayor and Aldermen of Newport at Carisbrook Castle upon the Swearing of Mr. Leigh the New Mayor. Folio, 1s 6d 1693

2087 TROUGHEAR (Thomas) Sermon preached at Northwood in the Isle of Wight. 8vo, 1s 1730

2088 WASHINGTON'S (H.) Farewell Sermon in the Chapel of West Cowes. 8vo, 1s 6d 1743

2089 JONES'S (Henry) *Victi*, or the Isle of Wight. A Poem. 4to, *three vignettes*, 2s 1766

2090 POETICAL Excursions in the Isle of Wight. 4to, *vignette of Carisbrook Castle*, 2s 1777

2091 THE Ladies Poetical Petition for a Winter Assembly at Newport in the Isle of Wight. 4to, 1s 6d *Newport*, 1806

2092 THE Isle of Wight, a Poem in three Cantos. 8vo, *plates*, 2s 1782

2093 STURCH'S (John) View of the Isle of Wight. 12mo, *map*, 1s 1778

2094 BURNING Shame or Punishment for bad Lawyers, a custom peculiar to Newport, Isle of Wight, a Poem by F. Nicholls. 8vo, *front.* 1s 6d 1812

2095 DURRANT'S Discourse at Newport to the Association of the Hampshire Independent Church. 8vo, 1s 1815

2096 PROCEEDINGS of a Court of Inquiry upon Lieut. Josiah Dornford and seven of the Crew of the Coast Guard Station at Freshwater for conniving at Smuggling. 8vo, 2s 1836

2097 HISTORY of Carisbrook Castle, with account of the imprisonment of King Charles I. *Plates by W. Westall.* royal 8vo, 2s 1839

2098 SABRINA, or the Pilgrims of the Isle, a Poem founded on Scenery in the Isle of Wight. 8vo, 2s *Ryde*, 1842

2099 TURNBULL on the Parochial Condition of Newport in the Isle of Wight. 8vo, 1s 1844

2100 THE Troubles of Brading, by the Vicar. 8vo, 1s *Ryde*, 1847

2102 HILLIER'S (Geo.) on Excavations on Brightstone and Bowcombe Downs, Isle of Wight. 4to, 2 *plates*, *privately printed*, 2s 1854

2103 ACCOUNT of the Public dinner given to Mr. C. Roach Smith at Newport, Isle of Wight, 28 Aug,, 1855, and Conversazione at Ryde the following day. 8vo, 1s 1855

2104 BEAL (Saml. Benoni), The Church of St. Thomas, Newport, Isle of Wight.—Elizabeth Stuart the Prisoner of Carisbrook, a poem, cr. 8vo, 1s 6d *Newport*, 1856

2105 QUARR Abbey, or the Mistaken Calling, a Tale (in verse) of the Isle of Wight in the XIIIth Century. By F. A. Trevelyan. 4to, *view of the abbey*, 2s 1862

2106 SHARPE'S (W. *Jun.*) Ramble from Newport to Cowes. 4to, *two plates*, 1s 6d

---

2107 KING'S (James), Poem on Leigh Park. 8vo, 1s 6d 1829

2108 HUNT'S Sermon at Lymington before the Associated Ministers of Hampshire. 8vo, 1s *Newport*, 1808

2109 WILKINSON'S (A.) Michaelmarsh and its Antiquities, together with Notices of the New Forest. 8vo, 2s 6d 1867

2110 HISTORICAL account of the making New Forest in Hampshire by King William the Conqueror and Richmond New Park in Surrey by King Charles the First. 8vo, *frontispiece of Rioters breaking into Richmond Park.* 7s 6d 1751

2110* ——————————— Another without the plate, 8vo, 3s 6d 1751

2111 ABSTRACT of all the claims on the New Forest in the County of Southampton, entered at the Lord Chief Justice in Eyre's Court at Lyndhurst and Winton in 1670, 8vo, 3s *Salisbury*, 1776

2112 NICHOLS (T.) Observations on the propagation and management of Oak Trees in general, more particularly applying to the New Forest. 8vo, 1s 6d *Southampton,* (1791)

2113 RUINS of Netley Abbey, a Poem (not by Keate) with a Short account of the Monastery. 4to, 2s 1765

2114 KEATE (George), Netley Abbey. An Elegy. 4to, 1s 1769

2115 COMPANION in a Visit to Netley Abbey, (by Hammond). 12mo, 1s 1800

2116 NETLEY Abbey, a Poem. 8vo, 1s 6d *Newport,* 1804

2117 BULLARD'S Companion in a Visit to Netley Abbey. 12mo, 1s 1828

2118 KELL'S (Rev. E.,) Netley Abbey, with an Account of the recent Excavations and Discoveries. 4to, *plates,* 2s 6d 1863

2119 WEBB'S (B. *of Odiham*), Essay on Education (*dedicated to the Gentlemen Educated there*). 8vo, 1s 1782

2120 LOWTH'S (Bishop), Sermon at Petersfield (in opposition to the dissenters opening a meeting house). 8vo, 1s 1722

2121 MANT (Rev. R.), Exhortation to diligent and constant prayer, in Buriton Church, Sunday, Sept. 23, 1804. 8vo, printed for the use of the Parishioners. 1s 6d *Petersfield*
Probably the earliest publication of Bp. Mant's.

2122 BINNEY'S (T.), Discourse at Petersfield before the Hampshire Independent Ministers. 8vo, 1s 1827

2123 ACT for enlarging the 9th of Queen Anne for repairing the Highways from Petersfield to Portsmouth. Folio, 2s 1725

2124 HARTSHORNE (Rev. C. H.), History and Architecture of Porchester Castle. 8vo, *woodcuts,* 2s 1846

2125 RYLAND'S Sermon at Portsea before the Ministers of the Baptist Churches. 8vo, 1s 1811

2126 GRIFFIN'S Sermon at Portsea on the death of the Rev. David Bogue, D.D., tutor of the Missionary Academy, Gosport. 8vo, 1s 6d 1825

2127 GUYER'S Sermon at Ryde on the death of the Rev. John Griffin of Portsea. 8vo, 1s *Portsea,* 1834

2128 AYLOFFE (Sir Jos.), Historical description of the ancient Painting, representing the Encampment at Portsmouth in 1545, at Cowdary, Sussex. 4to, 1s 6d 1778

2129 AN Impartial Account of the Portsmouth Disputation, with some just Reflections on Dr. Russell's Pretended Narrative. 12mo, 2s 1699
These two Tracts contain some curious particulars of the state of Religious Parties in Portsmouth at that time.

2130 WORREL'S (William), Sermon preached for the Reformation of Manners at Portsmouth, Nov. 24, 1699. 4to, 2s 1700

2131 SERMON in Portsmouth at the Funeral of Capt. George Pickerin, commander of a Swedish Man of War. 4to, 2s 1704

2132 A PLAIN and True Account of the Divisions in Portsmouth. 4to, 3s. *Privately Printed* 1711

2133 BROWNE (Simon), Jewish and Popish zeal described and compared, a Sermon preached at Portsmouth, Nov. 5, 1715. 8vo, 1s 6d 1715

2134 NORMAN (John), Sermon preached at Portsmouth, with Remarks on the Vicar's Sermon at the opening of the Organ 27 July. 8vo, 2s 1718

2135 LOWTH (W.), Answers to Remarks of Mr. John Norman of Portsmouth on a Sermon at Petersfield on Episcopacy. 8vo, 1s 6d 1723

2136 MEADOW'S (S.), Sermon on the death of the Rev. Mr. Daniel Whitewood of Portsmouth Common. 8vo, 1s. 1765

2137 MAXWELL'S (Arch.), Answer to Mr. Kirkland's Essay on Fevers. 8vo, 1s 6d *Portsmouth,* 1768

2138 PORTSMOUTH, a Descriptive Poem in two Books by Archibald
Maxwell. 8vo, 2s   *Ports.* 1755

2139 PORTSMOUTH Guide. 12mo, *curious folding view,* 2s *Portsm.* 1775

2140 TRIAL of James Hill, otherwise James Hind or James Actzen for
setting fire to the Rope House in Portsmouth Dock Yard. Folio,
5s   1777

      Hill was employed by the American Minister in Paris.

2141 JOHN the Painter's Ghost, how he appeared on the night of his Execution to Lord Temple (and circumstances relating to it), in verse.
4to, 2s   1777

2142 ENQUIRY into the Nature of the Titles conferred at Portsmouth
and the Camps by Geo. III., shewing the Origin and Ancient
Privileges of Knights Banneret. 8vo, 2s   1779

2143 ROWLES'S Funeral Sermon on the Rev. John Lacy of Portsmouth
Common. 8vo, 1s 6d   1781

2144 SHORT Essay on the Modes of Defence best adapted to the Situation
and Circumstances of this Island (relating to the fortifications of
Portsmouth and Plymouth). 8vo, 1s 6d   1785

2145 ANSWER to the "Short Essay." 8vo, 1s 6d   1785

2146 A BROAD Hint to Nobody, or the Child whipt with its own Rod,
published by Isaac Carter, Minister of God's word at Portsmouth,
with Poem entitled Minter's puzzle for religious drones, old maids,
and rickety children. 8vo, 2s   1794

2147 TRIAL of the Mutineers of H. M. ship Temeraire in Portsmouth
Harbour. 8vo, *ports.* 1s 6d   1802

2148 HISTORY of Portsmouth, with Accounts of Portsea, Gosport, and the
Isle of Wight. 12mo, 2s   *Portsmouth (about* 1802)

2149 BOGUE'S Sermon on the Death of Mr. Robt. Boyce Dods, of Haslar
Hospital. 8vo, 1s   1818

2150 PROPOSED Improvement of Portsmouth Harbour. 8vo, *plan,*
privately printed, 1s 6d   1823

2151 REPORT of the Portsmouth and Portsea Literary Society, 1826—7
8vo, 1s

2152 GRIFFIN'S Sermon on the Death of J. S. Charrier, French-Master of
the Dockyard Academy. 8vo, 1s   *Portsmouth, n. d.*

2153 CHARTER of K. Chas. I. to the Corporation of Portsmouth. 8vo, 1s
Portsea, n. d.

2154 HODSON'S Sermon at Little Ravely on the Feast of the Dedication
of the Church. 8vo, 1s   1803

2155 BOGUE'S (D.) Sermon at Ringwood, before an Association of Mis-
isters. 8vo, 1s   1789

2156 HALL'S (Peter) Topographical Remarks on the Parishes of Ringwood,
Ellingham, Ibbesley, &c. 12mo, 1s   *Ringwood,* 1831

2157 ACCOUNT of the Barbarous and Bloody Murder by Esther Ives, cn
the Body of her Husband, at Rumsey. 4to, 2s 6d   1686

2158 PALMER (W. Stern). Farewell Sermon preached at the Independent
Chapel, Romsey. 8vo, 1s   *Romsey,* 1817

2159 SERVICE at the Setting Apart of the Revd. John Reynolds to the
Pastoral Office at Romsey. 8vo, 1s   *Romsey,* 1819

2160 WINTER (Rev. R.) Parental Retrospect, a Very Brief Memoir of
Rebecca Beddome, of Romsey. 12mo, *only a few printed,* 1s
Romsey, 1821

2161 SPENCE (Charles). Essay Descriptive of the Abbey Church of
Romsey. Small 8vo, 1s 6d   *Romsey, n. d.*

2162 WHITE'S (Rev. Gilbert) Naturalists' Calendar (kept at Selborne).
8vo, *plate,* 1s   1795

2163 ANCIENT Purse Found at Selborne Described by T. Douce, *plate*
Account of an Ancient Building at Southampton, by Sir H. C
Englefield, 3 *plates.* Observations on Mosaic Pavements, discovered at Thruxton, Bramdean, and Crondall, by Sir H. Colt
Hoare. 4to (*from the Archæologia*), 2s   1811
2164 OBSERVATIONS on a Piece of Antiquity found at Selborne. 4to,
plate (*from the Archæologia*), 1s   1811
2165 HISTORY and Antiquities of Silchester. 8vo, 1s 6d *Basingstoke*, 1821
2166 HISTORY and Antiquities of Silchester, the *Vindonum* of the Romans.
8vo, 2s   *Basingstoke*, 1823
2167 HISTORY and Antiquities of Silchester, in Hampshire, the *Vindonum*
of the Romans and the *Caer Segout* of the Ancient Britons. 8vo,
1s 6d   *Basingstoke*, 1829
2168 —————— Another Edition. 8vo, 1s 6d   1837
2169 BATT upon Batt, *a poem* upon the Parts, Patience, and Pains of
Barth. Kempster, Clerk, Poet, Cutler, of Holy Rood Parish Southampton, with his Vision, and an Account of the Ancient and Present
State and Glory of Southampton, by Dr. Speed. 8vo, 1s   1706
2170 —————— Another Edition. 4to, 2s   1680
2171 —————— Another Edition. 8vo, 1s   1711
2172 SOUTHAMPTON Guide ; or, Account of the Ancient and Present
State of that Town, &c. 12mo, 1s   1768
2173 SOUTHAMPTON Guide, to which is prefixed Southamptom Rooms,
a Satyrical Poem. 12mo, 1s   *South.* 1787
2174 EXTRACTS from Plays Adapted to Southampton Characters. 4to, 2s
about 1790
2175 TWO Acts for Taking Down and Rebuilding the Parish Church of
All Saints, Southampton, and for Purchasing Land for a Church
Yard. Fol. 1s 6d   1791—3
2176 WARNER'S (Rev. R.) Attempt to Ascertain the Situation of the
Ancient Clausentum (*Bittern, near Southampton*). 4to, *map and
vignette*, 2s   1792
2177 STRICTURES upon Strictures respecting the intended Canal from
the Town of Southampton to the City of Salisbury. 8vo, 1s 6d
Salisbury, 1793
2178 DIRECTORY for the Town of Southampton. 12mo, 1s 6d   1803
2179 KINGSBURY'S Sermon at Southampton on the Execution at Winchester of Robt. Avery, for Forgery. 8vo, 1s   1805
2180 BOGUE'S Sermon on the Death of Mr. James Whatman Lobb, of
Southampton. 8vo, 1s   *Portsea*, 1807
2181 BULLAR (John), Brief Notices of Local Antiquities in Southampton
and its Neighbourhood, and on Objects Worthy of Attention in an
Excursion round the Isle of Wight, by John Drew. 8vo, *map*, 1s
1846
2182 SOUTHAMPTON Guide for 1804, 1805—another enlarged by Bullar,
n. d., all 12mo, 6d each.
2183 SOUTHAMPTON Guide, *with manuscript notes by Mr. A. Hammond,
of Southampton.* 12mo, 2s
2184 COWPER (Capt. Cowper) on the Spithead Forts. 1s   1862
2185 ACCOUNT of the Foundation of the Public School at East Titherley
and Lockerley. 8vo, *not printed for sale*, 1s   1839
2186 NOTES of a Journey to Harmony Hall, at Tytherley, a Socialist
Community. 8vo, 6d   1842
2187 TITCHFIELD, a Poetical Essay, by J. Missing. 4to, 2s   1749
2188 LANGLEY'S (J., *Minister of West Tuderly*) Sermon before the
House of Commons. 4to, 2s   1644

2189 MANNYNGHAM'S (Thos.) Sermon at East Tysted, at the Funeral of
Sir John Norton, Bart. 4to, 1s. 6d   1687

2190 MANNYNGHAM'S Sermon at East Tysted, at the Funeral of Lady
Dorothy Norton, of Rotherfield. 4to, 1s 6d   1703

2191 LEFROY (Chr. Edward), Letter to Sir Tho. Baring, on the Subject
of Allotments of Land to the Poor at West Ham, Basingstoke.
8vo, 1s   1834

2192 BALL'S (J.) Funeral Sermon on John Fryer, son of Sir John Fryer,
at Wherwell. 8vo, 1s 6d   1725

2193 THE Phœnix Sepulchre and Cradle in the Holy Death of the Rt. Hon.
Isabella Theresa Lucy, Marchioness of Winchester, by J. D. 4to,
2s 6d   1691

2194 COPIE of a Letter written from Master T. M. neere Salisbury, to
Master H. A. at London, concerning the Proceeding at Winchester,
where the late L. Cobham, L. Gray, and Sir Griffin Marckham, all
attainted of High Treason, were ready to be executed. 4to, 5s 1603

2195 BUCKLER (Edward, *Minister of Calbourn, I. of W.*), *Salus Populi*,
or a Nation's Happinesse, a Sermon Preached at the Assises holden
at Winchester, July 22, 1658. 4to, 3s   1658

2196 BROWNE'S (Abr., *Prebend. of Winton*) Sermon at the Winchester
Assizes. 4to, 2s   1623

2197 TRUE and Exact Relation of a Great Overthrow given to the Cavaliers in Winchester, by Colonell Hurrey, Colonel Browne, and some
others of the Parliaments Forces. 4to, 5s   1642

2198 TRACTS Relating to Winchester, its History, etc., from 1642 to 1792,
in all 16 separate old 4to publications, *some rare, and not often
heard of*, 5s   1642—1792

    Here we have Corbet, the Puritan, of Winchester, his Discourse ; also
the Discourse to King Chas. II., after the Rye House Plot, when he went
to Winchester, and tarried there for a season.

2199 CAPTAIN BURLEY, his Speech at the place of Execution at Winchester, where he was Hanged, Drawn, and Quartered, for endeavouring to raise Forces to take away the King from the Isle of
Wight and a great rising in the City of Worcester. 4to, 5s   1648

2200 MANUAL of Prayers for the Use of the Scholars of Winchester College,
&c. 12mo, 1s   1681

2201 SHERLOCK (William), Sermon at the Funeral of the Rev. Rich.
Meggot, late Dean of Winchester, at Twickenham. 4to, 1s 6d 1693

2202 BARKER'S (R., *Rector of St. Maurice's*) Visitation Sermon in Winchester Cathedral. 4to, 1s   1707

2203 WEST (Richard), Assize Sermon in Winchester Cathedral. 4to, 1s
1707

2204 BAKER'S (S.) Sermon at Winchester, for the Victory at Mons. 8vo.
1s 6d   1710

2205 PLEA of the Fellows of Winchester College against the Bishop of
Winchester's Local and Final Visitorial Power over the said College.
4to, 6s   1711

2206 THE Genealogy of Christ as it is represented in the East Window in
the Collegiate Chappell at Winchester, a poem, by a young Gentleman of Winchester School (*Lowth, afterwards Bp. of London*), 8vo,
1s 6d   1729

2207 CLARKE (Dr. Ahured), Sermon in the Cathedral Church of Winchester, at the opening of the County Hospital. 4to, 1s   1737

2208 THE Law and Equity of the late Appointment of a Warden of Winchester Considered. 8vo, 1s 6d   1758

2209 DEFENCE of the Conduct of the Warden of Winchester College, in Accepting of that Wardenship, occasioned by a Letter to the Rev. Dr. Lowth and Written by Himself. 8vo, 1s 6d   1758

2210 AN IMPARTIAL By-stander's Review of the Controversy Concerning the Wardenship of Winchester College. 8vo, 1s 6d   1759

2211 LOWTH (Dr.), Answer to an Anonymous Letter, Concerning the late Election of a Warden of Winchester College. 8vo, 1s 6d   1759

2212 PETITION of the Citizens of Winchester, 1450, concerning the Ruinous State of the City. 4to, 4 *pages*, 1s   1755

2213 LOWTH (Robt.), Mons Catharinæ prope Wintoniam, Poema. 4to, 2s   1760

2214 ACCOUNT of the Supervision held at the College near Winchester, by the Warden and Supervisors of St. Mary Winton College, in Oxford, on 3 Sept., 1766, and some Proceedings consequent thereupon. 8vo, 2s   1767

2215 HAMPDEN (Rev. James), Remarks on some Proceedings at the time of the late Election at Winchester College, in the Case of the Masters and the School Fairly Stated. 8vo, 1s 6d   1767

2216 CONDUCT of the Bishop of Winchester as Visitor of Magdalen College Fully Stated. 8vo, 1s 6d   1770

2217 STATUTES and Constitutions for the Use of the County Hospital at Winchester. 4to, 1s 6d   *Winton*, 1772

2218 MONS Catharinæ, prope Wintoniam, Poemata. 4to, 1s 6d   1774

2219 WINCHESTER Guide. Small 8vo, *plates (no front.)*, 1s   *Winton*, 1780

2220 RENNELL'S Sermon in Winchester Cathedral, on the Violence of the French Revolution. 8vo, 1s   1793

2221 RENNELL'S (Prebendary) Sermon in Winchester Cathedral, on the Vice of Gaming. 8vo, 1s   1795

2222 STURGES' (Dr. John, Prebend.) Reflections on the Principles and Institutions of Popery with Reference to Civil Society and Government, occasioned by the Rev. John Milner's History of Winchester and Supplement to same, 2 tracts. 4to, 3s 6d   *Winchester*, 1799
This occasioned Milner's " Letters to a Prebendary."

2223 STURGES' Reflections on Popery, occasioned by the Rev. John Milner's History of Winchester. 8vo, 2s   *Winch.*, 1800

2224 HISTORICAL Account of the Cathedral at Winchester, with a Review of the Modern Monuments. 8vo, 2 *plates*, 1s 6d
Winchester, 1801

2225 SHORT View of the History and Antiquities of Winchester. 8vo, *frontisp.*, 1s *each*   *Winchester*, 1802, 1804, and 1812

2226 WINCHESTER Cathedral, Historical and Critical Account of, extracted from Dr. Milner and Review of its Modern Monuments. 8vo, *plate*, 1s   *Winchester*, 1807

2227 BELL (Anthony, *Land Agent, Winchester*), Letter to John Fitzgerald, Esq. 8vo, *privately printed*, 1s 6d   *Winchester*, 1808

2228 OBSERVATIONS on the Proposed Junction Canal between Winchester and the Basingstoke Canal. 8vo, 1s 6d   1808

2229 SHORT Description of St. Cross, near Winchester. 8vo, 1s
Winchester, 1814

2230 CLARKE'S (Rev. Lips.) Letter to Brougham in reply to the Strictures on Winchester College. 8vo, 1s 6d   1818

2231 BOWLES'S (Rev. W. L.) *Vindiciæ Wykehamicæ*, or a Vindication of Winchester College against Brougham. 8vo, 1s 6d   1818

2232 ZILLWOOD'S Sermon at the Opening of the New Chapel in the House of Correction, Winchester. 8vo, 1s   1820

2233 HISTORY of St. Cross, near Winchester. 8vo, *plate*, 1s   1822

2234 GARBETT'S (W.) Observations and Correspondence, occasioned by the Failure and Restoration of a principal Pier in Winchester Cathedral. 4to, 2s *Winch.*, 1824

2235 SHORT Description of the Hospital of St. Cross. 8vo, *plate,* 1s 1824

2236 MILNER'S (Dr.) Short Description of the Hospital of St. Cross. 12mo, 1s

2237 SHUTTLEWORTH'S (Dr.) Sermon before the Hampshire Society, at Winchester. 8vo, 1s 1825

2238 APOLOGY for those who object to the Lateral Position of an Organ in Winchester Cathedral. 4to, 2s 1825

2239 SOME Account of the System of Fagging at Winchester School, with Remarks by Sir Alex. Malet, Bart. 8vo, 1s 1828

2240 LETTER to Sir Alex. Malet touching the Expulsions from Winchester School. 8vo, 1s 1829

2241 BARING'S (W. Bingham) Letter to the Inhabitants of Winchester on his Conduct as a Magistrate, towards Mr. and Mrs. Deacle. 8vo, 1s 1831

2242 WILLIAMS'S (Rev. D.) Reply to Mr. Baring's Letter on the Arrest of Mr. and Mrs. Deacle. 8vo, 1s 1832

2243 MINIATURE Memorials of Winchester. 12mo, *plates,* 1s *Winchester,* 1834

2244 TOWNSEND'S (Charles) Winchester and a few other Compositions in Prose and Verse. 4to, *privately printed,* 3s *Winchester,* 1835
   Contains Notices of Preston, near Brighton, of which the author was curate.

2245 HISTORICAL and Descriptive Guide to the City of Winchester. 12mo, 1s 1836

2246 MILNER'S Historical Account of Winchester Cathedral, with Supplements. 12mo, 1s 1840

2247 SAVAGE (W.), Guide to the Antiquities of Winchester. 12mo, *woodcuts,* 1s 1851

2248 BAIGENT (F. J.), On the Church of St. John, Winchester, and the Paintings on the North Wall. 8vo, *coloured plates,* 1s 6d 1852

2249 WINCHESTER City Cross, a Report of the Proceedings at a Meeting of the City Cross Restoration Committee. 12mo, 1s 1865
   A curious question arose, whether the Effigy of William of Wykeham should have his crozier in his right hand, as Mr. G. G. Scott had placed it.

2250 WILLIAM Rufus, his Tomb in Winchester Cathedral, by F. W. Richards. 8vo, *plates,* 1s 6d 1870

2251 GODWIN (Geo.), Ancient Structures in Winchester and Romsey. 8vo, 1s

2252 DESCRIPTION of the City, College, and Cathedral of Winchester, Antiquities and Present State. 8vo, 3s *Winchester, W. Greenville,* n. d.

2253 MILNER'S Historical Account of Winchester Cathedral. 8vo, *two plates,* 1s

2254 EXAMPLES of inlaid Gothic Tiles. 4to, 24 facsimile size of the Originals in Winchester Cathedral, &c. 3s 6d *Nichols*

2255 WINCHESTER in the Thirteenth Century, Original Documents. (From No. 23 of the *Archæological Journal.*) 8vo, 1s

2256 DESCRIPTION of the Hospital of St. Mary Magdalen, near Winchester. Folio, *with 2 plates from the Vetusta Monumenta,* 4s 6d

2257 BAIGENT'S (F. J.) History and Antiquities of the Parish Church of Wyke, near Winchester. 8vo, *with plate of a remarkable Monumental Brass,* 2s 6d 1865

PRINTS AND DRAWINGS RELATING TO

Hampshire.

₀ *No order of less amount than one shilling sent by post, nor any Prints sent out on approval.*

1 **MAP of the County**, with Plan of Winchester and Arms, folio, *curious*, 1s 6d ... ... *Speed*, 1610
2 —— With Plan of Winchester in the corner, and Arms, folio, *curious*, 1s 6d ... *Saxton, amended by Lea*
3 —— Folio, *curious*, 1s ... ... *John Norden*
4 —— Folio, with Plan of Winchester and Arms in the margins, 1s 6d ... ... *J. Hondius*, 1620
5 —— (Old), folio, 6d ... ... *Morden*
6 —— With Roman Antiquities in the margins, 4to, 3d *Moll*, 1739
7 —— Large folio, *coloured*, 1s ... ... *T. Kitchen*, 1750
8 —— And the Isle of Wight, with Views of Silchester, Netley, Carisbrook, Calshot, and the Needles, on 5 sheets, *coloured*, 7s 6d ... ... *Isaac Taylor*, 1759
9 —— Another, *not coloured*, 6s ... ... *ib.*
10 —— Bird's-eye View Map, folio, *curious*, 6d... ... *Bickham*
11 —— Large sheet, 1s ... ... *E. Bowen*, 1777
12 —— Large folio, 1s ... ... *Faden*, 1796
13 —— Large folio, *coloured*, 1s ... ... *Cary*, 1805
14 —— Large sheet, *coloured*, 1s 6d ... ... *Greenwood*, 1829
15 **Antique Jewellery** found in Hampshire, 4to, *coloured*, 6d *Fairholt*
16 **Alresford** (Old) **Church**, 12mo, 3d 1811
17 **Alresford** (New) **Church**, 12mo, 3d 1811
18 **Alton Church**, royal 8vo, 3d
19 **Amport House**, 8vo, 3d—4to, *india paper*, 4d ... *Neale*
20 —— 4to, 4d ... ... *Prosser*
21 **Andover**, the Theatre, 4to, 6d ... ... *Woodfall*, 1804
22 **Avington Park**, 8vo, 3d ... ... *Storer*
23 —— 4to, 4d ... ... *Prosser*
24 **Barton Farm**, near Winchester, View of the Hessian Camp on Barton Farm, with explanation of the tents, and the army at divine service, by Wingodson, land surveyor, large sheet, clean, 7s 6d 1756
25 **Basing** (Old) **Church**, Timber Roof of, 4to, 6d ... *Weale*
26 **Basing House**, at the time of the Siege, 4to, 1s ... *Old print*
27 —— From an old print, 8vo, 6d
28 —— From an ancient Drawing, 4to, 4d 1795
29 —— In 1760, 4to, 4d
30 —— Being destroyed by the Roundheads in the Civil War, 4to, *proof before letters*, 1s ... ... *Cattermole*
31 **Basingstoke**, St. Michael's Church, folio, 1s... ... *O. Carter*
32 —— Town Hall and Corn Market, folio, 1s ... ... *ib.*
33 —— Holy Ghost Chapel, folio, 1s ... ... *ib.*
34 —— 4to, 3d ... ... *Grose*
35 —— 8vo, 3d ... ... *Parkyns*

36 **Basingstoke**, Holy Ghost Chapel, 4to, 6d ... ... *Prosser*
37 —— 8vo, 3d ... ... *Greig*
38 **Beaulieu**, Map of the Manor and Haven of Bewley, folio, *old and curious*, 2s
39 —— The Palace House, 4to, *proof*, 6d ... ... *Gilbert*
40 —— Great Hall, 4to, 3d... ... ... *Grose*
41 **Beaulieu Abbey**, N.W. View, folio, *proof before letters*, 1s 6d
          Coney
42 —— 4to, 3d ... ... *Grose*
43 —— 4to, 6d ... ... *Hearne and Byrne*
44 —— 4to, 6d ... ... *Prosser*
45 —— Refectory, 8vo, 3d—4to, 4d ... ... *Buckler*
46 —— Elevation of Refectory, 4to, 6d ... ... *Street and Le Keux*
47 —— Longitudinal Section of the Refectory, 4to, 6d *ib.*
48 —— Stone Pulpit at, 4to, 6d ... ... *Goodman*
49 —— Pulpit at, 8vo, 2d 1796
50 —— Elevation of the Pulpit in do., 4to, 6d ... ... *Le Keux*
51 —— Foliage on Pulpit, 4to, 6d ... ... *ib.*
52 —— Plan, Section, and Details of Pulpit, 4to, 6d ... *ib.*
53 —— Section of Staircase leading to Pulpit, 4to, 6d... *ib.*
54 **Belvedere**, Sir W. Fordyce's, 8vo, 3d ... ... *Cary*
55 **Bighton Church**, S.E., 8vo, 3d ... ... *Basire*
56 **Bishopstoke**, the County Cheese Market, 8vo, 3d ... *Brannon*
57 **Bishop's Sutton Church**, S.E. View, 8vo, 3d ... *Basire*
58 **Bishop's Waltham Church**, 12mo, 2d
59 **Bishop's Waltham**, Monument of Rev. C. Walters at, 8vo, 3d—
    4to, 4d ... ... *Hill*
60 —— Remains of the Hall, 12mo, 2d ... ... *Varrall*
61 —— Palace Ruins, 4to, 6d ... ... *Prosser*
62 —— Abbey, Exterior, 4to, 3d ... ... *Grose*
63 —— Interior, 4to, 3d ... ... *ib.*
64 **Blackbrook Place**, 8vo, 2d ... ... *Cooke*
65 **Boldre Church**, Two Views, 4to, 6d ... ... *Whitty*
66 **Bournemouth**, 4to, *india paper*, 6d ... ... *Ferrey*
67 —— From N.W., 8vo, 3d
68 **Bramshill House**, 8vo, 3d—4to, *india proof*, 6d ... *Neale*
69 **Bramshot Church**, 3 Views of, 8vo, 3d 1793
70 **Breamore House**, 4to, 4d ... ... *Prosser*
71 —— Another View, 4to, 4d ... ... *ib.*
72 **Broadlands**, 4to, 4d ... ... *Angus*, 1787
73 —— 8vo, *coloured*, 3d 1825
74 —— 8vo, 3d ... ... *Neale*
75 —— E. Front, 4to, 3d ... ... *ib.*
76 **Brookwood Park**, 8vo, 3d—4to, *india paper*, 6d ... *Neale*
77 **Bury Hall**, near Gosport, 4to, 6d ... ... *Stockman*
78 **Cadland Park**, 4to, 4d ... ... *Watts*
79 **Calshot Castle**, South View, oblong folio, 1s 6d ... *Buck*, 1733
80 —— 4to, 4d ... ... *Walker*
81 —— 8vo, 3d ... ... *Prout*
82 —— 4to, 3d ... ... *Sandby*
83 —— 8vo 3d ... ... *Brannon*
84 **Calshot Castle and Fawley Village**, folio, 1s
85 —— A Sloop, with a View of Calshot Castle, 4to, 6d *Serres*

86	**Cams Hall**, 8vo, 3d	*Neale*
87	**Chawton House**, W. Front, 4to, 3d	*Prosser*
88	—— S. Front, 4to, 4d	*ib.*
89	**Christchurch**, 8vo, 3d	*Westall*
90	—— Castle, 4to, 3d	*Grose*
91	—— The Haven House near, 4to, *proof*, 6d ...	*Gilbert*
92	—— Basso-relievos on a large Ivory Casket in the possession of Gustavus Brander, Esq., at Christchurch, folio, 1s *Carter*, 1785	
93	**Christchurch Priory**, 4to, 4d ... ... *Walker*, 1800	
94	—— General View, 4to, 4d	*Grose*
95	—— S. Side, 4to, 4d	*ib.*
96	—— E. View, 8vo, 3d	*Storer*
97	—— S.E. View, 4to, 6d...	*Rawle*
98	—— N.W. View, 4to, 6d	*Zornlin*
99	—— S.E. View, 4to, 6d	*ib.*
100	—— N.E. View, 4to, 6d	*ib.*
101	—— From the opposite side of the River, 4to, *proof*, 6d *Gilbert*	
102	—— N.W. View, folio, 1s—*proof before letters*, 1s 6d *Coney*	
103	—— Part of Nave, 8vo, 3d	*ib.*
104	—— Exterior of North Transept, 4to, 6d	*Rawle*
105	—— Rood Screen, 4to, 6d	*Le Keux*
106	—— Statues and Basso-relievos on the High Altar, folio, *fine*, 1s 6d	*Carter*
107	—— Countess of Salisbury's Chantry, 4to, 6d ...	*Roffe*
108	—— Countess of Shrewsbury's Chapel, 8vo, 3d ...	*ib.*
109	—— Church, Monument of Margaret, Countess of Salisbury, 4to, 6d ... ... *Le Keux*	
110	—— Monument of Sir John Chidioc, folio, 6d ...	*Basire*
111	—— Heads of Sir John Chidioc and Lady from their Monument, and 3 *other drawings*, 4to, 1s 6d	
112	**Cuffnells**, near Lyndhurst, 8vo, 3d	*Smith*
113	**Dogmersfield Park**, 4to, 4d	*Prosser*
114	—— 8vo, 3d	*Neale*
115	**Ellingham**, Moyle's Court, 8vo, 3d—4to, 4d ...	*1828*
116	**Elvetham**, 4to, 4d	*Schnebbelie*
117	**Emsworth**, 4to, 4d	*Comte*
118	**Farnborough Railway Station**, 4to, 4d	*Jobbins*
119	**Froyle Place**, 8vo, 3d	*Neale*
120	**Gosport**, Flag Ship saluting, 4to, 4d	*Finden*
121	—— Naval Hospital, bird's-eye view, 4to, 6d ...	*1751*
122	**Grange Park**, 8vo, 3d—4to, *india paper*, 6d ...	*Neale*
123	**Hackwood Park**, 4to, 4d ... ... *Sandby and Rooker*, 1775	
124	—— 8vo, 3d—4to, *india paper*, 6d	*Neale*
125	**Hamble**, West Elevation and Ground Plan of Sydney Lodge, folio, 6d	*Soane*
126	**Harmony Hall** (Owen's Place), 4to, *coloured*, 6d	
127	**Haslar Hospital**, 8vo, 3d	*1790*
128	—— 8vo, 3d—4to, *proof*, 6d	*Harwood*
129	—— View and Plan, folio, 6d...	*Miller*
130	**Hayling Island** and its Vicinity, Map of, royal 8vo, 3d	*Mogg*
131	**Hayling Manor House**, royal 8vo, 4d	
132	**Hayling (North) Chapel**, and old Vicarage House, royal 8vo, 4d	
133	**Hayling (South) Church**, 4to, 6d	*Scott*

134 **Hayling** (South), Old Vicarage House, royal 8vo, 4d
135 —— New Vicarage House, royal 8vo, 4d
136 **Herriard House**, 4to, 4d ... ... *Prosser*
137 **High Clere Castle**, 8vo, 3d ... ... *Burke*
138 —— Lake and Temple, 4to, 4d ... ... *Prosser*
139 —— Milford Water, 4to, 4d ... ... *ib.*
140 —— Andover Lodge, 4to, 4d ... ... *ib.*
141 —— Winchester Lodge, 4to, 3d ... ... *ib.*
142 **High Cliff**, Earl of Bute's, 4to, 4d ... ... *Watts*
143 —— 8vo, 3d ... ... *Cary*
144 **Hook** (The) Hornby's, 4to, 4d... ... ... *Prosser*
145 **Hursley Lodge**, 8vo, 3d ... ... *Neale*
146 **Hurst Castle**, 4to, 4d ... ... *Mossman*
147 —— Another View, 4to, 4d ... ... *Grose*
148 —— 4to, 6d ... ... *Dewint and Cooke*
149 —— And the Needles, 12mo, *india paper*, 3d
150 —— From Keyhaven, 4to, *proof*, 6d ... ... *Gilbert*
151 —— Land View, 4to, *old drawing*, 1s 6d ... ... *B. Lens*
152 **Hurstbourne Park**, 4to, 4d ... ... *Heath*
153 **Hyde Abbey**, 12mo, 3d ... ... *Greig*
154 —— Plate I., 4to, 4d ... ... *Grose*
155 —— Plate II., 4to, 4d ... ... *ib.*
156 —— Antiquities at, folio, 1s ... ... *Carter*, 1790
157 —— Plan of the Remains, folio, 1s ... ... *Basire*
158 —— Head of a Crozier of Bronze found at, 4to, *private etching*, 6d
H. W. King
159 **Kemshott Park**, 4to, 4d—8vo, 3d ... ... *Prosser*
160 **Kings Somborne**, Tomb of Will. de Brestowe, folio, 6d *Basire*
161 **Kings Worthy Parsonage**, 4to, 4d—8vo, 3d ... *Basire*
162 **Laverstoke**, Mr. W. Portal's, 4to, 4d ... ... *ib.*
163 **Lymington**, Brick Hovel near, 4to, 6d ... *Hearne and Byrne*
164 —— The Solent Sea Baths, 4to, *proof*, 6d ... ... *Gilbert*
165 **Manydown**, Withers' Seat, 4to, 4d ... ... *Prosser*
166 **Marchwood**, New Church of St. John, folio, 6d ... *Colling*
167 **Meon** (East) **Church**, W., 8vo, 3d—4to, 6d... ... *Burnett*
168 —— 4to, *engraver's proof*, 6d
169 **Meon** (East), Font and two of the Sides, *two plates*, 4to, 6d
Basire
170 **Merdon Castle**, 8vo, 3d ... ... *Grose*
171 —— 4to, 6d ... ... *Prosser*
172 **Milford Village**, 4to, *proof*, 6d ... ... *Gilbert*
173 **Mottesfont House**, 4to, 4d ... ... *Prosser*
174 —— Ancient Doorway and Piscina discovered in, 4to, 4d *ib.*
175 **Nateley Scures**, Church and Windows, 8vo, 3d—4to, 4d 1836
176 **Netley Abbey**, 8vo, 3d... ... ... *Parkyns*
177 —— 8vo, *aquatint*, 2d ... ... *I. Clark*
178 —— 4to, *private etching*, 4d ... ... *W. B. Rye*
179 —— 4to, 4d ... ... *Grose*
180 —— Different View, 4to, 4d ... ... *ib.*
181 —— 4to, 4d ... ... *Powell*
182 —— 4to, *fine*, 2s... ... ... *Westall and Cooke*
183 —— 8vo, 3d ... ... *Hinchliff*
184 —— Ruins, 4to, 6d ... ... *Prosser*

185 **Netley Abbey,** Another View, 4to, 6d ... ... *Prosser*
186 —— Folio, *outline,* 1s
187 —— Part of the Ruins, folio, 1s ... *Barrow and Stadler,* 1800
188 —— 4to, two different Views, *neat pencil drawings,* 1s 6d
189 —— Eleven Different Views, royal 4to, 5s ... *W. Westall,* 1828
190 —— East View, 8vo, 3d ... ... *Harding*
191 —— North East View, 4to, 6d ... ... *Carpenter*
192 —— N.E. View, 4to, 6d ... ... *Mrs. Selby*
193 —— S.E. View, 4to, 6d ... ... *ib.*
194 —— North View, oblong folio, 1s 6d... ... ... *Buck,* 1733
195 —— Interior, 4to, 6d ... ... *Adams*
196 —— Interior, folio, *fine etching,* 1s 6d ... ... *Coney*
197 —— Interior, 8vo, 3d ... ... *Harwood*
198 —— Interior, High Altar Window, 4to, 6d... ... *Carpenter*
199 —— Inside View, 4to, 3d ... ... *Tomkins*
200 —— Part of N. Transept, 12mo, 2d ... ... *Storer*
201 —— Part of S. Transept, 12mo, 2d ... ... *Greig*
202 —— E. side of S. Transept, 12mo, 2d ... ... *Greig*
203 —— East Window, 12mo, 2d ... ... *Storer*
204 —— East Window, 12mo, 2d ... ... *Greig*
205 —— East Window, 4to, 6d ... ... *Hart*
206 —— West Window, folio, 6d ... ... *Barney*
207 —— West Window, 4to, 6d ... ... *Hart*
208 —— West Window, 4to, 6d ... ... *Mimpriss*
209 —— West Window, 8vo, 3d ... ... *Westall*
210 —— West Window and Nave, 8vo, 3d ... ... *Brannon*
211 —— Choir, East Window, 8vo, 3d ... ... *Brannon*
212 —— Abbot's Kitchen, 4to, 4d ... ... *Grose*
213 —— Chapel and South Transept, folio, 6d ... ... *Westall*
214 —— Entrance Gate, folio, 6d ... ... *Westall*
215 —— The Garden, 4to, 6d ... ... *Hart*
216 —— Brass Plate found in, 4to, 6d ... ... *Basire*
217 —— Castle and Abbey, 8vo, 3d ... ... *Rawle*
218 **Netley Fort,** 4to, *aquatint,* 6d ... ... *Tomkins*
219 **New Forest Scenes,** *two of his peculiar drawings,* 4to, 1s
Rev. W. Gilpin
220 —— Monument of William Rufus, 8vo, 3d... ... 1786
221 —— Rufus's Stone, 8vo, 3d ... ... *Brannon*
222 —— Twelve Apostles' Oaks, 4to, 6d
223 **Newtown Park,** 4to. 6d ... ... *Ferrey*
224 **Newton Valence,** Manor House, 4to, 4d ... ... *Prosser*
225 **Norman Court,** 4to, 4d ... ... *ib.*
226 **Odiam Castle,** 4to, 4d ... ... *Grose*
227 —— S.E., 4to, 3d ... ... *Prosser*
228 —— N.W., 4to, 3d ... ... *ib.*
229 **Odiam Church,** Font, 4to, *private etching,* 4d ... *Windle*
230 **Ovington Church,** 12mo, 3d ... ... *Hamper,* 1807
231 **Petersfield,** the Market Place, 8vo, 3d ... ... *Bond*
232 —— Map of the Borough, folio, 3d ... ... *Dawson*
233 **Porchester Castle,** 8vo, 3d ... ... *Noble*
234 —— 4to, 6d ... ... *Prosser*
235 —— 4to, 4d ... ... *Grose*
236 —— Oblong folio, *neat etching,* 2s ... ... *About* 1750

327 **Porchester Castle,** 4to, 3d ... ... *Lambert*
238 —— Different View, 4to, 3d ... ... *ib.*
239 —— 4to, 4d ... ... *Prout*
240 —— Different View, 4to, 4d ... ... *ib.*
241 —— 8vo, 3d ... ... *Old view*
242 —— North West View, oblong folio, 1s 6d... ... *Buck,* 1733
243 —— Inside View, taken by an Officer, oblong 4to, 1s 6d
              Peak, about 1750
244 —— Outside View, folio, 1s ... ... *Peak*
245 —— With the Barracks inside, 8vo, 3d ... ... *Williams*
246 —— Inner Court, N., 4to, 6d... ... ... *Godfrey*
247 —— The Saxon Keep, folio, 6d ... ... *Storer*
248 —— Gate to, 4to, 4d ... ... *Grose*
249 —— Castle Chapel, 12mo, 2d... ... ... *Greig*
250 **Porchester Church,** 8vo, 3d ... ... *Grose*
251 **Portsea,** Monument to Admiral Kempenfelt and others, who sank
  in the Royal George, 4to, 1s 1803
252 **Portsmouth,** 8vo, 3d 1754
253 —— 8vo, 3d ... ... *Old print*
254 —— And Spithead, from Portsdown, 8vo, 3d ... *Busby*
255 —— From the Sea, with the Masts of the Royal George, 4to, 1s
       Lord Duncannon and W. Birch, 1789
256 —— Town and Harbour, folio, *coloured, curious,* 1s *Bowles*
257 —— West View, 4to, 6d 1750
258 —— 4to, 3d ... ... *Harwood*
259 —— From Gosport, 8vo, 3d ... ... *Old drawing*
260 —— West Prospect, oblong folio, 32 inches long, *curious,* 4s 6d
              Buck, 1749
261 —— West Prospect, oblong folio, *corner torn,* 1s 6d *Buck,* 1749
262 —— View from Saluting Platform, 4to, 4d... ... *Finden*
263 —— Harbour, with H.M. Ship "Active," 4to, 6d
          Stanfield and Wilmore
264 —— Harbour, entrance, 4to, 4d ... ... *ib.*
265 —— Harbour, 4to, *proof before letters,* 6d ... ... *Finden*
266 —— Rigging-hulk and Frigate, 4to, 4d ... ... *Finden*
267 —— Geometrical Plan and West Elevation of Portsmouth Dock-
  Yard, 26 by 18 inches, *small piece off margin,* 2s 6d
         Clevely and Canot, 1756
268 —— Elevation of the Commissioners' House in the Dock Yard,
  oblong folio, 6d ... ... *Wyatt*
269 —— Garden Front of do., folio, 6d ... ... *ib.*
270 —— Garrison Chapel, Exterior and Font, 4to, 6d ... *Miss Allen*
271 —— Chancel of do., 4to, 6d ... ... *ib.*
272 —— St. George's Chapel, folio, 2s *Ingram and Bourn, about* 1750
273 —— The Semaphore, 4to, *india paper,* 6d ... ... *Harwood*
274 —— 8vo, 3d ... ... *Finden*
275 —— Hulk off the Gun Wharf, 8vo, 3d
276 —— High Street, 8vo, 3d ... ... *Shury*
277 —— The Theatre, 4to, 1s ... ... *Woodfall,* 1805
278 —— Representation of the Forensic Court as it appeared 24 Oct.,
  1832, at the Trial of Henry Stanhope for the Murder of Adol-
  phus Fitzclarence by Duelling, folio, *coloured,* 1s 6d *Levi*
279 —— Map of the Borough, folio, 3d ... ... *Dawson*

[338]

280 **Portsmouth,** Plan showing the proposed Improvements in the
    Camber at Portsmouth, folio, large sheet, 1s 6d   *Owen,* 1838
281 —— Three Pencil Sketches of Portsmouth, 4to, 1s   *About* 1790
282 —— Views between Portsmouth and the Isle of Wight, with
    Shipping, the Solent, &c., 6 *water colour drawings,* 4to, 3s 1811
283 **Ridgeway Park,** 4to, *pencil drawing,* 1s
284 **Ringwood Church and School,** 8vo, 3d   1807
285 **Romsey Abbey,** 1818, folio, *fine,* 1s 6d   ...   ...   *Coney*
286 —— 8vo, 3d   ...   .   *Smith*
287 —— Folio, *fine mezzo.,* 1s 6d ...   .*Buckler,* 1804
288 —— View of, and Norman Doorway, 4to, 6d   *J. P. Swanwick*
289 —— W. End Elevation, 4to, 4d   ...   .   *Le Keux*
290 —— S. Transept Elevation, 4to, 4d ...   .   *Le Keux*
291 —— Interior View, East End, 4to, 6d   ...   ...   *Rawle*
292 —— Two Compartments on the S. Side of the Nave, 4to, 6d
                                                  Le Keux
293 —— Coffin found in, 8vo, 3d ...   . *Swaine,* 1840
294 —— Saxon Capitals and other Ornaments in the Church, folio, 6d
                                                  Carter, 1784
295 —— Crucifix on the Outside Wall, folio, 1s   ... *Carter,* 1781
296 **Rookesbury,** Rev. W. Garnier's, 4to, 6d   ...   ...   *Hewetson*
297 **Rotherfield Park,** 4to, 6d
298 —— S.E., 4to, 4d   ...   .   *Prosser*
299 —— N.W., 4to, 4d   ...   .   *ib.*
300 —— Lodge Entrance, 4to, 3d   ...   .   *ib.*
301 **St. Dennis Priory,** 12mo, 2d ...   .   *Greig*
302 —— Another View, 12mo, 2d   ...   .   *Greig*
303 —— 8vo, 3d   ...   .   *Sands*
304 —— 4to, 4d   ...   .   *Grose*
305 **Selbourne,** Temple (a Farm House at), 4to, 6d   ... *Lerpiniere*
306 **Shirley House,** 4to, 6d   ...   .   *Gauci*
307 **Silchester,** 4to, *private etching,* 6d ...   ...   *H. C. Pidgeon*
308 —— Walls, 12mo, 3d ...   .   *Old print*
309 —— Plan of, folio, 6d ...   .   *Stukeley*
310 —— Ground Plan of, founded on actual surveys made about 1745,
    4to, 6d ...   .   *Basire*
311 **Somerford Grange,** 4to, 4d   ...   . *Grose,* 1784
312 **Southampton,** 4to, 4d ...   .   *Finden*
313 —— 4to, 4d   ...   .*Walker,* 1795
314 —— From the West, 4to, 6d ...   .   *Sparrow*
315 —— 4to, *fine,* 1s 6d   ...   .   *Westall and Cooke*
316 —— From the Water, 8vo, 3d   ...   .   *Brannon*
317 —— From the Millbrook Shore, 8vo, 3d   ...   ...   *Brannon*
318 —— From the Itchen, 4to, 4d   ...   .   *Allen*
319 —— From Pear Tree Green, folio, 1s *Wilkinson and Mazell,* 1772
320 —— From the Round Hill, near the Four Posts, folio, 1s .
                                                  Bellers, 1774
321 —— St. Mary's Church Yard, 8vo, 3d   ...   ...   *Brannon*
322 —— St. Michel's Church, Font in, 12mo, 2d   ...   *Greig*
323 —— Trinity Church, 8vo, 3d ...   .   *Brannon*
324 —— The Bar Gate, 4to, 6d ...   . *Hearne and Byrne*
325 —— The Bar Gate, 8vo, 3d ...   .   *Brannon*
326 —— Interior of the Hall over do., 8vo, 3d ...   ...   *ib.*

327 **Southampton**, Bar Gate in 1670, 4to, 6d ... ... *Sargent*
328 —— Above Bar, 8vo, 3d ... ... *Brannon*
329 —— West Gate, 8vo, 3d ... ... *Rawle*, 1807
330 —— East Gate, 4to, 4d... ... ... *Grose*
331 —— South Gate and Tower, 4to, 4d... ... ... *ib.*
332 —— The South Gate, 8vo, 3d... ... ... *Brannon*
333 —— Watergate, 4to, 4d ... ... *ib.*
334 —— N.W. Walls of Town and Castle, 8vo, 3d ... *Brannon*
335 —— Arcade in the West Wall, 8vo, 3d ... ... *ib.*
336 —— High Street, 8vo, *coloured*, 6d ... ... *Ackerman*
337 —— High Street, 8vo, 3d ... ... *Brannon*
338 —— Bernard Street, 8vo, 3d ... ... *Brannon*
339 —— Andrew's Coach Manufactory, 8vo, 3d ... *Brannon*
340 —— Jesus Chapel, 8vo, 3d ... ... *ib.*
341 —— New Wesleyan Chapel, 8vo, 3d... ... ... *Brannon*
342 —— Victoria Spa Assembly Rooms, 8vo, 3d ... *Brannon*
343 —— The New Riding School, 8vo, 3d ... ... *Brannon*
344 —— Pier Gates, Club House, &c., 3d ... ... *Brannon*
345 —— The Quays, &c., 8vo, 3d... ... ... *Brannon*
346 —— Entrance to Docks, 8vo, 3d ... ... *Brannon*
347 —— The Pier, 4to, *india proof*, 6d ... ... *Harwood*
348 —— Itchen Ferry, 4to, *proof before letters*, 1s
349 —— Itchen, the River, and Royal Oak, 8vo, 3d ... *Brannon*
350 —— Dispensary and Collegiate School, 8vo, 3d ... *Brannon*
351 —— The Avenue, 8vo, 3d ... ... *Brannon*
352 —— The Common, 8vo, 3d ... ... *Brannon*
353 —— Statue of Dr. Watts, 8vo, 3d
354 —— Pear Tree Green, 8vo, 3d ... ... *Brannon*
355 —— Northiam Bridge, 8vo, 3d ... ... *Brannon*
356 —— Grammar School, 4to, 4d ... ... *Buckler*
357 —— The Theatre, 4to, 1s ... ... *Woodfall*, 1805
358 —— The Polygon, 8vo, 3d ... ... *Walker*, 1783
359 —— Southampton, Plan of, and the Polygon, folio, 1s
Mazell, 1771
360 —— Grove Place Lunatic Asylum, near Southampton, 8vo, 3d
Brannon
361 —— Regent's Park, near Southampton, 8vo, 3d ... *Brannon*
362 —— Map of the County round Southampton, 8vo, 3d *Brannon*
363 **Southampton Water**, 4to, 6d ... ... *Serres*
364 **South Sea**, oblong 4to, *proof before letters*, 9d
365 **Southsea Castle**, 4to, 3d ... ... *Grose*
366 **Southwick**, folio, bird's-eye view of the House and Grounds, 2s
Kip, 1700
367 **Southwick Park**, 8vo, 3d—4to, *proof on india paper*, 6d *Neale*
368 —— 4to, 4d ... ... *Prosser*
369 **Southwick Priory**, Ancient Chair at, 12mo, 2d ... *Storer*
370 **Spithead**, Men of War at, 4to, 4d ... ... *Finden*
371 —— 4to, 6d ... ... *Swaine and Parr*
372 —— British Fleet at Spithead, July, 1853, *very large wood cut*,
oblong folio, 1s ... ... *Illustrated London News*, 1853
373 —— The Russian Squadron at, two plates, 4to, 6d *Moses*
374 —— Representation of W. Tracey, of Portsea's, Plan for raising
the Royal George, 4to, 6d

375 **Spithead**, Explosion of the Wreck of the Royal George at Spithead, 4to, 6d ...   .   *Thomas*
376 **Stoneham** (North) **Park**, 4to, 4d   ...   .   *Prosser*
377 —— Belvedere Ledge, 4to, 3d   ...   .   *ib.*
378 **Strathfield Saye**, Duke of Wellington's, 4to, 6d ...   *Shury*
379 **Stratton Park**, 4to, 4d   ...   .   *Prosser*
380 —— 8vo, 3d—4to, *india paper*, 4d ...   .   *Neale*
381 —— Elevation of, folio, 1s   ...   .   *Darby*
382 —— Section of, folio, 6d   ...   .   *Woolfe*
382⁹ —— Plan of the Principal Floor, folio, 6d   ...   *ib.*
383 —— Lodge, 4to, 3d   ...   .   *ib.*
384 **Tangier Park**, 8vo, 3d ...   .   *Prosser*
385 **Thruxton**, Monumental Brass of Sir John Lysle, 1407, folio, 1s
                                                                                        Basire
386 —— Folio, 6d   ...   .   *Boutell*
387 —— Details of ditto, folio, 6d   ...   .   *ib.*
388 **Tichborne Church**, 8vo, 3d   ...   .   *Hamper*, 1807
389 **Tichfield House**, 4to, 4d   ...   .   *Grose*
390 —— House, Chapel at, 4to, 4d   ...   .   *Grose*
391 **Titchfield Place**, Gate-house, 4to, 6d   ...   ...   *Prosser*
392 **Upham Church**, S.E., 8vo, 3d
393 —— Young's Birth-place, 8vo, 3d
394 **Upton Grey**, 4to, 4d   ...   .   *Prosser*
395 **Waltham**, Bp. of Winchester's House, Plate I., 4to, 4d   *Grose*
396 —— Plate II., 4to, 4d ...   .   *ib.*
397 **Warblington Castle**, 4to, 4d ...   .   *Grose*
398 —— 4to, 4d   ...   .   *Sparrow*
399 **Warblington Church**, 8vo, 3d—4to, 4d   ...   ...   *Basire*
400 —— Church and Castle, royal 8vo, 4d
401 **Warnford**, King John's House at, 4to, 3d ...   ...   *Grose*
402 **Wellow Church**, Window in, 8vo, 3d

WINCHESTER CITY—

403 Prospect of, from the South, folio, 1s   ...   *Stukeley*, 1723
404 East Prospect, oblong folio, 31 inches, 5s...   ...   *Buck*, 1736
405 East Prospect, 4to, 6d   ...   .   *Old print*
406 East Prospect, 4to, *curious*, 6d   ...   .   *Old view*
407 View of City from the East, 4to, 6d   ...   ...   *Taylor*
408 Bird's-eye view, East Prospect, 4to, 6d   1750
409 North East View, folio, 1s ...   .   *Cave and Pass*
410 North East View, 4to, *proof*, 6d ...   ... *Robson and Roberts*
411 From the North East, 4to, 6d   ...   .   *Harwood*
412 South West Prospect, folio, 1s   ...   .   *Kirkall*
413 From St. Giles's Hill, royal 8vo, 6d   ...   ...   *Shury*
414 Antiquities found in a bed of Chalk near Winchester, 4to, 6d
                                                                                        Basire
415 Roman Antiquities found near, 8vo, 3d ...   ...   *Mills*
416 Bishop's Palace, 8vo, 3d   ...   .   *Old print*
417 —— 8vo, 3d ...   .   *Taylor*
418 The Castle, 4to, 4d ...   .   *Grose*
419 Catholic Chapel, Interior, royal 8vo, 6d ...   ...   *Shury*

420 Cheesehill Street, 4to, 6d—*proof before letters,* 9d
            O. Carter and Le Keux
421 Cheyney Court, 4to, 6d—*proof before letters,* 9d
            O. Carter and Tombleson
422 Colebrook Street, 4to, 6d—*proof before letters,* 9d
            O. Carter and Tombleson
423 College of Clergymen's Widows, 12mo, 3d ...   *Taylor*
424 County Hall, 8vo, 3d ... ... *Old print*
425 County Hospital, 12mo, 3d... ... ... *Taylor*
426 The Cross, as it appeared in 1741, folio, 1s 6d ... *Vertue*
427 —— Cross and other Antiquities, 4to, 6d ... *Pine*
428 —— Cross, 4to, 1s ... ... *Old view*
429 —— 8vo, 3d ... ... *Cave*
430 —— Folio, 1s ... ... *Owen B. Carter*
431 —— 8vo, 3d ... ... *Roffe*
432 —— 8vo, 3d ... ... *Bond*
433 —— 4to, 6d ... ...   *Roberts*
434 —— 8vo, 3d ... ...   *Taylor*
435 —— 4to, 6d—*proof before letters,* 9d *O. Carter and Tombleson*
436 —— Cross, 4to, 6d—*proof,* 9d ... *Turner and Powell,* 1800
437 —— 4to, 6d ... ... *Seago,* 1785
438 The Gaol, royal 8vo, 6d ... ... *Shury*
439 Grey Friars, 4to, 4d ... ... *Grose*
440 Guildhall, 8vo, 3d ... ... *Old print*
441 High Street, royal 8vo, 4d—*proof,* 6d ... ... *Shury*
442 House of W. Pescod, Esq., 8vo, 3d ... ... *Old print*
443 House of Edw. Sheldon, Esq., 8vo, 3d ... ... *Old print*
444 House of Henry Penton, Esq., 8vo, 3d ... ...   *ib.*
445 House of Mrs. Townsend, 8vo, 3d ... ...   *ib.*
446 King Arthur's Round Table, 4to, 6d ... ... *Old print*
447 —— 4to, 6d ... ... *Pass*
448 Magdalen Chapel, near Winchester, N.W. View, Paintings on
  the Walls, &c., on one plate, folio, 1s 6d ... *Basire*
449 —— Inside View, folio, 1s 6d ... ... *ib.*
450 —— Another, folio, 1s 6d ... ...   *ib.*
451 Old Cottage near, 4to, 6d ... ... *Delamotte,* 1815
452 Old Cottage at, 4to, 3d
453 The Palace, or King's House (now the Barracks), East View,
  oblong folio, 1s 6d... ... ... *Buck,* 1733
454 —— Folio, 6d... ... ...   *Hinton,* 1750
455 —— Royal 8vo, 6d ... ...   *Shury*
456 —— 12mo, 3d ... ...   *Cave*
457 —— East View taken on the spot by an Officer, oblong folio, 1s
                Peak, about 1750
458 —— Another View, folio, *proof before letters,* 1s
459 —— and the adjoining Offices as intended to have been finished
  by Sir Christopher Wren, 4to, 6d ... ... *Pass*
460 —— as it was designed to be built, 4to, 6d ... *Old print*
461 —— Balloon Ascent from, 8vo, 3d 1862
462 St. John's Street and Church, 4to, 6d—*proof before letters,* 9d
            O. Carter and Le Keux
463 St. John's House, North Prospect, 8vo, 3d ... *Old print*

464 Hospital of St. John the Baptist, Exterior, 4to, 6d *O. B. Carter*
465 —— Interior, 4to, 6d ... ... *ib.*
466 Hospital of St. John, Principal Court, 4to, 6d ... *O. B. Carter*
467 St. Thomas's Church, East Window, folio, *finely coloured,* 2s
Warrington and Rawlins
468 The Theatre, 4to, 1s ... ... *Woodfall,* 1805
469 West Gate, 2 Views, 8vo, 3d ... ... *Carter,* 1789
470 —— 4to, 4d ... ... *Prout*
471 —— 8vo, 3d ... ... *Greig*
472 —— 4to, 6d—*proof before letters,* 9d *O. Carter and Le Keux*
473 —— Looking West, 4to, 6d—*proof before letters,* 9d
O. Carter and Le Keux
474 Tower of Gatehouse, 4to, *proof on india paper,* 1s *Le Keux*
475 Specimens of Arches taken near the West Gate and Cathedral,
4to, 3d ... ... *Basire*
476 Wolvesley Palace, 8vo, 3d—4to, 4d 1819
477 Wolvesley Castle, Remains, 4to, 3d ... ... *Grose*
478 —— 4to, 6d—*proof before letters,* 9d *O. Carter and Le Keux*
479 —— 4to, *proof before letters,* 6d
480 —— Fragments from Wolvesley Castle, 4to, 3d... *Basire*
481 —— Chapel, 4to, 3d ... ... *Grose*
482 Winchester, and the Valley of the Itchen, from St. Catherine's
Hill, 4to, 6d ... ... *Bartlett*
483 Plan of Winchester, with the Hessian Camp, folio, 1s 6d
Baur, 1756
484 —— Plan of the City, large folio, 1s ...*Atkinson and Perry*
485 —— Plan of, 4to, 3d... ... ... *Roper*
486 —— Plan of the Borough, folio, 3d ... ... *Dawson*
487 Eleven neat Engravings on Wood relating to Winchester and
St. Cross, printed on 4to paper, 2s

WINCHESTER CATHEDRAL—

488 Cathedral, 8vo, 3d ... ... *Greig*
489 8vo, 3d... ... ... *Hawksworth*
490 Old View, 12mo, 2d ... ... *Vere*
491 Royal 8vo, 3d... ... ... *Whimper*
492 From Wolvesey Castle, 8vo, 3d ... ... *Storer*
493 North View, large folio, 1s 6d *Sold by I. Smith, about* 1710
494 N. View, oblong 4to, 6d ... ... *V. Gucht*
495 N.W. View, 8vo, 3d ... ... *Storer*
496 N.W. View, large folio, 1s 6d ... ... *Coney*
497 N.W. View, 4to, 6d—folio, 1s ... ... *Buckler*
498 North East View, 4to, 6d ... ... *Shury*
499 N.E. View, 8vo, 3d ... ... *Storer*
500 N.E. View, Exterior, folio, 6d ... ... *Vandergucht,* 1715
501 North East View, folio, 1s ... ... *Buckler*
502 S. View, Exterior, 8vo, 3d ... ... *Storer,* 1813
503 S. View, folio, 1s 6d... ... ... *D. King,* 1655
504 S.E. View, 4to, 6d—folio, 1s ... . *Buckler*
505 S.E. View, 8vo, 3d ... ... *Winkles*
506 S.E. View, Exterior, royal 8vo, 6d... ... ... *Shury*
507 S.E. View, 8vo, 3d ... ... *Greig*

508 S.W. View, 8vo, 3d ... ... *Storer*
509 View of North Side, Exterior, 4to, 6d ... ... *Le Keux*
510 Elevation of three Compartments, North Side, 4to, 4d *Roffe*
511 East End, Exterior, 4to, 6d ... ... *Sands*
512 West Front, 8vo, 3d ... ... *Storer*
513 View of West Front, 4to, 6d ... ... *Le Keux*
514 West Front, 4to, 6d—*proof before letters,* 9d ... *Le Keux*
515 W. Front, 8vo, 3d ... ... *Winkles*
516 Section and Plan of West Front, 4to, 4d ... ... *Turrell*
517 West Door, 8vo, 3d ... ... *Storer*
518 West Door, Interior, 8vo, 3d ... ... *Storer*
519 Elevation of Church and Tower, 4to, *proof,* 6d ... *Le Keux*
520 Half Elevation and Half Section of the Church and Tower, from
    N. to S., 4to, 6d—*proof,* 9d ... ... *Le Keux*
521 Arches and parts of the Tower, 4to, 4d ... ... *Hollis*
522 North Transept, folio, 1s ... ... *Coney*
523 North Transept, Exterior, 4to, 6d—*proof before letters,* 9d
                                                    Le Keux
524 N. Transept, Exterior, 8vo, 3d ... ... *Winkles*
525 N. Transept, Interior, 8vo, 3d ... ... *Winkles*
526 View in the North Transept, 4to, 6d—*proof before letters,* 9d
                                                    Sands
527 South Transept, folio, 1s ... ... *Coney*
528 South Transept, Interior, folio, 1s ... ... *Coney*
529 N. Transept, Interior, 8vo, 3d ... ... *Storer*
530 Elevation, Interior and Exterior, near the Altar, 4to, 4d
                                                    Le Keux
531 Interior, folio, *fine,* 1s 6d ... ... *Coney*
532 Interior, 4to, 6d ... ... *Basire,* 1809
533 Interior, 4to, 6d ... ... *Mackenzie and Havell*
534 Interior, 4to, *proof,* 6d ... ... *Radclyffe*
535 Part of Interior, 4to, 6d—*proof before letters,* 9d *Radclyffe*
536 Interior, to the West, 4to, 6d ... ... *Basire*
537 Interior, to the West, folio, 6d ... ... *Basire*
538 Interior, looking West, 4to, *proof on india paper,* 1s
                                               Cave and Basire
539 The Choir, 4to, *proof on india paper,* 1s ... *Cave and Basire*
540 View of the Choir, 4to, 4d ... ... *Basire*
541 Choir, 8vo, 3d ... ... *Winkles*
542 Interior of Choir, 4to, 6d—*proof before letters,* 9d
                                             O. Carter and Le Keux
543 Choir, looking East, 4to, 6d—*proof before letters,* 9d *Edwards*
544 Choir, looking West, 4to, 6d—*proof before letters,* 9d *Radclyffe*
545 North side of Choir, Exterior, 4to, 6d ... ... *Le Keux*
546 S. Aisle of Choir, and Bp. Fox's Tomb, 8vo, 3d ... *Winkles*
547 Entrance to Choir, with Inigo Jones's Screen, 4to, 6d *V. Gucht*
548 Part of the Stalls of the Choir, 4to, 4d—*proof,* 6d *Le Keux*
549 Altar, 4to, *proof before letters,* 9d ... ... *Le Keux*
550 Altar Screen, 4to, *proof,* 6d ... ... *Le Keux*
551 Section and Elevation East of the Altar Screen, 4to, 6d—*proof,*
    9d ... ... *Le Keux*
552 Parts of Altar Screen, Old Screen, and Fox's Chantry, 4to, 4d
                                                    Hollis

553	Altar End, folio, 6d	*Basire*
554	Nave, 4to, *proof*, 6d	*Edwards*
555	Nave, looking East, 8vo, 3d	*Winkles*
556	Across the Nave, showing Font and Wykeham's Tomb, 8vo, 3d	*Winkles*
557	Nave, one Compartment Externally and Internally, 4to, 6d	*Le Keux*
558	Presbytery, 8vo, 3d	*Winkles*
559	Font, 8vo, 3d	*V. Gucht*
560	Views of the Font, 4to, 6d	*Le Keux*
561	Font in the Nave, drawn in 1784, folio, 1s *Carter and Basire*	
562	—— Three Basso-relievos on the same, folio, 1s...	*ib.*
563	The Font, two Views on one plate, folio, 1s ... *Carter*, 1786	
564	—— Sculptures on three sides, folio, 1s	*ib.*
565	Font, South Side, 4to, 4d	
566	Font, two Views, 4to, 6d	*Le Keux*
567	Prior Silkstead's Chapel, where Isaac Walton was buried, 8vo, *proof*, 1s	
568	—— 4to, *proof before letters*, 9d	*O. Carter*
569	St. Peter's Chapel, Altar End and Exterior, folio, 6d	*Basire*
570	Lady Chapel, Elevation of three Compartments on the N. Side, 4to, *proof*, 6d	*Roffe*
571	Chests of the West Saxon Kings, and Tomb of Rufus, folio, 6d	*Vandergucht*, 1715
572	Monumental Effigies of Bishops Edington, Wykeham, and Waynfleet, 4to, 6d	*Edwards*
573	Monument of William of Wykeham, 4to, 6d ...	*Le Keux*
574	Tomb of William of Wykeham, folio, 1s 6d *Sherwin*, 1778	
575	William of Wykeham's Chapel, 4to, 4d—*proof before letters*, 9d	*Le Keux*
576	Tomb and Chantry of William of Wykeham, 4to, 1s	*Skelton*
577	Wykeham's Chantry, outside, and his Tomb, &c., 4to, 6d *Pass*	
578	Wykeham's Chantry, 4to, 6d—*proof*, 9d	*Radclyffe*
579	Bishop Waynfleet's Monument, folio, 6d	*Basire*
580	Bishop Waynfleet's Tomb at, 8vo, 3d	
581	Effigy of Bishop Waynfleet, folio, 6d	*Basire*
582	Shrine of Bishop Waynfleet, 4to, 1s	*Skelton*
583	Waynfleet's Chantry, 8vo, 3d	*Pass*
584	Groined Roof of Waynfleet's Chantry, and Plans of Clustered Columns, 4to, 6d—*proof*, 9d	*Roffe*
585	Crockets from Waynfleet's Monument, 4to, 4d ...	*Pugin*
586	Monument of Cardinal Henry Beaufort, Bp. of Winchester, folio, 1s	*Gaywood*, 1677
587	Monument of Cardinal Beaufort, folio, 1s ...	*Basire*
588	Beaufort's Chantry, 8vo, 3d...	*Cave*
589	Beaufort Chantry, with part of Fox's, Waynfleet's, and Langton's Chantries, 4to, 6d	*Turrell*
590	Beaufort and Waynfleet's Chantries, 4to, 3d ...	*Pass*
591	Bishop's Fox's Monument, folio, 6d	*Basire*
592	Shrine of Bishop Fox, 4to, 1s	*Skelton*
593	Shrine of Bishop Fox, 4to, *engraver's etching*, 6d	
594	Details of the Monuments of Bishops Fox and Waynfleet, folio, 1s	*Schnebbelie and Basire*

595 Monument of Richard, second son of William the Conqueror,
 folio, 6d 1677
596 Monument of King William Rufus, folio, 6d ... *Du Bosc*
597 Monument of William Rufus, folio, 1s 1677
598 Monument of Dr. Joseph Warton, 4to, 6d ... *Flaxman*
599 Monument of Dr. Joseph Warton, 4to, 6d ... 1806
600 Dr. Warton and Bp. Hoadley's Monuments, folio, 6d *Basire*
601 Side of an Ancient Tomb and two Effigies, 4to, 4d *Le Keux*
602 Monument of a Crusader, 12mo, 3d ... ... *Greig*
603 The Cloisters, folio, 6d ... ... *Havell*
604 The Well under the Cathedral, 4to, 6d
605 Inscriptions in the Cathedral, folio, 6d ... ... *Basire*
606 Carved Woodwork, 4to, 6d—*proof*, 9d ... ... *Turrell*
607 Capitals and Bases, 4to, 6d—*proof*, 9d ... ... *Ranson*
608 William of Wykeham and St. Paul, from the Stained Glass
 Window of Choir, folio, *coloured*, 1s ... ... *O. Carter*
609 St. Swithen, from the same, folio, *coloured*, 1s ... *ib.*
610 Twenty-five Plates of the Painted Windows in the Cathedral,
 4to, *finely coloured*, 10s 6d ... *O. Carter and Le Keux*
611 Paintings on the Wall of the South Side of St. Mary's Chapel,
 two plates, folio, 2s ... ... *Carter*, 1785
612 Paintings on the North Side of the same Chapel, folio, 1s *ib.*
613 Ancient Painting on the Wall of a Chapel, 4to, 6d
614 Painting on the North Wall of the North Transept, 4to, 4d—
 coloured, 6d... ... ... *Schnebbelie*
615 Plan and Sections of the Crypts, 4to, 3d ... ... *Roffe*
616 Ground Plan of the Cathedral, 4to, 3d—*proof*, 6d *Britton*
617 Ground Plan, showing the Groining, Sites of Tombs, &c., 4to, 3d
               Gladwin
618 Ground Plan, 8vo, 3d ... ... *Winkles*
619 Ground Plan, 8vo, 3d ... ... *Hardwick*
620 Conventual Kitchen, 4to, 6d—*proof before letters*, 9d
          O. Carter and Le Keux
621 The Deanery, 4to, 6d—*proof before letters*, 9d
          O. Carter and Le Keux

ST. MARY'S COLLEGE—

622 St. Mary's College, bird's-eye view, large folio, 2s
           D. Loggan, 1675
623 Bird's-eye View, 4to, 6d ... ... *Old print*
624 College, 4to, 6d ... ... *Alexander and Powell*
625 —— 4to, 3d ... ... *Taylor*
626 4to, *proof before letters*, 6d ... ... *Le Keux*
627 College, Bridge, and River, large folio, 2s
        Taylor and Lewis, 1805
628 Entrance to the College, 8vo, 3d ... ... *Bedford*
629 From the Meadow, 4to, *coloured*, 6d ... ... *Stadler*
630 From the Warden's Garden, 4to, *coloured*, 6d ... *Stadler*
631 Entrance, with the Warden's House, 4to, *coloured*, 6d *Havell*
632 College Gate and Warden's Lodge, 4to, 6d—*proof before letters*,
 9d ... ... *O. Carter and Le Keux*
633 Inside View, 4to, 6d—*proof*, 9d ... ... *ib.*

634 The Chapel, from the Warden's Garden, folio, 9d
Buckler and Barnett
635 Another, from the Middle Quadrangle, folio, 9d
Buckler and Barnett
636 The Chapel, 4to, 6d—*proof before letters*, 9d
O. Carter and Le Keux
637 Chapel, from the Great Court, 4to, *coloured*, 6d... *Bluck*
638 Chapel, from the Bridge, 8vo, 3d ... ... *Harwood*
639 Chapel, Interior, 4to, *coloured*, 6d... ... ... *Bennett*
640 Key to the East Window, restored in 1822, folio, 6d
641 The Hall, 4to, 6d—*proof before letters*, 9d
O. Carter and Le Keux
642 School, from the West of the Quadrangle, folio, 9d
Buckler and Barnett
643 School Room, Interior, 4to, *coloured*, 6d ... ... *Stadler*
644 College Tower, Library, and Mill, 4to, 6d—*proof before letters*,
9d ... ... *O. Carter and Tombleson*
645 Cloisters, 4to, *coloured*, 6d ... ... *Havell*
646 College Library, from the Cloisters, folio, 9d *Buckler and Barnett*
647 Library, Interior, 4to, *coloured*, 6d ... ... *Bennett*
648 A Scholar in Costume, 4to, *coloured*, 6d ... ... *Ackermann*
649 School of St. Mary's College, folio, *proof*, 1s 6d
Buckler and Barnett
650 Grammar School, 4to, 4d ... ... *Buckler*
651 The Trusty Servant, from an Old Painting, 12mo, 3d *Cave*
652 Trusty Servant, 8vo, 3d ... ... *Basire*

ST. CROSS HOSPITAL AND CHURCH—

653 Hospital of St. Cross, N.W. Exterior, folio, 1s—*proof before
letters*, 1s 6d ... ... *Coney*
654 8vo, 3d ... ... *Old print*
655 Different View, 4to, 4d ... ... *Grose*
656 N.E. View, royal 8vo, 6d ... ... *Shury*
657 N.E. View, 4to, 6d—*proof before letters*, 9d
O. Carter and Le Keux
658 View Inside Quadrangle, 4to, 6d ... ... *Hearne and Byrne*
659 Beaufort Tower, 12mo, 3d ... ... *Greig*
660 Interior of the Hall, 4to, *proof before letters*, 1s ... *Le Keux*
661 Sculptures in the Hospital, folio, 1s ... ... *Carter, 1790*
662 The Church of St. Cross, 4to, 3d ... ... *Grose*
663 —— Another View, 4to, 3d ... ... *Grose*
664 —— 4to, 6d ... ... *Johnson*
665 —— Folio, 1s... ... ... *Coney*
666 —— 8vo, 3d ... ... *Woolnoth*
667 N.W. View, 4to, 6d ... ... *Johnson*
668 E. End, 12mo, 2d ... ... *Storer*
669 E. End Section, 4to, 4d ... ... *Le Keux*
670 E. End Elevation, 4to, 4d ... ... *Le Keux*
671 Part of, with Bp. Compton's Inscription, 4to, 6d *Schnebbelie*
672 Interior, folio, 1s—*proof before letters*, 1s 6d ... *Coney*
673 Window at, two views, 4to, 3d ... ... *Basire*
674 Windows, 4to, 3d ... ... *Sands*

675 Chapel on N. Side of Chancel, 12mo, 2d ...   ...   *Storer*
676 N. Side of Chancel, Exterior, 12mo, 2d ...   ...   *Storer*
677 W. Door, 12mo, 2d ...   .   *Greig*
678 Double Arch, 12mo, 2d   ...   .   *Greig*
679 Pointed Arches in S. Transept, 12mo, 2d...   ...   *Greig*
680 Font at, 12mo, 2d   ...   .   *Storer*
681 Brass of John de Campden, Warden, 8vo. 3d   ...   *Boutell*
682 Mon. Brass of John Campden, folio, 1s   ...   *Carter,* 1792
683 Fragments from the Church, 4to, 3d   ...   ...   *Basire*
684 Nine Private Etchings of St. Cross Church and Hospital
    executed about 1763, 8vo, *curious,* 5s
685 Mill Dam near St. Cross, 4to, *proof before letters,* 1s   *Fox*

---

686 **Winchfield House,** 4to, 3d ...   .   *-Prosser*
687 —— and Hartley Row Station, 4to, 4d   ...   ...   *Jobbins*
688 **Worthy Park,** 4to, 4d ...   .   *Prosser*
689 —— The Lodge, 4to, 3d ...   .   *ib.*
690 **Yately Church,** Ancient Tiles in, 4to, 3d

Isle of Wight.

691   **MAP of the Island,** with Plans of Newport and South-
    ampton, folio, *curious,* 1s 6d ...   ...   *Speed,* 1610
692   —— by John Albin, *large sheet,* 1s   ...   *Neele,* 1807
693   —— 4to, 3d ...   .   *Brannon*
694 **Thirty-five Views in the Isle of Wight,** drawn and etched by
    Wm. Cooke, 1808, 8vo, 3s
695 **Alum Bay and the Needles,** 4to, 3d   ...   ...   *Brannon*
696 —— From the Needles, 4to, 6d   ...   ...   *Westall*
697 **Appley,** near Ryde, 4to, 3d ...   .   *Brannon*
698 **Apley House and Ryde Pier in the Distance,** 4to, 6d   *Harley*
699 **Appledurcombe,** 4to, 4d   ...   .   *Brannon*
700 —— 8vo, *coloured,* 3d ...   .   *Gendall*
701 —— 4to, 4d   ...   .   *Watts*
702 **Arreton Church,** 4to, 6d   ...   .   *Varley*
703 —— The Dairyman's Cottage, 4to, 6d   ...   *ib.*
704 **Barton Oratory,** S. and E. Fronts, 8vo, 3d   ...   *Fairholt*
705 **Beauchamp Cottage and the Orchard Undercliff,** 4to, *private*
    etching, 6d ...   .   *Cecil,* 1817
706 **Bembridge,** 4to, 3d ...   .   *Brannon*
707 **Binstead Church,** 12mo, 2d ...   .   *Greig*
708 —— Parsonage, 4to, 3d   ...   .   *Brannon*
709 **Binnel Point, St. Lawrence,** 4to, 6d   ...   *Childs*
710 **Black Gang Chine,** 8vo, 3d ...   .   *Rawle*
711 —— From the Beach, 4to, 3d   ...   ...   *Brannon*
712 —— Different, 4to, 3d ...   .   *ib.*
713 —— Looking outwards, 4to, 3d   ...   ...   *Cooke*
714 —— 4to, *fine,* 1s 6d ...   .   *Dewint and G. Cooke*

On Sale at Smith's, 36, Soho Square, London.

715	**Black Gang Chine**, 4to, 6d	*Englefield*
716	—— 8vo, 3d	*Baker*
717	—— 4to, *fine*, 6d	*Dewint and Cooke*
718	—— Wreck near, 4to, 3d ⏐	*Brandard*
719	**Bonchurch**, 4to, *fine*, 1s 6d	*Cristall and W. B. Cooke*
720	—— Part of, 4to, 6d	...*Malton,* 1785
721	—— The Eminence, 4to, 3d	*Brannon*
722	—— Village of, 4to, 6d	*Childs*
723	—— Eastdene Villa, &c., 4to, 3d	*Brannon*
724	—— Col. Hill's Seat, 4to, 3d	*Walker,* 1788
725	—— View near, folio, *aquatint*, 6d	*Lewis*
726	—— View in, 4to, 3d)	*Brannon*
727	**Bonchurch** (Old) **Church**, 4to, 6d	*Swanwick*
728	**Brading**, Little Jane's Cottage, 4to, 6d	*Varley*
729	**Brading Church**, 4to, 6d	*Swanwick*
730	**Brixton Church**, royal 8vo, 3d	
731	—— Folio, 6d	*Walmesley*
732	—— Folio, 6d	*Cartwright*
733	**Carisbrook Village**, 4to, 3d	*Brannon*
734	—— 12mo, 2d	*Mathews*
735	—— Entrance to the Village, folio, 6d	*Cartwright*
736	**Carisbrook Church**, 12mo, 2d	*Greig*
737	—— Another View, *aquatint*, folio, 6d	*Lewis*
738	—— 4to, 3d	*Tomkins*
739	—— &c., 4to, 6d	*Mrs. Selby*
740	—— Coffin of Princess Elizabeth, daughter of Charles I., 4to, 3d	
741	**Carisbrook Castle**, folio, 1s ...	*Menageot and Hulett,* 1755
742	—— 8vo, *india paper*, 3d	*Cooke*
743	—— 12mo, 2d	*Wallis*
744	—— 8vo, 3d	*Greig*
745	—— Plate I., 4to, 4d	*Grose*
746	—— Plate II., 4to, 4d	*Grose*
747	—— Plate III., 4to, 4d...	*ib.*
748	—— 4to, 6d	*Westall*
749	—— 4to, 4d	*Greig,* 1801
750	—— 4to, 1s	*Alexander and W. B. Cooke*
751	—— 4to, 3d	*Brannon*
752	—— 8vo, 3d	*Radclyffe*
753	—— 4to, *old view*, 3d	*Neigel*
754	—— 4to, *private etching*, 4d	*H. Wright*
755	—— Large folio, *coloured*, 1s 6d	*Hassell*
756	—— Folio, 6d	*Cartwright*
757	—— N.W. View, 8vo, 3d	1760
758	—— Part of, 4to, 6d	...*Malton,* 1785
759	—— North View, oblong folio, 1s 6d	*Buck,* 1733
760	—— From the Newport Road, 4to, 4d	*Comte*
761	—— From Calbourn Road, 4to, *fine*, 1s *Clennell and W. B. Cooke*	
762	—— From above the Gatcomb Road, 4to, 9d ...	*Westall*
763	—— From the South East Ramparts, 4to, 9d ...	*Westall*
764	—— Entrance to the Castle, folio, 1s	*Hulett,* 1753
765	—— Entrance, &c., 4to, *fine*, 1s ...*Alexander and Cooke,* 1814	
766	—— Entrance, 12mo, 2d	*Storer*
767	—— Gateway, 4to, 3d	*Sandby*

768 **Carisbrook Castle,** Entrance to Keep, 8vo, 2d ... *Evans*
769 —— Entrance to Keep, 4to, 3d
770 —— Within the Walls, 4to, 6d ... ... *Childs*
771 —— Chapel inside the Castle, 12mo, 2d ... ... *Wallis*
772 —— Plan of, 8vo, 3d
773 **Carisbrook,** Conference with Charles I., 4to, *proof before letters,* 1s
Cattermole
774 **Chale,** Ancient Tower on the Cliffs near, 4 views, folio, 6d
About 1760
775 **Chale Farm** (Winter Scene), 4to, 6d... ... ... *Cooke*
776 **Chale Church,** 12mo, 2d ... ... *Greig*
777 **Cowes,** 4to, 3d ... ... *Winkles*
778 —— 4to, 4d ... ... *Finden*
779 —— Sir J. C. Hippesley's Villa, 4to, 3d ... ... *Brannon*
780 —— Cottage Scene near, 4to, *fine,* 6d ... ... *Wilkinson*
781 **Cowes** (East) **Castle,** 4to, 3d ... ... *Brannon*
782 **Cowes** (West), 4to, 3d ... ... *Brannon*
783 —— (West), 4to, 3d ... ... *Rogers*
784 **Cowes Castle,** 4to, 4d ... ... *Grose*
785 —— 4to, *fine,* 1s... ... ... *Dewint and Cooke*
786 —— 4to, 4d ... ... *Sandby*
787 —— 4to, 4d ... ... *Sparrow*
788 —— 8vo, *india paper,* 3d ... ... *Cooke*
789 —— Westward of the Castle, 4to, 3d ... ... *ib.*
790 —— Castle and Parade, 4to, 3d ... ... *ib.*
791 **Cowes** (West) **Church,** 12mo, 2d ... ... *Wallis*
792 —— The Alarm winning the Ladies' Challenge Cup at Cowes,
Aug., 1830, 4to, *proof,* 6d ... ... *Gilbert*
793 **Culver Cliff,** 4to, 6d ... ... *Mrs. Selby*
794 **Culver Cliff,** with the Negro Servant, 4to, 6d ... *Varley*
795 **Dunose,** 4to, 3d ... ...*Laurie,* 1798
796 **Durdle Cove,** 4to, 6d ... ... *Webster and Cooke*
797 **Fairlee,** 8vo, 3d... ... ... *Tomkins,* 1794
798 —— 4to, 3d ... ... *Brannon*
799 **Fernhill,** 4to, 3d ... ... *Brannon*
800 **Freshwater Village and Church,** 12mo, 2d ... *Roberts*
801 **Freshwater Bay,** 4to, 3d ... ... *Brannon*
802 **Freshwater Cave,** 8vo, 3d ... ... *Smith*
803 —— Cavern, Entrance, 4to, 3d ... ... *Brannon*
804 —— Cave, Entrance to, 8vo, *drawing,* 1s ... *Tomkins,* 1795
805 —— Cliffs, 4to, 3d ... ... *Brannon*
806 **Gatcombe,** 4to, 3d ... ... *Brannon*
807 **Gatcombe Park,** 4to, 3d ... ... *Brannon*
808 **Godshill Church,** &c., 4to, 3d ... ... *Brannon*
809 —— Monument in, 12mo, 2d... ... ... *Storer*
810 **Medina Hermitage,** 4to, 3d ... ... *Brannon*
811 **Mirables,** near Niton, 4to, 3d ... ... *Brannon*
812 **Molleston Church,** 8vo, 3d ... ... *Greig*
813 **Needles** (The) **Rocks,** folio, 6d ... ... *Cartwright*
814 —— 4to, 3d ... ... *Brannon*
815 —— Folio, 6d ... ... *Walmesley*
816 —— From Allum Bay, 4to, 6d ... ... *Westall*
817 **Newchurch,** 12mo, 2d ... ... *Varrall*

818	**Newchurch**, Church, &c., near Ryde, 4to, 3d	...		*Brannon*
819	**Newport**, folio, *coloured*, 6d ...	...	... ...	*Harraden*
820	—— Distant View, 8vo, 3d ...	...	... ...	*Smith*
821	—— Distant View, 8vo, 3d ...	...	... ...	*Shury*
822	—— Town Hall, 8vo, 3d	...	... ...	*Barker*
823	—— The Old Hall, 12mo, 2d ...	...	... ...	*Greig*
824	—— Market-place, &c., 4to, 4d	...	... ...*Walker*, 1798	
825	—— Market-place, &c., 4to, 3d	...	... ...	*Brannon*
826	**Newport Church**, 12mo, 2d ...	...	... ...	*Greig*
827	**Newport**, View of the Camp near Newport, large folio, 2s 6d			
			Menagoet, about 1750	
828	**Niton**, 4to, 6d ...	... ...	... ...	*Mrs. Selby*
829	—— Scene between Niton and Sand Rock Spring, 4to, 6d			
				Mrs. Selby
830	—— View near, 4to, 3d	...	... ...	*Brannon*
831	—— Sand Rock Spring Cottage, 4to, 4d	...	...	*Brannon*
832	—— Star Inn, &c., 12mo, 2d ...	...	... ...	*Wallis*
833	**Norris Castle**, 8vo, 3d ...	...	... ...	*Butler*
834	—— 8vo, 3d	...	... ...	*Wallis*
835	—— 4to, 3d	...	... ...	*Brannon*
836	—— From the Water, 4to, 3d	...	...	*ib.*
837	**North Court House**, 4to, 3d ...	...	...	*Brannon*
838	—— 8vo, 3d	...	... ...	*Neale*
839	—— 8vo, *coloured*, 3d ...	...	... ...	*Ackermann*
840	**Northwood Park**, 4to, 3d	...	... ...	*Brannon*
841	**Orchard Cottage**, Niton, 8vo, *coloured*, 3d...	...		*Gendall*
842	**Osborne Palace**, 8vo, *india paper*, 3d	...	...	*Shaw*
843	—— Folio, *proof*, 1s ...	...	... ...	*Prior*
844	—— (The Old Mansion), 4to, 3d	...	... ...	*Brannon*
845	**Priory** (The), near Brading, 4to, 3d ...	...	...	*Brannon*
846	**Priory** (The), 4to, *etching*, 3d ...	...	...	*Cooke*
847	**Puckaster Cottage**, 4to, 3d ...	...	... ...	*Brannon*
848	**Puckaster**, House of J. Vines, *drawing*, 4to, 6d ...			*Lugar*
849	**Quarr Abbey** (East View), 4to, *private etching*, 4d			*Pellett*
850	—— Folio, 6d ...	...	... ...	*Harley*
851	—— 4to, 6d	...	... ...	*Swanwick*
852	**Ryde**, 8vo, 3d ...	...	... ...	... *Rawle*, 1806
853	—— 4to, *coloured*, 6d ...	...	... ...	...*Daniell*, 1823
854	—— Taken from the Water, 4to, 4d	...	...	*Brannon*
855	—— West of the Pier, 4to, 3d	...	... ...	*Brannon*
856	—— From the Pier, royal 8vo, 3d	...	... ...	*Shury*
857	—— Looking down towards the Pier, 4to, *coloured drawing*, 5s			
			W. Daniell, R.A.	
858	—— Eastward from the Pier, 4to, 3d	...	...	*ib.*
859	—— View near, 4to, 3d	...	... ...	*ib.*
860	—— Different, 4to, 3d ...	...	... ...	*ib.*
861	—— The Marina, near, 8vo, 3d	...	... ...	*Sherwood*
862	**Ryde Church**, 4to, 3d ...	...	... ...	*Brannon*
863	—— Church (Old), 12mo, 2d ...	...	... ...	*Wallis*
864	**St. Boniface**, 4to, 3d ...	...	... ...	*Brannon*
865	**St. Boniface Church**, 12mo, 3d	...	... ...	*Wallis*
866	**St. Catherine's Tower**, 4to, 4d	...	... ...	*Sparrow*
867	—— Light-house Point, 4to, 4d	...	... ...	*Combe*

868	St. Clare (Lady Vernon's), 4to, 3d	*Brannon*
869	St. Lawrence Village Church and Rock, folio, 6d	*Vivares*
870	St. Lawrence, View at, 4to, 6d	*Mrs. Selby*
871	—— Cottage, 4to, 3d	*Brannon*
872	St. Lawrence Church, 4to, *coloured*, 6d	*Atkinson*
873	—— 4to, *private etching*, 4d	*H. Wright*
874	—— 4to, 3d	*Brannon*
875	Sandown Bay and Culver Cliff, Dunnose Head, &c., folio, *coloured*, 1s	*Webster*
876	Sandown Fort, oblong folio, *drawing coloured*, 3s	*Grose ?*
877	Sandrock, 4to, 3d	*E. C.*
878	—— Chalybeate Spring, 4to, 3d	*Brannon*
879	—— Hotel, 4to, 3d	*ib.*
880	Scratchell's Bay and the Needles, folio, *fine, proof before letters*, 1s 6d	*Webster and Cooke*
881	—— 4to, 6d	*Childs*
882	—— 4to, 3d	*Brannon*
883	—— Different View, 4to, 3d	*ib.*
884	Shalfleet Church, 12mo, 2d	*Greig*
885	—— Sculptures in, 12mo, 2d	
886	Shanklin Town, 8vo, 3d	*Wood*
887	—— Near the Hotel, 4to, 3d	*Brannon*
888	Shanklin Church, 12mo, 2d	*Wallis*
889	—— 8vo, 3d	*Hay*
890	—— Chapel and Manor Farm, 4to, 3d	*Brannon*
891	Shanklin Chine, looking *outwards*, 8vo, 3d ...	*Cooke*
892	—— Looking *inwards*, 8vo, 3d	*Cooke*
893	—— From the Beach, 4to, 3d	*Brannon*
894	—— Different, 4to, 3d	*ib.*
895	—— Head of, 4to, 3d	*ib.*
896	—— Different, 4to, 3d	*ib.*
897	—— Chine, 4to, 6d	*Middiman*
898	—— Chine, 4to, 6d	*Mrs. Selby*
899	Shorwell, 4to, 3d	*Brannon*
900	Steephill, Part of, 4to, 6d	*Stowers, 1785*
901	—— 4to, 3d	*Brannon*
902	Steephill Castle, 8vo, 3d	*Stannard*
903	—— 4to, 3d	*Brannon*
904	Steephill Cliffs, 4to, 4d	*Middiman*
905	Swainston, 4to, 3d	*Cooke*
906	—— 4to, 3d	*Brannon*
907	—— 8vo, *coloured*, 3d	*Gendall*
908	Undercliff (The), 4to, *fine*, 1s	*Dewint and Cooke*
909	—— 4to, 3d	*Brannon*
910	—— Another View, 4to, 3d	*ib.*
911	—— Folio, 6d	*Griffiths*
912	—— Folio, 6d	*Harley*
913	Ventnor, bird's-eye view, 4to, 3d	*Brannon*
914	—— Beach at, 8vo, 6d	*Dewint and Cooke*
915	Vernon Cottage, Mr. E. V. Utterson's, 4to, 3d ...	*Brannon*
916	Westover House, 4to, 3d	*Brannon*
917	Whippingham Church, 4to, 6d	
918	—— 12mo, 2d	*Roberts*

919 **Whippingham Church**, 4to, *coloured*, 6d ... ... *Tomkins*
920 **Whippingham**, Sculptured Stone at, 4to, *private plate*, 4d
                                                          Burkitt
921 **White Cliff, Colwell, and Alum Bays**, folio, 1s ... *Cooke*, 1815
922 **Whitwell Church**, 12mo, 2d ... ... *Roberts*
923 **Wight, Isle of,** West End from the Sea, 4to, *coloured*, 6d ¦*Timms*
924 **Wilkes'** (John, *the Politician*), **Cottage,** near Sandown, 8vo, 3d
                                                          Rawle
925 **Wolverton Undercliff**, 4to, *coloured*), 6d ... *Tomkins*, 1790
926 **Wotton Common,** Cottage on, 4to, 3d ... ... *Brannon*
927 **Wootton Bridge and Fern Hill**, 4to, 3d ... ... *Brannon*
928 **Yarmouth**, 4to, 4d ... ... *Angus*, 1801
929 —— View Little Distant from the Shore, 4to, *proof*, 6d *Gilbert*
930 **Yarmouth Church**, 12mo, 2d... ... ... *Greig*
931 **Yaverland Church**, 4to, 6d ... ... *Parez*
932 —— 12mo, 2d ... ... *Greig*
933 —— Church, *pencil drawing*, 1s
934 —— Interior, folio, *proof before letters*, 1s
935 **Yaverland Parsonage**, 4to, 3d ... ... *Brannon*

ADDITIONS.

936 **Alton Town**, from Windmill Hill, 8vo, 3d... ... *Shury*
937 —— Church, 8vo, 3d ... ... *Shepherd*
938 **Basingstoke**, from Chapel Hill, 4to, 3d ... ... *Shury*
939 **Beaulieu Abbey**, 4to, 4d ... ... *Grose*
940 **Beaulieu Church**, 8vo, 3d ... ... *Shury*
941 **Bishopstoke Church**, 8vo, 3d... ... ... *Shury*
942 **Bishop's Waltham Town**, 8vo, 3d ... ... *Shury*
943 **Bishop's Waltham Abbey**, Interior, 8vo, 3d ... *Higham*
944 **Bishop's Waltham**, Remains of the Hall, 12mo, 3d *Greig*
945 **Bittern** from Bevois Mount, 8vo, 3d ... ... *Shury*
946 **Boldre Church**, 8vo, 3d ... ... *Shury*
947 **Broadlands**, Lord Palmerston's, 8vo, 3d ... ... *Shury*
948 **Brockenhurst Church**, 8vo, 3d ... ... *Shury*
949 **Calshot Castle**, 8vo, 3d ... ... *Tomkins*, 1794
950 —— 8vo, 3d ... ... *Smith*
951 —— 4to, 3d ... ... *Sandby and Ryder*, 1780
952 —— 8vo, 3d ... ... *Toms*
953 **Christchurch**, the Church, North Entrance, 8vo, 3d *Storer*
954 —— Nave, 8vo, 3d ... ... *Storer*
955 —— Draper's Chapel, 8vo, 3d ... ... *Storer*
956 —— Countess of Salisbury's Chapel, 8vo, 3d ... *Storer*
957 **Eaglehurst**, 8vo, 3d ... ... *Rawle*
958 **Emsworth**, Street of, 6vo, 3d... ... ... *Shury*
959 **Fareham**, West Street, 8vo, 3d ... ... *Shury*
960 **Fawley Church**, 8vo, 3d ... ... *Shury*
961 **Fordingbridge Church**, 8vo, 3d ... ... *Shury*
HAMPSHIRE.

962 **Hackwood Park**, 8vo, 3d ... ... *Shury*
963 **Hartford Bridge**, View in, 8vo, 3d... ... ... *Shury*
964 **Heckfield Park**, 8vo, 3d ... ... *Shury*
965 **Hurstbourne**, Lord Portsmouth's, 8vo, *proof*, 3d
966 **Hurst Castle**, 4to, 3d... ... ... *Tomkins*
967 **Issley Church**, New Forest, 8vo, 3d ... ... *Shury*
968 **Itchen Ferry**, 8vo, 3d ... ... *Shury*
969 —— Different View, 8vo, 3d ... ... *ib.*
970 **Lymington**, View of the High Street, folio, 1s
Ferrey and Haghe

971 —— Bath House, 8vo, 3d
972 **Lyndhurst**, from the Road to Sarum, 8vo, 3d ... *Shury*
973 **Lyndhurst Church**, 8vo, 3d ... ... *Shepherd*
974 **Millbrook**, Southampton, 8vo, 3d
975 —— Lunar Rainbow seen at, 8vo, 3d ... ... *White*, 1810
976 **Netley Abbey**, North East Aspect, 8vo, 3d ... *Cooke*, 1806
977 —— General South View, 8vo, 3d ... ... *Morris*
978 —— West View, 4to, 3d ... ... *Tomkins*
979 —— Towards the East from Transept, 8vo, 3d ... *Storer*, 1815
980 —— East Window, 8vo, 3d ... ... *Morris*, 1790
981 —— Lady Chapel, 8vo, 3d ... ... *Brannon*
982 —— Kitchen Fire Place, 8vo, 8d ... ... *Brannon*
983 —— South Transept, 8vo, 3d ... ... *Brannon*
984 —— Do., seen from the Nave, 8vo, 3d ... ... *ib.*
985 —— Interior, looking East, 8vo, 3d ... ... *Shury*
986 —— Do., looking West, 8vo, 3d ... ... *ib.*
987 —— Do., looking North, 8vo, 3d ... • ... *ib.*
988 **New Forest**, Twelve Apostles' Oaks, 8vo, 3d ... *Woods*
989 **Northam Bridge and Farm**, 8vo, 3d
990 **Otterburne Hill**, near Winchester, the Comet of 1811 seen at,
8vo, 3d ... ... *Cook*
991 **Porchester Castle**, 8vo, 3d ... ... *Shury*
992 **Portsmouth**, from the Parade, 8vo, 3d ... ... *Shury*
993 —— View from Gosport, 8vo, 3d ... ... *Shury*
994 —— View from Blockhouse Point, 8vo, 3d ... *ib.*
995 —— View from the Parade, 8vo, 3d ... ... *ib.*
996 —— Opposite the Gun Wharf, 4to, *coloured*, 6d ... *Ackermann*
997 —— View from the Platform, 4to, *coloured*, 6d ... *ib.*, 1818
998 —— View of the Town and Harbour, with the Fleet under Lord
Anson, folio, 3s 6d ... ... *C. Seton*, 1747
999 **Portswood House**, 8vo, 3d ... ... *Heath*
1000 **Redbridge Village**, 8vo, 3d ... ... *Woods*
1001 **St. Cross Hospital**, near Winchester, 8vo, 3d ... *Taylor*
1002 —— Inside View, 8vo, 3d ... ... *Shury*
1003 —— Church, Interior, 8vo, 3d ... ... *ib.*
1004 —— Part of the Nave, 8vo, 3d ... ... *Storer*
1005 —— Arches in S. Transept, 8vo, 3d ... ... *Greig*
1006 **Southampton**, from Millbrook, oblong 8vo, 3d ... *Old print*
1007 —— Do., to Illustrate Shakespeare's Henry V., 8vo, 3d
Harding
1008 —— From the Water, 4to, *tinted lithograph*, 6d ... *Hart*
1009 —— Little Distant, 4to, 3d ... ... *Powell*, 1800
1010 —— From Netley Beach, 8vo, 3d ... ... *Woods*

1011 **Southampton,** from Netley Fort, 4to, 3d ... ... *Medland*
1012 —— High Street, 8vo, 3d ... ... *Skelton*
1013 —— Do., 4to, *tinted lithograph,* 6d... ... *Piper and Ellis*
1014 —— Do., folio, *coloured lithograph,* 1s ... *Haghe and Buchan*
1015 —— Street, above Bar, 8vo, 3d ... ... *Lee*
1016 —— 4to, 6d ... ... *Brannon*
1017 —— All Saints' Church, 8vo, 3d ... ... *Thomas,* 1795
1018 —— St. Mary's Church, 8vo, 3d ... ... *Skelton*
1019 —— St. Michael's Church, 8vo, 3d ... ... *Skelton*
1020 —— 8vo, 3d ... ... *Shury*
1021 —— Pier, 8vo, 3d ... ... *Baily,* 1817
1022 —— Gateway of God's House, 8vo, 3d ... ... *Hall,* 1817
1023 —— Chapel of God's House, 8vo, 3d ... ... *ib.*
1024 —— Interior of a Saxon Building adjoining the Town Wall,
  8vo, 3d ... ... *ib.*
1025 —— Water Gate, 8vo, 3d—4to, 4d ... ... *Grose*
1026 —— Bar Gate, 8vo, 3d ... ... *Skelton*
1027 —— Gaol and Bridewell, 8vo, 3d ... ... *Shury*
1028 —— The Platform, 4to, *tinted lithograph,* 6d ... *Hart*
1029 —— Entrance to Floating Bridge, 8vo, 3d ... *Skelton*
1020 **Spithead,** from Priory Rocks, 4to, 3d ... ... *Tomkins*
1031 **Stony Cross,** New Forest, 8vo, 3d ... ... *Shury*
1032 **Titchfield Town,** 8vo, 3d ... ... *Shury*
1033 —— Place House, 8vo, 3d ... ... *ib.*
1034 **Twyford Church,** 8vo, 3d ... ... *Shury*
1035 **Winchester,** View near, 8vo, 3d ... ...*Westall and Finden*
1036 **Winchester Cathedral,** North West View, 8vo, 3d *Shury*
1037 —— 4to, 3d ... ... *Grose*
1038 —— Prior Silksteed's Chapel, with Izaak Walton's Tombstone,
  8vo, 3d ... ... *Lowry*

Isle of Wight.

1039 **Alum Bay and the Needles,** 4to, 3d ... ... *Tomkins*
1040 **Appley,** near Ryde, 4to, 3d ... ... *Cooke*
1041 **Appuldurcombe,** 4to, 3d ... ... *Cooke*
1042 —— 8vo, 3d ... ... *Barber*
1043 **Arreton,** Dairyman's Cottage, 8vo, 3d
1044 —— Tombstone of the Dairyman's Daughter, 8vo, 3d
1045 **Barnsley Wood,** 4to, 3d ... ... *Tomkins*
1046 **Binstead Church,** 4to, 3d ... ... *Tomkins*
1047 **Binstead,** Waterfall in the Gardens of Lord Downes, 4to, 6d
  Brooks
1048 **Black Gang Chine,** from the Beach, 4to, 3d ... *Cooke*
1049 —— Looking to Sea, 4to, 3d... ... ... *Tomkins*
1050 **Blackpool,** Ryde, Sea View from front of Residence, 4to, *tinted*
  lithograph, 6d ... ... *Day*

1051	**Bonchurch**, 4to, 3d	*Tomkins*, 1793
1052	—— Village, 8vo, 3d	*Cooke*
1053	—— The Church, 4to, 3d	*Tomkins*
1054	—— The Shute, 4to, 3d	*ib.*
1055	**Brading**, Church, &c., 8vo, 3d—4to, *proof*, 6d ...	*Harwood*
1056	**Brixton Church**, 4to, 3d	*Tomkins*
1057	**Brook Church**, 4to, 3d	*Tomkins*
1058	**Calborne Church**, 4to, 3d	*Tomkins*
1059	—— Mon. Brass of a Knight, 8vo, 6d	*ib.*
1060	**Carisbrook Village**, 8vo, 3d...	*Shury*
1061	—— Ancient Sepulchral Slab, 8vo, 3d	*Tomkins*
1062	**Carisbrook Castle**, little distant, 4to, 3d	*Tomkins*
1063	—— Castle from behind the Church, 8vo, 3d ...	*Morris*
1064	—— North View of Castle, 12mo, 3d	*Old print*
1065	—— Gateway of Castle, 8vo, 3d	*Woolnoth*
1066	—— 8vo, 3d	*Poole*
1067	—— The Keep, 4to, 3d	*Tomkins*
1068	—— 8vo, 3d	*Woolnoth*
1069	—— Interior of Castle, 4to, 3d	*Tomkins*
1070	**Chale Bay**, 4to, 3d	*Tomkins*
1071	—— In a Storm, 8vo, 3d	*Woods*
1072	—— Rocks near, 8vo, *coloured*, 3d	
1073	**Cowes** (West), 8vo, 3d	*Rawle*, 1806
1074	—— Castle and Harbour, 4to, 3d	*Cooke*
1075	—— Castle, 4to, 3d	*Tomkins*
1076	—— 8vo, 3d	*Toms*
1077	—— 8vo, 3d	*...Morris*, 1790
1078	**Cowes** (East), 8vo, 3d...	*Shury*
1079	—— Mr. Lambert's Cottage at, 8vo, 3d	
1080	—— 4to, 3d	*Cooke*, 1808
1081	**Culver Cliffs**, 4to, 3d	*Tomkins*
1082	**Dunnose**, 4to, 3d ... ... •••	*Tomkins*
1083	**Fairlee**, near Newport, 4to, 3d	*Tomkins*
1084	**Freshwater Village**, 8vo, 3d	*Barber*
1085	**Freshwater Church**, 4to, 3d	*Tomkins*
1086	**Freshwater Gate and Mainbench**, 4to, 3d ...	*Tomkins*
1087	—— Cave at, 4to, 3d	*ib.*
1088	—— Entrance to Cave, 4to, 3d	*ib.*
1089	—— Arched Rock at, 8vo, 3d	
1090	—— 4to, 3d	*Cooke*
1091	—— Rocks in the Bay, 8vo, 3d—4to, 4d	*Cooke*
1092	—— Lighthouse on the Cliff, 4to, 3d	*Cooke*
1093	—— The Cliffs, 4to, 3d	*ib.*
1094	**Froghill**, near Calbourne, 4to, 3d	*Tomkins*
1095	**Gatcombe Church**, Monument in, 4to, 3d	*Tomkins*
1096	**Gatcombe House**, 8vo, 3d	*Cooke*
1097	—— Folio, 1s	*Godfrey*
1098	**Godshill Village and Church**, 8vo, 3d	*Rawle*, 1806
1099	**Hermit's Hole**, Pathway to, 4to, 3d	*Tomkins*
1100	**Knowles**, looking West, 4to, 3d	*Tomkins*
1101	**Luccombe Chine**, 4to, 3d	*Tomkins*
1102	**Marine Villa** of Sir R. Worsley, 8vo, 3d—4to, 4d	*Cooke*

1103 **Marine Villa** of Sir J. Cox Hippesley, 8vo, *coloured*, 3d
Gendall
1104 **Medina River**, 4to, 3d ... ... *Tomkins*
1105 **Mirables**, from Cripple Path, 4to, 3d ... ... *Tomkins*
1106 —— Mrs. Arnold's House, 8vo, 3d—4to, 4d ... *Cooke*
1107 **Motteston Church**, 4to, 3d ... ... *Tomkins*
1108 **Needles** (The), from Scratchell's Bay, 8vo, 3d—4to, 4d *Cooke*
1109 **Nettleston**, 4to, 6d ... ... *Varley and Harley*
1110 **Newport**, Plan of, 8vo, 3d 1610
1111 —— Entrance into, 8vo, 3d ... ... *Tomkins*
1112 —— Viewed from Fairlee, 4to, 3d ... ... *ib.*
1113 **Newport Church**, 8vo, 3d ... ... *Greig*
1114 **Niton Church**, 12mo, 3d ... ... *Wallis*
1115 —— 8vo, 3d ... ... *Winkles*
1116 —— 4to, 4d ... ... *Tomkins*
1117 **Norris Castle**, 4to, 3d ... ... *Cooke*
1118 —— 8vo, *coloured*, 6d... ... ... *Gendall*
1119 —— 12mo, 3d ... ... *Wallis*
1120 **Northcourt House**, 4to, 4d ... ... *Angus*, 1796
1121 —— 8vo, *coloured*, 3d... ... ...*Gendall*, 1826
1122 **Northwood Church**, 4to, 3d ... ... *Tomkins*
1123 **Norton Cottage**, 4to, 3d ... ... *Tomkins*
1124 **Norton Lodge**, 4to, 3d ... ... *Tomkins*
1125 **Nunwell**, folio, 1s ... ... *Godfrey*
1126 **Ryde**, 4to, 3d ... ... *Tomkins*, 1793
1127 —— View in, 8vo, 3d... ... ... *Rawle*, 1806
1128 —— From St. John's, 8vo, 3d ... ... *Harwood*
1129 —— From the Sea, 8vo, 3d ... ... *Barber*
1130 **St. Catherine's**, 4to, 3d ... ... *Tomkins*
1131 —— Distant View of, 4to, 3d ... ... *ib.*
1132 **St. Clare's**, Lord Vernon's, 8vo, 3d ... ... *Barber*
1133 **St. Helen's**, 4to, 3d ... ... *Tomkins*
1134 **St. John's**, 4to, 3d ... ... *Cooke*
1135 **St. Lawrence**, from Undercliff, 12mo, 3d ... ... *Matthews*
1136 —— Church, 4to, 3d ... ... *Tomkins*
1137 —— 8vo, 3d ... ... *Jones*
1138 —— The Well, 4to, 3d ... ... *Harwood*
1139 **Shalfleet Church**, 4to, 3d ... ... *Tomkins*
1140 **Shanklin Town**, 8vo, 3d ... ... *Wood*
1141 —— Antique Chest at, 4to, 3d ... ... *Tomkins*
1142 —— The Chine, 4to, 3d ... ... *Harwood*
1143 **Shide Bridge**, 4to, 3d... ... ... *Tomkins*
1144 **Steephill Cottage**, 8vo, 3d—4to, 4d ... ... *Cooke*
1145 **Swainston**, 4to, 3d ... ... *Tomkins*, 1794
1146 **Thorley Church**, 4to, 3d ... ... *Tomkins*
1147 **Undercliff**, taken near Mirables, 8vo, 3d—4to, 4d *Cooke*
1148 **Ventnor Mill**, 4to, 3d ... ... *Tomkins*
1149 **West End of the Isle**, 4to, 3d ... ... *Tomkins*
1150 **Western Lines**, 4to, 3d ... ... *Tomkins*
1151 **Westfield House**, View in the Gardens, folio, *coloured*, 1s
E. A. Brooke
1152 **Westhill Cottage**, near Cowes, 4to, 3d ... ... *Cooke*
1153 **Westover**, 4to, 3d ... ... *Tomkins*

1154 **Westover,** folio, 1s ... ... *Godfrey*
1155 **Wolverton Church,** 4to, 3d... ... ... *Tomkins*
1156 **Wotton Church,** 4to, 3d ... ... *Tomkins*
1157 —— 12mo, 3d ... ... *Roberts*
1158 **Wotton River,** 4to, 3d ... ... *Tomkins*
1159 **Yarmouth,** 8vo, 3d ... ... *Cooke*
1160 **Yarmouth Castle,** 4to, 3d ... ... *Tomkins*
1161 **Above Sixty Engravings** of Hampshire and the Isle of Wight, not worth cataloguing separately, 2s

[Supplement]

HAMPSHIRE.

1 **Broadlands,** Carriage Front, 8vo, 3d ... ... *Prosser*
2 **Christchurch,** Drapers' Chapel in Church, 8vo, 3d ... *Storer*
3 **Foxlease,** 4to, 6d ... ... *Prosser*
4 **Freefolk Priors,** 8vo, 3d ... ... *Prosser*
5 **Grange** (The), folio, 1s ... ... *F. W. T(rench)*, 1823

6 **Isle of Wight,** Shanklin Chine, royal 8vo, 3d ... *Woods*
7 —— Fairlee, near Newport, folio, 1s ... ... *Godfrey*
8 —— Binnel Bay below Woolverton, royal 4to, *proof*, 1s *Cooke*
9 **Netley Abbey,** Interior, 4to, *proof before letters*, 6d
10 —— South East Aspect, 8vo, 3d ... ... *Cooke*
11 **Portsmouth from the Sea,** 4to, 1s 6d *J. M. W. Turner and Miller*
12 **Portsmouth Harbour,** 4to, *proof before letters*, 6d
13 —— The "Active" in the Harbour, 8vo, 3d... ... *Stanfield*
14 **Winchester City,** from the East, 4to, 6d ... *Bartlett and Taylor*
15 —— North East View, 4to, 6d... ... ... *Robson and Roberts*
16 —— West Gate, East View, 8vo, 3d
17 —— Bp. Morley's College, 8vo, 3d
18 —— The College Cloisters, 4to, *proof,* 6d ... ... *Havell*
19 **Winchester Cathedral,** 4to, 3d ... ... *Grose*, 1787
20 —— North East View, royal 4to, 6d ... ... *Pass*, 1798
21 —— North West View, 8vo, 3d ... ... *Carter*, 1789
22 —— Interior Beaufort's Tomb, &c., 4to, 6d ... ... *Le Keux*
23 **St. Cross Hospital,** Interior of Court, 4to, 3d—*proof*, 6d *Le Keux*
24 —— Bird's-eye View, 4to, 3d ... ... *Taylor*
25 **Warblington Castle,** 4to, 3d ... ... *Sparrow*

A

CATALOGUE

OF

DRAWINGS, AND BOOKS OF DRAWINGS,

TO BE SOLD

(*On Thurſday the 6th of May* 1802)

FOR THE ENDOWMENT OF A PARISH-SCHOOL,

AT BOLDRE, NEAR LYMINGTON, IN HAMPSHIRE.

To this CATALOGUE is added the Author's Account of the DRAWINGS contained in it; and of the Principles, on which they are executed.

———◆———

Non minus *otii*, quam *negotii* rationem extare oportere.
CIC.

———◆———

LONDON:

PRINTED FOR T. CADELL JUN. AND W. DAVIES, STRAND,

1802.

[Figure 24; 12.3 x 19.7 cm]

THE NEW FOREST

Its History and its Scenery

BY JOHN R. WISE

ARTIST'S EDITION

WITH 12 ETCHINGS BY HEYWOOD SUMNER

63 Illustrations by Walter Crane, engraved by W. J. Linton, and Two Maps

HENRY SOTHERAN & CO.

LONDON: 136 STRAND—36 PICCADILLY

MANCHESTER: 49 CROSS STREET

MDCCCLXXXIII

[Figure 25; 22.6 x 31.5 cm]

A HAND-BOOK

TO THE

Topography

AND

FAMILY HISTORY

OF

England and Wales:

BEING

A DESCRIPTIVE ACCOUNT OF TWENTY THOUSAND MOST CURIOUS AND RARE
BOOKS, OLD TRACTS, ANCIENT MANUSCRIPTS, ENGRAVINGS, AND
PRIVATELY PRINTED FAMILY PAPERS, RELATING TO THE
HISTORY OF ALMOST EVERY LANDED ESTATE AND OLD
ENGLISH FAMILY IN THE COUNTRY, INTERSPERSED
WITH NEARLY TWO THOUSAND ORIGINAL
ANECDOTES, TOPOGRAPAICAL AND
ANTIQUARIAN NOTES.

THE LABOUR PERFORMED BY

JOHN CAMDEN HOTTEN.

The Books, &c., now on Sale, each Article having a small Price affixed.

MÆRET QUI LABORAT.

LONDON:
JOHN CAMDEN HOTTEN, PICCADILLY.

[359]

[360]